Leon Gordenker, *International Aid and National Decisions: Development Programs in Malawi, Tanzania, and Zambia* (Princeton University Press, 1976).

Carl von Clausewitz, *On War,* edited and translated by Michael Howard and Peter Paret (Princeton University Press, 1976).

Gerald Garvey and Lou Ann Garvey, *International Resource Flows* (D. C. Heath, 1977).

Walter F. Murphy and Joseph Tanenhaus, *Comparative Constitutional Law: Cases and Commentaries* (St. Martin's Press, 1977).

Gerald Garvey, *Nuclear Power and Social Planning: The City of the Second Sun* (D. C. Heath, 1977).

Richard E. Bissell, *Apartheid and International Organizations* (Westview Press, 1977).

David P. Forsythe, *Humanitarian Politics: The International Committee of the Red Cross* (Johns Hopkins University Press, 1977).

Paul E. Sigmund, *The Overthrow of Allende and the Politics of Chile, 1964-1976* (University of Pittsburgh Press, 1977).

Henry S. Bienen, *Armies and Parties in Africa* (Holmes and Meier, 1978).

Harold and Margaret Sprout, *The Context of Environmental Politics: Unfinished Business for America's Third Century* (University Press of Kentucky, 1978).

Samuel S. Kim, *China, the United Nations, and World Order* (Princeton University Press, 1979).

S. Basheer Ahmed, *Nuclear Fuel and Energy* (D. C. Heath, 1979).

Robert Johansen, *The National Interest and the Human Interest: An Analysis of U.S. Foreign Policy* (Princeton University Press, 1979).

The War System

Other Titles in This Series

Westview Special Studies in Peace, Conflict, and Conflict Resolution

The War System: An Interdisciplinary Approach edited by Richard A. Falk and Samuel S. Kim

This anthology on the war system grew out of the authors' sense of dissatisfaction with the existing literature and their feeling that a rigorous social science approach that is also sensitive to values is both desirable and possible. The book is organized around several key assumptions. First, because the authors agree that the conditions of peace cannot be prescribed before the causes of war are subjected to a systematic etiological inquiry, it is largely diagnostic. Second, its systems approach to the causes of war is based on the assumption that war is a species of human conflict and that the etiology of war should deal with the entire range of human conflict, from interpersonal to international. Third, the belief that war does not have a single cause leads to the interdisciplinary approach — a synthesis of relevant contributions from all the disciplines dealing with human behavior. The essays are uniformly marked by the recognition of values within the context of empirical research.

Richard A. Falk is Albert G. Milbank Professor of International Law and Practice at Princeton University and director of U.S. participation in the World Order Models Project (WOMP). Samuel S. Kim, professor of political science at Monmouth College, is currently visiting professor of public and international affairs at Princeton University and visiting research political scientist at the university's Center of International Studies.

Written under the auspices of the
Center of International Studies,
Princeton University

A list of other Center of International Studies publications
appears at the back of the book.

The War System:
An Interdisciplinary Approach

edited by Richard A. Falk
and Samuel S. Kim

Westview Press / Boulder, Colorado

Westview Special Studies in Peace, Conflict, and Conflict Resolution

Copyright © 1980 by Westview Press, Inc.

Published in 1980 in the United States of America by
  Westview Press, Inc.
  5500 Central Avenue
  Boulder, Colorado 80301
  Frederick A. Praeger, Publisher

Library of Congress Cataloging in Publication Data
Main entry under title:
The War system.
    (Westview special studies in peace, conflict, and conflict resolution)
    Bibliography: p.
    1. War and society—Addresses, essays, lectures. I. Falk, Richard A. II. Kim, Samuel S., 1935-   III. Series.
HM36.5.W37   301.6'334   79-19566
ISBN 0-89158-569-9
ISBN 0-86531-042-4 pbk.

VRP/s 37.00 33.30 4/19/82

Printed and bound in the United States of America

Contents

vii

Tables and Figures

xi

Figures

Acknowledgments

An interdisciplinary study of this nature and scope reflects contributions of many scholars in diverse disciplines and fields concerned with human conflict behavior in general and with human war-prone behavior in particular. They are too numerous to enumerate here. Still, our deep gratitude goes to those scholars whose writings have been incorporated in this volume as "sample representatives" of what their particular disciplines can contribute to the study of war.

In a serious sense, this volume is an outgrowth of our teaching world order and peace studies courses over the years. Richard Falk expresses his gratitude to those of his Princeton students and colleagues who have shared the concerns that comprise this volume. Samuel Kim profited immensely from his colleagues who have joined him in team-teaching peace studies courses at Monmouth College. Specifically, he acknowledges his intellectual indebtedness to Guy Oakes (social science methodology), William Mitchell (anthropology), and Kenneth R. Stunkel (intellectual history and human ecology). Their influence on his peace-research thinking has found its way into this book.

Robert C. Johansen and Saul H. Mendlovitz—respectively president of the Institute for World Order and director of the World Order Models Projects (WOMP)—have been unsparing in their moral support for the project. In addition, Johansen's suggestions have been very useful in revising the structure of the book. For their continuing encouragement of our partnership in this and other projects, we are thankful.

This study has grown out of the institutional sponsorship of the Center of International Studies, Princeton University. We wish to thank the Policy Committee of the center for supporting this project. In particular, we are greatly indebted to Cyril E. Black, director of the center, for his encouragement of our work and for financial support of the project. We also happily acknowledge that it is largely his leadership that has made the center such a stimulating and congenial place in which to carry on collaborative work of this nature. June Garson typed several drafts of different parts of the book with her customary skill and élan. Our most sincere thanks go to Charlotte

Ebel who has so graciously and efficiently borne the main managerial burden of producing a book of this nature. During the summer of 1979 when both of us were away, she guided the manuscript through the copy-editing process at Westview Press, becoming in the process a co-worker of the project.

Finally, it was indeed our pleasure to work with Westview Press in the production of this book. We wish to thank Frederick Praeger, Miriam Gilbert, Douglas Beall, Lynne C. Rienner, Annette Frahm, and Lynn Lloyd for their help in guiding our manuscript so effectively through the various stages of the production process.

None of these debts absolve us, however, from taking full responsibility for whatever errors and defects may still remain; of course, we alone are **responsible for the normative thrust of the book.**

Richard A. Falk
Samuel S. Kim

The War System

General Introduction

Richard A. Falk
and Samuel S. Kim

War has long exerted a powerful fascination over the human imagination. Novelists, filmmakers, poets, and artists have probed various dimensions of war in an attempt to fix its place in the annals of human experience. War touches and agitates our deepest recesses, our rawest nerves, our wildest fantasies as individuals and as members of human society. War captures man's fondest dreams and worst fears. War is being fought not only by contending soldiers but also by contending political propagandists. As such, war has a fugitive reality in popular consciousness as well as a geopolitical dimension in national statecraft.

The pervasiveness of war through time and across space expresses its intimate connection with the social and political organization of life on this planet. War continues to act as the main motivating force of change in relations among sovereign states. There are no effective mechanisms of peaceful change in international society. The General Assembly does not possess the status of a supranational legislature. The United Nations is primarily a forum for interstate interaction among member states, lacking coercive authority and capabilities as well as financial independence. However, it is the main avenue open to those who have serious grievances about present global arrangements of human affairs. Of course, nonviolent movements of social change sometimes occur within individual countries, but their transnational impact has not posed any challenge to the war system.

Attitudes and opinions about war have been changing. The destructiveness of modern warfare and the prospects of nuclear holocaust have turned many people in the industrial societies against war except as a last act of self-defense for survival. Since World War I war has been losing, at least in the domain of public consciousness, much of its traditional legitimization as something just, adventurous, romantic, necessary, or profitable. The legitimacy of war as an instrument of national policy has suffered substantial symbolic slippage in our times, as reflected in the development of legal thinking on war from the League of Nations Covenant to the

Kellogg-Briand Pact of 1928, to the United Nations Charter, to the acceptance by consensus in 1974 of an agreed Definition of Aggression in the General Assembly. Yet patriotic linkage to war as a necessary evil still survives vestigially in the nuclear age, demanding that every good citizen ought to fight and die for his or her country in a war situation almost irrespective of its moral or strategic merits.

In other parts of the world where war served as a midwife in the transition from colonial to independent political status, the positive image of war as an instrument of change persists at both popular and official levels. In Third World countries the idea of "catching up" (modernization) has been extended to the domain of war-making capabilities, sometimes serving as a pretext for the militarization of domestic rule. Measured in terms of armed forces and military expenditures, for example, the most rapid acquisition of weaponry in the world since 1960 has occurred in the Third World.

The advent of nuclear weapons has encouraged a higher degree of verbal caution and doctrinal sophistication (and sophistry) in international relations. But militarization evolves unchecked both vertically and horizontally in the contemporary international system. A few statistical measurements of such military growth in the world indicate the basic trends: (1) *world military spending* — over $400 billion in 1977, a growth in yearly outlays of 15 percent above the 1970 level and 60 percent above the 1960 level after allowing for price inflation; (2) *world armed forces* (regular and paramilitary) — 36 million men; (3) *exports of major weapons to Third World countries* — an estimated $8 billion yearly in constant 1975 prices, almost three times such exports in 1970, over four times the volume in 1960; (4) *strategic nuclear stockpiles of the two superpowers* — 14,000 warheads, an increase of 8,000 since 1970; and (5) *military R&D* — $30 billion a year (and an estimated $336 billion since 1960), now engaging over half a million scientists and engineers (almost one-fourth of the entire scientific community) throughout the world and consuming more public research money than all research on energy, health, education, food, and other civilian needs combined (Sivard 1978). Note a corollary of such militarization: since World War II there have been more than 135 wars involving over 70 countries and leading to as many as 25 million deaths.

For these reasons it is now possible to speak of war as a social system or "the war system." By "the war system" we mean an all-embracing structure of mutually interlocking organizational and behavioral variables, in which violence or force is accepted and legitimized as the ultimate arbiter of social conflicts at all levels of human society. Viewed in this systemic perspective, it is not easy to disentangle "war" from its economic, social, psychological, cultural, and normative complex of interactions that has shaped human struggle over the course of centuries. There is no easy "fix" for war by way of dramatic gesture, such as a general and complete disarmament treaty or an abrupt renunciation of force as an instrument of national statecraft. Political communities have been war-conditioned over such an extended period of time in the course of their nation-building and nation-expanding processes that the deconditioning and delinking process will be long and difficult. How, where, and in what manner do we begin such a process?

Besides presenting a clear and continuing danger to human survival, the war system claims and diverts resources and energies from the more humane and just allocation of goods and values at a time of acute scarcity and resource depletion. The diversion of resources and the spreading technological mastery over the weaponry of mass destruction create an urgent need to inquire more thoroughly into the place of the war system in the modern world, including the degree to which arms races and the requirements of constant vigilance lock societies into a permanent war economy.

The transition from the war system to a peace system requires a comprehensive and systemic effort to understand war in all its dimensions. Until we accumulate a more definitive body of knowledge about the underlying causes of the war system we will fail to grasp the dual reality: that the elimination of war is profoundly difficult and yet that it can be done.

Assumptions and Approaches

The dominant spirit of this book is heuristic and preliminary. Still, our conceptual and methodological assumptions, our value preferences and approaches, and our criteria for selecting the materials need to be made explicit. To begin with, we reject some dominant myths and misconceptions related to the study of war. We reject the popular and still prevailing *pessimistic inevitability school* that is convinced that nothing much can be done to abolish the war system and that constructive effort should be directed toward its "rational" management rather than its abolishment. Historically, this school had its proponents in such social and political Darwinists as Gumplowicz, Ratzenhofer, Treitschke, and Steinmetz who felt that war contributed to societal and survival needs, making the recurrence of war inevitable and eternal. In our times, the influence of this school lingers in the general endorsement of balance of power politics and its connected deterrent doctrine of *si vis pacem, para bellum* ("if you want peace, prepare for war"). The inevitability school is obviously incompatible with peace research.

We also reject the *utopian blueprint school* that envisages a warless future achieved by the adoption of legal or constitutional blueprints for general disarmament or world government. This approach, which is most comprehensively sketched out in *World Peace Through World Law* by Glenville Clark and Louis B. Sohn (3rd ed., 1966), requires a heroic faith in the politically naive slogan that what is desirable is indeed possible. War as a cultural artifact of profound character cannot be eliminated by a legal fiat emanating from the constitution of world government; it can be eliminated only through a protracted process of transforming the most fundamental values, beliefs, attitudes, and myths that give contemporary societal groups their sense of cohesion, identity, and security. Furthermore, substituting a centralized bureaucracy for the war system could easily pave the way to global tyranny.

Finally, we reject the *monocausal school* that traces the origin of all wars to a single, paramount source. What is called the etiology of war is premised in this book on a complex reality that builds understanding by investigating all major structural and behavioral variables of the human situation. As such, no single perspective or causal paradigm is conceived as more than partial. Any attempt to assert that such and such is "the cause of war" seems to us conceptually misleading and prescriptively dangerous. Such a cause could be removed and yet war would persist. For these reasons, we find that little insight derives from such common assertions as "war is caused by instinctive human aggression," or "war is caused by the division of world society into sovereign states," or "war is an expression of a constant search for overseas markets and critical raw materials." Each of these assertions is sensitive to an aspect of the war system and if understood as part of a systemic image could be useful, but taken alone, it is simplistic and distorting.

The monocausal school makes the basic error of mistaking the part for the whole. The extension of such single-cause explanations from their appropriate restricted application to account for war as a whole is misleading. For illustrative purposes, an analogy of cancer to war may be helpful. As of now the scientists have pinpointed more than 1,000 agents as definite or suspected causes of cancer in man. Such agents (carcinogens) have been discovered, we are told, in the air we breathe, the water we drink, the food we eat, the clothes we wear, the drugs we take, etc. Therefore a total abolition of cigarette smoking would reduce, but would not eliminate, the incidence of cancer from human life.

What we are saying, in effect, is that the causes of war can be assessed only by putting together in a tentative synthetic framework the accounts of war derived from a series of disciplinary perspectives from different levels of human society. As our research expands and our knowledge accumulates, the etiological conception of war will be correspondingly revised and updated, narrowing the gap between theory and reality and, it is hoped, the gap between scholarly research and public policy.

One inquiry in this book consists largely of a heuristic process of searching various ways and means of formulating hypotheses about the causes of war and of testing them in as rigorous a manner as the modern social and behavioral sciences permit. In short, we are proposing to subject the causes of war to an interdisciplinary etiological approach, drawing upon insights and findings of relevant disciplines involved in the study of human behavior in general and human conflict behavior in particular. The monocausal approach has the appearance and attraction of being a short and simple way to peace, but it is, we believe, only a diversion.

Our interdisciplinary approach is based on the methodological assumption that war is one form that human conflict assumes under certain conditions. The etiology of war should accordingly be concerned about the entire range of human conflict ranging from interpersonal to international levels. In order to deepen our understanding of war as a multidimensional reality possessing a firm hold on individuals and societies, we are conceptually and analytically linking war with the entire range of conflicts that occur in social process at all levels of human interaction.

Such an interdisciplinary approach is clearly beyond the purview of a single scholar or a single social science discipline. Hence our aim is modest and preliminary: to present what the social sciences have currently to say about the war system. Even within this scope, our main concern is more diagnostic than prescriptive at this stage because of our assumption that the conditions of peace cannot be prescribed before the causes of war are subjected to a more careful and comprehensive interdisciplinary analysis. What we are seeking in this diagnostic analysis is the formation of a more adequate conception of war firmly grounded in the separate analysis of its philosophical, psychological, anthropological, sociological, economic, historical, political, legal, and moral dimensions. In this respect we are not mounting a case against war, but only trying to improve our understanding of what the war system is. Our hope is that with an empirical foundation that clarifies the causes of war and the nature of the war system it will be subsequently possible to think more meaningfully about the conditions of peace and the design of a viable peace system (Falk 1975; Mendlovitz 1975).

Despite this open, tentative, and heuristic spirit, our inquiry is guided by the normative commitment to the shaping of a more just and humane world order premised on the values of peace, economic well-being, social and political justice, and ecological balance. We are not concerned with merely knowing about the causes of war as an exercise in pure science. We are guided by, and committed to, the dominant spirit of peace research as an applied science and as a policy science. The inclusion of the materials from disciplines more concerned with questions of human values — law, philosophy, ethics, and theology — reflects normative aspects of our inquiry as an applied science. Still, what we hope to achieve in this inquiry is to provide a firm and sound empirical analysis of the causes of war, so that it can be helpful to the related necessary work of designing models of preferred worlds and images of transitional paths leading from here to there that include the shaping of warless security systems.

We see the study of war evolving through three distinct stages of development, each with a different approach: the monodisciplinary approach of traditional international relations, the interdisciplinary approach of peace research, and the transdisciplinary approach of world order studies. In the first stage, the study of war was preempted by students of international relations who jealously guarded the subject matter within narrow parameters of disciplinary autonomy. The peace research movement, which arose in the late 1950s and early 1960s out of a disenchantment over the intellectual self-isolation of traditional international relations, marked the second stage. Peace research differed from traditional international relations in the following respects: (1) it is more interdisciplinary (in fact, it served as a rendezvous point for various disciplines concerned with human conflict behavior); (2) it is more value-oriented, rejecting both the feasibility and desirability of value-neutral models; and (3) it is broader in its scope of inquiry, responding to the challenge of violence in any form anywhere; it probes the possibilities of dealing with conflicts in a comparative and interdisciplinary framework, moving up and down different levels ranging from international through intergroup to interpersonal and finally intrapersonal conflicts.

The transdisciplinary approach of world order studies — in which the value of peace is broadened and updated by relating it more closely with such other values as economic well-being, social and political justice, and ecological balance — is exemplified in the transnational research enterprise of the World Order Models Project (WOMP) of the Institute of World Order (Mendlovitz 1975). It is an outgrowth of the second stage development of peace research. It does not reject the interdisciplinary approach of peace research; it merely refines, expands, and synthesizes a loose juxtaposition of concepts, paradigms, and theories borrowed from various social science disciplines in the second stage development by developing its own concepts and models suited to the world-order modelling process. The futuristic orientation, the formulation of transition strategies, and the designing of preferred worlds: these are three hallmarks of the transdisciplinary approach. As may be easily inferred from our discussion thus far, this book falls in the second stage of the interdisciplinary approach, but our hope is that it will encourage the transition process from the second to the third stage.

The above discussion outlines our assumptions, values, and framework of inquiry. It also sets forth our bases for selecting materials for the book. Our two explicit criteria for selection were, of course, quality and relevance. Aside from these two criteria, however, we have been rather flexible and pluralistic in our choices. Some selections were chosen for methodological and others for substantive reasons; some employ quantitative methods and other qualitative analyses; some approach the study of human conflict behavior from the vantage point of a single discipline and others from an interdisciplinary perspective. Some focus on structural variables and others on process variables in the war system. Some evolve a causal analysis focusing on antecedent (independent) variables; others on intervening or dependent (outcome) variables. The inclusion of a particular piece does not necessarily indicate our endorsement or agreement with its method or conclusions. Our main goal is to present the best and most challenging research on the war system produced by the various disciplines concerned with human conflict behavior.

War and Knowledge

There are various forms of knowledge about war. An influential form of inquiry, initiated in grand style by Clausewitz (1976), concentrates on war as an instrument of national policy. War is the continuation of politics by other means. The Clausewitzian hypothesis thus accepts war as a normal phenomenon in relations among nation-states and the pursuit of a specific and putatively rational political goal is the only valid *casus belli*. According to such conceptualization, the etiology of war is misleading and irrelevant. The normative implication of the Clausewitzian hypothesis leads to the conclusion that the state has the right and the duty to wage a war if and when there is a political objective to be gained.

The knowledge we seek is different. We ask a central question: Why war? What features of human experience explain the roots of war? By examining the causes of war from different outlooks and perspectives can we begin to construct a more coherent picture that includes a judgment about the nature of war and its links to other modes of conflict? In the background of inquiry are the complex relations of thought to feelings or values and to action. We believe that knowledge unites these three realms. Our thought about war is motivated by a concern over the costs and horrors of war, a concern so great that it produces a commitment to its abolition. At the same

time, feeling and thought are shaped by the impulse to act, not to incorporate knowledge passively, but to put it to use in the world for the sake of
the values we affirm.

War and Ideology

In Marxist thought war is associated with capitalist compulsions — struggles to gain control over foreign markets and sources of raw materials. The
coercive character of politics is a reflection of class conflict. Therefore,
Lenin in particular believed that when the socialist revolution spreads, war
will disappear in a world of socialist polities. The conflicts between the
Soviet Union and its dependent allies, especially in Eastern Europe, suggest that the roots of war go deeper than class structure. The bitterness of
the Sino-Soviet dispute and the danger that it could escalate to war are
further indications that the shift from capitalism to socialism is insufficient
to rid the world of war. Nationalism, hegemony, and territorial claims persist; besides, "new classes" emerge in the socialist polity. As of now, the
organization of power at home and abroad, as well as its unequal distribution, seems to assure the persistence of war regardless of ideology.

War and Survival

The commitment to work for a peace system is also a reflection of
historical experience. With the development and spread of nuclear weapons
the status of war as an instrument of change has been delegitimized. In fact,
the development of huge weapons arsenals threatens the survival of human
civilization as we know it. In the event of World War III hundreds of
millions of casualties could result, as well as significant disruption of the
ecosystems of this planet. An apocalyptic cloud hangs over human destiny.
As nuclear weapons states move toward "normalizing" these weapons and
as nonnuclear states move ever closer to having their own weapons option,
the dangers of general war increase. This danger is further increased by the
sharpening struggle among states and regions for economic viability, including the realization by countries in the North that industrial prosperity
will depend on reliable access to Third World oil supplies in sufficient
quantities and at sustainable prices.

Whether the war system imperils particular forms of civilization, civilization in general, or the human species as a whole is a matter of dispute and
controversy. The unit of survival is not assured, yet it is evident that the
possibility of a general nuclear war is real and that its occurrence would
raise questions of civilizational and species survival. Therefore, these questions are implicit in a war system whose actors premise their security on a

readiness to use weapons of mass destruction to protect vital interests. The quick reaction requirements of nuclear deterrence produce a permanent crisis mentality among national leaders and advisors. The situation of formal peace is overshadowed by continuous preparations for war, including both the fear of nuclear devastation and the threat to devastate others. While the ordering of the planet requires sentiments of solidarity and structures of coordination, the war system fragments humanity along geopolitical lines. Human survival in the nuclear-ecological age calls for new conceptions of security freed from dependence on military instrumentalities.

War and History

War has been both a recurring feature of human experience and an evolving one. As technology changes the shape and role of war, coercive politics also changes. From the arrow and spear to the nuclear missile and precision-guided munitions is an evolution that exhibits continuities and discontinuities. Have the technological discontinuities yet become decisive?

The place of war in human experience is also shaped by cultural and political evolution. Attitudes toward war influence its forms. The Napoleonic *levée en masse* was a major shift, drawing the general population into war. To vindicate conscription of civilians, as distinct from earlier combat between professional armies, requires that the people believe in the war effort. War becomes linked to nationalism and national patriotism; civic virtue is associated with fighting for one's country. Wars must be made as popular as possible so that people will accept its costs, including loss of life, suffering, and devastation. It becomes important to feel "right," to regard the enemy as "wrong" and "evil," and to associate victory with moral vindication. To mobilize these one-sided sentiments (on each side) leads to propaganda efforts that collide in democratic societies with notions that the public media should report "the truth."

These various historical tendencies convert war from being an occasional crisis for society into a permanent structural element. Even during "peace," large military budgets and constant preparedness are demanded. A national security bureaucracy grows and forms links with powerful civilian sectors. A national security state tends to stress secrecy and subversion (Shawcross 1979). Intelligence agencies grow powerful, assume paramilitary roles, and further limit the sphere of political action in democratic societies.

The style, cost, scale, and magnitude of modern war all work to centralize power, expand the scope of the national bureaucracy, and endow government with militarist and authoritarian habits, prerogatives, and personnel. The war system as evolving, then, is a formidable influence on civic government at the national level and on the character of the state system. The interactions of states reinforce these tendencies by creating pressure in each society to be strong and vigilant in a military sense at all times. National security is largely defined in military and relational terms. The United States must not be perceived as falling behind the Soviet Union in any major dimension of military power, or else its policymakers are attacked by domestic critics as being "weak" or "appeasing" vis-à-vis the enemy. Since one can never be sure what an adversary society is doing or what new breakthroughs might come out of its weapons labs, it is arguably necessary to proceed on worst case assumptions that usually exaggerate the capabilities of the other side and rarely turn out to be realistic. Such reasoning is reinforced by the "closed" nature of Soviet society. Western planners, even if acting in good faith, are obliged to assume the worst of Soviet intentions and the best of Soviet capabilities. "When calculating the force required," Robert S. McNamara (1968:53) wrote, reflecting on his experience as a key strategic planner in the Kennedy and Johnson administrations, "we must be conservative in all our estimates of both a potential aggressor's capabilities and his intentions. Security depends upon assuming a worst plausible case, and having the ability to cope with it."

This process of interaction, although not an expression of full war potential, is perceived as a continuous "arms race." To achieve public support for this military posture the other side must be portrayed as dangerous and as eager to exploit any advantage. This is true especially at times when it is claimed that an even greater budgetary effort must be made by the United States to catch up. What is played out at the level of the superpower also occurs at other levels of interaction in the world, depending on tension levels that exist in different settings. The superpowers export not only their military hardwares to Third World countries but also their military thinking, behavior, and attitudes toward the need to exert authority by reliance on force.

War and Security

At the core of this evolving experience is the sense that war is so deeply embedded in our reality that nothing can be done about it. Actually, there is evidence in survey research showing a high correlation between military conservatism and the belief in the inevitability of war, on the one hand, and between war frequency and military expectations, on the other (see Chapter 4). At any rate, the quest for security by national societies is carried on within the limits set by the war system. As a result, the level of military capability, the willingness to fight, and the quality of alliance relations are central ways of manifesting strength. This elite consensus about security is itself a cause of war since it avoids inquiry into alternative forms of security that are associated with the emergence of a dependable peace system. The social psychologist Gordon W. Allport (1968:191) put it in the following terms: "The greatest menace to the world today are leaders in office who regard war as inevitable and thus prepare their people for armed conflict. For by regarding war as inevitable, it becomes inevitable. Expectations determine behavior."

It is important to consider security of individuals and groups from sociological, psychological, and anthropological perspectives. By doing so we notice that "security" in some social settings depends more on support, warmth, and love than on degrees of physical strength or on fighting ability. These deeper insights into the nature of human security suggest that our mechanical insistence that security and military strength are automatically correlated needs to be reexamined. In what situations of conflict are cycles of violence generated? What are the possibilities of shifting conflict to nonviolent forms of struggle? Is the role of nonviolence necessarily marginal to the experience of extralegal political struggle or can its sphere of influence be indefinitely expanded given the appropriate leadership and public support? Can we imagine nonviolent security systems eventually displacing altogether the reliance on weaponry and threats of destructive violence?

War and World Order

The state system has evolved into a specific type of world order in which war plays a central role. As we have suggested, the roots of war go deeply into the makeup of human social personality and of modern national societies. Yet for the past sixty years or so there has been a growing realization that general war among dominant states is a disaster even if something called "victory" emerges in the end. And in the nuclear age there is a further determination to avoid such general war by emphasizing the deterrent function of military power. This adaptation is one of doctrinal adjustments. But it still rests on the conviction that national security is achieved through military strength. The deterrence emphasis is quite compatible with traditional roles for war in those parts of the world (Asia, Africa, Latin America) where the danger of nuclear war seems minimal because the geopolitical stakes are more marginal than in Europe, Japan, or central Asia.

There are the beginnings of a social movement for the abolition of war. Can such a movement grow powerful without encompassing the elusive domains of human consciousness and culture, including belief and myth patterns? Are these patterns shifting to support new moves toward the elimination of war? Over what period of time do such patterns shift? Do we find that some of the great world civilizations are more prepared by their culture than others to move toward a peace system?

In the end, a world without war would produce a new type of world order. Such an evolution on the political level is the outer limit of our inquiry into the contemporary status of war, as well as the most distant expression of the evolutionary potential of the war system.

Part 1
Moral and Philosophical Inquiries

Introduction

Moralists and philosophers have long been fascinated by war. War reveals the behavior of social groups at the extremity. The willingness of societies to pursue their collective goals by recourse to war tells us a lot about the human species.

The status of war has been and remains morally ambiguous for most people. No major society has committed itself to a pacifist ethic. Every government claims at least the right to use force in self-defense, as well as to define what constitutes a situation of self-defense. More than this, in some circumstances war as an instrument of change enjoys popular backing. There continue to be "holy wars" and "just wars" in the modern world. Prominent moral philosophers, undaunted by the destructiveness of modern war, affirm the possibility of appropriate warfare under certain circumstances (Ramsey 1968; Walzer 1977).

In the West there is a very rich literature concerning the idea of just war, a concept whose endorsement implies the prohibition of unjust wars. Moral controversy has been centered on the definition of acceptable causes for just war, although the significance of the controversy is uncertain. Is it about the proper form of words to be used in a given historic epoch to justify recourse to war? That is, is it an insistence that justifications for war in the contemporary world rely on an argument of self-defense or "liberation" from colonialism or racist oppression?

Or, more substantively, does the content of the just war doctrine have an impact on what the decisionmaker of a government is likely to do in a situation where recourse to war is contemplated in a serious way? In any event, we note that moralists are concerned with clarifying the occasions on which it is permissible, according to rules of international law and prevailing ideas of justice, for a polity to make war.

But as Part 1 explores, moralists are also concerned with the means used to wage war. There is a classic distinction that goes back at least to Roman times between *jus ad bellum* and *jus in bello*. In the first instance, concern is about regulation of recourse to war and, in the latter instance, its conduct. Increasingly, philosophers have despaired of cutting effectively into the geopolitical discretion claimed by leaders of sovereign states to employ war as an instrument of statecraft. Instead, more serious attention is paid to the excesses of war, and to the role of law and morality in limiting the means of its conduct that inflict deliberate harm on the innocent, or rely on cruel tactics and weaponry that run beyond the claims of military necessity, or employ methods that so offend moral sensibilities that they should be forbidden even in situations where a belief in their effectiveness exists (e.g., torture).

In the first selection, a moral philosopher, Thomas Nagel, seeks to provide a rational case for relying on absolutist reasoning to condemn certain tactics of warfare. His concern is more with the structure of the argument than with its application to concrete cases. He seeks, above all, to combat the modern cult of efficiency that would relinquish moral concern if a reasonable defense of the challenged tactic or weapon could be made by way of its effectiveness. To argue that certain acts are wrong in war, even if they apparently contribute to victory, is to allow individuals to have some grounds to oppose under all circumstances the absolutist claims of the state. Granting that war involves deliberate, large-scale killing, it remains morally significant to prohibit and condemn "massacre," that is, the killing of the innocent. War amounts to massacre unless its goals are pursued in a discriminating manner that is associated with the defeating of the enemy on the battlefield.

The ground of violence and war in human experience has also engaged the moral and philosophical imagination. The biblical murder of Abel by his brother Cain suggests that violence and struggle existed from the beginning in Western civilization. Some have argued that the adoption of settled agriculture 5,000 or so years ago more than anything else led to the formation of coercive political arrangements and intergroup warfare. In any event, one approach to the elimination of war has centered on a critique of the modern state. Philosophical anarchism has, in a variety of forms, emphasized the necessarily exploitative and violent character of the state, with its class divisions and centralized bureaucracy exercising control over violent capabilities. Such analysis applies both to the political life of particular states and to the political conditions associated with systems of states. From this anarchist perspective the elimination of war can be achieved only as an incidental by-product of political decentralization at the state level. The selection by Richard Falk examines the anarchist orientation toward global reform.

Underneath such a focus is the wider conviction that it is not enough to confine the means by which wars are waged. Given the march of modern weaponry, and the use, development, and spread of nuclear weapons in particular, it seems necessary also to consider the morality of war per se. Such an appraisal may take inspiration either from an insistence that nonviolence forms an essential attribute of any real political breakthrough on every level of social organization or from the realization that the war system as related to current and future technology threatens the human species with a tragic, if not apocalyptic, destiny. Already there are many specialists who believe it likely that World War III will occur well before the end of the century. In such circumstances, it is not surprising that a renewed interest in anarchism is evident.

In effect, people are sensing that governance structures as we know them are locked into the war system, and that no decoupling can occur. To challenge these structures, then, will require a popular movement from below that promises more fundamental shifts than the elevation of enlightened leaders to power or the adoption of a progressive ideology and program. The anarchists promise new structures that are inherently antagonistic to the outlook and organization of the war system. To consider anarchism as a global strategy extends the therapy of decentralization to the world as a whole. It contrasts, also, with conventional wisdom on global reform that associates taming the war system with establishing some kind of world government, most likely a federalist polity that combines sufficient central guidance with the reassurance that sovereignty at the state level can persist. Anarchist thought is generally dialectical, breaking down the structure of the state as we know it but building up the cooperative and coordinating activities and roles of groups situated throughout the world, generally through a network of international institutions, resembling in role the specialized agencies of the United Nations, but augmented in function.

In addition to restructuring power is the issue of conflict strategy. There is no serious way to work for change unless it is accompanied by a willingness to engage in conflict. The fundamental moral dilemma here, as with war itself, is whether such conflict should be viewed as a test of wills and capabilities, or whether, in addition, it is a test of values. Margaret Fisher creatively explores this basic alternative in the third selection. She argues that an approach to conflict oriented around conventional approaches to risk and security is incapable of generating the political will required to challenge and transform existing patterns of reliance on violence. In the end, Fisher invokes a Gandhian example to contend that a dedication to truth and a reliance on nonviolence is an absolute precondition for avoiding catastrophe and building a positive, revolutionary process: "Is not the true 'power of the people' to be defined in terms of the building up of moral courage to the point where the majority of the people become immune both to threats of violence and to the temptation to indulge in violent acts?"

To overcome the war system, then, tests the limits of human potential, individually and collectively. It disregards reformist efforts to moderate or civilize war, or even to restrict its occurrence to permissible instances ("just causes"). The abolitionist quest, if not entirely sentimental, anticipates struggle: war against war, so to speak. It also grounds the struggle on a sublime stance: the total repudiation of violence as a means of combat despite the violence of current power wielders. And it envisions a new world order founded on truth and justice as the outcome of destroying the war system. It is not a serious position to condemn war but leave patterns of social, cultural, economic, and political oppression intact. To eliminate war is tantamount to the achievement of liberation. Such a goal seems distant, unrealizable, and yet the failure to pursue it appears to condemn human society to a process of decay and eventual disaster.

These are themes initiated in Part 1 and pursued further in Part 9 of the book.

1

War and Massacre[1]

Thomas Nagel

From the apathetic reaction to atrocities committed in Vietnam by the United States and its allies, one may conclude that moral restrictions on the conduct of war command almost as little sympathy among the general public as they do among those charged with the formation of U.S. military policy. Even when restrictions on the conduct of warfare are defended, it is usually on legal grounds alone: their moral basis is often poorly understood. I wish to argue that certain restrictions are neither arbitrary nor merely conventional, and that their validity does not depend simply on their usefulness. There is, in other words, a moral basis for the rules of war, even though the conventions now officially in force are far from giving it perfect expression.

I

No elaborate moral theory is required to account for what is wrong in cases like the Mylai massacre, since it did not serve, and was not intended to serve, any strategic purpose. Moreover, if the participation of the United States in the Indochinese war is entirely wrong to begin with, then that engagement is incapable of providing a justification for *any* measures taken in its pursuit — not only for the measures which are atrocities in every war, however just its aims.

But this war has revealed attitudes of a more general kind that influenced the conduct of earlier wars as well. After it has ended, we shall be faced with the problem of how warfare may be conducted, and the attitudes that have resulted in the specific conduct of this war will not have disappeared. Moreover, similar problems can arise in wars or rebellions fought for very different reasons, and against very different opponents. It is not easy to

Thomas Nagel, "War and Massacre," *Philosophy & Public Affairs* 1, no. 2 (winter 1972). Copyright © 1972 by Princeton University Press. Reprinted by permission of the author and Princeton University Press.

keep a firm grip on the idea of what is not permissible in warfare, because while some military actions are obvious atrocities, other cases are more difficult to assess, and the general principles underlying these judgments remain obscure. Such obscurity can lead to the abandonment of sound intuitions in favor of criteria whose rationale may be more obvious. If such a tendency is to be resisted, it will require a better understanding of the restrictions than we now have.

I propose to discuss the most general moral problem raised by the conduct of warfare: the problem of means and ends. In one view, there are limits on what may be done even in the service of an end worth pursuing — and even when adherence to the restriction may be very costly. A person who acknowledges the force of such restrictions can find himself in acute moral dilemmas. He may believe, for example, that by torturing a prisoner he can obtain information necessary to prevent a disaster, or that by obliterating one village with bombs he can halt a campaign of terrorism. If he believes that the gains from a certain measure will clearly outweigh its costs, yet still suspects that he ought not to adopt it, then he is in a dilemma produced by the conflict between two disparate categories of moral reason: categories that may be called *utilitarian* and *absolutist*.

Utilitarianism gives primacy to a concern with what will *happen*. Absolutism gives primacy to a concern with what one is *doing*. The conflict between them arises because the alternatives we face are rarely just choices between *total outcomes:* they are also choices between alternative pathways or measures to be taken. When one of the choices is to do terrible things to another person, the problem is altered fundamentally; it is no longer merely a question of which outcome would be worse.

Few of us are completely immune to either of these types of moral intuition, though in some people, either naturally or for doctrinal reasons, one type will be dominant and the other suppressed or weak. But it is perfectly possible to feel the force of both types of reason very strongly; in that case the moral dilemma in certain situations of crisis will be acute, and it may appear that every possible course of action or inaction is unacceptable for one reason or another.

II

Although it is this dilemma that I propose to explore, most of the discussion will be devoted to its absolutist component. The utilitarian component is straightforward by comparison and has a natural appeal to anyone who is not a complete skeptic about ethics. Utilitarianism says that one should try, either individually or through institutions, to maximize good and minimize evil (the definition of these categories need not enter into the schematic formulation of the view), and that if faced with the possibility of preventing a great evil by producing a lesser, one should choose the lesser evil. There are certainly problems about the formulation of utilitarianism, and much has been written about it, but its intent is morally transparent. Nevertheless, despite the addition of various refinements, it continues to leave large portions of ethics unaccounted for. I do not suggest that some form of absolutism can account for them all, only that an examination of absolutism will lead us to see the complexity, and perhaps the incoherence, of our moral ideas.

Utilitarianism certainly justifies *some* restrictions on the conduct of warfare. There are strong utilitarian reasons for adhering to any limitation which seems natural to most people — particularly if the limitation is widely accepted already. An exceptional measure which seems to be justified by its results in a particular conflict may create a precedent with disastrous long-term effects.[2] It may even be argued that war involves violence on such a scale that it is never justified on utilitarian grounds — the consequences of refusing to go to war will never be as bad as the war itself would be, even if atrocities were not committed. Or in a more sophisticated vein it might be claimed that a uniform policy of never resorting to military force would do less harm in the long run, if followed consistently, than a policy of deciding each case on utilitarian grounds (even though on occasion particular applications of the pacifist policy might have worse results than a specific utilitarian decision). But I shall not consider these arguments, for my concern is with reasons of a different kind, which may remain when reasons of utility and interest fail.[3]

In the final analysis, I believe that the dilemma cannot always be resolved. While not every conflict between absolutism and utilitarianism creates an insoluble dilemma, and while it is certainly right to adhere to absolutist restrictions unless the utilitarian considerations favoring violation are overpoweringly weighty and extremely certain, nevertheless, when that special condition is met, it may become impossible to adhere to an absolutist position. What I shall offer, therefore, is a somewhat qualified defense of absolutism. I believe it underlies a valid and fundamental type of moral judgment — which cannot be reduced to or overridden by other principles. And while there may be other principles just as fundamental, it is particularly important not to lose confidence in our absolutist intuitions, for they are often the only barrier before the abyss of utilitarian apologetics for large-scale murder.

III

One absolutist position that creates no problems of interpretation is pacifism: the view that one may not kill another person under any circumstances, no matter what good would be achieved or evil averted thereby. The type of absolutist position that I am going to discuss is different. Pacifism draws the conflict with utilitarian considerations very starkly. But there are other views according to which violence may be undertaken, even on a large scale, in a clearly just cause, so long as certain absolute restrictions on the character and direction of that violence are observed. The line is drawn somewhat closer to the bone, but it exists.

The philosopher who has done most to advance contemporary philosophical discussion of such a view, and to explain it to those unfamiliar with its extensive treatment in Roman Catholic moral theology, is G.E.M. Anscombe. In 1958 Miss Anscombe published a pamphlet entitled *Mr. Truman's Degree,*[4] on the occasion of the award by Oxford University of an honorary doctorate to Harry Truman. The pamphlet explained why she had opposed the decision to award that degree, recounted the story of her unsuccessful opposition, and offered some reflections on the history of Truman's decision to drop atom bombs on Hiroshima and Nagasaki, and on the difference between murder and allowable killing in warfare. She pointed out that the policy of deliberately killing large numbers of civilians either as a means or as an end in itself did not originate with Truman and was common practice among all parties during World War II for some time before Hiroshima. The Allied area bombings of German cities by conventional explosives included raids which killed more civilians than did the atomic attacks; the same is true of certain fire-bomb raids on Japan.

The policy of attacking the civilian population in order to induce an enemy to surrender, or to damage his morale, seems to have been widely accepted in the civilized world, and seems to be accepted still, at least if the stakes are high enough. It gives evidence of a moral conviction that the deliberate killing of noncombatants — women, children, old people — is permissible if enough can be gained by it. This follows from the more general position that any means can in principle be justified if it leads to a sufficiently worthy end. Such an attitude is evident not only in the more spectacular current weapons systems but also in the day-to-day conduct of the nonglobal war in Indochina: the indiscriminate destructiveness of antipersonnel weapons, napalm, and aerial bombardment; cruelty to prisoners; massive relocation of civilians; destruction of crops; and so forth. An absolutist position opposes to this the view that certain acts cannot be justified no matter what the consequences. Among those acts is murder — the deliberate killing of the harmless: civilians, prisoners of war, and medical personnel.

In the present war such measures are sometimes said to be regrettable, but they are generally defended by reference to military necessity and the importance of the long-term consequences of success or failure in the war. I shall pass over the inadequacy of this consequentialist defense in its own terms. (That is the dominant form of moral criticism of the war, for it is part of what people mean when they ask, "Is it worth it?") I am concerned rather to account for the inappropriateness of offering any defense of that kind for such actions.

Many people feel, without being able to say much more about it, that something has gone seriously wrong when certain measures are admitted into consideration in the first place. The fundamental mistake is made there, rather than at the point where the overall benefit of some monstrous measure is judged to outweigh its disadvantages, and it is adopted. An account of absolutism might help us to understand this. If it is not allowable to *do* certain things, such as killing unarmed prisoners or civilians, then no argument about what will happen if one doesn't do them can show that doing them would be all right.

Absolutism does not, of course, require one to ignore the consequences of one's acts. It operates as a limitation on utilitarian reasoning, not as a substitute for it. An absolutist can be expected to try to maximize good and minimize evil, so long as this does not require him to transgress an absolute prohibition like that against murder. But when such a conflict occurs, the prohibition takes complete precedence over any consideration of consequences. Some of the results of this view are clear enough. It requires us to forgo certain potentially useful military measures, such as the slaughter of hostages and prisoners or indiscriminate attempts to reduce the enemy civilian population by starvation, epidemic infectious disease like anthrax and bubonic plague, or mass incineration. It means that we cannot deliberate on whether such measures are justified by the fact that they will avert still greater evils, for as intentional measures they cannot be justified in terms of any consequences whatever.

Someone unfamiliar with the events of this century might imagine that utilitarian arguments, or arguments of national interest, would suffice to deter measures of this sort. But it has become evident that such considerations are insufficient to prevent the adoption and employment of enormous antipopulation weapons once their use is considered a serious moral possibility. The same is true of the piecemeal wiping out of rural civilian populations in airborne antiguerrilla warfare. Once the door is opened to calculations of utility and national interest, the usual speculations about the future of freedom, peace, and economic prosperity can be brought to bear to ease the consciences of those responsible for a certain number of charred babies.

For this reason alone it is important to decide what is wrong with the frame of mind which allows such arguments to begin. But it is also important to understand absolutism in the cases where it genuinely conflicts with utility. Despite its appeal, it is a paradoxical position, for it can require that one refrain from choosing the lesser of two evils when that is the only choice one has. And it is additionally paradoxical because, unlike pacifism, it permits one to do horrible things to people in some circumstances but not in others.

IV

Before going on to say what, if anything, lies behind the position, there remain a few relatively technical matters which are best discussed at this point.

First, it is important to specify as clearly as possible the kind of thing to which absolutist prohibitions can apply. We must take seriously the proviso that they concern what we deliberately do to people. There could not, for example, without incoherence, be an absolute prohibition against *bringing about* the death of an innocent person. For one may find oneself in a situation in which, no matter what one does, some innocent people will die as a result. I do not mean just that there are cases in which someone will die no matter what one does, because one is not in a position to affect the outcome one way or the other. That, it is to be hoped, is one's relation to the deaths of most innocent people. I have in mind, rather, a case in which someone is bound to die, but who it is will depend on what one does. Sometimes these situations have natural causes, as when too few resources (medicine, lifeboats) are available to rescue everyone threatened with a certain catastrophe. Sometimes the situations are man-made, as when the only way to control a campaign of terrorism is to employ terrorist tactics against the community from which it has arisen. Whatever one does in cases such as these, some innocent people will die as a result. If the absolutist prohibition forbade doing what would result in the deaths of innocent people, it would have the consequence that in such cases nothing one could do would be morally permissible.

This problem is avoided, however, because what absolutism forbids is *doing* certain things to people, rather than bringing about certain *results*. Not everything that happens to others as a result of what one does is something that one has *done* to them. Catholic moral theology seeks to make this distinction precise in a doctrine known as the law of double effect, which asserts that there is a morally relevant distinction between bringing about the death of an innocent person deliberately, either as an end in itself or as a means, and bringing it about as a side effect of something else one does deliberately. In the latter case, even if the outcome is foreseen, it is not murder and does not fall under the absolute prohibition, though of course it may still be wrong for other reasons (reasons of utility, for example). Briefly, the principle states that one is sometimes permitted knowingly to bring about as a side effect of one's actions something which it would be absolutely impermissible to bring about deliberately as an end or as a means. In application to war or revolution, the law of double effect permits a certain amount of civilian carnage as a side effect of bombing munitions plants or attacking enemy soldiers. And even this is permissible only if the cost is not too great to be justified by one's objectives.

However, despite its importance and its usefulness in accounting for certain plausible moral judgments, I do not believe that the law of double effect is a generally applicable test for the consequences of an absolutist position. Its own application is not always clear, so that it introduces uncertainty where there need not be uncertainty.

In Indochina, for example, there is a great deal of aerial bombardment, strafing, spraying of napalm, and employment of pellet- or needle-spraying antipersonnel weapons against rural villages in which guerrillas are suspected to be hiding, or from which small-arms fire has been received. The majority of those killed and wounded in these aerial attacks are reported to be women and children, even when some combatants are caught as well. However, the government regards these civilian casualties as a regrettable side effect of what is a legitimate attack against an armed enemy.

It might be thought easy to dismiss this as sophistry: if one bombs, burns, or strafes a village containing a hundred people, twenty of whom one believes to be guerrillas, so that by killing most of them one will be statistically likely to kill most of the guerrillas, then isn't one's attack on the group of one hundred a *means* of destroying the guerrillas, pure and simple? If one makes no attempt to discriminate between guerrillas and civilians, as is impossible in an aerial attack on a small village, then one cannot regard as a mere side effect the deaths of those in the group that one would not have bothered to kill if more selective means had been available.

The difficulty is that this argument depends on one particular description of the act, and the reply might be that the means used against the guerrillas is not: killing everybody in the village—but rather: obliteration bombing of the *area* in which the twenty guerrillas are known to be located. If there are civilians in the area as well, they will be killed as a side effect of such action.[5]

Because of casuistical problems like this, I prefer to stay with the original, unanalyzed distinction between what one does to people and what merely happens to them as a result of what one does. The law of double effect provides an approximation to that distinction in many cases, and perhaps it can be sharpened to the point where it does better than that. Certainly the original distinction itself needs clarification, particularly since some of the things we do to people involve things happening to them as a result of other things we do. In a case like the one discussed, however, it is clear that by bombing the village one slaughters and maims the civilians in it. Whereas by giving the only available medicine to one of two sufferers from a disease, one does not kill the other, even if he dies as a result.

The second technical point to take up concerns a possible misinterpretation of this feature of the position. The absolutist focus on actions rather than outcomes does not merely introduce a new, outstanding item into the catalogue of evils. That is, it does not say that the worst thing in the world is the deliberate murder of an innocent person. For if that were all, then one could presumably justify one such murder on the ground that it would prevent several others, or ten thousand on the ground that they would prevent a hundred thousand more. That is a familiar argument. But if this is allowable, then there is no absolute prohibition against murder after all. Absolutism requires that we *avoid* murder at all costs, not that we *prevent* it at all costs.[6]

Finally, let me remark on a frequent criticism of absolutism that depends on a misunderstanding. It is sometimes suggested that such prohibitions depend on a kind of moral self-interest, a primary obligation to preserve one's own moral purity, to keep one's hands clean no matter what happens to the rest of the world. If this were the position, it might be exposed to the charge of self-indulgence. After all, what gives one man a right to put the purity of his soul or the cleanness of his hands above the lives or welfare of large numbers of other people? It might be argued that a public servant like Truman has no right to put himself first in that way; therefore if he is convinced that the alternatives would be worse, he must give the order to drop the bombs and take the burden of those deaths on himself, as he must do other distasteful things for the general good.

But there are two confusions behind the view that moral self-interest underlies moral absolutism. First, it is a confusion to suggest that the need to preserve one's moral purity might be the *source* of an obligation. For if by committing murder one sacrifices one's moral purity or integrity, that can only be because there is *already* something wrong with murder. The general reason against committing murder cannot therefore be merely that it makes one an immoral person. Secondly, the notion that one might sacrifice one's moral integrity justifiably, in the service of a sufficiently worthy end, is an incoherent notion. For if one were justified in making such a sacrifice (or even morally required to make it), then one would not be sacrificing one's moral integrity by adopting that course: one would be preserving it.

Moral absolutism is not unique among moral theories in requiring each person to do what will preserve his own moral purity in all circumstances.

This is equally true of utilitarianism, or of any other theory which distinguishes between right and wrong. Any theory which defines the right course of action in various circumstances and asserts that one should adopt that course, ipso facto asserts that one should do what will preserve one's moral purity, simply because the right course of action *is* what will preserve one's moral purity in those circumstances. Of course utilitarianism does not assert that this is *why* one should adopt that course, but we have seen that the same is true of absolutism.

V

It is easier to dispose of false explanations of absolutism than to produce a true one. A positive account of the matter must begin with the observation that war, conflict, and aggression are relations between persons. The view that it can be wrong to consider merely the overall effect of one's actions on the general welfare comes into prominence when those actions involve relations with others. A man's acts usually affect more people than he deals with directly, and those effects must naturally be considered in his decisions. But if there are special principles governing the manner in which he should *treat* people, that will require special attention to the particular persons toward whom the act is directed, rather than just to its total effect.

Absolutist restrictions in warfare appear to be of two types: restrictions on the class of persons at whom aggression or violence may be directed and restrictions on the manner of attack, given that the object falls within that class. They can be combined, however, under the principle that hostile treatment of any person must be justified in terms of something *about that person* which makes the treatment appropriate. Hostility is a personal relation, and it must be suited to its target. One consequence of this condition will be that certain persons may not be subjected to hostile treatment in war at all, since nothing about them justifies such treatment. Others will be proper objects of hostility only in certain circumstances, or when they are engaged in certain pursuits. And the appropriate manner and extent of hostile treatment will depend on what is justified by the particular case.

A coherent view of this type will hold that extremely hostile behavior toward another is compatible with treating him as a person — even perhaps as an end in himself. This is possible only if one has not automatically stopped treating him as a person as soon as one starts to fight with him. If hostile, aggressive, or combative treatment of others always violated the condition that they be treated as human beings, it would be difficult to make further distinctions on that score *within* the class of hostile actions. That point of view, on the level of international relations, leads to the position that if complete pacifism is not accepted, no holds need be barred at all, and we may slaughter and massacre to our hearts' content, if it seems advisable. Such a position is often expressed in discussions of war crimes.

But the fact is that ordinary people do not believe this about conflicts, physical or otherwise, between individuals, and there is no more reason why it should be true of conflicts between nations. There seems to be a perfectly natural conception of the distinction between fighting clean and fighting dirty. To fight dirty is to direct one's hostility or aggression not at its proper object, but at a peripheral target which may be more vulnerable, and through which the proper object can be attacked indirectly. This applies in a fistfight, an election campaign, a duel, or a philosophical argument. If the concept is general enough to apply to all these matters, it should apply to war — both to the conduct of individual soldiers and to the conduct of nations.

Suppose that you are a candidate for public office, convinced that the election of your opponent would be a disaster, that he is an unscrupulous demagogue who will serve a narrow range of interests and seriously infringe the rights of those who disagree with him; and suppose you are convinced that you cannot defeat him by conventional means. Now imagine that various unconventional means present themselves as possibilities: you possess information about his sex life which would scandalize the electorate if made public; or you learn that his wife is an alcoholic or that in his youth he was associated for a brief period with a proscribed political party, and you believe that this information could be used to blackmail him into withdrawing his candidacy; or you can have a team of your supporters flatten the tires of a crucial subset of his supporters on election day; or you are in a position to stuff the ballot boxes; or, more simply, you can have him assassinated. What is wrong with these methods, given that they will achieve an overwhelmingly desirable result?

There are, of course, many things wrong with them: some are against the law; some infringe the procedures of an electoral process to which you are presumably committed by taking part in it; very importantly, some may backfire, and it is in the interest of all political candidates to adhere to an unspoken agreement not to allow certain personal matters to intrude into a campaign. But that is not all. We have in addition the feeling that these measures, these methods of attack are *irrelevant* to the issue between you and your opponent, that in taking them up you would not be directing yourself to that which makes him an object of your opposition. You would be directing your attack not at the true target of your hostility, but at peripheral targets that happen to be vulnerable.

The same is true of a fight or argument outside the framework of any system of regulations or law. In an altercation with a taxi driver over an excessive fare, it is inappropriate to taunt him about his accent, flatten one of his tires, or smear chewing gum on his windshield; and it remains inappropriate even if he casts aspersions on your race, politics, or religion or dumps the contents of your suitcase into the street.[7]

The importance of such restrictions may vary with the seriousness of the case; and what is unjustifiable in one case may be justified in a more extreme one. But they all derive from a single principle: that hostility or aggression should be directed at its true object. This means both that it should be directed at the person or persons who provoke it and that it should aim more specifically at what is provocative about them. The second condition will determine what form the hostility may appropriately take.

It is evident that some idea of the relation in which one should stand to other people underlies this principle, but the idea is difficult to state. I believe it is roughly this: whatever one does to another person intentionally must be aimed at him as a subject, with the intention that he receive it as a subject. It should manifest an attitude to *him* rather than just to the situation, and he should be able to recognize it and identify himself as its object. The procedures by which such an attitude is manifested need not be addressed to the person directly. Surgery, for example, is not a form of personal confrontation but part of a medical treatment that can be offered to a patient face to face and received by him as a response to his needs and the natural outcome of an attitude toward *him*.

Hostile treatment, unlike surgery, is already addressed *to* a person and does not take its interpersonal meaning from a wider context. But hostile acts can serve as the expression or implementation of only a limited range of attitudes to the person who is attacked. Those attitudes in turn have as objects certain real or presumed characteristics or activities of the person which are thought to justify them. When this background is absent, hostile or aggressive behavior can no longer be intended for the reception of the victim as a subject. Instead it takes on the character of a purely bureaucratic operation. This occurs when one attacks someone who is not the true object of one's hostility — the true object may be someone else, who can be attacked through the victim; or one may not be manifesting a hostile attitude toward anyone, but merely using the easiest available path to some desired goal. One finds oneself not facing or addressing the victim at all, but operating on him — without the larger context of personal interaction that surrounds a surgical operation.

If absolutism is to defend its claim to priority over considerations of utility, it must hold that the maintenance of a direct interpersonal response to the people one deals with is a requirement which no advantages can justify one in abandoning. The requirement is absolute only if it rules out any calculation of what would justify its violation. I have said earlier that there may be circumstances so extreme that they render an absolutist position untenable. One may find then that one has no choice but to do something terrible. Nevertheless, even in such cases absolutism retains its force in that one cannot claim *justification* for the violation. It does not become *all right*.

As a tentative effort to explain this, let me try to connect absolutist limitations with the possibility of justifying *to the victim* what is being done to him. If one abandons a person in the course of rescuing several others from a fire or a sinking ship, one *could* say to him, "You understand, I have to leave you to save the others." Similarly, if one subjects an unwilling child to a painful surgical procedure, one can say to him, "If you could understand, you would realize that I am doing this to help you." One could *even* say, as one bayonets an enemy soldier, "It's either you or me." But one cannot really say while torturing a prisoner, "You understand, I have to pull out your fingernails because it is absolutely essential that we have the names of your confederates"; nor can one say to the victims of Hiroshima, "You understand, we have to incinerate you to provide the Japanese government with an incentive to surrender."

This does not take us very far, of course, since a utilitarian would presumably be willing to offer justifications of the latter sort to his victims, in cases where he thought they were sufficient. They are really justifications to the world at large, which the victim, as a reasonable man, would be expected to appreciate. However, there seems to me something wrong with this view, for it ignores the possibility that to treat someone else horribly puts you in a special relation to him, which may have to be defended in terms of other features of your relation to him. The suggestion needs much more development; but it may help us to understand how there may be requirements which are absolute in the sense that there can be no justification for violating them. If the justification for what one did to another person had to be such that it could be offered to him specifically, rather than just to the world at large, that would be a significant source of restraint.

If the account is to be deepened, I would hope for some results along the following lines. Absolutism is associated with a view of oneself as a small being interacting with others in a large world. The justifications it requires are primarily interpersonal. Utilitarianism is associated with a view of oneself as a benevolent bureaucrat distributing such benefits as one can control to countless other beings, with whom one may have various relations or none. The justifications it requires are primarily administrative. The argument between the two moral attitudes may depend on the relative priority of these two conceptions.[8]

VI

Some of the restrictions on methods of warfare which have been adhered to from time to time are to be explained by the mutual interests of the involved parties: restrictions on weaponry, treatment of prisoners, etc. But that is not all there is to it. The conditions of directness and relevance which I have argued apply to relations of conflict and aggression apply to war as well. I have said that there are two types of absolutist restrictions on the conduct of war: those that limit the legitimate targets of hostility and those that limit its character, even when the target is acceptable. I shall say something about each of these. As will become clear, the principle I have sketched does not yield an unambiguous answer in every case.

First let us see how it implies that attacks on some people are allowed, but not attacks on others. It may seem paradoxical to assert that to fire a machine gun at someone who is throwing hand grenades at your emplacement is to treat him as a human being. Yet the relation with him is direct and straightforward.[9] The attack is aimed specifically against the threat presented by a dangerous adversary, and not against a peripheral target through which he happens to be vulnerable but which has nothing to do with that threat. For example, you might stop him by machine-gunning his wife and children, who are standing nearby, thus distracting him from his aim of blowing you up and enabling you to capture him. But if his wife and children are not threatening your life, that would be to treat them as means with a vengeance.

This, however, is just Hiroshima on a smaller scale. One objection to weapons of mass annihilation — nuclear, thermonuclear, biological, or chemical — is that their indiscriminateness disqualifies them as direct instruments for the expression of hostile relations. In attacking the civilian population, one treats neither the military enemy nor the civilians with that minimal respect which is owed to them as human beings. This is clearly true of the direct attack on people who present no threat at all. But it is also true of the character of the attack on those who *are* threatening you, viz., the government and military forces of the enemy. Your aggression is directed against an area of vulnerability quite distinct from any threat presented by them which you may be justified in meeting. You are taking aim at them through the mundane life and survival of their countrymen, instead of aiming at the destruction of their military capacity. And of course it does not require hydrogen bombs to commit such crimes.

This way of looking at the matter also helps us to understand the importance of the distinction between combatants and noncombatants, and the irrelevance of much of the criticism offered against its intelligibility and moral significance. According to an absolutist position, deliberate killing of the innocent is murder, and in warfare the role of the innocent is filled by noncombatants. This has been thought to raise two sorts of problems: first, the widely imagined difficulty of making a division, in modern warfare, between combatants and noncombatants; second, problems deriving from the connotation of the word "innocence."

Let me take up the latter question first.[10] In the absolutist position, the operative notion of innocence is not moral innocence, and it is not opposed to moral guilt. If it were, then we would be justified in killing a wicked but noncombatant hairdresser in an enemy city who supported the evil policies of his government, and unjustified in killing a morally pure conscript who was driving a tank toward us with the profoundest regrets and nothing but love in his heart. But moral innocence has very little to do with it, for in the definition of murder "innocent" means "currently harmless," and it is opposed not to "guilty" but to "doing harm." It should be noted that such an analysis has the consequence that in war we may often be justified in killing people who do not deserve to die and unjustified in killing people who do deserve to die, if anyone does.

So we must distinguish combatants from noncombatants on the basis of their immediate threat or harmfulness. I do not claim that the line is a sharp one, but it is not so difficult as is often supposed to place individuals on one side of it or the other. Children are not combatants even though they may join the armed forces if they are allowed to grow up. Women are not combatants just because they bear children or offer comfort to the soldiers. More problematic are the supporting personnel, whether in or out of uniform, from drivers of munitions trucks and army cooks to civilian munitions workers and farmers. I believe they can be plausibly classified by applying the condition that the prosecution of conflict must direct itself to the cause of danger, and not to what is peripheral. The threat presented by an army and its members does not consist merely in the fact that they are men, but in the fact that they are armed and are using their arms in the pursuit of certain objectives. Contributions to their arms and logistics are contributions to this threat; contributions to their mere existence as men are not. It is therefore wrong to direct an attack against those who merely serve the combatants' needs as human beings, such as farmers and food suppliers, even though survival as a human being is a necessary condition of efficient functioning as a soldier.

This brings us to the second group of restrictions: those that limit what may be done even to combatants. These limits are harder to explain clearly. Some of them may be arbitrary or conventional, and some may have to be derived from other sources; but I believe that the condition of directness and relevance in hostile relations accounts for them to a considerable extent.

Consider first a case which involves both a protected class of noncombatants and a restriction on the measures that may be used against combatants. One provision of the rules of war which is universally recognized, though it seems to be turning into a dead letter in Vietnam, is the special status of medical personnel and the wounded in warfare. It might be more efficient to shoot medical officers on sight and to let the enemy wounded die rather than be patched up to fight another day. But someone with medical insignia is supposed to be left alone and permitted to tend and retrieve the wounded. I believe this is because medical attention is a species of attention to completely general human needs, not specifically the needs of a combat soldier, and our conflict with the soldier is not with his existence as a human being.

By extending the application of this idea, one can justify prohibitions against certain particularly cruel weapons: starvation, poisoning, infectious diseases (supposing they could be inflicted on combatants only), weapons designed to maim, disfigure, or torture the opponent rather than merely to stop him. It is not, I think, mere casuistry to claim that such weapons attack the men, not the soldiers. The effect of dumdum bullets, for example, is much more extended than necessary to cope with the combat situation in which they are used. They abandon any attempt to discriminate in their effects between the combatant and the human being. For this reason the use of flamethrowers and napalm is an atrocity in all circumstances that I can imagine, whoever the target may be. Burns are both extremely painful and extremely disfiguring—far more than any other category of wound. That this well-known fact plays no (inhibiting) part in the determination of U.S. weapons policy suggests that moral sensitivity among public officials has not increased markedly since the Spanish Inquisition.[11]

Finally, the same condition of appropriateness to the true object of hostility should limit the scope of attacks on an enemy country: its economy, agriculture, transportation system, and so forth. Even if the parties to a military conflict are considered to be not armies or governments but entire nations (which is usually a grave error), that does not justify one nation in warring against every aspect or element of another nation. That is not justified in a conflict between individuals, and nations are even more complex than individuals, so the same reasons apply. Like a human being, a nation is engaged in countless other pursuits while waging war, and it is not in those respects that it is an enemy.

The burden of the argument has been that absolutism about murder has a foundation in principles governing all one's relations to other persons, whether aggressive or amiable, and that these principles, and that absolutism, apply to warfare as well, with the result that certain measures are impermissible no matter what the consequences.[12] I do not mean to romanticize war. It is sufficiently utopian to suggest that when nations conflict they might rise to the level of limited barbarity that typically characterizes violent conflict between individuals, rather than wallowing in the moral pit where they appear to have settled, surrounded by enormous arsenals.

VII

Having described the elements of the absolutist position, we must now return to the conflict between it and utilitarianism. Even if certain types of dirty tactics become acceptable when the stakes are high enough, the most serious of the prohibited acts, like murder and torture, are not just supposed to require unusually strong justification. They are supposed *never* to be done, because no quantity of resulting benefit is thought capable of *justifying* such treatment of a person.

The fact remains that when an absolutist knows or believes that the utilitarian cost of refusing to adopt a prohibited course will be very high, he may hold to his refusal to adopt it, but he will find it difficult to feel that a moral dilemma has been satisfactorily resolved. The same may be true of someone who rejects an absolutist requirement and adopts instead the course yielding the most acceptable consequences. In either case, it is possible to feel that one has acted for reasons insufficient to justify violation of the opposing principle. In situations of deadly conflict, particularly where a weaker party is threatened with annihilation or enslavement by a stronger one, the argument for resorting to atrocities can be powerful, and the dilemma acute.

There may exist principles, not yet codified, which would enable us to resolve such dilemmas. But then again there may not. We must face the pessimistic alternative that these two forms of moral intuition are not capable of being brought together into a single, coherent moral system, and that the world can present us with situations in which there is no honorable or moral course for a man to take, no course free of guilt and responsibility for evil.

The idea of a moral blind alley is a perfectly intelligible one. It is possible to get into such a situation by one's own fault, and people do it all the time. If, for example, one makes two incompatible promises or commitments — becomes engaged to two people, for example — then there is no course one can take which is not wrong, for one must break one's promise to at least one of them. Making a clean breast of the whole thing will not be enough to remove one's reprehensibility. The existence of such cases is not morally disturbing, however, because we feel that the situation was not unavoidable: one had to do something wrong in the first place to get into it. But what if the world itself, or someone else's actions, could face a previously innocent person with a choice between morally abominable courses of action and leave him no way to escape with his honor? Our intuitions rebel at the idea, for we feel that the constructibility of such a case must show a contradiction in our moral views. But it is not in itself a contradiction to say that someone can do X or not do X, and that for him to take either course would be wrong. It merely contradicts the supposition that *ought* implies *can* — since presumably one ought to refrain from what is wrong, and in such a case it is impossible to do so.[13] Given the limitations on human action, it is naive to suppose that there is a solution to every moral problem with which the world can face us. We have always known that the world is a bad place. It appears that it may be an evil place as well.

Notes

1. This paper grew out of discussions at the Society for Ethical and Legal Philosophy, and I am indebted to my fellow members for their help.

2. Straightforward considerations of national interest often tend in the same direction: the inadvisability of using nuclear weapons seems to be overdetermined in this way.

3. These reasons, moreover, have special importance in that they are available even to one who denies the appropriateness of utilitarian considerations in international matters. He may acknowledge limitations on what may be done to the soldiers and civilians of other countries in pursuit of his nation's military objectives, while denying that one country should in general consider the interests of nationals of other countries in determining its policies.

4. Privately printed. See also her essay "War and Murder," in *Nuclear Weapons and Christian Conscience,* ed. Walter Stein (London, 1963). The present paper is much indebted to these two essays throughout. These and related subjects are extensively treated by Paul Ramsey in *The Just War* (New York, 1968). Among recent writings that bear on the moral problem are Jonathan Bennett, "Whatever the Consequences," *Analysis* 26, no. 3 (1966):83-102; and Philippa Foot, "The Problem of Abortion and the Doctrine of the Double Effect," *The Oxford Review* 5 (1967):5-15. Miss Anscombe's replies are "A Note on Mr. Bennett," *Analysis* 26, no. 3 (1966):208, and "Who is Wronged?" *The Oxford Review* 5 (1967):16-17.

5. This counterargument was suggested by Rogers Albritton.

6. Someone might of course acknowledge the *moral relevance* of the distinction between deliberate and nondeliberate killing, without being an absolutist. That is, he might believe simply that it was *worse* to bring about a death deliberately than as a secondary effect. But that would be merely a special assignment of value, and not an absolute prohibition.

7. Why, on the other hand, does it seem appropriate, rather than irrelevant, to punch someone in the mouth if he insults you? The answer is that in our culture it is an insult to punch someone in the mouth, and not just an injury. This reveals, by the way, a perfectly unobjectionable sense in which convention may play a part in determining exactly what falls under an absolutist restriction and what does not. I

am indebted to Robert Fogelin for this point.

8. Finally, I should mention a different possibility, suggested by Robert Nozick: that there is a strong general presumption against benefiting from the calamity of another, whether or not it has been deliberately inflicted for that or any other reason. This broader principle may well lend its force to the absolutist position.

9. It has been remarked that, according to my view, shooting at someone establishes an I-thou relationship.

10. What I say on this subject derives from Anscombe.

11. Beyond this I feel uncertain. Ordinary bullets, after all, can cause death, and nothing is more permanent than that. I am not at all sure why we are justified in trying to kill those who are trying to kill us (rather than merely in trying to stop them with force which may also result in their deaths). It is often argued that incapacitating gases are a relatively humane weapon (when not used, as in Vietnam, merely to make people easier to shoot). Perhaps the legitimacy of restrictions against them must depend on the dangers of escalation, and the great utility of maintaining *any* conventional category of restriction so long as nations are willing to adhere to it.

Let me make clear that I do not regard my argument as a defense of the moral immutability of the Hague and Geneva conventions. Rather, I believe that they rest partly on a moral foundation, and that modifications of them should also be assessed on moral grounds.

But even this connection with the actual laws of war is not essential to my claims about what is permissible and what is not. Since completing this paper I have read an essay by Richard Wasserstrom entitled "The Laws of War" (forthcoming in *The Monist*), which argues that the existing laws and conventions do not even attempt to embody a decent moral position: that their provisions have been determined by other interests, that they are in fact immoral.

12. It is possible to draw a more radical conclusion, which I shall not pursue here. Perhaps the technology and organization of modern war are such as to make it impossible to wage as an acceptable form of interpersonal or even international hostility. Perhaps it is too impersonal and large-scale for that. If so, then absolutism would in practice imply pacifism, given the present state of things. On the other hand, I am skeptical about the unstated assumption that a technology dictates its own use.

13. This was first pointed out to me by Christopher Boorse.

2

Anarchism and World Order

Richard A. Falk

Mere anarchy is loosed upon the world.
> —W. B. Yeats, "The Second Coming"

We do not fear anarchy, we invoke it.
> —Mikhail Bakunin,
> *The Program of the International Brotherhood*

An Introductory Perspective

Anarchism has largely directed its thought and actions against the sovereign state, seeking primarily to bring about the radical reconstruction of economic, political, and social life within individual domestic arenas. In addition, however, like any radical movement that challenges fundamental organizing norms and structures, anarchism has wider implications. These wider implications extend the critique of the state as domestic institutional nexus to a critique of statism or the state system as a global framework for political organization. Nevertheless, surprisingly little attention has been given to anarchism as a perspective relevant to global reform.[1] This neglect is somewhat surprising because anarchists generally appreciate the extent to which their goals can be realized only by the transformation of the world scene as a whole.

This lack of attention can, however, be explained by several factors. First, it reflects the previously noted domestic focus of anarchism—indeed, of all modern revolutionary theory. Second, it probably reflects the popular association of anarchy with disorder, while by almost everyone's definition disorder is precisely the opposite of the primary desideratum of global reform, namely, a quantum leap in the capacities to maintain order. Even

Reprinted from *ANARCHISM*, edited by J. Roland Pennock and John W. Chapman, © 1978 by New York University, by permission of New York University Press.

an antistatist, progressive thinker such as Doris Lessing seems to associate anarchist potentialities of our present civilization, and the declining capacities of governments to sustain elementary order and reliability even within national boundaries, with still further disintegration.[2] This identification of anarchism with disarray is juxtaposed against a generally accepted conviction that global reform will entail the globalization of governmental structures rather than the destructuring of national governments. The League of Nations and the United Nations are generally viewed as positive experiments to the extent that they have constituted tentative steps toward world government, as failures because they have represented too little by way of bureaucratic centralism.[3] Alternatively, an anarchist might hold that the League and the United Nations present suitable pretexts for partially dismantling bureaucratic structures at the state level *without* building up a superstate to compensate at the global level. In other words, it is the weakness of global institutions as bureaucratic presence that would appeal to anarchists. (Of course, in actuality, these global institutions, in both their mode of creation and their mode of operations, have proven to be elitist in the extreme and therefore antithetical to the anarchist ethos.)[4]

Third, there is a lingering tendency, given plausibility by the pervasiveness of nongovernmental terror in contemporary life, to dismiss anarchism on moral grounds as a more or less explicit avowal of terrorism, and on political grounds as an absurdly romantic gesture of nihilistic sentiment whose only consequence is to strengthen the case for governmental repression. The belief that anarchists glorify terror has historical roots in the nineteenth century, especially in Russia, and was given widespread currency in Dostoevski's great novel *The Devils*, which recreated in fictional form the actual nihilism of Nechayev, an extremist follower of Bakunin.

Jean-Paul Sartre has for this reason, until very recently, avoided acknowledging his own anarchist affinity: "Then, by way of philosophy, I discovered the anarchist being in me. But when I discovered it I did not call it that, because today's anarchy no longer has anything to do with the anarchy of 1890."[5]

True, one form of individual resistance to state power is the use of random violence by self-styled anarchist revolutionaries for the avowed purpose of exposing the vulnerability of individuals or of the community as a whole. It is no accident when antibureaucratic radicals identify with anarchism as a means of registering their dissent from the prevailing forms of state socialism; typical in this regard was the unfurling of black flags from Sorbonne buildings liberated during the student uprisings of May 1968.[6] However, terrorism bears no inherent relationship to anarchist thinking; many pacifists, including Tolstoy, Gandhi, and Paul Goodman, have been associated with anarchist traditions of thought.[7]

Conversely, the mere adoption of terrorist tactics does not necessarily imply a disavowal of statist goals, as witness the manifold examples of terrorism by contemporary "liberation groups." The Palestine Liberation Organization, consumed by statist objectives, has embraced indiscriminate terror for apparently expediential reasons: to get a hearing for its grievances and to give its claims a potency allegedly unattainable through less extreme forms of persuasion or even through conventional warfare. Terrorism is a desperate strategy of a powerless (or unimaginative) claimant, but it is not a necessary component of the anarchist perspective.[8]

In this essay I regard the anarchist position as characterized mainly by its opposition to bureaucratic centralism of all forms and by its advocacy of libertarian socialism. This attempt to delineate the anarchist position is less drastic than the dictionary definition of anarchism as entailing the absence of government. My understanding of anarchist thought, admittedly a personal interpretation, suggests that the basic anarchist impulse is toward something positive, namely, toward a minimalist governing structure in a setting that encourages the full realization of human potentialities for cooperation and happiness. As such, the quest is for humane government, with a corresponding rejection of large-scale impersonal institutions that accord priority to efficiency and rely upon force and intimidation rather than upon voluntary patterns of cooperation to sustain order. This quest puts the anarchist into a posture of opposition to the modern state, especially the most successful and powerful states, but it is only the most extreme examples of anarchist thought that devote their main energy to negation rather than to their affirmative case for radical reform on all levels of social, economic, and political organization.

On this basis, I believe that the anarchist tradition has something important to contribute to the emergent dialogue on the tactics and shape of global reform. This contribution must be predicated on a response to each of the three issues just considered. In effect, (1) an anarchist concept of global reforms needs to be fully worked out; (2) anarchist ideas on "security" and "organization" must be set forth; and (3) anarchist thinking on the relevance of violence must be clarified in relation to its practical and moral consequences. This chapter seeks to take tentative constructive steps in these directions, after first considering two additional preliminary issues:

- What kind of "a vision" do anarchists propose for the future?
- Why is anarchism an attractive antidote (or complement) to mainstream thinking on global reform?

In a perceptive essay on the full sweep of anarchist thought, Irving Louis Horowitz observed that "it scarcely requires any feats of mind to show that modern industrial life is incompatible with the anarchist demand for the liquidation of State authority. Anarchism can be no more than a posture. It cannot be a viable political position."[9] The validity of such an assertion depends on what is meant by "modern industrial life" and by "the anarchist demand for the liquidation of State authority." For example, representatives from many and diverse disciplines now contend, independent of any concern with statist organization, that the modern industrial ethos as we have known it is not sustainable on ecological grounds.[10] The revival of interest in "benign" or "gentle" technology, and of lifestyles outside the money economy, provides further evidence that the momentum of industrial civilization may possibly be reversible.[11]

Indeed, one could reverse Horowitz's assertion and contend that any political perspective that does not propose doing away with modern industrial life is doomed to failure and futility, and is an exercise in bad faith. Furthermore, the anarchist demand is not directed at eliminating all forms of authority in human existence, but at their destructive embodiment in exploitative institutions associated with the modern bureaucratic state. Contrary to general impressions, nothing in anarchist thought precludes a minimum institutional presence at all levels of social organization, provided only that this presence emanates from *populist* rather than *elitist* impulses, and that its structure is deliberately designed fully to protect the liberty of all participants, starting with and centering on the individual. Indeed Bakunin, with his admiration of American federalism of the nineteenth century[12] and his tentative advocacy of a universal confederation of peoples, lent anarchist support to the globalist approach to world order challenges. As Bakunin put it in 1866: "It is absolutely necessary for any country wishing to join the free federations of peoples to replace its centralized, bureaucratic, and military organizations by a federalist organization based on the absolute liberty and autonomy of regions, provinces, communes, associations, and individuals."[13] In essence, the anarchist proposes dismantling the bureaucratic state and reconstituting a world society from the bottom up (what Bakunin calls a "universal world federation" and "directed from the bottom up, from the circumference to the center"), with constant accountability to the bottom. Paul Goodman has expressed in a modern idiom this anarchist view of creative reordering: "My own bias is to decentralize and localize wherever it is feasible, because this makes for alternatives and more vivid and intimate life. . . . On this basis of weakening of the Powers, and of substitution of function for power, it would be possible also to organize the world community, as by the functional agencies of the United Nations, UNICEF, WHO, somewhat UNESCO; and to provide *ad hoc* cooperation like the Geo-physical Year, exploring space, or feeding the Chinese."[14] Furthermore, anarchist thinking has a notable antiterritorial bias which tends to deride national frontiers as artificial and dangerously inconsistent with the wholeness of its humanist affirmations. [15]

But reverting to Horowitz's characterization once again, doesn't such an anarchist approach to global reform lie far beyond the horizon of attainability? And hence, how can anarchism reasonably be regarded as a viable possibility that could materialize in our lifetimes? One could answer these questions in several ways. To quote Bakunin once more, as he is discounting the failures of the revolutionary uprisings of 1848 in Europe, "Must we . . . doubt the future itself, and the present strength of socialism? Christianity, which had set as its goal the creation of the kingdom of justice in heaven, needed several centuries to triumph in Europe. Is there any cause for surprise if socialism, which has set for itself a more difficult problem, that of creating the kingdom of justice on earth, has not triumphed in a few years?"[16] In this view, the anarchist position is no less coherent or relevant merely because its prospects of realization are not proximate. Bureaucratic socialists, those who seek to seize state power rather than to decompose it, contemptuously dismiss anarchist or libertarian socialists as utopians, or worse, as reactionaries.[17] But the anarchist response is more credible than the challenge here presented. The anarchist quite properly contends that merely to seize power is to default upon the humanist content of socialism and to create a new form of despotism. The real revolution cannot be rushed, but neither can it be dispensed with. I think, in this regard, that Herbert Read is wrong when he says of anarchism that "if the conception of society which it thus arrives at seems utopian and even chimerical, it does not matter, for what is established by right reasoning cannot be surrendered by expediency."[18] I think it does matter, and anarchists generally act as if it matters, both by their arguments about the cooperative capacities of human society (which, incidentally, Read strongly endorses) and by their belief in the revolutionary possibility lying dormant within mass consciousness. Of course, Read correctly stresses the principled character of anarchist thinking, its unwillingness to corrupt its values merely for the sake of power. This high-mindedness distinguishes anarchism from bureaucratic socialism in theory and vindicates its ethical purism in practice. The contrast seems particularly great in view of the consistent betrayal of socialist ideals at each new opportunity — not only in the Soviet Union but even in China and Cuba.[19] In this regard, the anarchist refuses both the facile radicalism of the conventional Marxist (who would merely replace one form of exploitation and repression with another) and the facile gradualism of the liberal (who would acquiesce in the structure of exploitation and repression, provided its cruelest manifestations could be gradually diminished).

A further anarchist response to the counsel of patience claims that the revolutionary possibility is hidden from view in the evolving currents of popular consciousness. According to Bakunin, revolutions "make themselves; they are produced by the force of circumstance, the movement of facts and events. They receive a long preparation of the masses, then they burst forth, often seemingly triggered by trivial causes."[20] Thus, the revolutionary moment may be closer than we think; it may be building toward eruption; and it may enter the field of history with unexpected haste and fury. The Paris Commune of 1871 is a favorite illustration of this possibility.[21] A time of crisis enhances revolutionary prospects; it creates receptivity to new ideas, however radical; it exposes existing injustice; and it generates a willingness to take risks. Naturally, however, there is no available calculus for determining the most propitious moment for actually instituting an anarchist program of destructuring the state and replacing international statism with global confederation.

Finally, the anarchist is not obliged to wait for the days of triumph. Although his concept of the future is visionary and vital to his position, it is not detached in time from present possibilities for actualization.[22] As Howard Zinn writes, "The anarchist sees revolutionary change as something immediate, something we must do now, where we are, where we live, where we work. It means starting this moment to do away with authoritarian, cruel relationships—between men and women, between children and parents, between one kind of worker and another kind. Such revolutionary action cannot be crushed like an armed uprising."[23] Paul Goodman vividly makes the same point through his characterization of a well-known peace activist: "Best of all, in principle, is the policy that Dave Dellinger espouses and tries to live by, to live communally and without authority, to work usefully and feel friendly, and so positively to replace an area of power with peaceful functioning."[24] By conducting his life in this way, the anarchist can initiate a process of change that is virtually invulnerable to external pressures, criticisms, and threats. The anarchist posture is thus deepened through experience and engenders credibility for the seriousness of its claims about the future. Unlike the utopian who tends to dichotomize present and future, regarding one mode as suitable given present practicalities and another as desirable given future wishes, the anarchist integrates his present behavior with his future hopes. The anarchist correctly perceives that the future is the eventual culmination of the present and that liberty is an existential condition enabling degrees of immediate realization.

The anarchist thus joins immediate action with his program for drastic societal reform. Herbert Read expresses this dual commitment as follows: "Our practical activity may be a gradual approximation towards the ideal, or it may be a sudden revolutionary realization of that ideal, but it must never be a compromise."[25]

Of course, despite this attempt at refutation, there is still a measure of common sense in Horowitz's observation. Surely, anarchism may serve as no more than a posture, and its immediate impact may consist primarily in leavening the more deeply rooted political traditions of Marxism and liberalism. However, even in this ancillary capacity, anarchism can perform the highly positive function of providing a corrective for the bureaucratic and repressive tendencies of Marxist politics, and for the apologetics and rationalizations of liberal politics.[26] Therefore, I would argue that anarchist thought, correctly understood, is both a position *and* a posture.

Let us consider now our second preliminary question: Why is anarchism an attractive antidote (or complement) to mainstream thinking on global reform? Most proposals for global reform have uncritically affirmed the ordering contributions of the state to domestic life and have, in one or another form, sought to make those contributions available to the world as a whole. Indeed, the argument for global reform, at least since World War I, has assumed the strident tones of necessity. Since Hiroshima these claims of necessity have been pitched on an apocalyptic level and have been extended to embrace biosocial survival in light of the allegedly deepening ecological crisis—the crowding, poisoning, and straining of planetary facilities. The unexamined premise in world-order thinking has been that *only* governmental solutions can organize planetary life, that only existing governmental structures and their leaders can command the authority required for this essential undertaking, and that only argument and persuasion can release the political energy needed to overcome the inertia that sustains the state system in the face of the most unmistakable writing on the wall. A major variant to this line of reformist thinking is that persuasion must be supplemented by tragedy before enough political energy is released to achieve a world-order solution.

Generally, such advocacy of bureaucratic centralism is coupled with confidence in the moderating capacities of law and institutionalism. The ideal world order would still consist of a realm of states, but with the venom drawn by substituting "law" for "force." Conflict would remain, but war would disappear. Peaceful methods of resolving conflicts would be accepted since all states would be unanimously committed to upholding the federalist edifice.

This kind of mainstream "idealism" often coexists with "realism." Until the existing world system is reconstructed according to the principles of legalist architecture, one is thrown back into the state system with its logic of power and its reliance on force to achieve "security" and to "manage" change. The world-order idealist of tomorrow can easily justify being

Machiavellian today. Hence, the issue of "transition" emerges as critical, and it is a fascinating indictment of mainstream thinking that no sustained attention has been given to the central challenge of transition — namely, access to, and transformation of, state power.

The anarchist comes forward with a quite different set of ideas, easily adapted to the world-order debate: first of all, a skeptical regard for the state and an unwillingness to accept it as "a model" for achieving a just order on any level of social organization; second, a positive belief in the capacities of various other collectivities — communes, cities, provinces, regions, associations — to provide the creative impetus for reorganizing the human enterprise; third, a bias toward decentralization of wisdom, authority, and capability, coupled with an insistence upon the autonomy of smaller units and the absolute status of individual liberty; fourth, a structural critique of the present organization of power, wealth, and prestige coupled with a revolutionary set of demands that existing leaders of society would never voluntarily meet; fifth, a processive view of the future, based on embodying the vision of a new order in immediate personal and political activities; sixth, a substitution of "justice" for "order" as the primary test of the adequacy of a given arrangement of power in world society; seventh, a refusal to blueprint the future in a manner that precludes creativity within the eventual setting that will give rise to the revolutionary possibility itself.[27]

These seven elements of anarchist thinking can be positively adapted to movement for global reform. What is most impressive about anarchist thought, taken from a world-order perspective, is its blending of critique, vision, and transition strategy. In the words of George Woodstock, a close student of anarchism: "Historically, anarchism is a doctrine which poses a criticism of existing society; a view of a desirable future society; and a means of passing from one to the other."[28] Often, proposals for global reform have been sterile because they lacked one or more of these three essential elements (most typically, the transition strategy), or else presented one of them in unacceptable form (e.g., the vision as a blueprint). Despite this general attractiveness of anarchism as a world order perspective, the anarchist position also poses several difficulties that must be considered in the course of evaluating its possible relevance to a beneficial movement of global reform.[29]

Three Hard Questions for Anarchists

1. *Are not the preconditions for anarchist success insurmountable?* The great anarchist success stories have been episodic, short-lived (e.g., the Paris Commune of 1871, the anarchist collectives in parts of Spain during the

1930s, the May uprising in Paris in 1968). Nowhere have anarchists enjoyed a period of sustained success. Generally, anarchist success has generated an overpowering reaction of repression, as when the mercenary soldiery of Versailles crushed and massacred the Paris Communards in May 1871 only weeks after their extraordinary triumph. Anarchists view such failures as inevitable "first attempts"; Kropotkin calls "the Commune of Paris" the "child of a period of transition . . . doomed to perish," but "the forerunner of social revolution."[30] Murray Bookchin and Daniel Guérin make a similar assessment of the Paris uprising of 1968, regarding its occurrence as proof of the anarchist critique, its collapse as evidence that "the molecular movement below that prepares the condition for revolution" had not yet carried far enough.[31]

On a deeper level, anarchists understand that the prerequisite for anarchist success *anywhere* is its success *everywhere*. It is this vital precondition that is at once so convincing and so formidable as to call into question whether the anarchist position can in fact be taken seriously as a progressive alternative to state socialism.

Bakunin expressed the anarchist demand and rationale with clarity: "A federalist in the internal affairs of the country, he desires an international confederation, first of all in the spirit of justice, and second because he is convinced that the economic and social revolution, transcending all the artificial and pernicious barriers between states, can only be brought about, in part at least, by the solidarity in action, if not of all, then at least of the majority of nations constituting the civilized world today, so that sooner or later all nations must join together."[32] Or, as Daniel Guérin expressed it: "An isolated national revolution cannot succeed. The social revolution inevitably becomes a world revolution."[33]

In essence, not only is it difficult for anarchists to attain power, but once they manage to do so their "organic institutions" seem incapable of holding it. Their movements will be liquidated ruthlessly by statists of "the left" or "the right."[34] Given such vulnerability, it may even be a betrayal of one's followers to expose them to slaughter by mounting a challenge against the entrenched forces of statism in the absence of either the will or the capabilities to protect the challengers.[35]

There is a report of a fascinating conversation between Lenin and Kropotkin in May 1919 in which Lenin mounts such an argument in two ways. First, he makes his familiar point that "you can't make a revolution wearing white gloves. We know perfectly well that we have made and will make a great many mistakes. . . . But it is impossible not to make mistakes during a revolution. Not to make them means to renounce life entirely and do nothing at all. But we have preferred to make errors and thus to act. . . . We want to act and we will, despite all the mistakes, and will bring our socialist revolution to the final and inevitably victorious end."[36] Lenin here in effect acknowledges the errors that flow from using state power to secure the revolutionary victory from external and internal enemies, and he rebuffs the anarchist view that state power can be dissolved. Lenin's second rebuff of the anarchist position is his condescending view of its revolutionary power: "Do you really think that the capitalist world will submit to the path of the cooperative movement? . . . You will pardon me, but this is all nonsense! We need direct action of the masses, revolutionary action of the masses, that activity which seizes the capitalist world by the throat and brings it down."[37] Of anarchist concepts of "social revolution," Lenin says "these are children's playthings, idle chatter, having no realist soil underneath, no force, no means, and almost nothing approaching our socialist goals. . . . We don't need the struggle and violent acts of separate persons. It is high time that the anarchists understood this and stopped scattering their revolutionary energy on utterly useless affairs."[38] In sum, Lenin is arguing that the ends of anarchists must be pursued by mass violent revolution and secured through state power. The anarchist response is, of course, that the choice of such means perverts and dooms the ends. The antagonism of anarchists toward the Bolshevik Revolution has been vindicated many times over.[39] On the level of their discussion, it seems that both Lenin and Kropotkin are correct[40] — Lenin in saying that there is no other way to succeed, the anarchists by contending that such success is as bad as, if not worse than, defeat.

But, in my view, the strongest case for the feasibility of the anarchist position still remains to be argued. It is implicit, perhaps, in Kropotkin's own work on the origins of the modern state and on its feudal antecedents in the European cities of the eleventh and twelfth centuries.[41] Kropotkin's argument rests on the historical claim that a vital society of communes and free cities created by brotherhoods, guilds, and individual initiative existed earlier: "It is shown by an immense documentation from many sources, that never, either before or since, has mankind known a period of relative well-being for all as in the cities of the Middle Ages. The poverty, insecurity, and physical exploitation of labor that exist in our times were then unknown."[42] Drawing on non-Western experience as well, Kropotkin argues in effect that societal well-being and security based on anarchist conceptions of organic institutions (of a cooperative character) were immensely successful over a wide geographical and cultural expanse until crushed by the emergent states of the fifteenth and sixteenth centuries. Thus, there is a kind of prima facie case for plausibility of the anarchist model, although in a prestatal context.

But evidence of the anarchist potential for "success" does not end with medieval Europe. The direction of contemporary China, especially its antiparty, populist phase that culminated in the Cultural Revolution, contains strong anarchist elements.[43] Indeed, it was precisely on these grounds of repudiating "organization" and "bureaucracy" as a basis for communist discipline that China made itself so offensive to communist ideologues in the Kremlin.[44] China is, of course, a mixed case. In its foreign policy it places great stress on statist prerogatives. Nevertheless, in its domestic patterns the Chinese example lends some credibility to Bakunin's and Kropotkin's claim that there are nonbureaucratic roads to socialism, and gives the anarchist orientation renewed plausibility as a serious political alternative.[45]

Such plausibility can, it seems to me, be extrapolated in a poststatal context. Here, my argument, sustained by sources as dissimilar as Saul Mendlovitz and Henry Kissinger, is that we are undergoing a profound historical transformation that is destroying the organizational matrix of a global system based on territorial states.[46] That is, we are entering a poststatal period, although its character remains highly conjectural. Whatever the outcome, however, the anarchist stress on nonterritorial associations and communal consciousness seems highly relevant because of its basic compatibility with the inevitable shift in the relation of forces.

In sum, the anarchist case for radical reform (i.e., for social revolution) was *chimerical within* the confines of the state system. However, the state system is now being superseded. In this context, one set of plausible possibilities is the globalization of societal life in a way that allows cooperative organizational forms to flourish. That is, the anarchist vision (as epitomized in Bakunin's writings) of a fusion between a universal confederation and organic societal forms of a communal character lies at the very center of the *only* hopeful prospect for the future of world order.[47] Needless to say, such a prospect has slim chances for success, but at least the possibility is no longer chimerical, given the change of objective circumstances. The state system is not an implacable foe, for many economic, political, technological, and sociological forces are everywhere undermining its bases of potency, if unevenly and at an uncertain rate. Therefore, although the political precondition of scale imposed by anarchism still remains formidable, it may yet prove historically surmountable. It may be surmountable because the preparatory processes going on throughout the world during this historical period are creating more favorable global conditions for the anarchist cause than have hitherto existed for several centuries. This assessment arises from several distinct developments. Perhaps the most significant is the growing disenchantment with the values, goals, and methods of industrial society. This sense of disenchantment is coming to be shared by increasing numbers of citizens, particularly in the developed nations of the West, and is finding various forms of expression that reflect revised notions of necessity based on "limits to growth," notions of well-being based on intermediate technology and small-scale institutions, and notions of personal transcendence based on a new spiritual energy that repudiates both conventional religion and secular humanism. In this setting, the quest for an appropriate politics converges rather dramatically with the central tenets of anarchist belief. This modern sensibility realizes, at last, that the state is simultaneously *too large* to satisfy human needs and *too small* to cope with the requirements of guidance for an increasingly interdependent planet. This realization is temporarily offset by a rising tide of statism in many other parts of the world, where political independence is a forbidden fruit only recently tasted, but where the fruit will be poisoned, as everywhere else, by a world of nuclear weapons, ecological decay, and mass economic privation. The main *problematique* of our age is whether an appropriate politics of global reform, combining a centralized form of functional guidance with decentralized economic, social, and political structures, can be shaped by voluntary action, or whether it must be formed in a crucible of tragedy and catastrophe. Attentiveness to the anarchist tradition can be one part of an effort to achieve an appropriate politics *this* side of catastrophe. Obviously, the objective conditions which require such a reassessment of political forms are not by themselves sufficient to effect a transformation. Indeed, the very relevance of these ideas may lead their powerful opponents to regard them as even more dangerous now than in the past. Prudence and patience are essential in these circumstances. The crisis of the state system may yet require several decades to develop to the point where eruptions of spontaneous anarchist energies would not unleash a variety of devastating backlashes.

2. *Given the urgency of global reform, isn't the anarchist prospect too remote in time?* Even accepting the optimistic assessment of the preceding section, namely, that the hour of anarchism may coincide with the collapse of statism, restructuring of the world system would still appear to be developed for an unnecessarily and dangerously long period of several decades or more. Just as the emergence of the state system was a matter of centuries, so might the consolidation of a new system of political order require hundreds of years.[48] Two sets of questions call for judgment based on imponderables. First, how serious and pressing is the crisis? Is the fire close at hand, or still barely visible on a distant horizon? How can we know? Second, are any alternative means available through which the principal goals of global reform could be attained more reliably and rapidly than through anarchism? Do we have any responsible basis for selecting or rejecting these alternatives? In part, we are forced here to confront the most fundamental issues of politics, knowledge, and action. In the abstract, we do not know enough to choose or to act. Of course this same limitation bears on every school of political

thought, including those that defend the status quo or incline toward gradualism. But it has even greater bearing on a political position that proposes radical tactics and goals, especially if large-scale violence is likely to ensue. On the other hand, this line of reasoning may be deceptive. In a moment of crisis, to do nothing may be the most risky of all postures toward the future. It is generally better to jump from a sinking ship than it is to stay on board, even if one knows nothing about the prospects of rescue from the waters below. The collective situation of human society cannot be cast in such deceptive simplicity. The veil of ignorance is thick indeed when it comes to assessing policy alternatives for the future of world society.

But the argument from ignorance cuts the other way as well. We have no real way to assess the degrees of progress along the transition path. Perhaps the collapse of statism is closer than we think. As Paul Goodman wrote:

> It will be said that there is no time. Yes, probably. But let me cite a remark of Tocqueville. In his last work, *L'Ancien Régime,* he notes "with terror," as he says, how throughout the eighteenth century writer after writer and expert after expert pointed out that this and that detail of the Old Regime was doomed and must soon collapse; and yet *there was not a single man who foretold that there would be a mighty revolution.*[49]

In the face of such uncertainty, compounded by the many evidences of pressure on the state system, it makes political as well as moral sense to pursue a *principled set of conclusions* even if their realization cannot be immediately foreseen. In one sense Herbert Read is correct in saying that "the task of the anarchist philosopher is not to prove the imminence of a Golden Age, but to justify the value of believing in its possibility."[50]

Such a value depends on some degree of plausibility, but also on whether or not there are any preferable alternatives. Given the established bankruptcy of statist solutions on the Right and Left, given the vulnerability of the state system as a whole to catastrophic and, quite possibly, irreversible damage, and given the insufficiency of gradualist strategies of amelioration, the case for some variant of radical anarchism seems strong despite the inability of the anarchist to provide skeptics with a credible timetable.

In essence, the issue of urgency reinforces the anarchist case. The primary world order need is to find an alternative to statism. Anarchism, despite its limited political success during the statist era, provides the most coherent, widespread, and persistent tradition of antistatist thought. It is also a tradition that has generally been inclined toward world-order values: peace, economic equity, civil liberties, ecological defense. As such, it represents the most normatively acceptable sequel to the state system. Other sequels include imperial consolidation; world state; regional federation; intergovernmental functionalism.[51]

To affirm the relevance of the anarchist tradition is not to accept the adequacy of its current formulations but only of its general orientation. Advocates of an anarchist approach need to formulate the globalist implications of anarchism in a manner responsive to the current world-order crisis. As far as I know, this has not yet been done. Indeed, anarchism suffers from the tendency of other traditions of philosophical speculation generated during the statist era, namely, to concentrate upon the national question and to assume that the global question will disappear when all nations have correctly resolved their own domestic problems. As I have suggested, anarchists are more dependent than other reformers on supportive transnational developments; but their analysis of international events is usually identical to that of Marxists, on the level of critique, and highly impressionistic when it comes to making specific proposals. Thus, the claims of anarchism are not weakened by the urgency of the world crisis, but the need for a more historically sensitive interpretation and for a globally oriented formulation of anarchist response is essential.

3. *Does the receptivity of anarchism to violence undermine the moral basis of its claim to provide an ideology for global reform?* I am not discussing here the anarchist as "bomb-thrower," but neither do I identify anarchism with pacifist ethics. As a philosophical position anarchism adopts an equivocal view of violence as an agent of change. Although anarchists tend to rely on spontaneous militancy of a nonviolent character — most typically, the general strike or other forms of unarmed struggle and resistance — there is no prevailing anarchist view on the role of violence.

I think Howard Zinn has sympathetically, but reliably, presented the anarchist position on violence in this assessment:

> Some anarchists — like other revolutionaries throughout history . . . have emphasized violent uprising. Some have advocated, and tried, assassination and terror. . . . What makes anarchists unique among revolutionaries, however, is that most of them see revolution as a cultural, ideological, creative process, in which violence would be as incidental as the outcries of mother and baby in childbirth. It might be unavoidable — given the natural resistance to change — but something to be kept at a minimum while more important things happen.[52]

The question is whether, given the technology of destruction and the ruthlessness of statist leadership, this view of violence is adequate. It can be attacked from either side, as underestimating the role of violence for any serious revolutionary position, or as too willing to accept the moral Trojan horse of political violence.

Mainstream Marxists and neo-Marxists generally contend that revolution depends upon mass-based armed struggle. A recent formulation is "the political statement of the Weather Underground" released under the title *Prairie Fire:*

> It's an illusion that imperialism will decay peacefully. Imperialism has meant constant war. Imperialists defend their control of the means of life with terrible force. There is no reason to believe they will become humane or relinquish power. . . . To not prepare the people for this struggle is to disarm them ideologically and physically and to perpetuate a cruel hoax.[53]

The cruel hoax is, of course, the illusion that revolution can occur without armed struggle, that a revolution can be made with white gloves. But as Kropotkin soon perceived, once the white gloves have been thrown away, it becomes all too easy to adopt terror and torture.[54] In my view, the abuse of state power by socialism has reversed the presumption that violence is a necessary concomitant of revolution. On the contrary, it now seems a cruel hoax to promise humane outcomes from any revolutionary process that embraces violence with anything other than the utmost reluctance. Any genuinely radical position that purports moral (as well as political) credibility must, above all else, reject a cult of violence and justify the use of specific forms of violence in the most careful and conditional manner.

But what, then, of the revolutionary triumphs of China, Vietnam, and Cuba? Was not violence essential to their success, and did they not achieve a net gain by prevailing on the level of armed struggle? I would answer that, first of all, in each of these domestic contexts there were no options other than extremist ones. Second, reliance on violent tactics may yet doom these revolutionary societies to Stalinist or other repressive patterns of governance. Third, the struggle for global reform should not be confused with the struggle for reform within an individual nation, although the two undertakings are closely related.

In other words, it is not enough to acknowledge that the imperialists are also violent, nor even that anarchists are prepared to accept violence only reluctantly and as incidental to their purposes. Something more considered, more explicit, is needed, even though specific choices cannot always be anticipated or determined in the abstract.

At the same time, an unequivocal renunciation of violence is probably "a cruel hoax," given the realities of power. There may be no way, in particular situations, to remain aloof from armed struggle without acquiescing, oneself, to violence of at least equal proportions.

If anarchism is to qualify as a morally suitable ideology for global reform, it requires a considered analysis of the role of violence, with emphasis on:

- Necessity of recourse, as an instrument of last resort (the futility of nonviolent militancy having already been demonstrated beyond reasonable doubt);
- Discrimination in application (with no intentional subjection of innocent people to foreseeable risks of harm);
- Limitation of the form and degree of application (absolute prohibition on torture and cruelty).

Such a middle position is no guarantee against revolutionary excess, but this doctrinal stance may at least exert some influence when it comes to choosing tactics, strategies, and policies. Also, it provides a defense against both Leninist and pacifist critiques. Finally, it acknowledges what has been so agonizingly confirmed in recent decades, namely, that revolutionaries must protect their own programs from their own propensities to embrace "evil."

Violence in the context of global reform is even more problematic. If national struggles are waged successfuly in critical countries, then violence will not be necessary on a global level. On the other hand, if such struggles end inconclusively or are defeated, then no degree of global violence will help. Given both the preponderance of military power possessed by state institutions and the objectives of global reform, it is possible to renounce violence for the exclusive purpose of reform but to retain militant nonviolence as a tactic. Indeed, in the years ahead it will be vital for the forces of global reform to confront statist institutions, in order that the latter be forced to expose their destructive patterns of behavior to a wider public.

Some Conclusions

Several broad lines of conclusion emerge from the preceding discussion:

1. There are no serious obstacles to the adoption of an anarchist perspective toward global reform; there are, to be sure, unacceptable variants of the anarchist position, but they do not invalidate the main lines of anarchist thought as represented by Proudhon, Bakunin, and Kropotkin, and more recently exemplified by Guérin, Herbert Read, and Paul Goodman.

2. Anarchism impressively links its goals for revolutionary change within national societies with a vision of a transformed global society; the linkage is integral and progressive in terms of world order values commonly affirmed; as a consequence, anarchism deals with entrenched power and avoids the political sterility associated with legalistic and moralistic

blueprints of "a new world order," as well as the static images of the future characteristic of utopography.

3. Anarchist thought is alive to the twin dangers of socialism and capitalism if pursued within the structure of statism; its espousal of populist strategies of change gains some historical credibility from its affinity with Mao Tse-tung's efforts to avoid the decay of revolutionary momentum in contemporary China.[55]

4. Anarchist thought on organic institutions of cooperation is creatively freed from either territorial or statist constraints and draws inspiration from both prestatist (Kropotkin) and poststatist possibilities of moving dialectically toward decentralizing bureaucratic power while centralizing human function (Goodman); in this regard, images of global functionalism and political confederation of nations merge with the deconcentration of power and role of national governments; the state is understood to be both inhumanly large in its bureaucratic dimension, and inhumanly small in its territorial and exclusionary dimensions; this dualism implicit in anarchism is excellently adapted to the purposes of global reform.

5. Anarchist thought, although often perceived as oscillating between extremes of terrorism and pacifism, is capable of evolving from within its framework of values an intermediate interpretation of violence. Such an interpretation would bias action in the direction of militant nonviolence, without depending on either the "white gloves" of utopians or the torture chambers of state socialists and cultist advocates of violence.

6. As yet, there is no comprehensive and satisfactory formulation of an anarchist position on global reform, only fragments here and there; a well-integrated statement could help crystallize enthusiasm for global reform of a drastic, yet constructive kind in many parts of the world where the internal strains of an obsolescent and moribund statism are being rapidly translated into repression, militarism, imperialism, and interventionary diplomacy; for weak states, even genuine national autonomy requires a radical program of global reform.

For those who view our era as one of transition between the state system and some globalist sequel, the anarchist perspective becomes increasingly relevant and attractive. Of course, it remains to be tested as an ideology for hope and action, as well as a basis for social, economic, and political reconstruction. Maoism, as embodied in the China of the 1960s and 1970s, is a peculiar mixture of statism and populism that should be generally, although not fully, encouraging. As Franz Shurmann notes: "The very word 'Maoism' came to mean a kind of anarchist, ultraleft troublemaking-for-troublemaking's sake. And when the New Left began to clash with older communist parties, as in France, China was invoked as a new Marxist Rome sanctioning this path to revolution."[56]

Notes

1. For one notable exception see Thomas G. Weiss, "The Tradition of Philosophic Anarchism and Future Directions in World Policy" (mimeographed); I have treated the anarchist briefly and analytically in *A Study of Future Worlds* (New York: Free Press, 1975), pp. 214-19.

2. "We believed we were living in a peculiarly anarchist community." Doris Lessing, *Memoirs of a Survivor* (New York: Knopf, 1975), p. 81.

3. See depiction of Franklin Roosevelt's vision of a new world order based on the primacy of the United Nations in Franz Schurmann, *The Logic of World Power* (New York: Pantheon, 1974), pp. 13-17, esp. pp. 67-76.

4. Sir Herbert Read expresses the anarchist attitude toward order and efficiency in social relations as follows: "Anarchism implies a universal decentralization of authority, and a universal simplification of life. Inhuman entities like the modern city will disappear. But anarchism does not necessarily imply a reversion to handicraft and outdoor sanitation. There is no contradiction between anarchism and air transport, anarchism and the divison of labour, anarchism and industrial efficiency." Sir Herbert Read, *Anarchy and Order* (Boston: Beacon, 1971), p. 134. In other words, anarchist images involve reconstituting order in the world rather than eliminating it.

5. "Sartre at Seventy: An Interview," *New York Review of Books,* August 7, 1975, pp. 10-17, at p. 14. Because anarchists are viewed as extremists there is a temptation to avoid the label. Consider, for instance, this passage by E. M. Cioran: "From the moment your actions and your thoughts serve a form of real or imagined city you are its idolators and its captives. The timidest employee and the wildest anarchist, if they take a different interest here, live as its function: they are both citizens internally though one prefers his slippers and the other his bomb." *A Short History of Decay* (New York: Viking, 1975), pp. 75-76.

6. See interpretation by French anarchist Daniel Guérin in *Anarchism: From Theory to Practice* (New York: Monthly Review Press, 1970), pp. 155-59.

7. For consideration of pacifist ethos in relation to an anarchist orientation see Karl Shapiro, "On the Revival of Anarchism," in Irving Louis Horowitz, ed., *The Anarchists* (New York: Dell, 1964), pp. 572-81; also Howard Zinn's introductory essay in Read, *Anarchy and Order*, pp. ix-xxii.

8. The PLO's adoption of terror as a tactic can also be condemned as a consequence of its failure to initiate a mass movement of nonviolent struggle. Such a movement would not necessarily succeed, but its failure is far from assured.

9. Introduction to Horowitz, *The Anarchists*, pp. 15-64, at p. 26.

10. E.g., Barry Commoner, *The Closing Circle* (New York: Knopf, 1971); Edward Goldsmith and others, *Blueprint for Survival* (Boston: Houghton Mifflin, 1972); Donella Meadows and others, *The Limits to Growth* (Washington, D.C.: Potomac Associates, 1972); R. A. Falk, *This Endangered Planet: Prospects and Proposals for Human Survival* (New York: Random House), 1971.

11. Among those who have discerned and charted this new direction of human energy, perhaps Theodore Roszak is most notable. See *The Making of a Counter Culture*

(New York: Anchor, 1969); *Where the Wasteland Ends* (New York: Anchor, 1973).

12. Sam Dolgoff, ed., *Bakunin on Anarchy* (New York: Knopf, 1972), p. 107; Bakunin characterized the American system as "the finest political organization that ever existed in history." [Hereafter cited as *Bakunin.*]

13. *Bakunin*, p. 98; see also p. 152.

14. Paul Goodman, "The Ambiguities of Pacifist Politics," in Leonard I. Krimerman and Lewis Perry, eds., *Patterns of Anarchy* (New York: Anchor, 1966), pp. 125-36, at p. 127.

15. E.g., Bakunin's conceptions are based on federations of many different, overlapping units, including "regions, provinces, communes, associations, and individuals," p. 98.

16. *Bakunin*, pp. 121-22.

17. On dismissal see George Plekanov, "Anarchist Tactics: A Pageant of Futility, Obstruction, and Decadence?" in Krimerman and Perry, *Patterns of Anarchy*, pp. 495-99; for an anarchist response to these kinds of allegations see Guérin, *Anarchism*, pp. 41-69; Read, *Anarchy and Order*, pp. 22-23, usefully distinguishes between positive and negative roles for utopian projections of the future.

18. Read, *Anarchy and Order*, p. 129.

19. In general see Nadezhda Mandelstam, *Hope Against Hope* (New York: Atheneum, 1970); also on repression at Kronstadt by Soviet government see Guérin, *Anarchism*, pp. 102-05; Alexander Berkman, "Kronstadt: The Final Act in Russian Anarchism," in Horowitz, *The Anarchists*, pp. 495-506.

20. *Bakunin*, p. 155.

21. See Kropotkin's essay "The Commune of Paris," in Martin A. Miller, ed., *Selected Writings on Anarchism and Revolution by P. A. Kropotkin* (Cambridge, Mass.: MIT Press, 1970), pp. 119-32 [hereafter cited as *Kropotkin*]. For a comparable anarchist appreciation of the spontaneous character of the Paris risings of 1968 and their relationships to the experience of the Paris Commune a century earlier see Murray Bookchin, *Post-Scarcity Anarchism* (Berkeley, Calif.: Ramparts, 1971), pp. 249-70.

22. See Kropotkin's essay "Must We Occupy Ourselves with an Examination of the Ideal of a Future System?" in *Kropotkin*, pp. 47-116.

23. Howard Zinn, Introduction to Read, *Anarchy and Order*, p. xviii.

24. Goodman, "Ambiguities of Pacifist Politics," at p. 136.

25. Read, *Anarchy and Order*, p. 129.

26. Sartre ascribed a similar role to existentialism in relation to Marxism. Sartre, *Search for a Method*, tr. Hazel E. Barnes (New York: Vintage, 1968), pp. 3-34.

27. See Bookchin's discussion of spontaneous features of the Paris 1968 events, in Bookchin, *Post-Scarcity Anarchism*, pp. 250-52; Herbert Read, *Anarchy and Order*, p. 23, argues that blueprints of the future pervert the genuine utopian impulse to transcend present societal arrangements. Such blueprints are condemned as "an advance on the spontaneous sources of life itself. They presume to plan what can only germinate . . . such scientific utopias will certainly fail, for the sources of life when threatened are driven underground to emerge in some new wilderness."

28. George Woodstock, *Anarchism* (New York: World, 1962), p. 9.

29. By "beneficial" I mean a movement that realizes world-order values associated with peace, economic well-being, social and political justice, and ecological balance. For an elaboration of why these values have been preferred and of the interplay between them see Falk, *Future Worlds,* pp. 7-55.

30. *Kropotkin,* p. 127.

31. Bookchin, *Post-Scarcity Anarchism,* p. 258.

32. *Bakunin,* p. 118.

33. Guérin, *Anarchism,* p. 69.

34. See references in note 19; Woodstock, *Anarchism,* pp. 275-424.

35. Such allegations have been made with respect to Salvador Allende's efforts in the early 1970s to transform the societal base of Chile without dismantling the state apparatus with its strong links to the vested interests of the old order.

36. *Kropotkin,* p. 328.

37. *Kropotkin,* pp. 329-30.

38. *Kropotkin,* p. 330.

39. One of the earliest and most eloquent anarchist critics of the Soviet experience was Emma Goldmann. See her *My Disillusionment with Russia* (Garden City, N.Y.: Doubleday, 1923).

40. Kropotkin's position can be extrapolated from his general anarchist writings; he did not state the anarchist case in his conversations with Lenin.

41. See Kropotkin's excellent essay, "The State: Its Historic Role," in *Kropotkin,* pp. 211-64.

42. *Kropotkin,* p. 231.

43. See perceptive discussion in Schurmann, *Logic of World Power,* pp. 369-80.

44. Schurmann, *Logic of World Power,* p. 380.

45. For a skeptical interpretation of China's domestic experience see Donald Zagoria, "China by Daylight," *Dissent* (spring 1975), pp. 135-47.

46. For opposing interpretations on the durability of the state and the state system see Saul H. Mendlovitz, Introduction to Saul H. Mendlovitz, ed., *On the Creation of a Just World Order* (New York: Free Press, 1975), pp. vii-xvii; and Stanley Hoffmann, "Obstinate or Obsolete? The Fate of the Nation-State and the Case of Western Europe," *Daedalus* (summer 1966), pp. 862-915.

47. A general interpretation can be found in Robert Heilbroner, *An Inquiry into the Human Prospect* (New York: Norton, 1974); see also Falk, *Future Worlds,* pp. 417-37; Richard A. Falk, "A New Paradigm for International Legal Studies: Prospects and Proposals," *Yale Law Journal* 84 (1975):969-1021.

48. See Joseph R. Strayer, *On the Medieval Origins of the Modern State* (Princeton, N.J.: Princeton University Press, 1970).

49. Goodman, "Ambiguities of Pacifist Politics," p. 136; see also *Kropotkin,* pp. 121-24.

50. Read, *Anarchy and Order,* p. 14.

51. For consideration of world order option see Falk, *Future Worlds,* pp. 150-276; Falk, "A New Paradigm," pp. 999-1017.

52. Zinn, Introduction to Read, *Anarchy and Order,* p. xvii.

53. *Prairie Fire*, Political statement of the Weather Underground, 1974, p. 3.

54. See Kropotkin letter to Lenin, dated December 21, 1920, in *Kropotkin*, pp. 338-39.

55. See Schurmann, *Logic of World Power*, p. 369; generally, pp. 268-80.

56. Schurmann, *Logic of World Power*, p. 369.

3
Contrasting Approaches to Conflict

Margaret W. Fisher

Throughout recorded history, human responses to conflict have ranged widely from a zestful enjoyment of conflict situations as a test of personal strength and courage all the way to an anguished yearning to be free from the necessity for engaging in conflict. Culturally approved responses have at different times established modes for the conduct of conflict which molded whole societies. The significance of the selection of such a mode from the various possible approaches to conflict can be demonstrated by examining two which differ radically in their basic premises. These are the Gandhian approach through which satyagraha was evolved and a mode derived from a relatively new "science of efficient action" known as praxeology.

Gandhian satyagraha ("adherence to truth") asserts the relevance of moral values, defines ends in terms of engaging the adversary in a search for "truth," insists upon nonviolent means, and stresses the bonds of common humanity linking the opposing sides. A basic human capacity to both display and respond affirmatively to moral courage is assumed. Stemming from this assumption is the conviction that voluntary and unflinching acceptance of suffering—to the death, if need be—will ultimately arouse compassion in the most stony-hearted adversary, making reconciliation possible.

The praxeological approach, on the other hand, elevates efficiency above all other values, takes no account of any ethical, moral, or emotional aspects of conflict except insofar as they may affect efficiency, seeks either victory or the denial of victory to the opponent, restricts means only by criteria based upon expediency, and assumes a basic need to guard at all times against human depravity. So important is that branch of praxeological theory dealing with conflict that a special term, agonology

Reprinted by permission of the publisher and author from Joan V. Bondurant, ed., *Conflict: Violence and Nonviolence* (Chicago and New York: Aldine-Atherton Press, 1971), pp. 183-202.

("science of struggle"), has been proposed for it. That suggestion has been adopted here.

For the refinement of concepts as well as for the coinage of the terms satyagraha (from Sanskrit roots) and agonology (from Greek roots), we are heavily indebted to the seminal efforts of two men: Mohandas K. Gandhi (1869–1948), a deeply religious social reformer and political activist whose original profession was the law;[1] and Tadeusz Kotarbiński (1886–), a philosopher and logician whose academic career reflects a major interest in a scientific approach to the theory of knowledge.[2] Among the voluminous supplements to Gandhi's writings, an outstanding contribution has been made by Joan Bondurant.[3] Useful in conjunction with Kotarbiński's writings[4] is Norman Bailey's brief survey of the status of conflict theory, in the course of which he introduced the Polish philosopher to American social scientists.[5]

Kotarbiński's treatise on praxeology had its beginnings in an effort to raise the level of efficiency of Poland's factories. Broadening the scope of his inquiry in the hope of constructing a general theory of efficient action, Kotarbiński scanned a wide range of published materials (although he did not refer either to the Gandhian experience or to the Indian classic, the *Arthashastra,* which has reportedly been translated into Russian several times). Beginning with Polish folklore (which he found "unfortunate in its maxims justifying negligence, slovenliness, and laziness"), he went on to consult the works of moralists, writers of fables, literary figures, scientists, and thinkers from various fields from the Greek philosophers down to modern studies of business administration, game theory, and the like, with particular attention to the theory of events and the theory of complex wholes.

In all his reading Kotarbiński came upon no strictly praxeological literature, although he did find praxeological "motifs" of importance in sources as diverse as Aristotle, La Fontaine, Defoe's *Robinson Crusoe,* Karl Marx, and Talcott Parsons, to name but a few of the writers to whom he has accorded special mention. The one work he found that dealt with a general theory of conflict was a small book on chess by Dr. Emanuel Lasker, the German mathematician who once held the world chess championship for nearly three decades.[6]

From these researches Kotarbiński emerged with several sobering reflections. He concluded that all observations concerning the effectiveness of purposive action had already been made, leaving to the theorist only systematization and quantitative precision. He was "embarassed" that no distinct discipline had yet developed for formulating a grammar of action.[7] He confessed that he himself was not entirely free from doubt that general praxeological theory "had no content over and above vague generalities," and conceded that there might be some truth in the criticism that "the more general a given praxeological maxim the more trivial the idea it contains."[8] He appeared ready to accept praxeology as a codifier of truisms concerning practical behavior and to be satisfied if his own work contributed to the "registering and ordering of existing concepts."[9]

The two contrasting modes for dealing with conflict, agonology and satyagraha, evolved in entirely different ways. Kotarbiński's treatise on praxeology was based largely on the examination and analysis by a senior scholar — he was nearly seventy when it was published — of the practical wisdom of mankind available to him in libraries. Interestingly enough, one of the points upon which he laid emphasis was the importance of the "compulsory situation" as a prerequisite to progress. In a very real sense, satyagraha can be looked upon as the outgrowth of a "compulsory situation" in which Gandhi, as a young man in his early twenties, found himself. In the event, he proved a striking example of its creative potential.

The details of this compulsory situation are readily to be found in Gandhi's own autobiographical writings. For our present purposes, a few points are all that need to be made. First, the young Gandhi, as a London-trained barrister, arrived in South Africa totally unprepared for the racism that subjected him to crude attacks upon his self-esteem and violent assaults upon his person. His first impulse was to leave the country immediately, but he found the courage to reject this emotional response and to stay on.

The year he so unwillingly remained in South Africa proved to be a major turning point in his career. His activities, demonstrably very different from what they would have been had he stayed in India, set the pattern for much that was to follow. During this year Gandhi came to realize that his talents as a lawyer lay in his ability to persuade adversaries to compose their differences out of court rather than in the usual adversary proceedings.

This was also the year that Gandhi, who by his own account had never before engaged in reading anything not connected with his schoolwork or professional training, had the leisure to indulge in reading. Again unlike Kotarbiński, who had consulted the world's practical wisdom, Gandhi sought to find his way out of his difficulties in otherworldly wisdom. He studied and discussed with friends the scriptures of all the world's great faiths. He concluded that all religions contained at least a core of truth and accepted Christ, Daniel, and Socrates as models to be emulated. All three had voluntarily accepted an agonizing death and in so doing had powerfully affected men's minds and hearts down through the ages.

Important as these ideas were to the development of satyagraha, the most significant outcome of this unusual year may well have been the capacity he achieved for mastering anger. As he once put it: "I have learnt through bitter experience the one supreme lesson to conserve my anger and as heat conserved is transmuted into energy, even so our anger controlled can be transmuted into a power which can move the world."[10] The immediate result of this capacity was an increase in his personal effectiveness, enabling him to become a leader of men much older than himself. In later years it also served to bind to him disciples whom he particularly prized: young terrorists who, learning from him how to control anger, forsook violence for the more challenging effort of practicing the "nonviolence of the strong."

The end of Gandhi's obligatory year did not, however, terminate his stay in South Africa. He first postponed his return to India for one month to lead a fight against proposed legislation threatening Indian rights. Then the month lengthened into years as the local government, alarmed by the rapid growth of the Indian population, adopted new restrictive devices as earlier ones were weakened or eliminated. Throughout his efforts for Indians in South Africa, Gandhi was consciously preparing himself for greater labors in India. He undertook experiments of various kinds, within a "model" community which he established, aimed at developing maximum village self-sufficiency with respect to food, shelter, clothing, health, and education. When Gandhi, at 45, finally returned to his homeland, his achievements had already established his reputation. He was himself full of confidence in his plans for social and political reform and in satyagraha as a "sovereign remedy" for all of India's ills.

What was the nature of this remedy? The word satyagraha has been anglicized and has gained wide acceptance, but the tendency has been to narrow its meaning to nonviolent mass civil disobedience. Such campaigns were indeed the most dramatic of Gandhi's many experiments, but from the beginning the term encompassed other modes of protest, including both group and individual action in the form of such efforts as strikes, fasts, and demonstrations, whether or not laws were disobeyed in the process.

Gandhi's initial attempts to apply his remedy in India were remarkably successful. Twice his mere readiness to undertake such campaigns was enough by itself to bring about the capitulation of local authorities. Gandhi began to visualize not only the transformation of India, but through India, of the world. In this mood, he requested a friend to draw up a list, for every state in India, of cases of hardship arising either from laws or from the manner of their enforcement. Local leaders everywhere received encouragement from him to make their own experiments with satyagraha.

With more experience, however, his euphoria waned. Not all campaigns that were called satyagraha seemed to him worthy of the name. The high potential that he saw in it made him all the more anxious to preserve its character of "righteous struggle," in which, he wrote, "there are no secrets to be guarded, no scope for cunning, and no place for untruth."[11] He was particularly concerned by the ever-present danger of the eruption of violence. When, after some years of trial and error, Gandhi came at last to feel that he had "mastered the technique of satyagraha," he made it clear that for him it was a complete way of life, and no "mere technique of struggle." The civil disobedience campaigns, he said, were the "aggressive aspects" of satyagraha. Its "profound" and "permanent aspects" consisted in peaceful experimentation with constructive programs with which he hoped to bring about Hindu-Muslim unity and promote economic and social justice for India's most downtrodden.[12]

For Gandhi, then, a prior concern with conflict as a means for effecting change gave way for a time to preoccupation with conciliation and integration. This shift in emphasis made it all the more necessary that satyagraha should live up to its highest ethical potential and not be resorted to lightly. Indeed, a trend — not fully consistent — toward narrowing the use of civil disobedience became discernible. The initial encouragement to wide experimentation with satyagraha gave way to restrictions on who should lead such campaigns and then to reductions in the number of participants, until at one point Gandhi himself became for a time the sole satyagrahi.

There are difficulties in any attempt to make a concise statement on the essential ingredients of satyagraha as Gandhi saw them, in part because the record of his doings and sayings is overwhelmingly voluminous and in part because of the many contradictions that record contains. Gandhi, engaged as he was in a lifelong search for truth as disclosed through action, always considered words to be less important than action, whether the words in question were his own or another's. Consistency he valued perhaps even less than did Emerson, whom he delighted to quote. When followers, perturbed by contradictory positions he had taken, brought their dilemmas to him for resolution, Gandhi, more amused than otherwise, would advise them to heed only his latest statement. Indeed, in the last months of his life he went so far as to recommend that all his writings be burned, since he considered his life to be his message.

Fortunately, this drastic counsel was not followed, but it does leave us in a somewhat difficult position. These difficulties are not made any easier by Gandhi's characteristic refusal to accede to requests either to draw up general principles for satyagraha or to write a treatise on nonviolence. Action, not "academic writings," was his domain, Gandhi said. "What I understand, according to my lights, to be my duty, and what comes my way, I do." And again, "I can give no guarantee that I will do or believe tomorrow, what I do or hold to be true today."[13] With respect to satyagraha, however, Joan Bondurant has surmounted the difficulty boldly, abstracting general principles from an examination of selected campaigns. Her formulations have left all students of satyagraha in her debt, and the statements concerning satyagraha in Table 3.1 rely heavily upon her work.[14] The statements concerning agonology I have abstracted from Kotarbiński's discussion.[15]

TABLE 3.1 Objectives and Directives: Gandhian Satyagraha
and Agonology

Satyagraha	*Agonology*

Objective

| To achieve an agreement with the opponent acceptable to both sides, by engaging him in a search for "truth," using only nonviolent means. | To defeat the opponent, or at least to avoid being defeated, using whatever means may be expedient. |

Directives

Search for avenues of cooperation with the opponent on honorable terms; never take advantage of his difficulties.	Make the opponent's position as difficult as possible; make difficulties for both sides if they will embarrass the opponent more than they will you.
Protect the opponent's person and his resources.	Strike first at the opponent's most vital parts; use his resources against him.
Reduce your demands to a minimum consistent with truth.	Try to leave your opponent only one way out.
Avoid a static condition, but launch direct action only after exhausting all other efforts to achieve an honorable settlement.	Economize your resources, but ensure your own freedom of movement and restrict the opponent's even at some loss to yourself.
Never lie; hold nothing back; keep the opponent, the public, and participants informed as an integral part of the movement.	Deceive the opponent. In general, refuse to disclose your intentions, but disclose them occasionally; the opponent may be deceived, or his next move be made more predictable by you.
Extend areas of rationality.	Commit "irrational" acts at times to confuse the opponent.

Of course, no chart could do justice to the richness of the original discussions, both of which should be consulted.

The entries in this chart are illustrative rather than exhaustive and are not fully comparable in all respects. It could scarcely be otherwise. Satyagraha, which began as a means for securing the redress of grievances suffered by a disadvantaged group at the hands of the dominant elements in South African society, evolved into a complex technique of action which had the potential, for those who chose to practice it, of changing the quality of their lives through its emphasis on ethics in action. Agonology, on the other hand, was not only codified from centuries of largely unhappy human experience but was also generalized to cover a broad spectrum of situations: from games with only two contestants through sports involving teamwork all the way to warfare between coalitions of nation states.

Agonology employs a strategy of deceit, lays emphasis on economy insofar as it is a component of efficiency, but relies even more heavily on keeping options open if the two principles are in conflict. Satyagraha employs a "truth" strategy stressing honor and rejects out of hand all options inconsistent with truth and honor. And although it sometimes came about that what Gandhi's sense of honor demanded on a given occasion could change with changing circumstances, it must also be said that satyagraha in his hands represented an ideal so lofty that few, if any, actual campaigns were felt by him to have maintained their purity unsullied. The precepts of agonology, on the other hand, are familiar enough as wartime expedients made palatable, temporarily at least, by the fervor of an enhanced love of country. But these same precepts, when stripped of emotion as well as of ethics, and applied in cold blood to any and all types of "struggle," fall well below the standards of conduct of the hypothetical "man of goodwill." Kotarbiński's own considerable distaste is made clear. The Polish philosopher, himself the author of papers on ethics, has explicitly withheld his own endorsement from the practices he has listed, "since what may be good from the praxeological point of view may be justly condemned on ethical grounds."[16] His chapter on the technique of conflict begins and ends with protestations that what is important is to understand the ruses he describes in order to avoid being surprised and defeated by an unscrupulous opponent.

An element of paradox regarding conflict has attracted the attention of several scholars, among them Kotarbiński, although none, perhaps, has been more strongly attracted than the German sociologist Georg Simmel (1858–1918). The paradoxical statement was a favorite pedagogical device with Simmel, who used it habitually to shake up students' presuppositions and sharpen their critical faculties. In his discussion of conflict, however, Simmel's intention appears less to dazzle his audience than to expound his conviction that human life is inextricably enmeshed in a basic dualism.[17] Thus, without denying the destructive potential of conflict, Simmel calls attention to an essentially integrative function that it performs. In his view life oscillates constantly between such opposing tendencies as love-hate, cooperation-competition, harmony-discord, and the like. If the whole is to have any shape, if it is "to really *be* the whole," Simmel insists, then each element in the contrasting pair must be present to some degree, and therefore each is to be viewed as making a positive contribution toward sustaining group relations, always providing that violence is subjected to at least some restrictions. Otherwise, warns Simmel (citing Kant), open conflict would become a war of extermination. He comments in particular upon the need to refrain "at least from assassination, breach of word, and instigation to treason."[18]

Simmel's equilibrium model is outmoded, and in any event is unlikely to be persuasive to a generation that has been taught that apathy, not hate, is the true opposite of love. It is nevertheless a useful exercise to overturn entrenched notions and recognize that conflict can perform certain integrative functions. For example, a conflict situation can be expected to lead to a study of the adversary, from which might arise eventually an increase in mutual understanding. (The first by-product might equally well be an increase in misunderstanding, depending upon the degree of objectivity animating the study.) Where contact between peoples had previously been slight, it is also conceivable that understanding would in the end be better promoted through open conflict than through "peaceful coexistence," if the latter had been based primarily on ignorance combined with indifference. But these insights do not of themselves carry us very far. It is unreasonable to expect integration to arise automatically from conflict. Questions concerning the nature of the issue, the intensity and duration of the conflict, and the manner in which conflict is conducted would all need to be taken into consideration.

Kotarbiński's interest in paradox centers upon the paradoxical element inherent in praxeological directives. For example, the element of surprise is a special case of deception. It can take the form of deliberately deviating from what would normally be considered the rational course in order to confound the adversary's plans, which would be based upon the expectation of rational behavior. However, it can also take the form of telling one's true intentions, thereby confusing the adversary who, not knowing what to believe, may either be deceived or be led to adopt a course of action that could more readily be foreseen and hence forestalled.[19]

Similarly, the concept of retreat (which Kotarbiński generalizes as an evasion of struggle in such a way as to change the circumstances in which the opponent finds himself, with the intention of "ensnaring" him), also contains an element of paradox, in that retreat can serve the purpose of attack. A literal example is calculated flight. Metaphorical examples include nonappearance before a given jury, refusal to consent to the date of a trial, and rejection of the nomination of members of a court of arbitration.[20]

Even the most basic praxeological directive — "make the opponent's position as difficult as possible" — contains a paradox.[21] For if the adversary's difficulties are sufficiently increased the result may be that these very pressures will compel the adversary to seek ever more ingenious ways of coping with his problems, to his ultimate advantage.[22]

If we apply praxeological thinking to the conflict between nation states we find that agonology, at least in the hands of the Polish philosopher, becomes in large part a defensive strategy to be employed against an enemy assumed to be, by comparison with one's own side, richer, stronger, and less scrupulous. For praxeological formulations geared to offensive military strategy we turn from the philosopher to the strategist General André Beaufre, who has given special attention to types of strategy and the conditions under which each is appropriate.[23] I have abstracted Table 3.2 from his illuminating discussion. (The strategies listed in this chart are typical rather than exhaustive and are presented in very broad terms. However, the selection was Beaufre's own and the circumstances governing applicability cover a wide variety of cases. For the subtleties of Beaufre's strategic thinking his treatise should be consulted.)

It is of interest to note that two of the five strategies employ credible threats rather than overt violence, two employ violence sparingly, and the fifth, which is characterized by violence, can be assured of success only if victory can be both rapid and complete. The conditions suitable for Maoist strategy — protracted conflict at a low level of intensity — are, it should be added, the same as those appropriate for satyagraha. Granted that these conditions exist and remain stable — the major factor would appear to be the strength of the moral commitment — both types of protracted struggle would appear to have an excellent chance of prevailing eventually, unless defeated in an early stage through an overwhelming use of force. An interesting question arises as to the probable outcome if protracted war of the Maoist variety were to be confronted by satyagraha. The chart suggests that if the issues were equally important to both sides and each had the requisite freedom of action, victory should accrue to the side with the stronger moral commitment. One suspects that much might depend on leadership. The chart, of course, presupposes a praxeological framework throughout and tacitly assumes leadership of roughly comparable competence.

All struggle, unless it is abruptly terminated, rapidly takes on a "dialectical" quality. In a political or military struggle the "move" may not shift

TABLE 3.2 Selected Strategies and Their Uses

Typical Patterns of Strategy	Appropriate Circumstances		
	Resources	*Freedom of Action*	*Importance of Issue*
1. Direct threat (deterrent strategy)	Large	Large	Moderate
2. Indirect pressure	Large	Limited by deterrent	Moderate
3. Successive actions combining (1) and (2) with limited application of force	Limited	Restricted	Major, but each episode *appears* to be minor
4. Protracted conflict at low level of intensity	Limited, but *moral* commitment strong	Large	Major, and far greater than for opponent
5. Violent conflict aiming at *rapid* and *complete* military victory	Large	Large	Major, but less than completely vital to opponent

from one side to the other with the set formality of a game or sport, but contingency planning must always take into account the probable range of responses to be expected from the opponent to each move that one makes. The problems of leadership under a "truth" strategy would differ enormously from those facing leadership operating a strategy based upon deceit. Beaufre has graphically portrayed the task of the strategist as he sees it: "The strategist is like a surgeon called upon to operate upon a sick person who is growing continuously and with extreme rapidity and of whose detailed anatomy he is not sure; his operating table is in a state of perpetual motion and he must have ordered the instruments he is to use five years beforehand."[24]

The task for a leader like Gandhi would be incomparably simpler. Since it is an integral part of satyagraha to employ only ethical means and to make all plans public, he would have no problems with security. Neither would he worry overmuch about specific ends, since it is an article of faith that he could be confident of the results provided his means were kept pure. He would escape the problems associated with weaponry but would require a high caliber of human material, with a trained corps of secondary leaders. The satyagraha leader would also be completely free of the predicament lamented by Beaufre: that the praxeological strategist must these days devise a total strategy, but one which is also totally instrumental in the service of policy, which must be left largely to his superiors. Further, to be truly effective policy should be the expression of an underlying philosophy which in Beaufre's experience was all too often lacking. For a leader like Gandhi, strategy in a very real sense *is* philosophy. His attention as commander-in-chief, once the issue was clear, would be focused mainly on two things: making sure that his followers maintained the high standards set for them and bringing his persuasive powers to bear upon the most highly placed of his opponents, preferably through man-to-man contact.

By "a leader like Gandhi" is meant a leader with a firm belief in non-violence who cherishes such values as truth and honor. Nourishing Gandhi the man in his extraordinary career were dreams he had concerning India, whose "mission," in his belief, was no less than to show mankind how to rid itself of the scourge of war. In his personal life he strove to make himself worthy to lead India in the fulfillment of this high mission.

During the Second World War, as the Japanese forces approached India, Gandhi was able to muster wide support for the demand that the British "quit India" immediately. He stood nearly alone, however, in urging that the country should then rely solely on satyagraha for its defense. He expected that once the British had withdrawn, one of two things would happen. Either the Japanese, seeing that no enemy forces were left there, would leave India alone, or they would attempt to take over India. In the latter, rather more probable case, India would have the opportunity, hopefully under his leadership, of demonstrating the potential which he saw in satyagraha. His plans were predicated upon the avoidance of all violence and rejected any scorched-earth policy.

The course of events was much more commonplace, but Gandhi still retained the hope that India, once freedom was achieved, would base its national defense upon satyagraha. Again he was doomed to disappointment — a disappointment shared by idealists elsewhere. If India, even under the leadership of men Gandhi had himself selected, dared not give his ideals a trial, what were the chances elsewhere for a test of nonviolence as a substitute for war?

The argument for recourse to war when a nation or a civilization is faced with a threat to its values or its very existence is indeed seemingly unanswerable. But neither is there an answer to the argument that as weapons grow increasingly destructive, a resort to warfare poses a serious threat to the civilization it is intended to protect. Can this dilemma be resolved?

A cautiously qualified optimism is currently being expressed in several quarters that the frightfulness of the alternative will yet induce mankind to turn toward nonviolence. The search for "acceptable passage between the horns of our dilemma" led H.J.N. Horsburgh, of the Moral Philosophy Department at the University of Glasgow, to reexamine the claims of Gandhian satyagraha as a moral equivalent of war.[25] Few would disagree with his conclusion that nonviolence is much superior to violence in its effect upon the way of life to be defended. He is also able to make a persuasive case for considering nonviolence as at least not inferior to violence in effectiveness as measured by several important criteria, including the one upon which mankind is now so heavily staking its future—the ability to deter aggression. He sees no prospect that Gandhian satyagraha can hope to play an important role in determining the relations between nation states, but sees reason to expect that nations will turn toward a non-Gandhian type of nonviolence, that is, one based upon expedience. (This interesting and important study has much more to offer than can be indicated here. It deserves the careful attention of anyone interested in exploring the relative claims to effectiveness of violence and nonviolence.)

War does indeed seem now to be widely regarded with loathing. Conflict, however, is quite another matter and can most certainly not be eliminated. Is Kotarbiński not correct in holding that "struggle" (as opposed to warfare) should not be renounced because mankind needs the spur of the compulsory situation, indeed "needs threats to life and to those values without which life is not worth living?" His reading of history has convinced him that whenever such threats have ceased, stagnation sets in; people become "mere consumers," and their vigor atrophies. Men, in his striking phrase, are "like deep-water fish—accustomed to strong external pressure, so when they reach shallow water they perish, burst by internal forces."[26]

Warfare does provide such pressure. Is there a source, apart from war, which might provide it? Certainly Kotarbiński's own recommendation for "taming" struggle by channeling it into competition in sports, the arts, and industrial production does not meet his own requirements with respect to the need for threats against life and cherished values. It was once suggested that only an invasion from another planet could turn earth's population away from internecine strife. That hope—if hope it was—has proved illusory.

As the destructive potential not merely of warfare but also of the very technology on which we have long prided ourselves becomes ever clearer, mankind's dilemma grows sharper and the intractable questions require rephrasing. The question no longer is: Can mankind abolish war? It goes even beyond: Can warfare indeed abolish man? For some it becomes: Does man's technology indeed pose a threat to the continued existence of human life on this planet? To many the answer to that question seems self-evident and they ask most urgently: Can man be brought to realize the full extent of his predicament and take remedial action before the process of environmental deterioration becomes irreversible? These overriding, global questions bring us back to time-worn problems of intergroup conflict, but with a keener sense of urgency. The "compulsory situation" that Kotarbiński posits as essential to progress is now upon us, for we are confronted with a possibly fatal environmental crisis. Questions about the potential of weapons technology to destroy human life on the planet become intertwined with the even greater considerations of technological man's capacity to destroy his life-sustaining environment.

Faced with so dire a predicament the relative merits of competing modes for conducting conflict require profound reconsideration. At one extreme is the praxeological nightmare so graphically set forth by General Beaufre. Here the *potential* for violence is staggering, despite the explicit desire that it need never be employed. At the other extreme is the Gandhian solution, the product of a social philosophy as profoundly ethical as his novel technique for conducting overt conflict, a solution that looked to the eventual abolition of all "machinery."[27] (This was of course an utterly unattainable goal, presenting Gandhi with many problems. He did not classify such devices as handlooms as machinery and even urged the development of improved looms. He also jocularly granted temporary exemption to the printing press used in the publication of his attack upon other machinery!)

Where both these extremes are at fault, it would appear, is in failing to make appropriate utilization of science and technology. The Gandhian approach all but ignores science; the praxeological approach misuses it in continuing to devote excessive time, treasure, and human ingenuity to the development of weapons systems and industrial products that compound the magnitude of the environmental threat to human existence. It will not do to either ignore or misuse science. For science *is* "intrinsically more revolutionary than any ideology or political or social movement," as Roy Finch points out.

How then should we use science in these troubled times, when dissatisfaction abounds and the rumbles of a revolutionary groundswell portend imminent change? Today a rather hybrid form of praxeological thinking dominates approaches to conflict and to technologically generated environmental problems. Are we to move toward a more rigorous—and dehumanized—praxeology, or can we, through the mediation of science, develop a humanistic praxeology which can accommodate certain insights developed through the Gandhian approach? A step in this direction could be taken by redefining the central praxeological concept of "efficiency."

It is significant that the praxeological approach as developed by Kotar-biński with a *nonaffluent* society in mind displays a tendency to favor non-violent means as more "efficient" (cheaper). Under conditions of relative affluence, however, efficiency is more likely to be equated with time saving, thus easily diminishing, if not negating, the moderating effect of cost considerations on the escalation of violence. Once escalation has taken place, however, a serious impediment to its reversal arises from the reliance of the praxeological strategist on deceit. The sharpest point of contrast between satyagraha and agonology is not with respect to violence but with respect to "truth."

A philosophy of conflict adequate to our times could well center upon the basic kind of ethical consideration that, in holding that power lay in pursuing and asserting truth, led to the development of satyagraha. In calling for an effort to "understand the *objective* nature of morality," Roy Finch expresses the belief that to do so will require a "vast upheaval of thought, which has scarcely begun." Such a beginning, I would contend, was made by Gandhi, who also extended it further to an understanding (and application) of the *uses* of morality in situations of conflict.

In the "recycling" of ideas that bear upon the moral facets of our predicament, we would do well to discard outworn political doctrines. Seductive promises of inevitably assured ends seem currently to be effecting the rehabilitation of theories of conflict built into deterministic political philosophies and social ideologies—and this despite a long record of betrayal of humanistic impulses. Slogans such as "power to the people," as past experience indicates, can all too readily lead to the exploitation of the aggrieved by an abrasive handful who give primacy to politics and ideology over human values. Is not the true "power of the people" to be defined in terms of the building up of moral courage to the point where the majority of the people become immune both to threats of violence and to the temptation to indulge in violent acts?

To suggest that we begin with Gandhian nonviolence and satyagraha, that we supplement it with a redefinition of "efficiency," and that we make science serve a constructively creative purpose is to present a new set of intellectual and practical problems. But today's generation cannot lightly dismiss the possibility, whatever the odds, that in their lifetime our planet may become incapable of further supporting human life. A way must be found to direct the revolutionary potential of our science into ecology-oriented systems in which conflict theory takes its own innovative place. The essentially human process involved in that effort could not only avert catastrophe but also usher in a new renaissance.

Notes

1. For Gandhi's autobiographical writings see his *Satyagraha in South Africa,* available in several editions of which the most useful is in *The Collected Works of Mahatma Gandhi* (New Delhi: Government of India, Publications Division, 1968), vol. 29, pp. xviii-269; and *The Story of My Experiments with Truth* (Washington, D.C.: Public Affairs Press, 1948).

2. See Tadeusz Kotarbiński, *Gnosiology: The Scientific Approach to Knowledge* (New York: Pergamon Press, 1966), translated from the revised Polish edition (Warsaw, 1961) of a work first published in 1929.

3. See particularly Joan V. Bondurant, *Conquest of Violence: The Gandhian Philosophy of Conflict,* rev. ed. (Berkeley: University of California Press, 1965) (1st ed., Princeton University Press, 1958); and her article "Satyagraha versus Duragraha: The Limits of Symbolic Violence," in *Gandhi: His Relevance for Our Times,* ed. G. Ramachandran and T. K. Mahadevan, 2d ed. (New Delhi: Gandhi Peace Foundation, 1967), pp. 99-112.

4. Tadeusz Kotarbiński, *Praxiology: An Introduction to the Sciences of Efficient Action* (New York: Pergamon Press, 1965) (first Polish edition 1955). English and American spelling fluctuates between "praxiology" and "praxeology." I have adopted Norman Bailey's suggestion and have used "praxeology" except in citing the title of the English translation of this book.

5. Norman A. Bailey, "Toward a Praxeological Theory of Conflict," *Orbis* 11, no. 4 (winter 1968):1081-1112.

6. Kotarbiński cites an edition in German, *Kampf* (New York, 1907). Lasker's remarkable success is generally attributed to his ability to discover and exploit the temperamental weaknesses of his opponents through close study of their games.

7. Kotarbiński, *Praxiology,* p. 7.

8. Ibid., p. 12.

9. Ibid., p. 13.

10. From Gandhi's speech on the Noncooperation Resolution, at the Calcutta Congress, September 8, 1920 (*Collected Works,* vol. 28, p. 246).

11. *Satyagraha in South Africa,* p. xiv.

12. See his speech of August 13, 1924, in his *Collected Works*, vol. 25, pp. 56-63.

13. Written to a friend in February 1946. D. G. Tendulkar, *Mahatma: Life of Mohandas Karamchand Gandhi* (Bombay: Vithalbhai K. Jhaveri and D. G. Tendulkar, 1953), vol. 7, pp. 84-85.

14. Bondurant, *Conquest of Violence,* chap. 2.

15. Kotarbiński, *Praxiology,* chap. 13.

16. Ibid., p. 159.

17. Georg Simmel, *Conflict,* trans. Kurt H. Wolff, and *The Web of Group-*

Affiliations, trans. Reinhard Bendix (Glencoe, Ill.: Free Press, 1955), pp. 13 ff.

18. Ibid., p. 26.

19. Kotarbiński, *Praxiology,* pp. 170-171.

20. Ibid., pp. 171-172.

21. Ibid., p. 174.

22. Ibid., p. 206.

23. André Beaufre, *An Introduction to Strategy* (London: Faber and Faber, 1965), pp. 26-30. (First published in France by Armand Colin under the auspices of the Centre d'Etudes de Politique Etrangere, in 1963.) General Beaufre's long and varied experience includes serving as French representative on the NATO Standing Group in Washington.

24. Ibid., p. 46.

25. H.J.N. Horsburgh, *Nonviolence and Aggression: A Study of Gandhi's Moral Equivalent of War* (London, New York, Toronto, Bombay: Oxford University Press, 1968).

26. Kotarbiński, *Praxiology,* p. 193.

27. Gandhi, "Hind Swaraj" or "Indian Home Rule," *Collected Works,* vol. 10, pp. 6-68.

Part 2
Ethological and
Psychological Inquiries

Introduction

The League of Nations and the International Institute of Intellectual Cooperation (UNESCO's predecessor) invited Albert Einstein in 1932 to formulate a most significant issue of the time and to discuss it with a person of his own choice. In response Einstein renewed the old question, "Is there a way of delivering mankind from the menace of war?" as the most important problem facing humanity and chose Sigmund Freud as the person most qualified to answer the question. Freud's response, though disappointingly vague in its conceptual clarity and misdirected in its normative guidance (sharing some of the important characteristics of the instinctive theory of aggression as described and criticized in Chapter 4), adds another chapter to the annals of this perennial nature/nurture debate concerning human behavior in general and aggressive behavior in particular.

Those committed to the removal of war from history reject "the nature view" that war is inherent in human nature and adhere to some variant of the "the nurture view" that war is a reflection of conditioning and hence can be eliminated if the environment is suitably altered. This more optimistic view is embodied in the widely quoted Preamble to the UNESCO Constitution: "Since wars begin in the minds of men, it is in the minds of men that the defenses of peace must be constructed."

The selections in Part 2 are designed to illuminate three competing approaches to human aggression in current ethological and psychological inquiries into the causes of war. Few can deny that the war system has a biological base. However, the real problem is first to locate and define biological/etiological variables of human aggressive behavior and then to relate them in explanatory and predictive ways to the outset of war. The current state of research on the causes and correlates of war is marked by divergent paths of politically naive ethologists and biologically naive behavioral scientists. In short, little attempt has been made to formulate a conceptual thread that can analytically tie and link aggressive or violent behaviors of man at different levels of social organization.

The study of human aggression has long been influenced by some metatheoretical assumptions and beliefs about the basic nature of man. Fears of Hobbesian realists and hopes of Rousseauian idealists have all made their way into descriptive, explanatory, and prescriptive analyses of aggression. Some writers have contended that aggression is a manifestation of an innate instinct; others have contended that it is an inborn reaction to frustration; and still others have argued that it is a learned social practice responding to particular situations. Is aggression an innate instinct, an instigated drive, or a social practice?

The instinctive theory as espoused by Lorenz and his followers has the following characteristics: (1) aggression is a phylogenetically programmed and ineradicably instinctive behavior; (2) aggression is spontaneous (hydraulic model of energy motivation); (3) aggressive behavior is indispensable not only for the preservation of individuals and species in the service of evolutionary adaptation and survival but also for the mastery of creative human endeavors; (4) undischarged aggression leads to pathology; and (5) aggression cannot — and should not — be eliminated because catharsis serves as the only prescriptive remedy for human warfare even in the nuclear age.

Clearly, the instinctive theory of aggression is plagued by numerous conceptual, methodological, and empirical weaknesses. Yet the sweeping simplicity and skillful popularizing and ·mythologizing with which this grandiose pseudoscientific theory has been advocated by its proponents seem to have captured the malaise of our violence-afflicted times, attracting wide and uncritical acceptance by a large literate audience. Note the latest expression of this approach has taken the form of the "sociobiology" movement led by Edward O. Wilson (1975, 1978). Here the promise is made that "sociobiology can eventually be derived from the first principles of population and behavioral biology and developed into a single mature science." While sociobiology is more advanced in its theoretical construct and more prudent in its empirical generalization than Lorenzian ethology, it does share with the instinctive theory the genetic and evolutionary insistence that aggression is an aspect of "human nature."

Is there any general human nature that explains the recurring phenomenon of organized killing in human history? It may be reasonable to assume that genetic endowment or biological potential of man plays an unspecified role in setting the outer scope and limits of human behavior. But the concept of human nature, which assumes so much uniformity of human behavior in time and place, is hopelessly inadequate in explaining why some people are so peaceful and others so war prone or why the same people are peaceful and violent at different times under different situations.

Given the present conceptual and empirical status of the instinctive theory of human aggression, there seems no valid reason to believe that peace research can profit much from this particular approach. However, the instinctive theory along with other deterministic conceptions of human nature exerts an influence. These views deserve serious scrutiny because their policy and behavioral implications tend to be so regressive. Specifically, several normative questions warrant our attention. Do not these deterministic theories serve to legitimize the status quo of the war system? Do not such theories make the people participate in the future of war making by default, that is, by accepting what they are led to believe and expect is something inevitable? Do not these theories therefore present a formidable cognitive-psychological barrier to building a peace ideology or movement?

The response-to-frustration hypothesis of human aggression stands on sounder and firmer conceptual and empirical grounds than the instinctive deterministic group of explanations. It also promises a greater potential in generating more policy-relevant hypotheses for describing, explaining, and predicting violent behavior at other systemic levels of human society. The chapters by Ted Gurr and the Feierabends (Chapters 11 and 12 in Part 4), for example, are superb applications of frustration-aggression theory to the study of civil violence and internal conflict behavior.

In the original formulation of frustration-aggression hypothesis by the Yale School (Dollard et al. 1939), it was proposed that "the occurrence of aggressive behavior always presupposes the existence of frustration, and contrariwise, that the existence of frustration always leads to some form of aggression." Does frustration ("an interference with the occurrence of an instigated goal-response at its proper time in the behavior sequence") *always* lead to aggression? Recent research and experiment by Leonard Berkowitz and others have added some modifications and refinements to the original frustration-aggression hypothesis in three ways. First, frustration creates a *readiness* or predisposition (by arousing anger) toward aggressive acts. Second, aggressive responses do not occur even under such a state of readiness without aggression-evoking *cues*. That is, cues serve as mediating variables between frustration (cause) and aggression (outcome), revising the simple one-to-one relationship in the original formulation. A third revision of the frustration-aggression hypothesis restricts the deterministic quality implied in the adverb "always" by adding *learning experience* as another mediating variable affecting the individual's definition of the situation.

In spite of these revisions and modifications, the frustration-aggression hypothesis poses several problems. The tendency to simplify and reduce the determinants of human aggression into a single cause has resulted in defining "frustration" in such broad terms as to make the concept almost circular, in which the cause (frustration) and the outcome (aggression) can each be cited as evidence of the other. Studies of monkeys and children have shown that frustration as well as such other nonfrustrating causal variables as rivalry for possession of a prized object, jealousy for the attention of an individual, and intrusion of a stranger in the group provide additional explanations of fighting (Durbin and Bowlby 1968). Moreover, responses to frustration may take forms other than aggression, such as acceptance, submission, resignation, dependence, avoidance, alienation, and withdrawal.

Both the instinctive and frustration-aggression theories are conceptually flawed by their failure to take into account the role of perception (cognition) in human behavior. Both theories are also prone to conservative biases by sidetracking instrumental aggression. More seriously, neither model can cope with institutionalized violence (or what Johan Galtung has called "structural violence"), the most pervasive form of violence deeply embedded in the modern state system, in which privileged classes and groups commit indirect violence against societal underdogs through the operation of institutions and structures of society that legitimate and defend unequal distribution of societal wealth, income, and support. Given the prevalence of the displacement of aggression (scapegoating aggression) and the inherent tendency in aggression to move downward in a social and political hierarchy, this weakness in both theories is of great societal significance.

The social-learning theory of aggression as explained by Albert Bandura in Chapter 6 shifts the locus of causal analysis from inner determinants (instincts, needs, impulses, and drives) to outer determinants (social contexts and targets) in advancing the proposition that human aggression is learned social behavior. This approach implicitly repudiates the Hobbesian image of human nature projected by the instinctive theory of aggression. Based on the contrary assumption that man's basic nature is infinitely malleable, it argues with substantial empirical cogency that the so-called inner forces of human aggression cannot possibly account "for the marked variation in the incidence of a given behavior in different situations, toward different persons, at different times, and in different social roles." The heroic optimism underlying this approach is expressed in the belief and some experimental evidence that man's aggressive acts attributed inferentially to his inner stimuli can easily be changed in form and direction by varying external stimulus and reinforcement controls. To the extent that this theory can be validated, the task of building a peace ideology becomes greatly clarified. For the theory suggests the possibility of unlearning aggression as a learned social behavior—a first step in laying the human behavioral foundation for a just and viable peace system.

The ethological/psychological approach as highlighted in the three alternative theories of human aggression sheds much light on the biological and psychological potential of human behavior. However, we should be wary of attempting any major inductive leap from this grounding in individual behavior to higher levels of social organization. These studies of aggression in human beings do not address the level-of-analysis problem. The question still remains as to how, in what ways, and to what extent the influence of individual human behavior is expressed (rather than modified) in the larger social and institutional contexts of war making. Personal aggressiveness, whether primary or reactive, may be a necessary but not a sufficient condition for the onset of war. The real value of this ethological/psychological approach may lie, as some of our later selections in the book show, in using its rich repertoire as a generator of models, hypotheses, and paradigms for the analysis of human behavior in specifically delimited situations.

4

The Lorenzian Theory of Aggression and Peace Research: A Critique

Samuel S. Kim

Practically all the significant theories of war and peace in Western political thought have been postulated either implicitly or explicitly on certain images of human nature. The Hobbesian image of man as *homo homini lupus* — a vicious and cruel animal with no compassion for his fellows — has been shared in varying degrees by St. Augustine, Machiavelli, Luther, Malthus, Jonathan Swift, Dean Inge, Spinoza, Bismarck, Freud, Reinhold Niebuhr, and Hans Morgenthau in their attempts to explain societal defects or evils in terms of the allegedly innate nastiness in human nature (Waltz 1959). Even the struggle for power among nations has been explained by some "realists" in terms of *animus dominandi,* the notion that *Homo sapiens,* viewed as individuals or as nations, act like beasts of prey, driven by an insatiable lust for power.

The contemporary version of Hobbesianism is presented, however, in a "scientific" wrapper. In fact, its most eloquent spokesman, Konrad Z. Lorenz, is widely recognized as "the founder of modern ethology" (Eibl-Eibesfeldt and Wickler 1968:186). Lorenz's scientific stature has been further enhanced since he was awarded the Nobel Prize in Physiology/Medicine in 1973. When Sigmund Freud revised his conception of aggression in the aftermath of World War I,[1] there was little public excitement or even awareness of it. Yet, in recent years many books advancing the instinctive theory of aggression and war — Lorenz's *On Aggression* (1966) is the most celebrated example — have become run-away best sellers. Evidence is growing that the current vogue of Lorenzian ethology is not confined to the reading public.

Reprinted by permission of the publisher from Samuel S. Kim, "The Lorenzian Theory of Aggression and Peace Research: A Critique," *Journal of Peace Research* 13 (1976):253-276.

According to one British observer, Lorenz "has become to aggression what McLuhan is to communications, de Chardin to evolution, Marcuse to revolution" (Clare 1969:153). Robert Ardrey (1966:302-303), an ardent Lorenzian, argues that "the human goose is cooked" if Lorenz's book (*On Aggression*) does not take its place "among the landmarks of our thought." For Driver (1967), the Lorenzian ethology promises to be the most objective and valuable of the behavioral sciences. "The main promise that ethology seems to hold out to students of society and politics," observed Willhoite (1971:619), "is the possibility of developing a scientifically defensible conception of man's nature." Likewise, Tiger (1969:59) argues that "the approach of ethologists—if not ethology itself—must become part of the repertoire of any serious student of human behavior."

Some political scientists in the United States, without necessarily accepting the Lorenzian concept of human behavior in *toto,* have already begun pleading for greater receptivity to a biologically based approach. Somit (1968) calls for "a more biologically oriented political science," while Corning (1971) advances a bold proposal that "evolution be employed as a general theory to explain all human life, including political life." Thorson (1970:82) also argues in an attention-capturing book, *Biopolitics,* that contemporary political science should adopt a new paradigm that would consider man as "above all, a biological organism," who "is what he is because of and through the process of biological and cultural evolution." On the other hand, Alcock (1972:2) of the Canadian Peace Research Institute, while admitting that "the scientific investigation of war has not yet found its Galileo or Newton," nonetheless cites Lorenz along with Quincy Wright, Lewis Richardson, and Sigmund Freud as "early predecessors" in peace research and then asserts that "they have all shown that there could be a science of peace."[2]

If accepted without critical scrutiny, the application of the Lorenzian theory to the social sciences in general and to peace research in particular can be misleading and even dangerous. This paper challenges the Lorenzian theory on conceptual, methodological, and substantive grounds and draws up some broad policy implications for peace research. However, a few caveats are in order at the outset. The present critique should not be regarded as an apology for antievolutionary approaches in the social sciences. Nor should it be regarded as an instance of parochial resistance to cross-disciplinary approaches in peace research or as a traditional opposition to "scientific" method in political science. Rather, it is predicated on the belief that indiscriminate cross fertilization can be of little heuristic value to the advancement of peace research as a value-oriented policy science.[3]

The Lorenzian Theory

The core of the Lorenzian theory of human and animal behavior is the assertion that "aggression"—defined as "the fighting instinct in beast and man which is directed against members of the same species" (Lorenz 1966:ix)—is phylogenetically programmed and, therefore, ineradicably instinctive behavior. Aggression is not a learned reaction to social cues or environmental stimuli but a species-specific instinct man has inherited from his anthropoid ancestors in the service of evolutionary adaptation and survival. All the amazing paradoxes of human history would somehow fall into place, Lorenz would have us believe, "like the pieces of a jigsaw puzzle, if one assumes that human behavior, and particularly human social behavior, far from being determined by reason and cultural tradition alone, is still subject to all the laws prevailing in all phylogenetically adapted instinctive behavior" (1966:237; see also 1970:xii). In his enthusiasm for the popularization of ethology, Lorenz (1966:29) conveys the impression that this conceptual net can stretch so far and wide as to cover "the alarming progression of aggressive actions ranging from cocks fighting in the barnyard to dogs biting each other, boys thrashing each other, young men throwing beer mugs at each other's heads, and so on to bar-room brawls about politics, and finally to wars and atom bombs."

In order to make the ambiguous concept of "instinct" integral to his theory of human and animal behavior, Lorenz has reified it. Closely following the formulation of Tinbergen (1951), Lorenz views instinctive acts as rigidly stereotyped innate movements ("fixed action patterns") which are coordinated in the central nervous system. Lorenz flatly asserts that "the motor co-ordination patterns of the instinctive behaviour pattern are hereditarily determined down to the finest detail" (1970:313). Instinctive acts are thus neurophysiologically motivated and released in the internal system of the organism—"a virtually closed system" in Lorenz's (1970:323) own words—quite independently of the animal's experience and environment.[4]

Another salient feature of the Lorenzian theory is its insistence on the *spontaneity of aggression*. Like other theorists of instinct—Craig (1918), McDougall (1923), Freud (Fromm 1973), Tinbergen (1942), Storr (1970), and Eibl-Eibesfeldt (1972)—Lorenz also conceptualizes the progress of aggressive behavior as a sort of hydraulic mechanism analogous to the pressure generated by dammed-up water in a closed container. According to this hydraulic process—also referred to as an energy model of motivation—action-specific energy spontaneously accumulates in the instinct center of the animal, generating pressure for its discharge with rhythmic regularity. Sometimes, the organism does not even wait passively for the release of its aggressive energy, but actively seeks stimuli. The more extensive the period during which the aggressive energy is dammed up — or the more extensive the period during which an instinctive behavior pattern is passive — the lower the threshold value of its elicitory stimulus. "Following a more or less extensive period of 'damming,'" Lorenz asserted, "the entire motor sequence can be performed *without* demonstrable operation of an external stimulus" (1970:320; see also 1966:52-53).

Lorenz has advocated the concept of spontaneous aggression with conviction and consistency. "There cannot be any doubt, in the opinion of any biologically minded scientist," he (1964:49) asserted, "that intraspecific aggression is, in Man, just as much of a spontaneous instinctive drive as in most other vertebrates." In an interview in 1974, Lorenz reaffirmed his belief in the concept of spontaneous aggression: "I'm convinced of it [spontaneous aggression]. I cannot prove it in man. I can prove that in certain animals aggressivity follows all the rules of threshold-lowering and appetitive behavior. You can see an animal looking for trouble, and a man can do that too" (Evans 1974:90).

The Lorenzians view aggression as indispensable not only for the survival of the individual and the species but also for the achievement of creative human endeavors. For example, Lorenz (1966:48) asserts — and Eibl-Eibesfeldt (1972), Storr (1970), and Tiger (1970) share this view — that "aggression, far from being the diabolical, destructive principle that classical psychoanalysis makes it out to be, is really an essential part of the life preserving organization of instincts."

While Freud (1968) viewed the death instinct as being opposed by the instinct of Eros, Lorenz (1964, 1966) holds, as does Storr (1970), that aggression in man is "an essential component of personal friendship."[5] The Lorenzians also assert that, without aggression, nearly everything man does would somehow lose its creative and intellectual vigor. "Aggression is related to mastery," asserts Tiger (1970:216). For Storr (1970), aggression is the basis of intellectual achievement. "Our ordinary speech expresses the fact," observes Eibl-Eibesfeldt (1972:84), "that even culturally creative achievements are nourished by aggression." And Lorenz (1966:278) too asserts that aggression is indeed "indispensable for the achievement of the highest human goals."

Lorenz fully agrees with Freud (1962, 1968) that the failure to discharge "aggression, far from being the diabolical, destructive principle that classical pre–World War I period that repression of sexuality could lead to mental illness and later applied the same argument to the death instinct, Lorenz (1966:243) also argues that "present-day civilized man suffers from insufficient discharge of his aggressive drive." In support of his argument, Lorenz

(1966:244) cites Ute Indians who "suffer more frequently from neurosis than any other human group" because of undischarged aggression. As a result of "a devastating hypertrophy of aggression in the Utes," Lorenz (1966:245, 298) further argues that they are the most accident-prone and unhappy of all peoples. That the discharge of aggression is a healthy and normal process can also be discerned in Lorenz's (1970:99) assertion that "any physical defect (however small) is accompanied by pronounced disruption of the instinctive behavioural system."

Since the establishment of an ecological balance between population and land/resources is viewed by the Lorenzians as the most important survival function of intraspecific aggression, the Lorenzian theory becomes closely tied to the concept of territorial behavior. Lorenz concurs with Tinbergen (1968) that man behaves very much like a territorial species. Lorenz (1966) also agrees with the judgment of such authors as Calhoun (1961, 1962) and Leyhausen (1965) that high population density always leads to an increase in aggressive behavior in both humans and animals.

Attacking Marx for his "errors of forgetting the instincts," Lorenz flatly declares: "But it's almost always overpopulation that is at the root of all the 'malfunctions' of human social behavior" (de Towarnicki 1970:29). "When thousands, millions, of men are brought together," Lorenz continues, "aggression begins to get seriously out of hand" (de Towarnicki 1970:29). One of the major reasons for mounting aggression today "is quite simply that men in large cities are too crowded together." Tellingly, Lorenz mentions — at least in two separate interviews — the bus terminal on 42nd Street in New York City as prima facie evidence for his contention that crowding causes hostility and aggression (de Towarnicki 1970:29; Evans 1974:85).

Intraspecific aggression is seldom dangerous among the animals, the Lorenzians contend, because of the development of so-called threat behavior. However, man has failed to develop innate inhibitory mechanisms of diverting or ritualizing maladaptive aggression because he lacks major morphological weapons. The fate of humanity is now in a precarious situation, Lorenz argues, because of the growing tension between the spontaneous and instinctive drive for aggressive behavior and the destructive capability of remote control nuclear weapons. Furthermore, "anonymity of the person to be attacked greatly facilitates the releasing of aggressive behavior" (Lorenz 1966:283). Lorenz wonders whether "responsible morality" will be able to cope with such a rapidly growing burden of modern civilization.

Following James (1968) and Freud (1968), Lorenz finally proposes the ancient Greek conception of catharsis as the solution — that is, aggression can be and should be sublimated, redirected, or ritualized. This Lorenzian thesis is based on the assumption that human nature cannot be changed and the belief that aggressive drives cannot be suppressed but only diverted. The concept of catharsis refers specifically to a discharge of energy following an aggressive response, the process of which will in turn reduce the probability of any subsequent aggressive behavior. Even though his cathartic thesis is derived largely from the observations of displacement activities of cichlids and birds, Lorenz (1964:45; 1971:21) is convinced that human beings too exhibit many examples of cathartic process.

In a manner suggestive of James's (1968) "moral equivalent of war," the Lorenzians all propose competitive games, academic or artistic masteries, and cultural activities as cathartic outlets for discharging aggressive drives of individuals and nation-states (Lorenz, 1966; Eibl-Eibesfeldt, 1972; Storr, 1970). Eibl-Eibesfeldt (1972:77) asserts that one can drain off aggressive energy by watching a film with aggressive content. Lorenz (1966:287) argues, on the other hand, that sport functions as "a healthy safety valve for that most indispensable and, at the same time, most dangerous form of aggression" which he characterizes as "collective militant enthusiasm."[6] Sporting contests, in addition to providing an outlet for the collective militant enthusiasm of nations, have two additional effects that counter the danger of war: "They promote personal acquaintance between people of different nations or parties and they unite, in enthusiasm for a common cause, people who otherwise would have little in common" (Lorenz 1966:282).

Conceptual Critique

One obvious conceptual problem with the Lorenzian theory lies in the cavalier use of key terms that are not given an operational definition. To define aggression, as Lorenz does, as the intraspecific fighting instinct in beast and man simplifies the task of popularizing ethological thinking, to be sure. However, such a reductionism can hardly be achieved without emasculating the heuristic value of the concept. Like the doctrine of Original Sin, the Lorenzian view of aggression is a general, monocausal, and monoexplanatory proposition which is not susceptible to empirical verification in most contexts of human behavior. Moreover, such key terms as aggression, violence, and war are not only used interchangeably, but also as common referents for the aggressive behavior of both animals and humans at all levels of organic, social, and ecological organization. As the following discussion will show, Lorenz's propensity for anecdotal reasoning in support of his argument is a corollary of his zeal to popularize his theory of aggression.

The Lorenzians constantly speak of "instinctive" behavior as if the import and the scope of this category of behavior were self-evident. The reification of the concept of instinct does not necessarily establish its heuristic value.

Clinical and laboratory experiments in recent years have shown that the dichotomy between instinct and learning is misleading. It is not possible completely to exclude learning from early ontogenetic processes in the egg or *in utero*. Apparently even "instinctive" behaviors operate against a complex tangle of interaction which includes other genes as well as the influence of the external environment. Hence the concept of instinct has now become passé as more and more students of behavior have abandoned use of the concept as outmoded (Alland 1969; Barnett 1973; Scott 1973).[7]

To operationalize the concept of aggression is an extremely complex and hazardous task. The Lorenzian definition seems to have taken a conceptual short cut by merging aggression with instinct. However, such a simplistic reductionism has been achieved by relegating many relevant questions to limbo. For example, does the intraspecific fighting instinct cover the attitudinal (the latent) aspect as well as the behavioral (the manifest) aspect? To concentrate exclusively on the overt act alone would shed little light on the motivational state of the actor. On the other hand, the state of anger and frustration alone could not explain the form of its final expression. A special methodological caution is needed here to avoid equating the cause with the outcome of behavior.

From the standpoint of peace research, however, the most troubling aspect of the Lorenzian definition of human aggression is its weakness in dealing with institutionalized aggression — the injury, harm, and violence indirectly inflicted upon one group of individuals by another group of individuals through institutions and structures of society, or what Galtung (1969) terms "structural violence." The irony is that the greater the capability an actor possesses in terms of such coercive weapons as position, wealth, persuasive skills, and the like, the greater the probability that his "aggression" will be expressed in an indirect institutional or structural form rather than in a direct personal/physical form.

Even the widely accepted (non-Lorenzian) definition of aggression as "any behavior whose goal is the injury of some person or thing" (Berkowitz 1968a:168) raises the conceptual problem of attribution of intent. Strictly speaking, intent is not a behavioral attribute but a circumstantial inference deduced from any behavioral pattern which is, or appears to be, nonaccidental. This raises an interesting conceptual problem. Is an actor who attempts to injure some person or object seriously, but fails, as "aggressive" as an actor who unintentionally injures some person or thing? Clearly, lack of consensus on the extent of attribution of intent remains a major obstacle in operationalizing the concept of aggression.

To compound the conceptual problem, the determination of intent in "aggressive" behavior is subject to perceptual and judgmental distortions. Just as sociological reality is what people perceive or expect it to be (Allport

1950; Merton 1957), aggression too becomes a mirror image of each observer's belief system. Even a cursory observation of UN politics would show that aggression in the context of contemporary international politics means different things to different people. Culture and politics have shaped our perceptual apparatus to such an extent that even trained observers are not immune from projecting their own images onto "aggressive" behavior.

That both the status and image of the actor and the values and perspective of the observer seriously complicate the conceptualization of aggression can no longer be doubted. Most Americans use a double standard in judging "violent" behaviors of the police and student demonstrators (Blumenthal et al. 1971). Another empirical study suggests that "the actor must have no physical characteristics, such as clothing, beard, long hair, color, stigmata, and the like, that could affect the labeling process apart from the act itself" (Tedeschi et al. 1974:557-558). Similarly, a cross-cultural study of aggression shows a meaninglessness of describing one culture more or less aggressive than another given the difficulty of establishing a value-free external criterion of evaluation (Green and Santori 1969). In short, the classification process raises two difficulties: the conceptual problem of separating the objective reality of human behavior from the subjective assessment of the observer and the problem of separating the perspective of the actor from that of the observer.

However, animal aggression is relatively easy to observe and classify without such conceptual problems because of a limited number of natural weapons and a definable range of threat instruments. Animal aggression is also direct and physical and almost never accidental, occurring within a specific situational context in which the cause of conflict is rather obvious (Tedeschi et al. 1974; Washburn and Hamburg 1973). However, human aggression involving our natural morphological equipment constitutes a small portion of the total inventory of human aggressive behaviors.

The fact that there are different sources, contexts, stimuli, dimensions, instruments, expressions, and effects of aggression now seems to be indisputable. Yet Lorenz (1958:3) tenaciously adheres to the assumption that "beneath all the variations of individual behavior there lies an inner structure of inherited behavior which characterizes all the members of a given species, genus or larger taxonomic group." To Lorenz and his followers, who view aggression as a hydraulic process in which energy rhythmically accumulates and discharges, all the conceptual problems raised in the preceding pages are largely irrelevant. However, any monocausal and monoexplanatory model such as Lorenz's cannot account for all aggressive behaviors. Moreover, neurophysiological determinism embodied in the Lorenzian conceptualization ignores the sociopolitical structure of situations in which aggression finds its final expression. That the heuristic utility of the Lorenzian concept of aggression is limited is illustrated diagrammatically in Figure 4.1, which shows variables associated with typology of human aggression.

Methodological Critique

Independent of its conceptual difficulties and substantive weaknesses, the Lorenzian approach to aggression and war is flawed on methodological grounds alone. This is due to Lorenz's recurrent tendency to stray beyond the boundary of well-established scientific standards and procedures. Instead of the formulation of operational hypotheses that can be empirically verified, or the development of theses based on evidence, one finds an unrestrained mixture of metaphorical reasoning and dogmatic conviction, a pervasive confusion of analogy and homology, and an unabashed exercise in cross-species extrapolation and long inductive leaps. Most important, Lorenz fails to construct a relevant or testable paradigm for the study of war.

FIGURE 4.1   Variables Associated with Human Aggression

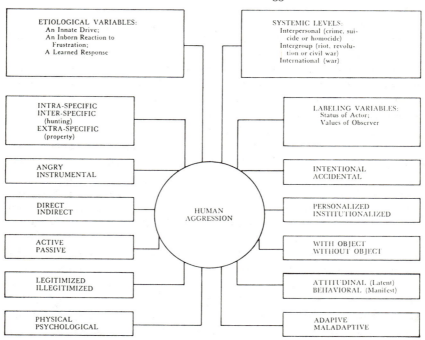

Invoking the authority of the Darwinian axiom that "we have a common origin with animals," Lorenz has wedded conceptually all kinds of animal and human behaviors based on superficial and semantic anthropomorphic comparisons. Thus, "all human rights have originated in a natural way, largely analogous to the evolution of social instincts in animals and man" (Lorenz 1966:84), while the urge for group membership has been "programmed in the pre-human phylogeny of man" (Lorenz 1966:265). "Like the triumph ceremony of greylag goose," Lorenz (1966:271) further extrapolates, "militant enthusiasm in man is a true autonomous instinct: it has its own appetitive behavior, its own releasing mechanisms, and, like the sexual urge or any other strong instinct, it engenders a specific feeling of intense satisfaction." In a 1940 paper entitled "Durch Domestikation verursachte Störungen arteigenen Verhaltens," Lorenz even equated the effects of civilization in human beings with the effects of domestication in animals (Lehrman 1953:354).

Lorenz and Ardrey are excessively freewheeling in their use of intraspecific and interspecific extrapolations. They habitually commit an anthropomorphic fallacy by describing animal behavior in human terms; they also reverse the process by describing human behavior in ethological terms. The ease with which they transfer observations of animal behavior into sociopolitical judgments about human beings contains far more of imaginative fantasy and magic label than of solid empirical observation and analysis. Lorenz (1966:217) is so convinced of his analogies between the social behavior patterns of wild geese and man that "all the truisms in our proverbs seem to apply equally to geese"; also the ritualized fighting of many vertebrates is "an impressive example of behavior analogous to human morality" (Lorenz 1966:110).

Consider the repeated argument of the Lorenzians that aggressive behavior of contemporary man — and his nation-states, too — can be understood only in terms of his phylogenetically programmed instinct, and that such an instinctual endowment can only be learned from animal studies. This argument "solves" the level-of-analysis problem by using one simple methodological linkage. As already discussed, the Lorenzian concept of aggression is difficult to employ at the systemic levels of large groups, nation-states, and the international system; hence, its methodological value for macropsychology, macroeconomics, and macropolitics — all of which are indispensable disciplines for peace research — is severely limited. By lumping together many different kinds and levels of behavior on the basis of phenotypic resemblances, however, the Lorenzians make a multilevel linkage. According to the Lorenzian methodology of "inductively determined facts,"[8] therefore, the cause of aggression in birds and fish is essentially the same as the cause of animal aggression (an intraspecific inductive leap),[9] just as the cause of animal aggression is essentially the same as the cause of human individual aggression (an interspecific inductive leap).[10] Likewise, the cause of individual aggression is essentially the same as the cause of group aggression (an intraspecific inductive leap), just as the cause of group aggression is essentially the same as the cause of international aggression (the final inductive leap).

It is indeed puzzling that a world-renowned scientist is so contemptuous of experimental research and so fond of impressionistic anecdotes and analogic word play.[11] Lorenz (1971:xix) candidly admits that he is "a very poor experimenter" but argues that "*induction,* the fundamental cognitive process of all science, which consists in the abstraction of a general law out of the observation of many special cases in which it prevails, is *not* absolutely dependent on the experiment." Likewise, he deplores the popularity of quantitative methods in science (Lorenz 1971:1). True, as a lifetime student and founder of modern ethology, Lorenz commands an encyclopedic knowledge of animal behavior. But his research stops short at *Homo sapiens,* for he has largely disregarded hundreds of relevant studies on human behavior in psychology, sociology, anthropology, social psychology, history, and political science. Yet, the two volume collection of Lorenz's lifetime work, published by Harvard University Press (Lorenz 1970, 1971), carries the misleading title *Studies in Animal and Human Behavior*, exemplifying his persistent propensity to advance arguments and claims far beyond available research or evidence. There is very little about *human* behavior in the two volumes, but obviously Lorenz is convinced that he has already learned from birds and fish everything that can be learned about human behavior.[12]

Furthermore, in all the writings of Lorenz (1958, 1964, 1965, 1966, 1970, 1971; Lehrman 1953) this writer has consulted, there is little reference to the growing literature of peace research including the well-known classics by Wright (1965) and Richardson (1960a, 1960b).[13] Instead, sources of "evidence" or "proof" of his observations of human aggression come exclusively from casual anecdotes. Just as the New York bus terminal is used as an "analogic proof" of his contention that crowding causes hostility and aggression, so his aunt's behavior is presented as an "anecdotal proof" of spontaneous human aggression. This anecdote merits a full citation, however, because it represents a typical example of Lorenz's analogic reasoning:

> Analogous behavior can be observed in human beings. In the good old days when there was still a Habsburg monarchy and there were still domestic servants, I used to observe the following, regularly predictable behavior in my widowed aunt. She never kept a maid longer than eight to ten months. She

was always delighted with a new servant, praised her to the skies, and swore that she had at last found the right one. In the course of the next few months her judgment cooled, she found small faults, then bigger ones, and toward the end of the stated period she discovered hateful qualities in the poor girl, who was finally discharged without a reference after a violent quarrel. After this explosion the old lady was once more prepared to find a perfect angel in her next employee.

It is not my intention to poke fun at my long-deceased and devoted aunt. I was able, or rather obliged, to observe exactly the same phenomenon in serious, self-controlled men, myself included, once when I was a prisoner of war. So-called polar disease, also known as expedition choler, attacks small groups of men who are completely dependent on one another and are thus prevented from quarreling with strangers or people outside their own circle of friends. From this it will be clear that the damming up of aggression will be the more dangerous, the better the members of the group know, understand, and like each other. In such a situation, as I know from personal experience, all aggression and intra-specific fight behavior undergo an extreme lowering of their threshold values. Subjectively this is expressed by the fact that one reacts to small mannerisms of one's best friends — such as the way in which they clear their throats or sneeze — in a way that would normally be adequate only if one had been hit by a drunkard (Lorenz 1966:55).

To be sure, this kind of anecdote is convenient and even useful in explaining — and popularizing — to the uninitiated the Lorenzian analysis of spontaneous and hydraulic process of aggression. But it can hardly be used as supporting evidence of the controversial concept. Lorenz makes no attempt to ascertain whether his aunt's behavior, or his own as a prisoner of war, is common to all men in all societies at all times. Heuristically, the anecdote is of little use because it has not been tested to meet the scientific standards of comparability in time and space. The biological potential of man does not ipso facto explain human behavior any more than one's IQ could predict its ultimate effect or outcome. The final expression of any biological potential, whether it be somatic or behavioral, depends largely on the ontogenetic history of an organism. Group aggression involves a complex chain of several behavioral components that cannot be treated as a uniform phenomenon. From the standpoint of peace research, therefore, it is more relevant to ask why some men, some groups, some cultures, and some nations are prone to violent behavior, and why others are peaceful, rather than to seek universal truth about man's nature.

Despite the modicum of his own research on *human* behavior or even reliance on the research of other students of human behavior, Lorenz advances sweeping pronouncements with the conviction of a man who has discovered the Truth. Repeatedly, he couches his argument in dogmatic terms, as if invoking the authority of Darwin would be sufficient to settle the issue. "To the humble [?] seeker of biological truth," he (1966:270) says, for example, "*there cannot be the slightest doubt* that human militant enthusiasm evolved out of a communal defense response of our prehuman ancestors" [italics added]. Similarly, "*there cannot be any doubt,* in the opinion of *any* biologically minded scientist that intraspecific aggression is, in Man, just as much of a spontaneous instinctive drive as in most other vertebrates" (Lorenz 1964:49; italics added).

On the other hand, critics of Lorenzian ethology are branded as antievolutionists if they point out discontinuities between animal and human *behaviors*, as fools who, having been influenced by the behavioralists (referring to American psychologists), refuse to admit that their own behavior obeys the laws of nature, or as followers of the dangerous American doctrine of equality if they believe in the malleability of human nature (Lorenz 1965, 1966, 1970, 1971; de Towarnicki 1970). Asserting that he has something to teach mankind, Lorenz finally concludes *On Aggression* with a prophetic message: "I am really being far from presumptuous when I profess my conviction that in the very near future not only scientists, but the majority of tolerably intelligent people, will consider as an obvious and banal truth all that has been said in this book about instincts in general and intra-specific aggression in particular, about the factors that build up the ever-increasing danger of human society's becoming completely disintegrated by the misfunctioning of social behavior patterns" (1966:276).[14]

Substantive Critique

Of the three alternative theories explaining the causation of aggressive behavior (biological-instinctual, response to frustration, and sociocultural learning), the substantive evidence in support of the Lorenzian theory of biological-instinctual determinism is weakest. A growing body of experimental/empirical literature in the social and behavioral sciences, including peace research, does not lend credence to the monocausal paradigm advanced by Lorenz and his followers. Aggressive behavior seems to be shaped by a plastic process involving an interwoven complex of internal, external, and experiential factors. Reflecting man's unique capability to expand and diversify his behavioral repertoire, human aggressive behavior expresses itself in a myriad of ways. There seems to be a discernible divergence, however, between the Lorenzian theory and human aggression and/or war: the higher one ascends on the phylogenetic scale in the animal kingdom, the farther one moves up the ladder of systemic levels of human behavior, the closer one reaches the core area of peace research, the more limited and insubstantial is the evidence supporting the Lorenzian theory.

Evidence for Animal Aggression

The lay public innocently assumes that Lorenz speaks for all students of animal behavior. Many of the social science critics have also accepted Lorenz's interpretation of animal behavior uncritically, even though they reject its application to humans (Barnett 1973; Berkowitz 1973; Nelson 1974). True, Lorenz stands on firmer ground in animal research. But his interpretation is not shared by all ethologists. In fact, his severe critics — S. A. Barnett, Sally Carrighar, J. H. Crook, Robert A. Hinde, J. P. Hailman, Daniel Lehrman, K. E. Moyer, T. C. Schneirla, J. P. Scott, and William Tavolga — have been his fellow professionals in animal behavior and closely related fields. Rejecting the nearly unanimous view of nonethological reviewers that Lorenz at least speaks authoritatively and reliably on animal behavior, one ethologist says that "*On Aggression* does not in fact represent the methods or opinions current in ethology" (Barnett 1973:75-76). Because of space limitations, this discussion is confined to a few illustrative examples of the salient substantive weaknesses in the Lorenzian theory of animal and human behavior with emphasis on aggression.

There is now increasing evidence in experimental literature on animal research that Lorenz has committed a double error. First, he oversimplifies the instinctive behavior of lower animals. Then, he overextrapolates from lower animals to animals high on the phylogenetic scale. In the interest of the completeness and the simplicity of his paradigm, Lorenz has considerably overlooked both phylogenetic and ontogenetic differences among various species. There appears to be no single instigation to aggression even among the lower animals. Instead, there are several kinds of aggression, the actual patterns of which differ from species to species.

The concept of prefixed innate behavior is also unsatisfactory because of the blurring line between developmental causation and hereditary causation. The straight-line relationship between gene and somatic characteristics is misleading since the organism is different at each different stage of its development (Lehrman 1953:346-347). Moreover, an experiment centering on the feeding behavior of sea gull chicks shows that "behavioral development is a mosaic created by continuing interactions of the developing organism and its environment" (Hailman 1969:106).

As we climb the evolutionary tree from lower animals to higher animals such as primates, which are closely related to man, aggressive behavior generally becomes less common. When it does occur, however, its causes are more complex, more numerous, less rigidly programmed by the genotype, and more influenced by ecological and experiential factors. Lorenz's characterization of primates as "irascible" does not seem to receive firm support from many primatologists who believe that the primates,

especially chimps, are on the whole peaceful and cooperative in their undisturbed natural environment, apart from the usual kinds of threat display. [15]

To say that aggressive behavior is rare and rather insignificant in the behavior of primates in their natural habitats is not to deny the fact that they
can become aggressive under certain conditions. However, there are different causal variables of animal aggression. The heritability of aggressiveness
in dogs and leghorn chickens has been demonstrated through selective
breeding (Corning 1973). It is also argued that frustration is as much a
source of aggression in animals as it is in children and adults (Berkowitz
1968b; Durbin and Bowlby 1968). The social conditions of rearing are also
believed to influence the probability of aggression in "intra-species encounters in mice, cats, dogs, monkeys, and other animals" (Hinde
1973:99). Despite the differences in emphasis on the etiological variables of
agonistic behavior, there is little doubt now that the causes of animal aggression are not as simple as the Lorenzians would have us believe and that
the stimuli evoking aggressive responses can be ecological, social, experiential, genetic, hereditary, hormonal, and even psychological (perceptual).

Can animal research shed light on human behavior in general and
human aggression in particular? By repeatedly stressing our common
origin with animals, the Lorenzians ignore the crucial fact that contemporary monkeys and apes are not the equivalents of human ancestors
(Washburn and Hamburg 1973:64). Without direct fossil evidence for the
evolution of *behavior,* we cannot make an inductive leap from contemporary
primates to our hominid ancestors nor from the latter to contemporary
man. Even in physiological attributes, contemporary man is unique. For
his brain has "enlarged from roughly 500 cc 1.75 million years ago to about
1450 cc at present" (Holloway 1968:43). Compared also with the ape or
monkey, the "social brain"—the parts in human brain that evolved in
response to social pressures and that today mediate appropriate social
behavior—has undergone a three-fold increase in size (Washburn and
Hamburg 1973:77).

The hazards of extrapolatory leap from animal to human behavior stem
from a large inventory of uniquely human characteristics of *Homo
sapiens:* greater survivability stemming from his greater adaptability and
lesser dependence on any particular environment; greater communicative
and symbolic skills; greater skill in the use of nonbiological tools and
weapons; greater and more generalized intellectual capacities; greater control over emotions; greater prevalence of organized violence; primacy of
social and cultural factors in the formation of hierarchy systems; greater diversity and range of instigating stimuli for aggression; greater variety and
dimension of manifestations of aggression; and greater cultural, social, and
psychological capacities to produce conflict or cooperation without direct

physical stimuli derived from the immediate sensory organs.

Evidence for Human Aggression and War

How much substantive evidence can we find in the empirical literature of peace research to support the Lorenzian theory of *human* aggression and war? It is beyond the scope of the present paper to review the entire literature; instead, we focus on a few crucial elements of the Lorenzian theory: instinctive-spontaneous-hydraulic process of aggression; indispensability of aggression for the preservation of individuals and species as well as for the mastery of creative human endeavors; pathology of undischarged aggression; territorial aggression; and catharsis as the prescriptive remedy for human warfare.

The Lorenzian theory of spontaneous aggression is aptly referred to as an energy model of motivation, but it is developed largely from the observations of some animal behavior—the hunting behavior of the dog, food begging of a young bird, fighting in a fish, courtship flights of a butterfly (Lehrman 1953). However, many students of animal behavior argue that there is no neurophysiological evidence for hydraulics in the brain (Alland 1969; Hailman 1969; Hinde 1973; Lehrman 1953; Schneirla 1966; Scott 1958). Experimental evidence is much weaker for spontaneous aggression in man. Most students of human behavior—psychologists, neurophysiologists, anthropologists, and social psychologists—reject the instinctive-hydraulic model; instead, they view aggression as one among many potential reactions to a variety of situations. It is indeed difficult to imagine how man's complex behavior patterns can be experimentally delineated with a simple mechanical model of physical energy.

The influence of learning and training on aggressive behavior, which has gained a considerable experimental support (Berkowitz 1973; Hunt 1973; Moyer 1971; Nelson 1974; Richter 1950; Scott 1958; Scott and Fredericson 1951; Tedeschi et al. 1974), also cast doubt on the notion of spontaneous aggression. For Scott and Fredericson (1951:306), training can overcome hereditary predispositions, and therefore "training includes by far the most important group of factors which affect agonistic behavior." In one study (Richter 1950), a complete inhibition of eating behavior was brought about by negative reinforcement in the form of sublethal doses of poison with the result that the subjects (rats) starved to death. That the physiological and emotional variables involved in aggressive behavior are different from those involved in sexual and ingestive behavior has been most cogently stated by J. P. Scott, who has done extensive research on aggression. "Thus we have a mechanism," Scott (1973:138) responds to Lorenz's notion of spontaneous aggression, "which prolongs and magnifies the effects of external stimulation but no mechanism for building up the first stimulation from within. There is no internal change corresponding to the change in blood sugar which results in hunger."

The Lorenzian argument that aggression has been adaptive in the evolutionary sense or that "collective militant enthusiasm, which is the prerequisite for war, is also the prerequisite for all higher human endeavor" is untenable. To validate such an argument, one would have to demonstrate that aggression has specifically contributed to the survival of *Homo sapiens*. If aggression has a quantifiable survival value, one would also find its distribution *universal in place and continuous in time*. Instead of producing a testable hypothesis or empirical or historical data, Lorenz merely restates the old Hobbesian cliché of war as the natural state of man. Even though there is no "fossil behavior," there is no accepted evolutionary theory which suggests killers are more adaptive than pacifists. "The survivors in the evolutionary rat race," observes Leach (1973:155), "are of two kinds—those which are disinclined to kill at all and those which are inclined to kill but are inhibited against killing members of their own kind."

It is difficult indeed to imagine how *homo homini lupus* whose life was so "nasty, brutish, and short" could have survived, multiplied, and even become the dominant species, while "99.9999 percent of all the species that have ever arisen are now extinct" (Corning 1971:355). The argument that many of man's charitable acts pass away uncompiled (Hunt 1973) and that the highest premium has been placed on cooperation throughout the five million or so years of man's evolution (Montagu 1973) still remains to be effectively rebutted. The oft-cited figure of fifty-nine million deaths from murders to world wars during the 126 years (from 1820 to 1945) in Richardson's (1960b:153) classic study cannot be used uncritically to support the Lorenzian thesis. Fifty-nine million deaths amount to about 1.6 percent of all deaths during the period;[16] moreover, 46.8 million (93.6 percent) of the total come from the upper four ranges in the eight-range scale of magnitude, showing a greater destructiveness of collective violence than individual aggression.

Besides, nation-states have varied so much in the frequency of their participation in wars during the period that Richardson (1960b:x, 176) argues that "none can be properly characterized as *inherently belligerent or inherently pacific*" [italics added]. Small and Singer (1970:152) also find that more than half the nations (77 out of 144) which were at one time or another members of the international system in the period 1816-1965 were able to escape international war entirely. A multivariate analysis of 652 primitive societies (taken from *A Study of War* by Quincy Wright) by Broch and Galtung (1966) shows that only 33 percent were "belligerent" in the sense that they were reputed to engage in aggressive warfare for economic and political exploitation. Even more tellingly, the level of belligerency increased with decreasing primitivity (i.e., increasing civilization).[17]

Whatever functions the wars of the distant past may have served, certainly modern war—even apart from its moral question—provides a poor survival or cathartic value. The soldiers in modern times are being constantly indoctrinated through positive and negative reinforcement to subordinate their individual impulses to the dictates of the state. Available studies of soldiers in combat (Allport 1950; Moskos 1969; Stouffer 1949; Shils and Janowitz 1948) have shown that the aggressive urge to fight the enemy was less commonly felt than individual self-interest—fear, concern for safety and survival, homesickness, anxiety for family welfare back home, job dissatisfaction, and boredom. The My Lai massacre is a pathological abnormality in the context of modern warfare. Levi (1966:151) finds that "in some armies more than half the men who were supposed to shoot did not pull the trigger." The refusal of Company A (of the 19th Light Infantry Brigade, 3rd Battalion of the U.S. Army in Vietnam) to obey the order to move out is also revealing (Moskos 1969).

A large-scale social science investigation conducted by the War Department's Information and Education Division during World War II revealed that many soldiers were engaged in "goldbricking"—that is, appearing to be busy without really accomplishing anything (Stouffer 1949). The German soldier during World War II gratified his primary needs through the primary group. As the war situation worsened for Germany with the corresponding disintegration of the primary group in the Wehrmacht, he progressively regressed into a narcissistic state in which moral and political symbols of the outer world were irrelevant to his first concern—"saving his own skin" (Shils and Janowitz 1948).

For the American soldier in Vietnam, the decisions of his government that brought him into combat were irrelevant and meaningless, and the paramount factor affecting his combat motivation was the operation of the rotation system (Moskos 1969). A typical American soldier in Vietnam may have spent no more than a few hours in actual fighting during his two-year term in the army, the greatest part of his service time being devoted to allelomimetic behavior, "behavior in which two or more individuals do the same thing at the same time, with some degree of mutual stimulation" (Scott 1969:130). Moreover, the ratio between front-line soldiers and rear-area supporters is rapidly changing in favor of the latter. In push-button and computerized wars, there is no survival or cathartic value.

Contrary to the Lorenzian assertion, there is no evidence in the studies of achievement motivation that aggression is indispensable for intellectual pursuit. In the best-known study of achievement motivation, McClelland and his associates (1953) concluded that there was no correlation between the instigation to aggression and achievement motivation. It has also been reported (*New York Times* 1971) that violent living conditions in the black ghettos of American cities impede a child's intellectual development. Based on their experimental study of ghetto school children in Washington, D.C., psychologists Gene Gordon and Dale Meers conclude that "the constant atmosphere of violence of the ghetto, absorbed into the unconscious in the form of fantasies, had arrested ego development," which is believed to be essential to reality perception or learning (cited in *New York Times* 1971).

Indeed there is much to be said for the hypothesis that aggression, far from being normal, healthy, or indispensable, is a pathological symptom. Mark and Ervin (1970) argue persuasively that the notion of spontaneous and self-generating aggression holds true only for people with specific brain abnormalities, some of which may be genetically inherited. Moyer (1971) also states that several types of brain dysfunction as well as low blood sugar are associated with pathological hyperirritability and aggressive behavior in humans. Frank (1968:46) mentions one type of brain fever — encephalitis lethargica — as being responsible for "a personality change characterized by marked destructiveness and impulsiveness." Fromm (1973:6) explains Hitler's "malignant aggression" in terms of necrophilia — "the passion to destroy life and the attraction to all that is dead, decaying, and purely mechanical."

Although evidence is still too tentative, several XYY chromosome studies in prisons "do demonstrate a variety of endocrinological, neurological, and other abnormalities which appear related to their [criminals'] deviant behavior" (Shah 1973:53). Likewise, Lauretta Bender (1973), a child psychologist who worked for more than three decades with disturbed children in New York City and State, observes that hostile aggression in a child is not a normal pattern of behavior, which infrequently occurs as a result of endogenous pathology in the context of disturbing social and environmental situations.

The experimental data and analyses presented above do not provide firm support for the Lorenzian thesis that undischarged aggression would have serious pathological effects. However, Lorenz relies on an unpublished lecture by Sydney Margolin to "prove" that the Ute Indians suffer more frequently from neurosis and accident-proneness than any other human group because of their undischarged aggression (1966:244-245). Omer C. Stewart (1973), who has studied the Ute Indians since 1930 and published most extensively on their ethnology, their history, and their adjustment to modern life, has shown how utterly erroneous Lorenz's account is of the Prairie Indians in general and of the Utes in particular. Pointing out numerous factual errors in Lorenz's account, Stewart (1973:224) concludes: "Like most other American Indians, the Ute have been victims of alcohol and under its influence have committed many criminal acts and have been careless with their own lives and the lives of others. But this has been true of the tribes of the Atlantic Coast states, the Chippewa of the Great Lakes, the Northwest Coast fishing Indians, etc." Stewart has also managed to have his statement of rebuttal approved by three other experts on the Ute: Elbert J. Floyd, John R. White, and Arthur L. Warner.

Although territorial behavior is not as simple or as unitary or universal a phenomenon as Lorenz and Ardrey make it to be, there is nonetheless strong evidence supporting the Lorenzian thesis in several studies of such nonhuman species as fish, birds, mice, insects, and some mammals (Calhoun 1961, 1962; Hoagland 1973; Tinbergen 1956). It has been observed experimentally in the behaviors of these animals that over-crowding causes a pathological breakdown in their normal social interactions including courtship, mating, and maternal behavior. However, man's nearest relatives among primates—the savannah monkeys, the chimpanzee, and the gorilla—do not show as much territorial behavior (Crook 1973; Scott 1973). In addition, caribou, elephants, sea otters, whale, and lemmings apparently have no territories, while such animals as gophers, prairie dogs, and marmots in the temperate zone have communal dwellings (Carrighar 1970).

Is there evidence for supporting "instinctive territorial aggression" in man? Actually, Lorenz and Ardrey do not make a clear conceptual distinction between *individual territorialism* and *group territorialism*. But the difference seems critical because of the inherent "biological" incompatibility between the two. In times of war, most men would have to give up their individual territorialism in defense of group territorialism, even though the two may be symbolically wedded through patriotic propaganda.

Most empirical studies have shown discernible correlations between geographical contiguity (common frontiers) and frequency of war involvement (Richardson 1960b; Singer 1972; Wright 1965). In Richardson's (1960b:297) study, for example, "the number of a state's external wars has a positive correlation of 0.77 with the number of its frontiers." However, common frontiers mean frequent contacts and interactions. Unless contact as a variable is clearly isolated from contiguity, we should not read too much into the positive correlation.[18] Besides, to say that most states would defend their territory when attacked is to avoid the more critical question: Why do some states *attack*, making it necessary for the attacked to *defend* their territory? It is not possible for all the states to attack and defend at the same time. In order to probe into this causal question, we have to examine Lorenz's repeated assertion that crowding or population density causes hostility and aggression.

Although available evidence is still meagre and fragmentary, it does seem to lean against the Lorenzian proposition that crowding necessarily

causes hostility and aggression. Man's territorial or "proxemic" behavior
under crowded conditions seems to vary widely depending on a multitude
of causal variables — ecological, social, cultural, sexual, circumstantial,
psychological (expectational), and political.

Since the high incidence of violent crime, street gangwars, juvenile delinquency, mental illness, and rioting as extreme expressions of interpersonal and intergroup aggression is found predominantly in overcrowded
American cities, it would be tempting to make a prima facie correlation between population density or crowding and aggressive behavior. However,
recent experimental studies (Ehrlich and Freedman 1973; Freedman et al.
1972) have produced some unexpected results. Crowding per se, with income level, malnutrition, noise, filth, and other related variables controlled, has no appreciable overall effect on crime, mental illness, competitiveness, and aggressiveness. Nonetheless, experiments showed that
males become somewhat more competitive, vindictive, and aggressive
while females became more lenient, tolerant, and cooperative under
crowded conditions.

In addition, the presence of females exerted some ameliorating influence
upon male aggressiveness. "Territoriality (personal space)," Freedman et
al. (1972:545) conclude, "seems to be largely a characteristic of the males of
a species rather than the females." Ehrlich and Freedman (1973:282) also
conclude their study by offering an interesting piece of advice for peace
research:

> All-male juries or cabinets or international conferences should probably be
> avoided, or at least be given spacious quarters. Better still, women should be
> included, not only to give them equal representation, but because apparently
> any negative effects of crowding disappear when the sexes are mixed. There is
> thus strong argument to eliminate the secretive meetings of men in back
> rooms deciding our fates — and bring them out into the open where their deci-
> sions are less likely to be aggressive.

Furthermore, available studies of war establish no correlation between
population density and war proneness. Instead of the expected correlation
between the degree of foreign conflict and population density, Haas
(1965:315) finds "a slight inverse relation" in his study of societal variables
contributing to foreign conflict behavior of nation-states. Finding no relationship between the rapid increase of world population from 1820 and
1949 and any proportionate increase in the frequency of, and losses from,
war, Richardson (1960b:167) concluded: "There is a suggestion, but not a
conclusive proof, that mankind has become less warlike since A.D. 1820."[19]

Singer (1972:267) too finds "no significant association between a nation's growth rate in population or density and its war-proneness" in his study of ninety-three international wars during the period 1816-1965. Population pressures may or may not lead to international conflict, Wright (1965: 1130) concluded his study, "depending upon a multitude of geographic, cultural, technological, physiological, political, military, psychological, and other factors in the particular situation."

Lastly, the Lorenzian catharsis prescription finds little support in the experimental literature. In fact, ample evidence points to the opposite direction — that is, the expression of aggression tends to strengthen subsequent aggressive response (Berkowitz 1962, 1968a, 1973; Eysenck 1955, 1966; Goldstein and Arms 1971; Moyer 1973; Singer 1971). Experiments with children have demonstrated that live and film models are equally effective in instigating aggression (Bandura et al. 1961, 1963; Lovibond 1967). The reinforcement influence works in such a way as to generalize from one kind of behavior to another through the common denominator — the attempt to injure some object or person. A laboratory experiment has shown, for example, that children exposed to aggressive adult models reproduced and generalized aggressive behavior to a new setting while children in the non-aggressive control groups exhibited virtually no imitative aggression (Bandura et al. 1961).[20]

The reinforcement potency of the modeling process in facilitating aggressive behavior was further confirmed in another experiment, in which children were exposed to film-mediated aggressive models. Moreover, this experiment produced significant sexual variables: boys, compared to girls, exhibited significantly more total aggression ($t = 2.69$, $p < .01$), more imitative aggression ($t = 2.82$, $p < .005$), more aggressive gun play ($z = 3.38$, $p < .001$), and more nonimitative aggressive behavior ($t = 2.98$, $p < .005$), while girls were more inclined to sit on the Bobo doll but refrained from punching it ($z = 3.47$, $p < .001$) (Bandura et al. 1963:8).

Similarly, experiments with adult audiences hardly support the contention of Eibl-Eibesfeldt (and of the TV and movie industry) that fantasy aggression works as a socially safe and vicarious outlet for the supposedly pent-up aggressive energy within the audience (Berkowitz and Rawlings 1963; Berkowitz et al. 1963). Instead of providing an easy and safe cathartic outlet, watching filmed violence increases the probability that someone in the audience will behave aggressively in a later situation. The more recent works prepared for the National Commission on the Causes and Prevention of Violence (1969) and for the Surgeon General (1972) on the impact of televised violence also present strong evidence, suggesting a causal relationship between witnessed violence and an observer's subsequent aggressive behavior.

Experimental data are equally damaging to Lorenz's proposal of aggressive sporting contests as a cathartic outlet. Eysenck (1966), drawing on his own earlier experiments as well as on those of others, states that there is a consistent tendency for persons aggressive in one context to be aggressive in another context. He concludes that there are positive correlations — as high as $+0.4$ for various groups — between instances and expressions of aggression. Goldstein and Arms (1971) conducted field interviews at the 1969 Army-Navy football game and also at an Army-Temple gymnastics meet (during the same month) in order to compare the hostility of spectators before and after the games, using the Buss-Durkee inventory with the possible range of hostility scores from 0 to 28. Results: regardless of the subjects' preferred team, post–football game hostility was greater than pregame ($F = 5.29$, df $= 1/144$, p $< .025$), showing little effect for preferred team ($F < 1.0$) or for the interaction effect ($F < 1.0$), while the premeet hostility mean of gymnastics spectators (12.00) was not significantly different from the postmeet hostility mean (12.71, t $= .66$, df $= 79$, p $< .20$), showing that hostility did not rise significantly as a result of observing a physically nonaggressive sport event. They arrive at the logical conclusion: regardless of team preference and the outcome of the game, watching an aggressive sport leads to an increase in hostility among spectators.

Several soccer riots and one soccer war in Latin America, the wanton destruction of train interiors by British football team supporters, and the behavior of players and spectators at professional hockey games in North America, to mention a few examples, are hardly reassuring to the Lorenzian assumption that sporting contests provide a healthy and cooperative outlet for the "collective militant enthusiasm" of nation-states. Lorenz's fallacy lies in his extrapolative equation of physical energy with psychological energy. If a drop in systolic blood pressure is a sign of physiological relaxation, a simple performance of physical activity or free aggression against any object or person does not work. This is because "the frustrated person (who wants, and is prepared, to attack his frustrater) may be primarily concerned with injuring the person who had provoked him" (Berkowitz 1968a:171). Even Tinbergen refuses to agree with Lorenz that redirected attack exhausts the aggressive urge. Aggressive behavior, Tinbergen (1968:1418) argues, has two simultaneous but opposite effects — a waning effect and a self-inflammatory effect — but the self-inflammatory effect often wins.

The basic flaw in Lorenz's catharsis thesis stems from his hydraulic conceptualization of human aggression. As the experimental evidence examined in this paper suggests, aggressive behavior is largely a learned habit which can be easily activated by cultural cues. Instead of deflating physical energy, aggressive competition tends to arouse stress and anxiety and to enhance the strength of an individual's aggressive potential unless checked by stronger inhibitions. The free and permissive expression of aggression weakens inhibitions, strengthens aggressive tendencies, provides more cues, and blunts perceptual and judgmental norms of the observer and the actor alike.

In the final analysis, the Lorenzian theory cannot account adequately for human aggression because it is insensitive to the relative importance of different causal variables, such as sex, age, social class and organization, culture, ecological habitat, frustration (deprivation) level, experiential factor, and inherited and/or learned predisposition of individuals. Indeed the popularity of the Lorenzian theory may lie in its diagrammatic simplicity and sweeping application. But the theory that assumes so much uniformity of human behavior in time and place cannot explain human aggressive behavior in sociopolitical contexts, let alone predict when wars will be fought or avoided, or who will win or lose, and why.

Policy Implications

Whether the present critique of Lorenzianism is valid or not might not matter much beyond the narrow confines of academic specialists were it not for the fact that Lorenz has mounted a pulpit to preach to mankind and that his message now attracts such a wide and uncritical acceptance among so large an audience. Capturing the malaise of our violence-afflicted times, the Lorenzians—especially Ardrey—have transformed Original Sin, Hobbesianism, and Darwinism into a political movement. In short, Lorenzianism as it is now propagated, believed, or practiced poses some serious policy and behavioral implications for peace research.

Ominously, Lorenzianism has appeared at a time when the rising tide of violence in human affairs seems to defy any logical or rational explanation. Is it not possible that Lorenz's thesis of man's innate depravity could easily be misused by those who rationalize the use of force as a healthy, necessary, or inevitable historical process? "War is," declared General Friedrich von Bernhardi in 1912, "a biological necessity . . . it is as necessary as the struggle of the elements in nature—it gives a biologically just decision since its decision rest [*sic*] on the very nature of things" (quoted in Clare 1969:163). Since Lorenz asserts with authority and conviction that aggression is integral to ambition, love, friendship, intellectual vigor, and other socially sanctioned attributes, a contemporary von Bernhardi could easily disguise himself as a Lorenzian in propagating militarism.

There is a clear and continuing danger that Lorenzianism without Lorenz could provide a "scientific" foundation upon which a new conservative-racial-militaristic ideology can be constructed.[21] Lorenz's biological determinism, his eufunctional view of aggression, his dualism on collective militant enthusiasm, his love of tradition,[22] his zeal for aggressive competition, his authoritarian attitude,[23] and his disregard of institutionalized aggression coupled with his unrestrained penchant for politicizing his theory of aggression—all of these would place Lorenz in the company of those who champion the political status quo at best and militarism at worst. However, the politicization of Lorenzianism reaches its peak in the writings of Ardrey (1966:316-317), a skillful popularizer of Lorenzianism who presents glorified views of white South Africa as "attaining peaks of affluence, order, security, and internal solidarity rivaled by few long-established nations" and of American military intervention in Indochina.

Man's behavior, including his war making or his war avoiding, is powerfully influenced by his belief and expectation. The belief in the inevitability of war or the expectation of omnipresent aggression may itself become a cause of war through a self-fulfilling prophecy. The notion that most people deplore war but expect it to continue and that the factor of expectancy becomes the indispensable condition of war (Allport 1950) has gained some additional support in recent years (Putney and Middleton 1962; Granberg 1969). Even in a cross-cultural survey of the warfare patterns of primitive peoples all over the world, "the strongest relationship that shows up is the positive correlation between *war frequency* and *military expectations*" (Naroll 1970:35).

The Lorenzian view that human aggression is instinctive, spontaneous, and unmodifiable[24] both enhances the old Hobbesian theme that war is natural and inevitable and encourages the fatalistic sense of low efficacy—the "nothing much we can do about it" attitude. We can hardly expect to make war obsolete if we refuse to believe it is a human invention or that it can be indeed abolished. Lorenzianism stands as a formidable conceptual barrier in the way of changing our attitudinal and behavioral orientation toward the nature of war.

Conclusion

The central point of the present chapter is that research on the causes and correlates of war cannot benefit from Lorenzianism in its present state of knowledge and conceptualization. As this chapter has attempted to show, the Lorenzian theory of aggression and war is seriously flawed on conceptual, methodological, and substantive grounds. The cavalier use of operationally ill-defined terms and concepts, the almost exclusive reliance on casual anecdotes, the disregard of empirical studies contradicting the monocausal paradigm, the inductive/extrapolative leaps to solve the level-of-analysis problem, the cross-species generalizations based on the uncritical merging of human and animal behavior, and the recurrent tendency to advance argument in finalistic terms with little supporting evidence—all these weaknesses warrant scientific disapproval of the Lorenzian theory.

Moreover, the Lorenzian approach raises some disturbing moral implications bearing on our social behavior as well as on our public policy. Because of its monocausal and monoexplanatory view of human aggression and war, its implicit association with war-prone attributes (militarism, conservatism, authoritarianism, nationalism, and racialism), and its inadequacy in the methodology and theoretical analysis of conflict resolution, the Lorenzian theory is not a useful model for the development of an applied science of war prevention. A naive and uncritical enthusiasm in embracing Lorenzianism can be a misleading and even dangerous pursuit. It is therefore clearly in the interest of peace that we should be vigilant, wary of the current voguish movement of Lorenzian ethology.

However, this is not to belittle contributions an ethological/biological approach could make to peace research. While ethological/biological theories do not adjust themselves easily to the revolutionary changes in the nature of war that have taken place in modern times, especially since Hiroshima, they nonetheless present a necessary challenge for our self-scrutiny as well as against the holistic paradigm of environmental determinism. By successfully delineating ways in which behavioral patterns can be shaped by constant and dynamic bio-environmental interactions and manners in which sign-stimuli of the environment work in eliciting certain sequences of motor action in animals under appropriate internal physiological conditions, the developmental school in ethology has shown legitimate ways of assimilating the work of the biological sciences into models, hypotheses, and explanations about human behavior in a specifically delimited situation. Specifically, this kind of ethological research can open up possibilities of exploring the types and effects of the biological inputs in a crisis decision-making process.[25]

Perhaps the widespread vogue of Lorenzianism should be greeted as an intellectual opportunity rather than feared as a threat to peace research. The current state of peace research, characterized as it is by completely divergent paths of politically naive ethologists and biologically naive behavioral scientists, is unhealthy. Before we can make a prudent, selective synthesis of whatever ethology has to offer, however, more and more social scientists engaged in peace research need to do ethological/biological research. This might open up a needed dialogue with those ethologists who have something more useful than Lorenzianism to offer. Failing that, we will have only ourselves to blame when the day comes, if it has not already, when Lorenzianism is propagated as the "gospel" of peace research.

Notes

1. The clearest—and the last—position Freud took on human aggression was stated in 1930, when he said: "In all that follows I adopt the standpoint, therefore, that the inclination to aggression is an original, self-subsisting instinctual disposition in man, and I return to my view that it constitutes the greatest impediment to civilization" (Freud 1962:69).

2. Most peace researchers would agree that Quincy Wright and Lewis Richardson have indeed made pioneering contributions to the development of peace research as a science. Singer and Small (1972:4) expressed a judgment in their important book on war that "the important turning point is marked by the rise of scientific (and therefore quantitative) analyses of war, manifested primarily in the work of Quincy Wright and Lewis Richardson beginning in the 1930s." However, the inclusion of Freud and Lorenz in this category by Alcock is mystifying. Perhaps, Alcock's conception of war, which appears to be a variant on the Lorenzian theme, may explain the mystery. "*War* is," Alcock (1972:199) states, "an overt action resulting from man's innate *aggressiveness.*"

3. This paper is premised on the acceptance of Galtung's conceptualization of peace research as "an effort to promote the realization of *values*" (Galtung 1969:190); furthermore, the values peace research seeks to promote refer not only to negative peace ("absence of violence") but also to positive peace ("social justice").

4. "The form of an instinctive behaviour pattern," to quote Lorenz's own words, "exhibits remarkable independence from all receptor process—not just independence from "experience" in the broadest sense of the term but also from stimuli which impinge upon the organism *during* performance of the pattern" (Lorenz 1970; see also Lorenz 1970:250, 314, 322, 348).

5. Lorenz's view on Freud's concept of aggression was stated in the following terms: "Freud—I'm simplifying a great deal—discovered the eternal instinctive drives, those not dependent on environment, in a time when the doctrine of the conditioned reflex was at its acme. If he had only that he would have deserved three Nobel prizes, but he generalized the properties of sexuality onto all the other instincts. Perhaps his fundamental error was to have made aggression the antagonist of life. He made it something of a devil" (de Towarnicki 1970:29).

6. "Militant enthusiasm," Lorenz (1966:268) defines, "is a specialized form of communal aggression, clearly distinct from and yet functionally related to the more primitive forms of petty individual aggression."

7. Lorenz himself seems to be admitting this point, when he wrote: "Many modern ethologists, particularly those publishing in English, contend that the term innate is not only useless, but heuristically harmful. They assume that phylogenetic adaptation and adaptive modification can be added to and mixed with each other in any behaviour mechanism, however minute and elementary. For this reason, they regard it as hopeless and even dangerous to try separating, in experiment or thought, innate and learned elements of behavior" (Lorenz 1965:102).

8. Lorenz repeatedly attempts to justify his approach as "inductive natural science." His approach "also provides convincing proof of the indispensable necessity for the broadest possible knowledge of concrete individual facts, collected

through *unprejudiced* observation and termed the *'inductive basis'* of a natural science" (Lorenz 1971:131). In a similar vein, he deplores "overestimation of the primacy of the entity over its components and underestimation of the relatively entity-independent component" (Lorenz 1971:125).

9. Carrighar (1970:42) contends that Lorenz's research with tamed animals such as geese induced by guard fences, and captive cichlid fishes in tanks, has enormously heightened their aggressiveness.

10. "The more distantly the animal is related to man," observe Washburn and Hamburg (1973:66), "the less the human perception of the situation is likely to correspond to that of the animal."

11. Ardrey's methodology is so crude and his analogic speculation so wild that *The Territorial Imperative* should be relegated to the category of pseudo–science fiction. To make a methodological critique of his work would seem superfluous. Even Lorenz (1970:xiv; Evans 1974:86) admits that Ardrey sometimes makes him "suffer" and "perspire."

12. To the question, "Does the study of the behavior of animals throw light on the behavior of man?" Lorenz responded: "If you know animals well, you know yourself reasonably well" (de Towarnicki 1970:4).

13. After comparing the Lorenzian theory of aggression with Freud's, Fromm (1973:20-21) also observed: "Lorenz, at least when writing *On Aggression,* seems not to have had any firsthand knowledge of Freud's work. There is not a single direct reference to his writings, and what references there are refer to what psychoanalytic friends told him about Freud's position; regrettably they are not always right, or they have not been accurately understood."

14. Lorenz reasserts his conviction in a 1970 interview: "Believe me, one day *everything* I've said will seem ordinary" (de Towarnicki 1970:30; italics added).

15. For substantiation of this point based on extensive field research by primatologists, see the following: Goodall 1965; Nishida 1970; Reynolds and Reynolds 1965; and Schaller 1965.

16. Singer and Small (1972:374), whose quantitative study of war identified 93 international wars in the period 1816-1965, count "the death of over 29 million military personnel, exclusive of civilians."

17. Singer and Small (1972) dispute the prevalent belief in the increase of the frequency of war. "Whether we look at the number of wars," they (1972:201) observe, "their severity or their magnitude, there is no significant trend upward or down over the past 150 years." However, they note that "most of the war in the [international] system has been accounted for by a small fraction of the nations, most of which would be found near the top of any hierarchy based on diplomatic status, military-industrial capability, or related indicators" (Singer and Small 1972:287).

18. Europe clearly emerges as the most war-prone region of the world, according to Singer and Small's study. However, the authors caution that this may be a consequence of their selection criteria (Singer and Small 1972:296). It should also be added here that European nations sharing common frontiers have had extensive interactions with each other.

19. While finding a strong tendency toward periodicity in the international

system's war experiences, Singer and Small (1972), as noted above, find no trend upward or downward in the frequency of international war during much the same period covered by Richardson.

20. Eysenck (1966) also shows numerous experimental studies which demonstrated with equal force the reinforcement power of the modeling process in facilitating antimilitaristic and antiwar attitude and behavior.

21. Willhoite (1971:629-630), who has examined the Lorenzian thought from the historical perspective of Western political philosophy, concludes that "Lorenz seems to have much in common with the conservative tradition in Western political thought."

22. For a well-highlighted position of Lorenz on tradition, see his interview with de Towarnicki (1970).

23. "I would venture to say," Lorenz expressed his somewhat authoritarian attitude in his interview with de Towarnicki (1970:27), "that in man there is a direct correlation between the hate among children and the lack of a dominant father."

24. Lorenz's view on this matter was stated as follows: "It is the spontaneity of the instinct that makes it so dangerous. If it were merely a reaction to certain external factors, as many sociologists and psychologists maintain, the state of mankind would not be as perilous as it really is, for, in that case, the reaction-eliciting factors could be *eliminated with some hopes of success*" (Lorenz 1966:50; italics added).

25. That this can be done fruitfully has been shown by Ole Holsti in his book *Crisis, Escalation, War* (1972), which explores the types and consequences of crisis-induced stress upon those aspects of individual and organizational performance that most directly bear upon the outcomes of foreign policymaking.

References

Alcock, N. Z. 1972. *The War Disease.* Oakville, Ontario: Canadian Peace Research Institute Press.

Alland, A. 1969. "Darwinian sociology without social Darwinism?" *Social Research 36,* 549-561.

Allport, G. W. 1950. "The role of expectancy." Pp. 43-78 in H. Cantril (ed.), *Tensions That Cause War.* Urbana: University of Illinois Press.

Ardrey, R. 1966. *The Territorial Imperative.* New York: Atheneum.

Bandura, A., D. Ross, and S. A. Ross. 1961. "Transmission of aggression through imitation of aggressive models." *J. of Abnormal and Social Psychology 63,* 575-582.

————. 1963. "Imitation of film-mediated aggressive models." *J. of Abnormal and Social Psychology 66,* 3-11.

Bandura, A., and R. H. Walters. 1963. *Social Learning and Personality Development.* New York: Holt, Rinehart & Winston.

Barnett, S. A. 1973. "On the hazards of analogies." Pp. 75-83 in A. Montagu (ed.), *Man and Aggression.* New York: Oxford University Press.

Bender, L. 1973. "Hostile aggression in children." Pp. 318-322 in C. Otten (ed.), *Aggression and Evolution.* Lexington, Mass.: Xerox College Publishing.

Berkowitz, L. 1962. *Aggression*. New York: McGraw-Hill Book Co.

_____. 1968a. "Aggression: psychological aspects." *International Encyclopedia of the Social Sciences 1,* 168-174.

_____. 1968b. "The study of urban violence." *American Behavioral Scientist* (March-April), 14-16.

_____. 1973. "Simple views of aggression." Pp. 285-295 in C. Otten (ed.), *Aggression and Evolution*. Lexington, Mass.: Xerox College Publishing.

_____, and E. Rawlings. 1963. "Effects of film violence on inhibitions against subsequent aggression." *J. of Abnormal and Social Psychology 66,* 405-412.

_____, R. Corwin, and M. Heironimus. 1963. "Film violence and subsequent aggressive tendencies." *Public Opinion Quarterly 12,* 300-306; 308-315.

Blumenthal, M. D., R. L. Kahn, and F. M. Andrews. 1971. "Attitudes toward violence." *Proceedings of the 79th Annual Convention of the American Psychological Association 6,* 836-837.

Broch, T. and J. Galtung. 1966. "Belligerence among the primitives: a re-analysis of Quincy Wright's data." *J. of Peace Research 3,* 33-45.

Calhoun, J. B. 1961. "Phenomena associated with population density." *Proceedings of the National Academy of Science 47,* 428-449.

_____. 1962. "Population density and social pathology." *Scientific American 206,* 139-148.

Carrighar, S. 1970. "War is not in our genes." *UNESCO Courier 8,* 40-45.

Clare, A. W. 1969. "Is aggression instinctive?" *Studies 58,* 153-165.

Corning, P. A. 1971. "The biological bases of behavior and some implications for political science." *World Politics 23,* 321-370.

_____. 1973. "Human violence: some causes and implications." Pp. 119-143 in C. R. Beitz and T. Herman (eds.), *Peace and War*. San Francisco: W. H. Freeman and Company.

Craig, W. 1918. "Appetites and aversions as constituents of instincts." *Biological Bulletin 34,* 91-107.

Crook, J. H. 1973. "The nature and function of territorial aggression." Pp. 183-220 in A. Montagu (ed.), *Man and Aggression*. New York: Oxford University Press.

de Towarnicki, F. 1970. "A talk with Konrad Lorenz." *New York Times Magazine* (July 5), 4-5, 27, 29-30.

Driver, P. M. 1967. "Toward an ethology of human conflict." *J. of Conflict Resolution 11,* 361-374.

Durbin, E.F.M., and J. Bowlby. 1968. "Personal aggressiveness and war." Pp. 81-103 in L. Bramson and G. W. Goethals (eds.), *War*. New York: Basic Books.

Ehrlich, P., and J. Freedman. 1973. "Population, crowding and human behavior." Pp. 274-282 in C. Otten (ed.), *Aggression and Evolution*. Lexington, Mass.: Xerox College Publishing.

Eibl-Eibesfeldt, I. 1972. *Love and Hate* (G. Strachan, trans.). New York: Holt, Rinehart & Winston.

_____, and W. Wickler. 1968. "Ethology." *International Encyclopedia of the Social Sciences 5,* 186-192.

Evans, R. I. 1974. "Lorenz warns." *Psychology Today* (November): 82-93.

Eysenck, H. J. 1955. *The Psychology of Politics*. New York: Praeger.

_____. 1966. "War and aggressiveness." Pp. 576-586 in J. K. Zawodny (ed.), *Man and International Relations*, Vol. 1. San Francisco: Chandler Publishing Company.

Frank, J. 1968. *Sanity and Survival*. New York: Vintage Books.

Freedman, J. L., A. S. Levy, R. W. Buchanan, and J. Price. 1972. "Crowding and human aggression." *J. of Experimental Social Psychology 8*, 528-548.

Freud, S. 1962. *Civilization and Its Discontents* (J. Strachey, trans. and ed.). New York: W. W. Norton & Co. (originally published in 1930).

_____. 1968. "Why war?" Pp. 71-80 in L. Bramson and G. W. Goethals (eds.), *War*. New York: Basic Books (originally published in 1932).

Fromm, E. 1973. *The Anatomy of Human Destructiveness*. New York: Holt, Rinehart & Winston.

Galtung, J. 1964. "A structural theory of aggression." *J. of Peace Research 1*, 95-119.

_____. 1969. "Violence, peace, and peace research." *J. of Peace Research 6*, 167-191.

Goldstein, J. H., and R. L. Arms. 1971. "Effects of observing athletic contests on hostility." *Sociometry 34*, 83-90.

Goodall, J. 1965. "Chimpanzees of the Gombe stream reserve." Pp. 425-473 in I. DeVore (ed.), *Primate Behavior*. New York: Holt, Rinehart & Winston.

Granberg, D. 1969. "War expectancy and the evaluation of a specific war." *J. of Conflict Resolution 13*, 546-549.

Green, R. T., and G. Santori. 1969. "A cross cultural study of hostility and aggression. *J. of Peace Research 6*, 13-22.

Haas, M. 1965. "Societal approaches to the study of war." *J. of Peace Research 2*, 307-323.

Hailman, J. P. 1969. "How an instinct is learned." *Scientific American 221*, 98-106.

Hinde, R. A. 1973. "The nature of aggression." Pp. 93-100 in C. Otten (ed.), *Aggression and Evolution*. Lexington, Mass.: Xerox College Publishing.

Hoagland, H. 1973. "Mechanisms of population control." Pp. 225-239 in C. Otten (ed.), *Aggression and Evolution*. Lexington, Mass.: Xerox College Publishing.

Holloway, R. L. 1968. "Human aggression." Pp. 29-48 in M. Fried, M. Harris, and R. Murphy (eds.), *War*. New York: The Natural History Press.

Holsti, O. R. 1972. *Crisis, Escalation, War*. Montreal: McGill-Queens Univ. Press.

Hunt, M. 1973. "Man and beast." Pp. 19-38 in A. Montagu (ed.), *Man and Aggression*. New York: Oxford University Press.

James, W. 1968. "The moral equivalent of war." Pp. 21-31 in L. Bramson and G. W. Goethals (eds.), *War*. New York: Basic Books (originally published in 1910).

Leach, E. 1973. "Don't say 'Boo' to a goose." Pp. 150-158 in A. Montagu (ed.), *Man and Aggression*. New York: Oxford University Press.

Lehrman, D. S. 1953. "A critique of Konrad Lorenz's theory of instinctive behavior." *Quarterly Review of Biology 28*, 337-363.

Levi, W. 1966. "On the causes of war and the conditions of peace." Pp. 146-155 in R. A. Falk and S. H. Mendlovitz (eds.), *Toward a Theory of War Prevention*. New York: World Law Fund.

Leyhausen, P. 1965. "The sane community—a density problem?" *Discovery 26*, 27-33.

Lorenz, K. Z. 1958. "The evolution of behavior." *Scientific American* (December), 3-12.

———. 1964. "Ritualized fighting." Pp. 39-50 in J. D. Carthy and F. J. Ebling (eds.), *The Natural History of Aggression*. London: Academic Press.

———. 1965. *Evolution and Modification of Behavior*. Chicago: University of Chicago Press.

———. 1966. *On Aggression*. New York: Harcourt, Brace & World, Inc.

———. 1970. *Studies in Animal and Human Behavior*, Vol. 1 (R. Martin, trans.). Cambridge, Mass.: Harvard University Press.

———. 1971. *Studies in Animal and Human Behavior*, Vol. 2 (R. Martin, trans.). Cambridge, Mass.: Harvard University Press.

Lovibond, S. H. 1967. "The effect of media stressing crime and violence upon children's attitudes." *Social Problems 15*, 91-100.

Mark, V. H., and F. R. Ervin. 1970. *Violence and the Brain*. New York: Harper & Row.

McClelland, D., J. W. Atkinson, R. A. Clark, and E. L. Lowell. 1953. *The Achievement Motive*. New York: Appleton-Century-Crofts.

McDougall, W. 1923. *An Outline of Psychology*. New York: Scribner's.

Merton, R. 1957. *Social Theory and Social Structure*. Glencoe, Ill.: Free Press.

Montagu, A. 1973. "The new litany of 'innate depravity,' or original sin revisited." Pp. 3-18 in A. Montagu (ed.), *Man and Aggression*. New York: Oxford University Press.

Moskos, C. C. 1969. "Why men fight: American combat soldiers in Vietnam." *Society 7*, 1-10.

Moyer, K. E. 1971. "The physiology of aggression and the implications for aggression control." Pp. 61-92 in J. J. Singer (ed.), *The Control of Aggression and Violence*. New York: Academic Press.

———. 1973. "The physiology of violence." *Psychology Today 7*, 35-38.

Naroll, R. 1970. "Does military deterrence deter?" Pp. 27-42 in K. Boulding (ed.), *Peace and the War Industry*. New Brunswick, N.J.: Transaction Books.

National Commission on the Causes and Prevention of Violence. 1969. *To Establish Justice, to Insure Domestic Tranquility: The Final Report of the National Commission on the Causes and Prevention of Violence*. Washington, D.C.: Government Printing Office.

Nelson, S. D. 1974. "Nature/nurture revisited I." *J. of Conflict Resolution 18*, 285-335.

New York Times. 1971. July 30.

Nishida, T. 1970. "Social behavior and relationship among wild chimpanzees of the Mahali mountains." *Primates 2*, 47-87.

Putney, S., and R. Middleton. 1962. "Some factors associated with student acceptance or rejection of war." *American Sociological Review 27*, 655-667.

Reynolds, V., and F. Reynolds. 1965. "Chimpanzees of Budongo forest." Pp. 368-424 in I. DeVore (ed.), *Primate Behavior*. New York: Holt, Rinehart and Winston.

Richardson, L. 1960a. *Arms and Insecurity*. Pittsburgh: The Boxwood Press.

_____. 1960b. *Statistics of Deadly Quarrels*. Pittsburgh: The Boxwood Press.

Richter, C. P. 1950. "Psychotic behavior produced in wild Norway and Alexandrine rats apparently by fear of food poisoning." Pp. 189-202 in M. L. Reymer (ed.), *Feelings and Emotions*. New York: McGraw-Hill Book Company.

Schaller, G. B. 1965. "The behavior of the mountain gorilla." Pp. 324-367 in I. DeVore (ed.), *Primate Behavior*. New York: Holt, Rinehart and Winston.

Schneirla, T. C. 1966. "Instinct and aggression." *Natural History* (December), 16-62.

Scott, J. P. 1958. *Aggression*. Chicago: University of Chicago Press.

_____. 1969. "Biological basis of human warfare: an interdisciplinary problem." Pp. 121-136 in M. Sherif and C. W. Sherif (eds.), *Interdisciplinary Relationships in the Social Sciences*. Chicago: Aldine Publishing Company.

_____. 1973. "That old-time aggression." Pp. 136-143 in A. Montagu (ed.), *Man and Aggression*. New York: Oxford University Press.

_____, and E. Fredericson. 1951. "The causes of fighting in mice and rats." *Physiol. Zool. 24*, 273-309.

Shah, S. A. 1973. "The XYY chromosomal abnormality." Pp. 37-60 in C. Otten (ed.), *Aggression and Evolution*. Lexington, Mass.: Xerox College Publishing.

Shils, E. A., and M. Janowitz. 1948. "Cohesion and Disintegration in the Wehrmacht in World War II." *Public Opinion Quarterly 12*, 300-306, 308-315.

Singer, J. D. 1972. "The 'correlates of war' project: interim report and rationale." *World Politics 24*, 243-270.

_____, and M. Small 1972. *The Wages of War 1816-1965: A Statistical Handbook*. New York: John Wiley & Sons.

Singer, J. L. 1971. "The influence of violence portrayed in television or motion pictures upon overt aggressive behavior." Pp. 19-60 in J. L. Singer (ed.), *The Control of Aggression and Violence*. New York: Academic Press.

Small, M., and J. D. Singer. 1970. "Patterns in international warfare, 1816-1965." *Annals of the American Academy of Political and Social Science* (September), 145-155.

Somit, A. 1968. "Toward a more biologically-oriented political science: ethology and psychopharmacology." *Midwest J. of Pol. Sc. 12*, 550-567.

Stewart, O. C. 1973. "Lorenz/Margolin on the Ute." Pp. 221-228 in A. Montagu (ed.), *Man and Aggression*. New York: Oxford University Press.

Storr, A. 1970. *Human Aggression*. New York: A Bantam Book.

Stouffer, S. A. 1949. "A study of attitudes." *Scientific American* (May), 3-7.

Surgeon General's Scientific Advisory Committee on Television and Social Behavior. 1972. *Television and Growing Up: The Impact of Televised Violence*. Washington, D.C.: Government Printing Office.

Tedeschi, J. R., R. B. Smith, and R. C. Brown. 1974. "A reinterpretation of research on aggression." *Psychological Bulletin 81*, 540-562.

Thorson, T. L. 1970. *Biopolitics*. New York: Holt, Rinehart & Winston.

Tiger, L. 1969. "The dangers of finding something out." *Encounter 33* (December), 59-63.

_____. 1970. *Men in Groups*. New York: Vintage Books.

Tinbergen, N. 1942. "An objective study of the innate behaviour of animals." *Bibliotheca Biotheoretica 1*, 39-98.

_____. 1951. *The Study of Instinct*. Oxford: Clarendon Press.

_____. 1956. "On the functions of territory in gulls." *Ibis 98*, 401-411.

_____. 1968. "On war and peace in animals and man." *Science* (June 28), 1411-1418.

Waltz, K. 1959. *Man, the State and War.* New York: Columbia University Press.

Washburn, S. L., and D. A. Hamburg. 1973. "Aggressive behavior in old world monkeys and apes." Pp. 63-81 in C. Otten (ed.), *Aggression and Evolution.* Lexington, Mass.: Xerox College Publishing.

Willhoite, F. H. 1971. "Ethology and the tradition of political thought." *Journal of Politics 33,* 615-641.

Wright, Q. 1965. *A Study of War.* Chicago: University of Chicago Press.

5

The Frustration-Aggression Hypothesis

Leonard Berkowitz

Frustration and Aggression

Most authorities today regard aggression as originating ultimately in response to some frustration. As we already have seen, this idea is not new. Freud had maintained in his earlier writings that aggression was the "primordial reaction" to the frustration occurring "whenever pleasure-seeking or pain-avoiding behavior was blocked" (cited in Dollard et al. 1939:21), and many psychoanalysts and psychiatrists prefer this view to his later formulation (e.g., Durbin and Bowlby 1939; Fenichel 1945; Saul 1956). But before going any further into this, some definitions are in order. The concepts "frustration" and "aggression" have many meanings in every-day life, and we should be clear as to how these terms are to be used in this chapter.

The course we shall follow is to adopt the relatively widespread and precise definitions employed by Dollard et al. in their now classic monograph *Frustration and Aggression* (1939). This work, a milestone in the application of the methods and concepts of experimental psychology to important social problems, also provides a helpful systematic foundation for the study of aggressive behavior. A "frustration" for these psychologists is "an interference with the occurrence of an instigated goal-response at its proper time in the behavioral sequence" (p. 7). To translate this technical terminology into simpler language, they present an illustration of a boy, James, who, on hearing an ice-cream vendor's bell, wanted an ice-cream cone (pp. 3-9). We can say that the boy is *instigated* to obtain this cone. A number of response sequences may be elicited as a result of this state of affairs. He runs toward his mother, thinking of the delights of the ice cream, and calls to her. When he reaches his mother he pleads for the cone, pulling her to the front door. These goal-oriented activities, or response sequences, will be terminated when James gets a cone (reaches his goal) and, making the goal response, eats the cone — that is, assuming the boy is not insatiable. The goal response is defined as the reaction reducing the strength of the instigation (p. 6).

But suppose that James does not get the ice cream. His mother may insist, for example, that he wait until dinnertime. The series of responses leading to the consumption of the cone is interrupted. There is an interference with the occurrence of the instigated goal response, and James cannot eat the ice cream. This interference is the *frustration*.

In this sense the term obviously refers to the condition or event bringing about the interruption in the response sequence and not to the emotional reactions resulting from this interference. The thwarting need not be caused by events outside the person, however. Responses from within the individual can produce this interference. Going back to our illustration (in so doing we depart from the letter but not the spirit of the Dollard et al. work), James's mother may have given him money from his allowance to buy the ice cream. But in going out of his house, James might have remembered that he was saving to buy a baseball glove. He is now in conflict, with his recollection of this other goal interfering with the sequence directed toward the attainment of the ice cream. These opposing responses can be regarded as frustrating to the extent that they do interrupt the other sequence.

Two phrases will constantly reoccur throughout the course of this discussion: *instigated response sequences* and *drives*. The former phrase more clearly implies an ongoing activity (which, however, may be internal to the organism), but both are meant to be synonymous here. When the writer speaks of a "frustrated drive" he generally refers to interference with some goal-directed activity, or the blocking of some response tendency that has been set into operation. It is important to keep this in mind because drives are not necessarily always active. The intensity of the sex drive in the adult, for example, probably is dependent upon both internal and external stimulation, with external cues doing much to activate and enhance the sexual strivings. If an individual does not attend to these cues, or if they do not have strong erotic significance for him, his sex drive will be at a relatively low level. Since this person has little sexually oriented activity, either internally or in overt behavior, any inability to have sexual intercourse would not interfere with many ongoing response sequences. Similarly, a man who has been without food for a number of hours will not necessarily become angry because he has missed a meal. He may be engaged in work — book writing, for example — and the activities involved in *this* work are not being thwarted. According to the present conception, anger would result only if goal-directed activity is blocked.

Brown and Farber distinguished among four kinds of frustrating conditions (although they preferred to define a *frustration* in terms of the hypothesized resulting internal state of an organism): (1) physical barriers; (2) delays "between the initiation and completion of the response sequence"; (3) "omission or reduction of a customary reward"; and (4) the eliciting "of a response tendency that is incompatible with the ongoing one." Although these conditions differ in several respects, Brown and Farber assumed all of them can arouse reaction tendencies that interfere with ongoing chains of responses. All presumably produce internal reactions capable of interrupting these response sequences. Thus, for them there is no useful distinction to be made between the production of a *conflict* and a *frustration* (Brown and Farber 1951:481). Both sets of events, in arousing incompatible reaction tendencies within the individual, are essentially similar.

The present writer agrees up to a point. Incompatible responses instigated within the individual can frustrate a particular course of action. There is, however, an important difference between these two concepts, at least as far as the aggressive reaction is concerned. If hostility is directed primarily toward the perceived locus of the frustration, as Dollard and his colleagues proposed (1939:39), it matters whether the interfering responses have been aroused principally by events within or outside the organism.

Dollard et al. defined *aggression* as any "sequence of behavior, the goal-response to which is the injury of the person toward whom it is directed" (p. 9). The behavior, they pointed out, need not be overt, but may occur in thoughts and fantasies, symbolic or direct attacks on inanimate as well as animate objects, or for that matter, may not seem to be aimed at any target at all (p. 10). Nevertheless, as just mentioned, there is an implicit tendency to attack the frustrating agent. Assertiveness and accidental injury to others are deliberately excluded from the category of aggressive acts, and no assumptions are made of a general, free-flowing destructive energy impelling nonhostile responses in the vein of what G. W. Allport (1954:356) has termed the "steam-boiler theory of aggression." This book generally employs the same definition of the term "aggression."

In one way or another, then, practically all present-day observers of human hostility contend that frustrations can produce an instigation to aggression. This is not to say that this instigation (*anger* in the present book) will necessarily be revealed in overt behavior. The individual obviously will inhibit his hostile reactions if he is anxious about the display of aggression and fears retaliation or punishment. As it is most frequently worded, the frustration-aggression hypothesis usually maintains that frustration often arouses or increases the *instigation* to aggression. Whether this instigation leads to open hostility depends upon other factors to be discussed later. Nor is it proposed that there are no consequences of frustration other than aggression. A person who is thwarted in his attempt to reach some goal may engage in any one (or several) of a variety of behaviors. His goals may change to those preferred at an earlier stage of life (goal regression); his ways of achieving the present goals may become more childlike (instrumental-act regression); he may exhibit fixation and not alter his behaviors at all; anxiety may make his actions more primitive and crude but without producing instrumental-act regression; or to be most optimistic, he may attempt to solve the problem posed by the interference.

The differences of opinion that do exist concerning the frustration-aggression hypothesis generally center about two problems. Some writers argue whether all aggression is the result of frustration, but most of the disputes in this area involve the question of whether every frustration increases the instigation to aggression. To put it succinctly, we ask, is frustration the necessary and sufficient condition for the arousal of aggression? The Dollard et al. formulation will be modified somewhat in dealing with these questions.

Is All Aggression the Result of Frustration?

"Nonfrustration" Causes of Aggression

Durbin and Bowlby listed three classes of "simple causes" of fighting, only one of which supposedly deals with frustrations. Drawing their evidence primarily from observations of children and apes, they argued that fights break out because of (1) disputes over the possession of external objects and (2) resentment at the intrusion of a stranger into their group, as well as because of (3) frustrations (1939:7-10). Karl Menninger, an explicit critic of the frustration-aggression thesis, was vehement in his opposition, claiming that the proposition is "nonsensical." He stated, "anyone who has had his toe stepped on, *which is certainly not a frustration*, knows how inadequate such a formula is" [italics mine] (1942:295).

Seward (1945) objected to the Yale conception largely on the basis of animal data. Frustration, for him, is not the only condition instigating aggression. Fighting also is aroused, he noted along with Durbin and Bowlby, by "stimulation from a strange animal of the same species." But where Durbin and Bowlby maintained that the stranger is attacked because of "resentment" at his intrusion — implying a vague sort of territorial defense — Seward suggested the aggression was produced by dominance strivings. As pointed out in the preceding chapter, Scott and Fredericson (1951) have also mentioned the sight of a strange animal as a cause of fighting[1] (although they do not attempt to explain why this should be), along with the sight of an animal running away, and slight pain.

The difficulty here obviously lies partly in the definition of frustration, and partly in a failure to consider instrumental aggression. The above writers clearly have a somewhat narrower conception of the term than do Dollard and his colleagues, and Brown and Farber. However, at the risk of losing rigor through an excessive broadening of the concept, all of the aggression-arousing conditions mentioned by these critics can be considered as instances of frustrations.

A child who fights with another over the possession of a toy undoubtedly is thwarted in his desire to possess the toy. This probably is so even if the child had not wanted it initially. Seeing the other with the toy could well have increased this object's attractiveness, or at least, by prompting the child to compare himself (not having a toy) with his peer (who has one), caused him to feel deprived relative to this other, producing resentment. Similarly, the stranger intruding into the group could be interfering with attempts (explicit and implicit) to attain either security in well-ordered relationships with familiar peers, or other goals, such as food, nesting sites, or dominant status. If there is resentment against a stranger, it probably arises because he is seen as a potential threat (i.e., potential obstacle to goal attainment). The organism, not being certain his goals can always be gained, may regard the stranger as another rival in a competitive world.

The objection raised by Menninger concerning the stepped-on toe has been brought up by others as well, and McDougall showed how this type of situation could be regarded as an obstruction to the gratification of an impulse (1926:62). If a man suddenly struck him in an unprovoked manner, the blow might not openly interfere with any activity at that moment, he pointed out, but it could nevertheless interfere with his "impulse of self-assertion." The exact nature of this impulse, of course, is unimportant; what is relevant here is the *interruption of an internal response sequence or the blocking of some drive.* Similarly, a person who steps on our toes might also arouse anger if this action interrupted or interfered with the internal responses oriented toward the preservation or attainment of security and comfort. People probably differ in the extent to which they will react with overt hostility to their toes being stepped on. It is a reasonable guess that the greatest annoyance will be exhibited by those most concerned with keeping or gaining security and comfort, in other words, those suffering the severest frustrations. Mild pain, the third aggression-arousing factor listed by Scott and Fredericson, may act as a frustration in just this way providing it interferes with some instigated response sequence.

We see, then, that these supposed exceptions turn out not to be exceptions at all. They can be understood as variations of the frustrating conditions mentioned by Brown and Farber.

Learned Aggression

There *are* some aggressive acts, however, that are not necessarily directly instigated by frustrations. During World War II, for example, many of our airmen participated in bombing raids against German and Japanese cities without feeling the slightest anger toward their civilian victims. (As a matter of fact, not a few of them felt better if they avoided thinking of the people living in the cities.) On the other side, Germans and Japanese inflicted injury and death in many instances toward those whom *they* did not hate. The aggression in this case was coldly and deliberately carried out as a matter of policy. It was *instrumental aggression* in the sense that the behavior was primarily oriented toward the attainment of some goal other than doing injury (such as winning the war). These actions supposedly would help the aggressors reach the goal. Competition in everyday life also produces this type of instrumental aggression. The businessman or politician who spreads lies about his rival believes that hurting the other (symbolically but nevertheless in a very real fashion) is necessary if he is to get what he wants. The rival may be hated in some cases, but such actions undoubtedly also are carried out at times in order to achieve certain noninjurious ends. Aggression in the service of dominance strivings also would be an instance of this instrumental aggression and therefore is not necessarily produced by frustrations.

The instrumental significance of hostile behavior is not always readily apparent. Bandura and Huston (1961) have demonstrated that children can acquire hostile modes of behavior merely by observing the aggressive actions of adults. They contend this is no "identification with the aggressor" (A. Freud 1937), whereby the child supposedly adopts the attributes of an aggressive, punishing agent, transforming himself from the victim to the agent of aggression, in order to alleviate anxiety. Rather, the children seemed to have learned the aggressive acts by imitating the adult's behavior. The quality of the adult-child relationship did not affect this learning in the Bandura-Huston experiments; a nurturant adult was copied as often as a less nurturant one. Nevertheless, the adult, in providing a model for the children to imitate, may have helped define the appropriate or at least permissible modes of behavior. He may have told them, in essence, that these actions might help them obtain whatever satisfactions they wanted from the situation.

Dollard and his colleagues excluded this type of hostile behavior from consideration in their discussion of the frustration-aggression hypothesis. They said simply and legitimately that they would not be concerned with learned aggression in their work. The aggression they deal with "reduces only the secondary, frustration-produced instigation, and leaves the strength of the original instigation unaffected" (1939:11). That is, the hostile responses that concern them have no purpose other than that of injuring the frustrater. Since this exclusion of learned aggression would also

eliminate consideration of those people who have learned to employ hostility frequently as a way of achieving their goals, and since consideration of
this type of hostility is necessary for a more complete understanding of aggressive behavior, instrumental aggression will be discussed in this book.

Anger as an Intervening Variable

A second criticism of the frustration-aggression hypothesis proposed by
Menninger deals with the motive force behind the hostile behavior. Where
does the aggressive energy come from that is provoked by the frustration,
he asked? (1942:295). The only answer, he believed, is that this behavior is
impelled by an aggressive instinct. However, the above discussion showed
that this is not a satisfactory solution to the problem, and some other explanation must be found.

The question does highlight one of the notable omissions in the Dollard
et al. formulation. The Yale psychologists attempted to deal with aggressive
reactions to frustration without referring to any emotional state, such as
anger, intervening between the thwarting and the hostile acts. Mowrer,
one of the original authors of *Frustration and Aggression,* later came to realize
that the neglect of these emotional responses raises more problems than it
solves. Even though the 1939 book drew its inspiration from psychoanalytic
theory, he remarked, "It was at the same time dominated, methodolog-
ically, by a strong behavioristic slant which required that frustration and
aggression be treated in a simple stimulus-response framework, which had
little or no place for the intervening variable of anger."[2]

Emotional arousal provides part of the answer to Menninger's question
concerning the source of the aggressive drive. As Brown and Farber (1951)
first proposed, the emotional state produced by some frustrating condition
can be regarded as a motivational construct. Anger (which always refers in
this book to the emotion) serves as a drive heightening the likelihood of aggressive behavior.

There does not seem to be any simple one-to-one relationship between
anger intensity and aggressive response strength, however. Other factors
intervene to affect the probability of aggressive reactions to frustration.
Chief among these, I believe, is whether or not a suitable aggression-
evoking cue is present in the situation.[3] In company with other writers
(e.g., Berlyne 1960:167), I maintain that *drives such as anger do not lead to the
drive-specific behaviors* (aggression in this case) *unless there are appropriate cues or
releasers.* These cues are stimuli bearing some degree of association with the
anger instigator, but they need not be physically present, nor is the association created only by physical similarity to the instigator. The thwarted individual may display hostile behavior after thinking of his frustrater. This
latter person, we can say, is present symbolically in the former's psy-

chological environment and, as a symbolic cue, evokes the aggressive responses. Similarly, a disliked object may become the target for displaced hostility because the frustrated individual subjectively equates the substitute with his tormenter (Berkowitz and Green 1962).

According to this conception, then, a frustration creates a predisposition to make hostile responses by arousing anger. Whether these responses are actually performed, however, depends in part upon the presence of suitable aggression-evoking cues. For the time being, I will propose that *the strength of the aggressive reaction to some thwarting is a joint function of the intensity of the resulting anger and the degree of association between the instigator and the releasing cue.* Extreme anger arousal may broaden the range of external objects capable of evoking aggression, perhaps because emotionality reduces the ability to discriminate among stimuli (Easterbrook 1959) and therefore, in effect, enhances the association between the instigator and other available objects.

A study by Weatherley (1962) has yielded findings consistent with the present reasoning concerning the importance of aggression-evoking cues. College women whose mothers had been either high or low in permissiveness toward aggression either were deliberately angered by the experimenter or received a kindlier treatment from him. After this a second person, supposedly unconnected with the experimenter, administered two sets of Thematic Apperception Test (TAT) cards, one containing strong cues for aggressive themes and the other low in "picture pull" for aggression. Maternal permissiveness toward aggression probably leads primarily to relatively weak internal restraints against aggression rather than to a strong, constantly active "aggressive drive." Thus, it is not surprising that the permissively reared students in the nonaroused condition gave no more aggressive responses to the TAT cards than did the less permissively trained women in this nonangered condition. The two nonaroused groups did not differ in the strength of their instigation to make aggressive responses. It was not until the women were provoked that significant differences emerged. But here too, relevant cues were necessary to activate the arousal predisposition created by the experimenter's insults. The students whose mothers had permitted aggression exhibited reliably more fantasy aggression than did the less-angered permissively treated group only to the high cue cards. Their aroused hostile inclinations were not revealed, even though their inhibitions were fairly weak, unless aggressive cues were present.[4]

Learning, obviously, can affect an individual's reaction to frustrating situations. Anger and relevant cues may exist, but nonaggressive response tendencies may be stronger than the inclinations to hostile actions and thus prevent the occurrence of overtly hostile behavior (Miller 1941; Sears 1941). The strengths of these nonaggressive tendencies can vary with prior learning experiences and with the intensity and persistence of the frustration-produced emotions. Some people habitually react to thwartings with renewed effort, while others may attempt to withdraw or seek help. In each of these cases, furthermore, if the initial (or primary) frustration reactions should fail to remove the obstacle, other responses may occur (Miller 1941).

The nature of the thwarting reaction depends, at least in part, upon the person's interpretation of the situation confronting him, and these interpretations can also be habitual responses. As will be discussed more fully later, the interpretation can govern which of the individual's instigations are blocked and the degree to which they are thwarted. He may or may not perceive another's criticism, for example, as an attack upon himself, and he may or may not judge this as a serious criticism or attack. The learned interpretation also can determine what emotions other than anger also are aroused. The individual may perceive some features of the frustrating situation as dangerous and thus believe he has to hide his hostility if he is to avoid punishment. Aggression anxiety is evoked in this situation, we might say. In other cases he may think any hostility on his part would be a violation of his moral standards, and consequently the aggressive reactions to any anger he feels also are inhibited, but this time by guilt feelings. Anger may be generated on each of these occasions arousing aggressive responses, but other emotional states evoked in these situations, such as anxiety or guilt, have produced stronger tendencies incompatible with aggression inhibiting overtly hostile behaviors.

Learning experiences probably also affect the nature of the responses made to anger. When angered, a seventeenth-century French nobleman might automatically reach for his sword, a nineteenth-century cowboy for his gun, and a twentieth-century Englishman for a pen so that he could write a letter to the London *Times*. These stereotypes, of course, are not too accurate, but they at least illustrate how learning governs the exact form of the aggressive reaction. It also may be that if a person has been given the appropriate training experiences his anger alone could serve as the stimulus to other emotional states, which in turn give rise to aggression-inhibiting tendencies. Thus, followers of certain religious movements may have learned to become ashamed of the anger they might feel in any situation.

The assessment of anger intensity from behavioral observations obviously requires the consideration of previous learning. A person who displays violently hostile actions upon being frustrated may do this because (1) he is in an intense emotional state, i.e., his anger level is very high, and/or (2) he has learned to perform violent actions in response to provocations. Some of his aggressive behavior, in other words, is due to acquired aggressive habits.

Reassociation of Aggressive Responses with Stimuli
Other than Those of Anger

Brown and Farber (1951) did not insist that frustration reactions are the only source of aggressive behavior. They believed originally innate responses to anger may become "functionally connected to almost any stimulus" (p. 490). Certainly, this "reassociation" must account for the instrumental aggression mentioned earlier. Some children seem to get into fights with their peers in order to attract attention from their otherwise indifferent mothers. The aggressive actions they engage in apparently have become "functionally connected" to their acquired drive to gain love and attention from their mothers so that arousal of this nonaggressive drive gives rise to the hostile behavior (I would add: in the presence of a relevant cue — the mother or stimuli associated with her). A similar "reconnection" process may explain an observation published by Scott. He reported (1958:59) that mice trained to fight with a series of easy victories never showed the emotional reactions characteristic of fighting in their species, but instead, quickly leaped upon their next victim. The hair-fluffing and other fighting signs may be fear (epinephrine) reactions primarily rather than norepinephrine anger responses. If so, all Scott's observation signifies is that the fear concomitants of fighting had diminished with continued victories. However, if these fighting signs are produced by anger, other emotional reactions, such as elation, elicited by the easy victories, could have become conditioned to the sight of other mice. These nonanger emotional reactions then may have been the drive conditions arousing the fighting behaviors. When another animal was introduced into the persistent victor's cage this emotional drive state was aroused, giving rise to the aggressive attacks.

Wurtz (1960) presented a hypothesis consistent with this line of thought in his reanalysis of data obtained by Sears, Pintler, and Sears (1946). The doll-play behavior of 150 nursery school boys and girls was scored for the intensity of aggression expressed by and to parent and child dolls (i.e., the dolls as either the fantasy agents or victims of aggression). For this sample more intense fantasy aggression was associated with the parent dolls, both as attacker and attacked, than with the child dolls. Wurtz accounted for these results by invoking the mechanism of classical conditioning. Supposedly because their hostile behavior had been punished relatively frequently by their parents, the instigation to aggression in these children presumably had come to be functionally connected with anxiety (anticipation of punishment), and both of these drive states, in turn, were associated with their parents. Arousal of the aggressive drive would activate the anxiety, but similarly, anxiety would be the stimulus to aggressive responses.

Parents and their symbols, such as dolls resembling them, might evoke anxiety reactions in the children which then would elicit the fantasy aggression. More direct overt hostility, of course, would be inhibited by this anxiety, and Wurtz concluded: "In fantasy as compared with real life, anxiety functions more as a stimulus than as an inhibitor" (p. 136).

This interesting notion certainly merits further investigation. Other explanations of the Wurtz findings are also available. For one, if anxiety associated with parents does account for the differences in the doll-play aggression, this anxiety could have produced the intense hostility because it operated as a frustration more than because it had become functionally connected to aggression. Nevertheless, this study at least can illustrate how the "reassociation" of aggression with some drive other than anger might take place.

Does Every Frustration Lead to Some Form of Aggression?

Dollard et al. (1939) stimulated controversy on the very first page of their classic monograph. Providing a preview of their theoretical model, the authors presented a sweeping two-part generalization as their basic postulate. The first part, stating that "the occurrence of aggressive behavior always presupposes the existence of frustration," has already been discussed. In the second half of the statement, the Yale psychologists proposed that "the existence of frustration always leads to some form of aggression" (p. 1). Needless to say, this latter phrase drew the fire of many critics (e.g., Levy 1941; Maslow 1941).

Two years after the publication of the book, in a symposium on the frustration-aggression hypothesis, Miller admitted that the basic generalization "was unclear and misleading." There was an implication, he pointed out, strong enough to override later statements in the book to the contrary, that "frustration has no consequences other than aggression." He suggested that a better phrasing was: "Frustration produces instigations to a number of different types of responses, one of which is an instigation to some form of aggression" (1941:338). Nevertheless, this rewording did not alter the basic supposition that every frustration increased the likelihood of overt hostility. The specific nature of any one frustration was important only with respect to the intensity of the drive that was blocked and the degree of interference with the response sequences. Both of these factors supposedly were positively related to the resulting instigation to aggression. Otherwise, no distinctions were made among qualitatively different forms of frustration. It was this point that several critics attacked.

Many of their criticisms will be discussed in the following pages. Surprisingly, though, few questions were asked about one of the more obvious problems in the Yale thesis. If every frustration increases the probability of aggression, what are the characteristics of those situations producing stronger fear than aggressive reactions? These situations also can be defined as obstructing drive satisfaction, but in what way do they differ from the frustrations eliciting relatively strong anger? Another modification of the Dollard et al. formulation will be proposed in attempting to answer these questions. To anticipate, it seems likely that the conditions arousing fear are perceived and interpreted differently from the situations producing anger. Another set of intervening processes omitted by the 1939 group, the individual's *interpretation* of the situation confronting him, therefore must be considered.

Types of Frustrations and Aggressive Behavior

Many of the critics believed it was necessary to differentiate among various classes of frustrations if aggressive reactions were to be predicted. Not every thwarting, they argued, necessarily arouses anger. Rosenzweig (1944) proposed a fairly elaborate classification scheme, implying that each category would produce a different reaction. Frustrations were divided into *primary* and *secondary* frustrations, the former referring only to the existence of an active need, such as hunger, the latter involving obstructions in the path to a goal, and thus coming closer to the present definition of frustration. These secondary frustrations were further differentiated in terms of the nature of the obstacle. The obstruction might be *passive,* representing "impassibility without itself being threatening" (as an illustration of this, Rosenzweig cited the case of a hungry man confronting a locked door to a room containing food when he has no key), or the obstacle might be *active,* in which there is not only an obstruction to need satisfaction, but also a threat "to the immediate security of the organism." Finally, the obstacle may be *external* or *internal,* either within or outside the individual (pp. 381-382).

Rosenzweig looked at frustration primarily from a clinical viewpoint and therefore was most concerned with active internal obstacles to need satisfaction. Frustrations of this sort were involved in the conflict situations emphasized by psychoanalytic theory (p. 382). *Ego-defensive* reactions, including hostility, presumably occur only in response to threats to the ego, i.e., only as a reaction to active secondary frustrations. His threefold division of ego-defensive reactions is well known and forms the basis of the Rosenzweig Picture-Frustration Study, a widely used (though with uneven success) projective test. When the individual is frustrated there may be (1) *extrapunitive* responses in which he "aggressively attributes the frustration to external persons or things"; (2) *intropunitive* responses in which he "aggressively attributes the frustration to himself"; or (3) *impunitive* responses which "avoid blame altogether."

Maslow (1941, 1943) also argued that distinctions should be drawn among qualitatively different kinds of frustrations. Like Rosenzweig, he felt *deprivations* (Rosenzweig's primary frustrations) must be differentiated from other forms of thwarting. However, unlike this other writer, he set up only one other category, *threats,* frustrations of the organism's "basic needs." The psychologically harmful effects usually attributed to frustration in general, he maintained, are really due specifically to threats. Deprivations alone supposedly are less likely to produce aggressive reactions.[5]

The words may be different in the Rosenzweig-Maslow line of thought, but operationally, their arguments and those of Dollard et al. seem to yield essentially the same predictions regarding aggressive behavior. The Yale group hypothesized that the strength of the instigation to aggression varies directly, among other things, with the "strength of instigation to the frustrated response" (1939:28). The stronger the drive whose satisfaction is being blocked, the more intense the aggressive reactions and, consequently, the greater the likelihood that some hostility will be revealed openly. This continuum of "strength of instigation to the frustrated response" is involved in Maslow's distinction between threats and deprivations. He defined threats in terms of obstacles to the satisfaction of the organism's basic needs, drives presumably of greater intensity than those involved in deprivations. Thus, if investigation shows that threats do provoke aggressive actions where deprivations do not, this may well be due to the interference with the stronger instigations. Since the resulting anger is more intense in this case, the hostile responses are more likely to be manifested in overt behavior.

Dimensional Aspects of Frustrations

The basic difficulty with the Rosenzweig-Maslow (and similar) formulations is that they have established discrete categories where, in actuality, there is a continuous dimension. "Threats" vary in degree; "basic needs" vary in the urgency with which they must be satisfied. To go back to Rosenzweig's illustration of the hungry man confronted by a locked door to a room containing food, the extent of threat represented by the door is a function of his degree of starvation. Not only can privations be threatening, but this is no dichotomy of either "threat" or "no threat." What is central here, clearly, is the intensity of the frustrated drive, rather than the qualitative nature of the frustration. It is not necessary to multiply concepts by differentiating among frustrations in some absolute and arbitrary manner. Drive strength or other aspects of the thwarting can be abstracted out and treated as a continuous variable in predicting aggressive responses.

This procedure, which of course is the one employed by Dollard and his colleagues, is more parsimonious, and logically more defensible, than the type of theorizing that invokes several concepts where only one can do. We can see this advantage in the analyses of several studies. The Yale group, for example, has reported that relatively minor deprivations can provoke aggressive reactions if they are repeated often enough (1939:31). Instead of resorting to the argument that the hostility arose when the deprivations became threats (since there are no a priori specifications of the operations defining these constructs, the argument can be tautological), Dollard et al. accounted for this finding with only one concept. They contended that the instigational effects summated with repeated frustrations (pp. 31-32). In another investigation, Graham, Charwat, Honig, and Weltz (1951) found that physical attacks directed against the individual were more likely to produce strong aggressive reactions in him than were less direct attacks. The researchers pointed out that the former direct attacks may be regarded as threats, while the latter indirect hostility supposedly is not in this category of frustration. However, rather than arbitrarily dividing a continuum of frustrations into discrete classes, as this scheme implies, they also proposed an alternative and preferable analysis. In line with the Yale model, Graham and her coworkers suggested that the different forms of hostility directed against the subject varied in the degree to which they interfered with such strivings as the drive for self-enhancement. The person receiving a physical blow suffered a greater interference in satisfying these drives than the person receiving indications of mild dislike. Their interpretation, then, is a special case of the more general supposition regarding the relationship between degree of interference with response sequence and the strength of the instigation to aggression (Dollard et al. 1939:30-31).

The "Arbitrariness" of Frustrations

Some attacks on the contention that every frustration increases the instigation to aggression are not based on a distinction between threats and deprivations. These objections still differentiate among classes of frustrations, however. In one of the studies employed to buttress the Dollard et al. formulation, Doob and Sears (1939) had presented their subjects with written descriptions of sixteen frustrating situations they supposedly had previously encountered. The subjects were asked to say what their reactions had been. Examining these situations, Pastore (1952) concluded that the frustrations were unreasonable or arbitrary. He felt it was the arbitrary nature of the thwartings that had produced the frequently reported aggressive reactions. To test this hypothesis, Pastore repeated the investigation by giving some of his subjects descriptions of arbitrary frustrations (e.g., "You're waiting on the right corner for a bus, and the driver intentionally passes you by.") Other subjects were told of frustrations that judges agreed were nonarbitrary (e.g., "You're waiting at the right corner for a bus. You notice that it is a special on its way to the garage.") As expected, significantly stronger aggressive reactions were indicated by the subjects in the arbitrary frustration condition. Pastore proposed on the basis of this that the arbitrariness of the frustration was an important determinant of the intensity of the resulting aggression. Frustration per se did not necessarily arouse hostility. A. R. Cohen (1955) more recently has obtained the same findings, using a similar procedure.

These studies, nevertheless, do not unequivocally demolish the Yale contention for a number of reasons. The subjects receiving the nonarbitrary treatment may have inhibited their aggressive reactions, as Pastore himself suggested (1952:731), because they had learned that society frowns upon hostile responses to "reasonable" frustrations. Rothaus and Worchel (1960) reported data apparently supporting this possibility. Employing the same type of questionnaire descriptions, their subjects were asked to indicate not only how they themselves would respond to the frustrations, but also how another person, identified only by initials, would react. This latter question was designed to be a "projective" measure of aggressive tendencies within the subject himself. The results showed, as Pastore had found, significantly stronger manifestations of hostility after arbitrary than after nonarbitrary frustrations. However, there also was a significantly greater number of hostile feelings reported in response to the projective than to the nonprojective items following the nonarbitrary frustrations, presumably indicating inhibited aggression in the "reasonable" frustration condition.

One of the difficulties with this conclusion, though, is that the above investigators utilized only questionnaire descriptions of hypothetical situations. As I noted elsewhere (1958:269), the procedure employed in these studies is particularly susceptible to the intrusion of the subjects' own psychological theories and to verbal control over behavior. They may have responded to the questionnaires in terms of what they believed their reactions *should* be, or (as in the Rothaus and Worchel study) the way they *thought* most people would behave, but not necessarily the way they and others actually would react. Definitive investigations of the possibility that qualitatively different classes of frustrations produce different reactions must utilize real (though experimentally controlled) frustrations, not hypothetical ones presented in questionnaires.

But perhaps the most important flaw in Pastore's criticism of the Dollard et al. thesis has to do with his conception of the frustrating situations. He assumed that the response sequences in the arbitrary and nonarbitrary frustration conditions were blocked to an equal degree objectively but that there were differences in the subjects' interpretation of the thwartings. This assumption is not necessarily correct. I will try to show later that the subjects in the arbitrary frustration condition actually may have had more of their response sequences blocked (assuming this study represents what would happen in real life), perhaps because they had not expected the interference.

Cognitive Factors in Frustrations

These variables, the extent to which an obstruction is arbitrary and/or unexpected, do point, however, to a notable area of omission in the Yale formulation. Dollard and his colleagues, it will be recalled, were strongly behavioristic in their approach, and as such, were reluctant to consider the individual's inner state in their theorizing. They believed it was preferable scientifically to develop hypotheses utilizing only variables that could be observed directly. As a consequence, explicit references to emotions were omitted, as we already have seen, and so were any considerations of thought processes. Modern behavior theory can accommodate these factors, but their omission in 1939 resulted in several gaps in the study of hostility. Perhaps the most striking of these "holes" was left by the failure to regard man as a thinking animal whose perception and understanding of his environment could affect his reactions to it.

Suppose, to take Pastore's illustration, a person who has been waiting on a street corner for a bus sees one pass him by. His reaction to this frustration will depend partly upon his interpretation of the situation. A paranoid, believing himself persecuted, might take this as a personal affront, while another man, knowing the driver on this route, could attribute his failure to stop to some good reason. The Yale group had postulated a relationship between the intensity of the instigation to aggression and the strength of the thwarted drive. Since a strong drive (for self-esteem) is blocked in the case of the paranoid, relatively intense anger should result. The paranoid's perception of the situation had determined which of his drives were thwarted, and thus affected the operation of the principles specified by Dollard and his collaborators.

Consideration of individual differences in these intervening cognitive responses, of course, is unnecessary for predicting frustration reactions when there are unambiguous obstructions to the satisfaction of drives most people possess, such as drives for self-enhancement or self-preservation. News of an impending atomic bomb explosion in their city coming from a very reliable source undoubtedly would disturb (to say the very least) nearly everyone living in it. We could predict that people would flee the city without inquiring into the way different groups understand the news. Most people undoubtedly would interpret the information in much the same manner. On the other hand, in order to anticipate reactions to a man running down the street carrying a gun in his hand, we would have to foretell the interpretations elicited in the passersby. Will they think he is a policeman, criminal, or lunatic? Taking the intervening cognitions into account significantly improves predictions primarily when the stimulus situation is so complex and/or ambiguous that a great variety of interpretations is possible. Since many social situations are fairly ambiguous, it is not unusual to find widely discrepant reactions in them; they are understood differently by the people involved.

Frustrations Producing Fear

One of the above examples raises a very important problem bearing on the question of whether all frustrations evoke anger. It also documents the desirability of considering cognitive and emotional responses to frustrations before predicting the behavioral outcome. An atomic bomb attack must be regarded as a frustration to the people who survive (assuming we can view this type of situation merely as psychologists). According to investigations made following the Hiroshima and Nagasaki atomic bombings (Janis 1951:4-66), the dominant reaction among survivors shortly after the attack was acute fear rather than anger against the United States. These people had suffered very serious interferences with their drives, but instead of responding with extreme hostility toward those directly responsible for these thwartings, most of the victims displayed strong signs of anxiety and depression. These fear reactions persisted in a sizeable proportion of the populace of the two cities for many days after the bombings. Janis's valuable review of the effects of air warfare reveals that German and British civilians subjected to very heavy bombing raids apparently reacted in a somewhat similar fashion, so the actions of the Japanese cannot be attributed to their unique characteristics (pp. 98-125).

Evidence from England, Germany, and Japan does indicate there was a rise in aggressive attitudes after air attacks. But much of this feeling seems to have been directed against other people in the victims' own country, particularly their leaders and other authorities, and not as much as we might expect toward the enemy (pp. 126-152). This last seemingly paradoxical set of findings concerning the target of aggression will be discussed more fully later. The most important matter for the present concerns the reasons for the strong fear. The relationship between frustration and aggression cannot be fully understood without knowledge of the conditions determining whether the dominant reaction to a frustration is fear rather than anger.

As the remaining section of this chapter will attempt to show, there are at least two important aspects of fear-producing situations. Fear is stronger than anger in such situations because of two qualities of the obstruction: (1) *fearful events signify noxious consequences,* and as a result of these events the individual anticipates either physical or psychological damage to himself; (2) *the frustrated individual sees himself as having low "power" relative to that of the frustrating agent.* The more vulnerable or less powerful he feels, i.e., the less able he is to control the frustrating agent or punish it for the injury he has received, the more fear predominates over anger.

As mentioned earlier, Scott and Fredericson (1951) have proposed that slight pain produces aggressive responses in mice and rats, while severe pain presumably gives rise to escape and avoidance behaviors. This hypothesis can serve as a takeoff point, but it must be altered somewhat. Physical pain is not absolutely necessary for the arousal of fear. Anticipation of severe pain or serious loss can have the same effect. An observer of the bombing attacks upon England (MacCurdy, cited in Janis 1951:103) has singled out the "experience of suddenly facing danger in the immediate vicinity" as the most critical determinant of an air raid's emotional impact. People who had undergone "near misses," who had faced but narrowly escaped death, for example, seemed to show the most acute and persistent fear symptoms. More fortunate individuals not directly witnessing the destructive fury of an air attack, who had seen danger only from afar, sometimes exhibited anxiety when the signs of potential danger became apparent. They became afraid when the warning siren sounded or the enemy planes were heard overhead, but this emotion usually did not persist after the raid had ended. Typically, they then experienced relief and a feeling of successful escape. Other independent observations tend to support this emphasis upon direct exposure to grave danger as a major cause of fear reactions, particularly when these extremely threatening experiences are relatively unfamiliar and unexpected (Janis 1951:98-125).

Noxious stimulation and fear. This elaborate discussion leads to an obvious and fairly simple point. *The intensity of the fear produced by a frustrating situation is a direct function of the intensity of the noxious stimulation experienced in the situation or anticipated because of it.* Moreover, we can suggest tentatively, *the noxious stimulation is frustrating, producing anger as well as fear.* However, *as the intensity of the noxious stimulation increases, either directly or in the perceived likelihood of its occurrence, fear rises more rapidly in intensity than does anger.* The relatively rapid increase in fear can be seen in the previously cited relationship between the pain inflicted on mice and the intensity of their aggressive acts. Anger was the dominant emotional state when the frustration was mild pain, but fear became dominant as this pain was increased.

A somewhat similar explanation can be used to account for the strong persistent fear reactions in people narrowly escaping danger during World War II. Very heavy bombing attacks and many "near misses" would naturally have aroused a good deal of fear. These responses then could have become strongly conditioned to a wide variety of cues: the thought of the enemy, the sound of airplane engines, the time of day at which air raids generally commenced, etc. As a consequence of this conditioning, these cues alone would have elicited strong fear reactions upon some later occasion. From the point of view of the people just missing death, *further injury or even death would have seemed all too likely.* Those who had not had these narrow escapes, on the other hand, did not have strong fear responses conditioned to environmental stimuli, and later, they could easily have disregarded thoughts of future harm. Danger became subjectively less probable. The sound and sight of air raids, or the anticipation of these attacks, did not "hurt" as much. Along these lines, Janis hypothesized that many people have learned to alleviate their fears of death, injury, and severe personal loss "by developing, to varying degrees of inner conviction, a feeling of personal invulnerability" (1951:173). Narrow escapes from extreme dangers apparently seriously weaken, if not eliminate entirely, this protective mechanism. The feeling of invulnerability is broken down, and as a consequence, the individual now consciously faces the imminent prospect of harm.[6]

This theme of fear and helplessness was continued in Janis's later analysis of stress reactions in surgical patients (1958). On the basis of psychoanalytic observations supported by a questionnaire survey, he suggested that patients provided with adequate preoperative information are stimulated to rehearse the danger situation mentally (setting into operation the "work of worrying"), which then causes them to find effective reassurances with which to control their fear. Anticipating the dangers, but also thinking of the reassurances, the adequately prepared patient presumably is less likely to feel helpless and extremely vulnerable when he actually enters the danger situation than the patient not having this information or the one who before this had defensively cloaked himself with "blanket immunity." As a consequence, the prepared patient apparently is less inclined than the others to develop either extreme depression and anxiety or a hostile resentment against those (e.g., doctors and nurses) whom he believes have let him down.

Frustrating situations also would "hurt" if they deprived the individual of a strongly held value or threatened the imminent loss of this value. A person who develops "stage fright" just before he is to make a speech, for example, probably expects this behavior to result in negative evaluations of him. His speech may not come up to his own standards, and/or the audience may think he was inept. The frustrating situation threatens harm to the value, a favorable self-concept.

The major feature of this analysis, then, is its emphasis upon the degree of harm the individual actually suffers or anticipates. However, a qualification of sorts may be necessary. Whether fear becomes the dominant emotion, at least in some situations, may not depend entirely on the absolute amount of hurt the person experiences. Rather, *the extent to which this emotion is stronger than anger may be a function of the individual's perceived power to control or hurt his frustrater relative to the frustrater's power to control or harm him.* He is more strongly afraid than angry when he believes he can receive serious harm from the frustrating agent, but is relatively unable to hurt him in return.

This reasoning seems to be consistent with observations of mob behavior. The usual explanation given for lynch mobs, such as the one that terrorized the Negro community in Leeville, Texas, in 1930 (Cantril 1941), is that frustration-produced hostility in the whites was vented against the minority-group members. By striving for increased social status, by competing with the whites for jobs, the Negroes presumably threatened, and hence frustrated, the dominant group. But not only did the Negroes arouse hostility, it also was safe to attack them; the lynch mob members probably felt, for one reason or another, that they were fairly immune from punishment for any aggression they might express. They saw themselves as having more power than the Negroes and as being relatively invulnerable to any dangers associated with attacking them. Thus, overall, while the Negroes may have been threatening, they did not have too much ability to hurt the whites in retaliation, and anger was stronger than fear in the whites.

A mob in panic obviously has an altogether different relationship to the frustrating agent. In this case, the mob members perceive themselves as less powerful than this agent and, therefore, feel extremely vulnerable to the dangers the agent represents. He can hurt them more than they can hurt him. They can lose their lives and most valued possessions, but cannot seriously threaten the frustrater in return. Fear becomes stronger than anger and people flee. Cantril has described just this state of affairs in his analysis of the panic reactions to Orson Welles's famous 1938 broadcast, "The Invasion from Mars" (Cantril 1958). Those who accepted the broadcast as news, and ran from what they believed to be the oncoming Martians, apparently thought these monsters were endangering their lives and everything they held dear. Their highly cherished values were threatened and no certain elimination of the threat was in sight (p. 300).

Conclusions

Our general conclusion, then, is to support the essential validity of the Dollard et al. formulation with some modifications. These alterations are largely brought about through the introduction of two classes of variables held to intervene between the objective situation and the individual's reaction to it: *anger* and *interpretation*.

There are some obvious advantages to considering the emotional state, anger, when dealing with the question of frustration reactions. Research has indicated that the physiological concomitants of anger can perhaps be differentiated from those of fear (Ax 1953; Schachter 1957). Thus, physiological indices of these emotional states could be employed as dependent variables in testing hypotheses concerning the effects of various types of thwarting conditions upon emotional responses. (This is one way of assessing, for example, whether fear actually rises more rapidly in intensity than does anger with increasing severity of noxious stimulation, as was hypothesized earlier.) Going further, the emotion could be manipulated and "held constant" by means of direct physiological measurements of this state in determining how other factors affect the degree to which anger leads to open hostility. Clearly, observations of these emotional reactions will increase our understanding of the nature of the frustration-aggression relationship.

The present view of this relationship is fairly similar to that advanced by Dollard and his colleagues, on one hand, and by McDougall, on the other. In common with these writers, I should like to propose that every frustration increases the *instigation* to aggression, but this instigation is here termed *anger*. It also may be, as an up-to-date reinterpretation of McDougall's formulation would maintain, that anger is the primary, inborn reaction to thwarting.

Many critics have disputed this point. Learning experiences undoubtedly can influence the nature of the reactions to obstructions, as Brown and Farber have stressed, and N. E. Miller (1941) and R. R. Sears (1941) acknowledged. Some ways in which frustration reactions could be altered through learning have been described earlier. Briefly, it was suggested that these prior experiences can determine whether there are any response tendencies that are stronger than the frustration-produced aggressive inclinations, and if so, the nature of these nonaggressive reactions. One of the ways in which learning might operate to alter the response probabilities is through affecting the individual's interpretation of the thwarting situation. Earlier training, of course, also can affect the form of the person's responses to his emotions, for example, whether he will curse his instigator, try to invoke a magic spell, punch him in the nose, or challenge him to a duel. Aggression may be the innately determined response to anger, but the exact form of this aggression, and perhaps even its vigor and intensity, may be affected if not molded entirely by past experiences. This previous learning also will govern the form and strength of the behavioral reactions to the nonanger emotions elicited in the frustration situation.

Whiting (1944), a colleague of the authors of *Frustration and Aggression* at Yale University Institute of Human Relations, came close to my theoretical inclinations in his description of the behavior of the Kwoma of New

Guinea. This anthropologist noted that the members of this tribe customarily exhibit four different patterns of reaction to frustration: submission, dependence, and avoidance, as well as aggression. Which pattern is displayed seems to vary with the age of the individual. Young children, for example, supposedly characteristically respond to thwarting with increased dependence upon their elders. Nevertheless, Whiting's observations suggest that the primary emotional response to frustrations in the newborn is a general bodily reaction resembling what Sears, Maccoby, and Levin (1957) termed *rage* or *anger*. Along with these later writers, he contended that this is the innately dominant response to frustration and that it is modified by later learning. The present approach would suggest that later learning experiences (1) affect the individual's definition of the situation, and so determine which, if any, goal-directed actions are blocked, (2) determine whether any other response tendencies are aroused that are stronger than the elicited aggressive acts, and (3) affect the exact nature and intensity of these acts.

The following chapters also will have more to say about the nature of aggression. This is particularly true in the discussion of "hostility catharsis." Our understanding of the instigation to aggression obviously is incomplete without consideration of the conditions decreasing the strength of this instigation. Furthermore, the frustration-aggression model leaves the problem of "aggressive personalities" unsettled. How do they get that way, we want to know? Do they continually experience frustrations or is their anger hidden (repressed) but still active? On the other hand, is their aggression, as we already have suggested, not necessarily always impelled by anger, and if so, what role does anger have in their behavior? These and other questions concerning the "aggressive drive" remain. Before they can be dealt with there must be a more comprehensive discussion of the factors affecting hostile reactions to frustration.

Notes

1. H. F. Harlow (in a personal communication) maintains this is a relatively rare occurrence.

2. Reprinted with permission from O. H. Mowrer, *Learning Theory and Behavior* (New York: John Wiley & Sons, Inc., 1960), p. 404.

3. This formulation makes explicit what is only implicit in the *Frustration and Aggression* monograph. Thus, by suggesting that cues are necessary to elicit aggressive actions we can explain why the strongest hostile responses in the absence of inhibitions supposedly are directed toward the perceived source of the frustration (Dollard et al. 1939:39), and why progressively weaker aggressive responses theoretically are evoked by objects having less and less similarity to the frustrater (Miller 1948).

4. Research into the effects of electrical stimulation of chicken brains (von Holst and von Saint Paul 1962), published after the present manuscript went to press, further highlights the importance of situational cues in evoking aggressive behavior. In these experiments stimulation of a certain region of the fowl brain led to organized patterns of aggressive behavior primarily when relevant cues ("an enemy, real or artificial") were present. An electrically stimulated rooster would attack a small stuffed predator or the rooster's keeper, but would exhibit "only motor restlessness" when "all substitutes for an enemy" were lacking.

5. Most writers actually are in agreement on this point. Deprivations, as defined by Maslow and Rosenzweig, do not seem to involve the frustration of ongoing goal-directed activities. Dollard et al. (1939) and the present writer stress the importance of considering whether the response sequence has been "activated," i.e., set into operation or instigated. As discussed earlier in this chapter, a man who has been without food for some time is not angered if he is engaged in non-food-related activities and does not want food.

6. The present formulation has the advantage of explaining why many frightened people also report experiencing some anger. Kardiner and Spiegel (1947) maintained that all the war trauma cases they observed not only had strong fear and anxiety, but also aggression "with or without the accompanying affect of rage." But where they contended that aggression and rage arose in an attempt to master the danger situation, the present view argues that both fear and anger may be results of the frustrations inherent in the danger situation, with fear increasing more rapidly in intensity as the noxious, harmful nature of the frustration increases. The fear may also be frustrating, further increasing anger.

References

Allport, G. W. 1954. *The nature of prejudice.* Reading, Mass.: Addison-Wesley.

Ax, A. 1953. The physiological differentiation of fear and anger. *Psychosom. Med.* 15:433-442.

Bandura, A., and Huston, A. C. 1961. Identification as a process of incidental learning. *J. abnorm. soc. Psychol.* 63:311-318.

Berkowitz, L. 1958. The expression and reduction of hostility. *Psychol. Bull.* 55:257-283.

————, and Green, J. A. 1962. The stimulus qualities of the scapegoat. *J. abnorm. soc. Psychol.*

Berlyne, D. E. 1960. *Conflict, arousal, and curiosity.* New York: McGraw-Hill.

Brown, J. S., and Farber, I. E. 1951. Emotions conceptualized as intervening variables—with suggestions toward a theory of frustration. *Psychol. Bull.* 48:465-495.

Cantril, H. 1941. *The psychology of social movements.* New York: Wiley.

————. 1958. The invasion from Mars. In E. Maccoby, T. M. Newcomb, and E. L. Hartley (eds.), *Readings in social psychology.* (3rd ed.) New York: Holt, Rinehart & Winston.

Cohen, A. R. 1955. Social forms, arbitrariness of frustration, and status of the agent of frustration in the frustration-aggression hypothesis. *J. abnorm. soc.*

Psychol. 51:222-226.

Dollard, J.; Doob, L.; Miller, N.; Mowrer, O.; and Sears, R. 1939. *Frustration and aggression.* New Haven: Yale.

Doob, L., and Sears, R. 1939. Factors determining substitute behavior and the overt expression of aggression. *J. abnorm. soc. Psychol.* 34:293-313.

Durbin, E.F.M., and Bowlby, J. 1939. *Personal aggressiveness and war.* New York: Columbia.

Easterbrook, J. A. 1959. The effect of emotion on cue utilization and the organization of behavior. *Psychol. Rev.* 66:183-201.

Fenichel, O. 1945. *The psychoanalytic theory of neurosis.* New York: Norton.

Freud, A. 1937. *The ego and the mechanisms of defence.* London: Hogarth.

Graham, F. K.; Charwat, W. A.; Honig, A. S.; and Weltz, P. C. 1951. Aggression as a function of the attack and the attacker. *J. abnorm. soc. Psychol.* 46:512-520.

Janis, I. L. 1951. *Air war and emotional stress: psychological studies of bombing and civilian defense.* New York: McGraw-Hill.

———. 1958. *Psychological stress: psychoanalytic and behavioral studies of surgical patients.* New York: Wiley.

Kardiner, A., and Spiegel, H. 1947. *War stress and neurotic illness.* New York: Hoeber-Harper.

Levy, D. M. 1941. The hostile act. *Psychol. Rev.* 48:356-361.

McDougall, W. 1926. *An introduction to social psychology.* (Rev. ed.) Boston: Luce.

Maslow, A. H. 1941. Deprivation, threat, and frustration. *J. abnorm. soc. Psychol.* 48:364-366.

———. 1943. Conflict, frustration, and the theory of threat. *J. abnorm. soc. Psychol.* 38:81-86.

Menninger, K. 1942. *Love against hate.* New York: Harcourt, Brace & World.

Miller, N. E. 1941. The frustration-aggression hypothesis. *Psychol. Rev.* 48:337-342.

———. 1948. Theory and experiment relating psychoanalytic displacement to stimulus-response generalization. *J. abnorm. soc. Psychol.* 43:155-178.

Pastore, N. 1952. The role of arbitrariness in the frustration-aggression hypothesis. *J. abnorm. soc. Psychol.* 47:728-731.

Rosenzweig, S. 1944. An outline of frustration theory. In J. McV. Hunt (ed.), *Personality and the behavior disorders.* New York: Ronald.

Rothaus, P., and Worchel, P. 1960. The inhibition of aggression under nonarbitrary frustration. *J. Pers.* 28:108-117.

Saul, L. J. 1956. *The hostile mind.* New York: Random House.

Schachter, J. 1957. Pain, fear, and anger in hypertensives and normotensives: a psychophysiological study. *Psychosom. Med.* 19:17-29.

Scott, J. P. 1958. *Aggression.* Chicago: Univ. of Chicago Press.

———, and Fredericson, E. 1951. The causes of fighting in mice and rats. *Physiol. Zool.* 24:273-309.

Sears, R. R. 1941. Nonaggressive reactions to frustration. *Psychol. Rev.* 48:343-346.

Sears, R. R.; Maccoby, E. E.; and Levin, H. 1957. *Patterns of child rearing.* Evanston, Ill.: Row, Peterson.

Sears, R. R.; Pintler, M. H.; and Sears, P. S. 1946. Effect of father separation on preschool children's doll play aggression. *Child Develpm.* 17:219-243.

Seward, J. P. 1945. Aggressive behavior in the rat. III. The role of frustration. *J. comp. Psychol.* 38:225-238.

von Holst, E., and von St. Paul, U. 1962. Electrically controlled behavior. *Scientific Amer.* 206:50-59.

Weatherley, D. 1962. Maternal permissiveness toward aggression and subsequent fantasy aggression. *J. abnorm. soc. Psychol.* 65:1-5.

Whiting, J.M.W. 1944. The frustration complex in Kwoma society. *Man* 44:140-144.

Wurtz, K. R. 1960. Some theory and data concerning the attenuation of aggression. *J. aborm. soc. Psychol.* 60:134-136.

6

The Social Learning Theory
of Aggression

Albert Bandura

Until recently, most personality theories depicted behavior as impelled by inner forces in the form of needs, drives, and impulses, often operating below the level of consciousness. Since the principal causes of behavior resided in forces within the individual, that is where one looked for explanations of man's actions. Although this view enjoyed widespread professional and popular acceptance, it did not go unchallenged.

Theories of this sort were criticized on both conceptual and empirical grounds. Because the inner determinants were typically inferred from the behavior they supposedly caused, the result was pseudoexplanations. Thus, for example, a hostile impulse was deduced from a person's irascible behavior, which was then attributed to the action of the inferred impulse. In a similar manner, various traits and dynamics, which represent the descriptive constructs of the assessor, frequently become entities within the individual that supposedly cause his behavior. Different personality theories proposed diverse lists of motivators, some containing a few all-purpose drives, others embracing a varied assortment of specific drives.

The conceptual structure of psychodynamic theories was further criticized for disregarding the tremendous complexity of human responsiveness. An internal motivator cannot possibly account for the marked variation in the incidence of a given behavior in different situations, toward different persons, at different times, and in different social roles. One can predict with much greater accuracy the expression of aggressive behavior from knowledge of the social contexts (for example, church, school, ghetto sidewalk, athletic gymnasium), the targets (for example, parent, priest, teacher, or peer), the role occupied by the performer (for example, policeman, soldier, teacher, sales clerk), and other cues that reliably signify

Albert Bandura, *Aggression: A Social Learning Analysis,* © 1973, pp. 39-53. Reprinted by permission of Prentice-Hall, Inc., Englewood Cliffs, New Jersey.

potential consequences for aggressive actions, than from the assessment of the performer (Bandura 1960; Bandura and Walters 1959). When diverse social influences produce correspondingly diverse behaviors, the inner cause implicated in the relationship cannot be less complex than its effects.

It should be emphasized here that it is not the existence of motivated behavior that is being questioned, but rather whether such behavior is at all explained by ascribing it to the action of drives or other inner forces. The deficiencies of this type of simplistic analysis can be illustrated by considering a common activity, such as reading printed matter, which has the qualities of a highly motivated behavior. People spend large sums of money purchasing reading material; they expend effort obtaining it from libraries; they engage in reading for prolonged periods; and they become emotionally upset over being deprived of reading material (as when their daily newspaper is not delivered through an oversight or when a library is unable to locate a desired book in its collection). Following the common practice of inferring drives from prepotent behaviors, one could ascribe the activated reading to the force of a reading drive. However, in predicting what a person reads, when he chooses to read it, and the order in which different contents are read, one would appeal not to drives, but rather to the stimulus inducements and consequences of reading, and to a variety of specific factors that influence reading behavior. On the stimulus side, one would want to know the person's reading assignments, their deadlines, the type of information he requires to deal effectively with projects he has undertaken, and the presence of other reading instigators; on the consequences side, knowledge about the contents the person finds rewarding and those he dislikes and the effects of reading or ignoring certain materials would constitute important controlling influences. There is a marked difference between ascribing motivating properties to social inducements and acquired incentives, a quality that is easily demonstrable, and invoking acquired drives, a concept that has been found lacking in explanatory power (Bolles 1967).

Although the conceptual adequacy of psychodynamic formulations was debatable, their empirical limitations could not be ignored indefinitely. They provided intriguing interpretations of events that had already happened, but they lacked power to predict how people would behave in given situations (Mischel 1968). Moreover, it was difficult to demonstrate that persons who had undergone psychodynamically oriented treatment benefited more than untreated cases (Bandura 1969; Rachman 1971). Acquisition of insight into the underlying impulses, through which behavioral changes were supposedly achieved, turned out to represent more of a social conversion than a self-discovery process. As Marmor (1962), among others, pointed out, each psychodynamic approach had its own favored set of inner causes and its own preferred brand of insight. The presence of these determinants could easily be confirmed through suggestive proving and selective reinforcement of clients' verbal reports in self-validating interviews. For these reasons, advocates of differing theoretical orientations repeatedly discovered their favorite motivating agents, but rarely found evidence for the hypothesized causes emphasized by proponents of competing views. The content of a particular client's insights and emergent "unconscious" could therefore be better predicted from knowledge of the therapist's belief system than from the client's actual social learning history.

It eventually became apparent that if progress in the understanding of human behavior was to be accelerated, more stringent requirements would have to be applied in evaluating the adequacy of explanatory systems. Theories must demonstrate predictive power, and they must accurately identify causal factors, as shown by the fact that varying the postulated determinants produces corresponding changes in behavior.

The attribution of behavior to inner forces can perhaps be likened to early explanatory schemes in other branches of science. At one time diverse chemical reactions were supposedly caused by movements of a material substance called "phlogiston," physical objects were internally propelled by intangible essences, and physiological functioning was ascribed to the action of humors.

Developments in learning theory shifted the focus of causal analysis from hypothesized inner determinants to detailed examination of external influences on responsiveness. Human behavior was extensively analyzed in terms of the stimulus events that evoke it and the reinforcing consequences that alter it. Researchers repeatedly demonstrated that response patterns generally attributed to underlying forces could be induced, eliminated, and reinstated simply by varying external sources of influence. These impressive findings led many psychologists to the view that the causes of behavior are found not in the organism, but in environmental forces.

The idea that man's actions are under external control, though amply documented, was not enthusiastically received for a variety of reasons. To most people it unfortunately implied a one-way influence process that reduced man to a helpless reactor to the vagaries of external rewards and punishments. Popular descriptions of the potential for social influence conjured up macabre associations of *1984* and *Brave New World,* in which people are manipulated at will by occult technocrats. By associating the term *behaviorism* with odious images of salivating dogs and animals driven by carrots and sticks, critics of behavioral approaches skillfully employ Pavlovian conditioning procedures on their receptive audiences to endow this point of view with degrading properties. The fact that valuation of places, persons, or things is affected by one's emotional experiences, whether they be fearful, humiliating, disgusting, mournful, or pleasurable, does not mean that such learning outcomes reflect a base animal process. To expect people to remain unaffected by paired experiences is to require that they be less than human. Moreover, to be sensitive to the consequences of one's actions indicates intelligence rather than subhuman functioning. Nevertheless, promoters of various causes often lobby against social practices they do not like by designating them as Pavlovian or as harrowing precursors of *1984*.

The view that behavior is environmentally determined also appeared to contradict firm but ill-founded beliefs that people possess generalized personality traits leading them to behave in a consistent manner, however variable the social influences might be. Fortunately for survival purposes, cultural practices are much too diverse to produce undiscerning generalized traits (Mischel 1968). A person who behaved in a church the same way he acted in a nightclub would be a forced recipient of an extended rest in a psychiatric facility. A high degree of behavioral flexibility is required if a person is to deal effectively with the complexities of ever-changing environmental demands.

A more valid criticism of extreme situational determinism is that, in a vigorous effort to avoid spurious inner causes, it neglected determinants of man's behavior arising from his cognitive functioning. Man is a thinking organism possessing capabilities that provide him with some power of self-direction. People can represent external influences symbolically and later use such representations to guide their actions; they can solve problems mentally without having to enact the various alternatives; and they can foresee the probable consequences of different actions and alter their behavior accordingly. These higher mental processes permit both insightful and foresighted behavior. By managing the stimulus determinants of given activities and producing consequences for their own actions, people are able to control their own behavior to some degree. As will be illustrated later, cognitive and self-regulative influences often serve important functions in causal sequences. To the extent that traditional behavioral theories could be faulted, it was for providing an incomplete rather than an inaccurate account of human behavior.

In the social learning view, man is neither driven by inner forces nor buffeted helplessly by environmental influences. Rather, psychological functioning is best understood in terms of continuous reciprocal interaction between behavior and its controlling conditions. Early attempts to incorporate both individual and environmental determinants in personality theory simply depicted behavior as caused by these two sets of influences. The problem with this type of formulation is that it treated response dispositions and the environment as independent entities. Contrary to this assumption, the environment is only a potentiality, not a fixed property that inevitably impinges upon individuals and to which their behavior eventually adapts. Behavior partly creates the environment and the resultant environment, in turn, influences the behavior. In this two-way causal process the environment is influenceable, just as the behavior it controls is.

In examining social interactions, Raush (1965) found that the immediately preceding act of one person was the major determinant of the other person's response. In approximately 75 percent of the instances, hostile behavior elicited unfriendly responses, whereas cordial acts seldom did. Aggressive children thus created through their actions a hostile environment, whereas children who displayed friendly interpersonal modes of response generated an amicable social milieu. With little effort one could readily identify individuals who predictably create negative social climates wherever they go. People thus play an active role in constructing their own reinforcement contingencies through their characteristic modes of response.

A complete theory of aggression, whatever its orientation, must explain how aggressive patterns of behavior are developed, what provokes people to behave aggressively, and what maintains their aggressive actions. These major issues are treated at length in subsequent chapters. The remainder of this chapter is devoted to a general discussion of social learning principles of how patterns of behavior are acquired and how their expression is continuously regulated by the interplay of self-generated and external sources of influence.

Development of New Modes of Behavior

Patterns of behavior can be acquired through direct experience or by observing the behavior of others. The more rudimentary form of learning, rooted in direct experience, is largely governed by the rewarding and punishing consequences that follow any given action. People are repeatedly confronted with situations with which they must deal in one way or another. Some of the responses they try prove unsuccessful, while others produce more favorable effects. Through this process of differential reinforcement, successful modes of behavior are eventually selected from exploratory activities, while ineffectual ones are discarded.

Although behavior can be shaped into new patterns to some extent by rewarding and punishing consequences, learning would be exceedingly laborious and hazardous if it proceeded solely on this basis. Most of the intricate responses people display are learned, either deliberately or inadvertently, through the influence of example. Indeed, virtually all learning phenomena resulting from direct experiences can occur on a vicarious basis through observation of other people's behavior and its consequences for them. Man's capacity to learn by observation enables him to acquire complex patterns of behavior by watching the performances of exemplary models. Emotional responses toward certain places, persons, or things can also be developed by witnessing the affective reactions of others punished for their actions. And, finally, the expression of previously learned responses can be socially regulated through the actions of influential models.

The preceding remarks are not meant to imply that new modes of behavior are fashioned solely through experience, either of a direct or observational sort. Biological structure obviously sets limits on the types of aggressive responses that can be successfully perfected, and genetic endowment influences the rate at which learning progresses.

Regulatory Functions

A comprehensive theory of behavior must explain not only how response patterns are acquired, but how their expression is regulated and maintained. In social learning theory, human functioning relies on three regulatory systems. They include antecedent inducements, response feedback influences, and cognitive processes that guide and regulate action. Human aggression is a learned conduct that, like other forms of social behavior, is under stimulus, reinforcement, and cognitive control. These control functions will be discussed separately for explanatory purposes, although in reality they are closely interrelated.

Stimulus Control

To function effectively a person must be able to anticipate the probable consequences of different events and courses of action and regulate his behavior accordingly. Without a capacity for anticipatory or foresighted behavior, man could not profit much from experience. Information about probable consequences is conveyed by environmental stimuli, such as verbal communications; pictorial cues; distinctive places, persons, or things; or the actions of others.

In the earliest years of development, environmental events, except those that are inherently painful, exert little or no influence on infants and young children. As a result of paired experiences, direct, symbolic, or vicarious, formerly neutral stimuli begin to acquire motivating and response-directive properties. Environmental stimuli gain the capacity to activate physiological reactions and emotional behavior through association with evocative events. Such learning often occurs on the basis of direct experience. People come to fear and to avoid individuals who are commonly associated in their experience with pain or distress. Through a similar learning process they become easily angered by the sight or thought of individuals with whom they have had hostile encounters.

Social characteristics generally acquire evocative power through processes that are more subtle and complex than is commonly believed. Emotional responses are frequently acquired on the basis of vicarious rather than direct experiences. The emotional responses exhibited by others toward certain people tend to arouse in observers strong emotional reactions that can become conditioned to the same targets. It is not uncommon for unpopular minority groups or nationalities to become endowed with anger-evoking potency in the absence of personal contact through exposure to modeled animosity. Emotion-arousing words and pictures that conjure up hostile reactions likewise often function as the vehicle for symbolic conditioning of hatreds.

The emotional responses that become established to paired events can be evoked not only by direct experience, observation of another's affective expression, and symbolic stimuli, but also by provocative thoughts. People can easily make themselves nauseous by imagining revolting experiences. They can become sexually aroused by generating erotic fantasies. They can frighten themselves by fear-provoking thoughts. And they can work themselves up into a state of anger by ruminating about mistreatment from offensive provocateurs. The cognitive capacities of humans thus enable them to invest things with positive or negative valence by pairing them repeatedly with thought-produced emotions. This self-arousal process is illustrated in a husband's slaying of a friend who kissed his wife at a New Year's Eve party (*Portland Press-Herald* 1963). The husband had brooded almost incessantly about the kiss over a period of two years. As Thanksgiving approached he further intensified his anger by imagining his foe enjoying a family Thanksgiving dinner while his own family life was irreparably ruined. Shortly after observing how easy it was to kill a man from seeing Oswald shot on television, the brooding husband sought and shot his former friend.

The preceding discussion has shown how things can become invested with response-activating properties on the basis of paired experiences. Environmental cues also acquire response-directing functions when they are associated with differential response consequences. The same actions can produce markedly different results depending upon the time, the place, and the persons toward whom they are expressed. Insulting an irascible aggressor, for example, will have painfully different effects from treating a submissive individual in the same manner. People therefore pay close attention to cues that signify probable consequences, and they partly regulate their behavior on the basis of such information. Stimuli indicating that given actions will be punished or unrewarded tend to inhibit their performance, whereas those signifying that the actions are permissible or reward-able facilitate their occurrence. The following quotation provides a telling example of an autistic boy who freely expressed destructive behavior with his lenient mother but rarely did so in the presence of his father, who tolerated no aggression.

> Whenever her husband was home, Billy was a model youngster. He knew that his father would punish him quickly and dispassionately for misbehaving. But when his father left the house, Billy would go to the window and watch until the car pulled out. As soon as it did, he was suddenly transformed. . . . "He'd go into my closet and tear up my evening dresses and urinate on my clothes. He'd smash furniture and run around biting the walls until the house was destruction from one end to the other. He knew that I liked to dress him in nice clothes, so he used to rip the buttons off his shirts, and used to go in his pants" (Moser 1965:96).

Social behavior is extensively regulated by verbal cues. We influence people's actions in innumerable situations by suggestions, requests, commands, and written directives. Often these operate in subtle ways. To take a common example, parents are quick to issue commands to their children, but they do not always see to it that their requests are heeded. Children are therefore inclined to ignore demands voiced in mild or moderate tones. The parents' mounting anger usually serves as the cue that they will enforce compliance, so that only shouts produce results. Because of the differential signal value of parental directives, many households are run at a fairly high decibel level.

Of the numerous cues that influence how people will behave at any given moment, none is more ubiquitous or effective than the actions of others. People applaud when others clap, they exit from social functions when they see others leaving, they wear their hair like others, they dress alike, and on countless other occasions their behavior is prompted and channeled by the power of example. Modeling influences play an especially important role in the rapid contagion of aggression. The actions of others acquire response-directing properties through selective reinforcement in much the same way as do physical and symbolic cues in nonsocial forms. When behaving like others produces rewarding outcomes, modeling cues become powerful determinants of analogous behavior; conversely, when imitative actions are treated negatively but dissimilar behavior proves rewarding, models' responses prompt divergent performances in observers.

In everyday life the likely consequences of a given course of action depend upon the presence of several factors, including combinations of temporal, social, and situational features. It may be permissible to aggress toward a peer during a physical contact sport, for example, but punishable to do so at other times or in other settings. When subtle variations in stimulus events carry diverse outcomes for similar conduct, it is easy to misjudge what effects aggressive actions will have. Moreover, the force of activating circumstances may at times prompt a person to behave aggressively without paying much heed to subsequent consequences.

Reinforcement Control

A second control system involves behavior feedback influences, mainly in the form of reinforcing consequences. An organism that responded foresightedly on the basis of informative environmental cues but remained unaffected by the results of its actions would be too obtuse to survive for long. In fact, behavior is extensively controlled by its consequences. Responses that cause unrewarding or punishing effects tend to be discarded, whereas those that produce rewarding outcomes are retained and strengthened. Human behavior therefore cannot be fully understood without examining the regulatory influence of reinforcement.

Reinforcement control of behavior is most convincingly demonstrated by intrasubject replication. In these types of studies interpersonal modes of response, many of long standing, are successively eliminated and reinstated by altering the effects they produce. The susceptibility of behavior to reinforcement control is further shown by the fact that even subtle variations in the frequency and patterning of outcomes result in different types of performances. Those who have been rewarded each time they respond are likely to become easily discouraged and to give up quickly when their efforts fail. On the other hand, individuals whose behavior has been reinforced intermittently tend to persist for a considerable time despite setbacks and only occasional success.

In the minds of most people, reinforcement is usually equated with tangible rewards and punishments. Actually, human behavior is largely sustained and modified by symbolic reinforcers. As a result of repeated association with primary experiences, social reactions in the form of verbal approval, reprimands, attention, affection, and rejection acquire powerful reinforcing functions. Such interpersonal reinforcers assume a prominent role in regulating the interactions of everyday life, including aggressive responsiveness. Similarly, after accomplishments become a source of personal satisfaction, knowledge that one has done well can function as a reward that sustains activities independently of social or material incentives. Many forms of behavior (such as communicative and motor skills) that enable an individual to deal effectively with his environment likewise persist with little external support because they produce desired results. Finally, the sensory experiences that are naturally produced by the behavior itself can be effective in modifying and maintaining it over a long period. One rarely has to resort to extrinsic rewards to get people to read interesting books, to watch entertaining television programs, or to play pleasing musical selections.

Vicarious reinforcement. Human functioning would be exceedingly ineffi-cient, not to say dangerous, if behavior were influenced only by directly ex-perienced consequences. Fortunately, one can profit greatly from the ex-periences of others. People repeatedly observe the actions of others and the occasions on which they are rewarded, ignored, or punished. Observed reinforcement influences behavior in much the same way as outcomes that are directly experienced (Bandura 1971a; Kanfer 1965). Observed rewards generally enhance, and observed punishments reduce, similar behavior in observers.

Observed consequences also provide reference standards that determine whether particular outcomes will assume positive or negative value. The same compliment, for instance, is likely to be punishing for persons who have seen similar performances by others more highly acclaimed, but rewarding when others have been less generously praised. Thus, through social comparison processes, observation of other people's response out-comes can drastically alter the effectiveness of direct reinforcements. Since both direct and vicarious reinforcement inevitably occur together in every-day life, the interactive effects of these two sources of influence on human behavior are of much greater significance than their independent control-ling power.

Self-reinforcement. At the highest level of psychological functioning, in-dividuals regulate their own behavior by self-evaluative and other self-produced consequences (Bandura 1971a). In this process people set them-selves certain standards of conduct and respond to their own behavior in self-satisfied or self-critical ways in accordance with their self-imposed demands. Comparative studies show that people can manage their own behavior by self-reinforcement as well as or better than through conse-quences arising from external sources.

After a self-monitored reinforcement system has been established, a given action produces two sets of consequences — a self-evaluative reaction as well as some external outcome. These two sources of reinforcement can occur in several different patterns. Sometimes people are rewarded socially or materially for behavior that they devalue. Anticipation of self-reproach for personally repudiated actions provides an important motivating in-fluence to keep behavior in line with adopted standards in the face of oppos-ing influences. There is no more devastating punishment than self-contempt. Under conditions in which self-devaluative consequences outweigh the force of rewards for accommodating behavior, external in-fluences prove relatively ineffective. On the other hand, when external inducements, whether rewarding or coercive, prevail over self-reinforcing influences, individuals exhibit cheerless compliance. Humans, of course, possess facile cognitive capacities for reconciling distressing conflicts. Devalued actions can be, and often are, justified so that losses in self-respect are minimized as long as the self-deception remains convincing.

An opposite type of conflict between external and self-produced consequences arises when people are punished for engaging in activities they value highly. The rebels, the dissenters, and the nonconformists often experience this type of counterinfluence. Here, the relative strengths of self-approval and external censure determine whether the behavior will be discarded or maintained. If the negative sanctions are relatively weak, socially disapproved but personally valued actions will be readily expressed. If the threatened consequences are severe, however, transgressive behavior is apt to be inhibited under high risk of penalty and freely performed in the absence of prohibitive agents. There are individuals whose sense of self-worth is so strongly linked to certain convictions that they will submit to prolonged maltreatment rather than accede to social practices they regard as unjust.

External reinforcement exerts its greatest influence when it is consonant with self-produced consequences — as when rewarded actions are a source of self-pride, and punished ones are self-censured. Indeed, people strive actively to achieve and to maintain such conditions. They do this by selectively associating with persons who share similar standards of conduct, thus ensuring social support for their own system of self-evaluation. Some of the most drastic changes in behavior are achieved in large part by modifying a person's basis for self-evaluation. By legitimizing aggression and dehumanizing potential victims, individuals who have been strictly socialized against brutalizing and slaying people can be led to do so in military situations without experiencing tormenting self-devaluative consequences. A later chapter presents the various antidotes for self-contempt. Among those who fully adopt the new standards of conduct, skillfully executed carnage may even serve as a basis for self-commendation.

Cognitive Control

If human behavior could be fully explained in terms of external inducements and response consequences, there would be no need to postulate any additional regulatory mechanisms. However, actions are not always predictable from these external sources of influence. Man's cognitive capacities tremendously increase the information he can derive from his experiences and thus partly determine how he will be affected by them. There are several ways in which cognitive functioning enters into the regulation of human behavior. These are discussed next.

Cognitive representation of reinforcement contingencies. Popular portrayals of behavioral approaches would lead one to believe that people can be easily conditioned and manipulated without their awareness. This melodramatic sketch receives little support in numerous studies of how awareness of reinforcement contingencies affects the process of behavior change. In fact, repeated paired stimulation generally fails to produce conditioned emotional responses as long as the connection between stimulus events goes unnoticed. The responses that get conditioned are to a large extent cognitively induced rather than directly elicited by external stimuli. Response consequences similarly have weak effects on behavior when the relationship between one's actions and outcomes is not recognized. On the other hand, awareness of conditions of reinforcement typically results in rapid changes in behavior, which is indicative of insightful functioning. People who are aware of what is wanted and who value the contingent rewards change their behavior in the reinforced direction; those who are equally aware of the reinforcement contingencies but who devalue the required behavior or the reinforcers show little change; those who remain unaware achieve, at best, small increments in performance even though the appropriate responses are reinforced whenever they occur.

Human behavior is regulated to a large extent by anticipated consequences of prospective actions. Individuals may accurately assess the customary effects of given activities but fail to act in accordance with existing conditions or reinforcement because of hope that their actions may eventually bring favorable results. Many a social reformer has sustained his efforts in the face of repeated failures by the belief that the rightness of his cause will ultimately produce desired changes. Sometimes people lead themselves astray by inaccurate expectations when they wrongly assume that certain changes in their behavior will alter future consequences. The deterrent value of threatened punishment, for example, is weakened when lawbreakers misjudge their chances of escaping apprehension for antisocial acts. Judgment of consequences can also be seriously impaired by intoxicants. Felonies are typically committed (72 percent) under the influence of alcohol (Shupe 1954). Under laboratory conditions drunk subjects are more willing to risk punitive attack than sober ones (Shuntich and Taylor 1972).

The notion that behavior is controlled by its immediate consequences holds up better under close scrutiny for anticipated consequences than for those that actually impinge upon the organism. In most instances customary outcomes are reasonably good predictors of behavior because the consequences that people anticipate for their actions are accurately derived from, and therefore correspond closely to, prevailing conditions of reinforcement. However, belief and actuality do not always coincide because anticipated consequences are also partly inferred from observed response consequences of others, from what one reads or is told, and from a variety of other cues that, on the basis of past experiences, are considered reliable forecasters of likely outcomes. When actions are guided by anticipated consequences derived from predictors that do not accurately reflect existing contingencies of reinforcement, behavior is weakly controlled by its actual consequences until cumulative experiences produce more realistic expectations.

In some of the more severe behavior disorders, psychotic actions are so powerfully controlled by bizarre subjective contingencies that the behavior remains essentially unaffected by its external consequences. This process is vividly illustrated in a patient's account of his psychotic experiences in an insane asylum during the early nineteenth century (Bateson 1961). The narrator had received a scrupulously moralistic upbringing, according to which actions ordinarily viewed as fully acceptable were judged by him to be sinful and likely to provoke the wrath of God. Consequently, many innocuous acts elicited dreadful apprehensions of hellish torment; these in turn motivated and maintained self-torturing rituals for hours on end, designed to forestall the imagined disastrous consequences. Reduction in acute distress accompanying the nonoccurrence of subjectively feared, but objectively nonexistent, threats powerfully reinforced the self-punitive defensive behavior. Given fictional contingencies with a powerful internal reinforcing system, the patient persisted in his atonement rituals even in the face of severe external punishment and blatant disconfirming experiences. The attendants' punitive measures were pale compared to the feared Hadean torture imaginally represented in visions of clanking iron and massive flames fanned by huge forge bellows. When the prophecies of divine inner voices failed to materialize, the disconfirming experiences were discounted as tests by the Almighty of the strength of his religious convictions.

Instances of bizarre thought control of grotesque murders occur from time to time. In one such case reported by Reich and Hepps (1972), a student became convinced that his commune companions were, in fact, conspirators from another planet plotting to destroy his mind with LSD. Seeking refuge in Europe, he fled in terror from city to city in the belief that he was escaping a Nazi scheme to exterminate him. Upon arriving in Tel Aviv, he concluded that the Nazis had already taken over and were gassing the population. While sitting in a sidewalk cafe resignedly drinking what he thought was poisoned wine, he interpreted an overheard conversation between Israeli soldiers as Nazis boasting about their kill rates. Enraged by imagined massacres, the student drew a knife, killing a soldier and wounding two other persons.

Cognitive guidance of behavior. Cognitive processes play a prominent role in the acquisition and retention of response patterns as well as in their expression. The memory trace of momentary influences is short-lived, but such experiences often have lasting behavioral effects. This is made possible by the fact that transitory external events are coded and stored in symbolic form for memory representation. Patterns of behavior that have been observed and other experiences long past can thus be reinstated by visualizing them or by representing them verbally. These internal models of the outside world can serve as guides to overt action on later occasions. It will be recalled from the earlier discussion of learning processes that internal representations of patterned behavior are constructed from observed examples and from informative feedback to one's trial-and-error performances.

Cognitive functioning is especially important in observational learning in which a person reads about or observes a pattern of behavior, but does not perform it overtly until appropriate circumstances arise. Evidence will be cited later to illustrate how modeled activities are acquired in symbolic form without behavioral enactment, how they can be strengthened by mental rehearsal, and how they provide the basis for action on later occasions given suitable inducements.

Thought control of action through mental problem solving. Man's efforts to understand and to manage his environment would be exceedingly wearisome if optimal solutions to problems could be arrived at only by performing alternative actions and suffering the consequences. Actually, most problem solving occurs in thought rather than in action. Man's higher mental capacities, for example, enable him to design sturdy dwellings and bridges without having to build them until he hits upon a structure that does not collapse. Alternative courses of action are generally tested in symbolic exploration and either discarded or retained on the basis of calculated consequences. The best symbolic solution is then executed in action.

The three major systems by which behavior is regulated do not operate independently; most actions are simultaneously controlled by two or more of the component influences. Moreover, the various systems are closely interdependent in acquiring and retaining their power to determine behavior. In order to establish and to maintain effective stimulus control, for example, the same actions must produce different consequences depending on the cues that are present. Stimulus and cognitive influences, in turn, can alter the impact of prevailing conditions of reinforcement. Certain stimuli can acquire such powerful control over defensive behavior that people avoid renewed encounters with feared or hated persons, places, or things. In instances in which the original threats no longer exist, their self-protective behavior is insulated from realistic reinforcement influences.

Even when the things one dislikes or fears are not completely avoided, cues having strong emotion-arousing potential provoke defensive behaviors that predictably create adverse reinforcement contingencies where they may not ordinarily exist. To the extent that an individual's distrust of certain people leads him to behave in ways that provoke hostile counterreactions from them, their negative valence is further strengthened and it, in turn, prompts actions that produce reciprocal negative reinforcement. Both processes thus support each other.

The way in which beliefs and conscious recognition of environmental contingencies can enhance, distort, or even negate the influence of reinforcing consequences has already been amply documented and needs no further illustration. Cognitive events, however, do not function as autonomous causes of behavior. Their nature, their emotion-arousing properties, and their occurrence are under stimulus and reinforcement control. Analysis of cognitive control of behavior is therefore incomplete without specifying what influences a person's thoughts. Detailed exposition of social learning theory falls beyond the scope of this book, but the principles are presented in other sources (Bandura 1969, 1971b).

References

Bandura, A. 1960. Relationship of family patterns to child behavior disorders. Progress Report, Stanford University, Project No. M-1734, United States Public Health Service.

———. 1969. *Principles of behavior modification.* New York: Holt, Rinehart and Winston.

———. 1971a. Vicarious and self-reinforcement processes. In R. Glaser (ed.), *The nature of reinforcement.* New York: Academic Press, pp. 228-78.

———. 1971b. *Social learning theory.* New York: General Learning Press.

———, and Walters, R. H. 1959. *Adolescent aggression.* New York: Ronald Press.

Bateson, G. (ed.). 1961. *Perceval's narrative: A patient's account of his psychosis, 1830-1832.* Stanford, Calif.: Stanford University Press.

Bolles, R. C. 1967. *Theory of motivation.* New York: Harper & Row.

Kanfer, F. H. 1965. *Vicarious human reinforcement: A glimpse into the black box.* In L. Krasner and L. P. Ullmann (eds.), *Research in behavior modification.* New York: Holt, Rinehart and Winston, pp. 244-67.

Marmor, J. 1962. Psychoanalytic therapy as an educational process: Common denominators in the therapeutic approaches of different psychoanalytic "schools." In J. H. Masserman (ed.), *Science and psychoanalysis,* Vol. 5, *Psychoanalytic education.* New York: Grune & Stratton, pp. 286-99.

Mischel, W. 1968. *Personality and assessment.* New York: Wiley.

Moser, D. 1965. Screams, slaps and love. *Life,* May 7, 90A-101.

Portland (Me.) Press-Herald. 1963. It looked easy on TV, says the man held in killing here. November 28, p. 1.

Rachman, S. 1971. *The effects of psychotherapy.* Oxford and New York: Pergamon Press.

Raush, H. L. 1965. Interaction sequences. *Journal of Personality and Social Psychology* 2:487-99.

Reich, P., and Hepps, R. B. 1972. Homicide during a psychosis induced by LSD. *Journal of the American Medical Association* 219:869-71.

Shuntich, R. J., and Taylor, S. P. 1972. The effects of alcohol on human physical aggression. *Journal of Experimental Research in Personality* 6:34-38.

Shupe, L. M. 1954. Alcohol and crime: A study of the urine alcohol concentration found in 882 persons arrested during or immediately after the commission of a felony. *Journal of Criminal Law, Criminology and Police Science* 44:661-64.

Part 3
Cultural and
Anthropological Inquiries

Introduction

In Part 2 we have noted the hazard of attempting a great inductive leap forward from man's individual to international behavior in the study of war. Anthropology promises, at least in theory, to provide an intermediate level of analysis between man's behavioral potential and its final expression in war making through the study of man's symbolic system called "culture." Kenneth E. Boulding (1967:16), in rejecting the instinctive theory of aggression, has instead suggested "the concept of a cultural instinct," defining it as "a body of coded information which is passed on from generation to generation, suffering mutation and selection, just as the coded information in the gene is passed on, except that cultural evolution is much more subject to mutation and proceeds at a much more rapid rate than the evolution of the genetic structure." The potential contributions that anthropology could make to the study of war — or perhaps more accurately to the effective execution of war — were even recognized by the U.S. government when it mobilized a group of outstanding American anthropologists during World War II to study the national character of the enemy societies (Japan and Germany).

The cultural or anthropological approach to the study of war is based on the assumption that all members of a given society or culture share the same culturally patterned characteristics of behavior and that it is possible to delineate these patterns of persistent regularity and consistency in the relationship of one member's behavior to another as well as to the culture as a whole. Based on such a premise anthropologists claim that the understanding of culture — or national character in the context of modern times — is essential to the understanding of such specific material as Japanese kamikaze operations or the Soviet defense of Stalingrad. For our illustrative purposes, a passage from Ruth Benedict's (1946:25) wartime study of Japanese culture and national character deserves to be quoted:

After the air battles were over, the Japanese planes returned to their base in small formations of three or four. A Captain was in one of the first planes to return. After alighting from his plane, he stood on the ground and gazed into the sky through binoculars. As his men returned, he counted. He looked rather pale, but he was quite steady. After the last plane returned he made out a report and proceeded to Headquarters. At Headquarters he made his report to the Commanding Officer. As soon as he had finished his report,

however, he suddenly dropped to the ground. The officers on the spot rushed
to give assistance but alas! he was dead. On examining his body it was found
that it was already cold, and he had a bullet wound in his chest, which had
proved fatal. It is impossible for the body of a newly-dead person to be cold.
Nevertheless the body of the dead Captain was as cold as ice. The Captain
must have been dead long before, and it was his spirit that made the report.
Such a miraculous feat must have been achieved by the strict sense of responsibility that the dead Captain possessed.

Human cognition is perhaps a most potent determinant of human
behavior. Anthropologists can therefore make an important contribution to
the enhancement of cross-cultural (and cross-national and cross-
ideological) communications in war making or peacemaking by clearly
defining such culturally transmitted definitions of social variables
as: strength and weakness; conflict and cooperation; hero and villain; victory and defeat; ascribed and achieved statuses; justice and injustice;
equality and hierarchy; submission and dominance; dependence and independence; and legitimate and illegitimate authority. These variables all
relate to both behavioral and structural attributes of any organized human
society. To the extent that anthropologists can clearly and accurately depict
the symbolism associated with each of these behavioral and structural attributes, our task of transforming the war system into a peace system
becomes clarified.

What is the relationship between warfare and the evolution of human
society? Or what is the role of warfare in the successive transformation of
human and subhuman cultures? In what respects does social conflict play a
eufunctional and a dysfunctional role in man's evolutionary process? Which
set of variables, behavioral or structural, plays a greater role in warmak-
ing? Do primitive societies provide us with any helpful evidence of the
kinds of experimentation in social order that can be applied to our present
challenge of working toward the establishment of a new world order with
justice? Anthropologists are supposed to deal with such questions in a cross-
cultural, nonethnocentric, and evolutionary spirit. Anthropological field
work is often claimed to give an understanding of small-scale living models
of human evolution from which we can draw relevant hypotheses about
man's capacity for adaptive or maladaptive behavior.

In spite of the great promise anthropology holds in store for peace
research, however, the performance of anthropologists has been on the
whole insignificant. The low saliency of anthropology is clearly revealed in
a recent UNESCO (1973:21) survey of institutions and individuals involved in peace and conflict research throughout the world. The contributions of anthropologists to such leading international and interdisciplinary
journals in the field of peace research as *Journal of Peace Research* and *Journal*

of Conflict Resolution have been marginal. Writing in 1968, three noted American anthropologists had to admit: "Anthropology, despite its unique strengths in biological, paleontological, archaeological, cultural, linguistic, ecological, and psychological specialties, has been strangely inarticulate on the subject of war" (Fried et al. 1968:xiii). It was against this backdrop that a major scholarly conference on "War: Its Causes and Correlates" was organized under the aegis of the Ninth International Congress of Anthropological and Ethnological Sciences in 1973, which eventually led to the publication of two important volumes embodying much of current anthropological inquiry into the causes of war (Nettleship, Givens, and Nettleship 1975; Givens and Nettleship 1976).

Our selections in Part 3 highlight the possibilities and limitations of cultural and anthropological inquiries into the causes of war. Levine's chapter is a sophisticated and sensitive inquiry into all aspects of social conflict—its structures, patterns, sources, manifestations, and consequences—but curiously shies away from linking this analysis to contemporary society or from suggesting some concrete hypotheses to be formulated and applied to international conflict. Applying a more rigorous quantitative method, Otterbein examines three variables—social structure, political organization, and intersocietal relations—of some fifty societies for their possible effect on the occurrence of internal war. One of his main conclusions is that the frequency of external war does not influence the frequency of internal war. Some readers will no doubt question the contemporary relevance and policy application of this study in the development of a science of war prevention, but in contrast, anthropologist Raoul Narroll's (1966) careful survey of primitive tribes has yielded a number of results that are relevant to modern deterrence theory. For one, he finds that the *si vis pacem, para bellum* doctrine—"if you want peace, prepare for war"—does not work among primitive tribes.

Fabbro's study of seven peaceful societies is rich in heuristic and normative power. Note that this piece, following the modern functional approach to world order, has reformulated the "swords into plowshares" approach into the "plowshares into peace" approach by asking the unconventional question, "Why do men live in peace?" Furthermore, Fabbro uses the expanded concept of peace. He examines the seven societies on fourteen attributes, seven of which are subsumed under structural violence. Note also his conclusion with normative implications: that there is no basic incompatibility between positive and negative peace and that "the very idea that the presence of one is the 'price' paid for the absence of the other may simply be a manifestation of Western—although now becoming global—culture and its concomitant hierarchical world view."

There are several hazards and problems in cultural and anthropological inquiries into the causes of war that need to be noted. Anthropological research even with a most sophisticated statistical method or a most comprehensive conceptual net cannot hope to capture all the variables that make up a given culture. This problem becomes even more serious and complicated when we try to describe foreign cultures. Notwithstanding their novel claims for a nonethnocentric and evolutionary perspective, Western anthropologists can hardly avoid the influence of their own cultural filter in the study of non-Western cultures.

The attempt to solve the above problem through field work may enable anthropologists to capture all the fish in a given culture, but creates a problem of different sorts. Surely the value of anthropology for the study of war lies in its contribution as an applied behavioral and social science, but the typical scale or size of sample in such field work is so small as to call into question its relevance to large-scale human affairs characteristic of the modern state system. If a primitive society has managed to substitute feasting, sorcery, games, or something else as a functional or moral equivalent of warfare, for example, what would be its counterpart in a modern society? In short, field work establishes a measure of empirical integrity in cultural analysis but leaves us with the methodological problem of comparing apples with oranges.

Moreover, anthropological research needs to be as contemporary as possible if it is to gain some credibility and relevance for the study of war in our times. The quoted passage from Ruth Benedict's classic, *The Chrysanthemum and the Sword,* already seems rather incongruous with contemporary Japanese culture. In the age of "global village," there can be no island culture enjoying a splendid isolationism. Virtually every significant national culture is now under a variety of cross pressures from internal and external sources. Learning from history can easily become a dangerous business, as shown by the role of the so-called Munich syndrome in the perpetuation of the war system in the United States. In sum, then, anthropological studies of national cultures can become a double-edged sword that can cut either way: positively to see other people as they see themselves, or negatively to see them as mirrors of our own outmoded images and stereotypes.

In order to minimize the above-mentioned problems and to present as undistorted (and updated) a picture of man's cultural and symbolic behavior as possible, we require an interdisciplinary participation and partnership of a wide range of social science and other humane and biological disciplines concerned with all aspects of human behavior at all levels of human organization. The selections below should be read with the openness required of an interdisciplinary approach.

7

Anthropology and the
Study of Conflict

Robert A. LeVine

Ethnographers have long been recording instances of warfare, feuding, factionalism, and sorcery, but theoretical attention to social conflict is relatively new in anthropology. Recent theoretical work by anthropologists on this subject has been influenced primarily by the structural-functional theory of social systems and indirectly by the psychoanalytic theory of personality (including behavioristic revision in the frustration-aggression hypothesis).

At the present writing there appear to be two schools of anthropological thought on the subject of conflict. One is that of Max Gluckman and V. W. Turner, of the University of Manchester, who see patterns of social conflict as eufunctional for the maintenance of social systems. The "silver-lining" approach of Gluckman is exemplified by the titles of some of his well-known BBC lectures (1955): "The Peace in the Feud" and "The Bonds in the Colour-Bar." The theoretical position of this school of thought is that conflicts within and between small social units promote the solidarity of larger social units (particularly the society as a whole), that rebellions against occupants of political positions serve to emphasize the value of those positions to society, and that expressions of hostility in ritual serve as symbolic reaffirmations of the unchallenged moral order within which the rituals occur. On the assumption that the study of conflict within African societies is the most direct route to the understanding of their cohesive forces, Turner (1957) has devised the "social drama," a case-history approach to community conflict as a method of ethnographic recording and presentation.

The other school of thought is that of Bernard J. Siegel and Alan R. Beals of Stanford University. They have challenged the theory that patterns of continual conflict in nonliterate societies are socially eufunctional:

Reprinted by permission of the publisher and author from Robert A. LeVine, "Anthropology and the Study of Conflict," *Journal of Conflict Resolution* 5 (1961):3-15.

It is difficult to interpret conflict of this kind in terms of a crystalline model of structure and function. In fact, so dubious is the functional value of such behaviors, that it appears probable that such organizational types would have little survival value in the face of new and critical problems and stresses (1960a:107).

Siegel and Beals are concerned primarily with the causes of conflict rather than with its functions. They view social conflict as a maladaptive outcome, produced by the interaction of strains — sensitive points of potential disruption within the social system — and stresses — alteration in pressures external to the system. The latter include acculturative pressures. They have distinguished different types of factionalism, defined as "overt, unregulated (unresolved) conflict which interferes with the achievement of the goals of the group" (1960a:108), and attempted to identify the antecedent conditions leading to different forms and intensities of factionalist dispute. Their discussion of strain shows the influence of psychoanalytic formulations concerning aggression and its inhibition and displacement, but the emphasis is on structural factors as causes of strain.

In contrast to Gluckman and Turner, who have limited themselves to analyses of conflict in particular African societies, Siegel and Beals have attempted a broadly cross-cultural formulation applicable to all human societies and testable in laboratory studies of groups as well as in the field (1960b). Another major difference between the two schools of thought is that Siegel and Beals study conflict as a product of culture change, while Gluckman concentrates on conflict as an aspect of stable social systems.

With this recent flurry of anthropological activity on the theory of conflict, we can reasonably expect advances of an empirical and analytic nature to be made in this problem area during the next few years on both sides of the Atlantic. Regardless of what turns anthropological approaches to conflict take, there are certain aspects of its cross-cultural variations which cannot be ignored, and an attempt has been made to summarize these in the following conceptual framework.

Structural Levels of Conflict

In any cross-cultural study of conflict, the level or levels of social structure under examination must be made explicit even if not held constant. There are, as Siegel and Beals (1960b) have pointed out, kinds of conflict which spread to several structural levels, and which may be thought of as "pervasive," but it is necessary to distinguish the levels before one can determine whether or not a kind of conflict is pervasive. The following structural levels can be thought of as applicable to virtually all societies.

1. *Intrafamily*. Interpersonal conflict within the domestic family group,

including sibling rivalry, intergenerational conflict, husband-wife antagonism, would be found at this level.

2. *Intracommunity*. Since the small local community is an identifiable territorial unit in most nonurban societies, it is possible to make comparisons at this level. Intergroup conflict within local communities, as between factions based on neighborhood, descent, class or caste, or associational ties (or some combination of them), is included here as well as interpersonal conflict which cuts across families but does not involve groups.

3. *Intercommunity*. This covers the entire range of levels above the single local community but within one ethnolinguistic entity. The number of levels and size of the interacting units are extremely variable cross culturally and depend on total population size and degree of political centralization. The following are examples of levels in the category for which ethnographers have reported conflict: (a) local communities, each operating autonomously, in conflicts against one another; (b) allied clusters of local communities; (c) nonlocalized social groups such as lineages, clans, and associations which are mobilized for purposes of conflict from among residents of several local communities; (d) autonomous states or chiefdoms of a single ethnolinguistic group; (e) provinces or chiefdoms within a national organization, in conflict against each other or against the central state. A single ethnolinguistic group may have conflict at a number of intercommunity levels, with temporary alliances among the groups and subgroups. The Nuer as described by Evans-Pritchard (1940) are a good example of this.

The great cross-cultural variability in sociopolitical organization at supracommunity levels raises the question of what kinds of units should be used for comparison. The answers which anthropologists have given to this question are as variable as the phenomena under study. Fortes and Evans-Pritchard, while admitting that "the designation of autonomous political groups is always to some extent an arbitrary matter" (1940:22), insist on the total ethnolinguistic entity as the unit of comparison. Murdock (1949:86) has argued for using units which are roughly similar in size and scale, regardless of which structural level is chosen. Schapera (1956:8) disagrees with Murdock and asserts that what should be compared is the *political community*, by which he means the autonomous self-governing group, even though this may be a tiny hunting band in one society and a great kingdom in another. Leach (1954) has presented the case against treating ethnolinguistic groups as isolated units and has argued for studying the wider intercultural environment. This great range of views among anthropologists boils down to a fundamental problem which must be faced by anyone doing a systematic cross-cultural study of conflict: whether to make an arbitrary a priori selection of a structural unit, such as "the local com-

munity" or "the total social system," and then try to find its nearest
equivalent in the societies being studied or to adjust the comparative
perspective to the structure of the societies being studied. The latter can be
done by using a functional unit, e.g., the permanent decisionmaking unit
of maximal size, or by attempting to capture the entire relevant milieu internal and external to the groups being examined.

4. *Intercultural.* This level involves interaction between ethnolinguistic
groups or their members. In the case of stateless societies, the ethnolinguistic group may be so loosely organized that its component
segments are never involved in collective action, but the fact that it is
linguistically, culturally, and territorially distinct from other such groups
justifies a distinction in levels between its internal and external relations.
What is often referred to as intertribal conflict occurs at this level. It can remain a significant dimension of cleavage even when a central political
authority is superimposed over several ethnolinguistic groups, and even
when they lose their territorial distinctness, as in some of the new nations of
Africa.

The sections that follow concern five aspects of conflict at any structural
level: the culture patterns which can be viewed as indicators of conflict,
their attitudinal concomitants, their sources or causes, their functional
value, and the culture patterns involved in the control and resolution of
conflict. One of the central problems in the cross-cultural study of conflict is
the amount and kind of variation in these aspects at different structural
levels within one social system. While this is still something of an open
question, we can reasonably expect to find a heavier reliance on informal
mechanisms for conflict control and resolution at the lowest structural levels
(intrafamily and intracommunity) and a greater use of politico-legal means
of conflict resolution at the higher structural levels, if there are any means
at all (Whiting 1950). This variation in itself justifies distinguishing among
structural levels in empirical studies of conflict.

Conflict-indicating Culture Patterns

What are the overt cultural manifestations of conflict? The view taken
here is that universal or institutionalized forms of aggressive behavior provide the categories for comparing societies in terms of conflict. The meaning of aggression in this context is interpersonal behavior consciously
directed toward injuring a person (or group) or interfering with his attainment of goals. While the psychoanalytic notion of aggression as behavior
which can be directed against the self may be a valid one, it leads into so
controversial an area of interpretation of culture patterns that the omission
of this aspect of aggression from comparative discussion appears operationally useful at this point. The following five categories are culturally pat-

terned forms of aggressive behavior which can be taken as indicators of social conflict, without making any assumptions about their functional value.

1. *Physical aggression.* This would include warfare, i.e., armed combat between groups, and feuding, a highly regulated, limited form of warfare, in the case of intergroup relations. At the interpersonal level, homicide, brawls, and dueling (a socially acceptable and limited form of interpersonal combat) are indicators. Although homicide and brawls may be deviant behavior, there is reason to believe that they are culturally patterned (Bohannon 1960) and are therefore as useful as any other type of physical aggression as conflict indicators. Property destruction, as in arson and theft of valued goods, may be a physical expression of conflict between persons or groups. Cultures can be compared with respect to differences in frequency of a type of physical aggression and in its intensity (e.g., average seriousness of injury, number of persons killed, value of goods destroyed or stolen).

2. *Public verbal dispute.* Public insult and accusation of wrongdoing, litigation, and debate fall into this category. The use of such behavior patterns as indicators of conflict may require an estimate by the investigator of the aggressive intent and emotional intensity of the participants. Litigation, for example, may represent a nonaggressive alternative to physical attack, but in societies with extremely high rates of litigation, the judicial process appears to be used for aggressive purposes. In one sense, any cultural pattern which pits individuals against one another as adversaries with conflicting interests can be viewed as social conflict, although it may be a highly eufunctional form of it. In the context of aggressive behavior, however, it seems desirable to have independent measures of the degree to which patterns of public verbal dispute actually do involve aggressive intent.

3. *Covert verbal aggression.* This covers malicious gossip, privately expressed suspicions of witchcraft and sorcery, and the use of malevolent magic. While magic is not entirely verbal, it involves the manipulation of verbal and nonverbal symbols, and does not ordinarily entail face-to-face combat or encounter. The frequency of these patterns of covert verbal aggression appears to be a sensitive index of conflict at the intrafamily and intracommunity levels in many nonliterate societies (Naroll 1959). . . .

4. *Breach of expectation.* Failure to perform acts which are valuable to other persons or groups and which they have come to expect as the result of past performance may be a form of aggression. The refusal to participate in cooperative endeavors at the intracommunity level, described by Beals in this issue, is an example of this. Examples of other forms are refusal to obey commands in social relationships which involve obedience and withholding of goods in economic transactions. Since the expectations involved are

often traditional, behavior of this kind is commonly found in situations of
culture change.

   5. *Avoidance and separation.* This is different from breach of expectation in
that contact and communication between conflicting persons or groups are
cut off to a greater degree and also in that avoidance and separation are
more likely to be institutionalized in relatively stable cultures. Culture patterns in this category can be found at every structural level. They include
avoidance relationships between categories of kin (e.g., the father-son
avoidance described by Skinner in this issue), the erection of fences or other
barriers between neighbors, emigration of individuals or groups from a
community or region, segregation of groups, secession of political units,
and the breaking off of diplomatic relations. It must be emphasized again
that the functional consequences of the culture patterns listed, or the extent
to which they are the least disruptive alternatives available, are not being
assessed at this point. Without considering function, it seems reasonable to
assume that avoidance and separation represent reactions to aggressive
motivation or incompatibility of interests (which could lead to aggression)
experienced by the actors in the social situation and are therefore indicators
of conflict. It is in this category, however, that we confront those culture
patterns which, while indicative of actual or potential conflict, may be so
successful in preventing more disruptive forms from occurring that they
must be considered under the heading of conflict control as well.

Attitudinal Concomitants of Conflict

   Social conflict appears to be regularly accompanied by certain feelings
and beliefs of individuals who are participating in the conflict or who are
members of participating groups. Although these feelings and beliefs are
culturally patterned, they can be measured independently of the overt
manifestations of conflict discussed above and often *must* be measured independently because they are less likely to be recorded by ethnographers who
do not have a specialized interest in conflict. Furthermore, there is an advantage to research in keeping overt patterns of conflict analytically distinct
from individual attitudes, viz., retention of the freedom to find concomitant variations between the two sets of variables. The interview schedule
presented in this issue by Campbell and LeVine has been devised with this
advantage in mind.

   Two types of attitudinal concomitants of conflict are conceived here: (a)
Hostility, i.e., aggression in the form of a latent disposition to take aggressive action or in the form of fantasy aggression. In both forms hostility
is a symbolic activity of the individual and can be measured by taking a
sample of the relevant symbolic activity, as through an interview or

psychological test. For example, an individual responding to such an instrument may express hatred of others, a desire to kill or injure them, and a description of how he would do it if he had the chance, even though his overt behavior does not exhibit this tendency. (b) Negative images, i.e., beliefs concerning other individuals or groups which involve an unfavorable evaluation of them. Such images are likely to be compounded of distorted perceptions of them and a selection of unfavorable traits from among their actual attributes. Where relatively stable groups are in conflict the negative images may become elaborate and well-organized stereotypes which condition intergroup behavior. This is conspicuous at the intercultural level, where cultural differences provide material for negative evaluation, but it undoubtedly goes on at other levels as well. . . .

Sources of Social Conflict

What are the causes of conflict in human social systems? Whatever they are, it is safe to assume that not all of them are peculiar to *Homo sapiens*, since aggressive behavior is found widely among the vertebrates and is presumably adaptive in a broad range of environments. It may also be said that human social life inevitably entails frustrations and incompatibilities between individuals which engender conflict in all societies. No matter how valid such universal propositions are, a cross-cultural perspective bids us to pay attention to the determinants of differences in amount and kind of conflict among human populations. While we may assume that all societies have patterns of social conflict, it is the variations across societies (and over time in particular societies) that we want to explain and predict.

The subject of determinants of social conflict has been dealt with by Siegel and Beals in their discussions of strains and stresses (1960a, 1960b) and is treated in this issue by Gulliver, Beals, and Skinner. At this point, then, I shall simply indicate three categories of factors which seem to be determinants of cross-cultural variations in social conflict.

1. *Economic.* Competition for scarce resources is often mentioned as a source of conflict, and there can be no question that the degree of scarcity of valued goods varies greatly among societies and in the histories of particular societies. In some groups, conflict arises over land, as Gulliver describes in this issue; in others, there is competition for employment opportunities and/or for the prestige goods rather than subsistence resources. Competition for positions of status and authority, while not strictly economic, is similar in form to economic competition. This category of conflict determinant can be found at all structural levels.

2. *Structural.* At least two types of variables are involved here. (a) Demographic variables, such as proximity which, by increasing the

amount of contact between competitive persons or groups, with other things being equal, increases the amount of conflict between them. LeVine (1960b) has found a relationship between the proximity of co-wife residence in polygynous families and the frequency of witchcraft and sorcery accusations, and has argued that frequency of intrafamily contact of this kind influences the level of covert, verbal aggression. (b) Role or status ambiguity which, in potentially competitive situations, allows competition to become so intense that conflict results. This appears to be the case at all structural levels, and at the intercommunity and intercultural levels, tends to be correlated with a lack of authoritative means for resolving conflicts.

3. *Psychological.* Although all aggressive behavior may be linked to individual motivation, there are some cross-cultural variations in conflict which do not seem to be adequately accounted for in terms of economic and structural hypotheses and which require psychological explanations. Two types of psychological variables are relevant here. (a) Environmental conditions in childhood, e.g., training by parents, which reinforce aggressive behavior patterns or which create intrapersonal conflicts that produce hostile attitudes in the individual. For example, in some societies, physical aggression is encouraged in childhood while in others it is discouraged, and this appears to have important consequences for the reaction in adulthood of individuals who have been trained differently. (b) Adult stresses and frustrations other than those arising from competition for scarce resources. These include biopsychological variables which have been hypothetically linked to increments in the aggressive behavior of individuals, e.g., nutritional deficiencies, such as hypoglycemia, and sexual frustration. Also included here are the phenomena of culture stress (Naroll 1959) and the psychological stress resulting from acculturation.

The Functional Value of Conflict

Are aggressive patterns of behavior and their attitudinal concomitants adaptive (eufunctional) or maladaptive (dysfunctional) for the survival and operation of social systems? It is clear that no single answer can be given which will hold for all such patterns in all social systems. In some contexts, conflict is disruptive, while in others it appears to have a facilitating effect. The problem is to assess disruption and facilitation in some relatively objective fashion.

Two ways of assessing the functional value of social conflict suggest themselves. One is in the terms of the effects of conflict on the solidarity of groups at various structural levels. Behavior which reduces group solidarity is dysfunctional, that which promotes it is eufunctional. Although it might seem that conflict could never promote group solidarity, one must take into account effects at different structural levels. It has often been pointed out in sociological discussions that open conflict between groups aids the internal cohesion of the groups, and this is illustrated by Lewis in his description of interclan feuding in Morocco in this issue. The observation that hatred and unfavorable stereotypes of outgroups help maintain feelings of solidarity within the ingroup is commonplace in discussions of ethnocentrism. On the other hand, it has been a major point of Gluckman and Turner that schism and fission at the local level can promote cohesion in a wider system of social relationships. All such propositions can be formulated as cross-culturally testable hypotheses if cohesion or solidarity at a certain level is measured by the absence or lesser degree of conflict at that level. The first generalization mentioned above would become: the more frequent or intense a conflict-indicating culture pattern at the intercultural or intercommunity levels, the less frequent or intense will be a conflict-indicating culture pattern at a lower intercommunity level at one of the two intracommunity levels. A parallel formulation is possible for the attitudinal concomitants of conflict. The second generalization can be reformulated for cross-cultural testing as: the more frequent or intense a conflict-indicating culture pattern at an intracommunity or low intercommunity level, the less frequent or intense will it be at a higher structural level. Putting the two hypotheses together, we would expect to find an inverse relationship between conflict variables at different structural levels.

A second way of assessing the functional value of social conflict is by the development of a transcultural ranking of the degree of disruptiveness of the various conflict-indicating culture patterns. If it were possible to establish in some intersubjectively plausible manner that, e.g., certain patterns of physical aggression, breach of expectation, and avoidance and separation are more disruptive than certain patterns of public verbal dispute and covert verbal aggression or that some patterns of physical aggression are more disruptive than others, then it would be possible to rank societies along a dimension of the disruptiveness of the conflict patterns which they exhibit at a given structural level. A hypothetical example would be a ranking of societies in terms of the frequency of litigation or witchcraft accusations at the intracommunity level and another ranking of the same societies with respect to the frequency of intracommunity homicide. If it were agreed that litigation and witchcraft accusations are less disruptive than homicide, then a functional hypothesis, i.e., a hypothesis which sees one form of conflict as a functional alternative to another would be that the two series of rankings are inversely related. By organizing cross-cultural data in this way, it would be possible to find out if different conflict-indicating culture patterns, varying in their disruptiveness at a given structural level, are functional substitutes for one another. If it turns out that they are, then one can compare societies in terms of the relative disruptiveness (dysfunctionality) of their solution to the same functional problem.

Patterns of Conflict Control and Resolution

In societies with specialized central political structures, mechanisms for the resolution and control of internal conflicts tend to be conspicuously identified with the explicit functions of political offices. However, among the empirical contributions which anthropology has made to the study of political organization, none is of greater significance than the discovery that there are viable and stable societies which lack both central government and specialized political roles. The problem of how conflict is controlled and resolved in these stateless societies, analogous in many ways to problems of international regulation, has been the object of considerable attention from social anthropologists during the twenty years since the publication of Fortes and Evans-Pritchard's *African Political Systems* (1940). The following discussion continues this concentration on stateless societies, in a review of the mechanisms for conflict resolution which have been found in anthropological research.

Most theoretical analyses of stateless political systems have been primarily concerned with intercommunity structural levels within ethnolinguistic groups; the internal authority system of the local community has received less attention than it deserves. This is unfortunate, because the available evidence suggests that the mechanisms for resolving conflicts within small, face-to-face groups are quite different from those operating between groups, just as conflict resolution within organized national states is different from that found at the uncentralized international level. In this discussion, patterns of conflict resolution within local communities will be taken up first and then those operating at intercommunity levels. It should be noted that "the local community" is an abstraction which is not approximated as a distinct, stable, and cohesive entity in a number of stateless societies. Nevertheless, if thought of as a territorial unit greater than the domestic family, e.g., a village, hamlet, or neighborhood, with not more than 1,500 persons (Murdock 1949) and with at least some collective activity in cases of internal or external conflict, it is applicable to the vast majority of societies under consideration here.

In such communities, internecine violence tends to be rare, and, when it does occur, is quickly terminated. Several factors—social, economic, psychological, and political—are involved in the control and resolution of physical conflict in the local community.

First, there is the economic interdependence of its residents. Since the community is often an important subsistence unit, requiring the cooperation of its members for their joint survival, they are highly motivated to get on and restrain their aggressive impulses toward one another. An hypothesis involved here is that the frequency of internecine violence will vary inversely with the need for economic cooperation.

Second, there is the acceptance by community residents of an internal system for the making of community decisions regarding economic, judicial, military, and religious affairs. Among the decisions arrived at by this socially accepted process are those involving the application of sanctions to individuals who break the peace of the group. Sanctions include: the inflicting of injury, banishment, permitted retaliation, payment of compensation, ridicule, expression of disapproval, and supernatural cursing. The agencies which may legitimately apply sanctions may be formal, e.g., a council, hereditary headman, or magico-religious practitioner, or they may be informal, e.g., an assembly of elders or adult males or even the unassembled community in its entirety. The degree to which the power to sanction is concentrated in the hands of a few wealthy, wise, or aged individuals or diffused among the mass of residents of the community is also variable from one society to another. Regardless of its particular structure, this system of sanctions tends to maintain order in the group by stimulating in group members anticipation of painful or anxiety-arousing consequences for serious aggressive acts.

Third, there is often a related set of supernatural sanctions against violent conflict within the community. Particularly when the community is coterminous with a localized descent group, there is likely to be a belief in ancestor spirits or ghosts who automatically punish murderers through disease regardless of whether community agencies take any action. Under such circumstances, the use of classificatory kinship categories equates murder of a member of the local descent group with fratricide or parricide, which is believed to deserve supernatural intervention. The belief in supernatural punishment for intracommunity homicide, insofar as it relieves human agents of the task of applying sanctions, helps to avoid the perpetuation of conflict that may occur when community residents pronounce the verdict and perform the punishment themselves. In many societies supernatural belief systems play an important role in the maintenance of community order.

Fourth, there is the individual inhibition of aggression and the conformity to cultural rules which result from the socialization of the child. This is what Radcliffe-Brown referred to in his preface to *African Political Systems* (1940:15-16) when he stated, "Within small communities there may be little or no need for penal sanctions. Good behavior may be to a great extent the result of habit, of the conditioning of the individual by his early upbringing."

Fifth, there is emigration from the local community as an alternative to violent conflict within it. In nomadic societies and agricultural groups with abundant land, local communities often shed their dissident members, who simply join another community of the same society. This solution is usually satisfactory to all concerned while it is possible, but should a land shortage develop and emigration become impossible, the community might not have adequately developed internal mechanisms for conflict resolution, with a resultant rise in internecine violence. Such a process is under way in many societies with rapidly increasing population densities.

These, then, are the factors which act to prevent disruptive violence within the local communities of stateless societies: economic interdependence, a legitimate decision system capable of applying sanctions, supernatural sanctions, effective socialization, and the emigration of dissidents. Not all of the factors are found in all societies and they are combined and relied upon in varying degrees in different parts of the world, but some of them will be found to be operating in any particular situation.

The maintenance of intercommunity order in stateless societies, involving as it does the interaction of politically integrated units, presents a different set of problems from the maintenance of internal order in local communities. On the intercommunity level there is a much greater crosscultural range of variation in the amount of order actually achieved. At one end of the continuum there are contiguous local communities which have a common military-judicial decision system under a single chief or council where the probability of organized intercommunity violence is virtually nil. They constitute what Deutsch (1954) calls *a politically amalgamated security community*. At the other end of the continuum are local communities which engage in sporadic violence and prolonged feuds against one another and which exist in a condition of mutual hostility and tension. Under such conditions the most unity ever achieved is in the form of temporary military alliances to fight clusters of villages in another area. In between these two types there are many intermediate forms of interaction with varying probabilities of intercommunity violence.

In outlining some patterns of conflict control among local communities, I shall give primary attention to the factors which community decision-makers must take into consideration when tempted to involve their group in military activity against other local communities. The control patterns and decision factors are as follows:

1. *Mutual military deterrence.* This has been stressed by Fortes and Evans-Pritchard (1940), who see certain African stateless systems as being in a state

of equilibrium which serves to maintain a modicum of order ("ordered anarchy") in the absence of a central government. Equilibrium is achieved by a balance of power between territorial segments of the same order and by temporary military alliances between such segments for battles against segments of the next highest order. These alliances have been referred to as "fusion" but it must be understood that the fusion is military and does not involve political amalgamation of the temporarily allied segments. In this "balanced opposition of segments" military retaliation is a primary mechanism for the control of overt conflict. Although the effectiveness of this mechanism may have been exaggerated, there can be no doubt that mutual military deterrence does operate between local groups in stateless societies, particularly in the absence of strong integrating mechanisms. Where communities are roughly equivalent in size and power, decision-makers have to consider the possibility that their attack will bring on counterattacks by forces of equal or slightly superior strength and create a situation of prolonged and indecisive tension between the communities.

2. *The inclusion of other communities in the primary descent group.* Where local communities are coterminous with localized descent groups, particularly patrilineages, it is often the case that the male members of contiguous communities recognize a common ancestor and apply classificatory kinship terms to one another. This involves an extension of integrating mechanisms within the community to other communities, but in diluted form. Since persons in other communities are close lineage-mates, killing of one of them is equivalent to fratricide or parricide and is punishable by the ancestor spirits if reparations are not paid. Judicial agencies internal to each community may function jointly on occasion to enforce the payment of compensation. The greater the distance between the communities, the less likely this is to occur. Organized but attenuated violence may occur among communities whose members are so linked, e.g., the participants may recognize a rule of using clubs rather than spears. In the African societies which have this type of system, a number of communities may be linked by this extension of localized lineage regulations. Beyond the perimeter of the cluster of communities recognizing such bonds are other such clusters connected with the first in a similar but even more tenuous fashion. Genealogical connections among the clusters may be traced, but kinship terms are not used and supernatural sanctions not operative. Conflict with spears between clusters is quite possible and occurs fairly frequently. Within this territorial unit, however, it is recognized that violent conflict may be terminated by the payment of compensation for homicide. In actuality, compensations may be rarely paid, but it is recognized as the proper procedure for handling homicide and conflict between the clusters. Middleton and Tait (1958:9) call this maximal unit within which compen-

sation can be paid the *jural community,* and refer to the armed hostilities which are carried on within it as the *feud* as distinguished from *warfare,* which cannot be terminated by compensation and is carried on *between* jural communities. The jural community is not always a territorial unit, but it tends to be in those societies which have the feud. In such societies it may be a territorial unit encompassing as many as 65,000 residents. Beyond its boundaries no permanent integrative ties exist.

Where a system like the one described above exists, community decision-makers, before committing themselves to military action in response to provocation by another community, must consider (a) the lineage relationship between the two groups, (b) supernatural sanctions which might result from the action, and (c) the spatial distance between the two groups. Such considerations most often act to mitigate hostilities between local groups which are closer in either space or descent, or both, and to perpetuate open conflict with groups which are more distant. In this situation, integration and the maintenance of order on the intercommunity level tends to be a reflection or extension of the internal system of the community itself, and its effectiveness falls off sharply as distance from the community increases.

3. *Loyalties to descent and other groups outside the local community.* In contrast to the balance of power position, Colson (1953:210) suggested that divided loyalties of individuals between territorial and kinship groups might be a factor in the maintenance of order in segmentary lineage societies; Gluckman (1955:10-20) has elaborated this point and analyzed Nuer social control in terms of it. The latter emphasizes the pacifying effects of dispersal of the patrilineal kin group.

> Now if the vengeance group is scattered it may mean, especially in the smaller districts, that the demand for community solidarity requires that a man mobilize with the enemies of his agnates. And in the opposite situation such an emigrant member of the group which has killed may be living among the avengers, and be liable to have vengeance executed upon him. I suggest . . . that his exposure to killing exerts some pressure on his kin to compromise the affair. . . . Conversely, if a man of the group demanding vengeance resides among the killers, he has an interest in securing that his kin accept compensation instead of insisting on blood for blood (1955:11-12).

It should be noted that both Fortes and Evans-Pritchard recognized the potentially pacifying ties of kin group dispersal and cognatic relationships occasioned by exogamy, but considered them less important than segmental opposition for the maintenance of order. Regardless of which view has greater empirical validity, the Colson-Gluckman concept of divided loyalties must take its place beside the Fortes-Evans-Pritchard balance of power notion as a theoretical position on the resolution of conflict in "ordered anarchies."

Thus, intermarriage between local communities and the dispersal of kin groups among them may, under certain circumstances, establish enduring connections which tend to prevent conflict between them. In general, such cross-cutting ties seem to be more effectively pacifying in situations where men have shifted their residence (in uxorilocal or neolocal marriage, non-marital emigration) away from the localities in which their kin groups predominate, than they are when women are uprooted by virilocal marriage.

Murphy has formulated this in general terms:

> I would propose as a statistically testable hypothesis that matrilocal societies must repress open aggression in order to insure cohesion and continuity. If we take any matrilocal and matrilineal or bilateral society as our model, the system of residence tends to disperse males at least throughout the local community. Thus, any male will have close ties of kinship and economic interdependence with his housemates, his natal household, the households of his maternal uncles, and the households of his brothers. The same is true of patrilocal societies from the viewpoint of the women, but males are the principal political role-players in all human societies. Any conflict involving men therefore becomes a matter of deep community concern. . . . In short, when the residence and kin groups of the male do not coincide, he acquires multiple commitments that may come into conflict [1957:1033].

Murphy reports that among the Mundurucú of Brazil, men are members of patrilineal descent groups but marriage is matrilocal so that they leave their home communities and take up residence in those of their wives. Under these conditions, the married warriors of any village are faced with the fact that an attack on another village would bring them into armed conflict with men of the same patrilineal affiliation. These extracommunity ties are so dispersed that the Mundurucú are able to maintain what Deutsch (1954:41) would call a "pluralistic security community" in which stable expectations of interunit peace are maintained in the absence of political amalgamation. In contrast, other Brazilian tribes practicing *patrilocal* descent are reported by Murphy to have considerable internecine violence.

Other examples of cross-cutting ties in stateless societies resulting from the scattering of kin group members are given by Goody (1957) for the LoDagaba, Morgan (1901) for the Iroquois, Warner (1937) for the Murngin, and Colson (1953) for the Plateau Tonga, to mention but a few. Evans-Pritchard (Peristiany, pp. 27-28) has pointed out the pacifying effects of regiments, clans, and age sets which cross-cut localities and each other among the Kipsigis. The unifying consequences of cross pressures and multiple group affiliations have been recognized by numerous sociologists and political scientists in their analyses of complex societies (Lipset 1959; Simmel 1956).

These three patterns of intercommunity control of violence are merely a sampling from among the many which exist in stateless societies. Extracommunity loyalties of males may be based on age-group organizations and military regiments as well as on descent groups and may form pacifying networks of cross-cutting ties. Ritual connections and trade relations between local communities or clusters of communities may also serve to reduce the probability of internecine violence in the total social structure. In this issue, Kopytoff describes an unusual pattern of intercommunity conflict resolution which is new in the ethnographic literature on the subject, and we can expect other patterns, as yet unknown to anthropology, to turn up as empirical investigations in this area progress.

More comparative analysis is necessary before we understand the relative effectiveness of various mechanisms for controlling intercommunity conflict in the absence of political amalgamation. It may prove valuable to think in terms of "security communities" and to bear in mind the parallel between international relations and the interaction of politically integrated units at any level. Hoebel (1954:331) recognized this parallel in stating, "International law, so-called, is but primitive law on the world level." Keesing and Keesing (1956:18) have used the concept of "security community," developed by Deutsch (1954) for the study of international relations, in their analysis of the unstable central political organization of Samoa. Applications of such concepts to stateless societies may also be useful in future comparative analysis.

References

Beals, A. R. 1961. "Cleavage and Internal Conflict: An Example from India," *Journal of Conflict Resolution* 5:27-34.

Bohannan, P. J. 1960. *African Homicide and Suicide.* Princeton, N.J.: Princeton University Press.

Campbell, D. T., and LeVine, R. A. 1961. "A Proposal for Cooperative Cross-Cultural Research on Ethnocentrism," *Journal of Conflict Resolution* 5:82-108.

Colson, E. 1953. "Social Control and Vengeance in Plateau Tonga Society," *Africa* 23:199-211.

Deutsch, K. W. 1954. *Political Community at the International Level.* Garden City, New York: Doubleday and Company.

Evans-Pritchard, E. E. 1940. *The Neur.* London: Oxford University Press.

Fortes, M., and Evans-Pritchard, E. E. 1940. *African Political Systems.* London: Oxford University Press.

Gluckman, M. 1955. *Custom and Conflict in Africa.* Glencoe, Ill.: The Free Press.

Goody, J. 1957. "Fields of Social Control among the LoDagaba," *Journal of the Royal Anthropological Institute* 87:75-104.

Gulliver, P. H. 1961. "Land Shortage, Social Change, and Social Conflict in East Africa," *Journal of Conflict Resolution* 5:16-26.

Hoebel, E. A. 1954. *The Law of Primitive Man.* Cambridge, Mass.: Harvard University Press.

Leach, E. R. 1954. *Political Systems of Highland Burma,* London: G. Bell.

LeVine, R. A. 1960a. "The Internalization of Political Values in Stateless Societies," *Human Organization* 19:51-58.

————. 1960b. "Witchcraft and Marital Relations in East Africa: A Controlled Comparison." (Paper presented at American Anthropological Association meeting.)

Lipset, S. M. 1959. "Some Social Requisites of Democracy: Economic Development and Political Legitimacy," *American Political Science Review* 53:69-105.

Middleton, J., and Tait, D. (eds.). 1958. *Tribes Without Rulers: Studies of African Segmentary Systems.* London: Routledge and Kegan Paul.

Morgan, L. H. 1901. *League of the Ho-De-No-Sau-Nee or Iroquois, I.* New York: Dodd, Mead and Co.

Murdock, G. P. 1949. *Social Structure.* New York: Macmillan.

Murphy, R. F. 1957. "Intergroup Hostility and Social Cohesion," *American Anthropologist* 59:1018-35.

Naroll, R. 1959. "A Tentative Index of Culture Stress," *International Journal of Social Psychiatry* 5.

Peristiany, J. G. 1939. *The Social Institutions of the Kipsigis.* London: Routledge and Sons.

Schapera, I. 1956. *Government and Politics in Tribal Societies.* London: C. A. Watts and Co.

Siegel, J., and Beals, A. R. 1960a. "Conflict and Factionalist Dispute," *Journal of the Royal Anthropological Institute* 90:107-117.

————. 1970b. "Pervasive Factionalism," *American Anthropologist* 62:394-417.

Simmel, G. 1956. *Conflict and the Web of Group Affiliations.* Glencoe, Ill.: The Free Press.

Skinner, E. P. 1961. "Intergenerational Conflict Among the Mossi: Father and Son," *Journal of Conflict Resolution* 5:55-60.

Turner, V. W. 1957. *Schism and Continuity in an African Society: A Study of Ndembu Village Life.* Manchester, England: Manchester University Press.

Warner, W. L. 1937. *A Black Civilization.* New York: Harper & Bros.

Whiting, B. B. 1950. *Paiute Sorcery.* Viking Fund Publications in Anthropology, No. 15, New York.

8
Peaceful Societies

David Fabbro

Introduction

The majority of work in peace research has been directed toward gaining an understanding of the sources and dynamics of direct and structural violence. Elaboration of the social preconditions of peace has all too often been neglected, viewed as an abstraction and/or utopia, or been of a purely theoretical nature. This paper is an attempt to arrest this underdevelopment by directing attention toward a number of concrete examples of peaceful societies.

Criteria of Peace

There are a number of levels or intensities of peace which members of a society may experience. In ascending order of comprehensiveness these would include:

1. The society has no wars fought on its territory;
2. The society is not involved in any external wars;
3. There are no civil wars or internal collective violence;
4. There is no standing military-police organisation;
5. There is little or no interpersonal physical violence;
6. There is little or no structural violence;
7. The society has the capacity to undergo change peacefully; and
8. There is opportunity for idiosyncratic development.

An example of a study using criterion 1 is provided by Melko (1973); this work is interesting as it is one of the few attempts to study peace, but it is disappointing because of its reliance on a behavioural definition of peace.

Reprinted by permission of the publisher from David Fabbro, "Peaceful Societies: An Introduction," *Journal of Peace Research* 15 (1978):67-83.

Because no consideration is given as to the justice of such peace it becomes a study of stable empires and states rather than an analysis of social structures and organisations which minimise both direct and structural violence. The seven societies considered in this paper fulfil criteria 1 to 5. The societies selected represent the first seven to meet these criteria from a collection of possible societies drawn from various works which make reference to societies lacking in warfare or other forms of violence (Benedict 1935; Davie 1929; Fromm 1974; Mead 1961; Otterbein 1970; Sipes 1973).

In terms of their social structure many of these societies correspond to the first level of development in Fried's (1967) schema of political evolution: egalitarian band society. That is, they generally lack formal patterns of ranking and stratification, place no restriction on the number of people capable of exercising power or occupying positions of prestige, and have economies where exchange is based on generalised reciprocity (Fried 1967:28-35). As such it can be argued that these societies do not experience certain types of structural violence.

The similarities between the societies examined cannot simply be attributed to the occupation of a common ecological niche (Service 1966:3). Neither can their similarity be solely attributed to a common mode of production — hunting and gathering — as at least two of the sample have an agricultural base.

External Factors

Before considering the internal characteristics of these societies it is necessary to consider possible external influences upon them. For example, Sipes (1973) rejected several societies from one of his samples because their peacefulness appeared to be based on the presence of stronger and more aggressive neighbours. Although all these societies are bounded by more complex and powerful neighbours it would be misleading to assume that this is the sole reason for their peacefulness. In relation to external war it should be noted that all but one of these societies lack some of the major structural prerequisites for engaging in it: a coercive hierarchy and leadership, and a surplus to support a nonproductive military organisation. Admittedly warfare is only one form of externally directed physical violence and less organised forms such as feuding and raiding are possible at this level of social organisation (Fried 1967:99-101). Indeed the Siriono, for example, at one time engaged in acts of violence against white colonisers. But external stimuli capable of eliciting violent responses from a society raise issues of a different, although related, order than those to which this preliminary paper is directed.

Internal Factors

A number of questions have been developed in order to demonstrate various aspects of these societies, and, where sources allow, to extract the same type of information for each society.

General

1. In what type of natural habitat does the society reside?
2. How is subsistence gained?
3. What is the prevailing ideology-cosmology–world view of the society? What are the core or paramount norms which act as the basis of regulation in social intercourse?
4. On what basis is the society integrated?

Direct Violence

5. What are the major characteristics of the child socialisation process?
6. Does physical violence exist? If so, what forms does it take?
7. What conflict resolution processes exist? Are they institutionalised or informal?

Structural Violence

8. Is there any division of labour and if so does it lead to specialisation?
9. Are there any forms of socially coercive organisations which are capable of gaining compliance on the basis of power?
10. Are there any forms of hierarchy? If so are they exclusive or restrictive?
11. Who participates in decisionmaking concerning the society as a whole? Is such participation direct or mediated?
12. Who exercises social control?
13. What forms does social control take?
14. Are there any forms of discrimination which militate against an equal distribution of self-respect between individuals?

The Societies

The Semai of Malaya

(1) The Semai Senoi live in western Malaya and are subdivided into eastern and western groups. Their habitat is a mixture of lowland tropical rain forest and mountain ridges. (2) The Semai gain their subsistence by hunting, trapping, fishing, and some swidden — slash and burn — agriculture. Some gathering of wild food consisting mainly of fruit is also

carried out. They also have domesticated animals such as hens, ducks, and goats.

(3) The religious system of the Semai is complex but does not give rise to any religious leaders or elite. Central to social organisation and the regulation of interpersonal relations is the concept of *punan*. Implicit in *punan* is the idea that making someone unhappy, especially by frustrating desires, increases the probability of that person suffering physical injury. The notion of *punan* pervades their whole lifestyle and influences matters such as child rearing and sexual relations.

(4) The band is the largest form of social organisation; each one being composed of a number of nuclear families. In the west the predominant settlement pattern is a cluster of small houses which together form a homestead. The houses of the western Semai generally have between five and twenty-four inhabitants while the eastern Semai live communally in long houses which may have as many as fifty residents.

(5) Semai children enjoy a considerable amount of freedom in their behaviour. If a child does not wish to engage in some activity parents do not force it to do so; such action would be *punan*. Generally children learn through voluntary imitative play. When children misbehave, adults invoke the threat of evil spirits or the occurrence of certain evil happenings to gain compliance with their wishes. Where physical punishment is used it consists of a pinch on the cheek or a tap on the hand. All child rearing practices are geared toward the personal internalisation of norms of conduct. This is especially so with children who display aggressive behaviour. In such cases the Semai deliberately do not punish such behaviour physically and so personal experience of violence is very limited. Moreover it is very difficult for children to rebel against their parents because adults do not object if a child does not wish to do something.

(6) Physical violence is more or less unknown in Semai society. Apparently between 1956 and 1967 a number of cases of murder and attempted murder occurred but this appears to have arisen because of the political turbulence in Malaya in general at this time. Also the Semai apparently abandoned the very old or sick during times of scarcity but this was done reluctantly. According to Dentan (1968:59) violence appears to terrify the Semai who meet force with passivity or flight.

(7) Conflict resolution processes do exist in Semai society but they are not particularly formalised. In a dispute one party usually suffers (that is, is taken to suffer) *punan*. The victim has two courses of action available. The *punan* may be endured or the offender may be asked for compensation. Generally the offender pays it. In a dispute where both parties feel in the right they may appeal to a respected elder; but, should one of the parties

think the judgement unjust it can be ignored. Disputants who become angry manifest such feelings by avoiding the other party. Generally, most quarrels are conceived of by the participants as being a personal matter.

(8) There is some division of labour in Semai society but mainly in relation to hunting which is a male activity. Men, women, and children help to clear the forest for agriculture. Men and women too old to hunt supplement the diet by fishing. Domestic activities such as basket weaving or carrying water are performed by women. Both men and women plant crops but only women harvest the rice. Both sexes cook and winnow grain. There does not appear to be any specialisation of labour in Semai society; even the headman must gain his own subsistence.

(9 and 10) There is no specifically political organisation within Semai bands. All elders are accorded respect on two grounds. Firstly, they have the largest amount of experience and as such are valuable sources of information. Secondly, most young people and young married couples move frequently between homesteads. Thus it is the elders who provide continuity and stability within each homestead. The foremost male elder is regarded as the headman of the group. As with all other elders, however, young people may ignore his advice. The headman keeps the peace — when disputes cannot be solved by the parties directly involved — by conciliation rather than coercion. If the headman is to function efficiently he must be respected; one who is not respected will find people turning to another elder for advice. People only recognise the headman's authority in specific situations: in the mediation of a dispute, as a group representative in external matters, and in the west, in deciding upon the selection and apportionment of land. The position of headman appears to be held by males only.

(11 and 12) Theoretically all adults participate in decisionmaking and social control. Women are not formally prevented from being influential within the group but in general they apparently feel embarrassed about participating in discussions about matters of general concern. In practice a few women are influential in discussions but the majority appear to abstain. Both social control and decisionmaking are implemented through the medium of public opinion. Usually it is the older men who have the greatest influence on public opinion but paradoxically such elders are often regarded with suspicion by the rest of the group and so their authority is probably less than would appear at first sight. Another person who has a major influence on public opinion is the one who enjoys popularity. Such popularity accrues to an individual who shares what can be afforded without appearing to calculate the cost of such generosity. (13) The main sanction is embarrassment; when public opinion goes against an individual that individual is "embarrassed" (Dentan 1968:69). Sanctions other than public opinion do not appear to exist. Strong internalised norms of

behaviour combined with the influence of public opinion appear to make deviance very uncommon.

(14) Self-respect appears to be fairly evenly distributed among the Semai. Children have great freedom of action and can if they wish ignore adult instructions. Men and women seem to enjoy equal sexual license with divorce and separation as frequent occurrences. It should be noted, however, that there appear to be informal barriers which prevent women from fully participating in group decisionmaking and neither do women hold the position of headman.

The Siriono of Eastern Bolivia

(1) The Siriono live in the tropical rain forest centred on eastern Bolivia. (2) They are seminomadic aborigines who practice some swidden agriculture but are primarily hunter-gatherers. (3) The kinship system is based on the matrilineal extended family. A band—the highest level of social integration—is composed of a number of nuclear families who all occupy a communal hut. Each family has an area in the hut where the parents' hammocks are hung. (4) Sorcery is more or less unknown to the Siriono. Reciprocity does exist between families but it is generally forced; and, there is a general reluctance to share food which has not been produced cooperatively.

(5) It is usually females who look after children although both parents spend a lot of time playing with their children. Holmberg characterises child rearing practices as: "informal, random and haphazard" (1966:203). Reward and punishment techniques are used but there is little or no physical punishment. Apparently Siriono mothers almost always cry after they have been angry with their children. Both sexes are taught early to contribute to the family economy. From about eight years of age boys accompany their fathers when hunting, while girls help with household tasks. (6) Physical violence does occur among the Siriono but fighting with weapons and clubs is rare. Males seldom express direct aggression against other males. Neither do males beat their wives but there are apparently quarrels among women, frequently culminating in fighting with digging sticks. At one stage the Siriono engaged in violence against white colonisers although it did not continue for long and did not become an institutionalised feature of Siriono society. (7) Various conflict resolution processes exist but usually disputes are settled by those who start them. An exception to this general rule arises at drinking feasts—a regular feature of social life—when quarrels are settled by wrestling matches. Any other type of fighting is frowned upon and is usually stopped by nonparticipant men and women. There are no formal agencies of social control and the chief does not interfere in disputes. The final form of conflict resolution is fission. In

this instance one of the parties to the conflict will leave the band temporarily or permanently and join another group or alternatively a number of families may leave a band and establish a new one.

(8) The Siriono do practice division of labour to a small extent. Hunting is a male occupation whereas food gathering and horticulture are joint pursuits. There is no occupational specialisation, and there are no nonproductive sectors in the society. Even the chief must provide for himself. (9 and 10) Leadership which exists among the Siriono is based solely on the personal qualities of the incumbent. It appears, however, to be held by males only. (11) Participation in decisionmaking does not appear to arise because there are very few collective enterprises requiring decisions. Husband and wife or wives appear, in the given situation, equal in prestige even if this is only indicated by the fact that women start quarrels as frequently as do men. (12) Social control appears to be based on individual action toward the offender; calling for satisfaction by reference to group norms rather than group action against the offender. "Justice is an informal and private matter. . . . Generally speaking it would seem that the maintenance of law and order rests largely on the principle of reciprocity (however forced), the fear of the supernatural, sanctions and retaliation, and the desire for public approval" (Holmberg 1966:153).

(13) Norms of behaviour appear to be flexible as evidenced by the lack of recognition in the culture of sexual offences or theft. (14) Self-respect appears to be fairly evenly distributed. Individuals may ignore the advice of a chief if they wish. Sexism does exist as shown by the informal exclusion of women from the leadership position. Females do, however, have sexual license and hold their own drinking feasts and dances. Holmberg does not offer any evidence that women are subservient to their husbands or men in general.

The Mbuti Pygmies of the Ituri Forest

(1) The pygmies live in the equatorial forest belt of central Africa. (2) The Mbuti are hunter-gatherers with the emphasis on hunting. Some bands use nets for trapping game while others rely on individual hunting with bows and arrows. (3) Their myth system is in one sense very pragmatic. According to Barrington Moore, "they have made for themselves no oppressive taboos and have about as light hearted an attitude toward their own social regulation as it is possible to have and still maintain the degree of social cohesion necessary for their particular form of society" (1972:18). They have a great feeling of identification with the forest. It is viewed as the benevolent provider of life, all good things, and the protector from the malevolence of nonforest peoples. Rituals associated with birth, puberty, sickness, and death all symbolically express the identification be-

tween forest and pygmy which is also expressed in interpersonal relations through cooperation and mutual aid.

(4) Mbuti bands are composed of several nuclear families. Their kinship system is relatively undeveloped. The extended family is the largest blood-tie group, but the Mbuti use kinship terms to relate to both blood relatives and friends. (5) Babies are breast-fed for between eighteen months and three years. Once a child has been weaned he or she may demand and expect to be disciplined by any adult. From an early age children are encouraged to imitate adult activities. By the age of six both girls and boys contribute to the general economy by helping with camp chores. From nine years of age onwards children participate in hunting in bands which use nets. At this age the form of punishment changes; ridicule replacing physical punishment. "The whole process of child training is characterised by informality and by emphasis on the child's responsibilities to the band as a whole" (Turnbull 1965:306).

(6) Mbuti bands do not appear to experience much interpersonal violence. Fighting does take place between husbands and wives. The violence which does occur has a peculiar property which mitigates lethality.

> The human body is in a sense, *boru*. . . . It is a term seldom used, but the concept affords a firm basis for a code of respect for the body, abuse or mutilation of which may drive away the *pepo* causing death. Thus physical violence as a means of settling a dispute is abhorred as sacrilege. A sound thrashing is perfectly in order, but any violence that produces blood causes an opening through which *pepo* may escape. (Turnbull 1966:250)

(7) Various conflict resolution processes exist. The most common form is third-party intervention. Young married couples, older married couples, or elders may intervene depending on the nature of the dispute. If any one of these mediators fails then the band as a whole may take part in mediation. Individuals may also mediate in a dispute. One major form of this is intervention by the "clown." The clown is often unmarried but entitled to respect because of prowess in a skill and also because he possesses a certain amount of impartiality. Generally he mediates through the voice of ridicule or he may be singled out by the parties to the dispute as the source of their difference which he accepts without letting it get him down. Should reconciliation at the band level fail it may split into two sections or a family may join another band.

(8) Some division of labour exists in Mbuti society but it is not well defined and does not lead to specialisation. Men, women, and children all participate in the hunt in bands using nets. In archer bands, men hunt without the aid of women and children. All individuals help with the gathering of vegetable foods. There are no unproductive people in Mbuti

bands. (9) Political organisation is not differentiated from general social life. The only distinction which the Mbuti make is in respect to their dealings with the Negro cultivators who live in villages on the edges of the forest. (10 and 11) It is only in relation to the village that leadership exists. One particular individual who is a past master at trickery but who is willing to appear subservient to the villagers acts as leader in the exchange relationship. In the village the other pygmies refer to him as the leader but on returning to the forest his leadership ceases. Life in the forest does not produce leadership although older people and those who are considered foremost — by virtue of their prowess — in a particular activity have influence in the band in general. Almost every adult has the right to express himself in almost any activity. It is interesting to note that even in the Negro villages during a crisis all members of the band present participate in decisionmaking even where villagers have poisoned a pygmy to bring about the desired results of sorcery. In this situation the leader does not make the decision to return to the forest, neither does the victim or the immediate family; the whole band does. The reaction of the pygmies to this threat provides an insight into their general outlook: "The pygmy attitude is ambivalent: they do not believe in supernatural powers of this order . . . their reaction is not one of fear, even when their fellows die, nor is it coloured by the desire for revenge, nor even of anger or hatred" (Turnbull 1965:304).

(12) All members of a band ultimately exercise social control through the medium of public opinion. (13) The major form of sanction related to norm breaking is ridicule and the appeal to the need for mutual cooperation. (14) It would seem that self-respect is fairly evenly distributed between members of Mbuti bands. Women have an equal voice with men in all major decisions. The early encouragement of children to contribute to the general economy probably militates against the effect of feeling inadequate in an adult world. There is, however, one major drawback: marriages are arranged by parents. To offset this constraint the Mbuti practice divorce which does not appear to cause much dislocation in the lives of the individual or of the band.

The Kung Bushmen of the Kalahari Desert

(1) The Kung live in the Kalahari desert of southern Africa. The desert has a mean average height of 3,000 feet above sea level. It is covered in wind-blown sand to a depth of three to four hundred feet. There are some water holes and a variety of drought-resistant plants, plus numbers of small and large game. (2) The Kung are hunter-gatherers. They have few material artifacts, the main ones being bows and arrows and digging sticks. (3) The kinship system is of a patrilineal extended family type. When the old father dies, however, that particular extended family ceases to exist;

dependents who are left are usually supported by close blood relatives. A band is composed of a number of nuclear families who usually have some blood tie.

(4) The Kung myth system is comparatively well developed. There are two gods, a greater and a lesser one. Neither god is inherently good or evil. The greater god created the world, animals, plants, women, and then men. The Kung pray spontaneously and, in part, it reflects the major preoccupations of life: hunger, sickness, and death. The great god, however, gave healing powers to medicine men who exist solely to cure people and do not engage in witchcraft or sorcery. Social norms that are emphasised are the institutionalised patterns of sharing and their determined striving for cooperation and harmony.

(5) Kung parents are protective, gentle, and permissive in their child training. Parents do not make demands on children to help with work, Marshall maintains, because there are few household tasks to perform because of their low level of technology (1965:264). Lee, on the other hand, maintains that few demands are made on children to contribute to the general economy because a modest work effort by adults produces enough food to support all the members of a band (1968a:39). Children are always kept within sight of adults because of the dangers arising from predators and becoming lost in a featureless landscape. Children are, however, encouraged to imitate adult activities. Marshall sums up child development: "They usually fall in with group life and do what is expected of them *without* uncertainty, frustration, or fear; and expression of resistance or hostility toward their parents, the group, or each other are very much the exception" (1965:264).

(6) Physical violence appears to be rare in Kung society. According to Thomas, the Bushmen deplore bravery and in their legends the heroes are the animals which survive through trickery and deception rather than force (1969:32). The Kung do practice infanticide occasionally and it generally occurs when a woman is already nursing one child. (7) Conflict or wrongdoing is usually judged and controlled through public opinion which is usually expressed through conversation. Occasionally an individual may try to obtain revenge personally and this method is ostracised by them. The headman is not a formalised judge of the people in a band. Neither can he punish a wrongdoer.

(8) Division of labour exists mainly along age and sex lines and does not, with the exception of medicine men, give rise to specialisation. The major division occurs over hunting, which is a male activity. Although women gather four-fifths of the food requirement it is the men who are accorded esteem for the production of the remaining fifth in the form of meat. This situation has arisen, according to Lee, because hunting is a less predictable

activity than gathering (1968a:40).

(9) There does not appear to be any dividing line between political, social, or religious life. (10) Leadership does exist in Kung bands. Usually it is an inherited position which passes from father to son. But in certain circumstances people may turn away from a headman because another may be more suited. The areas of leadership are, however, circumscribed. The headman personifies the rights of a band over a given geographical area but does not own the land in a private individual capacity. Every family has an inalienable right to the resources on the land. (11) The headman's authority extends only to the coordination of the band's movements in relation to the use of resources. Apart from the decision to move the camp it is individuals who decide on various questions. There is strong informal pressure on men to go and hunt, but it is the individual who decides with whom and where to hunt. Within hunting groups there is no leadership. (12) All the adult members of a band exercise social control, which is usually done through the medium of public opinion. (13) Norms appear to be fairly rigid in Kung society. The very ethos of mutual dependency appears to forestall much norm breaking. (14) Self-respect seems to be fairly evenly distributed. Divorce is a characteristic feature of marital life although adultery is severely condemned. Sexism does exist in several forms: whereas a man may have more than one wife, women only take one husband at a time. Neither do females appear to hold leadership positions or receive acknowledgement commensurate to the amount of food which they provide.

The Copper Eskimo of Northern Canada

(1) The area which the Copper Eskimo inhabit is part of the arctic tundra. The subsoil is permanently frozen, being covered with snow during the winter months. Temperatures range from $-47°$ F to $+70°$ F in August. (2) Seals and caribou were the most abundant game animals which provided not only meat but also skins for clothing and equipment. Migratory game birds, musk oxen, squirrels, foxes, some brown bears, and salmon, lake trout, and tom cod also supplemented the diet.

(3) The Copper Eskimo conceive of the world as a flat, unbroken expanse of land and sea. Above this real world, supported at its four corners by wooden pillars is another flat level abounding in animals. Above this is another level for the sun, moon, and stars, which are semispiritual beings — the sun being a woman, the moon a man, and the stars either animal or human spirits before they ascended into the sky (Jeness 1922:179). The world of human existence is partly composed of spirits which may be benign or malevolent. All people have a soul — *nappan* — which is conceived of as the vital life force. The Copper Eskimo practice propitiation of these spirits by offering food and drink. Many phenomena and unusual events

are attributed to the intervention of spirits. Such an outlook means the Copper Eskimo is "a true Epicurean, holding that life is a short and uncertain thing at the best, and that the wise man will grasp at what pleasures he can in his course without stopping to ponder over those things that do not directly affect his immediate welfare" (Jeness 1922:229). Relationships between individuals are based on the idea that in theory all the members of a group — a composition of a number of nuclear families — are free and equal. The Copper Eskimo are intolerant of restraint upon individual behaviour. Such values mean that their society is a tolerant one. Only individual acts which have a direct effect upon the community as a whole are evaluated in terms of being morally good or bad. The foremost virtues of Copper Eskimo society are: peacefulness, good name, courage, energy, patience and endurance, charity toward both the young and the old, and loyal cooperation. Fair dealing and truthfulness are of secondary importance only while sexual relations are hardly considered as coming within the scope of group consideration. (4) Bands are composed of a number of nuclear families which usually have some blood ties. The composition of a band changes over time.

(5) Children are suckled for three to four years and sometimes for as long as five. Rarely is the child away from its parents during this stage and the mother usually carries it with her wherever she goes. Copper Eskimo children display a certain amount of deference to adults but such behaviour does not imply passivity. Children usually address adults as their equals and will join in any conversation that is taking place and do not hesitate to interrupt and correct their parents (Jeness 1922:169). In general parents do not use corporal punishment in child rearing although "a child may receive a thump with a fist or a blow from the snow duster in the passion of the moment when it will often try to retaliate" (Jeness 1922:169). Usually, however, the shame of public disapproval is sufficient to control a child's behaviour. From the age when children start to move about on their own until puberty they are left without adult interference to a great extent.

(6) Various forms of physical violence have been documented among the Copper Eskimo. They practice infanticide for material and social reasons — both the parents of a newborn child must wish to bring it up, otherwise the child is abandoned. Some physical punishment is used in child rearing but it is not consistently used as part of an established practice. Homicide does occur and Rasmussen (1932:17) intimates that it is quite frequent, a point reinforced by Palmer (1965:322). Physical violence also occurs among marriage partners although men appear to use it more frequently. Much of the violence appears to be spontaneous rather than premeditated. (7) Conflict resolution processes in Copper Eskimo bands are generally informal and take place at the interpersonal level. Only in

rare instances will the band as a whole engage in joint action against an individual, leading to that person's exclusion from the group. The only remedy for minor offences such as theft or the abduction of a wife is for the individual to extract personally compensation or vengeance. It is fairly common for murderers to go unpunished but where they are punished it is always a close relative of the deceased who is responsible for retribution. This situation does not, however, lead to a hereditary vendetta system.

(8) Division of labour occurs mainly along age and sex lines. Heavier work and hunting tend to devolve on males while women are responsible for all the domestic tasks. Some younger women do, however, hunt. In the caribou drives all the band participates either in the killing or the beating. Specialisation appears to extend only to shamanism and even here individual shamans have to provide the bulk of their own material needs. (9 and 10) There appear to be no socially coercive organisations basing their compliance on power in Copper Eskimo bands. Similarly there is no hierarchy. Certain individuals may have influence but it is restricted in application and declines with old age. (11) All adults appear to participate directly in general group discussions; women apparently being as vociferous as men in the dance house and on caribou drives. (12 and 13) Only in extreme cases where an individual's behaviour becomes a threat to the group as a whole will collective action ensue; in all other situations people mind their own business even to the extent of quietly standing by and witnessing a robbery or a murder (Jeness 1922:235).

(14) It appears that all men have a relatively equal amount of self-respect as do women between themselves. While, according to Jeness, "marriage involves no subjection on the part of the woman" (1922:162), he mentions cases where wives are beaten by their husbands for failing to perform, in the husbands' opinion, their tasks sufficiently quickly. But in general women participate as freely as do men in various aspects of social life. Shamanism, for example, is open to women as well as men.

The Hutterites of North America

(1) The Hutterites live in North America in both the United States and Canada in temperate grassland areas. (2) They maintain themselves by mixed agricultural production. The surplus which they produce is sold and used to buy in various types of equipment and clothing and to establish new colonies. (3 and 4) Hutterites are extremely religious in a Western sense. Their religious belief system is the basis of their whole material culture. Absolute authority resides in a supernatural being — God — who created everything. It is thought that human nature has a natural carnal tendency which can only be overcome by continued submission to God's will through communal living. "Self-surrender, not self-development is the divine order"

(Hostetler and Huntington 1967:15). Natural carnality is overcome by teaching children the divine discipline, and until they are capable of self-control, obedience to elders. Male dominance in the culture is reflected in the creation of the universe. The male is thus the righteous example and women are required to be submissive and obedient to men.

(5) The socialisation of children cannot be characterised in terms other than authoritarian. The premise of child development is that they are expected to behave badly because they have not yet learned to cope with their carnal desires. Part of the punishment for misdemeanour is the instilling of the need to try harder in the future. This does not mean that there is no physical punishment, the reverse is in fact prevalent. "Punishment is usually physical, arbitrary, and inconsistent, and, from the child's point of view, often unpredictable" (Hostetler and Huntington 1967:61). Much of the child's life is spent in hands other than those of its parents: with babysitters, adults in general, the kindergarten, the German school, and the English school. Children do not take their meals with adults—who eat communally—but are fed at home.

(6) The only physical violence in Hutterite communities occurs—apart from the disciplining of children by adults—between the children. This plays an important role in the socialisation of the children as Hostetler and Huntington point out.

> Much of the children's play is physically rigorous and often rough. . . . They fight hard, quickly and quietly. They vie with one another, showing no physical fear of jumping off high places or pushing one another in front of the tractor. Adults generally ignore the children's dangerous games. . . . The free play of school children reinforces community values: the children learn to ignore physical discomfort and fear of injury and to minimise the importance of the body; the changing play groups teach the unpleasantness of being excluded (1967:72-73).

(7) Given that a Hutterite colony is structured hierarchically, conflict resolution processes tend to be a set of decisions handed down from above. The preacher often has the task of smoothing over differences. The executive council also adjudicates in interpersonal disputes. Some potential conflict situations are structured in a random fashion as for example when a colony divides to create a new one. Who stays and who goes is done by selection from a hat. (8) There is a definite division of labour on age and sex lines. Women work predominantly in the communal kitchen and look after the hens and geese. During the busy harvesting period they also help in the fields. Men work solely with the larger animals and the land. In the kitchen and in the fields there is a hierarchy; and with the men there is also specialisation of labour. (9) It appears that Hutterites do not differentiate

political and social activities and forms. Their distinction is between worldly (material) existence and spiritual life.

(10) Only baptised males are eligible for departmental positions such as cattleman, pigman, or shoemaker. Between five and seven of the baptised men are elected to form an executive council. These men hold the key colony positions including first and second preacher, householder, and field manager. The executive makes decisions concerning colony life. The preacher holds the highest leadership position but his actions are subject to review by the council. The preacher has no formal training and is elected by lot from nominations of his own colony. He does not gain full power until after several years of proven leadership; he can be removed should his conduct meet with general disapproval. (11) All baptised males of a colony exercise social control, although it is often delegated to the preacher or executive for more minor breaches of norms. (12) Similarly all baptised males participate in decisionmaking on major policies and determine who will hold the leadership positions. (13) Norms of behaviour are very rigid. This is offset to an extent by the propensity of the Hutterites to forgive individuals for misdemeanours, even where the individual has left the colony to live in the world outside. The deciding factor in forgiveness appears to be repentance on the part of the individual concerned.

(14) The distribution of self-respect appears to be highly skewed. The Hutterite ideology creates its own feudal structure. God is at the top, then men who preside over women, who together control children, all of whom dominate nature. As was seen above, child training is authoritarian and punishment can be arbitrary. Women do not participate in deciding colony affairs either by voting or by holding leadership positions. Sexism exists in a blatant form where women are believed to be intellectually and physically inferior to men and, whereas men reflect some of God's glory, women have weakness (Hostetler and Huntington 1967:30). This has given rise to male and female subcultures. While men attempt to avoid confrontation with the colony's power structure, women often complain because they have little to lose. The net result is a condition where a woman "often projects her annoyance and mildly dislikes men as a group" (Hostetler and Huntington 1967:30).

The Islanders of Tristan da Cunha

(1) They inhabit the island of Tristan da Cunha which is located in the South Pacific Ocean. It includes two smaller islands within reach of rowing boat. It has a mild wet windy climate. (2) The economy of Tristan has taken three distinct forms since its initial colonisation in the early nineteenth century. During the nineteenth century it was based primarily on barter with passing ships, fresh vegetables and meat being traded for items

which the islanders could not produce themselves. From about 1915 to 1940, with the end of sailing ships, Tristan was almost totally isolated from the outside world. In this period a subsistence economy was developed based on fishing, farming, gathering, and earlier hunting. Gradually after 1945 a money economy was introduced via a South African fishing company and later by various public works instituted by the British government. The islanders have always been dependent on the outside for items such as rope, canvas, wood, flour, sugar, salt, tea, and coffee. While at one stage the introduction of a money economy appeared to threaten the core values of the community, the islanders have managed to adopt it to their own ends. "The islanders refused to become 'chained to the labour market.' They refused to give up their subsistence economy with its network of reciprocal relations and its independence. These were values that they would not sacrifice for all the affluence and prosperity" (Munch 1971: 306-307).

(3) The islanders have many bilateral kinship ties with neither the male or female line taking precedence. This gives rise to many self-selective labour exchange relationships. The founding ethos of the community was based on the principles of equality, communal ownership, cooperation, and freedom from government control. These founding values are still the predominant ones on the island although communal ownership no longer exists.

(4) Most of the inhabitants are Christians but this does not appear to have a great effect on social organisation (Munch 1964:371; Munch 1971:136—for two different examples). (5) Child-rearing practices on the island have a peculiar nature.

> The importance attached to the avoidance of open violent display of aggressive feeling among Tristan people is well seen in the ways in which children are taught. . . . Paradoxically it is through threats or acts of physical punishment that children are inculcated with the importance of non-violent behaviour (Loudon 1970:307).

Parents go to great lengths to remove what they characterise as willful behaviour in children. One of the basic aims in child rearing is to instill patience so that immediate gratification of desires is not expected. To gain this end parents will tease and provoke children into displays of willful behaviour and then physically punish it. There is a graded use of physical punishment which tends to increase in severity with increasing age of the child.

(6) Apart from the physical punishment of children the only other physical violence on Tristan occurs between husband and wife. Further-

more there is no theft, misdemeanour, or disturbances. (7) When some conflicts have arisen on the island individuals have intervened. On only one occasion did an outsider act in this capacity: in 1908 when an Anglican clergyman intervened in a dispute which was not purely internal to the island (Munch 1971:80-81). In fact many of the disputes which arose during the nineteenth century occurred between existing inhabitants and newcomers—generally from shipwrecks. Among the islanders themselves there is little need for third-party intervention and there are even norms militating against it because esteem is accorded to the person who minds his own business and leaves others to do as they please (Munch 1970:1302). Public opinion takes a distinct form on Tristan which Loudon has termed "public teasing," which basically is making jokes at another's expense. Although Loudon identifies this as one of the legitimated forms of hostility, it is interesting to note the issues over which it arises. "Characteristics and tendencies particularly liable to expose people to public ridicule are what may be termed cowardice, laziness, stupidity, and credulity, but above all boastfulness and self importance and over-readiness to push oneself forward" (Loudon 1970:315)[1]—that is, basically all those aspects of personal behaviour which the ethos of the community would define as normatively bad. It is interesting to note the sexism in this situation; women are neither the butt of such teasing nor do they participate in it.

(8) In principle every household is economically self-sufficient. The islanders do, however, cooperate on various tasks. There are those tasks such as crewing a boat which demand cooperation and others such as berry picking to reduce the tedium. All cooperation is reciprocal. Division of labour exists on age and sex lines but does not appear to lead to occupational specialisation.

(9) Political organisation only exists on Tristan insofar as it has relations with the outside world. Internally there is no leadership or organisation based on power. A person may influence others by example rather than dictum (Munch 1970:1303). There is evidence that political organisations have been formed on two occasions. The first occurred in Britain after evacuation because of volcanic activity. Initially it was a spontaneous outburst against a bureaucrat from Whitehall who maintained that they might not be able to return to Tristan. A petition was then sent to the government and when no reply was forthcoming the islanders held a public meeting. Even in this case they had received encouragement and moral support from outsiders (Munch 1964:374). The second time was after the return to Tristan when all those men working on the new dock spontaneously walked out—under threat of dismissal—in order to travel to Nightingale Island to collect guano.

(10) As was mentioned previously there is no universally recognised

hierarchy on Tristan. Church authorities often tried to establish some form of authority but it was usually short-lived and always ignored where possible (Munch 1964:371). (11) Munch also mentions two cases when individuals from within the community attempted to establish themselves as leaders. The islanders spontaneously thwarted these two attempts by simply ignoring the self-styled leaders: "They had received the most severe denunciation this atomistic and pacific community would hand out to anybody: they were ignored, isolated, denied a status in the community, not by communal decree but simply as a consequence of the withdrawal of individual reciprocal relationships" (Munch 1974:256).

(12 and 13) Social control exists only insofar as all the inhabitants of Tristan abide by the norms of the founding charter. The main sanction of social control rests with the withdrawal of individual reciprocal relations. (14) Only tentative comments can be made on the distribution of self-respect. One would expect there to be equality between men as all have similar tasks to perform with similar resources. Munch does mention one of the more "prominent" families in relation to the meeting in England. Women and children may suffer in this respect. They do not participate in fishing expeditions and women cook for men even during cooperative ventures such as the thatching of a house.

Discussion

The attributes selected for examination in these societies are presented in summary form in Table 8.1. Although there are differences between these groups a number of patterns emerge from this preliminary sample. It is, however, necessary to consider some other aspects of these societies in order to gain some insight into their internal dynamics.

All of these groups are essentially small, local, face-to-face communities, although some of them exist within a larger cultural milieu—there are, for example, some 40,000 Mbuti Pygmies. The small size of all these societies is a major contributory factor in their open and basically egalitarian decisionmaking and social control processes.

The five traditional groups all experience a changing composition in their membership in the short term. This "flux" derives in part from seasonal-ecological variables and in certain cases from need for collective activity to maintain boundary distinctions (Turnbull 1968a:135).[2] But conflicts within these groups are also partly responsible for personnel changes, fission being used as a dissociative conflict resolution form. The changing composition of these traditional societies is partly responsible for the lack of lineal leadership. To maintain such a system of control would not only be difficult given the large geographical area which these groups cover but in

TABLE 8.1   Common Factors of Peaceful Societies

Groups / Items	Semai	Siriono	Mbuti	Kung	Copper Eskimo	Hutterites	Tristan
1 Habitat	Tropical Rain Forest	Tropical Rain Forest	Tropical Rain Forest	Hot Desert	Arctic Tundra	Temperate Grassland	Temperate Grassland
2 Subsistence	Hunting-Gathering, Swiddening	Hunting-Gathering, Swiddening	Hunting-Gathering	Hunting-Gathering	Hunting, some Gathering	Mixed Agriculture	Mixed-Subsistence Agriculture
3 Cosmology	Ideational*	Ideational	Ideational	Ideational	Ideational	Ideational	Idealistic
4 Integration	Kinship & Interest	Kinship & Interest	Kinship & Interest	Kinship & Interest	Kinship & Interest	Interest & Kinship	Interest & Kinship
5 Socialisation	Permissive	Permissive	Permissive	Permissive	Permissive	Authoritarian	Authoritarian
6 Physical Violence	Little, Lethal	Little, non-lethal	Little, non-lethal	Little, Lethal	Some, Lethal	Some, non-lethal	Some, non-lethal
7 Conflict Resolution	Individual & Group	Individual some Group	Individual & Group	Individual & Group	Individual some Group	Group	Individual
8 Division of Labour	Yes	Yes	Yes	Yes	Yes	Yes + Specialisation	Yes
9 Coercive Organisation	No	No	No	No	No	Perhaps	No
10 Hierarchy	Yes, non-restrictive for males	No	No	Yes, non-restrictive for males	No	Yes, non-restrictive for males	No
11 Decision	All adults	All adults	All adults	All adults	All adults	All male adults	All adults
12 Social Control	All	All	All	All	All	All male adults	All adults
13 Forms of Social Control	Usually psychic	Usually psychic	Usually psychic	Usually psychic	Psychic & Physical	Psychic	Psychic
14 Discrimination	Yes	Yes	Yes	Yes	Yes	Yes	Yes

* Used in Sorokin's (1962: 55-102, Vol. I) sense.

certain circumstances it would stand in the way of "economic" necessity in terms of the production and distribution of food (Fried 1967:106).

The traditional groups produce little or no surplus. As such, material inequality between individuals on a long-term basis is impossible. As a corollary, leadership remains on the level of personal authority rather than coercive power because there is no surplus to appropriate and utilise. According to Fried (1967:117), however, the first step in the establishment of power-based leadership is the creation of a centre for the redistribution of material surplus for the benefit of the society as a whole (as per the Mountain Arapesh, Mead 1961:34) rather than an appropriation centre for personal-sectional advancement. What these groups do produce, however, is distributed equitably. In this context the cases of Tristan da Cunha and the Hutterites are of importance. Although the domestic mode of production on Tristan undoubtedly keeps the surplus small, the more specialised techniques employed by the Hutterites create a larger one and yet no great material inequality exists within them. The Hutterites in fact hold their surplus collectively and use it for the benefit of the group as a whole. It is interesting to note that both of these groups were "created"; they were established in the historical past with specific social structures designed to achieve definite goals.

The differences in child-rearing practices between the traditional and created societies are open to a number of possible — and contradictory — explanations. Firstly, it could be argued that the latent "violence" of the created societies — the existence of surplus which does not produce material inequality — manifests itself in their authoritarian child-rearing methods. Alternatively, their violent socialisation ways are a product of their historical background. Their respective conceptions of human nature — natural carnality or willful behaviour — are only a reflection of their Western European Christian origin which emphasises control rather than development and as such directly influences the way they rear their children. Another possible explanation derives from their mode of subsistence. Both Tristan da Cunha and the Hutterites have sedentary farming lifestyles which are incompatible with independent adventurous personalities which permissive child socialisation processes tend to create.

Fortunately this sample of peaceful societies is not solely composed of hunting-gathering groups. If it were so composed then the absence of large structural inequalities might simply be attributed to this particular level of sociocultural development. The cases of Tristan da Cunha and the Hutterites demonstrate that it is possible for a society to produce a surplus and still retain a fairly egalitarian social structure which is not maintained by the use or threat of physical violence.

Conclusion

Any points derived from this small sample of peaceful societies must necessarily be tentative. The attributes of the groups considered, however, do not point toward a basic incompatibility between social justice or equality on the one hand and an absence of physical violence on the other. The very idea that the presence of one is the "price" paid for the absence of the other may simply be a manifestation of Western — although now becoming global — culture and its concomitant hierarchical world view.

Much more work is needed on the study of peaceful patterns of social organisation in terms of increasing the sample and perhaps more importantly of locating groups where there is sufficient information for longitudinal studies. Also, comparisons with societies which are physically violent but have basically similar social structures would possibly aid in identifying factors critical in the production of peace. This area of study has links with various other approaches, in particular the study of futures (e.g., Targ 1971, Weiss 1975). This type of information would not only provide insights into how various groups have "achieved" a relatively peaceful lifestyle but also, and perhaps more importantly, would demonstrate that peace is not a utopian and by implication unobtainable goal.

Notes

The groundwork for this chapter was carried out while I was an undergraduate in the School for Independent Studies, University of Lancaster 1974-1975. Many thanks go to my supervisor of that time, David Osterberg. My thanks also go to my current supervisor Paul Smoker whose comments encouraged me to rework parts of the original. Also for various personal friends whose support has encouraged me to stay with the original idea.

1. A number of authors of works used here (Dentan 1968; Loudon 1970; Chance 1966; Hostetler and Huntington 1967) display a common tendency to use some form of neo-Freudian drive reduction model of human aggression. Thus, even these peaceful societies, according to this approach, have violence ready to break out. Such a theory of course does little to explain the variance in the distribution of violence between egalitarian band societies and nation-states for example. When dealing with such macro categories of social organisation, hierarchy and compulsive organisation appear to account for a more significant amount of the variance.

2. Contrary to the argument maintaining some form of instinctual disposition to possess land as a part of human inheritance these least complex of societies are not generally territorial in the sense of maintaining an exclusive monopoly over an area of land. Other groups may come and go, and in times of shortage an incumbent band may share the food and water resources with another less fortunate group (Fried 1967:94-98; Lee and Devore 1968a:12).

References

Balicki, A. 1968. "The Netsilik Eskimos: Adaptive Processes." Pp. 78-82, in Lee and Devore (eds.), *Man the Hunter*. Chicago: Aldine.

Benedict, R. 1935. *Patterns of Culture*. London: Routledge & Kegan Paul.

Broch, T., and J. Galtung. 1966. "Belligerence among the Primitives." *Jnl. Peace Research* 3:33-45.

Chance, N. A. 1966. *The Eskimo of North Alaska*. New York: Holt, Rinehart & Winston.

Coon, C. S. 1972. *The Hunting Peoples*. London: Cape.

Davie, M. R. 1929. *The Evolution of War: A Study of Its Role in Early Societies*. Port Washington, New York: Kennikat Press, 1968.

Dentan, R. K. 1968. *The Semai: A Non-Violent People of Malaya*. Holt, Rinehart & Winston.

Dole, G. E., and R. L. Carneiro (eds.). 1960. *Essays in the Science of Culture: In Honour of Leslie A. White*. New York: T. Y. Crowell.

Forde, D. C. 1963. *Habitat, Economy and Society: A Geographical Introduction to Ethnology*. New York: Dutton & Co.

Fourie, L. 1960. "The Bushmen of South-West Africa." Pp. 87-95 in S. and P. Ottenberg (eds.), *Cultures and Societies of Africa*. New York: Random House.

Fried, M. H. 1967. *The Evolution of Political Society: An Essay in Political Anthropology*. New York: Random House.

Friedl, E. 1975. *Women and Men: An Anthropologist's View*. New York: Holt, Rinehart & Winston.

Fromm, E. 1973. *The Anatomy of Human Destructiveness*. New York: Holt, Rinehart & Winston.

Galtung, J. 1969. "Violence, Peace and Peace Research." *Jnl. Peace Research* 6:167-191.

Gardener, P. M. 1968. "Discussion: Primate Behaviour and the Evolution of Aggression." Pp. 338-344 in Lee and Devore (eds.), *Man the Hunter*.

Gjessing, G. 1967. "Ecology and Peace Research." *Jnl. Peace Research* 4:125-139.

Godlier, M. 1975. "Modes of Production, Kinship, and Demographic Structures." Pp. 3-27, in M. Bloch (ed.), *Marxist Analyses and Social Anthropology*. London: Malaby Press.

Holmberg, A. R. 1966. *Nomads of the Longbow: The Siriono of Eastern Bolivia*. Natural History Press.

Honigman, J. J. 1968. "Interpersonal Relations in Atomistic Communities." *Human Organisation* 27:220-229.

Hostetler, J. A. 1974. *Hutterite Society*. Baltimore and London: The Johns Hopkins University Press.

———, and G. E. Huntington. 1967. *The Hutterites of North America*. New York: Holt, Rinehart & Winston.

Jeness, D. 1922. *The Life of the Copper Eskimo*. Report of the Canadian Arctic Expedition 1913-1918, Vol. XIIa. Ottawa: F. A. Acland.

———. 1946. *Material Culture of the Copper Eskimo*. Report of the Canadian Arctic Expedition 1913-1918, Vol. 16. Ottawa: E. Clouter.

Lee, R. B. 1968a. "What Hunters Do for a Living: Or How to Make Out on Scarce

Resources." Pp. 30-48, in Lee and Devore (eds.), *Man the Hunter*.

_____. 1968b. "Discussion: Predation and Warfare." Pp. 157-158, in Lee and Devore (eds.), *Man the Hunter*.

_____, and I. Devore (eds.). 1968. *Man the Hunter*. Chicago: Aldine.

_____, and I. Devore. 1968a. "Problems in the Study of Hunter-Gatherers." Pp. 3-12, in Lee and Devore (eds.), *Man the Hunter*.

Lenski, G. 1966. *Power and Privilege: An Essay in the Theory of Social Stratification*. New York: McGraw-Hill.

Loudon, J. B. 1970. "Teasing and Socialisation on Tristan da Cunha." Pp. 293-331, in P. Mayer (ed.), *Socialisation: The Approach from Anthropology*. London: Tavistock.

Marshall, L. 1965. "The Kung Bushmen of the Kalahari Desert." Pp. 241-278, in J. L. Gibbs (ed.), *Peoples of Africa*. New York: Holt, Rinehart & Winston.

Mead, M. 1961. *Cooperation and Conflict among Primitive Peoples*. Boston: Beacon Press.

_____. 1972. *Culture and Commitment: A Study of the Generation Gap*. London: Panther Books Ltd.

_____. 1973. "Warfare Is Only an Invention Not a Biological Necessity." Pp. 112-118, in C. R. Beitz and T. Herman (eds.), *Peace & War,* San Francisco: Freeman & Co.

Institute Press.

Moore, B., Jr. 1972. *Reflections on the Causes of Human Misery and upon Certain Proposals to Eliminate Them*. London: Allen Lane, The Penguin Press.

Munch, P. A. 1964. "Culture and Superculture in a Displaced Community: Tristan da Cunha." *Ethnology* 3:369-376.

_____. 1970. "Economic Development and Conflicting Values: A Social Experiment in Tristan da Cunha." *American Anthropologist* 72:1300-1318.

_____. 1971. *Crisis in Utopia: The Ordeal of Tristan da Cunha*. New York: T. Y. Crowell.

_____. 1974. "Anarchy and Anomie in an Anarchistic Community." *Man* 9:243-261.

Otterbein, K. F. 1970. *The Evolution of War: A Cross-Cultural Study*. Human Relations Area Files Press.

Palmer, S. 1965. "Murder and Suicide in Forty Non-Literate Societies." *Jnl. Criminal Law, Criminology, and Police Science* 56:320-324.

Rasmussen, K. 1932. *Intellectual Culture of the Copper Eskimo*. Report of the Fifth Thule Expedition to Arctic North America, Vol. IX. Copenhagen: Gyldendalske Boghandel, Nordisk Forlag.

Sahlins, M. 1974. *Stone-Age Economics*. London: Tavistock.

Schapera, I. 1930. *The Khoisan Peoples of South Africa: Bushmen and Hottentots*. London: Routledge & Kegan Paul, 1965.

Service, E. R. 1966. *The Hunters*. Englewood Cliffs, N.J.: Prentice-Hall.

Sipes, R. G. 1973. "War, Sports and Aggression: An Empirical Test of Two Rival Theories." *American Anthropologist* 75:64-86.

Sorokin, P. 1962. *Social and Cultural Dynamics*. 4 vols. New York: Bedminster Press.

Sweet, L. E. 1973. "Culture and Aggressive Action." Pp. 325-344, in C. M. Otten (ed.), *Aggression & Evolution*. Lexington, Mass.: Xerox College Publishing.

Targ, H. R. 1971. "Social Science and a New Social Order." *Jnl. Peace Research* 8: 207-220.

Thomas, E. 1969. *The Harmless People*. Penguin.

Turnbull, C. M. 1965. "The Mbuti pygmies of the Congo." Pp. 279-318, in J. L. Gibbs (ed.), *Peoples of Africa*. New York: Holt, Rinehart & Winston.

————. 1966. *Wayward Servants: The Two Worlds of the African Pygmy*. London: Eyre & Spottiswoode.

————. 1968a. "The Importance of Flux in Two Hunting Societies." Pp. 132-137, in Lee and Devore (eds.), *Man the Hunter*.

————. 1968b. "Discussion: Resolving Conflicts by Fission." P. 156, in Lee and Devore (eds.), *Man the Hunter*.

————. 1968c. "Discussion: Primate Behaviour and Human Aggression." Pp. 338-343, in Lee and Devore (eds.), *Man the Hunter*.

Watanabe, H. 1968. "Subsistence and Ecology among Northern Food Gatherers." Pp. 69-77 in Lee and Devore (eds.), *Man the Hunter*.

Weiss, T. G. 1975. "The Tradition of Philosophical Anarchism and Future Directions in World Policy." *Jnl. Peace Research* 12:1-17.

Wright, Q. 1964. *A Study of War*. Chicago: University of Chicago Press (abridged ed.).

9
Internal War:
A Cross-Cultural Study

Keith F. Otterbein

Internal war, or warfare between culturally similar political communities, is widespread. But it is neither well understood nor adequately described, because ethnological discussions of warfare usually fail to discriminate between internal war and external war (warfare between culturally different political communities). Three factors may be examined as possibly influencing the occurrence of internal war: social structure, political organization, and external relations that culturally similar political communities have with culturally different ones. Fraternal interest groups, such as are produced by patrilocal residence or polygyny, can engage in warfare by making attacks upon individuals in neighboring political communities. On the other hand, a centralized political system presumably has officials who are the sole initiators of war and who can prevent groups from making unauthorized attacks. And lastly, external war—the most violent form of intersocietal relations—should produce cohesiveness and thereby eliminate internal war between culturally similar political communities. This chapter reports a cross-cultural study of internal war in which hypotheses derived from each of these considerations were tested with a sample of fifty societies.[1]

Methodology

Measures

Internal war, the dependent variable, was defined as warfare between political communities within the same cultural unit. A political community is "a group of people whose membership is defined in terms of occupancy of

Reproduced by permission of the author and the American Anthropological Association from Keith F. Otterbein, "Internal War: A Cross-Cultural Study," *American Anthropologist* 70 (1968):277-289.

a common territory and who have an official with the special function of announcing group decisions—a function exercised at least once a year" (Naroll 1964a:286).[2] Warfare was defined as armed combat between political communities. A cultural unit is composed of contiguous political communities that are culturally similar.[3] External war, one of the independent variables, was defined as warfare between culturally different political communities, i.e., political communities that are not members of the same cultural unit.[4] Two aspects of external war can be measured separately: political communities of a cultural unit can either attack or be attacked by culturally different political communities. Since for internal war the unit of analysis was the whole cultural unit rather than any single political community, it was not possible to make this differentiation.

Ethnographic data were used to code the variables of internal and external war on three-point scales as "continual," "frequent," and "infrequent or never." If the data included statements that warfare was a constant state of affairs within a cultural unit, that the political communities of the cultural unit were constantly attacking other peoples, and that the cultural unit was constantly being attacked by neighboring peoples, the respective variables were coded as "continual" warfare. Internal war was coded as "frequent" if the sources stated that although the political communities within the cultural unit frequently fought with each other, periods of peace occasionally occurred. The first measure of external war (attack) was coded as "frequent" if the sources stated that the political communities within the cultural unit frequently attacked other peoples, but that this was not an annual affair. The second measure of external war (being attacked) was coded as "frequent" if the sources stated that the cultural unit was frequently attacked by neighboring peoples, but that this did not occur every year. Internal war was coded as "infrequent or never" if warfare was described as being uncommon, rare, or nonexistent. Both aspects of external war were coded as "infrequent or never" if the cultural unit was described as having peaceful relationships with neighboring peoples, as being socially or geographically isolated, or as having a history of virtually no war. For purposes of analysis in the present study, societies coded as "continual" or "frequent" were grouped together.

In addition to external war, three other independent variables were used: the existence of fraternal interest groups, the party who initiates war, and the degree of centralization of the political community. The procedures used in indexing fraternal interest groups are identical to those followed in a previous study of feuding:

Two factors which should lead to the formation of fraternal interest groups are a marital residence pattern in which the new family lives with or near the groom's relatives and the presence of polygyny; both indices were derived from the codings given by Murdock, in the Ethnographic Atlas (1962:117-118). A society was considered to be *patrilocal* if the residence pattern was listed as patrilocal (P),[5] avunculocal (A), virilocal (V), ambilocal, where the majority of couples lives with the groom's relatives (D), or where a common household is not established but the men of the community either remain in their natal households or live in special men's houses (O). Societies were coded as *other* if the residence pattern was matrilocal (M), uxorilocal (U), neolocal (N), or ambilocal, where the residence was not consistently with the kin of either spouse but was determined by personal circumstances (B, C). The symbols in column 14 of the Atlas (1962:116) were used to code for the presence of polygyny (P, Q, R, and S or E, F, and G with either p, q, r, or s following) and its absence (E, F, G, M, N, and O) (Otterbein and Otterbein 1965:1471).

War can be initiated either by officials or by some other member of the political community. If the ethnographic sources state that only officials or a council of the political community can initiate attacks and that they can prevent unauthorized individuals from going to war, the initiating party is coded as an "official." If, in addition to officials, any member of the political community can initiate an attack — usually a raid organized to seek revenge or honor — then the initiating party is coded as "anyone."

The degree of centralization of each political community was measured by using Service's scale of four types of sociopolitical systems (1962), each of which is structurally more complex than the preceding type. These types are "bands" (which are typically patrilocal hunting groups), "tribes" (which are characterized by pantribal sodalities), "chiefdoms" (which have chiefs with redistributive functions), and "states" (which possess governments with the legitimate use of force). Although ethnographic data were used to code each society for one of the four types, for the purposes of analysis "bands" and "tribes" were grouped together and considered to be "uncentralized political systems," while "chiefdoms" and "states" were considered to be "centralized political systems."

Sample

The universe from which the sample was drawn consisted of the first 628 societies listed in the Ethnographic Atlas (Murdock 1962-1964),[6] a series of installments in the journal *Ethnology*. This listing was used in preference to the World Ethnographic Sample (Murdock 1957), which lists 565 societies, because bibliography is provided for each society only in the Ethnographic Atlas. A further reason for using the Ethnographic Atlas, although both lists contain coded data for each society on a number of variables, is that this atlas provides more variables, some of which are revisions of the variables in the World Ethnographic Sample. A list with a larger number of variables was preferred, for at a future time either I or some other researcher may want to correlate the warfare variables with other ethnographic variables.

The societies in the Ethnographic Atlas are grouped into sixty culture areas, ten for each of "six major ethnographic areas": Africa, Circum-Mediterranean, East Eurasia, Insular Pacific, North America, and South America (1962:114). After each society was drawn for the sample, using a table of random numbers, it was recorded by culture area. References for each society were compiled from the Ethnographic Atlas, from regional ethnographic bibliographies, from my personal knowledge and that of my colleagues and students, and from the microcard edition of the Human Relations Area Files. A society was dropped from the sample for any one of four reasons: (1) if only foreign language references could be found (I intended to use student assistants and wanted to avoid the problem of finding good translators); (2) if source materials were not in the library of the University of Kansas, my personal library, or the microcard edition of the Human Relations Area Files; (3) if the society was a peasant community or a modern nation, although for several societies — Egyptians, Albanians, Japanese, Thai, Javanese, and Aymara — I used tribal peoples within the nation or data from the earliest available accounts, such as thirteenth-century Java and Japan; (4) if data on military organization, tactics, and causes of war were not in the sources (societies, however, which do not engage in warfare were not excluded from the sample). These four rejection criteria alter the nature of the universe to which one can legitimately generalize; the universe becomes all societies, excluding peasant communities and modern nations, for which there are data on warfare in the English language and for which source materials were available in Lawrence, Kansas, during the spring of 1965.

The references and source materials for each society were examined in the order that the societies were drawn. The data, if sufficient, were recorded on preliminary code sheets. After a society was coded, no more societies from that culture area were used. If a society was dropped, the next society drawn from that culture area was used. This procedure was followed for fifty societies; hence, there is one representative society for fifty of the culture areas and none for ten. The sample was limited to one society per culture area in order to reduce the possible influence of diffusion on correlations[7] and in order to insure a wide variety of types of military organization. The culture areas represented and the societies in the sample are listed with codings in Table 9.1. Of the fifty societies, thirty were first choices for their culture area, ten were second choices, seven were third, two were fourth, and one was sixth. Twenty-six societies in nine

TABLE 9.1 Societies and Codings

Cul- ture Area	Region	Society	Internal War¹	External War (attacking)	External War (attacked)	Initi- ating Party²	Polit- ical System³
Aa:	African Hunters	Dorobo (2*), 1920†	I	I	I	§	T
Ab:	South African Bantu	Ambo (19), 1910	C	I	I	O	S
Ac:	Central Bantu	Ila (1), 1920	C	C	C	A	T
Ad:	Northeast Bantu	Gisu (9), 1900	F	I	F	A	T
Ae:	Equatorial Bantu	Amba (1), 1950	C	I	I	n.d.	T
Af:	Guinea Coast	Mende (5), 1930	F	n.d.	n.d.	O	C
Ag:	Western Sudan	Mossi (2), 1950	I	F	I	O	S
Ah:	Nigerian Plateau	Tiv (3), 1920	C	F	I	n.d.	T
Ai:	Eastern Sudan	Ingassana (4), 1920	I	C	I	O	T
Aj:	Upper Nile	Nandi (7), 1910	I	C	F	O	T
Ca:	Ethiopia and the Horn	Somali (2), 1950	C	F	I	O	T
Cd:	North Africa	Egyptians (2), 1250BC	‡	F	F	O	S
Ce:	Southern Europe	Albanians (1), 1900	C	I	F	A	T
Cj:	Semitic Near East	Mutair (5), 1930	C	I	F	O	C
Eb:	Central Asia	Kazak (1), 1910	C	n.d.	n.d.	A	T
Ec:	Arctic Asia	Yukaghir (6), 1900	I	C	C	O	T
Ed:	East Asia	Japanese (5), 1200	F	I	I	O	S
Ee:	Himalayas	Tibetans (4), 1920	C	F	I	A	T
Eg:	South India	Toda (4), 1900	‡	I	I	§	T
Eh:	Indian Ocean	Andamanese (1), 1870	F	I	I	A	B
Ei:	Assam and Burma	Sema (16), 1910	F	F	I	O	C
Ej:	Southeast Asia	Thai (9), 1600	‡	C	C	O	S
Ib:	Western Indonesia	Javanese (2), 1300	F	F	I	O	S
Ic:	Eastern Indonesia	Toraja (5), 1900	n.d.	n.d.	n.d.	A	T
Id:	Australia	Tiwi (3), 1920	F	I	I	A	B
Ie:	New Guinea	Orokaiva (9), 1920	C	I	I	A	T
If:	Micronesia	Marshallese (3), 1850	F	I	I	O	C
Ig:	Western Melanesia	Kurtatchi (3), 1930	C	C	C	A	T
Ih:	Eastern Melanesia	Lau (4), 1850	F	I	I	O	S
Ii:	Western Polynesia	Tikopia (2), 1930	‡	I	I	§	T
Ij:	Eastern Polynesia	Hawaiians (6), 1800	F	I	I	O	S
Na:	Arctic America	Copper Eskimo (3), 1920	I	I	I	§	B
Nb:	Northwest Coast	Comox (14), 1880	C	F	F	A	B
Nc:	California	Monachi (23), 1870	I	I	I	A	C
Nd:	Great Basin and Plateau	Wishram (18), 1860	n.d.	F	F	O	T
Ne:	Plains	Plains Cree (19), 1850	I	C	C	A	B
Nf:	Prairie	Fox (7), 1830	n.d.	C	C	A	T
Ng:	Eastern Woodlands	Cherokee (5), 1750	I	C	C	A	T
Nh:	Southwest	Santa Ana (12), 1800	I	I	C	O	T
Ni:	Northwest Mexico	Papago (1), 1800	I	F	C	O	T
Nj:	Central Mexico	Aztec (2), 1520	‡	F	I	O	S
Sb:	Caribbean	Motilon (3), 1940	C	I	I	n.d.	B
Sc:	Guiana	Saramacca (6), 1750	I	C	C	O	C
Sd:	Lower Amazon	Mundurucu (1), 1820	I	C	I	O	T
Se:	Interior Amazonia	Jivaro (3), 1930	F	C	C	A	T
Sf:	Andes	Aymara (2), 1500	C	F	F	A	S
Sg:	Chile and Patagonia	Tehuelche (4), 1800	F	F	F	A	B
Sh:	Gran Chaco	Abipon (3), 1800	F	F	F	O	B
Si:	Mato Grosso	Trumai (2), 1900	I	I	F	n.d.	B
Sj:	Eastern Brazil	Timbira (4), 1820	C	C	C	O	T

* Ethnographic Atlas number
† Approximate time level to which the ethnographic data pertain
‡ One political community in cultural unit

§ No military organization
¹ War: C = continual; F = frequent; I = infrequent.
² Initiating Party: O = official; A = anyone.
³ Political System: B = band; T = tribe; C = chiefdom; S = state.

unrepresented culture areas were dropped, fifteen being from five culture areas in the Circum-Mediterranean. In all, sixty-one societies were dropped from the sample for one or more of the reasons cited.[8]

The five variables coded for use in this study were taken from a list of twenty-six variables designed to cover many aspects of primitive war. In selecting the fifty societies, I conducted the preliminary coding. Without prior knowledge of my codings, students in a political anthropology class and a research assistant perused the sources and recorded on code sheets the pages on which data were to be found. Information they found was used to verify or, in some instances, to modify the original codings.

Results

The independent variables that have been proposed as factors influencing the occurrence of internal war can be grouped under three categories — social structural variables, political variables, and intersocietal variables.

Social Structural Variables

Two recent cross-cultural studies have demonstrated the significance of fraternal interest groups as determinants of intrasocietal conflict. In the first of these studies, Van Velzen and Van Wetering (1960) test the hypothesis that societies with fraternal interest groups are less peaceful than societies without fraternal interest groups. Since fraternal interest groups are localized groups of related males, they can resort to aggressive measures when the interests of their members are threatened. These anthropologists use patrilocal residence as an index of the presence of fraternal interest groups because it results in a settlement pattern in which related males live near each other. Matrilocal residence, on the other hand, results in a social structural condition in which related males are scattered over a large area and are unable readily to support each other's interests. The hypothesis is examined with five indices of peacefulness vs. nonpeacefulness, and it is shown that it is valid for each index. In the second study, Otterbein and Otterbein (1965:1473) test the hypothesis that "societies with fraternal interest groups are more likely to have feuding than societies without fraternal interest groups." The presence and absence of fraternal interest groups were indexed as in the present study, and feuding was indexed by the occurrence of blood revenge following a homicide. The hypothesis was confirmed.

In societies characterized by feuding, blood revenge is often taken by a small group of men who lie in ambush and kill an unsuspecting relative of the man whose act of homicide is being avenged. The victim is usually alone and has little chance of escape. The ambushers are of necessity sufficiently armed and organized so that they can be referred to collectively as a military organization; for some degree of organization is required for the warriors to arrange an ambush secretly, to remain in hiding silently, and to spring an attack at the appropriate moment.

Such ambushing tactics are used in warfare as well as in feuding. Warfare and feuding can be distinguished if feuding is defined as blood revenge occurring within a political community and warfare as armed combat occurring between political communities. Thus, if the members of such an ambushing military organization make an attack upon someone who is a member of their own political community, they are feuding or initiating a feud; if the next day these warriors ambush a member of another political community, they are engaging in an act of war. If the existence of fraternal interest groups, which can form small-scale military organizations, is related to feuding, as has been demonstrated in a cross-cultural study, then it seems reasonable to infer that the existence of fraternal interest groups will also produce warfare between political communities.

The first hypothesis tested in this study is similar to the one tested in the feuding study: societies with fraternal interest groups are more likely to have internal war than societies without fraternal interest groups.[9] The relationship between patrilocal residence and internal war is shown in Table 9.2.[10] Although the correlation is positive, it is not significant.[11]

The hypothesis can also be tested by using the presence of polygyny as an index of fraternal interest groups. Polygyny usually produces a situation in which at least some men have a large number of sons: before the sons are married, they probably live in their father's household; if they are married, they probably live near their father. Previous research indicates that polygyny is as good an index of fraternal interest groups as is patrilocal residence, for the same degree of correlation was obtained between polygyny and feuding as between patrilocality and feuding (Otterbein and Otterbein 1965:1473-1474). The relationship between polygyny and internal war is shown in Table 9.3. The data confirm the hypothesis; the correlation is higher than in Table 9.2 and it is significant. The interrelationship of the two indices is shown in Table 9.4. Although there is a significant correlation, it is clear that different indices are being used.

Political Variables

Fraternal interest groups, it has been argued, lead to internal war because the leaders of such groups of related males will, apparently upon their own initiative, organize a war party that will ambush members of other political communities. In a case study of a changing political system, Gearing (1962:85-105) has described the difficulties that Cherokee leaders had in the eighteenth century preventing unauthorized war parties from at-

TABLE 9.2   Patrilocal Residence and the Occurrence of Internal War

	Internal War		
	Continual or Frequent	Infrequent	
Other	8	6	14
Patrilocal	20	8	28
	—	—	—
	28	14	42

$\phi = 0.14$ $X^2 = 0.86$ n.s.

TABLE 9.4   Correlation between the Two Indices

	Polygyny		
	Present	Absent	
Other	3	14	17
Patrilocal	18	15	33
	—	—	—
	21	29	50

$\phi = 0.35$ $X^2 = 6.27$ $0.01 < p < 0.02$

TABLE 9.3   Polygyny and the Occurrence of Internal War

	Internal War		
	Continual or Frequent	Infrequent	
Polygyny absent	13	11	24
Polygyny present	15	3	18
	—	—	—
	28	14	42

$\phi = 0.31$ $X^2 = 3.93$ $P < 0.05$

TABLE 9.5   Political Complexity and the Initiation of War

	Initiating Party		
	Anyone	Official	
Centralized political systems	2	14	16
Uncentralized political systems	16	10	26
	—	—	—
	18	24	42

$\phi = 0.48$ $X^2 = 9.73$ $p < 0.01$

tacking neighboring Indians and colonists. It was not until a certain degree of centralization occurred that the chiefs were able to prevent an individual warrior from raising a war party and going on a raid. On the basis of Gearing's research, it seems reasonable to hypothesize that the higher the level of political complexity, the less the likelihood of war being initiated by anyone in the political community. This hypothesis is strongly confirmed (see Table 9.5). Apparently centralized political systems are able to prevent unauthorized parties, which would include fraternal interest groups, from engaging in war.

In societies in which any group within the political community can initiate war, I have assumed that leaders of fraternal interest groups to a large extent are the initiating parties. The following hypothesis allows the testing of this assumption: uncentralized political systems are more likely to have war initiated by anyone rather than by an official of the political community if fraternal interest groups are present. The hypothesis is confirmed for both indices of fraternal interest groups (see Tables 9.6 and 9.7).

TABLE 9.6   Political Complexity, Patrilocal Residence, and the Instigation of War

	Patrilocal			Other		
	Initiating Party			Initiating Party		
	Anyone	Official		Anyone	Official	
Centralized political systems	2	10	12	0	4	4
Uncentralized political systems	11	4	15	5	6	11
	13	14	27	5	10	15

Patrilocal: $\phi=0.64$; $X^2=10.99$; $p<0.001$.   Other: $\phi=0.43$; $X^2=2.73$;   n.s.
Difference between ϕ's not significant.

Having demonstrated that there is a strong relationship between uncentralized political systems and the initiation of war by anyone, particularly if fraternal interest groups are present, I infer that uncentralized political systems are probably characterized by a greater amount of internal war than are centralized political systems. This leads to the prediction that the lower the level of political complexity, the more likely the political communities within the cultural unit are to war with each other. As shown in Table 9.8, the direction of the correlation is opposite of that predicted; rather, the data imply that the more complex the political system, the more likely internal war.

The relationship, however, is not significant. There are two possible reasons for this relationship: first, the fact that unauthorized groups are prevented from waging war does not mean that fraternal interest groups cannot engage in warfare if so directed by officials of the political community; second, in centralized political systems the existence of internal war does not depend on fraternal interest groups, for such political systems usually have efficient military organizations that are just as likely to fight

TABLE 9.7   Political Complexity, Polygyny, and the Instigation of War

	Polygyny present			Polygyny absent		
	Initiating Party			Initiating Party		
	Anyone	Official		Anyone	Official	
Centralized political systems	0	5	5	2	9	11
Uncentralized political systems	9	3	12	7	7	14
	9	8	17	9	16	25

Polygyny present: $\phi=0.68$; $X^2=7.79$; $p<0.01$.   Polygyny absent: $\phi=0.33$; $X^2=2.72$;   n.s.
Difference between ϕ's not significant.

TABLE 9.8   Political Complexity and the Occurrence of Internal War

	Internal War		
	Continual or Frequent	Infrequent	
Centralized political systems	10	3	13
Uncentralized political systems	18	11	29
	—	—	—
	28	14	42

$\phi = -0.15$ $X^2 = 0.89$ n.s.

TABLE 9.9   Initiating Party and the Occurrence of Internal War

	Internal War		
	Continual or Frequent	Infrequent	
Initiating party:			
Official	12	8	20
Anyone	13	3	16
	—	—	—
	25	11	36

$\phi = 0.23$ $X^2 = 1.89$ n.s.

with neighboring political communities of the same cultural unit as with culturally different peoples (see *Intersocietal Variables* and Table 9.14).

I have shown, thus far, that it is characteristic of uncentralized political systems that anyone can initiate war. This is particularly the case if fraternal interest groups are present. I have also shown that uncentralized political systems in and of themselves are not prone to more internal war than are centralized political systems; in fact, they are prone to less. Thus it seems that it is the existence of unauthorized raiding parties, rather than the absence of a centralized political system, that leads to internal war. The following hypothesis allows the testing of this conjecture: societies in which anyone can initiate war are more likely to have internal war than societies in which an official initiates war. The data are presented in Table 9.9. The correlation is positive, but it is not significant.

Although neither the relationship between internal war and centralized political systems nor the relationship between internal war and unauthorized raiding parties is significant, it is possible that there is a functional relationship between internal war and some interaction of the two independent variables. If we control for level of political complexity, the magnitude of the relationship between the type of initiating party and the frequency of internal war in uncentralized political systems is increased in comparison with the relationship found in Table 9.9; the correlation also becomes significant (see Table 9.10).

For centralized political systems the direction of the relationship is reversed. Although there are not enough cases to draw any definite conclusions, it appears that centralized political systems in which an official is the only one who can initiate war are more likely to engage in internal war than are centralized political systems in which anyone can initiate war. The data seemingly provide support for the interpretation that in uncentralized political systems wars are initiated by unauthorized parties and officials are the parties who try to maintain peace, while in centralized political systems

TABLE 9.10   Initiating Party, Political Complexity, and the Occurrence of Internal War

	Uncentralized Political Systems			*Centralized Political Systems*		
	Internal War			*Internal War*		
	Continual or Frequent	*Infrequent*		*Continual or Frequent*	*Infrequent*	
Initiating party:						
Official	3	6	9	9	2	11
Anyone	12	2	14	1	1	2
	—	—	—	—	—	—
	15	8	23	10	3	13

Uncentralized: $\phi = +0.54$; $X^2 = 6.63$; $p = 0.01$.   Centralized: $\phi = -0.27$; $X^2 = 0.97$;   n.s.
Difference between ϕ's is significant: $p < 0.05$.

TABLE 9.11   Patrilocal Residence, Political Complexity, and the Occurrence of Internal War

	Uncentralized Political Systems			*Centralized Political Systems*		
	Internal War			*Internal War*		
	Continual or Frequent	*Infrequent*		*Continual or Frequent*	*Infrequent*	
Other	5	6	11	3	0	3
Patrilocal	13	5	18	7	3	10
	—	—	—	—	—	—
	18	11	29	10	3	13

Uncentralized: $\phi = 0.27$; $X^2 = 2.08$;   n.s.   Centralized: $\phi = -0.30$; $X^2 = 1.17$;   n.s.
Difference between ϕ's not significant.

wars are initiated by officials.

I have already demonstrated that the existence of fraternal interest groups, just as the existence of a political system in which anyone can initiate war, is a factor influencing the frequency of internal war (see Tables 9.2 and 9.3). We should also test for a functional relationship between internal war and some interaction of fraternal interest groups and level of political complexity. We can hypothesize that internal war will be found in uncentralized political systems characterized by fraternal interest groups; on the other hand, the presence of fraternal interest groups in centralized political systems — since such groups are prevented from engaging in war without authorization — should have no effect on the frequency of internal war. Tables 9.11 and 9.12 provide the evidence supporting this hypothesis, although the differences between the coefficients are significant only when the index of fraternal interest groups is polygyny (see Table 9.12).

As in Table 9.10, for centralized political systems the direction of the

TABLE 9.12   Polygyny, Political Complexity, and the Occurrence of Internal War

| | Uncentralized Political Systems | | | Centralized Political Systems | | |
| | Internal War | | | Internal War | | |
	Continual or Frequent	Infrequent		Continual or Frequent	Infrequent	
Polygyny absent	6	10	16	7	1	8
Polygyny present	12	1	13	3	2	5
	18	11	29	10	3	13

Uncentralized: $\phi = +0.56$; $X^2 = 9.15$; $p < 0.01$.   Centralized: $\phi = -0.32$; $X^2 = 1.31$; n.s.
Difference between ϕ's is significant: $0.01 < p < 0.02$.

TABLE 9.13   Instigators of Internal War in Uncentralized Political Systems

| | Uncentralized Political Systems | | |
| | Internal War | | |
	Continual or Frequent	Infrequent	
Official:			
Neither polygyny nor patrilocality	2	4†	6
Either polygyny or patrilocality	0*	1	1
Both polygyny and patrilocality	1*	1	2
Anyone:			
Neither polygyny nor patrilocality	1*	1	2
Either polygyny or patrilocality	4*	1	5
Both polygyny and patrilocality	7*	0	7
	15	8	23

* Indicates that internal war is accurately predicted.
† Indicates that absence of internal war is accurately predicted.

relationship is reversed. It appears that centralized political systems without fraternal interest groups are more prone to internal war. A possible interpretation is that since societies without fraternal interest groups lack conflict — specifically feuding — within the political communities, their officials are more willing and able to engage in internal war.

If only uncentralized political systems are considered, either the existence of a political system in which anyone can initiate war or the presence of fraternal interest groups can be used to predict internal war. Since the magnitude of the correlations in the left sections of Tables 9.10 and 9.12 are nearly identical, it is difficult to say which independent variable is the better predictor of internal war. The two variables were combined in Table 9.13 in order to determine whether a more sophisticated analysis would lead to a more accurate prediction of internal war. Using this table we can accurately classify 74 percent of the societies (17 of 23 societies). On the other hand, slightly more accurate predictions can be made with either of the predictor variables alone: using only the type of initiating party as a predictor we can accurately classify 78 percent of the societies (18 of 23 societies); using only fraternal interest groups, indexed by polygyny, as a predictor we can accurately classify 76 percent of the societies (22 of 29 societies). It remains for future research, using a larger sample, to determine which variable is the better predictor of internal war.

Intersocietal Variables

Sociologists (Coser 1956), social psychologists (Sherif et al. 1961), and anthropologists (Otterbein and Otterbein 1965) have argued that intergroup conflict creates cohesion within the contending groups. We may state as a hypothesis that if the groups under consideration are composed of culturally similar political communities, they will unite to fight political communities that are culturally different. (Armed combat between culturally different political communities is referred to as external war.) If culturally similar political communities unite to engage in external war, then internal war will be infrequent. Since external war, the independent variable, can be analyzed in three different ways (see Table 9.14), there are three variations of the hypothesis to be tested. Neither the first of these variations — the more frequently the political communities of a cultural unit attack other societies, the less frequently they war with each other — nor the

TABLE 9.14   Relationship of External War to Internal War*

| | Contingency Table Cells | | | | | | |
	A	B	C	D	ϕ	X^2	p
Frequency of attacking:†	13	9	13	5	0.14	0.75	n.s.
Uncentralized political systems	10	7	7	4	0.05	0.06	n.s.
Centralized political systems	3	2	6	1	0.29	1.03	n.s.
Frequency of being attacked:†	11	8	15	6	0.14	0.80	n.s.
Uncentralized political systems	9	7	8	4	0.11	0.31	n.s.
Centralized political systems	2	1	7	2	0.11	0.15	n.s.
Intersocietal situations:‡	16	11	10	3	0.17	1.20	n.s.
Uncentralized political systems	12	9	5	2	0.13	0.45	n.s.
Centralized political systems	4	2	5	1	0.19	0.44	n.s.

* For the dependent variable cells A and C represent the societies with continual or frequent internal war and cells B and D represent societies with infrequent internal war.

† For the independent variable cells A and B represent societies with continual or frequent external war and cells C and D represent societies with infrequent external war.

‡ For the independent variable cells A and B represent societies that continually or frequently war when continually or frequently attacked, societies that infrequently war when continually or frequently attacked, and societies that attack continually or frequently while only being infrequently attacked (these are cells A, B, and D of Table 15); cells C and D represent societies that infrequently attack other societies and are themselves infrequently attacked (cell C of Table 15).

second — the more frequently a cultural unit is attacked, the less frequently the political communities within the cultural unit war with each other — is confirmed (see Table 9.14). Although the correlations are positive, they are not significant. Before testing the third variation, it is necessary to test an auxiliary hypothesis, since both the independent and dependent variables of the hypothesis will be used to construct a measure for indexing external war.

The assumption made by many writers that revenge and retaliation play a prominent role in war can be submitted to empirical test if it is formulated as follows: the more frequently the political communities of a cultural unit are attacked, the more frequently they will attack other societies. As shown in Table 9.15, the assumption, thus formulated, is strongly confirmed. Cell B of Table 9.15 represents societies that continually or frequently war when continually or frequently attacked; cell A represents societies that infrequently war when continually or frequently attacked; cell D represents societies that attack continually or frequently while only being infrequently attacked; cell C represents societies that infrequently attack other societies and are themselves infrequently attacked. Cells A, B, and D, if combined, represent an intersocietal situation in which culturally different political communities engage in warfare. Cell C represents an intersocietal situation in which external war infrequently occurs. The dichotomy between cells A, B, and D and cell C can be used to construct a measure for indexing external war. Using this measure as an independent variable, a third variation of the hypothesis can be formulated: the more frequently the political communities of a cultural unit war with other societies, the less likely they are to war with each other. This variation, like the first two, is not confirmed (see Table 9.14).

Because none of the three variations of the hypothesis was confirmed, an attempt was made to see if external war could have an influence upon in-

TABLE 9.15   Frequency of Attacking
or Being Attacked

	Frequency of attacking		
	Infrequent	*Continual or Frequent*	
Frequency of being attacked:			
Continual or Frequent	5	18	23
Infrequent	15	9	24
	20	27	47

$\phi = 0.41$ $X^2 = 7.98$ $p < 0.01$

ternal war, if the level of political complexity was held constant. Since a centralized political system has an official who can prevent unauthorized parties from engaging in war (see Table 9.5), the official presumably can ally his political community with a neighboring political community and direct the military organization to unite forces with the military organization of the new ally. On the other hand, an uncentralized political system lacks officials with power and authority to control the activities of its warriors, and consequently the officials are unable to form alliances with neighboring political communities. Therefore, when an uncentralized political community is threatened by external war, its officials are unable to form alliances; but when a centralized political system is threatened, alliances can be formed. If this argument is valid, there should be no relationship between external and internal war for uncentralized political systems, but for centralized political systems there should be an inverse relationship between external and internal war. However, for none of the three variations of the hypothesis do the data support this argument (see Table 9.14).

Although case studies do not prove or disprove general hypotheses, examples are available that illustrate that the existence of external war does not necessarily reduce the frequency of internal war nor cause centralized political communities within the same cultural unit to unite. A study of a Yoruba war in the nineteenth century (Ajayi 1964) shows that the jealous officials of various warring Yoruba states were more fearful of each other than of culturally different political communities, the Fulani and Dahomey. Even when Yorubaland was invaded by these enemies, the officials could not put aside their jealousies and come to the aid of the state that was bearing the brunt of the attack. In fact, as Ajayi's analysis clearly demonstrates, several Yoruba states allied themselves with the Fulani and Dahomey in order to obtain help in their attempts to defeat other Yoruba states.

Conclusion

Three categories of variables have been examined in this study for their possible influence upon the occurrence of internal war. The same three sets of categories were utilized in a cross-cultural study of feuding (Otterbein and Otterbein 1965). If the results of these studies, conducted with two independently drawn samples, are compared in terms of these categories it will be possible not only to discuss the results of this study of internal war, but also to draw some general conclusions concerning the relationship between fraternal interest groups, political organization, and armed combat.[12]

In these two studies, the existence of fraternal interest groups, as indexed by either patrilocal residence or polygyny, was found to be a factor influencing the frequency of both feuding and internal war. The hypotheses in these studies can be combined to read: societies with fraternal interest groups are more likely to have both feuding and internal war than societies without fraternal interest groups. Such groups form small-scale military organizations that attack enemies who are either members of the same or of a neighboring political community within the cultural unit. (Although the tabulations are not presented in this study, there is no relationship between fraternal interest groups and external war.)

In both studies it was found that level of political complexity had no significant influence upon either feuding or internal war. That is, centralized political systems are just as likely to be characterized by feuding and internal war as are uncentralized political systems. However, at this point the similarity of results between the two studies ceases. When the relationship between fraternal interest groups and feuding is controlled for level of political complexity, no significant difference between uncentralized and centralized political systems occurs. But when the relationship between fraternal interest groups and internal war is controlled for level of political complexity, a significant difference occurs between uncentralized and centralized political systems. Thus fraternal interest groups were found to be a factor directly influencing the frequency of internal war only in uncentralized political systems; in centralized political systems the presence of fraternal interest groups was inversely related to internal war. To summarize, in uncentralized political systems fraternal interest groups are a determinant of both feuding and internal war, whereas in centralized political systems fraternal interest groups are a determinant of feuding but not internal war. It has been argued in both studies that officials in uncentralized political systems are unable to prevent fraternal interest groups from engaging in either feuding or internal war; on the other hand, it is difficult to understand why officials in centralized political systems—who apparently can prevent unauthorized raiding parties, including fraternal interest groups, from engaging in internal war—would permit fraternal interest groups to engage in feuding.

The answer to this difficulty was sought in the type of relationship that a political community has with its neighbors. Warfare, the most violent form of intersocietal relationship, was chosen, on theoretical grounds, as the factor most likely to produce cohesion within the contending groups. War (which would include both internal and external war, since a distinction between these was not made in the feuding study) was found to have no relationship to feuding, nor were external and internal war found to be related. However, when the relationship between war and feuding was controlled for level of political complexity, a strong relationship between war and the absence of feuding was found in centralized political systems, but in uncentralized political systems war and feuding were positively correlated. Apparently officials in centralized political systems intervene to prevent the development of feuding only when the society is engaged in war. On the other hand, controlling for level of political complexity does not affect the relationship between external and internal war. In other words, both uncentralized and centralized political systems within a cultural unit engage in internal war with the same frequency as they do external war. Seemingly officials in centralized political systems do not unite, and thereby eliminate internal war, when engaged in external war.

The discrepancy in results between the feuding and internal war studies stems, I believe, from the difference between the units of analysis used in the studies. In the feuding study the focus is upon single political communities, and in the present study the focus is upon all the political communities within a particular cultural unit. The difference corresponds to the distinction made by Bohannan between unicentric and multicentric power systems (1963:283-284). A political community, by definition, has a single center of power, the degree of power varying with the type of political system. A grouping of political communities constitutes a system with multiple centers of power. Since feuding, by definition, occurs within a political community, it likewise occurs within a unicentric power system, but warfare, which by definition occurs between political communities, is characteristic of multicentric power systems. In a single political community or unicentric power system there is an official who, if he has sufficient power, can and will, if he perceives that the inter–political community situation demands it, intervene between feuding fraternal interest groups. Roberts (1965:209) has argued that in societies with "higher political integration" (most of the centralized political systems in the two studies would fall in this category), officials are reluctant to test the limits of their authority except under demanding circumstances. On the other hand, in a grouping of political communities or a multicentric power system there are as many officials as there are political communities. Each official exercises authority only within his political community; he can only control, in centralized political systems, or attempt to control, in uncentralized political systems, the activities of the military organization(s) of his political community. The only condition, ruling out conquest, under which internal war would cease would be that in which all the officials within the cultural unit formed alliances between their political communities and prevented their military organizations from attacking one another's political communities. Although this can theoretically occur when the political communities are attacked by a culturally different political community, the fear that one's political community will become subordinated or incorporated into another political community often prevents alliances from occurring. An official may also fear that he will become politically insignificant or be assassinated by his ally. Rather than form an alliance he may prefer to witness the defeat of a rival political community at the hands of a culturally different political community. Such conditions prevailed in the nineteenth-century Yoruba war described above.

Notes

1. I am indebted to my wife, Charlotte Swanson Otterbein, for advice on statistical procedures and for helpful comments and criticisms on this chapter. I am also indebted to Raoul Naroll for advice on sampling procedures.

2. This is Naroll's definition of a territorial team. The term "political community" is preferable because it is difficult to conceptualize large states as teams.

3. A cultural unit apparently differs from Naroll's cultunit that by definition seemingly cannot include more than one state: "People who are domestic speakers of a common distinct language and who belong either to the same state or the same contact group" (1964a:286). The cultunit concept was not employed since it was felt desirable for the purposes of this study to have a definition that would include culturally similar states, such as the Yoruba, within the same unit.

4. A similar distinction between external and internal war has been made by Ember and Baldwin (1965:5).

5. Capital letters in parentheses are code symbols used in column 16 of the Ethnographic Atlas.

6. Only four of the cultural units in this study differed from a society drawn from the Ethnographic Atlas. The cultural unit for the Mutair was the Bedouin tribes of Saudia Arabia, for the Comox it was the Coast Salish, for Santa Anna it was the Rio Grande pueblos, and for the Trumai it was the refugee groups in the upper Xingu River basin.

7. Not only was the sample drawn to reduce the possible influence of diffusion, but after the study was completed the linked pair method (Naroll 1964b) was used in order to rule out the possibility that diffusion through borrowing, dialect differentiation, or migration from societal fission rather than functional relationships between the variables could have produced the correlations. The method, which tests for resemblances among neighboring societies in terms of selected variables, was used to determine whether the seven variables employed in this study varied independently of geographical propinquity. The procedure followed consisted of plotting each society on a world map using the degrees of latitude and longitude given in the Ethnographic Atlas. A north-south alignment of societies was obtained by dividing the world into vertical strips 15° in width, and an east-west alignment was obtained by dividing the world into horizontal strips of the same width. Details of how to employ the method for obtaining the phi coefficient of association and the associated chi-square value are to be found in Naroll (1964b). Using the north-south alignment, the phi coefficients, the chi-square values, and the probability levels using one-tailed tests of significance are as follows for each variable: internal war, Φ

= 0.36, X^2 = 5.36, 0.01 <p< 0.05; attacking, Φ = 0.13, X^2 = 0.79, n.s.; attacked, Φ = 0.06, X^2 = 0.19, n.s.; initiating party, Φ = 0.13, X^2 = 0.66, n.s.; political system, Φ = −0.19, X^2 = 1.90, n.s.; residence, Φ = −0.01, X^2 = 0.01, n.s.; polygyny, Φ = 0.10, X^2 = 0.47, n.s. Using the east-west alignment, the phi coefficients, the chi-square values, and probability levels are as follows: internal war, Φ = 0.14, X^2 = 0.86, n.s.; attacking, Φ = −0.22, X^2 = 2.24, n.s.; attacked, Φ = 0.02, X^2 = 0.00, n.s.; initiating party, Φ = 0.03, X^2 = 0.03, n.s.; political system, Φ = 0.17, X^2 = 1.49, n.s.; residence, Φ = 0.07, X^2 = 0.24, n.s.; polygyny, Φ = 0.10, X^2 = 0.47, n.s. Only one of the fourteen correlations is significant at the 0.05 level. Thus only one of the variables, internal war, can conceivably be influenced by diffusion, and this interpretation is not conclusive since the other alignment test is not significant. Therefore, it can be concluded that it is highly unlikely that the results of this study can be attributed to the influence of diffusion.

8. Of the sixty-one societies dropped, sixteen were dropped because only foreign language references were found, sixteen because the sources were unavailable, five because the society was a peasant community or a modern nation, and twenty-four because data on military organization, tactics, and causes of war were not in the sources. It should be noted that even if foreign language references had been used (most would not have been available in Lawrence, Kansas) and if all sources had been available, many of the societies would still have been dropped because of lack of data on war. It is also to be noted that sources on seventy-four societies were perused in order to locate fifty societies for which there were sufficient data on warfare.

9. A recent cross-cultural study by Frank W. Young tests the hypothesis that "local warfare predicts in some measure the highly institutionalized types of male solidarity, and if community conflict is absent solidarity is also likely to be absent" (1965:71). Although this hypothesis is similar to the fraternal interest group hypothesis, it differs in two respects: First, I attribute internal war (and also feuding) to the unauthorized attacks of small groups of related males, whereas Young (1965:70) considers "the forms of armed conflict that, as a unit, actively involve all or nearly all the men of the community." Second, I view fraternal interest groups as producing internal war; Young, on the other hand, reverses the direction of causality and examines the influence of warfare upon male solidarity.

10. For all contingency tables values of Φ and X^2 are presented. Statements of significance or probability level are based upon the value of the X^2 statistic (with d.f. = 1) in those cases where N > 20; where N ⩽ 20, such statements are based upon Fisher's exact test. All significance statements are based upon two-tailed tests.

11. The disproportionate distribution of cases for both variables affects the size of the coefficient of correlation and thus could be one reason for the lack of significance (Ferguson 1959:198-199).

12. For a more detailed comparison of these two studies see Otterbein (1968).

References

Ajayi, J. F. Ade. 1964. The Ijaye War, 1860-5: a case study in Yoruba wars and politics. In *Yoruba Warfare in the Nineteenth Century.* J. F. Ade Ajayi and Robert

Smith. London: Cambridge University Press.

Bohannan, Paul. 1963. *Social anthropology.* New York: Holt, Rinehart & Winston.

Coser, Lewis A. 1956. *The Functions of Social Conflict.* Glencoe: The Free Press.

Ember, Melvin, and Carol R. Baldwin. 1965. The conditions that favor matrilocal and patrilocal residence. Presented at the American Anthropological Association Annual Meetings, November 19, 1965.

Ferguson, George A. 1959. *Statistical Analysis in Psychology and Education.* New York: McGraw-Hill Book Company.

Gearing, Fred. 1962. Priests and warriors. *American Anthropological Association Memoir* 93.

Murdock, George P. 1957. World ethnographic sample. *American Anthropologist* 59:664-687.

_____. 1962-1964. Ethnographic atlas. *Ethnology* 1-3.

Naroll, Raoul. 1964a. On ethnic unit classification. *Current Anthropology* 5:283-312.

_____. 1964b. A fifth solution to Galton's problem. *American Anthropologist* 66:863-867.

Otterbein, Keith F. 1968. Cross-cultural studies of armed combat. *Buffalo Studies* 4:91-109.

Otterbein, Keith F., and Charlotte S. 1965. An eye for an eye, a tooth for a tooth: a cross-cultural study of feuding. *American Anthropologist* 67:1470-1482.

Roberts, John M. 1965. Oaths, autonomic ordeals, and power. *American Anthropologist* 67(6), pt. 2:186-212.

Service, Elman R. 1962. *Primitive Social Organization.* New York: Random House.

Sherif, Muzafer, et al. 1961. *Intergroup Conflict and Cooperation: The Robbers Cave Experiment.* Norman, University of Oklahoma, Institute of Group Relations.

Van Velzen, H.U.E. Thoden, and W. Van Wetering. 1960. Residence, power groups and intrasocietal aggression. *International Archives of Ethnography* 49:169-200.

Young, Frank W. 1965. *Initiation Ceremonies: A Cross-Cultural Study of Status Dramatization.* New York: Bobbs-Merrill Company.

Part 4
Sociopsychological Inquiries

Introduction

Sociopsychological inquiries into the causes of war and the conditions for peace may be seen as part of the larger interdisciplinary development of the behavioral approach in the study of international relations. As an offshoot of both sociology and psychology, social psychology strives toward the formulation of general propositions about human social (intergroup) behavior grounded in empirical observations, making use of a variety of available methods and tools such as public opinion and survey research, field interviews, content analysis, and simulations and other laboratory experiments. The social psychology of international relations is an interdisciplinary endeavor largely concerned with the human dimensions of state interaction. In short, it purports to be an applied social science of international behavior.

The assumptions and approaches associated with the social psychology of international relations can be specified. First, war is conceptualized as a particular and lethal species of social conflict; hence, its root cause is being sought in the causal role of social interaction between "predispositional" (attitudinal) and "situational" (societal) variables. This approach belongs to what Kenneth N. Waltz (1959) has called "the second image" explanation of war in his three-image typology of international conflict. To put it differently, the causal analysis is grounded neither in human nature removed from social context nor in the international system separated from human context. Instead it is related to the internal societal defects, pressures, and stresses that may be externalized in international hostility and conflict behavior.

Second, the primary focus of the social psychology of international relations still centers on human behavior. Unlike the ethological-psychological inquiries we have already reviewed, however, this approach takes sufficient note of cognitive and societal variables in its explanation of human conflict. National behavior is assumed to be an aggregate transformation of a variety of behaviors on the part of many individuals of different roles, interests, and influence in the society, thereby helping to shift a given social system from a condition of peace to a state of war. War is thus conceptualized as a function of sociopsychological dynamics located within the separate states that together comprise international society. The underlying methodological assumption here is that the real characteristics of the international system can be more accurately delineated by reference to the behavioral characteristics of individual state actors rather than through a macroanalysis of the system as a whole.

Third, attempts to capture the analytically elusive state behavior center on describing and explaining certain national and international images of conflict and cooperation within national society as relevant socio-psychological variables in foreign policy processes. "If men define situations as real," observed W. I. Thomas (1928:572), the dean of American sociologists, "they are real in their consequences." This noted statement, which is claimed as having now become "a theorem basic to the social sciences" (Merton 1949:179), is also one of the central analytical assumptions guiding sociopsychological research in international relations. Hence, there is great stress on the potential relevance of sociopsychological research in such areas as cognition, learning, motivation, and personality as they relate to the problems of state interaction. The articles by Robert Jervis (Chapter 19) and by Kenneth E. Boulding (Chapter 22), though subsumed under different headings later in the book, easily qualify as socio-psychological inquiries into foreign and international relations.

Finally, the social psychology of international relations firmly links human behavior to societal and organizational context. Such analytical linkage is based on the assumption that man's behavior reflects not only his own individual attributes but also the group norms and values of the social system to which he belongs. Viewed in this light, statism as the embodiment of the character of the national social structure with all of its concomitant images about the power, purpose, and authority of the state in the modern international system is regarded as a major determinant in the causation of war.

What are the necessary and sufficient conditions for the causation of intergroup conflict? R. M. Williams (1947) advanced four such conditions: intergroup visibility, intergroup contact, intergroup competition, and intergroup differences in values and behavioral patterns. The chapter by Ross Stagner, one of the pioneers in the sociopsychological approach to the problems of war and peace, centers on social conflict in the framework of a homeostatic conception of human nature. He is concerned with the cognitive or perceptual factors determining the direction of human conflict behavior based on the premise that people's national and international (in-group and out-group) images tend to be highly personalized. Ethnocentrism is stressed as an important psychological barrier to international cooperation. Stagner's conclusion calls for *"diluting sovereignty* by building up groups and institutions of a supranational character."

Employing the response-to-frustration theory of human aggression, Ted Gurr as a political scientist adopts a sociopsychological framework in his theoretical and empirical analysis of the causes and conditions of civil violence within the structure of the nation-state. The relationship between attitudinal and societal variables is examined in terms of systemic frustration called "relative deprivation"—actors' perceived discrepancy between their expectations and capabilities. Gurr persuasively argues that relative deprivation constitutes the necessary precondition for violent civil conflict but its likelihood and magnitude of resulting in overt civil violence are determined through a funnel of mediating societal and institutional variables. Much of the chapter centers on Gurr's elaboration of eleven proportions that identify the general causes of civil violence.

The chapter by the Feierabends is a comparative cross-national study of conflict behaviors in eighty-four polities for the period 1948-1962. Like Gurr's study, this study also adopts and tests the response-to-frustration model. The key hypothesis is that political stability is a function of relative lack of systemic frustration (the discrepancy between social wants and social satisfaction, in the Feierabends's terms), or conversely political instability as measured by violent or aggressive behavior is a function of systemic frustration. Note that the study confirms the hypothesized relationship between the level of systemic frustration and the level of political instability. Furthermore, the Feierabends equate their frustration index with the modernity index and then conclude that the global instability level increased sharply during the fifteen years under study based on the aggregation of frustration index data of the eighty-four countries.

While sociopsychological inquiries represent more useful, relevant, and contemporary tools than the other types of inquiries into the causal analysis of war examined earlier in the book, they still leave some problems unresolved. The question of the proper unit or level of analysis—and the closely related question of generalizing or extrapolating from one situation to another—remains for consideration. Is there a necessary causal chain of interaction between internal and external conflict behaviors of nation-states? Rudolph J. Rummel's (1968) empirical analysis concluded that national attributes were not highly predictive of national involvement in foreign conflict. Similarly, Michael Haas's (1968) study negates the hypothesis that national stress or strain usually precedes involvement in international conflict. Note also how the hypothesized relationship between foreign conflict and a number of societal and institutional variables comes out in another study by Haas included in Part 5 (Chapter 15). Closer to home and to our recent experience, would it not be more tenable to argue that internal stress in American society was mainly an *outcome* or *effect*, rather than a prior *cause*, of its aggressive conflict behavior in Indochina? In view of such contrary evidence, the Feierabends's measurement and resulting generalization of the global instability level based on systemic frustrations within the boundaries of the eighty-four polities are debatable.

Moreover, the sociopsychological framework shares the dominant bias in contemporary social science research against work that explicitly employs a normative frame of reference as á way of defining social problems to be researched. This tends to constrain the potential contribution of social psychology to peace research as a policy science. Note, for example, that the normative and prescriptive implications of the studies by Gurr and the Feierabends are left curiously unspecified for the elimination of the war system. Note also how their "rigorous empirical methodology" steers them in the direction of overt physical violence, overlooking the role and reality of structural violence within and between polities of nation-states.

One may also argue that social psychology is too generalized a field of human social behavior to contribute much to a careful study of war-making processes. If we are to take the "minds of men" approach within the heuristic framework of the social psychology of international relations, the question as to *whose* minds are most immediately relevant in the initiation of foreign conflict behavior remains virtually unexplored. Surely, there is no such thing as the "one man, one vote" formula in the modern war-making process. Hence, survey research on the people's images, prejudices, and stereotypes is of only indirect value. Our attention needs to be more sharply focused on the role of "war makers," or on the principal role of what Richard J. Barnet (1972) has called in the context of American foreign policy "the national security managers," men who structure the presidential choices by controlling and interpreting the information that reaches him. The cognitive, social, and bureaucratic variables impinging on the behaviors of the national security managers throughout the world open up a potentially most promising path for sociopsychological research on war and peace in our times. Obviously, the diverse governmental settings in the countries of the world make it essential to initiate a serious inquiry into comparative styles of war making.

10

Personality Dynamics
and Social Conflict

Ross Stagner

"Wars begin in the minds of men," asserts the UNESCO charter. This is, of course, a view widely held outside of our profession as well as within it. Mr. George F. Kennan, distinguished analyst of foreign policy, has also stressed the psychological determinants of American activities. In 1954 he wrote, "It is precisely these subjective factors — factors relating to the state of mind of many of our own people — rather than the external circumstances, that seem to constitute the most alarming component of our situation. It is such things as the lack of flexibility in outlook, the stubborn complacency about ourselves and our society, the frequent compulsion to extremism, the persistent demand for absolute solutions . . . it is these things in the American character that give added gravity to a situation which would in any case be grave enough" (Kennan 1954:32).

We may appropriately enough note that Mr. John Foster Dulles, whose rigidity Kennan was implicitly criticizing, had in 1938 taken a stand on the same basis as Kennan. Dulles wrote, "There has been a grave misconception of the nature of peace. Peace has been identified with the status quo, stability and rigidity" (Dulles 1939:ix). And elsewhere he stated, "The human race craves certainty and precision. . . . It treats the world as a basket in which are placed packages, each wrapped, labeled and tied in its separate container." (Dulles 1939:156). "The ambitious and dynamic powers bitterly resent a dominant world philosophy under which peace and international morality are equated with the preservation of rigidities which for long operated, as they believe, to protect selfishness and to prolong inequities" (Dulles 1939:162-163).

Some readers may suspect that I have chosen this quotation from our late secretary of state because of his emphasis on the craving for certainty and

Reprinted by permission of the publisher from Ross Stagner, "Personality Dynamics and Social Conflict," *Journal of Social Issues* 17 (1961):28-44.

related rigidity. This suspicion is justified. I want to deal with problems of social conflict in the framework of a homeostatic conception of human nature, and an emphasis on perception as a major process. Let me remind you of only a few basic assumptions which will assume considerable importance in the analysis.

A Homeostatic Conception of Human Nature

According to this view, the dominant principle in the behavior of living organisms is the maintenance of certain vital constancies of the internal environment — that is, the steady states of oxygen, food, water, and other essentials for survival. In the service of these constancies man creates a predictable environment, in the physical world by way of agriculture, housing, economic systems, and the like; in his personal world by way of the perceptual constancies. He learns to adapt to the changing aspects of physical reality, *distorting* sensory inputs to correspond to the most probable physical object. He creates a *constant* perceptual environment, and as far as possible he stabilizes the physical and social milieu within which he lives. Some individuals even come to value the ideological environment which they associate with survival and mobilize energy to resist change in this structure of institutions, beliefs, and values (Stagner 1961:69-86).

The specific application of this thesis which I shall propose in this paper is that man comes to value his nation, or other social group, as an essential part of his environment, and mobilizes energy to protect it. Further, as a part of this process, he distorts the input of information in such a fashion as to protect valued aspects of his social environment, and these distortions contribute in no small degree to the intensity and bitterness of social conflicts. The rigidity referred to by Messrs. Kennan and Dulles is a key aspect of this distortion.

In this connection it is important, I think, to clarify a source of confusion which sometimes creeps into discussions of homeostasis. Man needs a *predictable environment,* a stable milieu, within which he can function. But this is not to say that he wants to make the same responses over and over. It is not uniformity of behavior, but an environment within which he can anticipate the consequences of behavior, which is essential.

In an agrarian civilization, man's need for such a stable environment was largely met by the uniformity of physical laws, the weather and the seasons, plants and lower animals. But as men multiplied and lived closer together, their very spontaneity and unpredictability as individuals compelled the creation of bureaucracy as a device for imposing some order upon chaos — for improving the stability of the milieu. Strong men imposed rules on their fellows to obtain predictability: but the strong man did not expect to, and generally did not, conform to the rules. As Dalton (1959) has pointed out, the efficient executive is one who knows when to ignore or circumvent rules. And unquestionably, man will go on trying to evade bureaucratic controls, just as he has always sought to master the limitations imposed by physical and biological laws.

Ethnocentrism

It was over sixty years ago that Hobson, a British social scientist, wrote, "The actual direct efficient forces in history are human motives." Yet, despite sporadic efforts, psychologists as a group have contributed relatively little to the understanding of social conflict.

Some efforts, of course, have been made in this direction. The Society for the Psychological Study of Social Issues (SPSSI) established in 1936 a Committee on War and Peace. In recent years, the American Psychological Association has created a committee to study the place of psychology in the maintenance of world peace. I should like to urge all of you to cooperate with this committee with suggestions, with questions, with research proposals.

I would like to hark back for just a moment to the work of the SPSSI Committee on War and Peace, whose labors were rudely interrupted by Pearl Harbor. A major conclusion had early been reached by this committee, on the basis of a careful study of the writings of historians, economists, and political scientists—viz., that the major psychological factor involved in the occurrence of international war was the attitude complex called "nationalism" (Stagner et al. 1942). The political scientists, for example, stressed the phenomenon of sovereignty; disputes could not be settled peacefully because nations recognized no higher authority to which they could be submitted. Blackstone's famous *Commentaries* referred to sovereignty as "the supreme irresistible, absolute, uncontrolled authority." Clearly persons who hold such a view cannot tolerate the notion of yielding to a court of justice; equally clearly there is an element here of psychotic delusions of grandeur. Similarly, in economic discussions of war, stress was placed on a struggle for competitive advantage, with ruthless disregard for the welfare of other nations, through policies of economic nationalism (Stagner et al. 1942).

The defining features of nationalism are generally considered to be two in number: an exaggerated glorification of the nation, its virtues, its benefactions, its right to superiority; and an exaggerated denigration of nations perceived as being in opposition, these nations generally being seen as bad, cruel, vicious, and untrustworthy.

When we look at this description, we readily observe that a similar pattern appears in other forms of social conflict. During the religious wars in Europe 300 years ago, a comparable glorification of one's in-group and vilification of the out-group were common; and anti-Semitism in this country shows this pattern in less bizarre form. The white supremacists of our southern states, and in extreme the Afrikaners of South Africa, hold similar delusions of racial grandeur and of the inferiority of colored races. Partisans of labor unions and of industrial owners do not show quite the same extremes of grandeur and hostility, but certainly many of them suggest that all virtue is on their side, all stupidity, violence, or greed on the other. It seems, therefore, that this bipolar attitude of grandeur and evil is a psychological feature of all social conflicts. It is unfortunate that we have no generally accepted term for labeling this pattern. Ethnocentrism is undoubtedly the most appropriate term, but it has become identified with religious and racial prejudice. I shall use ethnocentrism to identify this general trend toward group centeredness, and nationalism for its specific form in international conflict, on which I shall focus.

The central problem, from the point of view of personality theory, is how the motives and perceptions of individuals influence their decisions on social issues. Psychoanalytic writers on these problems, such as Glover, Hopkins, Durbin and Bowlby, and Alix Strachey, have tended to emphasize the decisive influence of motivation, frequently in the form of a "death instinct." In opposition, I wish to stress the perceptual approach to these questions.

Hostility as a Critical Factor in Social Conflicts

Let me first deal with the argument that the decisive consideration in major social conflicts is the level of aggressive drive or hostility. I propose to argue that this is not an important consideration and indeed that it can, in some degree, be ignored as both a theoretical and a practical problem.

As a theoretical problem aggression has mainly been conceptualized in one of two ways: first, as an instinctive drive, as in the nineteenth-century "instinct of pugnacity" associated with the names of McDougall and James; and its modern variant, the "death instinct" proposed by Freud and still advocated by some orthodox analysts. Secondly, aggression has been conceptualized as a derivative of frustration—largely in a means-end relationship, proposed by John Dollard and the Yale School, and also in a tension-release formulation by Norman Maier (Dollard et al. 1939; Maier 1949).

A hereditary conception of aggression leads nowhere with regard to social conflict. If man is born with a given potential for aggression, we must apparently assume that in the course of his life he will act out this potential in some form. But aggression, as even the Freudians agree, may be channeled into face-to-face hostility, into competitive behavior, and even into work, or it may be vented in group competition and conflict of a nonviolent nature. Thus the theory cannot logically lead to any kind of prediction about the occurrence of violent social conflict, whether between nations, or classes, or races.

A similar conclusion must be reached with respect to the frustration-aggression hypothesis. This view is somewhat more directly relevant to problems of social interaction because it carries an important, sometimes unstated, assumption that the preferred outlet for aggression will be an attack on the frustrating agent. This would suggest that, if large numbers of individuals find themselves being frustrated by, let us say, communist tactics, they will become hostile to communists. The inadequacy of this approach is suggested by the fact that most of the applications of the theory to social problems make use of displaced aggression, as in the famous study of southern lynchings, in which it appeared that a drop in the price of cotton led to more aggressive outbursts. But opposed to this we have the observation of criminologists that crimes of violence for the entire population increase in times of prosperity, not in times of depression. It thus appears that the crucial question is not, What led to the increase in aggressive acts? The question must be phrased: What variables determine the direction to be taken in expressions of hostility? It seems likely that the groups perceived as "bad" and therefore suitable for attack, and preferably "weak," hence not in a position to retaliate, will be the objects of aggression.

As a practical problem neither an instinctivist nor an environmentalist theory of aggression has much value from the point of view of blunting or disarming social conflicts. Both the Freudians and the Yale School advocate reducing frustrations to a socially tolerable minimum, especially for young children; but this seems to be based on concern for the mental health of the individual more than for social health.

As a concrete example, let me say that many people suppose the level of hostile tension experienced by the leaders of the Soviet Union to be a factor of great importance as regards the possible outbreak of World War III. It is assumed that these men may allow, or even order, acts which will precipitate a nuclear war. But does the level of aggression have anything to do with such a decision? On the hereditary assumption, we must conclude that their tension levels are already determined and what we do is irrelevant. If we look at the problem in terms of a frustration theory, we must certainly conclude that the men in the Kremlin are not hungry, they are not cold and wretched, and they have tremendous gratifications for any drive toward power which may motivate them. Can we suppose, then, that their *personal* level of frustration is relevant to a decision on international policy? I think not.

There is, of course, the theory of leader behavior expressed variously by Plato, by Machiavelli, and by more recent advisors to rulers: if your people are aggressive, encourage them to hate a foreign enemy, thus displacing their hatred from yourself. But even on this kind of theorizing, it must be clear that the crucial consideration becomes this: What are the perceptual factors determining the *direction* of aggression? The level of aggressive tension then becomes a remote rather than an immediate factor — not to be ignored, but not open to practical manipulation if we seek to reduce the probability of organized violence.

In opposition to those views of social conflict which stress drive, therefore, I want to talk about the decisive role of perception. Essentially, what I shall say is that for both theoretical and practical reasons, we should focus on how members of groups perceive other groups and their goals and tactics. To quote Kenneth Boulding (1959:120), "the people whose decisions determine the policies and actions of nations do not respond to the 'objective' facts of the situation, whatever that may mean, but to their 'image' of the situation."

The Decisive Role of Perception

Perception can operate in the service of creating a predictable environment in at least three ways. First, it can magnify certain information inputs, giving them greater weight; and secondly, the obvious corollary, it can diminish the importance of other cues. Finally, actual distortions may occur in quality and magnitude. The phenomena of size constancy, for example, require that the individual differentiate among cues of apparent size, and weight them in such a fashion as to give the closest approximation to the assumed "real object."

Perception in social affairs shows the same attributes. The real virtues of our nation are magnified; our sins are blocked out. The evils of the enemy are exaggerated, and his virtues ignored. Finally, cues indicative of behavior contrary to our expectations are often distorted to support the rigid percepts already organized. The great British statesman, Edmund Burke, said a long time ago, "We can never walk surely but by being sensible of our blindnesses." We must recognize our tendency to exclude certain information from consciousness. Another early insight on this topic comes from the Greek historian, Thucydides, who commented that, "Different eyewitnesses give different accounts of the same events, speaking out of partiality for one side or the other, or else from imperfect memories." Since memory distortions seem to obey the same dynamic principles as perceptual distortions, it appears that most erroneous reports stem from dynamic influences within the personalities of the reporters.

But let us not assume that only reporters and historians are guilty of partiality. Diplomats, presidents, and prime ministers likewise have their blind spots, their distortions, their misperceptions. So does the famous "man in the street." Each tends to see reality only in the manner which is compatible with his own motives and past experiences.

I propose this assertion as a starting point for my discussion of social conflict: social conflicts are rational if we grant the accuracy of the way in which the participants perceive the issues. It is easy enough for the detached observer to see the irrationality of both sides, let us say, in the Spanish-American War of 1898, in the 1959 steel strike, or in the religious wars of three hundred years ago. But if we learn to look at the matters in controversy as they were seen by the participants, it becomes clear that perceptual distortion was a fundamental process. Once given these misperceptions, given a distorted reality, the behavior of the participants was reasonable.

I shall propose, in other words, that the behavior of the communist is rational once we grant his way of perceiving Western democracy; the behavior of the white supremacist is rational if we accept his way of perceiving the Negro; the behavior of the steelworkers' union is rational if we grant this way of perceiving the companies' proposals in changes in work rules, and so on.

This view, in effect, says that it is inappropriate for psychologists to label other people as "good" or "bad," even if we do it in fancy terms like authoritarian aggression, autistic hostility, unresolved Oedipus complexes, and the like. I suggest that the problem of psychological theory is not to pin labels on those persons who hold attitudes with which we disagree, but to analyze the processes by which certain distorted perceptions become established and to consider ways in which these ways of seeing reality might be modified.

Such an approach does not eliminate any occasion for concern with needs, desires, emotions, and conflicts. It does shift the focus of theoretical exploration from the motivational state itself to the effects of motivation on perceiving — recognizing, of course, that any distinction between the two processes is logical, not functional.

We must be concerned not solely with the processes of perceptual distortion and rigidity, but also with content. Many perceptual distortions are strictly interpersonal and have no social implications. Some relate to religious, racial, or industrial conflicts, others to national problems. I should like to illustrate my remarks primarily with reference to questions of international hostility.

Whittlesey (1942) reproduced a propaganda map issued by Nazi Germany early in the campaign against Czechoslovakia. It visualized that small nation as a dagger aimed at the heart of Germany, with bombers readily capable of saturating the German nation. What it ignored was the much greater extent to which Czechoslovakia was at the mercy of Germany, a fact which became apparent in 1938. One need not assume that the German author was aware of this distortion; consider the excitement in the United States today over the situation in Cuba, which is even less capable of mounting an assault on our country. Looked at from the other side, note that Americans approve strongly of the ring of air bases we have built around Russia, many of which are as close to that nation as Cuba is to ours.

The perceptual distortion here arises from the fact that we perceive our nation and its purposes as good and pure, hence our bases are no threat to anyone. Russia, on the other hand, is obviously bad, cruel, and untrustworthy, hence Russian bases are a great menace to world peace. Please do not interpret my remarks as implying that a Russian base in Cuba would be innocent and virtuous; what I do want to observe is that objectively similar events look quite different when viewed through nationalistic spectacles.

We should also remember that a policy of secrecy is no monopoly of the Soviet Union. Just after World War II our futile efforts to keep the A-bomb secret aroused antagonism even among our allies. It was undoubtedly perceived as extremely threatening by the Russians—as, indeed, we find their secrecy so alarming that we risk air flights over their territory to penetrate the curtain. Perhaps such efforts at secrecy are always interpreted as threats because of the phenomenon which Else Frenkel-Brunswik christened "intolerance of ambiguity"—the very common mechanism which treats an unclear situation as potentially dangerous. The individual who is extremely anxious is likely to show this intolerance of ambiguity in extreme form. This, clinicians tell us, leads to both perceptual rigidity and behavioral rigidity. It gives rise to the sharp polarization of good and bad which is so characteristic of nationalism, and to the inflexibility deplored by Mr. Kennan and Mr. Dulles.

The significance of this intolerance of ambiguity as regards foreign policy questions can readily be illustrated by a report by Lane (1955). In the Korean War of 1950-1953, clear-cut choices were represented by "get out of Korea entirely" or by "bomb China and Manchuria," whereas an ambiguous policy was represented by "keep on trying to get a peaceful settlement." In a national sample, the high authoritarian cases chose either of the clear-cut choices much oftener than the middle choice; the low authoritarian cases avoided the extreme policies.

Perhaps this is a good point at which to say that I consider such findings to be important regardless of one's emphasis on leaders or on the general population as determinants of policy. Leaders have personalities too, and there is every reason to believe that they can be impatient, can seek for and push the quick, clear-cut alternative, can shy away from policies which appear weak and vacillating. Similarly, the populace can prod the government in certain directions. Our concern with perceptual dynamics is thus not tied to either alternative view of policy determination.

Rigidity on the part of a dominant group is perceived by others as an arbitrary frustration and so gives rise to exceptionally strong hostility. The inflexible policy of apartheid in South Africa is arousing violence on the part of the natives. Despite the examples of Algeria, Cyprus, and other former colonies, the Afrikaners cling blindly to their delusion that tyranny can work. Few of us will have doubts as to the tragic violence so elicited.

I have noted above the tendency to personalize the nation, to deal with it as a hero or as a villain. Sometimes the personalization is in terms of a specific individual: Churchill, Stalin, DeGaulle, Eisenhower; sometimes in terms of a mythical personage such as Uncle Sam. While psychologists have often deplored this because of the obvious distortion involved, I think we must accept it as inevitable. After all, our patterns of cognition are derived from experience—unless we wish to accept some Kantian absolutes. Since our experience of active agents has almost exclusively been with people, it is scarcely possible that we would think of nations except in a personalized way. Certainly it is easier to build myths of grandeur and virtue about a nation-hero than about the oddly assorted characters we see on the bus going to work. And it is easier to project vicious, violent attitudes onto a foreign leader than onto the total foreign population which, even the relatively naive citizen realizes, must be much like ourselves. It is also true that the leader of a nation is more dangerous than the average citizen. By the demands of his social role, he must be more defensive of national honor, more suspicious of national enemies, more alert to exaggerate trivial actions into major threats. Should he underestimate a foreign danger he would be derelict in his duty. But by his actions he tends to magnify these delusions of persecution which are so widely held among the citizens.

The dilemma of the two world powers today is that each is afraid to give up the ability to destroy the other. The best escape route available today seems to be this: the control of these destructive devices must be placed in other hands, so that Russia and the United States can withdraw gracefully from their hazardous positions. I think this is entirely possible; we have done little to explore the techniques for accomplishing it. Creative thinking along this line is urgently needed. C. E. Osgood (1959) has offered an intriguing suggestion in his recent article "On winning the real war with communism."

The solution, according to the political scientists, calls for giving to an international force a monopoly on the instruments of violence. We clearly dare not allow sovereignty—with its concomitant right to unlimited violence—to the small countries of the world. As in the days of our own Wild West—at least as portrayed on TV—we must have a Wyatt Earp or Matt Dillon who will deny to small nations the right to shoot up the town. But such a plan can work only if the United States and the USSR will support it. Our picture of the Communists, and theirs of us, makes such cooperation difficult.

The legal authority must not only have a monopoly of violence, but he must also be perceived as impartial. This calls for a body of law, a set of rules acceptable to the contesting parties, which he enforces. Labor unions would not give up what they considered the sovereign right to violence until law enforcement was less purely a defense of managerial rights. Religious wars continued until both Protestants and Catholics came to perceive the government as an impartial arbiter. Can we turn to international law as a body of doctrine which could provide this framework of impartiality? Unfortunately, nobody today knows just what international law is. Clearly we shall not be able to provide for peaceful settlement of national disputes until we get some legal framework within which the participants can expect to receive justice.

Some Principles of Perception

Before taking up the problem of what can be done to foster such a development let me return to the question of theory for a moment. I said that personification of the nation, while it is a distortion of reality, seems inevitable. In terms of the conceptualization I am offering, the individual's awareness of his nation is qualitatively similar to his perception of another person. This suggests that we may utilize the same principles of perception which have become well-accepted in our observations of physical objects and in face-to-face personal relations.

There are two possible approaches to this problem. One places emphasis on stimulus generalization or perceptual equivalence. That is, one may simply generalize from perceptions of persons to a percept of the nation as a person. This is known as the *generalization hypothesis*. A second approach stems from psychoanalytic theory and involves the notion that emotions such as hostility may be repressed as regards persons near at hand, but are expressed toward foreign groups or personified nations. Christiansen (1959) has suggested that this be called the *latency hypothesis,* since its distinctive feature is that latent emotions are directed toward out-groups.

The empirical evidence, as collected both in this country and abroad, seems to favor the generalization hypothesis. An excellent study, within the limits of attitude scales and questionnaires, has recently been published in

Norway by Christiansen (1959). He finds that persons who report aggressive behavior toward their fellows also endorse aggressive policies toward other nations by Norway. Persons reporting generally cooperative behavior endorse less aggressive policies. Those inclined to be self-critical and intropunitive are likely to assume that Norway may have committed errors in international dealings, whereas the extrapunitive individual usually assumes that Norway was right and the other nation guilty. I reported somewhat parallel findings on American subjects 20 years ago (Stagner 1944a), and other researchers, e.g., Harry Grace (1949), have confirmed this.

The latency hypothesis, on the other hand, would predict a negative correlation between manifest behavior toward close associates and preferred behavior toward foreign nations, racial minorities, and so on. This follows from the fact that the displaced emotion, either affection or hostility, leaves its opposite to govern behavior and perception. Thus the boy who resolves his Oedipus complex by repressing hostility to his father will presumably show affection and positive attitudes at home, but will project bad, tyrannical characteristics onto the evil rulers of foreign nations.

Limited evidence favoring the latency hypothesis is reported by Christiansen using the Blacky Pictures and the Rosenzweig P-F test as devices for getting at latent emotions. On the whole he confesses to disappointment that the evidence is not clear-cut. Similar, slightly favorable evidence has been reported by Krout and Stagner (1939), Lasswell (1930), and others. No one has reported strong support for this point of view.

The complexity of the problem is exaggerated by variations in what may be called the range of stimulus generalization. This is important in connection with the role of reference groups in defining "good" and "bad" nations or social groups. The anthropologists tell us that isolated cultures quite commonly hold to the view that "only we are human." The Hebrews' perception of the Gentiles, like the Greek view of the barbarians, illustrates this. Growing up in an ethnocentric culture, we become alert to trivial cues which identify the in-group, but which enable us to label and reject the out-group. Various studies suggest that anti-Semites are more accurate at detecting Jewish facial characteristics than are their more tolerant peers. Whether this alleged sensitivity can hold up realistically is unimportant. The individual *believes* that he can perceive major differences between his fellows and the out-group; his gradient of generalization, and his responses of friendship and cooperation, are thus limited in scope. There is reason to believe, however, that some individuals are unable to perceive these allegedly differentiating cues and thus may generalize responses of acceptance to humans beyond the in-group. These persons may manifest the cognitive style which George Klein (1951) has called "levelling"; i.e., they tend to iron out differences and to see *all* humans as basically similar.

A second factor which appears to play a part in the choice of such reference groups is also perceptual-cognitive in character. Helen Peak and her students (Peak et al. 1960) have been working with a cognitive style which they call *opposition*. Each of us, I am sure, knows one or more persons who have a consistent tendency to "see the other side" of any issue. They enjoy playing the devil's advocate; and often enough they are not playing. In contrast to this, of course, we have the response-set of *acquiescence,* which has received so much attention in the aftermath of the "Authoritarian Personality" and F-scale studies. A distribution of cases on a hypothetical continuum from extreme acquiescence to extreme opposition would, of course, reveal a skew toward the acquiescent end. And this confirms everyday experience; most children within a nation grow up to accept the nation's leaders as a reference group. But occasionally we get individuals who insist upon looking at the other side, who are not convinced that the policies of their nation are always just, the leaders necessarily paragons of virtue and wisdom. Such critics may become mere cranks and chronic objectors; they may, indeed, find some foreign reference group which is more acceptable. But another common outcome is that they choose an idealistic reference group and perhaps contribute to the development of a body of advocates of an internationalist position. Peak cites some evidence to indicate that oppositionists are also "levellers"; they would thus be more likely to perceive all human beings as basically alike.

I assume that I need not expand on the application of this idea to parallel social conflicts. How did the Reformation start? Because some people rejected the leaders of the Catholic Church. How did feudalism begin its decline? When some individuals saw the possibility of rejecting feudal leaders and organizing a different social structure. Men such as Martin Luther, John Calvin, Descartes, and Spinoza were undoubtedly characterized by the tendency to ponder automatically the opposite of statements posed to them. (This does not suggest that such men reacted favorably to questioning of their own dogmas. On the contrary, such persons are often quite intolerant of "opposite thinking" when it is focused on their views.)

Given these facts regarding the ways in which decisionmakers may act on biased information, and the psychological processes which lead to biasing, one must ask: what can we do about it? The physical scientists have already made it possible for all men to *die* together. The task of the social scientists is to seek ways by which we can *live* together.

In this chapter, I can only suggest a line of approach. Let me mention a couple of suggestions which seem quite futile, and some which appear to have promise.

First of all, I see no point in the recommendation, offered in all seriousness by some psychoanalysts, that government leaders ought to be analyzed. Can we imagine a megalomaniac like Hitler, on the threshold of power, taking off a few years to be analyzed? Can we suppose the United Nations would demand that a Prime Minister come in for psychotherapy? Or that he would obey? I think not.

Secondly, I see little value in communications which focus on the horrors of war, and the devastation which would result from atomic war. It is clear that past decisionmakers have in general found war and violence distasteful, but these alternatives have seemed to them less painful than the situations facing them. That is, if the communist perceives capitalism as a deadly menace, he must eventually come to the point at which he will risk nuclear war because he is so hostile to the bad capitalist nations; the citizen of a capitalist nation must also come to such a point when he perceives communism as an intolerable threat.

Turning to the positive side, I would stress first the importance of *diluting sovereignty* by building up groups and institutions of a supranational character. As we cede a little bit of sovereignty to the International Postal Union, we get used to the idea that our nation cannot act in a completely unilateral manner, without regard to other nations and their rights. More spectacular and more beneficial, of course, is the UN venture in the Congo. This enables people all over the world to get used to the idea that force might be removed from nationalistic controls and used for the welfare of the entire human race.

We need a much larger staff of persons who are agents of such supranational agencies. Ernst Haas (1958), in his recent book, *The Uniting of Europe,* shows the major contributions of the European Coal and Steel Community (ECSC) to developing an internationalist point of view. He speaks of the "spill-over" process, i.e., that men whose duty it is to run the ECSC organization efficiently find themselves forced to expand international cooperation in areas peripheral to the organization itself. I am reminded here of the observations reported by Melville Dalton (1959), describing industrial managers who, in their quest for personal power, go beyond assigned roles (treaties?) to activate new functions. Dalton's findings support Haas; they indicate that the creation of a few more supranational structures like ECSC may help tremendously in the task defined by Haas as "redirecting the loyalties and expectations of political actors" from one level of government (the national) to another (the European).

A more frequent suggestion is that we exchange more visitors with other countries. While this can be hardly undesirable, I think the benefits may easily be exaggerated. Unless personal motives become engaged in the perception of other persons and other nations, the effects are likely to be minimal.

We should keep in mind the rigidity of perceptual constancy, and the effectiveness of perceptual defense. Mere communication without involvement has little effect. A recent proposal by the well-known semanticist S. I. Hayakawa (1960), for example, argues that we could make progress toward peace simply by listening, i.e., by inviting Russian speakers over and letting them state their case, if we were allowed to do likewise. It seems to me unlikely that this would have any effect.

The French have a phrase, *le dialogue des sourds* — "the dialogue of the deaf" — to refer to the fact that two people may talk to each other without either hearing what the other is trying to communicate. Clearly such dialogues make up a major portion of what passes for social communication. Consider, for example, the Negro-white colloquy in the southern United States. The Negro is talking about education to fit him for job opportunities, the opening up of these opportunities, the chance to participate in economic and political affairs. The white speaks of violence, immorality, and other social problems. Neither listens to what the other has to say. We have had, of course, a more dramatic instance of the same kind in the recent interchanges between the United States and the Soviet Union over disarmament. The Russians speak in favor of complete disarmament, the Americans ask about controls and inspections. Since all of you are familiar with the defects of the Russian argument, let me point out a weakness in our own approach. The Russians propose that reports of violations of arms agreements go to the UN Security Council; we object that this would enable them to veto any resolution of condemnation. This utterly misses the point that we have been trying frantically, via U-2, RB-47, and heaven knows what other devices, to get information from inside Russia. If a UN inspection team reported a violation, does it matter who is condemned? We would have obtained vital information; effective counteraction must be taken by the United States, not by the UN.

Unless we take account of the different realities perceived by ourselves and the Russians, increased communication may lead only to increased *misunderstanding*. Let me cite a very simple case. The Yalta agreements provided for "free democratic elections" in Poland, Czechoslovakia, and other satellite nations. Ultimately we learned that these were to be "free and democratic" as in Russia, i.e., the voter was free to vote for the Communist slate or not to vote. The Russians were not hypocritical; the words did not convey the same "reality" to them as to us.

I hope I am making my point clear. I am trying to say that perceptual distortions and perceptual rigidities block communication between groups in conflict. Further, man's craving for a stable, predictable environment tends to force ambiguous data into the existing perceptual structure. All of you remember the Irishman who, when told that Ireland was neutral in the last war, said, "Yes, I know we are neutral, but who are we neutral against?" Thus many Americans assumed that a neutral India must be against us. Fortunately, it has become more clear in recent months that India is neutral against communism; however, this is not the crux of the matter. The psychological phenomenon here takes the form of a demand for a clearly structured environment, one with a minimum of ambiguities. It has variously been discussed by Osgood (1955) as a need for congruity, by Festinger (1957) in terms of consonance and dissonance, and by Newcomb (1953) as a case of symmetry of meaning. Osgood points out that if an approved source, say ex-President Eisenhower, issues a statement favorable to a disapproved object, such as communism, incompatible responses are activated, and conflict occurs. Congruity is achieved by becoming less favorable to Eisenhower or more favorable to communism. However, there is another solution which is often adopted; this is to refuse, in effect, to receive the communication. The technique effectively blocks channels and makes possible the "dialogue of the deaf."

Let me say just a word about the role of *consciousness* in adaptation. Studies of subliminal perception make it clear that the organism can utilize information fed in under conditions operationally defined as unconscious, i.e., when the subject could not report verbally that he had received the information (Miller 1939). But such utilization is at a very low level of efficiency. Material of which one is consciously aware can be used more effectively in guiding behavior; Norman Maier (1931) has shown that problem solving goes on more expeditiously when the experimenter calls attention to significant cues. Finally, we have the widespread belief of clinicians that the resolution of a neurotic conflict requires that all of the significant components of the conflict become available to consciousness. If we are on firm ground in our assertion that social conflicts must be resolved — as they were initiated — in the minds of men, then it follows that men must become conscious of aspects of the aspects of the social conflict which heretofore they have refused to see. Whether nondirective or directive psychotherapy is appropriate here we cannot say at this moment, but my prediction is that a vigorously directive approach will be necessary for effective treatment.

Is an attempt to understand the Russians, and to seek ways in which we might establish peaceful coexistence, a sign of national weakness? I do not think so. I am reminded of the fact that, 300 years ago, suggestions of religious tolerance were denounced as evidence of moral weakness. Today we consider religious *intolerance* a sign of moral decay. I think we may reach a point at which the delusions of national pride and national persecution will be looked upon with the same tolerance — when they no longer threaten us with the holocaust of nuclear war.

How Can Our Civilization Survive?

The illusory nature of perceived reality, our tendency to build up a dream world based on wishful thinking, was brilliantly described by Matthew Arnold:

> The world, which seems
> To lie before us like a land of dreams,
> So various, so beautiful, so new,
> Hath really neither joy, nor love, nor light.

Unconsciously we have deceived ourselves into the belief that we can have more chromium on our cars and fewer teachers in our schools; that we can afford the luxuries of nationalism and race prejudice, and dispense with the sacrifices of comfort and ego expansion needed to resolve these social conflicts. But repression means wandering the dark, denying ourselves the information essential to a problem solution. To complete Arnold's familiar passage,

> We are here, as on a darkling plain
> Swept with confused alarms of struggle and flight
> Where ignorant armies clash by night.

This is the problem facing social psychologists: to devise methods by which we can break the darkness, enlighten the ignorant armies. At all levels of society there are psychological barriers to clear understanding of the social conflicts which plague us. Can we marry the skills and insights of social and clinical psychologists to aid this clarification? This is the specific version, for our profession, of the great question facing the West today: How can our civilization survive?

References

Boulding, Kenneth E. 1959. "National images and international systems," *Journal of Conflict Resolution* 3:120-131.

Christiansen, Bjorn. 1959. *Personality and Attitudes Toward Foreign Policy.* Oslo: University of Oslo Press.

Dalton, Melville. 1959. *Men Who Manage.* New York: John Wiley & Sons.

Dollard, John, et al. 1939. *Frustration and Aggression.* New Haven: Yale University Press.

Dulles, John Foster. 1939. *War, Peace and Change.* New York: Harper & Bros.

Durbin, E.F.M., and Bowlby, John. 1939. *Personal Aggressiveness and War.* New York: Columbia University Press.

Festinger, Leon. 1957. *A Theory of Cognitive Dissonance.* Evanston, Ill.: Row, Peterson and Co.

Grace, Harry A. 1949. *A Study of the Expression of Hostility in Everyday Professional, and International Verbal Situations.* New York: Columbia University Press.

Haas, Ernst B. 1958. *The Uniting of Europe.* Stanford: Stanford University Press.

Hayakawa, Samuel I. 1960. "Formula for Peace: Listening," *New York Times Magazine,* July 31, 10-12.

Janis, Irving L. 1959. "Decisional conflicts: a theoretical analysis," *Journal of Conflict Resolution* 3:6-27.

Kennan, George F. 1954. "The illusion of security," *Atlantic Monthly,* August, 31-34.

Klein, George S. 1951. "The personal world through perception," in Robert R. Blake and Glenn Ramsey (eds.), *Perception: an Approach to Personality.* New York: Ronald Press.

Krout, Maurice H., and Stagner, Ross. 1939. "Personality development in radicals: a comparative study," *Sociometry* 2:31-46.

Lane, Robert F. 1955. "Political personality and electoral choice," *American Political Science Review* 49:173-190.

Lasswell, Harold D. 1930. *Psychopathology and Politics.* Chicago: University of Chicago Press.

Levinson, Daniel J. 1957. "Authoritarian personality and foreign policy," *Journal of Conflict Resolution* 1:37-47.

Maier, Norman R. F. 1931. "Reasoning in humans. II. The solution of a problem and its appearance in consciousness," *Journal of Comparative Psychology* 12:181-194.

———. 1949. *Frustration.* New York: McGraw-Hill Book Co.

Miller, James G. 1939. "Discrimination without awareness," *American Journal of Psychology* 52:562-578.

Newcomb, Theodore M. 1953. "An approach to the study of communicative acts," *Psychological Review* 60:393-404.1.

Osgood, Charles E. 1959. "Suggestions for winning the real war with communism," *Journal of Conflict Resolution* 3:295-325.

Osgood, Charles E., and Tannenbaum, Percy. 1955. "The principle of congruity in the prediction of attitude change," *Psychological Review* 62:42-55.

Peak, Helen, et al. 1960. "Opposite structures, defenses and attitudes," *Psychological Monographs* 74, No. 8.

Stagner, Ross. 1944a. "Studies in aggressive social attitudes. I.," *Journal of Social Psychology* 20:109-120.

———. 1944b. "Studies in aggressive social attitudes. III.," *Journal of Social Psychology* 20:129-140.

———. 1961. *Psychology of Personality* (3rd. ed.). New York: McGraw-Hill Book Co.

Stagner, Ross, Brown, Junius F., Gundlach, Ralph H., and White, Ralph K. 1942. "Analysis of social scientists' opinions on the prevention of war," *Journal of Social Psychology* 15:381-394.

Strachey, Alix. 1957. *The Unconscious Motives of War.* New York: International Universities Press.

Whittlesey, Derwent. 1942. *German Strategy of World Conquest.* New York: Farrar & Rinehart, Inc.

11

Psychological Factors in Civil Violence

Ted Gurr

Until recently many political scientists tended to regard violent civil conflict as a disfigurement of the body politic, neither a significant nor a proper topic for their empirical inquiries. The attitude was in part our legacy from Thomas Hobbes's contention that violence is the negation of political order, a subject fit less for study than for admonition. Moreover, neither the legalistic nor the institutional approaches that dominated traditional political science could provide much insight into group action that was regarded by definition as illegal and the antithesis of institutionalized political life. The strong empirical bent in American political science led to ethnocentric inquiry into such recurring and salient features of American political life as voting and legislative behavior. The American Revolution and Civil War appeared as unique events, grist for exhaustive historical inquiry but unlikely subjects for systematic comparative study or empirical theory. Representative of the consequences of these attitudes is a recent judgment that political violence "by its very nature [is] beyond any simple or reasonable laws of causation."[1]

This chapter proposes, first, that civil violence *is* a significant topic of political inquiry and, second, not only that it is capable of explanation, but that we know enough about the sources of human violence to specify in general, theoretical terms some of the social patterns that dispose men to collective violence.

The proposition that civil violence is important as a genus is widely but not yet universally accepted, even by scholars concerned with some of its forms, revolution in particular.[2] This is the case, one suspects, because revolutions have traditionally been regarded as the most significant form of civil strife, because the universe of such events has been defined by

Ted Gurr, "Psychological Factors in Civil Violence," *World Politics* 20, no. 2 (January 1968). Copyright © 1968 by Princeton University Press. Reprinted by permission of the author and Princeton University Press.

reference to their consequences rather than their common characteristics or preconditions, and because the older theoretical generalizations have emphasized primarily the processes of such events and categorization of their concomitants at a low level of generality.[3] But the evidence both of recent history and of systematic attempts at specifying the incidence of civil strife suggests that revolutions are but one of an extraordinarily numerous variety of interrelated forms of strife;[4] that some of these forms, among them coups d'état, guerrilla war, and massive rioting, can alter political processes and social institutions as drastically as any of the classic revolutions; and that the forms themselves are mutable, or rather, that by reifying our arbitrary distinctions among forms of strife we have overlooked some fundamental similarities.[5] Examination of those special conditions and processes that lead from turmoil to revolution provides a partial understanding of revolution per se, but for a sufficient explanation we require a more general theory, one capable of accounting for the common elements of that much larger class of events called civil strife.

The resort to illicit violence is the defining property that distinguishes these collective events from others. We can regard this as just a definitional point,[6] but it has a crucial theoretical consequence: to direct attention to psychological theories about the sources of human aggression.

Some types of psychological theories about the sources of aggressive behavior can be eliminated at the outset. There is little value in pseudo-psychological speculation about revolutionaries as deviants, fools, or the maladjusted. Psychodynamic explanations of the "revolutionary personality" may be useful for microanalysis of particular events but scarcely for general theory. Aggression-prone victims of maladaptive socialization processes are found in every society, and among the actors in most outbreaks of civil violence, but they are much more likely to be mobilized by strife than to be wholly responsible for its occurrence. Nor can a general theory of civil strife rest on culturally specific theories of modal personality traits, though it might well take account of the effects of these traits. Some cultures and subcultures produce significantly more aggression-prone than cooperative personalities, but an explanation of this order says little of the societal conditions that elicit aggression from the aggression-prone, and nothing at all of the capacity for civil violence of even the most apparently quiescent populations.

The only generally relevant psychological theories are those that deal with the sources and characteristics of aggression in all men, regardless of culture. Such psychological theories do not directly constitute a theory of civil strife. They do offer alternative motivational bases for such a theory and provide means for identifying and specifying the operation of some crucial explanatory variables. As is demonstrated in the following section, one or another of these theories is implicit in most theoretical approaches to civil strife that have no explicit motivational base, although only one of them appears highly plausible in the light of empirical evidence.

Psychological Theories of Aggression

There are three distinct psychological assumptions about the generic sources of human aggression: that aggression is solely instinctual, that it is solely learned, or that it is an innate response activated by frustration.[7] The instinct theories of aggression, represented, among others, by Freud's attribution of the impulse to destructiveness to a death instinct and by Lorenz's view of aggression as a survival-enhancing instinct, assume that most or all men have within them an autonomous source of aggressive impulses, a drive to aggress that, in Lorenz's words, exhibits "irresistible outbreaks which recur with rhythmical regularity."[8] Although there is no definitive support for this assumption, and much evidence to the contrary, its advocates, including Freud and Lorenz, have often applied it to the explanation of collective as well as individual aggression.[9] The assumption is evident in Hobbes's characterization of man in the state of nature and is perhaps implicit in Nieburg's recent concern for "the people's capability for outraged, uncontrolled, bitter, and bloody violence,"[10] but plays no significant role in contemporary theories of civil strife.

Just the opposite assumption, that aggressive behavior is solely or primarily learned, characterizes the work of some child and social psychologists, whose evidence indicates that some aggressive behaviors are learned and used strategically in the service of particular goals — aggression by children and adolescents to secure attention, by adults to express dominance strivings, by groups in competition for scarce values, by military personnel in the service of national policy.[11] The assumption that violence is a learned response, rationalistically chosen and dispassionately employed, is common to a number of recent theoretical approaches to civil strife. Johnson repeatedly, though not consistently, speaks of civil violence as "purposive," as "forms of behavior *intended* to disorient the behavior of others, thereby bringing about the demise of a hated social system."[12] Parsons attempts to fit civil violence into the framework of social interaction theory, treating the resort to force as a way of acting chosen by the actor(s) for purposes of deterrence, punishment, or symbolic demonstration of their capacity to act.[13] Schelling is representative of the conflict theorists: he explicitly assumes rational behavior and interdependence of the adversaries' decisions in all types of conflict.[14] Stone criticizes any emphasis on violence as a distinguishing or definitional property of civil strife on grounds that it is only a particular means, designed to serve political ends.[15]

The third psychological assumption about aggression is that it occurs primarily as a response to frustration. A "frustration" is an interference with goal-directed behavior; "aggression" is behavior designed to injure, physically or otherwise, those toward whom it is directed. The disposition to respond aggressively when frustrated is considered part of man's biological makeup; there is an innate tendency to attack the frustrating agent. Learning can and does modify the tendency: what is perceived to be frustrating, modes of aggressive response, inhibition through fear of retaliation, and appropriate targets are all modified or defined in the learning process, typically but not solely during socialization.

Frustration-aggression theory is more systematically developed, and has substantially more empirical support, than theories that assume either that all men have a free-flowing source of destructive energy or that all aggression is imitative and instrumental. Moreover, the kinds of evidence cited in support of theories of the latter type appear to be subsumable by frustration-aggression theory, whereas the converse is not the case.

One crucial element that frustration-aggression theory contributes to the study of civil violence concerns the drive properties of anger. In the recent reformulation of the theory by Berkowitz, the perception of frustration is said to arouse anger, which functions as a drive. Aggressive responses tend not to occur unless evoked by some external cue, but their occurrence is an inherently satisfying response to that anger.[16] Similarly, Maier has amassed extensive evidence that the innate frustration-induced behaviors (including regression, fixation, and resignation, as well as aggression) are for the actor ends in themselves, unrelated to further goals and qualitatively different from goal-directed behavior.[17]

To argue that aggression is innately satisfying is not incompatible with the presence of learned or purposive components in acts of individual or collective aggression. Cues that determine the timing, forms, and objects of aggression are learned, just as habits of responding aggressively to moderate as well as severe frustration can be learned. The sense of frustration may result from quite rational analysis of the social universe. Leaders can put their followers' anger to rational or rationalized uses. If anger is sufficiently powerful and persistent it may function as an autonomous drive, leading to highly rational and effective efforts by both leaders and the led to satisfy anger aggressively. The crucial point is that rationalization and organization of illicit violence are typically subsequent to, and contingent upon, the existence of frustration-induced anger. Collective violence may be a calculated strategy of dispassionate elite aspirants, and expectations of gains to be achieved through violence may be present among many of its participants. Nonetheless the implication of frustration-aggression theory is that civil violence almost always has a strong "appetitive," emotional base and that the magnitude of its effects on the social system is substantially dependent on how widespread and intense anger is among those it mobilizes.

If anger implies the presence of frustration, there is compelling evidence that frustration is all but universally characteristic of participants in civil strife: discontent, anger, rage, hate, and their synonyms are repeatedly mentioned in studies of strife. Moreover, the frustration assumption is implicit or explicit in many theoretical analyses of the subject. Smelser's concept of "strain" as one of the major determinants of collective behavior, particularly hostile outbursts and value-oriented movements (revolutions), can be readily reformulated in terms of perceived frustration.[18] So can Willer and Zollschan's notion of "exigency" as a precursor of revolution.[19] Ridker characterizes the consequence of failure to attain economic expectations as "discontent," analogous in source and consequence to anger.[20] In Davies' theory of revolution, the reversal of a trend of socioeconomic development is said to create frustration, which instigates revolution.[21] Galtung's theory of both intranational and international aggression recognizes that "the external conditions leading to aggression . . . probably have to pass through the minds of men and precipitate as perceptions with a high emotive content before they are acted out as aggression."[22]

In none of these approaches to theory, however, has frustration-aggression theory been systematically exploited nor have its variables been taken into account.[23] The primary object of this chapter is to demonstrate that many of the variables and relationships identified in social psychological research on the frustration-aggression relationship appear to underlie the phenomenology of civil violence. Juxtaposition of these two diverse types of material provides a basis for an interrelated set of propositions that is intended to constitute the framework of a general theory of the conditions that determine the likelihood and magnitude of civil violence. These propositions are of two types, whose proposed relationships are diagrammed in Figure 11.1: (1) propositions about the operation of *instigating variables,* which determine the magnitude of anger, and (2) propositions about *mediating variables,* which determine the likelihood and magnitude of overt violence as a response to anger.[24]

This approach does not deny the relevance of aspects of the social structure, which many conflict theorists have held to be crucial. The supposition is that theory about civil violence is most fruitfully based on systematic knowledge about those properties of men that determine how they react to certain characteristics of their societies.

FIGURE 11.1   Variables Determining the Likelihood and Magnitude of Civil Violence

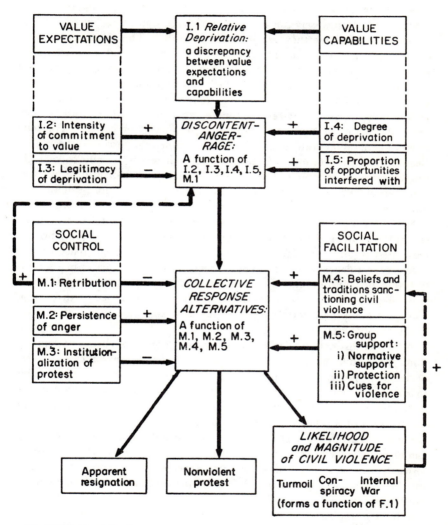

a. The direction(s) of proposed effects on magnitude of civil violence are indicated by + and −.

Relative Deprivation: Variables Determining
the Magnitude of Anger

My basic premise is that the necessary precondition for violent civil conflict is relative deprivation, defined as actors' perception of discrepancy between their *value expectations* and their environment's apparent *value capabilities*.[25] Value expectations are the goods and conditions of life to which people believe they are justifiably entitled. The referents of value capabilities are to be found largely in the social and physical environment: they are the conditions that determine people's perceived chances of getting or keeping the values they legitimately expect to attain. In a comparable treatment, Aberle defines relative deprivation as "a negative discrepancy between legitimate expectation and actuality," viewing expectations as standards, not mere prophecies or hopes.[26] For purposes of general theoretical specification I assume that perceived discrepancies between expectations and capabilities with respect to any collectively sought value — economic, psychosocial, political — constitute relative deprivation. The extent to which some values may be more salient than others is a subject of theoretical and empirical inquiry not evaluated here.

Relative deprivation can be related to the concept of frustration by extending Yates's distinction between the frustrating situation and the frustrated organism.[27] A frustrating situation is one in which an actor is, by objective standards, thwarted by some social or physical barrier in attempts to attain or continue enjoyment of a value. The actor can be said to be frustrated, however, only when he is aware of interference or thwarting. The awareness of interference is equivalent to the concept of relative deprivation as defined above.

A further distinction is necessary between two general classes of deprivation: those that are personal and those that are group or category experiences.[28] For given groups, and for some classes of societies, it is possible to identify events and patterns of conditions that are likely to be widely seen as unjust deprivation. Such events may occur abruptly — for example, the suppression of a political party or a drastic inflation — or slowly, like the decline of a group's status relative to other social classes. Such conditions can be called *collective frustrations*[29] to distinguish them from such unexpected *personal frustrations* as failure to obtain an expected promotion or the infidelity of a spouse, which may be relatively common but randomly incident in most populations.

Whether empirical research ought to focus on conditions defined as collectively frustrating or directly on perceived deprivation is an operational question whose answer depends on the researcher's interest and resources, not upon the following theoretical formulation. Survey techniques permit more or less direct assessment of the extent and severity of relative deprivation.[30] To the extent that the researcher is prepared to make assumptions about measurable conditions that are collectively frustrating in diverse nations, cross-national aggregate data can be used in correlational studies.[31]

The basic relationship can be summarized in a proposition analogous to and assuming the same basic mechanism as the fundamental theorem of frustration-aggression theory:[32]

> *Proposition I.1:* The occurrence of civil violence presupposes the likelihood of relative deprivation among substantial numbers of individuals in a society; concomitantly, the more severe is relative deprivation, the greater are the likelihood and intensity of civil violence.

This proposition may be truistic, although theories were noted above which attempt to account for civil strife without reference to discontent. Moreover, relative deprivation in some degree can be found in any society. The usefulness of the basic proposition is best determined by reference to the set of propositions that qualify it. These propositions specify the conditions that determine the severity and in some cases the occurrence of deprivation, whether or not it is likely to lead to civil violence, and the magnitude of violence when it does occur. The fundamental question, which is susceptible to a variety of empirical tests, is whether the proposed precise relationship between severity of deprivation, as determined by variables I.2 through I.5, and magnitude of violence does hold when the effects of the mediating variables M.1 through M.5 are taken into account.

Definitions and Qualifications

Civil violence and relative deprivation are defined above. If relative deprivation is the perception of frustrating circumstances, the emotional reponse to it tends to be anger. Obviously there are degrees of anger, which can usefully be regarded as a continuum varying from mild dissatisfaction to blind rage. The severity of relative deprivation is assumed to vary directly with the modal strength of anger in the affected population; the determinants of strength of anger are specified in propositions I.2 to I.5, below.

The concept of magnitude requires elaboration. Various measures of quantity or magnitude of aggression are used in psychological research on the frustration-aggression relationship — for example, the intensity of electric shocks administered by frustrated subjects to a supposed frustrater, numbers of aggressive responses in test situations, or the length of time frustrated children play destructively with inanimate objects. A consideration of theory, however, suggests that no single measure of magnitude of aggression is prima facie sufficient. Assuming the validity of the basic frustration-aggression postulate that the greater the strength of anger, the greater the quantity of aggression, it seems likely that strong anger can be satisfied either by inflicting severe immediate damage on the source of frustration or by prolonged but less severe aggression, and that either of these tactics is probably more or less substitutable for the other. Which alternative is taken may very well be a function of opportunity, and while opportunities can be controlled in experimental situations, in civil violence they are situationally determined. Hence neither severity nor duration alone is likely to reflect the modal strength of collective anger or, consequently, to constitute an adequate measure of magnitude of civil violence.

Moreover, there are evidently individual differences — presumably normally distributed — in the strength of anger needed to precipitate overt aggression. Hence the proportion of a population that participates in collective violence ought to vary with the modal strength of anger: discontent will motivate few to violence, anger will push more across the threshold, rage is likely to galvanize large segments of a collectivity into action. This line of argument suggests that magnitude of civil violence has three component variables: the degree of participation within the affected population, the destructiveness of the aggressive actions, and the length of time violence persists.

Frustration-aggression theory stipulates a set of variables that determine the strength of anger or discontent in response to a given frustration. Dollard and others initially proposed that the strength of instigation to aggression (anger) varies with "(1) the strength of instigation to the frustrated response, (2) the degree of interference with the frustrated response, and (3) the number of frustrated response-sequences."[33] The first of these variables, modified in the light of empirical evidence, provides the basis for propositions about characteristics of value expectations that affect the intensity of anger. The second and third variables, similarly modified, suggest several propositions about value capabilities.

Before the propositions are presented, two qualifications of the classic behaviorist conceptualization of frustration as interference with specific, goal-directed responses must be noted. First, it appears from examination of specific outbreaks of civil violence that abrupt awareness of the likelihood of frustration can be as potent a source of anger as actual interference. The Vendée counterrevolution in eighteenth-century France was triggered by the announcement of military conscription, for example.[34] A survey of twentieth-century South African history shows that waves of East Indian and Bantu rioting historically have coincided with the parliamentary discussion of restrictive legislation more than with its actual imposition. The Indian food riots in the spring of 1966 were certainly not instigated by the onset of starvation but by its anticipation.

Second, it seems evident that the sense of deprivation can arise either from interference with goal-seeking behavior or from interference with continued enjoyment of an attained condition. As an example from psychological experimentation, frustration is often operationalized by insults; it seems more likely that the insults are a threat to the subjects' perceived level of status attainment or personal esteem than they are an interference with behavior directed toward some as-yet-unattained goal. Several examples from the history of civil violence are relevant. A study of the coup d'état that overthrew the Perón regime in Argentina states that the crucial events that precipitated the anti-Perónists into action were Perón's public insults to the Catholic hierarchy and isolated physical depredations by his supporters against Church properties — events symbolizing an attack on the moral foundations of upper-middle-class Argentine society.[35] In Soviet central Asia, according to Massell, the most massive and violent resistance to Sovietization followed systematic attempts to break Muslim women loose from their slavish subordination to Muslim men.[36] The two kinds of interference may have differential effects on the intensity and consequences of anger; the point to be made here is that both can instigate violence.

Consequently, analysis of the sources of relative deprivation should take account of both actual and anticipated interference and human goals, as well as of interference with value positions both sought and achieved. Formulations of frustration in terms of the "want:get ratio," which refers only to a discrepancy between sought values and actual attainment, are too simplistic. Man lives mentally in the near future as much as in the present.[37] Actual or anticipated interference with what he has, and with the act of striving itself, is a volatile source of discontent.

Value Expectations

The propositions developed here concern the effects on perceived deprivation of the salience of an expectation for a group, rather than the absolute level of the expectation.[38] The first suggestion derived from psychological theory is that the more intensely people are motivated toward a goal, or committed to an attained level of values, the more sharply is interference resented and the greater is the consequent instigation to aggression. One can, for example, account for some of the efficacy of ideologies in generating civil violence by reference to this variable. The articulation of nationalistic ideologies in colonial territories evidently strengthened preexisting desires for political independence among the colonial bourgeoisie at the same time that it inspired a wholly new set of political demands among other groups. Similarly, it has been argued that the desire of the nineteenth-century European factory worker for a better economic lot was intensified as well as rationalized by Marxist teachings.

Experimental evidence has suggested qualifications of the basic proposition which are equally relevant. One is that the closer men approach a goal, the more intensely motivated toward it they appear to be.[39] This finding has counterparts in observations about civil violence. Hoffer is representative of many theorists in noting that "discontent is likely to be highest when misery is bearable [and] when conditions have so improved that an ideal state seems almost within reach. . . . The intensity of discontent seems to be in inverse proportion to the distance from the object fervently desired."[40] The intensity of motivation varies with the perceived rather than the actual closeness of the goal, of course. The event that inflicts the sense of deprivation may be the realization that a goal thought to be at hand is still remote. The mechanism is clearly relevant to the genesis of post-independence violence in tropical Africa. Failure to realize the promises of independence in the Congo had extraordinarily virulent results, as is evident in a comparison of the intensive and extensive violence of the uprisings of the "Second Independence" of 1964-1965 with the more sporadic settling of accounts that followed the "First Independence" of 1960.[41]

The proposition relates as well to the severity of discontent in societies in the full swing of socioeconomic change. The rising bourgeoisie of eighteenth-century France, for example, individually and collectively had a major commitment to their improving conditions of life, and great effort invested in them. Many felt their aspirations for political influence and high social status to be close to realization but threatened by the declining responsiveness of the state and by economic deprivations inherent in stumbling state efforts to control trade and raise taxes.[42]

Although much additional evidence could be advanced, the relationships cited above are sufficient to suggest the following proposition and its corollaries:

Proposition I.2: The strength of anger tends to vary directly with the intensity of commitment to the goal or condition with regard to which deprivation is suffered or anticipated.

I.2a: The strength of anger tends to vary directly with the degree of effort previously invested in the attainment or maintenance of the goal or condition.

I.2b: The intensity of commitment to a goal or condition tends to vary inversely with its perceived closeness.

It also has been found that, under some circumstances, anticipation or experience of frustration tends to reduce motivation toward a goal. This is particularly the case if frustration is thought to be justified and likely.[43]

Pastore, for example, reports that when subjects saw frustration as reasonable or justifiable, they gave fewer aggressive responses than when they perceived it to be arbitrary. Kregarman and Worchel, however, found that the reasonableness of a frustration did not significantly reduce aggression and that anticipation of frustration tended not to reduce anger but rather to inhibit external aggressive responses.[44]

The low levels of motivation and the moderate nature of interference that characterize these studies make generalization to "real," collective situations doubtful. If applied to a hypothetical example relevant to civil strife — say, the effects of increased taxation on a population under conditions of varying legitimacy attributed to the action — the experimental findings suggest three alternatives: (1) that anger varies inversely with the legitimacy attributed to interference; (2) that anger is constant, but inhibition of its expression varies directly with legitimacy; or (3) that no systematic relationship holds between the two. If the sources of legitimacy are treated in Merelman's learning-theory terms, the first of these alternatives appears most likely: if legitimacy is high, acceptance of deprivation (compliance) provides symbolic substitute rewards.[45] It may also be that the first alternative holds in circumstances in which legitimacy is high, the second in circumstances in which it is moderate. The first relationship can be formulated in propositional form, with the qualification that evidence for it is less than definitive:

Proposition I.3: The strength of anger tends to vary inversely with the extent to which deprivation is held to be legitimate.

Value Capabilities

The environment in which people strive toward goals has two general characteristics that, frustration-aggression theory suggests, affect the intensity of the anger: the degree of interference with goal attainment and the number of opportunities provided for attainment.

Almost all the literature on civil strife assumes a causal connection between the existence of interference (or "frustration," "cramp," or "disequilibrium") and strife. "Discontent" and its synonyms are sometimes used to symbolize the condition of interference without reference to interference per se. A direct relationship between degree of interference and intensity of strife is usually implicit but not always demonstrated. Rostow has shown graphically that poor economic conditions — high wheat prices, high unemployment — corresponded with the severity of overt mass protest in England from 1790 to 1850.[46] Variations in bread prices and in mob violence went hand in hand in revolutionary France.[47] There is correlational evidence that the frequency of lynchings in the American South,

1882-1930, tended to vary inversely with indices of economic well-being.[48] From cross-national studies there is suggestive evidence also — for example, Kornhauser's correlation of − .93 between per capita income and the Communist share of the vote in sixteen Western democracies in 1949.[49] The Feierabends devised "frustration" measures, based on value capability characteristics of sixty-two nations, and correlated them with a general measure of degree of political stability, obtaining a correlation coefficient of .50.[50]

As far as the precise form of the relationship between extent of interference and intensity of aggression is concerned, the experimental results of Hamblin and others are persuasive. Three hypotheses were tested: the classic formulation that instigation to aggression varies directly with the degree of interference and the psychophysical hypotheses that aggression ought to be a log or a power function of interference. The data strongly support the last hypothesis, that aggression is a power function of degree of interference — i.e., if magnitude of aggression is plotted against degree of interference, the result is a sharply rising "J-curve." Moreover, the power exponent — the sharpness with which the J-curve rises — appears to increase with the strength of motivation toward the goal with which interference was experienced.[51] It is at least plausible that the J-curve relationship should hold for civil strife. Compatible with this inference, though not bearing directly on it, is the logarithmic distribution curve that characterizes such cross-polity measures of intensity of civil violence as deaths per 100,000 population.[52] It also may account for the impressionistic observation that moderate levels of discontent typically lead to easily quelled turmoil but that higher levels of discontent seem associated with incommensurately intense and persistent civil violence. In propositional form:

Proposition I.4: The strength of anger tends to vary as a power function of the perceived distance between the value position sought or enjoyed and the attainable or residual value position.[53]

Experimental evidence regarding the hypothesis of Dollard and others that the greater the number of frustrations, the greater the instigation to aggression is somewhat ambiguous. Most people appear to have hierarchies of response to repeated frustration, a typical sequence being intensified effort, including search for alternative methods or substitute goals, followed by increasingly overt aggression as other responses are extinguished, and ultimately by resignation or apparent acceptance of frustration. Berkowitz suggests that most such evidence, however, is congruent with the interpretation that "the probability of emotional reactions is a function of the degree to which all possible nonaggressive responses are blocked, more than to the interference with any one response sequence."[54]

The societal equivalents of "all possible nonaggressive responses" can be regarded as all normative courses of action available to members of a collectivity for value attainment, plus all attainable substitute value positions. Relevant conditions are evident in the portraits of "transitional man" painted by Lerner and others. Those who are committed to improving their socioeconomic status are more likely to become bitterly discontented if they have few rather than many prospective employers, if they can get no work rather than some kind of work that provides a sense of progress, if they have few opportunities to acquire requisite literacy and technical skills, if associational means for influencing patterns of political and economic value distributions are not available, or if community life is so disrupted that hearth and kin offer no surcease from frustration for the unsuccessful worker.[55] All such conditions can be subsumed by the rubric of "opportunities for value attainment," with the qualification that perception of opportunities tends to be more crucial than actual opportunities.

Much evidence from studies of civil strife suggests that the greater are value opportunities, the less intense is civil violence. The argument appears in varying guises. Brogan attributes the comparative quiescence of mid-nineteenth-century English workers vis-à-vis their French counterparts in part to the proliferation in England of new cooperatives, friendly and building societies, and trade unions, which provided positive alternatives to violent protest.[56] The first of the American Negro urban rebellions in the 1960s occurred in a community, Watts, in which by contemporary accounts associational activity and job-training programs had been less effective than those of almost any other large Negro community. Cohn explains the high participation of unskilled workers and landless peasants in the violent millenarian frenzies of medieval Europe by reference to the lack of "the material and emotional support afforded by traditional social groups; their kinship groups had disintegrated and they were not effectively organised in village communities or in guilds; for them there existed no regular, institutionalised methods of voicing their grievances or pressing their claims."[57] Kling attributes the chronic Latin American pattern of coup d'état to the lack of adequate alternatives facing elite aspirants with economic ambitions; political office, seized illicitly if necessary, provides opportunity for satisfying those ambitions.[58]

More general observations also are relevant. Economists suggest that government can relieve the discontents that accompany the strains of rapid economic growth by providing compensatory welfare measures — i.e., alternative means of value satisfaction.[59] Numerous scholars have shown that migration is a common response to deprivation and that high emigration rates often precede outbreaks of civil violence. In a cross-national study of correlates of civil violence for 1961-1963, I have found a rather consistent association between extensive educational opportunities, proportionally large trade union movements, and stable political party systems on the one hand and low levels of strife on the other, relationships that tend to hold among nations whatever their absolute level of economic development. Education presumably increases the apparent range of opportunity for socioeconomic advance, unionization can provide a secondary means for economic goal attainment, and parties serve as primary mechanisms for attainment of participatory political values.[60] Hence:

> *Proposition I.5:* The strength of anger tends to vary directly with the proportion of all available opportunities for value attainment with which interference is experienced or anticipated.

The Mediation of Anger: The Effects of Social Control and Social Facilitation

For the purpose of the theoretical model I assume that the average strength of anger in a population is a precise multiple function of the instigating variables. Whether or not civil violence actually occurs as a response to anger, and its magnitude when it does occur, are influenced by a number of mediating variables. Evidence for these variables and their effects is found both in the psychological literature and in studies of civil violence per se. It is useful to distinguish them according to whether they inhibit or facilitate the violent manifestation of anger.

Social Control: The Effects of Retribution

The classic formulation is that aggression may be inhibited through fear of "such responses on the part of the social environment as physical injury, insults, ostracism, and deprivation of goods or freedom."[61] Good experimental evidence indicates that anticipation of retribution is under some circumstances an effective regulator of aggression.[62] Comparably, a linear relationship between, on the one hand, the capacity and willingness of government to enforce its monopoly of control of the organized instrumentalities of force and, on the other, the likelihood of civil violence is widely assumed in the literature on civil strife. Strong apparent force capability on the part of the regime ought to be sufficient to deter violence, and if violence should occur, the effectiveness with which it is suppressed is closely related to the likelihood and intensity of subsequent violence. Smelser states that a major determinant of the occurrence of civil strife is declining capacity or loyalty of the police and military control apparatus.[63] Johnson says that "the success or failure of armed insurrection and . . . commonly even the decision to attempt revolution rest . . . upon the attitude (or the revolutionaries' estimate of that attitude) that the armed forces will adopt toward the revolution."[64] In Janos's view, the weakening of law-enforcement agencies "creates general disorder, inordinate concrete demands by various groups, and the rise of utopian aspirations."[65] Military defeat is often empirically associated with the occurrence of revolution. Race riots in the United States and elsewhere have often been associated with tacit approval of violence by authorities.[66] Paret and Shy remark that "terror was effective in Cyprus against a British government without sufficient political strength or will; it failed in Malaya against a British government determined and able to resist and to wait."[67]

It also has been proposed, and demonstrated in a number of experimental settings, that if aggression is prevented by fear of retribution or by retribution itself, this interference is frustrating and increases anger. Maier, for example, found in animal studies that under conditions of severe frustration, punishment increased the intensity of aggression.[68] Walton inferred from such evidence that a curvilinear relationship ought to obtain between the degree of coerciveness of a nation and its degree of political instability, on the argument that low coerciveness is not frustrating and moderate coerciveness is more likely to frustrate than deter, while only the highest levels of coerciveness are sufficient to inhibit men from civil violence. A permissiveness-coerciveness scale for eighty-four nations, based on scope of political liberties, has been compared against the Feierabends' political stability scale, and the results strongly support the curvilinearity hypothesis.[69] Bwy, using a markedly different measure of coerciveness — one based on defense expenditures — found the same curvilinear relationship between coerciveness and "anomic violence" in Latin America.[70] Some theoretical speculation about civil strife implies the same relationship — for example, Lasswell and Kaplan's stipulation that the stability of an elite's position varies not with the actual use of violence but only with ability to use it,[71] and Parsons' more detailed "power deflation" argument that the repression of demands by force may inspire groups to resort to increasingly intransigent and aggressive modes of making those demands.[72]

One uncertainty about the curvilinear relationship between retribution and aggression is whether or not it holds whatever the extent of initial deprivation-induced anger. It is nonetheless evident that the threat or employment of force to suppress civil violence is by no means uniform in its effects, and that it tends to have a feedback effect that increases the instigation to violence. Such a relationship is diagrammed in Figure 11.1 and is explicit in the following proposition and its corollary:

Proposition M.1: The likelihood and magnitude of civil violence tend to vary curvilinearly with the amount of physical or social retribution anticipated as a consequence of participation in it, with likelihood and magnitude greatest at medium levels of retribution.

M.1a: Any decrease in the perceived likelihood of retribution tends to increase the likelihood and magnitude of civil violence.

These propositions and corollaries, and all subsequent propositions, hold only, of course, if deprivation-induced anger exists. If the modal level of collective discontent is negligible, a condition that holds for at least some small, although few large, collectivities, the mediating variables have no inhibiting or facilitating effects by definition.

The propositions above do not exhaust frustration-aggression evidence about effects of retribution. Experimental evidence further indicates that a delay in the expression of the aggressive response increases its intensity when it does occur.[73] Observations about civil violence also suggest that the effects of feared retribution, especially external retribution, must take account of the time variable. The abrupt relaxation of authoritarian controls is repeatedly associated with intense outbursts of civil violence, despite the likelihood that such relaxation reduces relative deprivation. Examples from recent years include the East German and Hungarian uprisings after the post-Stalin thaw, the Congo after independence, and the Dominican Republic after Trujillo's assassination.

A parsimonious way to incorporate the time dimension into frustration-aggression theory is to argue that in the short run the delay of an aggressive response increases the intensity of anger and consequently the likelihood and magnitude of aggression, but that in the long run the level and intensity of expectations decline to coincide with the impositions of reality, and anger decreases concomitantly. Cognitive dissonance theory would suggest such an outcome: men tend to reduce persistent imbalances between cognitions and actuality by changing reality, or, if it proves intransigent, by changing their cognitive structures.[74] The proposed relationship is sketched in Figure 11.2.

One example of experimental evidence to this point is the finding of Cohen and others that once subjects became accustomed to certain kinds of frustration—withdrawal of social reinforcement in the experimental situation used—they were less likely to continue to seek the desired value or condition.[75] One can, moreover, speculate that the time scale is largely a function of the intensity of commitment to the frustrated response or condition. The effects of South Africa's apartheid policies and the means of their enforcement offer an example. These policies, which impose substantial and diverse value deprivations on nonwhites, especially those in urban areas,

FIGURE 11.2   Displacement of Instigation to Violence over Time

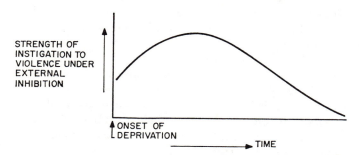

were put into effect principally in the 1950s. Violent protests over their implementation were repressed with increasing severity, culminating in the Sharpeville massacre of 1960 and a series of strikes and riots. By the mid-1960s, when deprivation was objectively more severe than at any time previously in the twentieth century, levels of civil strife were very low, inferentially the result of very high levels of deterrence (feared retribution). Since deprivation remains severe and has affected a wide range of values, avoidance of violence in this case probably would require the maintenance of very high and consistent deterrence levels beyond the active life span of most of those who have personally experienced the initial value deprivation. Any short-run decline in the perceived likelihood or severity of retribution, however, is highly likely to be followed by intense violence. In propositional form:

Proposition M.2: Inhibition of civil violence by fear of external retribution tends in the short run to increase the strength of anger but in the long run to reduce it.

M.2a: The duration of increased anger under conditions of inhibition tends to vary with the intensity of commitment to the value with respect to which deprivation is suffered.

Social Control: The Effects of Institutionalized Displacement

On the evidence, the effects of repression in managing discontent are complex and potentially self-defeating in the short run. Displacement theory suggests means that are considerably more effective. Several aspects of displacement theory are relevant for civil violence. Among Miller's basic propositions about object and response generalization is the formulation that the stronger the fear of retribution relative to the strength of anger, the more dissimilar will the target of aggression be from the source of interference and the more indirect will be the form of aggression.[76] With reference to object generalization, Berkowitz has proposed and demonstrated that hostility tends to generalize from a frustrater to previously disliked individuals or groups.[77] A counterpart of this thesis is that displaced aggressive responses tend to be expressed in previously used forms.

Examples of object generalization in civil violence are legion. Several studies have shown positive relationships between poor economic conditions and lynchings of Negroes in the American South.[78] An initial reaction of urban white colonialists to African rural uprisings in Madagascar in 1947 and Angola in 1961 was vigilante-style execution of urban Africans who had no connections with the rebellions. English handweavers, when their livelihood was threatened by the introduction of new weaving machines, destroyed thousands of machines in the Luddite riots of 1811-1816, but almost never directly attacked the employers who installed the machines and discharged superfluous workers.[79]

Object generalization is a crucial variable in determining who will be attacked by the initiators of particular acts of civil violence, but is only peripheral to the primary concern of the theory, the determination of likelihood and magnitude of violence as such. Most important in this regard is the psychological evidence regarding response generalization. Experimental evidence suggests that only a narrow range of objects provides satisfying targets for men's aggressive responses, but that almost any form of aggression can be satisfying so long as the angry person believes that he has in some way injured his supposed frustrater.[80]

By extension to the collectivity, insofar as adequate response displacement options are available, much anger may be diverted into activity short of civil violence. The evidence is diverse and extensive that participation in political activity, labor unions, and millenarian religious movements can be a response to relative deprivation which permits more or less nonviolent expression of aggression. Studies of voting in the United States show that politicians in farm states are rather consistently voted out of office after periods of low rainfall and that the occurrence of natural disasters may lead to hostility against officials.[81] Extremist voting—which may be regarded as nonviolent aggression—in nine European countries during the Depression has been shown to correlate $+.85$ with the percentage of the labor force unemployed.[82] Studies of labor movements repeatedly document the transformation of labor protest from violent to nonviolent forms as unionization increases. Comparative and case studies similarly document the development of aggressive millenarian religious movements as a response to natural disaster or political repression, in places and eras as diverse as medieval Europe, colonial Africa, and among the indigenous peoples of the Americas and the South Pacific.[83]

This is not to imply that displacement is a sole or exclusive function of such institutions. Their instrumental functions for participants (Proposition I.5) can be crucial: peaceful political and union activism are alternative means to goals whose attainment by other means is often impaired; religious chiliasm provides hope and belief for those whose social universe has been destroyed. But insofar as men become accustomed to express discontents through such institutional mechanisms, the likelihood that anger will lead to civil violence is diminished. In propositional form:

Proposition M.3: The likelihood and magnitude of civil violence tend to vary inversely with the availability of institutional mechanisms that permit the expression of nonviolent hostility.

Social Facilitation: Cognitive Factors

Experimental, developmental, and field studies of the effects of rewarding individual aggression demonstrate that habitual aggression may be developed and maintained through intermittent rewards and may also be generalized to situations other than those in which the habits were acquired.[84] A number of experiments indicate that the presence of cues or stimuli associated with anger instigators is necessary for most aggressive responses to occur. A summary proposition is that "a target with appropriate stimulus qualities 'pulls' (evokes) aggressive responses from a person who is ready to engage in such actions either because he is angry or because particular stimuli have acquired cue values for aggressive responses from him."[85]

For members of a collectivity a variety of common experiences can contribute to the acquisition of aggressive habits and the recognition of aggression-evoking cues. Among them are socialization patterns that give normative sanction to some kinds of aggressive behavior; traditions of violent conflict; and exposure to new generalized beliefs that justify violence. The literature on civil violence suggests at least four specific modes by which such experiences facilitate violent responses to deprivation. They can (1) stimulate mutual awareness among the deprived, (2) provide explanations for deprivation of ambiguous origin, (3) specify accessible targets and appropriate forms of violence, and (4) state long-range objectives to be attained through violence.

Subcultural traditions of violent protest are well documented in European history. The frequency with which Parisian workers and shopkeepers took to the streets in the years and decades following the great *journées* of 1789 is one example. At least 275 food riots, most of them similar in form and sequence, took place in rural England between 1725 and 1800 in close correlation with harvest failures and high food prices.[86] Hobsbawm points out that in southern Italy "every political change in the nineteenth century, irrespective from what quarter it came, automatically produced its ceremonial marches of peasants with drums and banners to occupy the land," while in Andalusia "millenarian revolutionary waves occurred at roughly ten-year intervals for some sixty or seventy years."[87] Lynching as a Southern white response to Negro transgressions and the mobbing of white policemen by Negroes are comparable expressions of subcultural traditions that facilitate civil violence.

The theoretical point is that the initial occurrences of civil violence among some homogeneous group of the deprived — those events that set the pattern — tend to be nonrational responses to extreme deprivation. If violence provides a satisfactory outlet for tensions or if it motivates authorities to remedy the sources of deprivation, civil violence tends to become a sanctioned group activity. The fact that normative support for violence thus develops does not mean that violence subsequently occurs without instigation. Deprivation remains a necessary precondition for violence; the strength of anger at which it is likely to occur is lowered.

A related source of attitudinal support for collective violence is the articulation of ideology or, more generally, what Smelser calls generalized belief among the deprived. Such beliefs, ranging from rumors to fully articulated ideologies, are said to develop in situations characterized by social strain that is unmanageable within the existing framework for social action.[88] It is evident that in many social settings relative deprivation is manifest but its sources obscure. In psychological terms, no cues associated with the anger instigator are present. The agency responsible for an unwanted tax increase is apparent to the most ignorant villager; the causes of economic depression or of the disintegration of traditional mores are often unclear even to economists and sociologists. A new ideology, folk belief, or rumor can serve to define and explain the nature of the situation, to identify those responsible for it, and to specify appropriate courses of action.

Moreover, there usually are a number of competing generalized beliefs circulating among the deprived. Those most likely to gain acceptance tend to be those with substantial aggressive components, i.e., those that rationalize and focus the innate drive to aggression. Cohn's comparative study of the waves of chiliastic excitement that swept medieval Europe in times of plague and famine, for example, documents the fact that the heresies that most effectively mobilized the deprived were those that suited or could be molded to their states of mind: "when . . . eschatological doctrines penetrated to the uprooted and desperate masses in town and country they were re-edited and reinterpreted until in the end they were capable of inspiring revolutionary movements of a peculiarly anarchic kind."[89]

Some of these observations can be summarized in this proposition and its corollary:

Proposition M.4: The likelihood and magnitude of civil violence tend to vary directly with the availability of common experiences and beliefs that sanction violent responses to anger.

M.4a: Given the availability of alternative experiences and beliefs, the likelihood that the more aggressive of them will prevail tends to vary with the strength of anger.

Social Facilitation: Sources of Group Support for Violence

A classic subject of social psychological theory is the extent to which some social settings facilitate overt aggression. It is incontrovertible that individuals tend to behave in crowds differently from the way they act alone. The crowd psychologies of scholars such as Le Bon and Sorokin have emphasized the "unconscious" nature of crowd behavior and its "de-individuating" effects.[90] It appears more fruitful to examine experimentally identified variables that contribute to the "crowd behavior" phenomenon. From this point of departure one can distinguish at least three modes by which groups affect individuals' disposition to violence: (1) by providing normative support, (2) by providing apparent protection from retribution, and (3) by providing cues for violent behavior.

1. *Normative support.* There is good experimental evidence that individuals alone or in poorly cohesive groups are less likely to express hostility than those in highly cohesive groups. Members of highly cohesive friendship groups respond to external frustrations with greater hostility than randomly formed groups. Similarly, if individuals believe that their peers generally agree with them about a frustrater, their public display of antagonism more closely resembles their privately expressed antagonism than if they do not perceive peer agreement.[91]

Theoretical and empirical studies of civil violence repeatedly refer to the causal efficacy of comparable conditions. Social theorists describe the perception of anonymity and of universality of deprivation characteristic of riotous crowds. Hopper's classic picture of group interaction under conditions of relative deprivation in the early stages of the revolutionary process is relevant: by participating in mass or shared behavior, discontented people become aware of one another; "their negative reactions to the basic factors in their situations are shared and begin to spread. . . . Discontent . . . tends to become focalized and collective."[92] Comparative studies of labor unrest show that the most strike-prone industries are those whose workers are relatively homogeneous and isolated from the general community.[93]

Some of the efficacy of revolutionary brotherhoods and tightly knit bands of rebels in prosecuting civil violence can be interpreted in terms of the reinforcement of mutual perception of deprivation and the justification of violence as a response to it.

2. *Protection from retribution.* Groups appear capable of reducing fears of external retribution for violence in at least three ways. Crowd situations in particular provide members with a shield of anonymity. In an experimental study by Meier and others, two-thirds of subjects who were prepared to join a lynching mob said, inter alia, that they would do so because in the crowd they could not be punished. The same relationship is apparent in the handful of studies made of riot participants: crowd members usually feel insulated from retribution.[94]

Organized groups can provide apparent protection from retribution by acquiring sufficient force capability to prevent the agents of retribution—i.e., military and internal security forces—from effectively reaching them. Increases in the relative force capability of a deprived group may also reinforce rationalization for violence by raising hopes of success or may merely facilitate the expression of rage by providing desperate men with the means to strike at tormentors who had previously been unassailable.

A third aspect of group protectiveness is the perceived effect of hierarchical organization and the presence of highly visible leaders. Leaders of revolutionary organizations, in addition to their other manifest functions, not only foment but assume responsibility for illicit violence. Their followers tend to see such leaders as the likely objects of retaliatory efforts and hence feel less personal risk.

3. *Cues for violence.* The transition from anger to aggression is not automatic or even abrupt. Laboratory studies of imitative behavior repeatedly document the significance of aggression-releasing cues provided by social models. The act of punishing aggression itself can serve as a model for imitation by the person punished. Aggression-releasing cues need not necessarily originate with high-status persons. Polansky and others found that when frustrations were imposed on groups of children, "impulsive" but low-status children were both initiators and ready followers of aggressive behavioral contagion. On the other hand, not any aggressive model evokes aggression from angered subjects; the models that evoke greatest aggression are those associated with the subjects' present situation or with settings in which they were previously aggressive.[95]

Angry crowds of men also appear to require some congruent image or model of violent action before they will seize cobblestones, rope, or rifles to do violence to fellow citizens. Such models may be symbolic: invocation of a subcultural tradition of violence by a leader, or articulation of a new generalized belief that is explicit in its prescription of violence. In general, however, a "call to arms" or an appeal to a tradition of violence appears less effective by itself than when accompanied by the sight or news of violence. The calculated use of terrorism by rebels can have such an effect, and so can a soldier's random shot into a crowd of demonstrators. Many specific cases of civil violence have been set off by comparable acts of violence elsewhere. "Revolutionary contagion" is evident in the 1830 and 1848 waves of European revolutionary upheavals and in the post-Stalin uprisings in Eastern Europe and Siberia. The same phenomenon is apparent in the initiation of innumerable cases of small-scale, unstructured violence. Series of riots in rural France and England have graphically been shown to spread outward from one or a few centers, riots occurring in the furthest villages days or weeks after the initial incident. Such patterning is evident, to mention a few cases, in the French Corn Riots of 1775, the "Plug-Plot" riots around Manchester in 1842, and the incidence of farmers' protest meetings and riots in Brittany in the summer of 1961.[96] The demonstration effect apparent in such series of events appears to have affected their form and timing more than the likelihood of the occurrence of strife. The people who responded to the events were already angered; they probably would have erupted into violence in some form sometime in the proximate future.

These three modes of group facilitation of civil violence can be summarized in propositional form:

> *Proposition M.5:* The likelihood and magnitude of civil violence tend to vary directly with the extent to which the deprived occupy organizational and/or ecological settings that provide (1) normative support through high levels of interaction, (2) apparent protection from retribution, and (3) congruent models for violent behavior.

The Forms of Civil Violence

The theoretical framework comprising the ten propositions is formally restricted to physically violent collective behavior. It is likely that it is as applicable to a still larger class of events, including those characterized by the threat of violence or by high levels of verbal aggression — for example, bloodless coups, demonstrations, and political strikes. Violent events tend to be more salient for the political system, however, and for most operational purposes constitute a more workable and clearly defined universe.

I have not discussed the propositions with reference to specific forms of civil violence on grounds that all of the variables specified are relevant to each form specified in current typologies.[97] It is nonetheless likely that the propositions are of differential weight for different forms, and it is useful to demonstrate how variations in form may be generally accounted for in the context of the theoretical model. The first question to be asked is how detailed a listing of forms one should attempt to account for. A series of factor analytic studies provide a systematic, empirical answer to that question. In each of eleven studies, data on the incidence and characteristics of various types of strife were collected and tabulated, by country, and the "country scores" (number of riots, assassinations, deaths from civil violence, coups, mutinies, guerrilla wars, and so on, in a given time period) were factor analyzed. Whatever the typology employed, the period of reference, or the set of countries, essentially the same results were obtained. A strong *turmoil* dimension emerges, characterized by largely spontaneous strife such as riots, demonstrations, and nonpolitical clashes, quite distinct from what we may call a *revolutionary* dimension, characterized by more organized and intense strife. This revolutionary dimension has two components, appearing in some analyses as separate dimensions: *internal war,* typically including civil war, guerrilla war, and some coups; and *conspiracy,* typically including plots, purges, mutinies, and most coups.[98] Events within each of the three types tend to occur together; events within any two or all three categories are less likely to do so. The implication is that they are substantively distinct forms of strife for each of which separate explanation is required.

Two complementary approaches to accounting for these three basic types of civil violence can be proposed within the context of the theoretical model. The first is that the two major dimensions, turmoil and revolution, reflect the varying class incidence of deprivation among societies. The defining characteristic of "turmoil" events is mass participation, usually rather spontaneous, disorganized, and with low intensity of violence; the forms of "revolution" reflect organized, often instrumental and intense, application of violence. The ability to rationalize, plan, and put to instrumental use their own and others' discontent is likely to be most common among the more skilled, highly educated members of a society—its elite aspirants. Thus if the incidence of mass deprivation is high but elite deprivation low, the most likely form of civil violence is turmoil. But if severe discontent is common to a substantial, alienated group of elite aspirants, then organized, intensive strife is likely.

The forms of revolution differ principally in their scale and tactics: internal wars are large-scale, and their tactics are typically to neutralize the regime's military forces; conspirators, usually few in number, attempt to subvert the regime by striking at its key members.

The differences between internal war and conspiracy can be accounted for by several characteristics. If severe deprivation is restricted largely to elite aspirants, the consequence is likely to be "conspiracy" phenomena such as plots, coups d'état, and barracks revolts. If discontent is widespread among substantial numbers of both mass and elite aspirants, the more likely consequence is large-scale, organized violence — civil and guerrilla war. The strategic position of the discontented elite aspirants may be relevant as well. If they are subordinate members of the existing elite hierarchy, they are likely to attack the regime from within, hence coups, mutinies, and plots. If they are instead excluded from formal membership in the elite though they possess elite qualities — acquired, for example, through foreign education — they must organize violent resistance from without. These are essentially Seton-Watson's explanations for the relative frequency of conspiracy in underdeveloped societies compared with the frequency of massive revolutionary movements in more developed states. In summary, "it is the combination of backward masses, extremist intellectuals and despotic bureaucrats which creates the most conspiratorial movements."[99]

These observations are of course only the beginning of an accounting of the forms of civil strife. They are intended to demonstrate, however, that such a theoretical explanation not only is compatible with but can be formulated within the framework of the theoretical model by showing the loci of deprivation in a society. They can be stated thus in propositional form:

Proposition F.1: The characteristic form of civil violence tends to vary with the differential incidence of relative deprivation among elite aspirants and masses: (1) *mass deprivation* alone tends to be manifested in large-scale civil violence with minimal organization and low intensity; (2) *elite-aspirant deprivation* tends to be manifested in highly organized civil violence of high intensity.

F.1a: Whether organized and intense civil violence is large-scale or small-scale is a joint function of the extent of mass deprivation and the strategic access of deprived elite aspirants to the incumbent political elite.

Conclusion

I have advanced eleven general propositions about the variables operative in generating and structuring violent political unrest. They are based on the assumption that the frustration-aggression mechanism, however culturally modified, is the source of most men's disposition to illicit collective violence. The propositions do not constitute a theory of the revolutionary process or of the outcomes of strife, but of the conditions that determine the *likelihood* and *magnitude* of strife. On the other hand, the variables stipulated by the propositions are not irrelevant to revolutionary processes. Process models can be formulated wholly or partly in terms of changing patterns of weights on the component variables.

It is likely that most "causes" and "correlates" of the occurrence and intensity of civil strife can be subsumed by these variables, with one exception: foreign intervention. This exception is no oversight but simply recognition that decisions to intervene are external to domestic participants in civil strife. The effects of foreign intervention can be readily interpreted by reference to the model, however: intervention on behalf of the deprived is likely to strengthen group support (M.5) and may, as well, heighten and intensify value expectations (I.2). Foreign assistance to a threatened regime is most likely to raise retribution levels (M.1), but may also alter aspects of value capabilities (I.4, I.5) and strengthen justification for violence among the deprived, insofar as they identify foreigners with invaders (M.4).

The framework has not been elaborated merely to provide a satisfying theoretical reconstruction of the general causes of civil violence. It is intended primarily as a guide for empirical research using the techniques of both case and comparative studies. The framework stipulates the variables for which information should be sought in any thorough case study of the origins of an act of civil strife.[100] For purposes of comparative analysis it stipulates relationships that should hold among cultures and across time. Its most important objectives are to encourage empirical validation of its component propositions in a variety of contexts by a variety of operational means, and specification of their separate weights and interacting effects in those contexts.[101]

Notes

This chapter is a revision of a paper read to the panel on "The Psychology of Political Unrest," at the Annual Meeting of the American Psychological Association, New York, September 2-6, 1966. Harry Eckstein's careful and helpful evaluation of draft versions of this paper is gratefully acknowledged. Others who have provided useful, though not always satisfiable, criticism of the theoretical model include Leonard Berkowitz, Alfred de Grazia, Mohammed Guessous, Marion J. Levy, Jr., John T. McAlister, Jr., Mancur L. Olson, Jr., Joel Prager, Bryant Wedge, and Oran R. Young. Theoretical work was supported by an award from a National Science Foundation institutional grant to New York University and by the Center for Research on Social Systems (formerly SORO) of American University.

1. Arnold Forster, "Violence on the Fanatical Left and Right," *Annals of the American Academy of Political and Social Science,* CCCLXIV (March 1966), 142.

2. For example, Lawrence Stone, "Theories of Revolution," *World Politics,* XVIII (January 1966), 159-76, advances the curious argument that collective violence generally cannot be the object of useful theorizing because it is at the same time both

pervasive and somehow peripheral.

3. The emphasis on processes is evident in the major theoretical analyses of the "classic" revolutions, including Lyford P. Edwards, *The Natural History of Revolutions* (Chicago, 1927); Crane Brinton, *The Anatomy of Revolution* (New York, 1938); George S. Pettee, *The Process of Revolution* (New York, 1938); Louis R. Gottschalk, "Causes of Revolution," *American Journal of Sociology*, L (July, 1944), 1-9; and Rex D. Hopper, "The Revolutionary Process: A Frame of Reference for the Study of Revolutionary Movements," *Social Forces*, XXVIII (March, 1950), 270-79.

4. A great many counts of the incidence of civil strife events have recently been reported. Harry Eckstein reports 1,632 "internal wars" in the period 1946-1959 in "On the Etiology of Internal Wars," *History and Theory*, IV, No. 2 (1965), 133-63. Rummel and Tanter counted more than 300 "domestic conflict events" per year during the years 1955-1960, including an annual average of 13 guerrilla wars and 21 attempted overthrows of government: see Raymond Tanter, "Dimensions of Conflict Behavior Within Nations, 1955-60: Turmoil and Internal War," *Peace Research Society Papers*, III (1965), 159-84. Most important to the argument that civil strife is a single universe of events are results of Rudolph Rummel's factor analysis of 236 socioeconomic and political variables, including nine domestic conflict measures, for a large number of nations. Eight of the conflict measures — e.g., number of riots, of revolutions, of purges, of deaths from group violence — are strongly related to a single factor but not significantly related to any others, strong empirical evidence that they comprise a distinct and interrelated set of events. See *Dimensionality of Nations Project: Orthogonally Rotated Factor Tables for 236 Variables*, Department of Political Science, Yale University (New Haven, July 1964), mimeographed.

5. The "French Revolution" was a series of events that would now be characterized as urban demonstrations and riots, peasant uprisings, and a coup d'état. It is called a revolution in retrospect and by virtue of the Duc de Liancourt's classic remark to Louis XVI. The American Revolution began with a series of increasingly violent urban riots and small-scale terrorism that grew into a protracted guerrilla war.

6. The universe of concern, civil violence, is formally defined as *all collective, nongovernmental attacks on persons or property, resulting in intentional damage to them, that occur within the boundaries of an autonomous or colonial political unit.* The terms "civil strife," "violent civil conflict," and "civil violence" are used synonymously in this article. The universe subsumes more narrowly defined sets of events such as "internal war," which Harry Eckstein defines as "any resort to violence within a political order to change its constitution, rulers, or policies" (in "On the Etiology of Internal Wars," 133), and "revolution," typically defined in terms of violently accomplished fundamental change in social institutions.

7. Bryant Wedge argues (in a personal communication) that much human aggression, including some civil strife, may arise from a threat-fear-aggression sequence. Leonard Berkowitz, however, proposes that this mechanism can be subsumed by frustration-aggression theory, the inferred sequence being threat (anticipated frustration)-fear-anger-aggression, in *Aggression: A Social Psychological Analysis* (New York, 1962), chap. 2. It may be conceptually useful to distinguish the two mechanisms; it nonetheless appears likely that most variables affecting the out-

come of the frustration-aggression sequence also are operative in the postulated threat-aggression sequence.

8. Konrad Lorenz, *On Aggression* (New York, 1966), xii.

9. Sigmund Freud, *Civilization and Its Discontents,* trans. Joan Riviere (London, 1930); Lorenz, chaps. 13, 14. Freud's instinctual interpretation of aggression is advanced in his later works; his early view was that aggression is a response to frustration of pleasure-seeking behavior. For a review and critique of other instinct theories of aggression, see Berkowitz, chap. I.

10. H. L. Nieburg, "The Threats of Violence and Social Change," *American Political Science Review,* LVI (December 1962), 870.

11. A characteristic study is Albert Bandura and Richard H. Walters, *Social Learning and Personality Development* (New York, 1963). For a commentary on instrumental aggression, see Berkowitz, esp. 30-32, 182-83, 201-02.

12. Chalmers Johnson, *Revolutionary Change* (Boston, 1966), 12, 13, italics added.

13. Talcott Parsons, "Some Reflections on the Place of Force in Social Process," in Harry Eckstein, ed., *Internal War: Problems and Approaches* (New York, 1964), 34-35.

14. Thomas C. Schelling, *The Strategy of Conflict* (Cambridge, Mass., 1960), 4.

15. P. 161.

16. The most influential and systematic statement of the theory is John Dollard and others, *Frustration and Aggression* (New Haven, 1939). Two important recent syntheses of the evidence are Berkowitz, *Aggression,* and Aubrey J. Yates, *Frustration and Conflict* (New York, 1962). Also see Leonard Berkowitz, "The Concept of Aggressive Drive: Some Additional Considerations," in Berkowitz, ed., *Advances in Experimental Psychology,* Vol. II (New York, 1965), 307-22.

17. Norman R. F. Maier, *Frustration: The Study of Behavior Without a Goal* (New York, 1949), 92-115, 159-61. Maier postulates a frustration threshold that may open the way to any of four classes of "goal-less" behavior of which aggression is only one. His findings have not been related adequately to the body of research on the frustration-aggression relationship. One can suggest, however, that the nonaggressive responses— fixation, regression, and apparent resignation—can be treated as more or less innate responses in a response hierarchy which are resorted to in the absence of aggression-evoking cues.

18. Neil J. Smelser, *Theory of Collective Behavior* (New York, 1963).

19. David Willer and George K. Zollschan, "Prolegomenon to a Theory of Revolutions," in George K. Zollschan and Walter Hirsch, eds., *Explorations in Social Change* (Boston, 1964), 125-51.

20. Ronald G. Ridker, "Discontent and Economic Growth," *Economic Development and Cultural Change,* XI (October 1962), 1-15.

21. James C. Davies, "Toward a Theory of Revolution," *American Sociological Review,* XXVII (February 1962), 5-19.

22. Johan Galtung, "A Structural Theory of Aggression," *Journal of Peace Research,* II, No. 2 (1964), 95.

23. Ivo K. and Rosalind L. Feierabend, in "Aggressive Behaviors Within Politics, 1948-1962: A Cross-National Study," *Journal of Conflict Resolution,* X

(September 1966), 249-71, have formally equated political instability with aggressive behavior and have derived and tested several hypotheses about stability from frustration-aggression theory. They have attempted no general theoretical synthesis, however.

24. The term "instigating" is adapted from the behavioristic terminology of Dollard and others. Instigating variables determine the strength of instigation, i.e., stimulus or motivation, to a particular kind of behavior. Mediating variables refer to intervening conditions, internal or external to the actors, which modify the expression of that behavior.

25. The phrase "relative deprivation" was first used systematically in Samuel A. Stouffer and others, *The American Soldier: Adjustment During Army Life,* Vol. I (Princeton, 1949), to denote the violation of expectations. J. Stacy Adams reviews the concept's history and some relevant evidence and suggests that feelings of injustice intervene between the condition of relative deprivation and responses to it, in "Inequity in Social Exchange," in Berkowitz, ed., *Advances in Experimental Psychology,* 267-300. The "injustice" aspect is implicit in my definition and use of relative deprivation as *perceived* discrepancy between what people think they will get and what they believe they are entitled to. The Stouffer concept has been related to levels of social satisfaction and to anomie, but has not, so far as I know, been associated with the discontent-anger-rage continuum in the frustration-aggression relationship.

26. David F. Aberle, "A Note on Relative Deprivation Theory," in Sylvia L. Thrupp, ed., *Millennial Dreams in Action: Essays in Comparative Study* (The Hague, 1962), 209-14. Bert Hoselitz and Ann Willner similarly distinguish between expectations, regarded by the individual as "what is rightfully owed to him," and aspirations, which represent "that which he would like to have but has not necessarily had or considered his due," in "Economic Development, Political Strategies, and American Aid," in Morton A. Kaplan, ed., *The Revolution in World Politics* (New York, 1962), 363.

27. Yates, 175-78.

28. Aberle, 210.

29. The Feierabends use the comparable term "systemic frustration" to describe the balance between "social want satisfaction" and "social want formation."

30. Hadley Cantril's work offers examples, especially *The Pattern of Human Concerns* (New Brunswick, 1965).

31. This approach is exemplified by the Feierabends' work and by Bruce M. Russett, "Inequality and Instability: The Relation of Land Tenure to Politics," *World Politics,* XVI (April 1964), 442-54.

32. The basic postulate of Dollard and others is that "the occurrence of aggressive behavior always presupposes the existence of frustration and, contrariwise, that the existence of frustration always leads to some form of aggression" (p. 1). It is evident from context and from subsequent articles that this statement was intended in more qualified fashion.

33. Ibid., 28.

34. Charles Tilly, *The Vendée* (Cambridge, Mass., 1964).

35. Reuben de Hoyos, personal communication.

36. Gregory Massell, "The Strategy of Social Change and the Role of Women in Soviet Central Asia: A Case Study in Modernization and Control," Ph.D. diss., Harvard University, 1966.

37. For this kind of approach, see Daniel Lerner, "Toward a Communication Theory of Modernization: A Set of Considerations," in Lucian W. Pye, ed., *Communications and Political Development* (Princeton, 1963), 330-35.

38. This general statement of theory is concerned with specification of variables and their effects, not with their content in specific cases; hence the conditions that determine the *levels* of expectation and changes in those levels are not treated here, nor are the conditions that affect perceptions about value capabilities. For some attempts to generalize about such conditions see Ted Gurr, "The Genesis of Violence: A Multivariate Theory of Civil Strife," Ph.D. diss., New York University, 1965, esp. chaps. 6-8. For empirical evaluation or application of the theory, it is of course necessary to evaluate in some way levels of expectation in the population(s) studied. Some approaches to evaluation are illustrated in Ted Gurr with Charles Ruttenberg, *The Conditions of Civil Violence: First Tests of a Causal Model,* Center of International Studies, Princeton University, Research Monograph No. 28 (Princeton, 1967); and Ted Gurr, "Explanatory Models for Civil Strife Using Aggregate Data," a paper read at the Annual Meeting of the American Political Science Association, 1967.

39. See Berkowitz, *Aggression,* 53-54.

40. Eric Hoffer, *The True Believer* (New York, 1951), 27-28.

41. Compare Crawford Young, *Politics in the Congo* (Princeton, 1965), chap. 13, with commentaries on the Kwilu and Stanleyville rebellions, such as Renée C. Fox and others, "'The Second Independence': A Case Study of the Kwilu Rebellion in the Congo," *Comparative Studies in Society and History,* VIII (October 1965), 78-109; and Herbert Weiss, *Political Protest in the Congo* (Princeton, 1967).

42. See, among many other works, Georges Lefebvre, *The Coming of the French Revolution* (Princeton, 1947), Part II.

43. Value expectations are defined above in terms of the value positions to which men believe they are justifiably entitled; the discussion here assumes that men may also regard as justifiable some types of interference with those value positions.

44. Nicholas Pastore, "The Role of Arbitrariness in the Frustration-Aggression Hypothesis," *Journal of Abnormal and Social Psychology,* XLVII (July 1952), 728-31; John J. Kregarman and Philip Worchel, "Arbitrariness of Frustration and Aggression," *Journal of Abnormal and Social Psychology,* LXIII (July 1961), 183-87.

45. The argument is that people comply "to gain both the symbolic rewards of governmental action and the actual rewards with which government originally associated itself" and rationalize compliance with "the feeling that the regime is a morally appropriate agent of control" (Richard M. Merelman, "Learning and Legitimacy," *American Political Science Review,* LX [September 1966], 551). The argument applies equally well to compliance, including acceptance of deprivation, with the demands of other social institutions.

46. Walt W. Rostow, *British Economy of the Nineteenth Century* (Oxford, 1948), chap. 5.

47. George Rudé, "Prices, Wages, and Popular Movements in Paris During the French Revolution," *Economic History Review,* VI (1954), 246-67, and *The Crowd in*

History, 1730-1848 (New York, 1964), chap. 7.

48. Carl Hovland and Robert Sears, "Minor Studies in Aggression, VI: Correlation of Lynchings with Economic Indices," *Journal of Psychology,* IX (1940), 301-10.

49. William Kornhauser, *The Politics of Mass Society* (New York, 1959), 160.

50. "Aggressive Behaviors Within Polities."

51. Robert L. Hamblin and others, "The Interference-Aggression Law?" *Sociometry,* XXVI (1963), 190-216.

52. Bruce M. Russett and others, *World Handbook of Political and Social Indicators* (New Haven, 1963), 97-100.

53. There is a threshold effect with reference to physical well-being. If life itself is the value threatened and the threat is imminent, the emotional response tends to be fear or panic; once the immediate threat is past, anger against the source of threat tends to manifest itself again. See note 7 above, and Berkowitz, *Aggression,* 42-46.

54. Leonard Berkowitz, "Repeated Frustrations and Expectations in Hostility Arousal," *Journal of Abnormal and Social Psychology,* LX (May 1960), 422-29.

55. See, for example, Daniel Lerner, *The Passing of Traditional Society* (Glencoe, 1958).

56. Denis W. Brogan, *The Price of Revolution* (London, 1951), 34.

57. Norman R. C. Cohn, *The Pursuit of the Millenium,* 2d ed. rev. (New York, 1961), 315.

58. Merle Kling, "Toward a Theory of Power and Political Instability in Latin America," *Western Political Quarterly,* IX (March 1956), 21-35.

59. Ridker, 15; Mancur Olson, Jr., "Growth as a Destabilizing Force," *Journal of Economic History,* XXIII (December 1963), 550-51.

60. Gurr with Ruttenberg.

61. Dollard and others, 34.

62. For summaries of findings, see Richard H. Walters, "Implications of Laboratory Studies of Aggression for the Control and Regulation of Violence," *Annals of the American Academy of Political and Social Science,* CCCLXIV (March 1966), 60-72; and Elton D. McNeil, "Psychology and Aggression," *Journal of Conflict Resolution,* III (September 1959), 225-31.

63. Pp. 231-36, 261-68, 332, 365-79.

64. Chalmers Johnson, *Revolution and the Social System* (Stanford, 1964), 16-17.

65. Andrew Janos, *The Seizure of Power: A Study of Force and Popular Consent,* Center of International Studies, Princeton University, Research Monograph No. 16 (Princeton, 1964), 5.

66. See, for example, H. O. Dahlke, "Race and Minority Riots: A Study in the Typology of Violence," *Social Forces,* XXX (May 1952), 419-25.

67. Peter Paret and John W. Shy, *Guerrillas in the 1960's,* rev. ed. (New York, 1964), 34-35.

68. *Frustration,* passim.

69. Jennifer G. Walton, "Correlates of Coerciveness and Permissiveness of National Political Systems: A Cross-National Study," M.A. thesis, San Diego State College, 1965.

70. Douglas Bwy, "Governmental Instability in Latin America: The Preliminary Test of a Causal Model of the Impulse to 'Extra-Legal' Change," paper

read at the Annual Meeting of the American Psychological Association, 1966.

71. Harold Lasswell and Abraham Kaplan, *Power and Society: A Framework for Political Inquiry* (New Haven, 1950), 265-66.

72. "Some Reflections on the Place of Force."

73. J. W. Thibaut and J. Coules, "The Role of Communication in the Reduction of Interpersonal Hostility," *Journal of Abnormal and Social Psychology,* XLVII (October 1952), 770-77.

74. See Leon Festinger, *A Theory of Cognitive Dissonance* (Evanston, 1957).

75. Arthur R. Cohen and others, "Commitment to Social Deprivation and Verbal Conditioning," *Journal of Abnormal and Social Psychology,* LXVII (November 1963), 410-21.

76. Neal E. Miller, "Theory and Experiment Relating Psychoanalytic Displacement to Stimulus-Response Generalization," *Journal of Abnormal and Social Psychology,* XLIII (April 1948), 155-78.

77. *Aggression,* chap. 6.

78. See note 48 above.

79. Rudé, *The Crowd in History,* chap. 5. The high levels of verbal aggression directed against the employers suggest that displacement was involved, not a perception of the machines rather than employers as sources of deprivation. In the Luddite riots, fear of retribution for direct attacks on the owners, contrasted with the frequent lack of sanctions against attacks on the machines, was the probable cause of object generalization. In the Madagascar and Angola cases structural and conceptual factors were responsible: the African rebels were not accessible to attack but local Africans were seen as like them and hence as potential or clandestine rebels.

80. Some such evidence is summarized in Berkowitz, "The Concept of Aggressive Drive," 325-27.

81. A critical and qualifying review of evidence to this effect is F. Glenn Abney and Larry B. Hill, "Natural Disasters as a Political Variable: The Effect of a Hurricane on an Urban Election," *American Political Science Review,* LX (December 1966), 974-81.

82. Kornhauser, 151. For interview evidence on the motives of protest voting, see Hadley Cantril, *The Politics of Despair* (New York, 1958).

83. Representative studies are Cohn; James W. Fernandez, "African Religious Movements: Types and Dynamics," *Journal of Modern African Studies,* II, No. 4 (1964), 531-49; and Vittorio Lanternari, *The Religions of the Oppressed* (New York, 1963).

84. Summarized in Walters.

85. Leonard Berkowitz, "Aggressive Cues in Aggressive Behavior and Hostility Catharsis," *Psychological Review,* LXXI (March 1964), 104-22, quotation from 106.

86. Rudé, *The Crowd in History,* 19-45.

87. E. J. Hobsbawm, *Social Bandits and Primitive Rebels,* 2nd ed. (Glencoe, 1959), 63-64.

88. Chap. 5.

89. P. 31.

90. Gustave Le Bon, *The Psychology of Revolution* (London, 1913); Pitirim Sorokin, *The Sociology of Revolutions* (Philadelphia, 1925).

91. Representative studies include J.R.P. French, Jr., "The Disruption and

Cohesion of Groups," *Journal of Abnormal and Social Psychology,* XXXVI (July 1941), 361-77; A. Pepitone and G. Reichling, "Group Cohesiveness and the Expression of Hostility," *Human Relations,* VIII, No. 3 (1955), 327-37; and Ezra Stotland, "Peer Groups and Reactions to Power Figures," in Dorwin Cartwright, ed., *Studies in Social Power* (Ann Arbor, 1959), 53-68.

92. Pp. 272-75, quotation from 273.

93. Clark Kerr and Abraham Siegel, "The Isolated Mass and the Integrated Individual: An International Analysis of the Inter-Industry Propensity to Strike," in Arthur Kornhauser and others, eds., *Industrial Conflict* (New York, 1954), 189-212.

94. Norman C. Meier and others, "An Experimental Approach to the Study of Mob Behavior," *Journal of Abnormal and Social Psychology,* XXXVI (October 1941), 506-24. Also see George Wada and James C. Davies, "Riots and Rioters," *Western Political Quarterly,* X (December 1957), 864-74.

95. See Walters; Norman Polansky and others, "An Investigation of Behavioral Contagion in Groups," *Human Relations,* III, No. 3 (1950), 319-48; and Leonard Berkowitz and Russell G. Geen, "Film Violence and the Cue Properties of Available Targets," *Journal of Personality and Social Psychology,* III (June 1966), 525-30.

96. Rudé, *The Crowd in History;* Henri Mendras and Yves Tavernier, "Les Manifestations de juin 1961," *Revue française des sciences politiques,* XII (September 1962), 647-71.

97. Representative typologies are proposed by Johnson, *Revolution and the Social System,* 26-68; Rudolph J. Rummel, "Dimensions of Conflict Behavior Within and Between Nations," *Yearbook of the Society for General Systems Research,* VIII (1963), 25-26; and Harry Eckstein, "Internal Wars: A Taxonomy," unpublished (1960).

98. Two summary articles on these factor analyses are Rudolph J. Rummel, "A Field Theory of Social Action With Application to Conflict Within Nations," *Yearbook of the Society for General Systems Research,* X (1965), 183-204; and Tanter. What I call internal war is referred to in these sources as subversion; I label conspiracy what these sources call revolution. My terminology is, I believe, less ambiguous and more in keeping with general scholarly usage.

99. Hugh Seton-Watson, "Twentieth Century Revolutions," *Political Quarterly,* XXII (July 1951), 258.

100. For example, it has been used by Bryant Wedge to analyze and compare interview materials gathered in the study of two Latin American revolutions, in "Student Participation in Revolutionary Violence: Brazil, 1964, and Dominican Republic, 1965," a paper read at the Annual Meeting of the American Political Science Association, Chicago, Ill., 1967.

101. Studies based on this theoretical model and using cross-national aggregate data include Ted Gurr, *New Error-Compensated Measures for Comparing Nations: Some Correlates of Civil Strife,* Center of International Studies, Princeton University, Research Monograph No. 25 (Princeton, 1966); Gurr with Ruttenberg; Gurr, "Explanatory Models for Civil Strife"; and Gurr, "Why Urban Disorders? Perspectives From the Comparative Study of Civil Strife," *American Behavioral Scientist* (forthcoming).

12
Aggressive Behaviors Within Politics, 1948-1962: A Cross-National Study[1]

Ivo K. Feierabend[2]
and Rosalind L. Feierabend[3]

A recent trend in behavioral research is the systematic and empirical analysis of conflict behaviors both within and among nations. External conflict behaviors among nations are typified by wars, embargoes, interruption of diplomatic relations, and other behaviors indicative of aggression between national political systems. Internal conflict behaviors within nations, on the other hand, consist of such events as demonstrations, riots, coups d'état, guerrilla warfare, and others denoting the relative instability of political systems.

There are a few studies which have attempted systematic empirical analyses of internal conflict, more or less broadly based in cross-national studies (Kling 1959; LeVine 1959; Davies 1962; Eckstein 1962, 1964; Feierabend, Feierabend, and Nesvold 1963; Haas 1964; Russett 1964; Nesvold 1964; Hoole 1964; Conroe 1965; Walton 1965). Furthermore, cross-national inquiry, as a method, is being used by many researchers (Cattell 1949, 1950, 1951; Rokkan 1955; Lerner 1957, 1958; Lipset 1959, 1960; Inkeles 1960; Deutsch 1960, 1961; Deutsch and Eckstein 1961; Fitzgibbon and Johnson 1961; McClelland 1961; Cantril and Free 1962; Cantril 1963, 1965; Banks and Textor 1963; Almond and Verba 1963; Russett et al. 1964; Gregg and Banks 1965; Merritt and Rokkan 1966; Singer and Small 1966; Rokkan forthcoming). All of these efforts have in common an interest in abstracting relevant dimensions on which to compare large numbers of nations. Some (McClelland 1961; Cantril and Free 1962; Cantril 1963, 1965; Almond and Verba 1963) are concerned with measuring

The original version of this article appeared under the title "Aggressive Behaviors Within Politics, 1948-1962: A Cross-National Study," by Ivo and Rosalind Feierabend published in *Journal of Conflict Resolution* 10, no. 3 (September 1966):249-271, and is reprinted herewith by permission of Sage Publications, Inc., and of the authors.

psychological dimensions. Others (especially Banks and Textor 1963; Russett et al. 1964) are directed toward a large-scale empirical assessment of the interrelationships among all available ecological variables — political, economic, and societal. A very few (Rummel 1963, 1965, 1966; Tanter 1964, 1966; Hoole 1964; Feierabend, Feierabend, and Litell 1966) attempt to discover the structure of the complex universe of internal or external conflict behavior through factor analysis.

The studies here described are directly concerned with the measurement of political instability and, furthermore, with a search for the correlates of internal conflict behaviors. As a first step, a theoretical framework is adopted to aid in the analysis of the problem.

Theoretical Framework

Although political instability is a concept that can be explicated in more than one way, the definition used in this analysis limits its meaning to aggressive, politically relevant behaviors. Specifically, it is defined as the degree or the amount of aggression directed by individuals or groups within the political system against other groups or against the complex of officeholders and individuals and groups associated with them. Or, conversely, it is the amount of aggression directed by these officeholders against other individuals, groups, or officeholders within the polity.

Once this meaning is ascribed, the theoretical insights and elaborations of frustration–aggression theory become available (Dollard et al. 1939; Maier 1949; McNeil 1959; Buss 1961; Berkowitz 1962). Perhaps the most basic and generalized postulate of the theory maintains that "aggression is always the result of frustration" (Dollard et al. 1939:3), while frustration may lead to other modes of behavior, such as constructive solutions to problems. Furthermore, aggression is not likely to occur if aggressive behavior is inhibited through devices associated with the notion of punishment. Or it may be displaced onto objects other than those perceived as the frustrating agents.[4]

The utility of these few concepts is obvious. Political instability is identified as aggressive behavior. It should then result from situations of unrelieved, socially experienced frustration. Such situations may be typified as those in which levels of social expectations, aspirations, and needs are raised for many people for significant periods of time, and yet remain unmatched by equivalent levels of satisfactions. The notation

$$\frac{\text{social want satisfaction}}{\text{social want formation}} = \text{systemic frustration}$$

indicates this relationship. Two types of situations which are apt to produce high levels of systemic frustration are investigated in this research, although certainly many other possibilities are open to study.

In applying the frustration-aggression framework to the political sphere, the concept of punishment may be identified with the notion of coerciveness of political regimes. And the constructive solution of problems is related to the political as well as the administrative, entrepreneurial, and other capabilities available in the environment of politics. The notion of displacement may furthermore be associated with the occurrence of scapegoating against minority groups or aggression in the international sphere or in individual behaviors.

The following general hypotheses are yielded by applying frustration-aggression theory to the problem of political stability:

1. Under a situation of relative lack of systemic frustration, political stability is to be expected.
2. If systemic frustration is present, political stability still may be predicted, given the following considerations:
   a.   It is a nonparticipant society. Politically relevant strata capable of organized action are largely lacking.
   b.   It is a participant society in which constructive solutions to frustrating situations are available or anticipated. (The effectiveness of government and also the legitimacy of regimes will be relevant factors.)
   c.   If a sufficiently coercive government is capable of preventing overt acts of hostility against itself, then a relatively stable polity may be anticipated.
   d.   If, as a result of the coerciveness of government, the aggressive impulse is vented or displaced in aggression against minority groups and/or
   e.   against other nations, then stability can be predicted.
   f.   If individual acts of aggression are sufficiently abundant to provide an outlet, stability may occur in the face of systemic frustration.
3. However, in the relative absence of these qualifying conditions, aggressive behavior in the form of political instability is predicted to be the consequence of systemic frustration.

A more refined set of hypotheses concerning socially aggressive behaviors and frustration can be achieved by interpreting the frustration-aggression hypothesis within the framework of theories of social and political action and political systems (Merton 1949; Parsons and Shils 1951; Lasswell 1951; Almond 1960; Parsons et al. 1961; Deutsch 1963; Easton 1965a, 1965b; Gurr 1965).

Methodology

The methodology of the studies is indicated by the scope of the problem. Concern is not with the dynamics underlying stability in any one particular country but with the determinants of stability within all national political systems. As many cases as possible, or at least an appropriate sample of cases, must be analyzed. Thus the present studies are cross-national endeavors in which data are collected and analyzed for as many as eighty-four polities. (The eighty-four nations are listed in Table 12.1.) The cross-national method is here conceived in similar terms as the cross-cultural studies of anthropology (Whiting and Child 1953; Murdock 1957; Feierabend 1962).

A crucial aspect of the research is the collection of relevant cross-national data. Although data are available on ecological variables of political systems through the Yale Political Data Program, the Dimensionality of Nations Project, and the Cross-Polity Survey, data collections on the political stability dimension are scarcer.

In order to carry out the research, data on internal conflict behaviors were collected for eighty-four nations for a fifteen-year period, 1948-1962. The data derive from two sources: *Deadline Data on World Affairs* and the *Encyclopaedia Britannica Yearbooks*. They are organized into a particular format in which each instability event is characterized according to country in which it occurs, date, persons involved, presence or absence of violence, and other pertinent characteristics (Feierabend and Feierabend 1965a). The data are on IBM cards, creating a storage bank of some 5,000 events.[5]

Study 1: The Analysis of the Dependent Variable: Political Stability

With Betty A. Nesvold, Francis W. Hoole, and Norman G. Litell

In order to evaluate the political stability-instability continuum, data collected on internal conflict behavior were scaled. The ordering of specific instability events into a scale was approached from the viewpoint of both construct validity and consensual validation (Nesvold 1964).

A seven-point instrument was devised, ranging from 0 (denoting extreme stability) through 6 (denoting extreme instability). Each point of the scale was observationally defined in terms of specific events representing differing degrees of stability or instability. An illustration may be given of one item typical of each position on the scale. Thus, for example, a general election is an item associated with a 0 position on the rating instructions. Resignation of a cabinet official falls into the 1 position on the scale; peaceful demonstrations into the 2 position; assassination of a significant political figure into the 3 position; mass arrests into the 4 position; coups d'état into the 5 position; and civil war into the 6 position.

Consensual validation for this intensity scale was obtained by asking judges to sort the same events along the same continuum. The level of agreement among judges on the distribution of the items was fairly high (Pearson r = .87). Other checks performed on the reliability of the method were a comparison of the assignment of items to positions on the scale by two independent raters. Their level of agreement for the task, involving data from eighty-four countries for a seven-year time period, was very high (Pearson r = .935).

Using this scaling instrument, stability profiles for the sample of eighty-four nations were ascertained for the seven-year period, 1955-1961. Countries were assigned to groups on the basis of the most unstable event which they experienced during this seven-year period. Thus countries which experienced a civil war were placed in group 6; countries which were prey to a coup d'état were placed in group 5; countries with mass arrests were assigned to group 4, and so on. The purpose of this assignment was to weight intensity (or quality) of instability events equally with the frequency (or quantity) of events.

Following the allotment to groups, a sum total of each country's stability ratings was calculated. Countries were then rank ordered within groups on the basis of this frequency sum total. The results of the ratings are given in Table 12.1.[6]

In this table, it may be seen first of all that the distribution is skewed. Instability is more prevalent than stability within the sample of nations, and the largest proportion of countries are those experiencing an instability event with a scale weighting of 4. Furthermore, there is an interesting combination of countries at each scale position. The most stable scale positions, by and large, include modern nations but also a sprinkling of markedly underdeveloped polities and some nations from the Communist bloc. Again, the small group of extremely unstable countries at scale position 6 comprise nations from Latin America, Asia, and the Communist bloc. The United States, contrary perhaps to ethnocentric expectations, is not at scale position 1 although it is on the stable side of the scale.

Another approach to the ordering of internal conflict behavior was based upon frequency alone (Hoole 1964).[7] The frequency of occurrence of thirty types of internal conflict behaviors was determined for the eighty-four countries for the time period 1948-1962. Analysis in terms of frequency was used in three different ways:

1. A global instability profile for all types of events, for all countries, was drawn to show changes in world level of instability during the time period under study. As may be seen in Figure 12.1, instability has been on the increase in recent years, reaching one peak in the late 1950s and an even

TABLE 12.1   Frequency Distribution of Countries in Terms of Their Degree of Relative Political Stability, 1955-1961 (stability score shown for each country)

0 STABILITY	1	2	3	4	5	6 INSTABILITY
				France 499		
				U. of S. Africa 495		
				Haiti 478		
				Poland 465		
				Spain 463		
				Dom. Rep. 463		
				Iran 459		
				Ceylon 454		
				Japan 453		
				Thailand 451		
				Mexico 451		
				Ghana 451		
				Jordan 448		
				Sudan 445		
				Morocco 443		
				Egypt 438		
				Pakistan 437		
				Italy 433		
				Belgium 432		
				Paraguay 431		
				USSR 430		
			Tunisia 328	Nicaragua 430		
			Gr. Britain 325	Chile 427		
			Portugal 323	Burma 427	India 599	
			Uruguay 318	Yugoslavia 422	Argentina 599	
			Israel 317	Panama 422	Korea 596	
			Canada 317	Ecuador 422	Venezuela 584	
	Norway 104		U. S. 316	China 422	Turkey 583	
	Netherlands 104		Taiwan 314	El Salvador 421	Lebanon 581	
	Cambodia 104	W. Germany 217	Libya 309	Liberia 415	Iraq 579	
	Sweden 103	Czech. 212	Austria 309	Malaya 413	Bolivia 556	
	Saudi Ar. 103	Finland 211	E. Germany 307	Albania 412	Syria 554	Indonesia 699
	Iceland 103	Romania 206	Ethiopia 307	Greece 409	Peru 552	Cuba 699
	Philippines 101	Ireland 202	Denmark 306	Bulgaria 407	Guatemala 546	Colombia 681
	Luxembourg 101	Costa Rica 202	Australia 306	Afghanistan 404	Brazil 541	Laos 652
N. Zea. 000			Switzer. 303		Honduras 535	Hungary 652
					Cyprus 526	

higher level in the early 1960s.

2. Frequencies of particular types of instability behaviors were compared for the entire sample of countries. The range of frequencies was from 18 (execution of significant persons) to 403 (acquisition of office). When the events were rank ordered in terms of frequency of occurrence and the rank ordering divided into quartiles, the first quartile, with the highest frequency of occurrence (1,555 occurrences) included events denoting routine governmental change (such as acquisition of office, vacation of office, elections, and significant changes of laws). The second quartile (704 occurrences) appeared to be one of unrest, including such events as large-scale demonstrations, general strikes, arrests, and martial law. The third quartile (333 occurrences) indicated serious societal disturbance, in the form of coups d'état, terrorism and sabotage, guerrilla warfare, and exile. And the fourth quartile (150 occurrences) consisted primarily of events connoting violence: executions, severe riots, civil war. Thus an inverse relationship was revealed between the frequency of occurrence of an event and the in-

FIGURE 12.1   Frequency of Variables by Year, 1948-1962

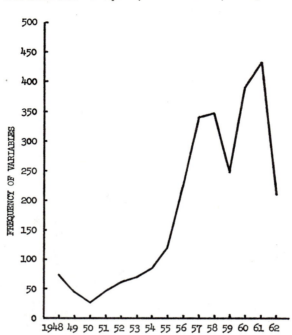

tensity of violence which it denotes.

3. Finally, countries were compared for the relative frequency of occurrence of all thirty instability behaviors during this time period. The range was from 136 events (France) to 1 event (Switzerland). The median of this distribution was represented by Laos and Burma, with 28 and 26 events, respectively.

An additional refinement in the understanding of political instability is achieved by factor analysis, which reduces the large number of observed variables to a smaller number of underlying dimensions. Four previous factor analyses of internal conflict behaviors have been performed. Rummel (1963), factor analyzing nine types of internal conflict behaviors for a three-year time period (1955-1957), emerged with three underlying dimensions: turmoil, revolution, and subversion. Tanter (1964, 1966), replicating the Rummel variables for the years 1958-1960, found a two-factor solution: turmoil and internal war. Recently, Rummel (1966) factor analyzed thirteen variables obtained from Eckstein's collection of internal conflict behaviors (Eckstein 1962) for the time period 1946-1950. This factor analysis again yielded three dimensions, which Rummel identifies with the three dimensions of the 1963 factor solution, namely, revolution, subversion, and turmoil. Hoole (1964) factor analyzed thirty variables collected over a fifteen-year time span, 1948-1962, from a single source (see note 5), and emerged with five major and five minor factors. The five major factors were labelled: demonstrations, change of officeholder, riots, guerrilla warfare, and strikes.

Most recently, Feierabend, Feierabend, and Litell (1966), using Hoole's thirty variables for the fifteen-year period 1948-1962 and the complete data bank derived from two sources, performed a factor analysis with a principal components solution and an orthogonal Varimax rotation. (See Table 12.2 for the rotated factor matrix.) Nine factors emerged. The first three of these, ranked according to importance in terms of the amount of variance accounted for after rotation, were labelled, first, a turmoil dimension (characterized by violence and mass participation); second, a palace revolution–revolt dimension (distinguished by a marked lack of mass support); and, third, a power struggle–purge dimension (connoting violent upheavals and changes of office within regimes). It will be noted that there is definite correspondence between the first two factors revealed in this analysis and the factors discovered by both Rummel and Tanter.

Looking at the variables with the highest loadings on each factor, we see that the first factor comprises strikes of all types; demonstrations and riots, large and small, violent and severe; and also mass arrests and terrorism. One could say that it denotes serious, widespread disturbance, anomie, popular mass participation, and some governmental retaliation.

The second factor presents a sharp contrast to this mass turmoil dimension. It encompasses revolts, coups d'état, martial law, arrests of politically prominent leaders, and governmental action against specific groups. These events do not connote mass participation but rather extreme instability created by highly organized and conspiratorial elites and cliques. And the third factor presents yet another divergent pattern, including acquisition and loss of office, arrests and executions of politically significant figures, and some punitive action. Mass turmoil is not evident, as on the first factor; neither is the situation one of revolt and coup d'état. This is an instability dimension of violent internal power struggles, purges, depositions, and changes within ruling parties and cliques, which nevertheless remain in power.

The nine factors in combination account for 71.5 percent of the total variance. After rotation the three first factors combined account for over half of the common variance (53 percent). The remaining six factors, accounting in combination for less than half of the common variance, seem to

TABLE 12.2   Rotated Factor Matrix of Domestic Conflict Measures

VARIABLES	Mass partic- ipation —Tur- moil	Palace revo- lution —Re- volt	Power strug- gle— Purge	Riot	Elec- tion	Dem- on- stra- tion	Im- pris- on- ment	Civil war	Guer- rilla war- fare
1. Elections	29	-02	09	-18	70*	-10	-17	-05	-23
2. Vacation of office	38	08	74*	-14	20	-11	-15	-25	09
3. Significant change of laws	38	41	41	-01	31	15	-16	-23	-11
4. Acquisition of office	29	06	75*	-19	15	-04	-25	-19	22
5. Crisis within a nongovernmental organization	40	13	12	-21	04	-09	62*	07	-23
6. Organization of opposition party	08	10	-02	02	56*	36	19	-39	-10
7. Repressive action against specific groups	46	61*	27	01	-03	16	12	04	12
8. Micro strikes	67*	00	-15	-26	-16	05	12	03	23
9. General strikes	73*	13	04	-42	09	-06	03	08	-18
10. Macro strikes	43	-22	-11	-35	15	-17	-33	-12	-19
11. Micro demonstrations	61*	19	-02	02	20	59*	10	03	02
12. Macro demonstrations	73*	-01	00	26	06	19	18	-21	03
13. Micro riots	46	11	-06	68*	27	-03	-03	-15	11
14. Macro riots	69*	28	-04	33	20	02	04	-08	-05
15. Severe macro riots	64*	-03	-04	53*	11	-19	-02	-20	14
16. Arrests of significant persons	09	64*	54*	07	-14	-06	23	-10	-01
17. Imprisonment of significant persons	-14	12	49	17	-05	16	38	-33	-22
18. Arrests of few insignificant persons	42	09	05	-08	07	75*	07	07	21
19. Mass arrests of insignificant persons	52*	33	14	54*	-12	-02	-01	05	01
20. Imprisonment of insignificant persons	26	-08	09	08	-12	34	64*	-03	-14
21. Assassination	17	40	23	06	24	23	-07	-10	56*
22. Martial law	11	71*	03	03	15	09	-27	-06	-08
23. Execution of significant persons	-08	01	54*	31	-26	14	-04	31	05
24. Execution of insignificant persons	01	-10	63*	32	-07	12	-02	47	-02
25. Terrorism and sabotage	62*	28	12	-21	13	-01	10	07	38
26. Guerrilla warfare	04	42	07	-19	19	-35	25	21	55*
27. Civil war	-14	25	31	14	45	08	-08	60*	02
28. Coup d'état	03	69*	07	01	-02	12	-40	07	-32
29. Revolts	06	75*	-01	11	07	-01	-10	32	16
30. Exile	-09	40	00	03	-36	32	-19	-13	04
Percentage of common variance	23.37	16.30	13.20	9.67	8.33	8.00	7.99	6.76	6.40 = 100.0
Percentage of total variance	23.33	11.11	7.52	6.77	5.89	5.32	4.18	3.82	3.62 = 71.46

* Asterisks indicate loadings >.50. Decimals omitted from loadings.

reveal the following patterns: a specific riot dimension; an election dimension; two factors connoting mild, limited unrest; and, finally, two separate dimensions of civil war and guerrilla warfare, respectively, the extreme forms of political instability.

Study 2: The Relation of Social Frustration and Modernity to Political Stability

With Betty A. Nesvold

Once the data for the dependent variable, political stability, were collected, factor analyzed, and scaled, the major step of seeking correlates of instability became feasible. In this attempt, two generalized and related hypotheses were investigated. (1) *The higher (lower) the social want formation in any given society and the lower (higher) the social want satisfaction, the greater (the less) the systemic frustration and the greater (the less) the impulse to political instability.* (2) *The highest and lowest points of the modernity continuum in any given society will tend to produce maximum stability in the political order, while a medium position on the continuum will produce maximum instability* (Nesvold 1964).

These hypotheses embody the basic propositions of the frustration-aggression theory, as well as insights gained from the literature on processes of modernization (Lerner 1958; Deutsch 1961; Cutright 1963). In the first hypothesis, the discrepancy between social wants and social satisfactions is postulated to be the index of systemic frustration. The relationship is represented as follows:

$$\frac{\text{want satisfaction low}}{\text{want formation high}} = \text{high frustration}$$

$$\frac{\text{want satisfaction low}}{\text{want formation low}} = \text{low frustration}$$

$$\frac{\text{want satisfaction high}}{\text{want formation high}} = \text{low frustration}$$

A variety of social conditions may satisfy or leave unsatisfied the social wants of different strata of the population within social systems. In our present century the process of modernization is certain to create new wants and aspirations, as well as to lead in the long run to their satisfaction.

The notion of modernity denotes a very complex set of social phenomena. It includes the aspiration and capacity in a society to produce and consume a wide range and quantity of goods and services. It includes high development in science, technology, and education, and high attainment in scores of specialized skills. It includes, moreover, new structures of social organization and participation, new sets of aspirations, attitudes, and ideologies. Modern affluent nations, with their complex of economic, political, and social systems, serve best as models of modernity to nations emerging from traditional society. In these transitional nations, the growing, politically relevant strata of the population are all participants in modern life. Lerner (1957), for one, states categorically that once traditional societies are exposed to the modern way of life, without exception they desire benefits associated with modernity.

The acquisition of modern goals, although an integral aspect of modernity, is hardly synonymous with their attainment. The notion of "the revolution of rising expectations" (Lerner 1958), also termed "the revolution of rising frustrations," points to the essentially frustrating nature of the modernization process. The arousal of an underdeveloped society to awareness of complex modern patterns of behavior and organization brings with it a desire to emulate and achieve the same high level of satisfaction. But there is an inevitable lag between aspiration and achievement which varies in length with the specific condition of the country. Furthermore, it may be postulated that the peak discrepancy between systemic goals and their satisfaction, and hence the maximum frustration, should come somewhere in the middle of the transitional phase between traditional society and the achievement of modernity. It is at this middle stage that awareness of modernity and exposure to modern patterns should be complete, that is, at a theoretical ceiling, whereas achievement levels would still be lagging far behind. Prior to this theoretical middle stage, exposure and achievement would both be lower. After the middle stage, exposure can no longer increase, since it already amounts to complete awareness, but achievement will continue to progress, thus carrying the nation eventually into the stage of modernity. Thus, in contrast to transitional societies, it may be postulated that traditional and modern societies will be less frustrated and therefore will tend to be more stable than transitional societies.

The most direct way to ascertain systemic frustration is through field work in the many countries, administering questionnaires (see Inkeles 1960; Doob 1960; Cantril 1963, 1965; Almond and Verba 1963). For the purpose of this study, an inexpensive and very indirect method was adopted.

The highly theoretical notions of want satisfaction and want formation were translated into observable definitions. For this purpose, available collections of cross-national statistical data were consulted and a few statistical items were chosen as appropriate indicators. The following selection of indicators was made: GNP and caloric intake per capita, physicians and telephones per unit of population were singled out as indices of satisfaction: newspapers and radios per unit of population were also included. Many other indicators denoting material or other satisfactions could have served the purpose. The selection was guided by parsimony as well as availability of data.

The indicators, of course, have different significance in referring to the satisfaction of different wants. Furthermore, their significance may vary at different levels of relative abundance or scarcity. A great deal of theorizing is necessary to select and use the indicators wisely. For example, it is possible that a country with many physicians and telephones may still be starving. Or, beyond a certain point, caloric intake cannot measure the satisfaction of some other less basic needs than hunger, while GNP per capita may do so.

For want formation, literacy and urbanization were chosen as indicators. This selection was influenced by the notion of exposure to modernity (Lerner 1958; Deutsch 1961). Exposure to modernity was judged a good mechanism for the formation of new wants, and literacy and city life were taken as the two agents most likely to bring about such exposure.

These eight indices (GNP, caloric intake, telephones, physicians, newspapers, radios, literacy, and urbanization) were used to construct both a frustration index and a modernity index. The modernity index was formed by combining scores on all of the eight indicators. Raw scores were first transformed into standard scores and then a mean standard score was calculated for each of the eighty-four countries on the basis of the available data. The frustration index was a ratio. A country's combined coded score on the six satisfaction indices (GNP, caloric intake, telephones, physicians, newspapers, and radios) was divided by either the country's coded literacy or coded urbanization score, whichever was higher.[8]

The data on the independent variables were collected for the years 1948-1955 whereas the stability ratings were made for the years 1955-1961. It was assumed that some lag would occur before social frustrations would make themselves felt in political aggressions, that is, political instabilities.

Results

The main finding of the study is that the higher the level of systemic frustration, as measured by the indices selected, the greater the political instability. The results are shown in Table 12.3. The stable countries are those which experience the least amount of measured systemic frustration. Conversely, the countries beset by political instability also suffer a high level of systemic frustration, although certain interesting exceptions occur.

Each indicator of want formation and satisfaction is also significantly related to political stability. The relationships between each indicator and stability are presented in Table 12.4. Another finding of interest in this table is that all eight indicators do not predict degree of stability with equal efficiency. Level of literacy is the best single predictor, as seen by the .90 degree of relationship (Yule's Q) between literacy and stability. Comparatively, GNP is one of the weaker predictors, along with percent of urbanization, population per physician, and caloric intake per capita per day.

These data on the predictors of political stability also determine empirical threshold values for each indicator. Above these values, countries are predominantly stable; below them, countries are predominantly unstable. The cutting point for each of the indicators was selected so as to

TABLE 12.3   Relationship Between Level of Systemic Frustration and Degree of Political Stability

| DEGREE OF POLITICAL STABILITY | INDEX OF SYSTEMIC FRUSTRATION | | | Total |
| | RATIO OF WANT FORMATION TO WANT SATISFACTION | | | |
	High systemic frustration		Low systemic frustration	
Unstable	Bolivia Brazil Bulgaria Ceylon Chile Colombia Cuba Cyprus Dom. Republic Ecuador Egypt El Salvador Greece Guatemala Haiti India Indonesia	Iran Iraq Italy Japan Korea Mexico Nicaragua Pakistan Panama Paraguay Peru Spain Syria Thailand Turkey Venezuela Yugoslavia 34	Argentina Belgium France Lebanon Morocco Union of South Africa 6	40
	2		20	
Stable	Philippines Tunisia		Australia New Zealand Austria Norway Canada Portugal Costa Rica Sweden Czech. Switzerland Denmark United States Finland Uruguay West Germany Great Britain Iceland Ireland Israel Netherlands	22
Total	36		26	62

Chi square** = 30.5, p = <.001   Yule's Q = .9653

* The number of cases in this and the following tables varies with the data available in the UN statistical sources. This table includes only those countries with data on all eight indices.
** All chi squares in this and the following tables are corrected for continuity in view of the small frequencies in the nonconforming cells.

reveal the maximum difference between stable and unstable countries.

From these empirical thresholds, a composite picture of the stable country emerges. It is a society which is 90 percent or more literate; with 65 or more radios and 120 or more newspapers per 1,000 population; with two percent or more of the population having telephones; with 2,525 or more calories per day per person; with not more than 1,900 persons per physician; with a GNP of 300 dollars or more per person per year; and with 45 percent or more of the population living in urban centers. If all of these

TABLE 12.4   Relationships Between the Eight Indicators of Systemic Frustration and Degree of Political Stability

A.   Literacy:

	% LITERATE		
	Low (below 90%)	High (above 90%)	Total
Unstable	48	5	53
Stable	10	19	29
Total	58	24	82

Chi square = 25.83; $p = <.001$
Yule's Q = .90

B.   Radios:

	PER 1,000 POPULATION		
	Low (below 65)	High (above 65)	Total
Unstable	45	6	51
Stable	9	20	29
Total	54	26	80

Chi square = 25.02; $p = <.001$
Yule's Q = .887

C.   Newspapers:

	PER 1,000 POPULATION		
	Low (below 120)	High (above 120)	Total
Unstable	48	5	53
Stable	6	10	16
Total	54	15	69

Chi square = 17.34; $p = <.001$
Yule's Q = .88

D.   Telephones:

	% OF POPULATION OWNING TELEPHONES		
	Low (below 2%)	High (above 2%)	Total
Unstable	35	6	41
Stable	7	18	25
Total	42	24	66

Chi square = 19.68; $p = <.001$
Yule's Q = .875

E.   Calories:

	PER CAPITA PER DAY		
	Low (below 2,525)	High (above 2,525)	Total
Unstable	39	10	49
Stable	8	20	28
Total	47	30	77

Chi square = 17.42; $p = <.001$
Yule's Q = .81

F.   Physicians:

	PEOPLE PER PHYSICIAN		
	Low (above 1,900)	High (below 1,900)	Total
Unstable	40	13	53
Stable	6	19	25
Total	46	32	78

Chi square = 11.41; $p = <.001$
Yule's Q = .81

G.   GNP:

	PER CAPITA (IN US DOLLARS)		
	Low (below 300)	High (above 300)	Total
Unstable	36	8	44
Stable	9	18	27
Total	45	26	71

Chi square = 14.92; $p = <.001$
Yule's Q = .80

H.   Urbanization:

	% OF POPULATION LIVING IN URBAN CENTERS		
	Low (below 45%)	High (above 45%)	Total
Unstable	38	6	44
Stable	11	15	26
Total	49	21	70

Chi square = 13.08; $p = <.001$
Yule's Q = .79

threshold values are attained by a society, there is an extremely high probability that the country will achieve relative political stability. Conversely, if gratifications are less than these threshold values, the more they fail to meet these levels, the greater the likelihood of political instability.

In order to investigate the relationship between modernity and stability, countries were rank ordered on the modernity index and the distribution was broken into three groups representing modern countries, transitional countries, and traditional countries. The cutting points for these three groups were to some extent arbitrary: the twenty-four countries which were highest on the modernity index were selected as the modern group. The traditional group was chosen to be equal in size to the modern group, while ranking at the opposite end of the modernity continuum. The remaining countries, falling between the modern and traditional groups, were designated transitional. The difficulty in determining the true state of the countries lies not so much in finding the cutting point for the modern group as in selecting the traditional one. Truly traditional countries do not report data and hence have no way of being included in the study. The countries designated traditional are simply less modern than those classed as transitional, but they have nonetheless been exposed to modernity.[9]

A mean stability score was calculated for each group of countries. The differences between the mean stability scores for the three groups were then estimated. According to the hypothesis, the difference in mean stability score should be greatest between the transitional group and either of the other two groups. The difference in mean stability score between modern and traditional countries should not be significant. The results are given in Table 12.5.

As may be seen in the table, the predicted difference between the stability level of modern and of transitional countries emerges as highly significant. The difference between modern and traditional countries is less but nonetheless also significant. And the difference between traditional and transitional countries does not reach significance. The difficulty in obtaining data on truly traditional countries undoubtedly contributes to the lack

TABLE 12.5   Relationship Between Modernity and Stability

Modernity level	N	Mean stability score	t	p^*	t	p^*
Modern countries	24	268				
			6.18	<.001		
Transitional countries	37	472			3.71	<.01
			1.53	>.05		
Traditional countries	23	420				

* Probability levels are two-tailed.

of significant difference between countries labelled in this sample as transitional and traditional.

In view of the lack of support in these eighty-four nations for the hypothesized curvilinear relationship between modernity and stability, the assumption may be made that all of the countries have been exposed to modernity. Hence want formation should be at a relatively high level throughout the sample. One might hypothesize that want formation reaches an early maximum with exposure to modernity, after which further awareness of the modern world can no longer increase desire for modernity. Under these conditions, the modernity index is also in fact a frustration index, indicating the extent to which these measured economic satisfactions are present within a society which may be presumed to have already been exposed to modernity.

To compare the relative efficacy of these two frustration indices, product-moment correlations were calculated between each index and stability. The results show that while both indices are significantly correlated with stability, the correlation between the so-called modernity index and stability is the higher of the two. The product-moment correlation between modernity and stability is .625; the correlation between the so-called frustration index and stability is .499. An *eta* calculated between the modernity index and the stability index, to show curvilinearity of relationship, is $\eta = .667$, which is not significantly different from the Pearson r of .625. Thus again the hypothesis of curvilinearity between modernity and stability is not supported.

Study 3: The Prediction of Changes in Political Stability over Time

With Wallace R. Conroe

In the previous study, stability, modernity, and the frustration index were all calculated as static measures. Each variable was represented by a single score, indicating an overall estimate of the level of the variable during the time period under study. The question raised in this study concerns the effect of relative rates of change over time in the ecological variables. It seeks to uncover dynamic relationships which would supplement the static ones.

The assumptions made in this study of dynamic trends are based on a view of change as essentially disruptive in character. The process of transition toward modernity, discussed in the previous study, is one during which, almost inevitably, goals and demands will exceed achievements. It is also a process during which former patterns of behavior, outdated technologies, established roles, statuses, and norms must all give way to new, unfamiliar patterns. The transitional personality is frustrated by his breakoff from the past and the uncertainty of the present.

To this picture of a society in ferment is now added the notion of the relevance of time. Insofar as the transitional process is a gradual one, there is a possibility that new patterns may be adopted and adjusted to before old ones are completely abandoned. There is also the further possibility that achievements may begin to approximate the level at which aspirations are set, before aspirations move even further ahead. Where the transitional process is rapid, however, the effect will be to decrease the possibility of adaptation, thus increasing the probability of disruption, chaos, and feelings of personal discontent. Furthermore, the more rapid the process of change, the greater the likelihood of opening new perspectives of modernity, that is, of creating higher and higher levels of aspiration, thus inevitably increasing the gap between aspiration and achievement, at least in the early stages.

Thus the hypothesis promulgated in this study is that: *the faster (the slower) the rate of change in the modernization process within any given society, the higher (the lower) the level of political instability within that society* (Conroe 1965).

As a first step in investigating this hypothesis, yearly changes in instability pattern for each of the eighty-four countries were calculated for the time period under study, 1948-1962. From the evidence accumulated on the global frequency of occurrence of instability events (Figure 12.1), it was clear that the world instability level increased sharply during the fifteen years, reaching its highest peak in the last six years. In order to compare countries as to their relative position on the instability continuum over time, the period was split in half and country instability scores were calculated for each seven-year period separately. The country scores for the second period tended to be higher than for the first one. A rank-order correlation between stability levels in the two seven-year periods for the eighty-four countries showed a moderate degree of relationship (Spearman r = .43). Not only was the instability level generally on the increase, but there was a tendency for countries to maintain their relatively stable or unstable positions over time.

As a further, more refined method of analyzing the stability-instability continuum over time, stability scores for the eighty-four nations were calculated on a year-by-year basis and plotted as a function of time. To characterize the time function, at least two measures were necessary: the slope of a best-fit line, indicating the average instability trend, over the fifteen-year period; and amplitude of change from year to year, as estimated by variance.

A calculation of the relationship between these two measures showed them to be independent and unrelated dimensions (Spearman r = .06). Of the two, only amplitude was related to static stability level as measured by the intensity scale (Spearman $r = .64$). This indicates that the meaning of instability as empirically ascertained in these studies is identified with the fluctuation of instability rather than with the average trend over time. Furthermore, it is the measure of amplitude and not the average trend over time which is directly related to rate of change in the independent variables. The average instability trend over time (increases or decreases) is related to the ecological variables only when combined with the data on yearly fluctuations in stability levels.

Turning to the predictors of instability, interest was in the effect of changes in levels of ecological variables upon changes in stability. The general hypothesis of this study was that rapid change will be experienced as an unsettling, frustrating societal condition and hence will be associated with a high level of internal conflict. To test the hypothesis, nine predictor indices were selected for study: caloric intake, literacy, primary and postprimary education, national income, cost of living, infant mortality, urbanization, and radios per thousand population. Data for these indices were collected for a 28-year period from 1935 through 1962. Plotting of the data revealed a consistent trend for substantially all countries in the sample to improve their position on all indices over time. Hence a yearly percent rate of change was calculated for each indicator.[10] These indicators are not identical to those of the previous study, although there is overlap. The new choice was determined by the availability of data for as many years as possible and for a maximum number of countries in the sample.

To summarize the results of the interrelationship between rates of change in the independent indices and rate of change in stability, it may be said that the higher the rate of change on the indices, the greater the increase in instability. A contingency table showing the relationship between mean rate of change on six or more of the nine indices and instability, as measured only by variation in pattern (amplitude), is given in Table 12.6.

As may be seen from the table, the countries experiencing a highly erratic instability pattern are those also undergoing a rapid rate of change in the ecological variables selected for study. On the other hand, countries experiencing political stability in the sense of a steady pattern are the static countries in which ecological change proceeds at a slower pace.

Furthermore, the rate at which modernization occurred from 1935 to 1962 is correlated with static stability level in the 1955-1961 time period (as measured in Study 1). A Pearson r of .647 was found between rate of change (calculated as a combined measure on six or more of the nine indices) and static stability score. Relationships were also calculated between rates of change on each of the nine independent indices taken separately and instability level, measured both as a static score and as a dynamic fluc-

TABLE 12.6 Relationship Between Mean Rate of Change on Ecological Variables and Rate of Change in Stability

MEAN RATE OF CHANGE ON ECOLOGICAL VARIABLES (PERCENT)	CHANGE IN STABILITY			TOTAL
	AMPLITUDE OF FLUCTUATIONS IN YEARLY STABILITY SCORES			
	Low change (amplitude)		High change (amplitude)	
Low change	Argentina Australia Austria Bulgaria Canada Chile Denmark Ecuador Finland France Guatemala Iceland Ireland Israel Italy Luxembourg	Mexico Netherlands New Zealand Norway Pakistan Philippines Spain Sweden Switzerland Taiwan Un. of S. Africa United Kingdom United States Uruguay West Germany	Belgium Cuba Greece Hungary Paraguay	36
		31	5	
High change	Ceylon Ghana India Syria Turkey	Bolivia Brazil Burma Cambodia Colombia Costa Rica Dom. Republic Egypt El Salvador Haiti Honduras Indonesia Iraq	Japan Korea Malaya Morocco Panama Peru Poland Portugal Thailand Tunisia USSR Venezuela Yugoslavia	31
		5	26	
Total		36	31	67*

Chi square = 30.0; p = <.001.

* The N on this and some of the following tables is reduced to include only those countries with data on six or more indices, from which to calculate the mean rate of change score.

tuation (variance measure) for the 1948-1962 period (see Table 12.7).

The pattern is somewhat the same for both sets of calculations, indicating primary education to be the best single predictor of instability and literacy the worst.[11] The most interesting finding is the inverse relationship revealed between rate of change in national income and instability. In the case of this indicator, the higher the rate of change, the greater the likelihood of stability. This finding may be understood when one contrasts the pattern of rate of change on national income to that for the nine indices taken together (see Tables 12.8 and 12.9).

TABLE 12.7 Rank-Order Correlations (RHO) Between Rate of Change on Ecological Variables and Rate of Change in Stability, 1948–1962

	N	Static stabil- ity	Dynamic stability (amplitude)
Primary education	70	.61	.57
Calories per capita per day	39	.49	.35
Postprimary education	30	.36	.41
Cost of living	72	.36	.21
Radios	82	.34	.31
Infant mortality rate	60	.33	.36
Urbanization	69	.17	.14
Literacy	82	.03	.01
National income	70	−.34	−.45

TABLE 12.8 Relationship Between Modernity Level and Mean Rate of Change on Ecological Variables

MEAN RATE OF CHANGE (PERCENT)	MODERNITY LEVEL				Total
	Traditional countries	Transitional countries		Modern countries	
Low change	Pakistan Philippines Taiwan	Bulgaria Chile Cuba Guatemala Hungary Italy Mexico Paraguay Spain Union of South Africa	Argentina Australia Austria Belgium Canada Denmark Finland France Iceland Ireland Israel	Luxembourg Netherlands New Zealand Norway Sweden Switzerland United Kingdom United States Uruguay W. Germany	34
	3	10		21	
High change	Bolivia Burma Cambodia Ghana Haiti India Indonesia Iraq Malaya Morocco	Brazil Ceylon Colombia Costa Rica Dom. Rep. Ecuador Egypt El Salvador Greece Honduras Japan	Korea Panama Peru Poland Portugal Syria Thailand Tunisia Turkey Venezuela Yugoslavia	USSR	33
	10	22		1	
Total	13	32		22	67

Chi square = 31.0; p = <.001 .

TABLE 12.9   Relationship Between Modernity Level and Rate of Change in National Income

RATE OF CHANGE IN NATIONAL INCOME (PERCENT)	MODERNITY LEVEL					Total
	Traditional countries		Transitional countries		Modern countries	
Low change	Burma Cambodia China Ghana Haiti India Iraq Jordan	Indonesia Malaya Morocco Pakistan Philippines Sudan	Bulgaria Colombia Costa Rica Dom. Rep. Ecuador Egypt El Salvador Guatemala	Honduras Lebanon Panama Poland Portugal Syria Tunisia Venezuela	E. Germany Ireland Switzerland USSR United Kingdom	35
		14		16	5	
High change	Taiwan		Brazil Chile Ceylon Cuba Greece Hungary Italy Japan Korea	Mexico Paraguay Peru Spain Thailand Turkey Un. of So. Africa Yugoslavia	Argentina Luxembourg Australia Netherlands Austria New Zealand Belgium Norway Canada Sweden Denmark United States Finland W. Germany France Iceland Israel	35
		1		17	17	
Total		15		33	22	70

Chi square = 17.8; $p = < .001$.

From Table 12.8 it is clear that all countries except the modern show a high rate of change on ecological variables. (This again confirms the point made earlier that no truly traditional countries are included in the sample. By definition, a traditional country should be characterized by lack of change.) The modern countries are those undergoing the least amount of change. They are also those experiencing the least amount of instability.

In Table 12.9, however, we find the situation reversed for growth in national income. On this indicator, it is the modern countries which show the highest rate of change over time. National income may be viewed as a variable with no intrinsic ceiling and one on which marked improvement will not occur until a country is well advanced toward modernity and has achieved a relatively high standard on other ecological variables, such as literacy, education, caloric intake, and infant mortality. Thus again it is the modern countries which are the most stable and which show the greatest growth rate in national income.

A final comparison between rate of change in modernization and instability level was made by grouping countries on instability in terms of both amplitude of yearly fluctuations and general trend in instability over time (variance and slope). Three groups of countries were distinguished: stable countries (in which yearly fluctuations are low and the trend over time is either stationary or improving); unstable countries (in which yearly fluctuations are high and the trend over time is either stationary or worsening); and indeterminate countries which represent conflicting combinations of trend and fluctuation. Four levels of rate of change were also distinguished. With these refinements, the relationship between rate of modernization and instability level over time appears more clearly (see Table 12.10).

The countries with the lowest rate of change are predominantly stable, as measured both by a low level of yearly fluctuations in instability and by a lack of any worsening trend toward instability over time. Conversely, the countries with the highest rate of change on the ecological variables are beset by instability, as measured both by yearly fluctuations in instability

TABLE 12.10   Relationship Between Mean Rate of Change on Ecological Variables and Change in Stability as Measured by Variance and Slope

MEAN RATE OF CHANGE ON ECO-LOGICAL VARIABLES	STABLE Low variance and either		INDETERMINATE Low variance/positive slope or high variance/negative slope		UNSTABLE High variance and either		Total
	negative slope	or zero slope			positive slope	or zero slope	
Low change	Norway New Zealand W. Germany Australia Denmark Iceland Israel	United States Canada Sweden Switzerland Netherlands Luxembourg	Great Britain Austria		Belgium		16
		13	2		1		
Moderately low change	Ireland Guatemala Bulgaria Taiwan	Finland Italy Chile Philippines	France Un. S. Africa Mexico Pakistan Greece	Argentina Uruguay Spain Ecuador	Cuba Paraguay Hungary		20
		8	9		3		
Moderately high change			Thailand Colombia Egypt Ceylon Poland	Costa Rica Ghana Turkey India	Peru Portugal Panama Brazil Haiti Iraq	Japan Yugoslavia Tunisia Burma USSR	20
		0	9		11		
High change	Syria		Korea Malaya		El Salvador Bolivia Venezuela Dom. Rep.	Cambodia Morocco Honduras Indonesia	11
		1	2		8		
Totals		22	22		23		67

levels and the absence of evidence of any improvement in trend toward stability over time. Furthermore, countries experiencing intermediate rates of change toward modernization are also intermediate in instability, showing some conflicting combination of fluctuation and trend over time.

In conclusion, one might speak of a syndrome which is exemplified by the modern group of nations. With interesting exceptions, they are relatively satisfied economically and relatively stable politically, no longer changing rapidly on many economic dimensions, although making sizable gains in national income. In contrast are the transitional nations, some moving more rapidly toward modernity than others but, by and large, all characterized by relative economic deprivation, a high rate of change on many economic dimensions but a low rate of growth on national income, and a strong tendency to political instability, finding overt expression in many diverse events such as strikes, demonstrations, riots, coups d'état, and even civil war.

The results of these studies are an encouraging indication that cross-national, correlational, and scaling methods can profitably be applied to complex areas such as the analysis of internal conflict behaviors. The scaling, as well as the identification of the dimensions of internal conflict behavior, show that these events can be classified and disentangled.

Furthermore, the results of the studies provide empirical corroboration for many current notions regarding the determinants of political instability. The fact that change may lead to unrest has been suggested. By applying postulates drawn from the frustration-aggression model to this area of internal conflict behavior, and by subjecting the area to empirical analysis, new insights are also obtained. On the basis of these findings, it may be suggested that one compelling reason for the greater stability of modern countries lies in their greater ability to satisfy the wants of their citizens. The less advanced countries are characterized by greater instability because of the aggressive responses to systemic frustration evoked in the populace. It could be argued simply that the increase in instability resulting from a change in ecological conditions is due to the disruptive effect of change. But it is also possible that the satisfaction of wants has a feedback effect, adding to the strength of the drive for more satisfactions. As wants start to be satisfied, the few satisfactions which are achieved increase the drive for more satisfactions, thus in effect adding to the sense of systemic frustration. It is only when a high enough level of satisfaction has been reached that a country will tend toward stability rather than instability.

Although exploratory in nature, the findings are sufficiently striking and persuasive to argue for continuing with additional designs. A large-scale series of studies utilizing a wider scope of ecological, psychological, and political variables, an inventory of other, complementary aggressive behaviors, and a longer time period should lead to more refined results.

Notes

1. This research was partially supported by a grant from the San Diego State College Foundation. A paper based on this article was delivered at the Annual Meeting of the American Psychological Association in Chicago, Illinois, September 1965 (Feierabend and Feierabend, 1965b).

2. Visiting associate professor, Department of Political Science, Washington University, St. Louis, 1966-1967.

3. Visiting research psychologist, Department of Psychology, Washington University, St. Louis, 1966-1967.

4. More recent analyses of aggression have placed increasing emphasis on the role of the stimulus in eliciting an aggressive response. (For a discussion of recent approaches, see Berkowitz 1965.)

5. The data bank of political instability events, including the *Code Index* to the bank, instructions to raters, etc., is available through the Inter-University Consortium for Political Research, Box 1248, Ann Arbor, Michigan.

6. These stability profiles correlate with the ordering of the same countries based on Eckstein's index, "Deaths from domestic group violence per 1,000,000 population, 1950-1962." The rank-order correlation between these two indices is Spearman $r = .69$. On the other hand, only a low correlation exists with Russett's index, "Executive stability: number of years independent/number of chief executives, 1945-1961." The rank-order correlation between these two indices is Spearman $r = .38$.

7. The data used in Hoole's 1964 study were gathered from a single source, *Deadline Data on World Affairs*. The data bank as presently constituted comprises two sources, *Deadline Data on World Affairs* and *The Encyclopaedia Britannica Yearbooks*.

8. The difficulty of dividing these highly correlated indicators should be noted. Each contains some error component due to the unreliable reporting of cross-national data. For an estimate of error in cross-national data, see Russett (1964) and Rummel (1963).

9. This modernity ranking, based on eight indices, is highly comparable to that of Russett et al. (1964) based on GNP alone. A Spearman r calculated between the two rank orderings is .92.

10. The yearly percent rate of change on the ecological variables was calculated by subtracting the lowest value of the variable in the twenty-eight year period from the highest value attained, dividing by the lowest value to convert to a percentage change, and then dividing by the number of years spanned to obtain the yearly percentage change.

11. This finding is in contrast to the high level of relationship obtained between literacy and static stability level reported in Study 1. The explanation may lie in the observed inconsistency in the literacy data reported over the longer time period in various sources.

References

Almond, Gabriel A., and James S. Coleman (eds.). *The Politics of the Developing Areas*. Princeton: Princeton University Press, 1960.

_____, and Sidney Verba. *The Civic Culture*. Princeton, N.J.: Princeton University Press, 1963.

Banks, Arthur S., and Robert B. Textor. *A Cross-Polity Survey*. Cambridge, Mass.: Massachusetts Institute of Technology Press, 1963.

Berkowitz, Leonard. *Aggression: A Social Psychological Analysis*. New York: McGraw-Hill, 1962.

_____. "The Concept of Aggressive Drive: Some Additional Considerations." In L. Berkowitz (ed.), *Advances in Experimental Social Psychology*, Vol. 2. New York: Academic Press, 1965.

Buss, Arnold H. *The Psychology of Aggression*. New York: Wiley, 1961.

Cantril, Hadley. "A Study of Aspirations," *Scientific American,* February 1963, pp. 41-45.

_____. *The Pattern of Human Concerns*. New Brunswick, N.J.: Rutgers University Press, 1965.

_____, and Lloyd A. Free. "Hopes and Fears for Self and Country," *American Behavioral Scientist,* 6, 2 (October 1962), 3-30.

Cattell, Raymond, H. Breul, and H. Parker Hartman. "An Attempt at More Refined Definition of the Cultural Dimensions of Syntality in Modern Nations," *American Sociological Review,* 16 (1951), 408-21.

_____. "The Principal Culture Patterns Discoverable in the Syntal Dimensions of Existing Nations," *Journal of Social Psychology* (1950), 215-53.

_____. "The Dimensions of Culture Patterns of Factorization of National Characters," *Journal of Abnormal and Social Psychology* (1949), 443-69.

Conroe, Wallace W. *A Cross-National Analysis of the Impact of Modernization Upon Political Stability*. Master's thesis, San Diego State College, 1965.

Cutwright, Philips. "National Political Development: Measurement and Analysis," *American Sociological Review,* 28 (April 1963), 253-64.

Davies, James C. "Toward a Theory of Revolution," *American Sociological Review,* 27 (January 1962), 5-19.

Deutsch, Karl W. *The Nerves of Government*. New York: Free Press, 1963.

_____. "Social Mobilization and Political Development," *American Political Science Review,* 55 (September 1961), 493-514.

_____. "Toward an Inventory of Basic Trends and Patterns in Comparative and International Politics," *American Political Science Review,* 54 (March 1960), 34-57.

_____, and Alexander Eckstein. "National Industrialization and the Declining Share of the International Economic Sector 1890-1959," *World Politics,* 13, 2 (January 1961), 267-299.

Dollard, John, et al. *Frustration and Aggression*. New Haven: Yale University Press, 1939.

Doob, Leonard W. *Becoming More Civilized: A Psychological Exploration*. New Haven:

Yale University Press, 1960.

Easton, David. *A Framework for Political Analysis.* Englewood Cliffs, N.J.: Prentice-Hall, 1965a.

———. *A Systems Analysis of Political Life.* New York: Wiley, 1965b.

Eckstein, H. (ed.). *Internal War.* New York: Free Press, 1964.

———. *Internal War: The Problem of Anticipation.* A report submitted to the Research Group in Psychology and the Social Sciences, Smithsonian Institution, Washington, D.C., January 15, 1962.

Feierabend, Ivo K. "Exploring Political Stability: A Note on the Comparative Method," *Western Political Quarterly (Supplement),* 15, 3 (September 1962), 18-19.

———, and Rosalind L. Feierabend. *Cross-National Data Bank of Political Instability Events (Code Index).* Public Affairs Research Institute, San Diego State College, January 1965a.

——— and ———. "Aggressive Behaviors Within Polities: A Cross-National Study." Paper delivered at the Annual Meeting of the American Psychological Association, Chicago, Illinois, September 1965b.

———, ———, and Norman G. Litell. "Dimensions of Political Unrest: A Factor Analysis of Cross-National Data." Paper delivered at the annual meeting of the Western Political Science Association, Reno, Nevada, March 1966.

———, ———, and Betty A. Nesvold. "Correlates of Political Stability." Paper delivered at the Annual Meeting of the American Political Science Association, New York City, September 1963.

Fitzgibbon, R. H., and Kenneth Johnson. "Measurement of Latin American Political Change," *American Political Science Review,* 55 (September 1961).

Gregg, Philip M., and Arthur S. Banks. "Dimensions of Political Systems: Factor Analysis of a *Cross Polity Survey,*" *American Political Science Review,* 59 (September 1965), 602-14.

Gurr, Ted. *The Genesis of Violence: A Multivariate Theory of the Preconditions of Civil Strife.* Ph.D. dissertation, New York University, 1965.

Haas, Michael. *Some Societal Correlates of International Political Behavior.* Stanford, Calif.: Studies in International Conflict and Integration, Stanford University, 1964.

Hoole, Francis W. *Political Stability and Instability Within Nations: A Cross-National Study.* Master's thesis, San Diego State College, August 1964.

Inkeles, Alex. "Industrial Man: The Relation of Status to Experience, Perception and Value," *American Journal of Sociology* (July 1960), 1-31.

Kling, Merle. "Taxes on the 'External' Sector: An Index of Political Behavior in Latin America," *Midwest Journal of Political Science* (May 1959), 127-50.

Lasswell, Harold D. *The Political Writings of Harold D. Lasswell.* Glencoe, Ill.: Free Press, 1951.

Lerner, Daniel. "Communication Systems and Social Systems: A Statistical Exploration in History and Policy," *Behavioral Science,* 2, 4 (October 1957), 266-75.

———. *The Passing of Traditional Society.* Glencoe, Ill.: Free Press, 1958.

LeVine, Robert A. "Anti-European Violence in Africa: A Comparative Analysis,"

Journal of Conflict Resolution, 3, 4, (December 1959), 420-29.

Lipset, Seymour H. *Political Man.* Garden City, N.Y.: Doubleday, 1960.

_____. "Some Social Requisites of Democracy," *American Political Science Review,* 53 (March 1959), 69-105.

Maier, Norman R. F. *Frustration: The Study of Behavior Without a Goal.* New York: McGraw-Hill, 1949.

McClelland, David. *The Achieving Society.* Princeton: Van Nostrand, 1961.

McNeil, Elton B. "Psychology and Aggression," *Journal of Conflict Resolution,* 3, 3 (September 1959), 195-293.

Merritt, Richard L., and Stein Rokkan. *Comparing Nations: The Uses of Quantitative Data in Cross National Research.* New Haven: Yale University Press, 1966.

Merton, R. K. *Social Theory and Social Structure.* New York: Free Press, 1949.

Murdock, George P. "Anthropology as a Comparative Science," *Behavioral Science,* 2, 4 (October 1957), 249-54.

Nesvold, Betty A. *Modernity, Social Frustration, and the Stability of Political Systems: A Cross-National Study.* Master's thesis, San Diego State College, June 1964.

Parsons, Talcott, and Edward A. Shils. *Toward a General Theory of Action.* Cambridge, Mass.: Harvard University Press, 1951.

_____, _____, K. Naegele, and J. Pitts, *Theories of Society.* New York: Free Press, 1961.

Rokkan, Stein. "Comparative Cross-National Research: II. Bibliography," *International Social Science Bulletin,* 1955, 622-41.

_____ (ed.). *Comparative Research Across Cultures and Nations,* forthcoming.

Rummel, Rudolph J. "Dimensions of Conflict Behavior Within Nations, 1946-59," *Journal of Conflict Resolution,* 10, 1 (March 1966), 65-74.

_____. "A Field Theory of Social Action and Political Conflict Within Nations," *General Systems Yearbook,* 10 (1965).

_____. "Dimensions of Conflict Behavior Within and Between Nations," *General Systems Yearbook,* 8 (1963), 1-50.

Russett, Bruce M. "Inequality and Instability: The Relation of Land Tenure and Politics," *World Politics,* 16, 3 (April 1964), 442-54.

_____, et al. *World Handbook of Social and Economic Indicators.* New Haven: Yale University Press, 1964.

Singer, J. David, and Melvin Small. "The Composition and Status Ordering of the International System: 1815-1940," *World Politics,* 18, 2 (January 1966), 236-82.

Tanter, Raymond. *Dimensions of Conflict Behavior Within and Between Nations, 1958-1960.* Monograph prepared in connection with research supported by National Science Foundation Contract NSF-GS224, 1964.

_____. "Dimensions of Conflict Behavior Within and Between Nations, 1958-60,' *Journal of Conflict Resolution,* 10, 1 (March 1966), 41-65.

Walton, Jennifer G. *Correlates of Coerciveness and Permissiveness of National Politica Systems: A Cross-National Study.* Master's thesis, San Diego State College, 1965

Whiting, John W., and Irvin L. Child. *Child Training and Personality: A Cross-Cu tural Study.* New Haven: Yale University Press, 1953.

Part 5
Sociological Inquiries

Introduction

In its broadest sense war may be regarded as a species of the genus "conflict." In a more restricted sense war is a form of social conflict behavior entailing a high degree of organized violence between groups of people (usually men) and nations. Sociology, as a social science discipline concerned with the study of human group activities in social situations, is therefore the most promising point of departure in the development of the etiology of social conflict. Approached in this way the domains of sociological inquiries should include all aspects of social conflict both as a sociological paradigm and a sociological phenomenon — its nature, its typology, its causation, its developmental processes, its functions, its effects, and its termination.

For sociology to become an active partner in any interdisciplinary approach to the study of war, however, it needs to be able to relate the manifestations of war to functions, types, and stages of the social process as well as to the ideologies, roles, interests, and institutions of the socially active groups. In short, what is called for is a development of the sociology of international (intersocietal) conflict that is capable of explaining the linkage or relationship, if any, between internal and external conditions, and between internal structures and external structures of nation-states in the causation of international war. Put simply, is there any causal linkage between domestic and foreign conflict behaviors of dominant actors in the contemporary international system?

Specifically, sociological inquiries should answer the following questions: In what ways and to what extent can societal conditions and structures be linked causally to the onset of international warfare? Is there, for example, any causal linkage between the types of political system (democratic, authoritarian, and totalitarian) and war-prone behavior? Is there any causal linkage between the types of economic system (feudal, capitalist, socialist, or communist) and war-prone behavior? Is there any causal linkage between the stages of economic development (traditional, transitional or developing, and developed) and war-prone behavior? Is there any causal linkage between societal stress or frustration indices as measured by depression, revolution, riot, strike, assassination, crime, and so on, and war-prone behavior?

The pioneering nineteenth-century sociologists of different ideological persuasions all used social conflict as the central explanatory variable in their research. Karl Marx's conceptualization of conflict as a derivative of the existing social and economic system as well as a catalytic agent of social and systemic change has indeed made a lasting theoretical and practical (revolutionary) contribution. Other social thinkers who were directly or indirectly connected with social Darwinism — Herbert Spencer, Gustav Ratzenhofer, Ludwik Gumplowicz, William Graham Sumner, and Walter Bagehot — all paid much attention to social conflict in their research. However, it was Georg Simmel, who by delinking conflict from both Marxist dialectical materialism and social Darwinism, gave a most comprehensive and independent formulation of the theory of conflict. Central to Simmel's ([1908] 1955) theory is that conflict is both constructive and integrative.

Max Weber's voluminous writings repeatedly stress the sociological importance of conflict as an agent of change and the political importance of conflict between ultimately irreconcilable values as a source of the need for the legitimization of power. Moreover, there is an important theoretical discussion of the category of conflict in the first chapter of his major sociological treatise, *Economy and Society* ([1922] 1978). However, the Weberian sociology of conflict has not exercised an influence on American research comparable to Simmel's. Those who had made American sociology come of age all followed Simmel's path in conceptualizing conflict as an ineradicable part of social structures.

In a more recent period, however, sociological research in general and American sociological research in particular have been remiss in conflict research. Growing out of a relatively peaceful period in American life, the dominant sociological approach was committed to the social consensus model, regarding social conflict as a sort of pathological deviance from the harmonious body polity. The rise of structural-functional theory in sociology under the leadership of the late Talcott Parsons typifies this approach. Sociology, in Parsons' (1951:552) view, is concerned *"with the phenomena of the institutionalization of patterns of value-orientation in the social system,* with the conditions of that institutionalization, and of changes in the patterns, with conditions of conformity with and deviance from a set of such patterns and with motivational processes in so far as they are involved in all of these."* Thus society is conceptualized as a unified and ongoing system of action, in which each component has some specific functions to perform in accordance with common value orientation.

The trend toward empiricism, which as in political science started at the University of Chicago in the 1920s and 1930s, steered sociological research into separate and divergent paths from conflict research. On the one hand, empirical sociological research moved in the direction of searching for value-neutral models, shying away from value-laden conflict or war issues.

On the other hand, empirical sociological research, even when focused on conflict, fragmented social reality into artificial elements (that is, empirically manageable boundaries of inquiry as in race conflict, industrial conflict, communal conflict, and so on) thereby inhibiting broad conceptualizations and theory building. In short, value-neutral empirical models have produced a shortage of macroanalyses of the type that characterized works of several seminal sociologists of the nineteenth and early twentieth centuries.

In the 1950s, however, a number of important sociological works challenging the dominent consensus model were published — Jessie Bernard (1957), Lewis Coser (1956), Ralf Dahrendorf (1959), and Max Gluckman (1956). The more serious and shattering challenge to the consensus model came in the United States during the 1960s in the form of antiwar demonstrations and urban riots. Note the establishment of the three national commissions to study social disorder: the President's Commission on Law Enforcement and Administration of Justice (1967); the National Advisory Commission on Civil Disorders (1968); and the National Commission on the Causes and Prevention of Violence (1969). Revealingly, the American Sociological Association became a Johnny-come-lately in 1972 when it too established a subcommittee to propose to its council "a program for action that could be aimed toward the investigation of war and peace."

The three selections included in Part 5 represent three different sociological analyses of conflict. The chapter by the late Quincy Wright, who had early transcended the boundary of his original training in the discipline of political science and international law and who had perhaps made the single greatest contribution to the development of conflict research as a normative science in our times, is a broad conceptual-methodological piece highlighting different dimensions of conflict in the study of war. Having defined war as a species of conflict in the sociological sense, Wright elaborates how conflict is related to, but also differs from, such variables as inconsistency, tension, competition, and cooperation. He then discusses the typology, development, solution, and methods of conflict. Wright thus presents a conflict model as a way of thinking about war.

The noted sociologist Lewis Coser, who, in his earlier work *The Functions of Social Conflict* (1956), had made an important contribution to the revival of sociological research on social conflict through his careful and critical assessment of Simmel's work, challenges in the essay chosen here what he calls "a remarkably tame and domesticated view of the social world," resulting from the excessive commitment of American social theorists to models of social harmony. Specifically, his essay centers on three social functions of violence: (1) violence as a form of achievement; (2) violence as a danger signal; and (3) violence as a catalyst.

Two of Coser's arguments in the essay deserve special consideration. First, Coser makes a cogent argument that violence can serve as a liberating force for the social underdogs by opening up a new channel of "achievement." If this interpretation were correct, it would pose a serious challenge to the liberal-pacifist assumption that war and peace (as well as violence and nonviolence) can be generalized into two independent and mutually exclusive categories in the social process. Second, can violence be said, as Coser contends, to possess an educational value for the insensitive political elites? To what extent and for how long did the social violence of the 1960s in American society work as an effective danger signal for the political elites that brought about some fundamental social and economic reforms? Coser's line of analysis of the role of violence becomes problematical when applied to the violence committed by such global underdogs as PLO commandos, although it must be pointed out that Coser does not extend his proposition to intersocietal conflict situations.

It may be obvious from the short and cursory synopsis above that international conflict or the linkage between domestic and foreign conflict behavior has not yet become a part of sociological research on conflict. Curiously enough, most works employing a linkage approach to conflict behavior were carried out by political scientists — Haas (1968), Midlarsky (1975), Rosenau (1969), Rummel (1963, 1968, 1973), Tanter (1966), and Wilkenfeld (1973). On the whole, the empirical findings of the studies by these political scientists tend to contradict the commonly accepted causal linkage between domestic and foreign conflict behaviors of nation-states. In his 1963 study based on data for seventy-seven nations in the mid-1950s, Rudolph Rummel concluded that foreign conflict behavior is generally unrelated to domestic conflict behavior. In his 1968 study designed to test the relationship between national attributes and foreign conflict behavior, Rummel (1968:213) again reached the conclusion that "the characteristics of a nation are not highly predictive of the intensity of its involvement in foreign conflict." Raymond Tanter (1966), in a work that replicated Rummel's 1963 study for a later period (1958-1960), also concluded that there was only a small relationship between domestic and foreign conflict behavior which increased with a time lag. In a similar vein, Manus I. Midlarsky (1975:178) concluded in his empirical study that "domestic social institutions were least successful in explaining the number of wars or 'onset' as a variable."

In the third selection for this part, Michael Haas, a political scientist, tests the hypothesis of the relationship between domestic and foreign conflict behavior. The thirteen tables in the chapter, which sum up the empirical findings of his study, deserve scrutiny. On the whole, his study does not suggest a correlation between domestic societal and political variables and foreign conflict behavior. Note here for comparative purposes that Haas in a later study (1968:243), in which three indicators of social change (domestic stress, strain, and use of military tools of statecraft) were intercorrelated with national aggressiveness, also concluded that "the hypothesis that stress precedes international military behavior is not well supported."

Two of Haas's findings in our selection are especially relevant. First, Haas's finding that the economically most- and, to a lesser extent, the least-developed countries show more significant foreign conflict behavior than do the underdeveloped and intermediate types may seem to contradict one of the key arguments of the Feierabends (Chapter 12). There need not be any incompatibility between the two studies, however, if the Feierabends do not extrapolate their equation of (domestic) systemic frustration index and the modernity index into foreign or global conflict behavior. Haas's finding on this matter enjoys the additional support of a high correlation between "have" countries as measured in UN assessments and their high foreign conflict behavior as shown in Table 15.3 of his chapter. Actually, there should be no surprise in this finding since it conforms to the reasonable inference from the history of international politics that major powers tend to be more warlike than minor ones. This point is more graphically demonstrated in Chapter 23 in Part 8. Second, the hypothesis that a direct relationship exists between population density and foreign conflict behavior is not supported in Haas's study; in fact, there is *a slight inverse relation,* as shown in Table 15.5. In another study of Japan's warlike behavior leading to World War II, Kenneth E. Boulding and Alan H. Gleason (1965:4) also concluded that the overpopulation argument for military expansion was "little more than a convenient myth which served to stimulate the laggards at home and to lull the gullible abroad."

Our brief survey and analysis of sociological inquiries call for several caveats. First, we need to be wary of extrapolating the finding of human behavior at one level to another. All the empirical studies employing the linkage approach do not support the causal relationship between domestic and foreign conflict behaviors of nation-states. Second, sociological research on conflict has not yet adopted Johan Galtung's expanded formulation of violence as encompassing structural features. The dominant approach is still focused on the direct violence of those who resist adverse structures, giving almost no attention to the indirect (structural) violence of those who administer society. A dialectical approach in which the two types of violence are conceptualized as two sides of the same coin in any hierarchical system is needed. And finally, there is a danger of overcorrecting the consensus (or cooperation) model by moving toward the opposite ex-

13

The Nature of Conflict

Quincy Wright

War is a species of conflict; consequently, by understanding conflict we may learn about the probable characteristics of war under different conditions and the methods most suitable for regulating, preventing, and winning wars.[1]

In the legal sense, war has been considered a situation during which two or more political groups are equally entitled to settle conflicts by armed force. Its essence is the legal equality of the parties and the obligations of impartial neutrality by outsiders. In this sense, the Kellogg-Briand Pact and the United Nations Charter have eliminated war. Procedures have been established to determine who is the aggressor if hostilities occur, and all states have bound themselves not to be neutral but to assist the victim of aggression and to give no aid to the aggressor.[2]

In the sociological sense, which is the sense of ordinary usage, war refers to conflicts among political groups carried on by armed forces of considerable magnitude. The street fight of two small boys, the forensic contention in a law court, the military suppression of mob violence in the state, the collision of two automobiles, and the combat of two stags are not war; but they are conflict. Perhaps an analysis of the broader concept will help better to understand the lesser.[3]

Conflict and Inconsistency

Conflict is sometimes used to refer to inconsistencies in the motions, sentiments, purposes, or claims of entities, and sometimes to the process of resolving these inconsistencies. Thus, if it is said that the values of the communist and democratic systems are in conflict, it may mean that it is impossible for a person rationally to believe in these two systems at the same

The original version of this article appeared under the title "The Nature of Conflict," by Quincy Wright published in *Western Political Quarterly* 4 (June 1951):193-209, and is reprinted herewith by permission of the University of Utah, copyright holder, and of the author.

time; or it may mean that some process of propaganda, education, synthesis, or war is going on for reconciling them or for superseding one by the other. The two meanings are not necessarily identical, because inconsistent systems of thought and action may coexist in different places for long periods of time. However, as contacts increase and the world shrinks under the influence of new inventions, such inconsistencies tend to generate processes of reconciliation or supersession and thus to constitute conflict in the second sense of the term.

The word conflict is derived from the Latin word *confligere* meaning "to strike together." Originally, it had a physical rather than moral connotation, though the English word has both. In the physical sense of two or more different things moving to occupy the same space at the same time, the logical inconsistency and the process of solution are identical. For example, the logical inconsistency of two billiard balls being in the same place at the same time is resolved by the conflict which results in their rolling to different positions.[4]

In an analysis of conflict, as used in the sociological sense and, in accord with the etymology of the word, it seems best to limit its meaning to situations where there is an actual or potential process for solving the inconsistency. Where there is no such process, conflict does not seem to be the proper word. If used to describe mere differences or inconsistencies in societies or value systems, it may induce the belief that peaceful coexistence is impossible. Where such differences have existed violent conflict has sometimes been precipitated when none was necessary. An example may, perhaps, illustrate this terminological distinction. Islam began a career of conquest in the seventh century with the thesis that it was the only true faith and was necessarily in conflict with all other religions. This was represented by the doctrine of the *Jihad,* or perpetual war of the "world of Islam" and the "world of war." According to Majid Khadduri, "The world of war constituted all the states and communities outside the world of Islam. Its inhabitants were usually called infidels, or better termed, unbelievers. In theory the believers were always at war with the unbelievers."[5]

Belief in the *Jihad* induced continuous attacks by the Arabs upon the Roman Empire and rising Christendom during the seventh and eighth centuries, and resulted in extensive Moslem conquests in the Near East, North Africa, and Spain. Christendom, however, reacted militantly in the Crusades of the eleventh, twelfth, and thirteenth centuries, turning on Islam with the doctrine of papal sovereignty of the world. The Ottoman Turks then took the leadership of Islam, and during the fifteenth, sixteenth, and seventeenth centuries were almost continuously at war with Christian Europe, conquering Constantinople, the Balkans, and Hungary, as well as most of the Arab countries. Turkish power then waned, and eventually the

Ottoman Empire broke up into national states, as did the Holy Roman Empire. Today Christian and Moslem states coexist and cooperate in the United Nations. Both the *Jihad* and the Crusades are things of the past. When, as a political measure, the Ottoman sultan, after entering World War I on the German side, proclaimed the *Jihad* on November 16, 1941, his action was repudiated by the Arab leader, Hussein ibn Ali, of Mecca, who had entered the war on the Allied side.[6]

Similarly, the identification of religious differences with conflict led to a century and a half of war between Protestants and Catholics in the sixteenth and seventeenth centuries, ended by the Peace of Westphalia which recognized the sovereignty of territorial states and the authority of the temporal monarch to determine the religion of his people if he wished. Since then Protestant and Catholic states have found it possible to coexist peacefully.

These bits of history suggest the question whether the inconsistency of democracy and communism makes conflict between the Western and the Soviet states inescapable. May it not be possible for communist and democratic states to coexist, even in this technologically shrinking world, as do Moslem and Christian states, Protestant and Catholic states? The answer may depend on the policy pursued by the governments or other regulatory agencies, rather than on the ideologies themselves. In 1858 Lincoln thought that "a house divided against itself cannot stand. A government cannot endure permanently half-slave and half-free." Three years later, however, in his first inaugural, he asserted that he had "no purpose, directly or indirectly, to interfere with the institution of slavery in the States where it exists. In your hands, my dissatisfied fellow citizens, and not in mine," he said, "is the momentous issue of civil war. The government will not assail you. You can have no conflict without being yourself the aggressor." Coexistence in the Union of diverse institutions of North and South then seemed to him possible. The Civil War occurred, and eventually emancipation was proclaimed. Some historians, however, think that emancipation could have been achieved peacefully if war had been avoided for ten years longer. They are not certain that "the inevitable conflict" really was inevitable.[7]

Historically, radical differences of religion, ideology, or institutions have tended to induce conflict. They do not, however, necessarily do so, nor does conflict if it occurs necessarily eliminate the differences. Consequently, it is unwise to identify inconsistencies of opinion with conflict. Coexistence of inconsistent opinions may, in fact, be an essential condition of human progress. It is through the contact and competition of differing opinions and methods, and the eventual synthesis of thesis and antithesis that history is created.

Conflict and Tension

It depends on the policies of governments whether inconsistencies of social ideologies develop into conflicts, but these policies are likely to be influenced by the amount of social tension which the inconsistencies have generated. Social tension has been defined as the condition which arises from inconsistencies among initiatives in the structure of a society.[8] Ideologies accepted by different groups within a society may be inconsistent without creating tension; but if initiatives or actions are taken by individuals or groups in accord with those inconsistent ideologies, and if these actions lead to contact, tension arises. The degree of intensity of tension tends to increase with decreases in the social distance between the groups and with increases in the amount of energy behind them. If the groups with inconsistent ideologies are in close contact, that is, if the society is closely integrated, the tension will be great. If the society is loose (as was, for example, the world society during the nineteenth century) such initiatives originating in different and widely separated nations may create little tension. It is also true that if the groups or nations within the society from which the inconsistent initiatives emerge are small and weak, tension will be less than if they are great and powerful.[9] In the present world of decreasing social distances, initiatives emerging from such different and inconsistent ideologies as democracy and communism, respectively supported by such great powers as the United States and the Soviet Union, can be expected to cause great tension.

Tension is more likely to develop into violent conflict if it is intense and if regulatory arrangements are ineffective.[10] The United Nations is a more effective regulatory arrangement than was the system of diplomacy of the nineteenth century, but tensions are so much greater today that serious conflict is more probable. Once conflict develops, the process by which anxiety and power accumulate in each of the conflicting groups tends to result in war.

The phenomena of inconsistency, tension, conflict, and war within a society may thus be considered distinct, but they constitute a series in which each succeeding term includes those that precede. In war, each inconsistent value system has integrated itself in order to maintain its position against the other; tensions have risen, the situation is recognized as conflict, and open violence is used or projected.[11] Relations of logical inconsistency in social ideas or institutions are likely to generate tension, which in turn leads to conflict and frequently to war.[12]

However, this progress is not inevitable. Social inconsistencies can coexist without tension, and tension can exist for a long time without conflict, just as conflict may be resolved without war. If regulatory procedures such as diplomacy, mediation, conciliation, consultation, arbitration, and adjudication are available and efficiently operated, then accommodation, adjustment, and settlement may be achieved at any point and the process stopped. If, however, tensions rise above a certain level, these procedures are likely to prove ineffective.

Conflict and Competition

Conflict, defined as opposition among social entities directed against one another, is distinguished from *competition,* defined as opposition among social entities independently striving for something of which the supply is inadequate to satisfy all. Competitors may not be aware of one another, while the parties to a conflict are. *Rivalry,* halfway between, refers to opposition among social entities which recognize one another as competitors. Conflict, rivalry, and competition are all species of *opposition,* which has been defined as a process by which social entities function in the disservice of one another. Opposition is thus contrasted with *cooperation,* the process by which social entities function in the service of one another.[13]

These definitions are introduced because it is important to emphasize that competition between organisms is inevitable in a world of limited resources, but conflict is not; although conflict in some form — not necessarily violent — is very likely to occur, and is probably an essential and desirable element of human societies.

Many authors have argued for the inevitability of war from the premises of Darwinian evolution — the struggle for existence among organic species from which only the fittest survive. In the main, however, this struggle of nature, is competition, not conflict. *Lethal* conflict among individuals or groups of animals of the *same species* is rare. Birds and some mammals monopolize nesting and feeding areas during the mating season and fight intruders of the same species. Males of such polygamous species as seals, deer, and horses fight other males to maintain their harems. Social animals, such as monkeys and cattle, fight to win or maintain leadership of the group. The struggle for existence occurs not in such combats, but in the competition among herbivorous animals for limited grazing areas, and for the occupancy of areas free from carnivorous animals; and in the competition among carnivorous animals for the limited supply of herbivorous animals on which they prey. Those who fail in this competition starve to death or become victims, not of attack by their own, but by other species. The lethal aspect of the struggle for existence does not resemble human war, but rather the business of slaughtering animals for food, and the competition of individuals for jobs, markets, and materials. The essence of the struggle is the competition for the necessities of life that are insufficient to satisfy all.[14]

Among nations there is competition in developing resources, trades, skills, and a satisfactory way of life. The successful nations grow and prosper; the unsuccessful decline. It is true that, because nations are geographically circumscribed and immovable, this competition may induce efforts to expand territory at the expense of others, and thus lead to conflict. This, however, is a product of civilization. Wars of territorial conquest and economic aggrandizement do not occur among animals of the same species or among the most primitive peoples. They are consequences of large-scale political and military organization and of legal relations defining property and territory. Even under conditions of civilization, however, it cannot be said that warlike conflict among nations is inevitable, although competition is.[15]

Conflict and Cooperation

Lethal conflict among individuals or groups of the same species, or war in a very general sense, is not a necessary factor of either animal or human life. Most psychologists seem to be in agreement on this.[16] However, opposition — both in the sense of conflict and of competition — is a necessary factor of human society no less important than cooperation. A society has been defined as a group manifesting sufficient cooperation internally and sufficient opposition externally to be recognizable as a unity.[17] This definition raises the question: Can there be a *world* society unless contact is made with societies in some other planet to which it can be opposed? It is perhaps premature to say there cannot be a society existing without external opposition and manifesting itself only by the cooperation of its members to achieve common ends. It would be difficult to discover such an isolated society among either primitive or civilized peoples; but, even in such an isolated society, there would be internal opposition because a society implies that its members have interests of their own as well as common interests, and in these individual interests they not only compete but also, on occasions, conflict.

Communism seeks, like the ant colony, completely to subordinate the individual to the society and thus to eliminate all oppositions within it. In a communist society — whether through heredity, education, or central control — all divergent initiatives of individuals and subgroups have been destroyed and all are, in theory, in complete harmony. There is no historic illustration of such a society, and it is probably inconsistent with the psychological characteristics of man. Among colonial insects guided by instinct, it is perhaps possible; but among man, having taken the road of reason, which is a function of the individual human mind, such a complete subordination of the individual to the group is impossible.[18] Human societies exist by the cooperation of individuals and subgroups, and the existence of the latter implies that they have some initiative, some autonomy. They cannot exist unless each defends some sphere of freedom. Such a defense implies conflict. A society in which there was no internal conflict would be one in which no individual or subgroup could formulate its own purposes and act to achieve them. A society of that character would be an entity guided by a single purpose and a single method. In short, it would not be a society at all. It would not even be a machine, because in a machine gears and other parts are opposed to one another. It would rather be an undifferentiated mass moving toward a single goal — perhaps more like an inflamed mob than any other social manifestation.[19]

Democratic societies, in accepting human rights, freedom of association, and a multiplicity of political parties, have institutionalized opposition. They regard it as no less important than cooperation. In England, "His Majesty's Loyal Opposition" is an essential feature of parliamentary government, and its leader receives a salary out of the annual budget. American party leaders recognize an opposition party as an essential, though sometimes unpleasant, feature of the Constitution.

Psychologists have suggested that the ability to consider conflicting alternatives of action at the same time distinguishes man from the animals. This mental conflict creates the possibility of choice, thus permitting man to escape the necessity of following a single course of action to which minds incapable of such internal conflict are bound.[20] The hesitancy of a man, suddenly faced by a wild bull and by the choice of fleeing to a fence, taking to a tree, or facing the animal and dodging, may save his life, provided he chooses rapidly and adequately. In the field of politics, the democratic state, within which the opposition of parties continually suggests alternatives of policy, has possibilities of choice and progress denied to the one-party state. The same is true in the economic field. Competition among many firms offers the consumer choices that may be denied the citizen under a totally planned economy.

Too severe and enduring conflicts in the individual mind may create neuroses, and over-intense conflicts can disrupt societies. Even democratic societies must keep their internal oppositions within bounds, or they will become anarchies. In general, they prohibit fraud and violence. The competition of business firms must be by fair methods, and the conflict of political parties must avoid violence. Although a society cannot exist without competition and conflict, and cannot progress without a good deal of both, it can exist without violence and war. However, even in the best regulated societies, eternal vigilance is the price of avoiding these disruptive manifestations of opposition.

Types of Conflict

As already noted, conflict can take place among different sorts of entities. *Physical conflict* by which two or more entities try to occupy the same space at the same time must be distinguished from *political conflict* by which a group tries to impose its policy on others. These two types of conflict can be distinguished from *ideological conflicts* in which systems of thought or of values struggle with each other, and from *legal conflicts* in which controversies over claims or demands are adjusted by mutually recognized procedures.[21]

War in the legal sense has been characterized by the union of all four types of conflict. It is manifested by the physical struggle of armies to occupy the same space, each seeking to annihilate, disarm, or capture the other; by the political struggle of nations to achieve policies against the resistance of others; by the ideological struggle of peoples to preserve or extend ways of life and value systems; and by the legal struggle of states to acquire titles, to vindicate claims, to prevent violence, or to punish offenses by recognized procedures of regulated violence.[22]

Is this identification of different sorts of conflict in a single procedure expedient? Might it not be wiser to deal with legal conflicts by adjudication; ideological conflicts by information, education, and persuasion; political conflicts by negotiation or appeal to international agencies, such as the United Nations Security Council or the General Assembly, leaving to war only resistance to armed aggression? Such discrimination is the objective of the United Nations, as it was of the League of Nations before it, the Hague system before that, and of customary international law even earlier. Practice has indicated that such a segregation of the aspects of conflict is difficult to achieve, but the effort should nevertheless be made.[23]

Tendency of Conflict

It has been emphasized by Clausewitz that there is a tendency for conflict to become war, and for war to become total and absolute in proportion as the parties are equal in power and determination, and are unaffected by outside influences. This tendency has four aspects—the unification of policy, the garrison state, total war, and the bipolar world.

The legal claims of the state come to be conceived as inherent in the value system and way of life of the people. These claims come to be formulated as national policy, and armed forces are developed as the only certain means of achieving this policy. Policy in the legal, moral, political, and military field becomes integrated at the national level.

This integration of policy, and of military preparation to maintain it, tends to integrate the state. Public opinion and moral values, as well as economic life and the maintenance of law and order, are placed under central authority; institutions of deliberation, freedom in the formulation and expression of opinion and the exercise of individual rights, are subordinated to the demands of national policy, of military preparation, and of national loyalty. The garrison or totalitarian state emerges in which the individual is in a large measure subordinated to the group.[24]

In such unification of the state, restraints on war tend to be abandoned. These restraints have existed because of the presence of religious, moral, aesthetic, economic, and legal opinions and interests that are independent of the government and have been influenced by similar opinions in outside countries. Once all elements of the state are united behind the national policy and the effort to achieve that policy by war, internal and external influences for moderation cannot penetrate the crust of the gigantic war machine in motion. War becomes unrestrained and total.[25]

Integration, however, does not stop with the nation, since alliances and coalitions are formed until the entire world is drawn in on one side or the other. Absolute war is fought in a bipolar world. There are no neutrals, and the forces of the world concentrated at two strategic centers lunge at each other in unrestrained fury, each demanding total victory and the annihilation or unconditional surrender of the enemy.[26]

This expansion of war is in fact but an aspect of the movement of conflict from the individual mind. The Constitution of UNESCO declares that wars begin in the minds of men. The psychologists assert that conflict in the individual mind is a human trait. Instead of the simple sensory-motor circuit of animals, whereby a stimulus of the senses at once induces appropriate action developed in the instincts or the experience of the animal, the circuit is interrupted in man at the seat of consciousness in the brain. Here ideal alternatives of action are set against one another, their advantages considered, and eventually a decision is made and action proceeds on the chosen course. Sometimes, however, decision fails; and the indecision gives rise to ambivalence, especially when each of the conflicting alternatives is highly charged emotionally. Such conditions are characteristic of the child who loves his mother as the source of his material comforts and yet, at the same time, hates her because she disciplines him to teach him the requirements of social life. To escape this ambivalence the child displaces his hatred upon a scapegoat—perhaps the father, perhaps a neighbor's child—but the habit of displacement to solve apparently insoluble conflicts is established. As the child becomes an adult in a local group he tends to find a scapegoat outside the group so that all can be harmony within. So with consciousness of the nation, all citizens displace their hatreds and animosities upon an external enemy who conveniently serves as scapegoat.

Similarly when coalitions are formed their maintenance depends in no small degree upon displacement of all sources of conflict among the allies upon the enemy. While the United States and Russia were desperately fighting the Axis, they could displace the hatreds causing differences among them on the common enemy.

The mechanism of displacement tends to enlarge all conflicts from the individual mind to the bipolar world, and the mechanism of projection tends to augment the vigor of these conflicts. Once group conflict develops, each group is stimulated by its anxieties about the other group to build its armaments and to prepare for strategic action. Its own preoccupation about the favorable conditions of attack is projected upon its antagonist. It sees every move of that antagonist as preparation for attack. This stimulates its own preparation. The enemy similarly projects his own aggressive dispositions, armaments mount, and eventually war emerges.

The tendency toward the expansion and intensification of war is further developed by the rational pursuit of balance of power politics. Each of two rivaling great nations seeks allies to maintain the balance, and smaller nations seek protection of one or other of the great. The number of uncommitted powers declines. Finally, all power in the world is gathered about one or the other pole. Once the world is bipolarized, each center of power anticipates war and begins to calculate the influence that time is having on its relative power position. There is a strong urge for the power against which time is running to start the fight. This may entail risk, but the risk may be greater if hostilities are postponed. Thus, psychological and political factors conspire to extend, enlarge, and integrate conflicts, and to precipitate war.[27]

Methods of Conflict

Conflict may be carried on by methods of coercion or persuasion. The former usually involves violence and has the character of physical conflict; the latter need not involve violence, though violence may be utilized as a method of persuasion, and is characteristic of political, ideological, and legal conflict.

In employing purely coercive or physical methods of conflict, each party may seek to destroy the other, to control him, or to occupy his territory. In war, the destruction or disorganization of the enemy's armed forces, communications, and sources of supply; the capture of his matériel and the imprisonment of the personnel of his forces; and the driving of the enemy from strategic points or from productive territory and the occupation of that territory are operations of this character, constituting what may be called the military front in war. These methods are also used by governments in conflict with criminals and by international organizations in operations of collective security.

Noncoercive or moral methods of conflict involve efforts by each party to isolate the other, to persuade him to change his policy, ideology, or claims, or to defeat him in accordance with the rules of the game. In war successful efforts to cut off the enemy's external trade and communications, to create an opinion opposed to him in other countries and governments, and to deprive him of allies, make for his isolation. Such efforts constitute the economic and diplomatic fronts in the war. Military methods may also contribute to such isolation — such as naval blockade and the destruction of the instruments of external trade and communication.

Persuasion may be conducted by propaganda utilizing symbols to influence the minds of the enemy's armed forces, his government, and his civilian population. In war, propaganda constitutes the psychological front. Persuasion is, of course, used in may types of conflict other than war, such as diplomatic conversations, political campaigns, and parliamentary debates.

In a certain sense, however, all methods of war, unless the total destruction of the enemy's population as well as his power is contemplated, are aimed to persuade the enemy's population and government. The object of war is the complete submission of the enemy. It is assumed that military methods aimed to destroy or control his armed forces and occupy his territories, economic measures designed to starve his population and reduce his resources, and diplomatic measures designed to destroy his hope of relief or support will, when sufficient, induce the enemy government and population to change their minds and submit to whatever terms are demanded.[28]

Defeat means formal abandonment of effort by the losing party to the conflict. It implies that all parties to the conflict have accepted certain rules and criteria by which victor and vanquished can be determined. In games such as chess, bridge, football, and tennis defeat is thus conventionalized, although in some, such as football, the conventions may permit coercive methods resembling war, but with less violence. Chess is a highly conventionalized war in which available forces, strategies, and tactics are strictly regulated by the rules. War itself may have a conventional character. Rules of war may prohibit certain kinds of action, and custom may even decree that forces or fortified places ought to surrender in certain circumstances even though such action is not physically necessary. War among primitive peoples often has a highly conventional character not unlike a game; and in the wars of the *Condottiere* in fifteenth century Italy and the sieges of the eighteenth century, war was highly conventionalized in Europe and regulated so as to moderate losses. In most wars, the formalities of surrender in-

struments, armistices, and peace treaties register defeat and victory symbolically, usually after the application of military, economic, diplomatic,
and psychological methods have persuaded one side that further resistance
is hopeless. The degree of formality, regulation, and symbolic representation in conflicts varies greatly from games to total war. However, the extent
to which war has been conventionalized at certain periods indicates
possibilities of limitation and avoidance of the trend toward absolute war by
means of rational considerations and suitable social organization.[29]

Under suitable conditions, war might be decided by highly intelligent
generals without any bloodshed. Each would calculate the best utilization of
materials and manpower, the best strategy and maneuvers of armed forces
both for himself and the enemy, each assuming—as in playing a game of
chess—that the other would similarly calculate and would follow the plan
most in his own interest. According to such calculations, victory for one
side and defeat for the other might be certain, and the defeated would surrender without any hostilities. However, it is highly improbable that war
will ever be so conventionalized that incalculable factors like courage,
morale, faulty intelligence, accidents of weather, and new inventions can
be eliminated. The party whose defeat seems certain by logical calculations
may yet believe it can win because of these factors, and so will not surrender without a trial of strength unless indeed the disparity in strength is
very great as in interventions by a great power in the territory of a very
weak power. In the course of time, such disparity may be presented by the
United Nations in its operations of collective security or international policing; but, as the Korean episode indicates, the United Nations cannot yet be
certain of overwhelming power against a dissident member. Even national
federations cannot always muster sufficient power to discourage rebellion,
in which case their policing operations assume the character of war—as
witness the American Civil War.

Consideration of the variety of methods by which conflict is conducted
suggests that appraisal of national power or capacity to win wars cannot be
based on any simple analysis. Capacity to win allies and persuade enemy
and neutral opinion by propaganda is no less important than capacity to
create a powerful war potential including the command of large armed
forces. Capacity to invent and to produce, which depends upon a high
development of science and technology, is no less important than capacity
to plan the strategy of campaigns and tactics of battle. Perhaps most important in statecraft is the capacity to analyze conflicts, to distinguish the important from the unimportant aspects, to view the world as a whole, to appreciate the influence of time and opinion, and to synthesize this knowledge
in order to forward the interests of the nation and of the world without
resort to violent methods, which often destroy more than they create and
which settle fewer conflicts than they initiate.

Solution of Conflicts

None of the methods by which conflict is carried on necessarily ends the conflict — unless, indeed, the conflict is completely conventionalized as in a game. Even total defeat in war may not remove the causes of conflict, and after a time the defeated may revive and renew the conflict.

A conflict is solved by *definitive acceptance* of a decision by *all* parties. In physical conflicts where all but one party are totally destroyed such decisions may be absolute; but if the conflict concerns ideas, policies, or claims, the words "definitive," "acceptance," and "all" have to be taken relatively. The rejected ideas, policies, or claims may be presented again. A decision may be accepted in a different sense by different parties. Finally, the direct parties to a controversy may not be the only parties interested. In the modern situation of widespread interdependence and general vulnerability to military and propaganda attacks from distant points, solutions of a dispute may not stand unless accepted by many states and groups in addition to the formal litigants.

In democracies, the relative character of decisions and settlements is both acknowledged and approved. In the United States, defeat of the Republicans by the Democrats in an election is accepted by the Republicans only on the assumption that they will have another chance in which the decision may be reversed. The opponents of legislation adopted by Congress often hope to acquire a majority and to repeal the law later. Democracy seeks to avoid once-for-all decisions which permanently reject certain alternatives, but rather seeks to facilitate temporary and relative decisions achieved by methods which avoid violence by keeping alive the hope of those defeated that eventually they may triumph. Only by the maintenance of such hope can minorities be persuaded to submit easily and can a spirit of tolerance be maintained.

Dictatorships that seek final decisions find it necessary to suppress minorities by force and are likely in time to be overthrown by revolution. Democratic institutions maintaining — at least to some degree — freedom of thought, expression, opinion, and association are not designed to suppress conflicts within the society but to encourage advocates of all policies, ideas, or claims to think that eventually they may win sufficient support to achieve their objectives.

Psychologists have discovered, however, that unresolved conflicts in the individual human mind may cause neuroses, incapacitating the individual for social life, or produce a displacement of animosities upon scapegoats resulting in serious social conflicts. A mature human personality is one which poses alternatives of action, reflects upon such conflicts, but eventually decides and acts, abandoning the rejecting course after commitment.[30]

It may be that while the definitive settlement of conflict is a vice in societies, it is a virtue in the individual mind. A more accurate description would perhaps avoid the dichotomy between psychic and social conflicts and would recognize that sociopsychological conflict may occur at a number of different levels. It may occur in the individual mind, in small societies like families, clubs, trade unions, and corporations; in large societies like nations, and in supranational groups like alliances, regional arrangements, international organizations, and the world community. It is perhaps a safe generalization that the smaller the group, the more necessary is decision; the larger the group, the more dangerous is decision. In the world as a whole, in which differences of religion, ideology, culture, economic system, and policy exist and are to be expected for a long future, definitive decision of conflicts that may arise because of these differences seems to be both improbable and undesirable. Variety is the essence of a progressive and interesting world. However, so long as these differences exist conflict is possible.[31]

There are four ways in which social conflicts can be relatively solved: (1) by negotiation and agreement resulting in settlement or adjustment in accord with the will of all the parties; (2) by adjudication and decision in accord with the will, perhaps guided by legal or moral principles, of an outside party; (3) by dictation or decision in accordance with the will of one party to the conflict; and (4) by obsolescence through agreement to disagree which may in time, as new issues arise, sink the conflict into oblivion and result in a settlement according to the will of no one.[32] It may be that while negotiation and obsolescence are least likely to result in speedy and definitive decisions, yet, for that very reason, they may be most suitable for dealing with controversy among the nations and alliances of the international community. In practice, settlement by dictation usually involves violence; and while it brings about social change and settles some conflicts, at least for the time, it is likely to precipitate new ones. Adjudication in the form of arbitration and judicial settlement has been used in international affairs; but has, on the whole, proved capable of settling only controversies in which both parties base their claims on formal principles of law and in which vital interests, such as national power and survival, and policies supported by widespread and intense public opinion, were only slightly involved.

With these considerations in mind, it is well for those responsible for the foreign policy of a nation in the presence of any conflict to ask in what degree decision is desirable, and to adjust the methods employed to conclusions on that point.

Conflict and Civilization

This discussion should indicate that conflict is a complicated subject and presents complicated problems to individuals, group leaders, and statesmen. Conflict is related to competition and to cooperation, but differs from both. There are many types of conflict — physical, political, ideological, and legal — but there is a tendency for conflict to become total and absolute, and to split the community of nations into halves which would destroy one another in absolute war. The shrinking of the modern world under the influence of new means of communication and transport and the increasingly destructive methods of warfare culminating in the airborne atomic bomb have augmented this tendency and have made war ominous for the future of civilization.

Conflict is carried on by many methods — coercive and noncoercive — and there are various procedures for settling conflicts; but among large groups no final decision of most conflicts is likely to be absolute, and it is perhaps undesirable that it should be.

It may be suggested that all champions of civilization, particularly of the American type should earnestly and hopefully search for means to obstruct the natural tendency of conflict under present-day conditions to integrate policies, to centralize authority both geographically and functionally, to bipolarize the world, and to precipitate absolute war between the poles. It is difficult to question the existence of that tendency manifested in two world wars and in the present "cold war." It is possible to describe the psychological, technological, sociological, and political factors which account for this tendency, but it is difficult to stem the tide. Nevertheless, the effort to do so is called for by our culture and may be required for the salvation of our civilization. It is worth recalling that, when faced by conditions resembling those of today, most civilizations have begun a fatal decline ending in death to be followed, after a period of dark ages, by a new civilization.[33] Since our civilization, differing from others, is worldwide, and therefore, without the roots of new civilizations on its periphery, the situation may be more ominous.

Notes

1. Quincy Wright, *A Study of War* (Chicago: University of Chicago Press, 1942), pp. 699, 956.

2. Ibid., pp. 8, 341, 891. See also the same author, "Neutrality and Neutral Rights Following the Pact of Paris," *Proceedings, American Society of International Law* (1930), p. 86; "International Law and International Politics," *Measure* (spring 1951).

3. Wright, *A Study of War*, pp. 9, 685.

4. Kurt Singer, "The Meaning of Conflict," *Australian Journal of Philosophy* (December 1949); *The Idea of Conflict* (Melbourne: Melbourne University Press, 1941), pp. 13 ff.

5. Majid Khadduri, *The Law of War and Peace in Islam* (London: Luzac, 1940), p. 20.

6. Naval War College, *International Law Documents* (Washington: Government Printing Office, 1917), pp. 17, 220.

7. George Fort Milton, *The Eve of Conflict: Stephen A. Douglas and the Needless War* (New York: Houghton Mifflin Company, 1934), p. 608. "There is no scientific validity in the phrase 'inherent contradiction' and 'inevitable conflict.' In so far as they are not just untrue, they merely express a pessimistic conviction that human beings will always fail to find a sensible method of resolving a dangerous situation." R.H.S. Crossman, "Reflections on the Cold War," *The Political Quarterly* 22 (January 1951):10.

8. Quincy Wright, "The Importance of the Study of International Tensions," *International Bulletin of the Social Sciences,* UNESCO (spring 1950), p. 90.

9. Ibid., p. 90; and Wright, "Measurement of Variations in International Tensions," in Bryson, Finkelstein, and MacIver, *Learning and World Peace,* 8th Symposium on Science, Philosophy and Religion (New York, 1948), p. 54.

10. Wright, *A Study of War,* p. 959. On factors making for extreme tensions, see pp. 1107 ff.

11. Ibid., pp. 684 ff.

12. Ibid., pp. 1410 ff. This process is illustrated in various forms of the duel.

13. Ibid., p. 1439. See also R. E. Park and E. Burgess, *Introduction to the Science of Sociology* (Chicago: University of Chicago Press, 1924), pp. 574 ff; W. F. Ogburn and M. F. Nimkoff, *Sociology* (New York: Houghton Mifflin Company, 1940), pp. 346, 369. Kurt Singer defines conflict as "a critical state of tension occasioned by the presence of mutually incompatible tendencies within an organismic whole the functional continuity or structural integrity of which is thereby threatened" ("The Resolution of Conflict," *Social Research* 16 [1949]:230).

14. Wright, *A Study of War,* pp. 42 ff., 497 ff.

15. Ibid., pp. 11, 36 ff.

16. Ibid., pp. 277, 1198. John M. Fletcher, "The Verdict of Psychologists on War Instincts," *Scientific Monthly* 35 (August 1932):142 ff.

17. Wright, *A Study of War,* p. 145.

18. Henri Bergson, *Creative Evolution* (New York: The Macmillan Company, 1944), p. 453.

19. Wright, *A Study of War,* pp. 517, 957; Georg Simmel, "The Sociology of Conflict," *American Journal of Sociology* 9 (1903):490; Park and Burgess, *Introduction,* pp. 1, 583; Robert Waelder, *Psychological Aspects of War and Peace,* Geneva Studies 10 (May 1939):17 ff.

20. Singer, "The Meaning of Conflict," pp. 5, 21 ff; Park and Burgess, *Introduction,* p. 578.

21. Singer, *The Idea of Conflict,* p. 14.

22. Wright, *A Study of War,* p. 698.

23. Ibid., pp. 720 ff., 1227 ff., 1332 ff.

24. H. D. Lasswell, "The Garrison State," *American Journal of Sociology* 46 (1941):455; *National Security and Individual Freedom* (New York: McGraw Hill, 1950); see also Wright, *A Study of War,* p. 306.

25. Wright, *A Study of War,* pp. 307 ff.; John U. Nef, *War and Human Progress* (Cambridge, Mass.: Harvard University Press, 1950), p. 464.

26. H. D. Lasswell, "The Interrelations of World Organization and Society," *Yale Law Journal* 55 (August 1946):889 ff.

27. Wright, "The Importance of the Study of International Tensions"; *A Study of War;* "Some Reflections on War and Peace," *American Journal of Psychiatry* 107 (September 1950):161 ff.

28. Wright, *A Study of War,* p. 317.

29. Nef, *War and Human Progress,* p. 464; Hoffman Nickerson, *Can We Limit War* (Bristol, 1933).

30. Singer, "The Meaning of Conflict"; "The Resolution of Conflict," *Social Research* 16 (1949):230 ff.

31. In a communication to the author dated January 12, 1951, Kurt Singer writes: "I am in fact inclined to emphasize the dangers of identifying conflicts within the mind and within a society still more than you do. . . . But even a modern democracy organized in an 'agnostic' state must be based on decisions — it requires a consensus and a common fund of values and norms, and even the 'agreement to disagree' on the rest and on the mode of settling such differences requires a decision of a very high order. . . . On the other hand I would not equate the individual personality with a monolithic structure and its decision with rigid centralization. In the richest personalities of our culture, Dante, Shakespeare, Goethe, Unity (Gestaltung) harbours more differences (e.g., Antique and Christian values) than any democracy could hope to manage and which are never reconciled once forever." Singer emphasizes the differences of "decisions" in a complex situation with respect to explicitness rather than with respect to duration. The latter distinction is also important. It may be the essence of science, as of democracy, to accept any solution only tentatively. Scientists know that in time new observations will force reconsideration of the best verified "laws"; and politicians know that in time new opinions will force legislation superseding established "laws."

32. Singer suggests that conflicts may be resolved by (1) integration and constructive action, (2) by sublimation and withdrawal, (3) by resolve contention and fighting, and (4) by regression and yielding ("The Resolution of Conflict," pp. 230 ff.).

33. Arnold J. Toynbee, *A Study of History* (Oxford: Oxford University Press, 1935), Vol. I, pp. 129 ff.; Vol. III, p. 167.

14

Some Social Functions of Violence

Lewis A. Coser

The folklore of psychology has it that animals in experimental studies display systematically different behavioral characteristics depending on the investigator. Rats described by American observers are seen as frenetically active, given to a great deal of motor activity, forever dashing in and out of mazes, always trying to get somewhere — though not always certain exactly where. In contrast, experimental animals seen through the lens of German investigators, apes, for example, seem given to long and intense periods of pensive deliberation and musing cogitation.

This jest highlights an important truth. There *are* systematic differences in the ways a particular scholarly community at a given moment in time chooses to approach the manifold data with which it is confronted. In sociology, for example, even if most American social theorists would readily agree in the abstract that conflict as well as order, tension as well as harmony, violence as well as peaceful adjustment characterize all social systems in varying degrees, social theory actually has settled mainly for a remarkably tame and domesticated view of the social world. This is so despite the fact that European social thinkers such as Marx, Weber, and Simmel, upon whose works so much of American theorizing depends for its inspiration, had an entirely different orientation.

It seems as if American social science, developing in a society which, its birth through revolution notwithstanding, has only known one major internal upheaval throughout its history, has failed to be sensitized to the pervasive effects of violence, conflict, and disorder which to the European thinker were facts that they could not but be acquainted with intimately. While to the European thinker the fragility of the social fabric and the brittleness of social bonds seemed self-evident experiences, American social science proceeded from a world view in which social violence was at best

Reprinted by permission of the publisher and author from Lewis A. Coser, "Some Social Functions of Violence," *The Annals of the American Academy of Political and Social Science* 364 (March 1966):8-18.

seen as a pathological phenomenon. As Arnold Feldman has recently argued: "Violence is conceived as being *incidental* to the basic character of social structures and processes. Indeed the very complexion of social structure ordinarily excludes the source of structural destruction."[1]

As long as American sociology confined its attention mainly to a limited view of the contemporary American scene, its neglect of conflict and violence was, perhaps, none too disabling, at least until recently. But at present, when sociology has happily awakened to the need of doing comparative studies of social structures in both geographical space and historical time, this domesticated vision of the social world can be severely hampering. In addition, it seems that even the proper study of American society can no longer profit from exclusive emphasis on models and constructs in which conflict and violence are deliberately or unwittingly minimized. Just as analyses of, say, contemporary South Africa, Latin America, or Southeast Asia, or of seventeenth-century England or nineteenth-century France, would be patently unrealistic if they ignored the functions of political violence, so it has become increasingly evident that such ignoring would be just as unrealistic in the study of the current racial scene in the United States.

For a number of years I have urged a correcting of the traditional balance in theoretical and empirical emphasis in studies of social conflict and social order and have suggested that it is high time to tilt the scale in the direction of greater attention to social conflict.[2] Though much of my work was more generally concerned with the wider topic of social conflict rather than with the somewhat narrower area of social violence, a number of propositions previously advanced apply to violence as well. There is no need, therefore, to reiterate them in this chapter. Instead, I shall focus selectively on but a few functions of social violence: violence as a form of achievement, violence as a danger signal, and violence as a catalyst. It is to be understood that this is by no means an exhaustive list of the functions of violence, nor will its dysfunctions be dealt with in this chapter.

Violence as Achievement

Certain categories of individuals are so located in the social structure that they are barred from legitimate access to the ladder of achievement, as Merton has argued in convincing detail.[3] Moreover, as Cloward and Ohlin[4] have shown more recently, certain categories of persons may find themselves in structural positions which effectively prevent them from utilizing not only legitimate channels of opportunity but criminal and illegitimate channels as well. I shall argue that when all such channels are barred, violence may offer alternate roads to achievement.

Cloward and Ohlin take as a case in point adolescents in disorganized urban areas who are oriented toward achieving higher positions and yet lack access to either conventional or criminal opportunity structures. "These adolescents," they argue,

> seize upon the manipulation of violence as a route to status not only because it provides a way of expressing pent-up angers and frustrations but also because they are not cut off from access to violent means by vicissitudes of birth. In the world of violence, such attributes as race, socioeconomic position, age, and the like are irrelevant; personal worth is judged on the basis of qualities that are available to all who would cultivate them. The acquisition of status is not simply a consequence of skill in the use of violence or of physical strength but depends, rather, on one's willingness to risk injury or death in the search for "rep."[5]

In the area of violence, then, ascriptive status considerations become irrelevant. Here, the vaunted equal opportunity, which had been experienced as a sham and a lure everywhere else, turns out to be effective. In the wilderness of cities, just as in the wilderness of the frontier, the gun becomes an effective equalizer. Within the status structure of the gang, through a true transvaluation of middle-class values, success in defense of the "turf" brings deference and "rep" which are unavailable anywhere else. Here the successful exercise of violence is a road to achievement.

Nor need we rest consideration with the case of juvenile delinquency. One can make the more general assertion that in all those situations in which both legitimate and illegitimate socioeconomic achievement seems blocked, recourse to aggressive and violent behavior may be perceived as a significant area of "achievement." This may help to explain the ideal of *machismo* in the lower classes of Latin America. Here, as in the otherwise very different violence in disorganized urban areas of American cities, men tend to feel that only prowess in interpersonal violence or in aggressive sexual encounters allows the achievement of personal identity and permits gaining otherwise unavailable deference. Where no social status can be achieved through socioeconomic channels it may yet be achieved in the show of violence among equally deprived peers.

Somewhat similar mechanisms may be at work in the intrafamilial aggression and violence of American lower-class fathers. These men tend to compensate for inadequate rewards in the occupational world at large by an aggressive assertion of male superiority within the little world of the family—as Donald McKinley has recently argued with much cogency.[6] The disproportionately high rate of interpersonal violence among Negro males may yield to a similar explanation. Since Negroes are assigned lowest position in all three major dimensions of the American status system — ethnicity, class, and education — and since their mobility chances are nil in the first and minimal in the second and third, it stands to reason that achievement in the area of interpersonal violence might be seen as a channel leading to self-regard and self-enhancement — at least as long as conflict with the dominant white majority seems socially unavailable as a means of collective action. This does not preclude that violent acting out may not also at the same time call forth a feeling of self-hatred for acting in the stereotypical manner in which the Negro is accused of acting by the dominant white.

Revolutionary violence, both in the classical revolutions of the past and in the anticolonialist liberation movements of the present, can also be understood in this manner. Participation in such violence offers opportunity to the oppressed and downtrodden for affirming identity and for claiming full manhood hitherto denied to them by the powers that be. Participation in revolutionary violence offers the chance for the first act of participation in the polity, for entry into the world of active citizenship. In addition, participation in acts of violence symbolizes commitment to the revolutionary cause. It marks to the actor, but also to his circle, the irrevocable decision to reject the *ancien régime* and to claim allegiance to the revolutionary movement. This has been well described by the late Frantz Fanon, an active participant in the Algerian movement of liberation and one of its most powerful ideological spokesmen. "For colonial man," he writes,

> violence incarnates absolute *praxis*. . . . The questions asked of militants by the organization are marked by this vision of things. "Where did you work? With whom? What have you done?" The group demands that the individual commits an irreversible deed. In Algeria, for example, where almost all of the men who called for the struggle of national liberation were condemned to death or pursued by the French police, confidence in a man was proportional to the degree of severity of his [police] case. A new militant was considered reliable when he could no longer return to the colonial system. It seems that this mechanism was at play among the Mau Mau in Kenya where it was required that each member of the group strike the victim. Hence everyone was personally responsible for victim's death. . . . Violence once assumed permits those who have left the group to return to their place and to be reintegrated. Colonial man liberates himself in and through violence.[7]

The act of violence, in other words, commits a man symbolically to the revolutionary movement and breaks his ties with his previous life and its commitments. He is reborn, so to speak, through the act of violence and is now in a position to assume his rightful place in the revolutionary world of new men.

Similar considerations may also account for the otherwise puzzling fact that women, normally much less given to violence than men, have played leading roles in classical revolutionary movements and in such modern liberation movements as that of Algeria. Here one may suggest that situations where the old norms have broken down differ significantly from normatively stable situations. In the latter, women, having internalized the acceptance of their lower status relative to men, tend to have low rates of active violence. Their suicide as well as their homicide rates are much lower than those of men. Being more sheltered in their lower status positions, women tend to have less motivation for aggression whether directed toward self or toward others. The situation is different, however, when the old norms are challenged, as in revolutions. Here many observers have noted high female participation rates in violent crowds and in street riots. In certain key revolutionary events, such as the March to Versailles of October 1790, and in later food riots, women were predominant. Writes the foremost student of revolutionary crowds, George Rudé, "On the morning of October 5 the revolt started simultaneously in the central markets and the Faubourg Saint-Antoine; in both cases women were the leading spirits."[8]

Revolutionary situations topple the status order and allow underdogs to aspire to equal participation. They provide the occasion for women to act like men. It is as if women were to say to themselves: "If all these extraordinary actions have become possible, then it is perhaps permissible to entertain the extraordinary idea that women need no longer accept their inferior status and can aspire to achieve a hitherto unattainable equality." Here, as in all the other cases considered, violence equalizes and opens to the participants access to hitherto denied areas of achievement.[9]

Violence as a Danger Signal

The late Norbert Wiener once remarked that cancer is so peculiarly dangerous a disease because it typically develops through its early stages without causing pain. Most other diseases, by eliciting painful sensations in the body, bring forth bodily signals which allow early detection of the illness and its subsequent treatment. Pain serves as an important mechanism of defense, permitting the medical readjustment of bodily balance which has been attacked by disease. It seems hardly far fetched to apply this reasoning to the body social as well.

A social dysfunction can, of course, be attended to only if it becomes visible, if not to the total community, at least to certain more sensitive and more powerful sectors of it. But the sensitive usually lack power, and the powerful often lack sensitivity. As Merton has phrased the issue, there are latent social problems, "conditions which are . . . at odds with values of the group but are not recognized as being so,"[10] which can become manifest, and hence subject to treatment, only when particular groups or individuals choose to take cognizance of them. Merton urges that it is the task of the sociologist to make latent social problems manifest; at the same time he stresses that "those occupying strategic positions of authority and power of course carry more weight than others in deciding social policy and so . . . in identifying for the rest what are to be taken as significant departures from social standards."[11] Granted that the social perceptions of those in power and authority may be influenced by social scientists calling attention to previously neglected problems, it would be an indulgence in unwarranted Comtean optimism to assume that such enlightenment will at all times be sufficient to alert them. It is at this point that the signaling functions of social violence assume importance.

Although there are individual, subcultural, and class variations in the internalized management and control of anger in response to frustration, I take it to be axiomatic that human beings — other than those systematically trained to use legitimate or illegitimate violence — will resort to violent action only under extremely frustrating, ego-damaging, and anxiety-producing conditions. It follows that if the incidence of violence increases rapidly, be it in the society at large or within specific sectors of it, this can be taken as a signal of severe maladjustment. I would further suggest that this signal is so drastic, so extremely loud, that it cannot fail to be perceived by men in power and authority otherwise not noted for peculiar sensitivity to social ills. This is not to say, of course, that they will necessarily respond with types of social therapy that will effectively remove the sources of infection. But I suggest that outbreaks of social violence are more apt than other less visible or sensitive indicators at least to lead them to perceive the problem.

To be sure, outbreaks of violence can be seen as mere manifestations of underlying conditions. Yet, perhaps because of this, they may lead power holders to effect a change in these conditions. Two illustrations will have to suffice. Conventional historical and sociological wisdom has it that the British Chartist movement of the first half of the last century and the often violent and destructive popular movements which preceded it were but manifestations of temporary imbalances brought by the Industrial Revolution upon the British social and political scene. These imbalances, it is argued, were progressively eliminated through a variety of social-structural changes, more particularly through an increase in structural differentiation which gradually provided the homeostatic forces that led to the restabilization of British society in the second part of the nineteenth century.[12] In this view, Chartism was a symptom of a temporary pathological condition, and its defeat highlighted the return to equilibrium and stability.

This view seems to be seriously deficient, if for no other reason than that it ignores the impact of Chartism and related movements on the political decisionmakers. It ignores, in other words, the determining contribution of this movement. Far from being but an epiphenomenal manifestation of temporary maladjustment, Chartism had a direct impact by leading to a series of reform measures alleviating the conditions against which it had reacted. Violence and riots were not merely protests: they were claims to be considered. Those involved in them assumed that the authorities would be sensitive to demands and would make concessions. And it turned out that they were right.[13]

Historians will hardly deny that the condition of the laboring poor, and more particularly the industrial working class, between the beginning of the Industrial Revolution and the middle of the nineteenth century was appalling. Nor is it subject to debate that for a long time these conditions were barely perceived by those in power. Finally, it is not to be doubted that legislative remedies, from factory legislation to the successive widening of the franchise and the attendant granting of other citizenship rights to members of the lower classes,[14] came, at least in part, in response to the widespread disorders and violent outbreaks that marked the British social scene for over half a century. Let me quote from Mark Hovell, one of the earliest, and still one of the best, of the historians of the Chartist movement. "The Chartists," he writes:

> first compelled attention to the hardness of the workmen's lot, and forced thoughtful minds to appreciate the deep gulf between the two nations which lived side by side without knowledge of or care for each other. Though remedy came slowly and imperfectly, and was seldom directly from Chartist hands, there was always the Chartist impulse behind the first timid steps toward social and economic betterment. The cry of the Chartists did much to force public opinion to adopt the policy of factory legislation in the teeth of the opposition of the manufacturing interests. It compelled the administrative mitigation of the harshness of the New Poor Law. It swelled both the demand and necessity for popular education. It prevented the unqualified victory of the economic gospel of the Utilitarians. . . . The whole trend of modern social legislation must well have gladdened the hearts of the ancient survivors of Chartism.[15]

The often violent forms of rebellion of the laboring poor, the destructiveness of the city mobs, and other forms of popular disturbances which mark English social history from the 1760s to the middle of the nineteenth century, helped to educate the governing elite of England, Whig and Tory alike, to the recognition that they could ignore the plight of the poor only at their own peril. These social movements constituted among other things an effective signaling device which sensitized the upper classes to the need for social reconstruction in defense of a social edifice over which they wished to continue to have overall command.[16]

My second example concerning violence as a danger signal will be brief since it deals with recent experiences still vivid in social memory: the civil rights movement and the war against poverty. The plight of the American Negro and of the urban poor until recently had a very low degree of visibility for the bulk of the white population and the decisionmakers on the American scene. Much of it was physically not visible in the sense that it took place in segregated areas not customarily visited by "good people." Much of it, on the other hand, though physically visible, was yet not socially perceived. The sociology of social perception, a sociology elucidating why people sometimes look and why they sometimes look away, it may be remarked in passing, still is to be written. Be that as it may, the shock of recognition, the jolt to conscience, occurred only when the Negroes, through by-and-large nonviolent action in the South and through increasingly violent demonstrations and even riots in the North, brought the problem forcibly to the attention of white public opinion and the white power structure. To be sure, a whole library of books has been written on the dehumanizing consequences of the racial caste system. Yet all this became a public issue only after a number of large-scale social conflicts, beginning in Montgomery, Alabama, helped to highlight the issue. No doubt, the slow process of structural differentiation might have taken care of the problem some time in the indeterminate future. In fact, something was done about it here and now mainly because Negroes, no longer satisfied with promises and having gained some advances, now raised their level of expectations, indicating in quite drastic a manner that they were no longer prepared to wait, that they wanted "Freedom Now." (I shall return to the topic in the last part of this chapter.) Much as one might deplore the often senseless violence displayed in such racial riots as those in Los Angeles, one cannot help feeling that they, too, constituted quite effective signaling devices, perhaps desperate cries for help after other appeals had been unavailing. They indicated a sickness in the body social which demands immediate remedy if it is not to undermine social order altogether.

Violence as a Catalyst

Marx once remarked: "The criminal produces an impression now moral, now tragic, and hence renders a 'service' by arousing the moral and aesthetic sentiments of the public." Marx here anticipated by many years similar formulations by Durkheim and Mead stressing the unanticipated functions of crime in creating a sense of solidarity within the community.[17] Here I shall argue a related idea, namely, that not only criminals, but law-enforcing agents also, may call forth a sense of solidarity against their behavior. More particularly, the use of extralegal violence by these officers may, under certain circumstances, lead to the arousal of the community and to a revulsion from societal arrangements that rest upon such enforcement methods.

It is common knowledge that the violence used by sheriffs and other Southern officers of the law against Southern Negroes engaged in protest activities and voting-registration drives has had a major impact upon public opinion and federal legislation. The fact is that such methods had been relied upon by Southern police for a very long time without any marked reaction against them. Why, then, did they suddenly become counter-productive? Two major factors seem to account for this reversal. First, modes of control involving the extralegal uses of violence worked well as long as the acts in question could be committed with a minimum of publicity and visibility. They became suicidal when they were performed under the glare of television cameras and under the observation of reporters for national newspapers and magazines.

Everett Hughes, in discussing the Nazi case, has argued that all societies depend for their maintenance on a certain amount of "dirty work" by shady agents of the powers that be, and he added that such dirty work is usually performed far from the sight of "good people."[18] Indeed, the usefulness of those doing the "dirty work" may well come to an end when it must be performed in full view of "good people." If, as Hughes argues, those who do the dirty work "show a sort of concentrate of those impulses of which we are or wish to be less aware," then it stands to reason that they cease to be useful if they have to operate in full view. The solid middle-class citizen of Nazi Germany seems, by and large, to have been unconcerned with what was being done to the Jews; even the early public degradation of Jews in city streets seems to have left them unaffected. But the Hitler regime showed very good judgment indeed in carefully hiding and camouflaging its later murderous methods. One may doubt that the death camps could have been operated except in secret. Similarly, solid middle-class citizens in both North and South may have been aware of the extralegal uses of violence habitually resorted to by Southern sheriffs and police. Yet as long as such knowledge did not intrude too much in their visual field, they remained unconcerned. Matters changed drastically when these inhuman methods were fully exposed to the public at large. Now visibility could no longer be denied. Had these officials become conscious of the changed circumstances under which they were now forced to operate, they might well have abandoned these methods in favor of more subtle means of intimidation. As it turned out, they were subject to the "trained incapacity" upon which Veblen and Kenneth Burke have commented. They adopted measures in keeping with their past training — and the very soundness of this training led them to adopt the wrong measures. Their past training caused them to misjudge their present situation.[19] The very exercise of violence which had been productive of "order" in the past now produced a wave of public indignation which undermined the very practice.

The matter of publicity, powerfully aided by the recent "communication revolution," though crucially important, is not the only one to be considered here. It is equally relevant to observe that violent tactics of suppression tend to be much less successful when used against people who are publicly committed to the principle of nonviolence. Violence by the police, even extralegal violence, may be approved, or at least condoned, when it can be justified by reference to the supposed actual or potential violence of the offending criminal. That is, such behavior seems to be justified or condoned when there exists, or seems to exist, a rough equivalence between the means used by both sides. A tooth for a tooth tends to be a maxim popularly applicable in these cases. But the matter is very different when the presumed offender is committed in principle to a politics of nonviolence. The nonviolent resisters in the South, as distinct from other cases where nonviolence was not based on principle, had consciously assumed the burden of nonviolence. That is, they had made a commitment to the public not to have recourse to violence. When violence was used against them, this hence came to be seen as a breach of a tacit reciprocal commitment on the part of those they opposed. What is ordinarily perceived as a multilateral relationship in which both sides actually or potentially use violence came now to be perceived as unilateral violence. This impression was still accentuated when acts of official or semiofficial violence were being directed against ministers, that is, against men who enjoy specific mandates and immunities as men of peace.

For these reasons, extralegal violence habitually used in the South to maintain the caste system turned out to be a most effective triggering device for measures to abolish it. One need, perhaps, not go so far as to argue, as Jan Howard has recently done,[20] that the very effectiveness of the nonviolent methods used depended on the assumption or expectation that it would encounter violent reactions that would arouse the public conscience. The violent reactions did not have to be anticipated. But it was nevertheless one of the latent functions of Southern violent response to the nonviolent tactics used to lead to the arousal of a previously lethargic community to a sense of indignation and revulsion.

Nor is the Southern case unique. Even in earlier periods extralegal violence on the part of law-enforcement agencies has often been suicidal.

The Peterloo Massacre of 1819 in Manchester, when a crowd of listeners to speeches on parliamentary reform and the repeal of the Corn Laws was charged by soldiers who killed ten and injured hundreds, became a rallying cry for the reformers and radicals. The wholesale massacre of participants in the French Commune of 1871 created a sense of intimate solidarity, but also of alienation from society at large, among large sectors of the French working class. In these latter cases the impact was not on the total society but only on particular sectors of it, but in all of them the show of violence on the part of officialdom was suicidal in so far as it transformed victims into martyrs who became symbols of the iniquity and callousness of the rulers.

Lest it be understood that I argue that unanticipated and suicidal uses of violence are limited to cases involving law-enforcement agents alone, let me remark, even if only in passing, that there are clearly other groups within society whose resort to violence may under specifiable circumstances bring forth similar suicidal consequences. In particular, when minority groups appeal to the public conscience and attempt to dramatize the fact that they are treated with less than justice and equity, their resort to violence may effectively hamper their cause. They must depend on their appeal on winning to their side previously indifferent and unconcerned sectors of the public. Resort to violence, however, even though it may serve as a danger signal, is also likely to alienate precisely those who are potential recruits for their cause. Hence groups such as the Black Muslims and other extremist Negro organizations may, if they resort to violence, bring about suicidal results by turning previously indifferent or potentially sympathetic bystanders into hostile antagonists.

Conclusion

The preceding discussion has identified and examined a series of cases in which violence may perform latent or manifest functions. The approach was meant to be exploratory and tentative rather than exhaustive and systematic. It is hoped, however, that enough has been said to show that the curiously tender-minded view of the social structure which has generally predominated in American social theory is seriously deficient and needs to be complemented by a more tough-minded approach.

Notes

1. Arnold S. Feldman, "Violence and Volatility: The Likelihood of Revolution," *Internal War,* ed. Harry Eckstein (New York: Free Press of Glencoe, 1964), p. 111.

See, also, Ralf Dahrendorf, *Class and Class Conflict in Industrial Society* (Stanford, Calif: Stanford University Press, 1959), and a series of later papers collected in the author's *Gesellschaft und Freiheit* (Munich: R. Piper, 1961).

2. Lewis A. Coser, *The Functions of Social Conflict* (Glencoe, Ill.: Free Press, 1956); Lewis A. Coser, "Social Conflict and the Theory of Social Change," *British Journal of Sociology* 8, no. 3 (September 1957):197-207; Lewis A. Coser, "Some Functions of Deviant Behavior and Normative Flexibility," *American Journal of Sociology* 68, no. 2 (September 1962):172-181; Lewis A. Coser, "Violence and the Social Structure," *Violence and War,* Vol. VI of *Science and Psycholanalysis,* ed. Jules Masserman (New York: Grune and Stratton, 1963).

3. Robert K. Merton, *Social Theory and Social Structure* (rev. ed.; Glencoe, Ill.: Free Press, 1957), chaps. 4 and 5.

4. Richard A. Cloward and Lloyd E. Ohlin, *Delinquency and Opportunity* (Glencoe, Ill.: Free Press, 1960).

5. Ibid., p. 175.

6. Donald G. McKinley, *Social Class and Family Life* (New York: Free Press of Glencoe, 1964).

7. Frantz Fanon, *Les Damnés de la Terre* (Paris: Francis Maspero, 1961), pp. 63-64.

8. George Rudé, *The Crowd in the French Revolution* (Oxford: Clarendon Press, 1959), p. 73.

9. I have dealt with this in a somewhat different framework in "Violence and the Social Structure."

10. Robert K. Merton, "Social Problems and Social Theory," *Contemporary Social Problems,* ed. Robert K. Merton and Robert A. Nisbet (New York: Harcourt and Brace, 1962), p. 709.

11. Ibid., p. 706.

12. Cf. Neil J. Smelser, *Social Change in the Industrial Revolution* (Chicago: University of Chicago Press, 1959), and the same author's *Theory of Collective Behavior* (New York: Free Press of Glencoe, 1963). In the latter work, social movements are seen as always involving the "action of the impatient" who "short-circuit" the process of social readjustment by "exaggerating reality," see pp. 72-73. In this perspective one might be justified in concluding that had impatient Christians not short-circuited the adjustment process in ancient Israel, the Jews would have readjusted in time — and spared the world the spectacle of much later impatient religious action.

13. Eric J. Hobsbawm, *The Age of Revolution* (London: Weidenfels and Nicholson, 1962), p. 111.

14. Cf. T. H. Marshall, *Class, Citizenship and Social Development* (New York: Doubleday Anchor Books, 1965).

15. Mark Hovell, *The Chartist Movement* (London: Longmans, Green, 1918), pp. 210-211. See also Edouard Dolléans, *Le Chartisme* (Paris: Marcel Rivière, 1949).

16. On the politics of rioting and crowd action see, among others, George Rudé, *The Crowd in History* (New York: John Wiley & Sons, 1964); *The Crowd in the French Revolution* by the same author, also his *Wilkes and Liberty* (Oxford: Clarendon Press, 1962); Eric J. Hobsbawm, *Labouring Men* (London: Weidenfels and Nicholson,

1964), and his earlier *Social Bandits and Primitive Rebels* (Glencoe, Ill.: Free Press, 1959).

17. For the relevant quotations from Marx, Durkheim, and Mead, see Coser, "Some Functions of Deviant Behavior."

18. Everett C. Hughes, "Good People and Dirty Work," *Social Problems* 10, no. 1 (summer 1962):3-11.

19. Kenneth Burke, *Permanence and Change* (New York: New Republic, 1936), p. 18.

20. In *Dissent* (January-February 1966).

15
Societal Approaches to the Study of War

Michael Haas

Introduction

Societal[1] conditions have been related to fluctuations of war and peace since the dawn of civilization. The factor cited most often as responsible for propensities to external aggression among preliterate peoples is the desire to preserve tribal solidarity (Wright 1942, I:78; Murphy 1957). Armed clashes of the ancient empires of Egypt, Assyria, Babylon, Persia, Macedon, and Rome were conscious attempts to suppress insurrections and external sources of potential imperial disunity (cf. Bozeman 1960). In the sixteenth and seventeenth centuries, when religious sentiments and dynastic claims were invoked to legitimize wars, more international aggression occurred than in any previous era of history (Sorokin 1937:297-298). But when conflicts between Protestants and Catholics and those between rival royal houses were resolved within the framework of the newly arising European state system, the use of force in international politics did not cease. The territorial state system, however, did make it possible for religious conflict to be resolved short of war, and by the end of the eighteenth century there was a fading away of dynastic quarrels. Meanwhile, nationalism and imperialism flourished in the nineteenth century to guide decisionmakers in the use of military means for seemingly just goals. Ideologies extolling particular forms of political and economic arrangements have been utilized in the twentieth century to sanction both internal and external war (Aron 1954).

Parallel with the changing course of international history, writings of prominent social theorists from Plato through Lenin have usually linked *societal conditions within states* to the aggressive behavior of states in foreign affairs. Yet in our own day societal factors are assigned a much lesser

Reprinted by permission of the publisher from Michael Haas, "Societal Approaches to the Study of War," *Journal of Peace Research* 2 (1965):307-323.

degree of attention than was formerly the case. It is more fashionable to speculate on the *psychological basis* of war and, alternatively, to treat international aggression as a product of the very *structure of the international system* (Waltz 1959).[2] According to those who focus on war as rooted in the minds of men, to use UNESCO's phrase, the individual decisionmaker of a state entering war must be better understood psychologically. Analysis of the process of arriving at a decision to go to war has pointed very often to such irrational aspects as overpreoccupation with hostility (Zinnes, North, and Koch 1961). The systemic approach, on the other hand, stresses that there may be features of the international environment which make war more probable than would otherwise be the case. For example, Lewis F. Richardson (1960:177) finds that the more boundaries a country has with other states, the more likely it is to participate in war. The imperial or hierarchically dominated international system, such as classical Rome succeeded in creating, doubtless has a higher potential for international tranquillity than does a system of many independent and sovereign states.

Fortunately, the newer approaches have stimulated much new theory and research on the subject of war. Advances in the societal level of analysis have emerged, although only very recently, and they are codified in the following discussion. Accordingly, it is the task of this chapter to examine changing foci in the societal level of analysis, to systematize the two main societal approaches, to indicate whether empirical findings require a modification of traditional theory, and to integrate the societal approach with both the psychological and systemic levels of analysis.

Early Theorists

Throughout writings of the theorists who relate domestic conditions of states to warlike behavior, various sorts of internal factors have been stressed in different periods of time. The most common argument is that war is a function of the type of government or of economic conditions.

Plato (n.d.:64-67) advises states wishing to avoid war to have a cohesive people and an economic system with a moderate level of consumption. Cohesion ensures a loyal citizenry, which is necessary to deter attacks, whereas moderate prosperity means that the state has little to gain economically from war and is not at the same time an attractive bait for states desiring the booty of war. Although Plato regards democracy as unstable and warlike, to such philosophers of the Enlightenment as Kant, Bentham, and Paine, the lesson which dynastic wars taught was that republics with representative institutions are much more peaceful than monarchical despotisms (Waltz 1959:82-83). Aristocratic elites are warlike and oppressive, so new elites must be installed, the argument went. By reducing the frustrations of governmental restrictions and by expanding the share in decisionmaking to encompass future soldiers, chances of war would decrease: there would be fewer internally generated political tensions to release externally, and no sane man would vote to go to a frivolous war which might mean his death.

The economic aspect of Plato's advice was also modified by later thinkers. The advocates of economic liberalism believed that preoccupation with the problems and benefits of industrialization would make a stable international environment more profitable. Indeed, according to classical economists and sociologists, conquests for economic gain characterize poor, agrarian countries, rather than industrial societies, where enrichment is secured most efficiently through extensive economic production and trade (Silberner 1946).

The overall consensus, then, was that democracy and capitalism would be harbingers of international tranquillity, but there was dissent from this view on the part of Karl Marx and Friedrich Engels. While they never analyzed war at length in any single work, their critique of previous theory was unusually devastating. The comprehensive scope of their succinctly presented theory of war merits special consideration.

Marxist Theory

According to the Marxian dialectical view, one economic system is far more peaceful than its antecedents, but that system has not yet arrived. War accompanies class struggles of precapitalist and capitalist societies, but in a communist world there are no classes, so there are no wars (Marx and Engels 1959). Under communism both aristocratic tyranny and bourgeois democracy will have been transcended; the most peaceful political system turns out to be one with no visible government at all. There will be no elites to compel men to fight, and there will be no states to attack or to defend.

Even as history progresses toward communism, war will be less of a problem. So even Marx acknowledges that capitalism is more peaceful than feudalism, and his reasoning goes as follows. Communism can emerge only when capitalism has developed to the fullest extent, whereupon capitalism's internal contradictions will be greatest, and it will collapse. And as capitalism is spread more globally its inner logic will demand that free trade be established everywhere. Separate national characteristics will vanish, and close economic and political cooperation between capitalists in many lands will give rise to a universal bourgeois culture. In a world of fewer differences and more interdependence among states, wars will decline.

At the same time war-breeding crises may occur due to internal contradictions of bourgeois economics. As Marx demonstrates in *Capital,*

Rodbertus was mistaken in assuming that crises result from such a worsening of economic conditions for the working class that the bourgeoisie has to embark upon war to escape from problems of social unrest inherent in a system of social stratification. Economically, the proletariat actually improves before crises, but because capitalism is not controlled centrally by altruistic men, more goods are manufactured for consumers to buy than their wages permit. Overproduction triggers economic collapses, which in turn on occasion lead to war. Why so? In bourgeois economics, Marx and Engels point out, there are only four ways of restoring to equilibrium an economic system with more supply than demand. Supply may be decreased (1) by destroying goods and (2) by wrecking means of production, but since such action diminishes future sources of profits, capitalists usually prefer to increase demand. (3) They exploit old markets more thoroughly, being careful that the proletariat does not become too powerful, or (4) they seize new markets through war. International violence may mean making colonial acquisitions or forcing other nations to adopt bourgeois methods.

Marx evidently foresaw that the operation of the dialectical process in history would mean that some day all states would become capitalist. To Lenin, the process should and could be shortened. By the early twentieth century, he commented (Lenin 1939), few of the four techniques for handling crises were available. Competition among giant economic units had advanced so far that all available markets had been exploited. Even with members of the upper proletariat "bribed" by the bourgeoisie with generous wages, these "trustworthy" internal markets were saturated with economic goods. Greed for more profits could be satisfied only by subjugation of other countries, in other words by stealing markets from capitalists of other lands. A stable international arena had become impossible as wars were fought by newly emerging capitalist states for divisions of economic spoils abroad. Unlike Marx, Lenin was suggesting that capitalism would entail more, not fewer, instances of international aggression.

The First World War, to Lenin, was an imperialist attempt to "seize lands and to conquer foreign nations, to ruin competing nations, to pillage their wealth," but it was also a war "to divert the attention of the labouring masses from the domestic political crises" (Lenin 1935:123). The effect of the war in ineptly ruled, discontented Russia was to exacerbate social unrest, and when Lenin came to power he withdrew from the war in order to consolidate the new socialist state. On observing the participation by socialists in the European conflict, Lenin realized that the war fulfilled another function, namely, "to disunite the workers and fool them with nationalism, to annihilate their vanguards in order to weaken the revolutionary movement of the proletariat." Why did revisionist socialists in Europe allow nationalist loyalties to override their ideological convictions that capitalist states are unworthy of support? To oppose entry into the war would have been interpreted as treason, and the socialist movement would have been discredited thoroughly. For Lenin the "betrayal of socialism" was possible where the proletariat had not become very class conscious. As he foresaw, when socialists attempted to set up workers' states in Europe after the war in Germany and in Hungary, the communist movement proved too weak.

As class conflicts have been minimized in the twentieth century by gradual acceptance of nationalist, socialist, and welfare-statist ideas, it is true that Marxist and Leninist theory may have lost much of its relevance as a diagnosis of modern problems. Indeed, as economic prosperity has risen throughout developed countries, attention to ideology has declined (Bell 1962). But the Marx who saw historical trends as superstructures varying with changes in social and economic conditions does remain influential. Subsequent theoretical analyses of war's interrelation with societal factors have done perhaps little more than to expand and to rephrase Marxist hypotheses.

Approaches in Societal Analysis

Though Marx is a pioneer in developing concepts and propositions in sociological theory, some ambiguity remains in his formulation. On the one hand, he talks of ruling classes as welcoming war to forestall impending revolution or to extend the scope of capitalism. On the other hand, the type of economic system is assigned primacy: capitalism requires antagonistic relationships between men in order to operate, whence come brutishness and the class struggle. These two ways of looking at the relation between internal factors and war involve very different kinds of analytical approaches. The focus on objectives invoked by elites or nonelites to legitimize the use of force is what may be referred to as the "functional" approach. The second approach, which searches for societal conditions disposing elites to perceive that aggression is necessary or legitimate, is the "prerequisites" approach. The functional approach is used to analyze individual cases; but, as will be seen shortly, it is not very useful in discovering regularities in behavior. The prerequisites approach concentrates on conditions shared by countries before war and lacking in countries avoiding war.

Functional Approach

According to functionalists, especially those prominent in the time of Bismarck, war is a technique of internal statecraft consciously employed when states find it necessary to increase stability or profitable to be victorious (Simmel 1955:92-93; Bernhardi 1914:17-18). In other words, war is justified in terms of its social consequences. Let us examine some of these arguments more carefully.

Because morale is an important component of national power, cohesive states are often in an advantageous position if they wish to go to war. Similarly, potential aggressors may avoid combat with states which have internal solidarity. On the other hand, countries may be so content internally that no excuse for international misbehavior will present itself. Apparently disagreeing with Chinese views on the subject at one time, Soviet Russian ideologists do not want internal social progress to be interrupted by wars with no constructive purposes (Khrushchev 1963:4). The new Soviet man is supposed to be more "humanistic" because socialist methods of economic production are not based on antagonisms.

Low stability is associated both with war and with peace, too. Societies with domestic difficulties can be confronted with war because of military weakness. When internal disputes broke out in Switzerland in 1802, Napoleon dispatched 20,000 men to obtain an "armistice," which brought the Alpine land under French domination (Maurice 1883:35). Large nation states with vexing domestic problems, modern Southeast Asian countries for example, would be difficult for another country to control by bayonets. In short, in some cases internal weakness invites war and in others it deters war.

War may have a different effect upon the elite and the nonelite groups in a society. One theory is that the masses alone improve their lot in wartime at the expense of the ruling classes. To ensure wartime cohesion, the elite may feel compelled to grant political and religious concessions and to distribute income more equitably (Silberner 1946). If the elite fails to provide tangible rewards, it may be overthrown by a more radically attuned counterelite, as in Russia in 1917. In class struggles of the Greek city-states a discontented faction out of power sometimes would make common cause with external enemies; the former would go on strike as foreign soldiers approached the city's gates, forcing the ruling faction to capitulate.

The alternative hypothesis, that the elite uses international aggression to its own selfish advantage, is a central theme in Marxist theory. Wars enable elites to emphasize patriotic feelings over class consciousness, hence delaying and obscuring class conflict and social revolution. Imminence of war can be a justification by elites for detecting potential dissenters and for discouraging opposition so that the country does not appear divided. A "garrison" state in constant readiness for war can easily make infringement of liberties seem acceptable, but the anxiety created by governmental surveillance may reduce internal solidarity, leading to even further restrictions. Because expert elite leadership is needed more in a crisis than in normal times, rulers also might consider it to their own best interest to make themselves indispensable by engineering a popularly supported war. Yet another function of war is as a safety valve to drain off tension that might be dangerous to the elite.

Finally, one could point out that war may be either beneficial or detrimental to both elites and nonelites. Victory may be profitable, and even defeat may have the latent function of triggering industrialization in order to recover what has been lost in territory or prestige.

In summary, there does not appear to be a single justification which cannot be argued for peace or for war under very similar circumstances. The functional approach does not lead very far scientifically. The underlying conditions which prompt war, rather than the verbal or behavioral rationale for war, may instead be linked more closely to the roots of international aggression. It is to these factors that we now turn.

Prerequisites Approach

Theory concerning necessary and sufficient societal conditions for international aggression has neither been codified nor tested until very recently. Types of political and economic systems have been discussed as prerequisites to war from Plato through Lenin, but two additional generic features of societies should also be mentioned: stress and strain. "Stress" is a force which threatens to disrupt the continued existence of a society; "strain" is a condition of imbalance in the structuring of a society such that nonconformity to basic cultural patterns is a rational response to socially induced frustrations.

For each of the types of societal factors there is a growing body of theory. Democratic, authoritarian, and totalitarian political systems have been claimed to have more or less congeniality to decisions to enter wars. The wealth of a country and the role of the government in an economy have been hypothesized to relate to propensities for international aggression. Stress conditions, such as economic depressions, revolutions, or very rapid social change, are assigned primacy by many theorists. And deviant behaviors, from riots, murders, and narcotic addiction to suicides, appear as well to be antecedent factors in accounting for wars.

Unlike the previous discussion on functional theory, however, much of prerequisite theory has been tested, and an empirical review of these studies is therefore possible. Because the increase in knowledge on this subject is due in part to advances in techniques of data processing, it may be useful to preview the statement of findings by enumerating the studies from which they are extracted.

Four of the studies are factor analyses. The first effort is a factor analysis of cultural variables for sixty-nine countries over the years 1837-1937 by Raymond Cattell (1949). Two studies factor analyzed indicators of internal and external conflict: Rudolph Rummel (1963) collected data for seventy-seven countries for the years 1955-1957, and Raymond Tanter (1964) replicated the study on eighty-eight countries for 1958-1960. The political variables of the *Cross-Polity Survey,* by Arthur Banks and Robert Textor (1963), were factor analyzed more recently by Phillip Gregg and Arthur Banks (1965). Using regression techniques, Michael Haas (1965) correlates the frequency of participation in war by ten countries since 1900 with unemployment, homicides, suicides, and death rates due to alcoholism. In addition, the present author reports below for the first time results of correlations between the data of Banks and Textor and those of Rummel and Tanter.

Political Systems

Historically the most prevalent form of government has been the inefficient despotism. If war is related to the form of government of a polity, then, we must contrast regimes which fall into the modal category, often called "authoritarian," with democracies on the one hand and totalitarian systems, the efficient despotisms, on the other hand.

In a study of the relation between forms of government and cooperativeness in League of Nations behavior, James Watkins (1942) found that democracies were much more active in positive roles during the League's existence than nondemocracies. Uncooperative League members subsequently were aggressors in World War II, whereas democratic states banded together cohesively within the Allied coalition.

Gregg and Banks (1965) report, however, that foreign conflict is independent of their "access" factor, which has high positive loadings for democratic characteristics and high negative loadings for features of authoritarian or totalitarian polities. "Number killed in foreign violence" has a .00 score, and "number of ambassadors expelled" has a – .06 loading. Because these findings were unexpected, the present author decided to test the same hypothesis using the *Cross-Polity Survey* data in a somewhat different fashion. The raw data decks contain a variable "foreign conflict," which is a composite of several types of diplomatic and military state behavior,[3] as well as six variables relevant to the degree of democracy — constitutional status, number of political parties, competitiveness of party systems, freedom of group opposition, representativeness of regimes, and degree of press freedom. Foreign conflict, accordingly, was cross run against each of the political systemic variables.

The most direct test of the nature of a political system as a factor affecting foreign conflict levels is supplied by the categorization of countries into "constitutional," "authoritarian," and "totalitarian" forms (Table 15.1).

TABLE 15.1   Foreign Conflict and Constitutional Status of Regimes (figures in percent)

Type of Regime (scope of elite powers)	Extent of Foreign Conflict				Total	(N)
	Significant	Moderate	Limited	Negligible		
Constitutional (limited)	8	11	36	44	99	(36)
Authoritarian (political)	18	12	24	47	101	(17)
Totalitarian (political-social) ...	13	7	40	40	100	(15)
$x^2 = 1.51$ C = .15						

Comparing percentages in Table 15.1, authoritarian regimes have the highest proportion of significant and moderate foreign conflict; totalitarian governments have somewhat more foreign conflict than constitutional systems. But the findings are not very pronounced; the contingency correlation (C) of the matrix, derived by a 1.51 chi-square (x^2) is only + .15, so the observed distribution closely resembles a random distribution. Most cases fall within the "limited" and "negligible" cells no matter how democratic or undemocratic the regime.

Similar results emerged from tests conducted with each of the remaining five political system variables. We must keep in mind, however, that a lack of *statistical* significance is more than offset by *socially* significant findings. In each of the six runs there was a slight but consistent tendency for democratic countries to have less foreign conflict than undemocratic political systems. The low correlation must be explained nevertheless. The years of the cross-sectional study are approximately 1955-1960, which are relatively calm years internationally; one would expect differences to be more striking in turbulent eras.

Economic Systems

Systematic studies of types of economic systems and international aggression have not yet made their appearance. A major stumbling block is that most of the categories in common parlance, the "grand alternatives" of feudalism, capitalism, socialism, and communism, are strictly ideal types. In reality economies have mixed characteristics, and it is difficult to classify them by using objective criteria. If we were to use as an index of socialism the expenditure of the government, as a percentage of gross national product, then India would turn out to be less socialist than the United States, and West Germany more socialist than Sweden (Russett et al. 1964, Table 11). Similar paradoxes would arise if welfare expenditures were treated as indicators of welfare statism (Russett et al. 1964, Table 15). The data, in short, may be noncomparable in terms of traditional concepts.

The distinction between "mature" and "developing" economies, which superficially resembles the familiar dichotomy between "have" and "have not" nations, leads to more fruitful results. According to Bert F. Hoselitz and Myron Weiner (1961:173), the most developed regions within India have had the greatest amount of overt conflict and violence. To test the theory that their observation is a more general relation across states in the world polity, *Cross-Polity Survey* raw data were utilized (Table 15.2). The findings are opposite such expectations. The most and, to a lesser extent, the least developed countries, which one might expect to have a high degree of economic stability, exhibit more significant foreign conflict than do the underdeveloped and intermediate types. But if the percentages of significant foreign conflict are combined with those for moderate foreign conflict, differences between the four categories nearly vanish.

Because Banks and Textor base their classification only in part on national wealth, a direct test of the have–have not theory is in order as an independent check on the findings of Table 15.2. Using United Nations assessments as an estimate of national wealth, "have" countries are highest in the "significant" foreign conflict classification, and the figures drop almost consistently in the first two columns (Table 15.3). The corresponding correlation is high enough to show that the results are probably not pro-

TABLE 15.2 Foreign Conflict and Level of Economic Development (figures in percent)

| Economic Development Status | Extent of Foreign Conflict | | | | Total | (N) |
	Significant	Moderate	Limited	Negligible		
Very Underdeveloped	12	15	23	50	100	(26)
Underdeveloped	8	15	54	23	100	(13)
Intermediate	7	14	29	50	100	(14)
Developed	17	6	39	39	101	(18)
$x^2 = 6.56$ C = .30						

TABLE 15.3 Foreign Conflict and International Financial Status (figures in percent)

| UN Assessment (percent of total dues) | Extent of Foreign Conflict | | | | Total | (N) |
	Significant	Moderate	Limited	Negligible		
High (1.5 +)	30	20	20	30	100	(10)
Medium (.25–1.49)	12	12	42	35	101	(26)
Low (.05–.24)	9	14	41	36	100	(22)
Very Low (.04)	7	13	20	60	100	(15)
$x^2 = 6.58$ C = .29						

duced by a coding artifact. Similar but weaker findings are obtained with gross national product figures, both total and per capita.

In the Cattell (1949) factor analysis consistent findings emerge. The "cultural pressure" factor, which has a + .63 loading for foreign clashes and a + .62 score for participation in war, also has positive loadings for standard of living (+ .35) and for per capita income (+..34).

Stress

Just as economic systems are related closely to war propensities,[4] economic stress precedes war in most cases. Cattell's "cultural pressure" factor has only a + .09 score for unemployment of 1932-1933, but the median product-moment correlation in Haas's study of ten countries over the years 1900-1960 between unemployment and war frequency is + .33 (Haas 1965).

Rural countries, however, differ greatly in their reaction to stress from states with large urban populations. Lacking an industrial base for prolonged or total war, rural states are much more aggressive in entering war as an immediate escape from sudden stress than are urban countries (Table 15.4). Nevertheless, rural nations are so often isolationist (cf. Rummel 1964) that they respond to few of their economic crises in a violent external manner. Urban countries are less immediately aggressive, but many of them find it convenient to eliminate the unemployment problem. And the effect of militarization by several countries has been to feed fears and suspicions of other states, thus triggering fateful arms races. However, not all militarizing states eventually go to war. Thus, Switzerland's militarization in the late 1930s possibly deterred Germany, so there is nothing necessarily inexorable about an arms race.

A second stress factor which may be related to war is "population pressure." According to some theorists an overcrowded population exerts such an impact upon a country's foreign policy that the state must seek additional territories in which to resettle its people more comfortably. In the

TABLE 15.4   Rural and Urban Responses to Unemployment Stress

Urbanization (percent of work force outside agriculture)	War Aggressiveness (9-point scale)	Years Elapsing Between Unemployment Peak and War	Military Expenses (percent of budget)
Low (0–40)	5.2	4.0	23.4
Mixed (40–60)	3.2	5.4	25.1
High (60–100)	4.1	5.3	32.5

Cattell (1949) study population density has a + .32 score on the "cultural pressure" factor, and urbanization has a + .78 loading; war participation, it will be recalled, had a + .62 position. In other words, war, population density, and urbanism are highly intercorrelated with the dimension of societal stress. Logically war could not of itself breed high population density or urbanization, so one might infer that urban population density is one antecedent to wars. Using the *Cross-Polity Survey* data it is possible to test these hypotheses more directly with current data (Table 15.5). The expectation of a direct relation between the variables would be confirmed if the degree of foreign conflict increases as populations become more dense; instead, a slight inverse relation is observed in Table 15.5. Although most of the cases do fall within the "limited" and "negligible" conflict cells, the tendency for less dense countries to have more foreign conflict, and vice versa, is not exactly a random result, the correlation based on a 4.50 chi-square being .24. However, the location of the "pressure" could be in countries overpopulated in the countryside or in cities, so a more refined measure of density is in order. First of all, urbanization is mapped against foreign conflict (Table 15.6), and the results are more consistent with earlier studies: the stress within overcrowded cities bears more relation to international conflict than the stresses associated with life in densely settled farmlands. The same conclusion is made from a separate run using the percentage of a country's population engaged in agriculture as the independent variable.

TABLE 15.5   Foreign Conflict and Population Density (figures in percent)

Density of Population (persons per sq. mile)	Extent of Foreign Conflict				Total	(N)
	Significant	Moderate	Limited	Negligible		
Very High (600+)	0	0	25	75	100	(4)
High (300–599)	10	10	30	50	100	(10)
Medium (100–299)	17	9	39	35	100	(23)
Low (0–99)	10	18	33	38	99	(39)
$x^2 = 4.50$ C = .24						

TABLE 15.6   Foreign Conflict and Urbanization (figures in percent)

Urbanization (percent of pop. in cities of 20,000 or more)	Extent of Foreign Conflict				Total	(N)
	Significant	Moderate	Limited	Negligible		
High (20+)	16	14	35	35	100	(49)
Low (0–19)	5	14	33	48	100	(21)
$x^2 = 2.92$ C = .20						

A third type of stress is an extreme amount of system conflict, as for example revolutionary disturbances. Since social conflict at more tolerable levels is treated as one of four types of strain, the discussion of this third factor is postponed until the first part of the following section, where it can be regarded as one end of the conflict-consensus continuum.

Strain

"Strain" may be defined formally as a malintegrated aspect of a system. Rules and standards in any culture are bound to contain some inconsistencies, and if a system contains many subcultures the violation of the dominant culture's goals is likely to be frequent. Strains are experienced in the form of conflicting role expectations, so strain begets deviant, or nonconformist, behavior. Conformity, after all, is unlikely if a person is expected to perform semicontradictory tasks, or if he is so uprooted socially that he has no clear set of social standards to which his observance will be rewarded socially. Similarly, if the means at hand to achieve desired goals, such as "success," are restricted socially a deviant interpretation of goals or even means would seem only rational. By definition the well-integrated society has minimal strain; informal social controls operate to keep rates of deviance at low levels. In stressful times, however, deviance skyrockets and becomes intolerable.

One way to classify types of social deviance may be adapted from a discussion by Talcott Parsons (1951, Chapter 7). One basic distinction is between active and passive deviance (Table 15.7). Social conflict is a special type of active deviance aimed directly at the rules governing social and political behavior; examples of domestic conflict behavior include strikes, riots, assassinations, ministry downfalls, purges, demonstrations, revolutions, and guerrilla warfare. If one's active nonconformity is directed at persons, rather than rules, the common manifestation is some form of assault, from fistfighting to homicide. Passive deviance may be directed as well either at social norms or at persons. The former are attempts to escape from constricting rules, manifest as bureaucratic rigidity and formalism to the use of such euphoric agents as narcotics and alcohol. The latter is illustrated by suicide and other forms of self-destructiveness.

TABLE 15.7   A Classification of Deviant Behavior (cells contain examples)

Attention Focus	Personality Types	
	Active	Passive
Norms	social conflict	escapism
Persons	assault	self-destructiveness

Social Conflict

Existing theory suggests that there must be a positive relation between war and domestic conflict behavior. It is generally the factor presupposed by representatives of the functional approach, including Marxists, who see class struggle at the foundation of the dialectical process of history.

Much of the evidence, nevertheless, does not permit such an easy inference. Longitudinally, Sorokin (1937) observes that "internal disturbances" cluster before, during, and after periods of war in ten European national groupings since the time of classical Greece and Rome. Lee (1931) traces the same pattern in China from antiquity. They concur that there are some periods of turbulence in which both internal and external conflict take place, while in other eras peace, stability, and economic developments proceed. Cross sectionally, several factor analyses have reported little relation between social conflict and international aggression. The first of these studies are the factor analyses of Cattell (1949), Rummel (1963), and Tanter (1964). In all three the correlations between war and domestic conflict are low,[5] and the loadings of social conflict variables are low on the factor dimension containing war. Does this mean that the degree of social conflict within a state is totally independent of its propensity to engage in foreign conflict? One would be tempted to infer that social conflict is unrelated to war, but the findings of the Gregg and Banks (1965) factor analysis do not allow such a facile conclusion. The third factor extracted in their study is named "Consensus," which refers to a conflict-consensus continuum. Although expulsion of ambassadors has a + .03 loading on this factor, the number killed in foreign wars has a − .33 score. To determine a satisfactory explanation for such lack of consistency in results, a more refined analysis is warranted.

Recalling that consistency of results is often more important for social theory than the significance or magnitude of overall findings, one consideration should be whether the correlations and factor loadings are predominantly positive or negative. In Rummel's study 89 of the 117 correlations between 9 indicators of internal conflict and 13 indicators of foreign conflict are positive; in Tanter's study 104 out of 117 are positive. The general positive relation between domestic and foreign conflict shows up in factor loadings of both studies, thus demonstrating after all a very considerable consistency with the Gregg and Banks factor analysis.

Another way of approaching the problem is to ask whether there are some types of social conflict which are linked to war while other types are not. One of the major distinctions in conflict theory concerns the arena in which it is expressed. Conflict which proceeds within legitimate institutional channels is expected to be eufunctional to a system, since adaptation of a system to changes in the environment requires an opposition between "old" and "new" ways of behaving (Simmel 1955; Coser 1956). Conflict outside the legitimate arena of politics can take two forms: some persons may attempt to displace existing institutions by revolution or guerrilla operations, or conflict may be expressed anomically by such devices as occasional riots. Rummel and Tanter empirically derive a similar formulation: their first factor is called the "internal war" dimension, while they lump the latter two types together into a single "turmoil" factor. "Internal war" includes such variables as revolutions, purges, domestic casualties, and guerrilla warfare; "turmoil" is composed of the anomic variables, riots, and demonstrations, which have high factor loadings, but the same dimension contains as well some variables with lower loadings which one would associate with more legitimate forms of conflict — strikes and government crises. A fifth variable, assassinations, falls in between the "turmoil" sub-dimensions. Rummel and Tanter distinguish also between categories of foreign conflict which correspond to the three types suggested for domestic conflict: legitimately channelled conflict is "diplomatic"; the attempt to subvert existing channels is the "war" dimension; and the "anomic" type is called "belligerency."[6]

It would seem useful to ask which of the nine possible sets of correlations is most consistently positive (Table 15.8). Anomic conflict, with only one exception, is positively associated with foreign conflict; legitimately and illegitimately channelled conflict is related less consistently to international conflict. One would expect internal war to overtax a society's capacity to engage in foreign military conflict, so the negative correlations between internal war and foreign conflict reveal that when conflict is stressful, war is less likely. Revolutions and guerrilla warfare are more prevalent in rural countries, which we have seen are less prone to international activity. At the same time, when conflict is routed into existing political machinery, that is, when a government is asked to cope with politicized problems, the very use of the legitimate arena of politics appears to reduce the probability that the foreign conflict arena will be entered as some sort of solution for

TABLE 15.8 Correlations Between Foreign Conflict and Domestic Conflict (figures in percent of correlations that are positive)

Type of Foreign Conflict	Type of Domestic Conflict		
	Legitimate	Anomic	Illegitimate
Diplomatic	91.5	100.0	72.9
Belligerent	54.2	96.7	83.3
Military	81.8	100.0	71.8

domestic social difficulties. Anomic reactions evidently constitute pressures which can make a decision to go to war more possible.

The Banks and Textor data permit independent checks on these hypotheses about social conflict. "Articulation by anomic groups" correlates in the expected direction (Table 15.9). There is a very slight relation between foreign conflict and both governmental stability (legitimate channel) and system stability (illegitimate channel), so we can again infer that all types of social conflict make war more probable, especially anomic conflict (Tables 15.10-11). Since the correlations are low, we know that social conflict is by no means a sufficient condition for foreign conflict.

Assault

Anomic actions, such as riots and demonstrations, often are associated

TABLE 15.9   Foreign Conflict and Articulation by Anomic Groups (figures in percent)

Extent of Articulation by Anomic Groups	Extent of Foreign Conflict				Total	(N)
	Significant	Moderate	Limited	Negligible		
Frequent	33	11	33	22	100	(9)
Occasional	3	10	34	52	100	(29)
Infrequent	17	8	33	42	100	(12)
Very Infrequent	8	0	46	46	100	(13)
$x^2 = 8.48$ C = .34						

TABLE 15.10   Foreign Conflict and Governmental Stability (figures in percent)

Degree of Stability	Extent of Foreign Conflict				Total	(N)
	Significant	Moderate	Limited	Negligible		
Very High	10	10	30	50	100	(20)
High	15	10	30	45	100	(20)
Moderate	0	10	50	40	100	(10)
Unstable	16	16	37	32	101	(19)
$x^2 = 3.46$ C = .22						

TABLE 15.11   Foreign Conflict and System Stability (figures in percent)

System Stability	Extent of Foreign Conflict				Total	(N)
	Significant	Moderate	Limited	Negligible		
High	10	5	45	40	100	(20)
Low	19	11	38	32	100	(37)
$x^2 = 1.42$ C = .15						

with violence directed at persons; indeed, political assassinations may represent the category of "assault" more than that of "social conflict," since the assassin's motives may at least in part be nonpolitical. If so, the stronger relation between anomic as opposed to the other two forms of conflict would vanish if the assaultive factor were partialled out.

One method of checking this suggestion is to use a second indicator of assault, namely, deaths due to homicides per 100,000 persons resident in a country. The "cultural pressure" dimension of Cattell's study, which has a high loading for foreign conflict, has only a + .01 score for homicide rates, while in the Haas study mean homicide rates correlate negatively with war participation (Table 15.12). This may not seem surprising when one considers that higher homicide rates characterize rural countries, which tend to have fewer dealings in international relations. Assault is not related to war propensity, contrary to the Marxist view that capitalists' dehumanization of man has made war a more congenial form of state behavior (Engels 1959:376). Moreover, rates of homicide are highest where capitalism is developed less fully.

Escapism

In an urban environment, the system of reciprocal expectations is structured so highly that behavior directed violently at occupants of certain roles is obviously maladaptive as a response to strain. Another person can always be found to assume the same role, observing the same rules of behavior, and the underlying conditions of strain will remain. Urban strain more commonly leads to passive deviance. If the regulations and rules are seen as the source of an individual's frustrations, and he realizes that he cannot change them, he may seek some form of escape from social reality. Indeed, *rapid* economic development appears to go hand in hand with an increasing death rate due to alcoholism, while in mature economies alcoholism death rates are on the decline (Haas 1965).

Given the findings concerning the importance of urban factors as antecedents of international military behavior, one would anticipate a positive correlation between war frequencies and alcoholism death rates. In Cattell's study alcoholism death rate has a + .10 loading on the "cultural pressure" dimension, and the Spearman correlation between the two factors is also positive in the Haas study (Table 15.12). In a separate computation, alcoholism death rates were divided by homicide rates within each country, and the resulting ratio was correlated with war frequency (Table 15.13). The correlation is positive again, so one can infer that as alcoholism replaces homicide as a major form of deviance, war becomes more probable, which is consistent with previous findings about the urbanization process.

TABLE 15.12   War as a Function of Deaths due to Deviant Behavior.

Type of Deviance	Spearman Correlation
Homicide	−.11
Alcoholism	.14
Suicide	.02

TABLE 15.13   War as a Function of Comparative Rates of Deviant Behavior

Deviance Ratio	Spearman Correlation
Alcoholism/Homicide	.14
Suicide/Alcoholism and Homicide	.29

Self-destructiveness

Passive deviance directed at oneself occurs when rules of behavior are so internalized that strain can only be conceived as resulting from personal inadequacy. In Cattell's "cultural pressure" factor there is a + .30 loading for suicide, and a positive but very low correlation with war participation is reported in the Haas study (Table 15.12). Suicide is prevalent in cultures which are predominately rural, as well as in urban cultures, so it would seem useful to distinguish between countries which have few suicides in relation to homicides and alcoholism deaths (rural) and, on the other hand, countries having few violent deviant alternatives to suicide (urban). The resulting correlation (Table 15.13) shows that as suicide becomes almost the exclusive violent form of deviance within a culture its propensity for war rises.

To conclude this section on strain as a precondition to international aggression, we have found that passive deviance is related more closely to war than active deviance. It is insufficient to know that strain is present in a society if one wishes to predict its chances of entering war: one should know the types of nonconformist reactions being selected and even the geographic location of the strains. A similar conclusion is reported in a study of mass society by William Kornhauser (1959). According to Kornhauser's calculations, voting for extremist parties, a form of social conflict in a legitimate channel (elections), correlates inversely with deaths due to suicides, alcoholism, and homicides. A resort to social conflict is possible for an individual who is integrated enough into the polity to try to use or to replace existing government institutions; assault, escapism, and self-destruction characterize persons who lack even family ties as a cushion for strain, Kornhauser speculates. In short, if social change is too fast, resulting in the breakdown of family life, institutional arenas for coping with new conditions may never implement reforms that would bring a solution to pressing social problems because no articulate spokesmen are able to plead for such reforms. Only maladaptive anomic outbursts or passive nonconformity will remain to satisfy short-term psychological needs. And if these anomic actions continue to increase, it appears that war becomes more and more probable.

Summary and Conclusion

Some of the pre-Marxist theory about war has been sustained in this codification of research: of the political systems, democracies are more peaceful than nondemocracies; but poorer countries are less prone to international conflict than are rich countries.

Stress is related to the genesis of international aggression, especially urban stress, but it can lead in several directions. In rural countries stress is associated with assaultive deviance, which is correlated negatively with war. If stress has an impact upon sections of a population that are politically mobilized, social conflict will follow, the incidence of which is almost independent of foreign conflict rates. If stress affects individuals by isolating them from social ties, withdrawal reactions develop, and war is more probable.

Because societal factors do exhibit a patterned relationship with war, it may be useful to suggest how the findings reported herein are relevant to the other two levels of analysis in the study of war — the psychological and the systemic.

In the study of the individual as a factor in international aggression, the current emphasis on irrationality could be broadened. Rather than paying exclusive attention to perceptions and calculations during international crises, one would want to know what conditioning factors explain how often crises themselves develop. A thorough study of decisionmakers would include their demographic background, the strata in the population to which they are responsive, and the social problems to which the regime adapts or fails to adapt. Indeed, the societal factors represent forces which an ordinary politician or foreign-policy maker must take into account if he wishes to remain in power. If stress has an impact within normal institutional channels, leaders can adjust directly to articulated demands, and war is unlikely to be one of those demands. But if stress is so severe that incoherent rumblings from the population must be decoded by policymakers, war appears to be an eventual response.[7] If a high degree of passive nonconformity is a necessary condition for war, however, it is not a sufficient condition. Knowing a country's suicide rate, one may be able only to predict its chance of engaging in war over the long run; changes in daily psychological states of decisionmakers appear to be more fruitful for short-term predictions of the day, or even the hour, in which a decision to go to war may be made. Some time will always elapse until societal conditions will have an impact on decisionmakers.

To integrate the societal with the systemic approach, several propositions seem plausible. An international system composed only of democratic countries would be more peaceful than one of autocracies, as would one of isolationist, poor states with little internal consensus. Urbanizing states are troublesome, particularly if their growth is so rapid that anomic, escapist, or self-destructive reactions rise in frequency. In other words, the systemic level of analysis may have to take into account the internal properties of international units and their collective homogeneity, whether the power distribution as a whole is unipolar, bipolar, or multipolar.

It would seem as well that more of the psychological and systemic factors should be plugged into the correlational and factor analytic studies. None of the correlations reported from these studies has approached a very high level, and this is perhaps more than the normal amount of attenuation in results when data are unreliable due to underreporting. Other factors are associated with the outbreak of international aggression than the ones discussed in the codification above. A future task is to employ multivariate regression analysis to ascertain what combination of factors will come closest to accounting for all of the variance in the "foreign conflict" variable. Due to the paucity of case studies, only bivariate analysis has been employed above. As further research in this field proceeds it will be possible to utilize more sophisticated regression techniques.

Notes

The author is grateful to a grant from the Office of Research Administration, University of Hawaii, for support in the preparation of the manuscript.

1. "Social" conditions are to be distinguished from "societal" ones: the former consist of characteristics of interpersonal, interactional systems; the latter is an aggregate feature of a large system composed of many social groups within a fixed territorial boundary (English and English 1958:506-507, 510).

2. At this point the reader may easily slip into the habit of regarding the relationships betwen variables discussed in the chapter as causal in nature. The cause-effect image is based on an old-fashioned mechanistic view of reality, and it is one which the author rejects as inapplicable to social phenomena. My interest is rather with the time phasing of statistically as well as logically related variables; though some of the descriptive language in the chapter may conjure a picture of "causes," the words are chosen merely for the sake of literary variety.

3. The exact weighting of diplomatic as opposed to military conflict behavior is not specified by Banks and associates, but it is derived evidently from the data of Rummel (1963) and Tanter (1964). The survey also fails to provide a precise guide to cutting points within some of the variables.

4. It should be pointed out that Richardson (1960:206-209) finds that an eco-

nomic rationale for international aggression shows up in but 29 percent of the wars between 1820 and 1949, and many of these situations involve clashes between imperial and colonial forces. Boundary issues and territorial designs, he asserts, are more frequent pretexts for the use of violent means in settling interstate disputes.

5. The highest correlation in the Rummel and Tanter studies is .20; one of Cattell's variables, "riots," exceeds that magnitude, having a + .48 correlation. Because many of the variables suffer somewhat from underreporting, it is no surprise that the results may be attenuated.

6. The "diplomatic" dimension includes expulsions or recalls of diplomats, protests, accusations; "war" includes military action, mobilizations, troop movements, and number killed in foreign violence; the variables on the "belligerency" dimension are antiforeign demonstrations, negative sanctions, and severance of diplomatic relations.

7. It may perhaps be no accident that dictatorships have more homicides, while democracies have more internally directed causes of death, such as suicides. Where informal social controls do hold back external misbehavior, restrictive governmental systems are unnecessary.

References

Aron, Raymond. *The Century of Total War.* Garden City: Doubleday, 1954.

Banks, Arthur S., and Textor, Robert B. *The Cross-Polity Survey.* Cambridge: M.I.T. Press, 1963.

Bell, Daniel. *The End of Ideology.* New York: Collier Books, 1962.

Bernhardi, Friedrich von. *Germany and the Next War.* Translated by Allen H. Powles. London: Arnold, 1914.

Bozeman, Abba B. *Politics and Culture in International History.* Princeton: Princeton University Press, 1960.

Cattell, Raymond B. "The Dimensions of Culture Patterns by Factorization of National Characters," *Journal of Abnormal and Social Psychology,* 44 (1949), pp. 443-69.

Coser, Lewis A. *The Functions of Social Conflict.* Glencoe: The Free Press, 1956.

Engels, Friedrich. *Anti-Dühring.* Moscow: Foreign Languages Publishing House, 1959.

English, Horace B., and English, Ava C. *A Comprehensive Dictionary of Psychological and Psychoanalytic Terms.* New York: Longmans, Green, 1958.

Gregg, Phillip M., and Banks, Arthur S. "Dimensions of Political Systems: Factor Analysis of *A Cross-Polity Survey.*" Paper presented to the Carnegie-IDRC Joint Study Group on Measurement Problems, Indiana University, March 1965.

Haas, Michael. "Social Change and International Aggression: A Correlational Study." Paper presented to the Conference on Mathematical Applications in Political Science, Dallas, July 1965.

Hoselitz, Bert F., and Weiner, Myron. "Economic Development and Political Stability in India," *Dissent,* 8 (1961), pp. 172-79.

Khrushchev, Nikita S. *The Worker* (New York), July 28, 1963.

Kornhauser, William. *The Politics of Mass Society*. Glencoe: The Free Press, 1959.

Lee, J. S. "The Periodic Recurrence of Internecine Wars in China." *China Journal of Science and Arts,* 14 (1931), pp. 111-15.

Lenin, V. I. *Imperialism*. New York: International Publishers, 1939.

_____. "The War and Russian Social-Democracy." *Selected Works,* V, pp. 123-30. Edited by J. Fineberg. New York: International Publishers, 1935.

Marx, Karl, and Engels, Friedrich. "Manifesto of the Communist Party," *Basic Writings on Politics and Philosophy*. Edited by Lewis S. Feuer. Garden City: Doubleday, 1959.

Maurice, J. F. *Hostilities Without Declaration of War*. London: Her Majesty's Stationery Office, 1883.

Murphy, Robert F. "Intergroup Hostility and Social Cohesion," *American Anthropologist,* 59 (1957), pp. 1018-35.

Parsons, Talcott. *The Social System*. Glencoe: The Free Press, 1951.

Plato. *The Republic*. Translated by Benjamin Jowett. New York: Random House, n.d.

Richardson, Lewis F. *Statistics of Deadly Quarrels*. Chicago: Quadrangle Books, 1960.

Rummel, Rudolph J. "Dimensions of Conflict Behavior Within and Between Nations." *General Systems,* 8 (1963), pp. 1-50.

_____. "Some Dimensions of International Relations in the Mid-1950's." Mimeographed, Dimensionality of Nations Project, Yale University, August 1964.

Russett, Bruce M., et al., *World Handbook of Political and Social Indicators*. New Haven: Yale University Press, 1964.

Silberner, Edmund. *The Problem of War in Nineteenth Century Economic Thought*. Translated by Alexander H. Krappe. Princeton: Princeton University Press, 1946.

Simmel, Georg. *Conflict*. Translated by Kurt Wolff. Glencoe: The Free Press, 1955.

Sorokin, Pitirim A. *Fluctuations of Social Relationships, War, and Revolution*. New York: American Book Co., 1937.

Tanter, Raymond. "Dimensions of Conflict Within and Between Nations, 1958-60." Unpublished Ph.D. dissertation, Indiana University, 1964.

Waltz, Kenneth N. *Man, the State, and War*. New York: Columbia University Press, 1959.

Watkins, James T. "Democracy and International Organization: The Experience of the League of Nations." *American Political Science Review,* 36 (1942), pp. 1136-41.

Wright, Quincy. *A Study of War*. 2 vols. Chicago: University of Chicago Press, 1942.

Zinnes, Dina A.; North, Robert C.; and Koch, Howard E., Jr. "Capability, Threat, and the Outbreak of War," in James N. Rosenau, *International Politics and Foreign Policy*. New York: The Free Press of Glencoe, Inc., 1961.

Part 6
Socioeconomic Inquiries

Introduction

The relationship between a state's internal socioeconomic structure and its external conflict behavior has been the main focus of socioeconomic inquiries into the causes of war. With the globalization of interstate conflict brought about in a large measure by the rise and spread of capitalism and anticapitalism on a worldwide scale, imperialism has come to play the dual role of being at once a general theory of international relations and a systemic manifestation of external conflict behavior of certain states. We shall focus in this part of the book on the former role of imperialism, especially on the economic theories of imperialism and on how these theories or schools of thought have explained the working of the war system.

Although many protagonists of varying ideological and academic persuasions have used the word "imperialism" in many different ways and for many different reasons, it has survived long enough in international relations research to prove its heuristic utility. Such durability, in spite of its odyssey through so many battles, is related to its usefulness in describing and explaining the recurring phenomena of social conflict behavior at different levels of human society. In addition to serving as a general theory of international relations, for example, the idea of imperialism has also been at the center of Marxist and neo-Marxist writings concerned with the historical development of social and political conditions within capitalist societies.

For our discussion we may accept imperialism in a broader sense as a general theory of relations between or among social groups, in particular nation-states and classes, in some hierarchical structure. Specifically, intellectual discourse on imperialism and war needs to say something about the following issues: (1) linkage between domestic and foreign policy of the nation-state; (2) reciprocal influence between politics and economics; (3) compatibility between imperialism and militarism; (4) specific forms of warlike behavior as functions of one socioeconomic system against another; (5) use of violence in both its behavioral and structural roles of penetrating, establishing, and maintaining "threat-submission" systems of interaction; (6) dependent or exploitative forms of interaction through exchange of unequal values; (7) legitimizing attempts on the part of dominant societal groups to minimize the costs of imperialism; and (8) delegitimizing attempts on the part of the victims of dominance to be free and independent.

In order to place the three selections in this part within a broader historical perspective, the theories of imperialism may be divided into five contending schools of thought. *The conservative school*—whose early proponents included Jules Ferry in France, Sir Charles Dike, Sir John Robert Seeley, Benjamin Disraeli, Lord Curzon, Cecil Rhodes, and Rudyard Kipling in England, Alfred Thayer Mahan, William McKinley, Albert Beveridge, Theodore Roosevelt, and other advocates of the Manifest Destiny in the United States—rationalized overseas empire building as being indispensable to preserving the social order at home, to securing and expanding overseas markets, and to civilizing and Christianizing "lesser breeds" of people beyond the pale of Western civilization.

The view of *the liberal school,* whose intellectual genealogy may be traced back to the old underconsumptionist school in economics represented by Malthus, Rodbertus, and Sismondi, was most eloquently expounded by the British economist John A. Hobson in his *Imperialism* ([1902] 1948). Hobson diagnosed imperialism in terms of surplus goods and capital seeking outlets in overseas markets. Imperialism is therefore a function of certain maladjustments—that is, underconsumption resulting from the maldistribution of consuming power—within the capitalist system, not the inevitable nor the rational means of disposing surplus revenues. For Hobson and his liberal followers, imperialism does not pay. What is called for is a more equitable distribution of income through social reform so as to obviate the necessity of opening up foreign markets. Hobson believed that trade unionism and socialism would serve as the natural antidotes to imperialism since they take away from the imperialist classes the surplus incomes which seek overseas outlets. In short, the liberal school believes that the link between capitalism and imperialism can be—and should be—cut through social reform.

Although *the Marxist school* presented the most influential causal analysis linking capitalism with imperialism and imperialism with war, it is indeed curious that Marx himself made little contribution to this development. It took the followers of Marx in the early twentieth century—Otto Bauer, Rudolph Hilferding, Rosa Luxemburg, and, of course, Lenin—to construct what came to be known as the Marxist theory of imperialism and war. The view of the classical Marxist school was most cogently stated by Lenin in his *Imperialism: The Highest Stage of Capitalism* ([1917] 1947). The Marxist school rests on a belief in economic determinism. The politics of imperialism is the natural expression of contradictions in the capitalist economic system. Lenin closely followed Hobson's diagnosis of imperialism but departed from the liberal school in stating that imperialist wars are absolutely inevitable as long as capitalism exists. Hence, Lenin's prescription is revolution, not reform.

However, Lenin's thesis of the inevitability of war generated considerable dispute among Soviet, Chinese, and Western Marxists in the wake of such new developments as the rise of nuclear weapons, the increasing military might of the Soviet Union, and the new imperative for peaceful coexistence in the post-Stalin foreign policy. Against this backdrop, the Twentieth Congress of the Communist Party of the Soviet Union (CPSU) virtually rejected the doctrine of the inevitability of war (Burin 1963). In his report to the Congress, Khrushchev made several important doctrinal points: (1) that Lenin's theory was evolved at a time when imperialism was an all-embracing world system and that antiimperialist forces were weak and disorganized; (2) that war is not only an economic phenomenon but also a product of political forces; and (3) that there are today mighty social and political forces (the socialist camp headed by the Soviet Union) to prevent the imperialists from unleashing war. In short, the Khrushchev doctrine amounts to a form of deterrence theory; that is, the existence of capitalism makes imperialist war a possibility, to be sure, but, thanks to the military might of the Soviet Union, not a probability and certainly not an inevitability. We need not dwell here on Sino-Soviet ideological polemics on this issue. Suffice it to say that there are now several contending schools of thought on the theory of imperialism and war even among the Marxists!

The military-industrial complex school may be regarded as a modern offshoot of the liberal school since its central thesis rests on the proposition that a powerful octopuslike coalition of domestic groups with vested interests in military spending and international conflict — professional soldiers, military industrialists, militarized civilian bureaucrats, and promilitary legislators — have rapidly risen to the position of dominance in the decision-making process, promoting antagonistic relations between nations in a self-serving and war-promoting manner. As early as 1919, the economist Joseph Schumpeter advanced a similar argument in his *Imperialism and Social Classes*, conceptualizing imperialism more in sociopsychological than in economic terms. For Schumpeter imperialism was basically the result of atavistic autistic behavior on the part of warrior classes in aristocratic feudal societies. Such autistic war-prone behavior, Schumpeter concluded following such nineteenth-century thinkers as Auguste Comte and Herbert Spencer, was bound to disappear with the growth of industrial capitalist economies, which were assumed to be more rational and peace loving. While Schumpeter's optimistic prognostication about the demise of military establishments under capitalism proved to be wrong, his sociopsychological theory of imperialism connects itself well with the military-industrial complex theory.

A more recent antecedent of the military-industrial complex school is found in what is pejoratively characterized by its critics as the "devil" theory of imperialism, an argument which received considerable vogue in the isolationist America of the 1930s, particularly in the Nye Committee of the U.S. Senate. In 1956 C. Wright Mills in his classic, *The Power Elite,* provided the conceptual base to link the military-industrial complex with an elite collusion theory. However, the term did not gain popular currency until 1961, when it was used in President Eisenhower's Farewell Address. Although this theory has posed a number of fundamental issues relating to social injustice and inequality as expressed by the social costs, economic costs, political-institutional costs, normative costs, and opportunity costs that the American military-industrial complex incurs, scholarly assessments of the theory were not available until the 1970s (Russett 1970; Sarkesian 1972; Rosen 1973). Assessments of similar phenomena in other states including the Soviet Union are not yet available, although some serious work is under way.

Finally, *the dependencia school* may be viewed as an adaptation and reformulation of Marxist thinking to explain the seemingly paradoxical development of *political independence* and *economic dependence* of Third World nations in the contemporary international system, with special reference to the Latin American situation. Developed by the writings of such socioeconomic theorists as Fernando Henrique Cardoso (1973), Samir Amin (1973, 1976, 1977), Andre Gunder Frank (1967, 1975), Harry Magdoff (1969), and Johan Galtung (1978), this major series of influential writings presents a sophisticated dialectical-structural analysis of linkages between imperialism and underdevelopment. Modern imperialism (or neoimperialism, although this term is generally avoided) is conceptualized as a new and more effective form of exploitation than old ones relying upon inefficient colonial rule; it is seen as a modern way of penetrating, linking, and perpetuating the exploitative center-periphery feudal structures both within and between nation-states.

Unlike old Marxists who viewed imperialism as a transient phenomenon in the progressive march of history toward communism, however, *dependencia* theorists see imperialist structures to be self-sustaining and self-perpetuating because of the development of harmony of interests between the centers (metropolitan elites and local elites) and of disharmony of interests between the peripheries (proletariats of centers and peripheries). Modern imperialists are too sophisticated to resort to the old inefficient means of gunboat diplomacy or war; they use structural penetration and linkage control to achieve imperial objectives more quietly and efficiently. Hence the main focus of the *dependencia* school is not so much on war in its narrow sense as on structural violence embedded in the modern imperialist system.

The first chapter in Part 6 can be accepted as an official view of the Soviet Union today on imperialism. It is excerpted from the book, *Marxism-Leninism on War and Army,* published in five Russian-language editions between 1957 and 1968 and translated into English in 1972 by Progress Publishers in Moscow. The book, written collectively by fourteen authors at Soviet military educational establishments, is addressed to "Soviet officers, generals, and admirals studying Marxist-Leninist teachings on war and the armed forces in general." As such, it does belong to the Marxist school — or the contemporary Soviet version of the Marxist school — already reviewed in this synoptic essay.

The chapter by the economic historian David Landes belongs to the liberal school. Landes rebuts the Marxist theory of imperialism by restating some old and familiar liberal arguments: (1) that imperialism does not pay for the capitalist system as a whole; (2) that the economic interpretation explains only part but not the whole of imperialism as claimed by many; and (3) that imperialism was necessary and profitable only for those groups of people who have managed to gain access to and influence the decision-makers of the nation-state. Landes explains away imperialism as "a multifarious response to a common opportunity that consists simply in disparity of power." "And power," he concludes, "like nature, abhors a vacuum."

The chapter by Johan Galtung, the dominant figure in contemporary transnational peace research, has proved to be at once influential and controversial. Note that Galtung's principal concern (value premise) in this chapter is not to deal with the causes of war as such but to conceptualize, explain, and counteract inequality as one of the major forms of structural violence embedded in contemporary imperialism. Clearly, this piece represents one of the most ambitious attempts to construct a morphology of international society by establishing functional-structural linkages between imperialism and underdevelopment. As such, it is an analysis that belongs within the *dependencia* school.

According to Galtung, contemporary imperialism in its neocolonialist manifestation sustains itself in feudal-vertical structures of interactions between and among four classes: the center in the Center; the periphery in the Center; the center in the Periphery; and the periphery in the Periphery. The problem of development/underdevelopment and dominance/dependence is thus structurally analyzed as a four-class relationship, as graphically shown in Figure 18.1. The chapter then elaborates two mechanisms (vertical and feudal), five types (economic, political, military, communication, and cultural), and three phases (colonialist, neocolonialist, and neo-neocolonialist) of imperialism.

for themselves how cogently each selection has clarified the eight issues set forth in the beginning of this essay. In evaluating the relevance of the imperialist literature several issues stand out. First, does economic determinism offer a better approach to the etiology of war because it avoids the hazards of such monocausal models as the instinctive theory of aggression and war? While economic causes have been an important factor in the past wars, there is no firm empirical evidence that they have been most prominent or decisive. Economic causes have figured directly in less than 29 percent of the wars from 1820 to 1929, according to Lewis Richardson's (1960b:210) statistical study of war.

Second, the linkage between imperialism and nationalism (or imperialism as an extension of modern nationalism) merits closer analysis than it has received in socioeconomic inquiries. The Chinese expansion of imperialism into another category—social imperialism—and recent intercommunist wars (the Sino-Soviet Border War of 1969, the Vietnamese-Cambodian War of 1978, and the Sino-Vietnamese War of 1979) all challenge the Marxist notion that war or imperialism is an exclusive monopoly of capitalist states. In a 1969 survey of world conflicts, for example, an empirical link between nationalism and war was shown: nationalist and ethnic conflicts accounted for about 70 percent of the cases, while other types of conflicts made up the balance (Rosen 1969). Finally, imperialism, if it is to retain its conceptual and normative value in peace research, needs periodic reformulation to keep abreast of behavioral and structural changes in the international system.

16

The Economic Foundations of Wars:
A Soviet View

Marxism-Leninism on War and Army

While engendering wars and determining their aims, politics is neither primary nor self-contained. It is determined by the vital interests of different classes evolved by the socioeconomic system of the exploiter state. This system, which has given rise to wars, is characterised by the domination of private ownership, the concentration of the bulk of the means of production in the hands of the exploiter classes, who exist by appropriating the surplus product created by the working people. This is what all class antagonistic formations have in common, what forms the common source of wars of the most varied type.

All wars in the past and present, those between exploiter states in pursuit of the selfish interests of slave owners, feudal lords, and the bourgeoisie, as also the uprisings and wars of the working people against whom they rose when their position had become unbearable and their patience had worn out, all these wars were caused by private ownership relations and the resultant social and class antagonisms in exploiter formations. However, this does not mean that the specific differences in the causes of wars have been abolished. Wars in each of the above formations and in definite historical epochs had their own, specific causes. Capitalism ushered in a new epoch in the history of wars. The basic law of capitalism is the production of surplus value. The aim of capitalist production is the constant, unlimited accumulation of profit. Capitalists cannot rest content with the mass of the surplus value being created by the proletariat of their own country. Their appetites are insatiable. They scour the world in search of high profits. Wars are a means of rapid enrichment for the capitalists and, hence, a constant travelling companion of capitalism. The system of the ex-

Reprinted from *Marxism-Leninism on War and Army (A Soviet View)* (Moscow: Progress Publishers, 1972), under the auspices of the United States Air Force (Washington, D.C.: Government Printing Office, 1974), pp. 31-39.

ploitation of man by man and the system of the destruction of man by man are two sides of the capitalist order. War is a means by which the bourgeoisie obtains new raw material sources and markets, robs foreign countries, and makes easy profits.

Capitalism created a world market for the first time in history and enlarged the number of objects over which wars were waged. Chief among them were colonies — sources of cheap raw materials and labour power, spheres for the export of goods and capital, and strongholds on international trade routes. For several centuries bourgeois Holland, Britain, France, Portugal, and other European states waged wars of conquest against weakly developed countries in order to make colonies of them. There were also wars between the capitalist countries themselves for a division of the world.

Naturally, some wars under capitalism were due also to other causes. The development of the productive forces of capitalism was obstructed in many countries by national oppression and political decentralisation. The epoch from the French bourgeois revolution of 1789-1794 to the Paris Commune of 1871 saw bourgeoisie-progressive, national liberation wars among other types of war. The main content and historical purpose of these wars were to overthrow absolutism and to destroy foreign oppression.

With the transition of capitalism to the imperialist stage, the bourgeois states became much more aggressive. This is explained by the economic features of imperialism, which is a decaying and moribund capitalism. At the turn of the century, leap-like development replaced the more or less regular spread of capitalism over the globe. This led to an unprecedented growth and intensification of all the contradictions of that system — economic, political, class, and national. The struggle of the imperialist powers for markets and spheres of capital investment, for raw materials and labour power, and for world domination took on extremely sharp forms. While imperialism ruled undividedly this struggle inevitably led to destructive wars. *The basic economic sources of these wars were rooted in the deepening conflict between the modern productive forces and the economic, and also political, system of imperialism.* This was the main cause of the armed clashes between imperialist powers.

The confines of old national states, without the formation of which capitalism could not have overthrown feudalism, became too narrow for it. The productive forces of world capitalism outgrew the limited framework of bourgeois states. The whole world merged into a single economic organism and was at the same time divided up among a handful of big imperialist powers. This contradiction found expression in the striving of the bourgeoisie to export capital and to win markets for commodities they cannot sell at home, to seize raw material sources and new colonies, to destroy competitors on world markets, and to conquer world domination and, hence, to unleash wars.

The conflict between the productive forces (with the national-imperialist limits imposed on their development) and the capitalist relations of production is strikingly expressed in the uneven, leap-like economic and political development of capitalist countries under imperialism. Thus, at the beginning of the century bourgeois countries which had launched out on industrial development only recently found themselves in a favourable situation and succeeded, by a sudden forward dash, to outstrip the old industrial capitalist states in a comparatively short time. After the Second World War the share and role of the individual capitalist states changed again and the unevenness of their economic development intensified.

Uneven development inevitably leads to abrupt changes in the alignment of forces in the world capitalist system. From time to time a sharp disturbance of the equilibrium occurs within that system. The old distribution of spheres of influence among the monopolies clashes with the new alignment of forces in the world. To bring the distribution of colonies in accord with the new balance of forces, there inevitably have to be periodical redivisions of the already divided world. Under capitalism armed violence is the only way of dividing up colonies and spheres of influence.

"Capitalism," Lenin said, "has concentrated the earth's wealth in the hands of a few states and divided the world up to the last bit. . . . Any further enrichment could take place only at the expense of others, as the enrichment of one state at the expense of another. The issue could only be settled by force — and, accordingly, war between the world marauders became inevitable."[1] *As a result of the social antagonisms inherent in capitalism and the operation of the law of the uneven, leap-like economic and political development of the capitalist countries under imperialism, the contradictions between the bourgeois states aggravate to the utmost, and this leads to a division of the capitalist world into hostile coalitions, and to wars between them.*

The First and the Second World Wars burst forth on this economic basis. The imperialists of all countries, the entire world system of capitalism were guilty of them. These wars had catastrophical results for the international bourgeoisie, promoted the formation of the world socialist community and the collapse of the colonial system of imperialism. However, the ruling circles of the imperialist states did not draw the necessary conclusions from them.

Reasons for the Greater Aggressiveness of the Imperialist States Today

Formerly the aggravation of the contradictions between these states or their coalitions was the main reason responsible for the striving of imperialist states to unleash wars. These contradictions continue to aggravate. However, the main contradiction now is that between the two opposing social systems — capitalism and socialism.

The contradictions between the two world systems are class contradictions. The socialist system greatly diminishes the sphere of imperialist exploitation and domination, creating conditions in which capitalism will lose the privileges it still enjoys. Socialism has a revolutionising influence on the working people in the capitalist countries, the colonies, and dependent countries.

Another reason for the growing aggressiveness of modern imperialism is that the contradictions between the imperialist states, on the one hand, and the colonies and recent colonies, on the other, have greatly aggravated. Under the influence of the example set by the Soviet Union — once a backward agrarian country and now a mighty industrial power — and that of the successes achieved by other socialist countries, the popular masses in Asia, Africa, and Latin America have launched a national liberation revolution. Deep antagonisms divide the imperialist states and the countries that have won national independence or are still fighting for liberation.

The imperialist predators are willing to resort to any means, fair or foul, to preserve and strengthen their colonial possessions. They attempt to suppress the national liberation struggle of the African peoples by force of arms, they unleash wars in the Southeast Asian countries, and organise reactionary coups in the Latin American states. Colonialism and neocolonialism are the direct and indirect cause of many conflicts threatening to plunge mankind into a new war.

The third cause is the exacerbation of the internal contradictions of capitalism after the Second World War. This is linked, first and foremost, with the continuing aggravation and deepening of the general crisis of capitalism, with the fact that the main contradiction of capitalist society, that between labour and capital, continues to grow. The transition from monopoly capitalism to state-monopoly capitalism, under which the monopolies merge with the state, intensifies the exploitation of the working people, makes science and technology and the growing productive forces serve the aim of enriching a handful of monopolists. Exploitation has never been as hideous as it is today. Even when business conditions are favourable, millions of people, workers, and intellectuals are unemployed, and peasants are ruined and evicted from their land. At the same time a small number of powerful monopolies are profiting from the exploitation of the working people, from the arms race and aggressive wars.

State monopoly capitalism is responsible for the unprecedented intensification of militarism, including the economic and ideological fields. Militarisation permeates the entire life of bourgeois society. The production of mass-destruction weapons eats up an enormous part of the national income of the bourgeois states. During the past twenty years U.S. military spending has increased more than forty-eight-fold over that in the two prewar decades. More than 75 percent of the total expenditure in the U.S. federal budget is directly or indirectly channeled to military needs. The growth in weapons production in the main imperialist states makes other countries spend large funds on strengthening their defence too.

The imperialist state is becoming a militaristic police state. The economic superstructure rising on the basis of finance capital and the politics and ideology of the finance oligarchy strengthen the state's aggressiveness. Under state-monopoly capitalism "big business," the political leaders and the top brass controlling the state, make it pursue a policy aimed at preparing a war against the Soviet Union and other socialist states.

The sharp diminution of the sphere of action of the imperialist forces and the extreme aggravation of the contradictions under state-monopoly capitalism make the economic and political development of the bourgeois countries ever more uneven. This is the fourth reason responsible for the greater aggressiveness of the imperialist states.

In recent years serious changes have taken place in the relation of forces within the capitalist world. This process is continuing. Intense exploitation of the working people through the system of state-monopoly capitalism, relatively small military spending over a long period of time, the high level of capital investments, and the comparatively rapid growth of labour productivity, the application of the fruits of scientific and technological progress, and the considerable material assistance given to them by the United States and some other countries have led to rapid economic advance in West Germany and Japan. For several years the West European countries and Japan outstripped the United States in economic growth rates. Lately, however, their roles have changed again.

This deepened the contradictions between the United States and the European capitalist countries and Japan. The competitive struggle in Western Europe has also taken on sharper forms, including the Common Market and other state-monopoly associations. New forms of international economic associations and new ways of dividing markets have emerged, as have also new centres of attraction and new hotbeds of contradictions. All this must be taken into account when the economic reasons for military clashes are investigated.

The triumph of socialist revolutions and the transition of a growing number of countries to the socialist road have greatly weakened imperialism. But, imperialism does not want to give up its positions without struggle. The class-social antagonisms between the two social systems are growing ever more distinct and at times assume very sharp forms.

The contradiction between capitalism and socialism is stronger than the interimperialist contradictions. It reflects all the contradictions of the epoch and leaves a deep mark on all major international events. It should be remembered that the growth of the forces of socialism and the upsurge of the class and national liberation struggle are attended by the growing aggressiveness of the monopoly bourgeoisie, which fights social progress by all and every means and attempts to preserve its class privileges and riches at all costs.

The advance of the world socialist system and other factors do much to exacerbate interimperialist contradictions. They exert a dual influence. On the one hand, they strengthen the will of the imperialist powers to unite, to create military, political, and other alliances on the other, they deepen the contradictions between them. This corroborates Lenin's statement that "two trends exist; one, which makes the alliance of all the imperialists inevitable; the other, which places the imperialists in opposition to each other — two trends, neither of which has any firm foundation."[2]

After the Second World War the first tendency naturally grew stronger in the course of the struggle waged by the imperialist powers against the socialist system. Imperialist states energetically strengthened their aggressive military blocs, signed bilateral pacts, etc. For the first time in history the main imperialist powers, the United States, Britain, West Germany, and others joined a single military alliance directed against the socialist system.

Naturally, the fact that there are two opposite tendencies in the development of the imperialist system makes every alliance of the capitalist countries contradictory and unstable. Such alliances (organisations) directed against the socialist countries and the national liberation movement do not resolve the economic and political contradictions between the individual capitalist countries in those alliances and within every one of them but, on the contrary, further deepen and aggravate them. Besides, the setting up of organisations involving a number of capitalist countries inevitably leads to a growth of the contradictions within these organisations and struggle against outsiders. At present, however, these interimperialist contradictions are dampened by the even sharper class antagonisms. That is why a war between the big imperialist states, though still possible, is far less likely now than it was before.

Thus, the world imperialist system is torn by deep and sharp antagonisms. These are contradictions between labour and capital and between the people and the monopolies, growing militarisation, the disintegration of the colonial system, the antagonisms between the young national states and the old colonial powers, and, most important, the rapid growth of world socialism that undermines and erodes imperialism, weakens it, and spells its doom.

In view of the above the imperialists intend to save capitalism through war, the danger of which is great at present and is threatening all the peoples of our planet. *It is precisely because capitalism at its highest stage has entered the period of its decline and ruin and is going through a new, third stage of its general crisis that its aggressive strivings are not decreasing but are incessantly growing.*

Imperialist aggression is spearheaded against the socialist community and only the strength of the countries in that community, notably that of the Soviet Union, prevents international reaction from unleashing a world military conflict. At the same time the antagonisms between the handful of highly developed imperialist powers and the young developing countries are growing sharper. The imperialists attempt with all the means at their disposal to hamper the peoples from carrying out radical changes in their social systems. With this aim in view they unleash local wars, instigate military coups, and organise plots and interventions.

Socioeconomic Conditions for the Establishment of Peace

War, as Marxism-Leninsm has shown scientifically, is not a permanent feature in history. The historical inevitability of transition of all or at least of the main countries to socialism creates the economic basis for banning wars from the life of society and for establishing eternal peace. Mankind has already attained a stage of development in which there are material prerequisites determining not only the possibility but also the objective need for the victory of the new, socialist system, under which the causes breeding wars and military conflicts will disappear. Lenin wrote: "Our aim is to achieve a socialist system of society, which, by eliminating the division of mankind into classes, by eliminating all exploitation of man by man and nation by nation, will inevitably eliminate the very possibility of war."[3]

The modern productive forces have created the material prerequisites and the objective need for the transition of mankind to socialism. Because of their high level of development and social character an extensive division of labour has been established between different countries, and close economic ties have been formed. The development of sea, land, and air transport has made it possible to cover distances between countries in no time.

Modern scientific and technological progress opens up broad prospects for the rapid development of the productive forces and for the radical improvement of the material conditions in all countries. The introduction of its enormous achievements on a mass scale, the extensive use of nuclear energy for peaceful purposes, and the comprehensive automation of production will give mankind unheard-of wealth, which we must not risk losing just to please a handful of warmongers.

However, the long-since-obsolete capitalist relations of production prevent the use of the enormous achievements made by production, science, and technology in the interests of all members of society, and also equal economic cooperation between the peoples.

Under capitalism already there is a clearly expressed tendency toward the setting up of a single world economy managed according to a common plan, a tendency that will undoubtedly develop further and will fully assert itself once socialism is established on a global scale. Socialism will remove the barriers between countries and nations imperialism has set up, and will unite mankind into a single workers' collective. The triumph of socialism in all countries will bring a social system "whose international rule will be *Peace,* because its national rules will be everywhere the same — *Labour!*"[4]

These prophetic words which were spoken by Marx as early as 1870, have been fully borne out by the peace-loving policy of the Soviet Union and other socialist countries, by the new relations between them. These are relations of fraternal cooperation and mutual assistance between countries, in which the leading role is played by the working class, and in which the working people themselves are the masters of their destiny and are building a new life without the bourgeoisie. The socialist community embodies the objective invincibility of mankind's movement toward eternal peace.

Now the world socialist system determines the main trend of human society's historical progress. The further transformation of the world socialist system into the decisive factor in mankind's social development will express not only the chief content, trend, and main distinctive features of history, but also the entire process of that development, all its paths and specific features.

But, until the economic basis of wars and their only source — imperialism — continue to exist, until imperialist policy and ideology are aimed at preparing and unleashing military conflicts, the economic and military might of the Soviet Union and the entire socialist community and the policy and ideology of the building and defence of socialism and communism will have to play an important part in preventing wars and reining in the aggressive imperialist forces.

Notes

1. V. I. Lenin, *Collected Works,* Vol. 28, p. 80.
2. V. I. Lenin, *Collected Works,* Vol. 27, p. 369.
3. V. I. Lenin, *Collected Works,* Vol. 24, pp. 398-99.
4. *The General Council of the First International, 1870-1871, Minutes* (Moscow, 1967), p. 328.

17
Some Thoughts on the Nature of Economic Imperialism

David S. Landes

One should distinguish from the start between the economic interpretation of imperialism and economic imperialism. The one is an explanation, an essentially monistic explanation, of an historical phenomenon. The latter is an aspect of the phenomenon itself: if imperialism is the dominion of one group over another, economic imperialism is the establishment or exploitation of such dominion for continuing material advantage. The definition assumes that economic imperialism is more than simple, once-for-all pillage; rather that it tries to cultivate relationships that yield a recurrent harvest of profit, as the ground its corn. Moreover, it makes no distinction between dominion established for economic motives and dominion that, for whatever reasons established, is maintained and exploited primarily for material ends. Finally, it does not confine imperialism to cases of formal rule or protectorate, but includes that "informal" dominion that is often far more effective and lucrative than direct administration.[1]

It is not easy to write about imperialism. So much has been written about it already. One would think that all this learned and not-so-learned polemic would have settled some issues; in particular, that the massive attacks by historians, sociologists, and even economists on the economic interpretation of imperialism would have long since buried it in the graveyard of historical myths. Yet cherished myths are not easily abandoned, and this one is at least as lively today as it was over a decade ago when Koebner, in a memorable article, wrote of the "international *communis opinio*" for which the economic interpretation of imperialism was an "accepted fact."[2]

Under the circumstances some will wonder why it is necessary to reexamine the question: those who are historically sophisticated are already enlightened; and those who accept the economic interpretation are imper-

David S. Landes, "Some Thoughts on the Nature of Economic Imperialism," *Journal of Economic History* 21 (1961):496-512. Reprinted by permission of the author and the publisher.

vious to reason and facts. To this I can only plead that if the target is old, the ammunition may be new; and a reconsideration may suggest a new way of looking at the entire problem.

The economic interpretation of imperialism has many faces. It goes back almost a hundred years and derives from a number of separate sources. Koebner distinguished three streams — the Marxian, Fabian, and American — and each of these is a blend of varied currents. All of them agree, however, on the essential: that the taproot of imperialism is the appetite for material gain; that this appetite grew appreciably in the nineteenth century as a result of structural changes in the industrial economies of Europe; and that modern imperialism is the work of monopoly capitalism. (There are some interesting variations at this point, some like Hobson stressing the role of high finance in promoting the drive for empire, others singling out industrial trusts and monopolies, still others equating the two.)

One should first do justice to this argument. In its intelligent versions (and it has been distorted to the point of caricature by polemicists pro and con), it does not pretend that only capitalism in its monopolistic stage produces imperialism; on the contrary, it specifically distinguishes between the "colonial policy of capitalism in its *previous* stages" and that of "finance capital." Nor does it attribute imperialist ambitions exclusively to monopoly capitalism; on the contrary, it recognizes the importance of "politico-social roots," though these in turn grow in and are nourished by economic ground.[3] Nor does it make the mistake of thinking that only imperialism consists in formal occupation of colonial territory. On the contrary, it is well aware of the existence of informal domination — too well aware, for it tends to see it almost everywhere.

If the economic interpretation of imperialism is not foolish, neither is it empty. There is no question of the great importance of material incentives to imperialism in any period, or of their special and increasing importance in the nineteenth century. We are all familiar with the stimulus given the drive for empire by the enormously increased productive capacity of a technologically transformed industrial system. From the first years of the century, the need and hence incentive to increase overseas outlets became acute for Britain: witness Popham's picaresque expedition to Buenos Aires in 1806; and Raffles' attempt to displace the Dutch in Indonesia after 1811.[4] And concomitant with this went a sharpening hunger for raw materials; it is no coincidence that even Victorian Britain abated its allegiance to free trade to protect the tin of Malaya from foreign interlopers.[5]

Clearly the economic interpretation is not a figment of doctrinaire imagination. It casts light on an important causal relationship, and the effort of certain anti-Marxists to dismiss it completely has only compelled them to erect other myths in its place. Its essential failing lies in the discrepancy between its pretensions and accomplishments. It explains part and claims to explain all — not every trifle and detail, but all that really matters. And this discrepancy, embarrassingly enough, is especially marked for the formal imperialism of the late nineteenth century. Nothing fits the economic interpretation so poorly as the partition of Africa (South Africa and the Congo excepted) — that frantic scramble of industrial, industrializing, and preindustrial European countries for some of the most unremunerative territory on the globe.

As is often the case, much of this explanatory inadequacy derives from the premises, explicit and implicit, on which the structure rests. There are at least three of these:

a. There is a cohesive business class — in Marxian terminology a bourgeoisie — conscious of a common economic interest.
b. Insofar as relations with other peoples are concerned, this economic interest lies in the furtherance of imperialism. For dominion, formal or informal, makes it possible to extract wealth from another society, either directly by expropriation on artifically favorable terms, or indirectly by exploiting the labor of the indigenous population. It is precisely in this ability to use force for gain where resides the advantage of imperialism over free contractual relations.
c. That this business class or bourgeoisie controls the state, whose officers of government are in effect its servants.

We need not tarry long on the first of these. Even the most rudimentary knowledge of European history makes clear how divided the so-called bourgeoisie was on any and every issue, economic or noneconomic. It could not agree as a class on tariff questions, the suffrage, the tax system, public works, or factory laws; why should it be expected to agree on colonial policy? In fact, as we shall see, it really did not matter whether or not the business class, or classes to be more precise, acknowledged as a group the material advantages of imperialism. The motor of imperialism lay elsewhere; and the sanction of the bourgeoisie, as well as of the rest of society, could as easily be gained on noneconomic as on economic grounds.

The second premise deserves more detailed examination, not only because it has given rise to its own myths but also because through it we may be able to arrive at a more exact understanding of the actual workings of imperialism.

To begin with, what is exploitation? Few words have been so freely bandied about; this one has come to be almost a battle cry. For most people the word simply means low wages, low in relation to profits, low in relation to wages in other places or occupations—the content is rarely precise, but the disapproval and moral stigma are inescapable.

For serious work as against polemic, this kind of imprecision simply will not do, and I would propose in its stead a definition linked to the exercise of political dominion, formal or informal: imperialist exploitation consists in the employment of labor at wages lower than would obtain in a free bargaining situation; or in the appropriation of goods at prices lower than would obtain in a free market. Imperialist exploitation, in other words, implies nonmarket constraint.[6]

So defined—and I submit that this is the only significant definition of the word—exploitation is by no means the universal concomitant of imperialism that it is frequently alleged or assumed to be. It makes no sense, for example, to talk of exploitation by oil companies in Venezuela or sugar refineries in Cuba when these not only pay a freely negotiated wage, but a wage distinctly higher than that prevailing in the sector of indigenous enterprise. (My own ironic experience has been that some of those who cry out most bitterly against exploitation are the first to complain about foreigners who spoil the market by tipping too generously or overpaying domestic servants.) Nor is it reasonable to decry as exploitation every fall in the price of coffee, cocoa, or palm oil even when due to the normal interplay of supply and demand.

Yet even in the strict sense, exploitation has been a widespread concomitant of imperialism. So far as labor is concerned, one has only to think of the discharge ticket system of Malaya, the head taxes of Africa, and such thinly disguised forms of bondage as the plantation gangs of Angola and the Congo. This recourse to constraint has been based partly on the assumption that force labor is more profitable than free—a dubious assumption, as Marx himself implied—even more, on the absolute shortage of voluntary labor. In primitive areas, especially those where nature requires little work for subsistence and where much of such work as has to be done is performed by women, it is often impossible to attract labor by means of money, at least at first; and even such labor as is recruited is relatively unresponsive to increasing reward (the supply curve bends backwards once income expectations are fulfilled).

It is similar with commodities: the most notorious example is the "Culture System" of the Dutch East Indies, under which the peasants of Java, and to a small extent Sumatra, were required to devote a part of their lands to certain cash crops and to deliver these to the government at fixed prices. Such institutional arrangements have been exceptional, however, partly because of the difficulty of compelling satisfactory performance from otherwise free native cultivators, and partly because the system is a closed preserve and does not generate wealth for the nationals of the imperialist power. Instead, the proceeds go to the occupying authorities, in lieu of tax payments, as it were, and to such enterprises as they choose to employ.[7] As a result, economic imperialism prefers direct occupation and cultivation of the soil, whether by plantation-sized estates or small homesteads; and if there is to be exploitation, it prefers exploitation of labor to forcible appropriation of commodities.

It is one thing, however, to note the existence of exploitation and its profitability, and another to argue or assume that it is always the most remunerative possible arrangement and that it constitutes therefore an implicit incentive to economic imperialism. There have been, on the contrary, numerous instances of abstention from dominion on the ground that it would not pay. The history of the British East India Company, for example, is full of this — the directors were inclined to look at territorial ambitions as a bottomless drain of men and money, to the intense frustration of some of their ambitious servants or they abstained on the ground that it was not necessary: businessmen in the field rarely lacked for native commercial cooperation, even in illicit ventures, and free bargaining generally proved more than lucrative enough.

Thus in the recruitment of labor: neither slavery nor the more subtle forms of bondage that followed it proved satisfactory for large-scale undertakings. The quality of performance was invariably low, and the quantity of labor offered was often inadequate. As a result, employers preferred when possible to find their manpower in the open market. In the Eastern hemisphere and certain parts of the Western, the most important source of labor for capitalist colonial enterprise was the teeming multitudes of the Orient. Tens of thousands of Indian coolies mined diamonds and harvested sugar in Natal, and immigration was halted only by the South Africans' fear of commercial competition (the Indian proved to have a talent for retail trade) and India's resentment of South African discrimination. Gangs of Chinese mined tin in Malaya and Sumatra, and cultivated sugar in Cuba and cocoa and rubber in Samoa.[8] These workers were generally recruited by contractors of their own nationality, men whose rapacity and cruelty far surpassed those of the white planters or European corporations who were the ultimate employers. One writer, generally sympathetic to Dutch rule in the Indies, described "this trade in human cattle" as follows:

> The coolie's agent or labour contractor receives all the expenses of importing him, including passage money, cost of engagement, commission, and medical examination, and the value of his wages at the rate of 1 florin 20 (two shillings) per diem, but the coolie himself receives only a fraction less than 4d. per

diem for food, and wages at the rate of 12s. 6d. per month. He must engage himself for at least a year: tempted by opium, driven by the physical distress that follows its discontinuance, and obliged to obtain all that he needs upon credit; clothed and fed at usurious prices by the stores run or leased by the labour agent himself; burdened with debts and with vices, he can no longer hope to escape from the mine, and only too often dies in abject poverty in sight of the natural treasure-house that has taken his life.[9]

In the acquisition of commodities, take that strangest and most evil of commodities, the human being reduced to chattel: the opposition to the abolition of the slave trade was just as strong among those African tribes that had made a business of taking and selling captives as it was among the European traders who bought and resold them. In 1850 the king of Dahomey rejected a British offer of a subsidy to give up the slave trade, on the ground that his people were too "manly" for agriculture and had laid waste by their raids all the arable land around.[10]

I am reminded here of that illuminating story of British reluctance to extend His Majesty's authority in West Africa. In 1807 the Ashanti pursued two enemy chiefs into the territory of the Fanti; these refused to give up the refugees and were themselves attacked and driven toward the coast town of Anamabo, where there was a British fort. In spite of the British commander's offer to mediate, the townspeople elected to fight and were slaughtered; the British garrison, which was also attacked, barely held out. At this point the Ashanti king negotiated a peace with Colonel Torrane, governor of Cape Coast. Torrane agreed to turn over the refugee chiefs, as well as up to half the Fanti who had sought asylum in the Anamabo fort; he and his council then turned the rest to profit by selling most of them as slaves. The best comment on the proceeding is that of the Ashanti king: "From the hour Governor Torrane delivered up Tchibbu [one of the fugitive chiefs] I took the English for my friends, because I saw their object was trade only and they did not care for the people. Torrane was a man of sense and he pleased me much."[11]

In the presence of such mutual esteem, imperialism was often an embarrassment. The hard-bitten sea captain of fiction, scouring exotic seas for any and all business — Have tub, will travel; no questions asked — is not a figment of the imagination. Many traders preferred to keep their activities secret, to conceal their profits or the way in which they made them. And the last thing they wanted was "nosy" officials and Her Majesty's law, hence numerous instances of appeals by missionaries for political intervention to defend the native from free enterprise.

As for businessmen at home, they entertained far less illusions about the profitability of colonial ventures than the adventurers, chauvinists, and statesmen who exhorted them to invest and become rich. Bismarck had to instruct his bankers to drum up interest in the South Pacific and Africa — to little avail.[12] Leopold's warm invitations to the financiers of Europe to fructify the resources of the Congo got a lukewarm response.[13] Bouet (the later Admiral Bouet-Willaumez), France's Popham, found the chambers of commerce of Le Havre, Nantes, and Marseilles despairingly indifferent to his campaign to establish French power in the Gulf of Guinea.[14] And so on. It was a veritable epic of obtuseness, or rationality, depending on the point of view. Insofar as the promoters of empire succeeded in whipping up the enthusiasm of business groups at home, they had their greatest success with those whose interests were remote from the acquisitions in question and those who had nothing to lose and possibly something to gain, manufacturers for example. And they had their least success with those made wary by experience, above all, with those who would have to prove their faith with cash.

At this point the economic interpretation of imperialism would argue that such abstinence was exceptional — a temporary aberration — and that increased international competition toward the end of the century encouraged European powers to seek closed rather than open markets. Here, too, the picture is not so simple as that. There were closed markets and preferential systems; but there were also large colonial areas where free trade prevailed, or where foreign enterprise was invited — reluctantly perhaps, but deliberately — to make up for the shortcomings or hesitations of home entrepreneurs, as in German Africa, where most of the trade remained in British hands.[15] Nor is this surprising: many of these territories were acquired not as a by-product or for the sake of economic expansion, but for political, military, or psychological reasons; their shape and size were a function not of rational market considerations but of negotiation and accident. Once one had them, one made the best of them; and the best rarely coincided with neat patterns of international economic rivalry.

What is more, those very monopolies and trusts that critics of economic imperialism have been wont to inveigh against were themselves forces for international cooperation: the bigger they got, the more they understood the advantage of sharing resources and markets rather than fighting over them. Oil is the best example of this trend, which would not have surprised Marx: even in so closed a colony as the Dutch East Indies, more than half the investment in extraction and refining came from Britain and France.

Indeed, one may well argue that in the long run, exploitation is no more a rational motor of imperialism in nonindustrial areas than it is in industrial ones; and that this same free contractual nexus that Marx felt to be indispensable to the development of capitalism in Europe is equally advantageous elsewhere, and while not all merchants, manufacturers, and planters dealing with or working in colonial areas were prepared to recognize this, many did. Ironically, the best examples of the latter are the great international bankers—Hobson's villains—who have always understood that prosperous, independent states make the best clients.

Related to this matter of exploitation is the general question: Did imperialism pay? Books have been written on the subject, which we can hardly do justice to here. Suffice it to say that most informal imperialism paid—in spite of occasional crashes and repudiations, if only because the use of power in such situations was minimal and the outlay of funds was based on essentially rational grounds. Formal imperialism, on the other hand, rarely paid (India, the East Indies, Malaya, and the Congo are egregious exceptions), for precisely the opposite reasons.[16]

Yet for some people imperialism has always paid: energetic traders, enterprising (corrupt?) officials, manufacturers of cheap, colorful wares. And in the last analysis that is what counts. The advocates of the economic interpretation have tried to prove too much. One does not need a business class or an economic system to create a demand for empire. All one needs is a few interested people who can reach the ears or pockets of those who command. It is sufficient for the others to stand passively by, absorbed by their own cares or convinced that their opinions are of no weight anyway—as often they were. For imperialism was in large measure built on the fait accompli—the Jameson raid is the most famous example with the state almost always ready to pull its nationals' chestnuts out of the fire. And it was ready to do this, at some risk and expense, not for material reasons, but for face; for nations as for men, *amour propre* is the most powerful of drives.

If ever it proved advisable, moreover, to whip up general support for these *faits accomplis,* this could usually be accomplished by appeals to lofty sentiments of prestige and humanity. To material interests, too, but I am inclined to think these less important: first, because people are better judges of their own than of national interests, and second, because they do not like to think they are acting for selfish reasons. Hence their powers of rationalization on the one hand, and credulity on the other, know no bounds. Nothing illustrates this sugar-coating better than the following sincere defense of the hut tax, the basis of forced labor in much of Africa:

> The direct taxation of the native is desirable in order to create in him a sense of responsibility, without which a settled condition of society is difficult to attain. It is essential to impress upon the native mind the fact that they can and must participate in the government of the country. This can only be done by getting them to contribute towards the expenses of administration. They are likely to value more highly a government for which they have to pay directly. Moreover, direct taxation fosters commerce, and settled habits of life. In

order to pay the hut tax or gun tax, or both, the natives must work. Commerce will be fostered in two directions: firstly, by providing labour for the extension of commercial enterprise; secondly, by supplying the natives with wages which will be spent increasingly upon the imports of European trade. There is, also, the broader question of political ethics — what the native receives he should pay for. The former government by tribal chiefs gave no security for life and property. This has been introduced by the British administration. It is only fair to ask the native to contribute to the cost of the benefits which he now enjoys.[17]

There is, of course, a big "if" here. To make this kind of economic imperialism effective, interested parties had to be able to call on power. And this brings us to the third premise of the economic interpretation, that the state was in the hands or service of the business class.

Once again, the facts belie the assumption. We have, to begin with, numerous instances of governments refusing to annex territory or bring pressure on weaker states in order to protect or further the material interests of their nationals. Britain in particular repeatedly rejected the importunities of empire builders and businessmen, partly on moral grounds, partly because of economic principle — the Liberals clung wistfully to the ideal of a free-trade, free-enterprise world well into the period of renewed territorial expansion — and not least because she was rich with empire already and could assume a disenchanted stance. The pique of Kimberley, frustrated in his desire to establish a protectorate over Zululand in 1884, is classic: "I see the cabinet do not want more niggers."[18] The correspondence of the Foreign Office is full of lamentations by conscientious consuls of the abuse of power and privilege by European fortune hunters in hapless quasicolonial lands; and of injunctions from London to observe that golden rule of international relations: treat the stranger as you would your own. The whole makes a fascinating story of an honorable effort to build policy on right rather than expediency. The attempt, for reasons to be examined, was condemned to failure from the start.[19]

Other countries were less scrupulous, but there other considerations often served to hamper collaboration between economic interests and the political arm. At least British diplomatic and military personnel recognized the principle of the state in the service of *legitimate* trade. When the Shah of Persia asked British support against Russian encroachment in 1884, the cabinet decided to ask the Shah to open the rivers of Persia to British trade as "an earnest of his good intentions." Dilke notes in his diary: "Not a bad touchstone." It was a typically British touchstone.[20]

Elsewhere, however, officials, while paying lip service to the importance of trade, were less than sympathetic to the activities and personalities of their compatriot entrepreneurs. French traders and chambers of commerce, for example, complain repeatedly of lack of cooperation from consular and naval officers, even of hostility. The following letter of April 1847, from Victor Régis of Marseilles, pioneer of the French palm-oil trade in West Africa, to Captain Bouet-Willaumez, Governor of Senegal, is indicative of a larger conflict:

> Do we want to confine ourselves to making Gabon a military station from which traders must be excluded? If such a policy has not been decided in principle, it exists in fact, and I am pained to conclude that we shall have to start all over with a war in the newspapers to enlighten the government on the consequences of the conduct of several officers towards trade. It is distasteful to me to resort to such an extreme measure, but I refuse [*je ne serais nullement disposé*] to submit to injustices.[21]

Nor is this conflict surprising. On the one side stood a gentleman or presumed gentleman, often drawn from a milieu traditionally hostile to business; on the other, tough, grasping men anxious to get rich as quickly as possible and get out. To those charged with maintaining order and securing territorial gains, the trader looked like a bull in a china shop. Even British officials — and there were none more sympathetic to commerce and cognizant of its importance as means and end — felt a certain impatience with the lesser vision of the money-makers. Listen to the tone of a letter from Harry Johnston, "Commissioner and Consul-General for the territories under British influence to the north of the Zambezi," to the British South Africa Company:

> There is nothing for it. You must make up your minds to trust me, for say one year, with the supreme direction of all things in British Central Africa. I must be able to say to one of your trading agents 'build a store here', 'Give six and threepence a pound for ivory', 'You are selling that cloth too dear', 'You must send an indent for twelve gross of brass pans', 'Supply Crawshay instantly with one dozen child's tops, 26 wax dolls, 3,000 yards of cotton, 30 packets of fancy stationery, five bales of imitation cashmere shawls, and send them off to Lake Mweru tomorrow'. I know as much about your African trade as your Moirs and your Ewings. It is twelve years ago to-day since I landed in Tunis and I have studied Africa ever since. Besides, for the first year or two in my great task of bringing five hundred thousand square miles of Central Africa under British control, the shop is only second to the sword. But it is a shop which must be wisely and judiciously managed, and its shopboys must not be allowed to baulk my efforts by cheating an African chief over damaged jam or pretending that half a crown and a rupee are just the same value. In plain words the African Lakes Company is loathed by everyone in the land. Its policy has been idiotic because its silly little frauds have not even profited it. However enough on this score. If you start your Trading Department in the

way I have sketched out, send out, with public or private instructions to work under my direction in all things, two good men of the accountant type, and for a change, just for a change, send Englishmen.[22]

One final point: even when one considers the numerous instances of collaboration between economic interests and the state, it would be a mistake to assume that there is a simple one-way pattern of influence. In fact, it was often business that was in the service of diplomacy, when necessary at some disadvantage to itself. Moreover, this relationship grew steadily more important in the course of the century, as the development of a world market for goods and capital, with its concomitant patterns of dependency, made economic pressure an ever more effective diplomatic weapon. I cannot do justice to the subject here, but nothing offers so instructive a commentary on the oversimplicity of the economic interpretation than the record of lending as an instrument of foreign policy in pre–World War I eastern Europe.[23]

The foregoing analysis of the complexity of imperialism, with its stress on what we may call countervailing forces—avoidance of or opposition to territorial expansion; conflicts between business ambitions, state policy and personnel; subordination of economic interests to diplomatic considerations—suggests a question: In view of all this tugging and hauling, how does one account for the remorseless if spasmodic advance of imperialism over the course of the century? Surely all these contradictory tendencies and hesitations are only the surface detail that characterizes any broad historical movement. Surely, once one cuts away the brush one finds firm ground—the ground of economic motivation that changes its form of expression but not its meaning. This is the argument advanced, for example, by Gallagher and Robinson, in their article on the "Imperialism of Free Trade": that dominion is essentially a device for the integration of new areas into the expanding industrial economy of Britain; and that the form of control—explicit or implicit, manifest or latent—simply reflects need and opportunity.[24]

While accepting this point about the persistence and indeed primacy of the economic pressures toward empire, especially informal empire, in nineteenth-century Britain, I would dissent from this interpretation on a ground already adduced: that it will account for only a part—an important but nevertheless insufficient part—of the facts. In particular, it will not account for a major historical phenomenon, the occupation of large areas of the world for noneconomic reasons. The correct observation that Africa was "the bottom of the [imperialist] barrel,"[25] far from disposing of the significance of this occupation, only heightens it.

A more general interpretation would seem desirable; and to that end I should like to hazard an equilibrium analysis that transcends place and circumstance. It seems to me that one has to look at imperialism as a multifarious response to a common opportunity that consists simply in disparity of power. Whenever and wherever such disparity has existed, people and groups have been ready to take advantage of it. It is, one notes with regret, in the nature of the human beast to push other people around — or to save their souls or "civilize" them, as the case may be. To be sure, there is such a thing as morality, and occasionally a nation or part of a nation, as in nineteenth-century Britain, develops ideals concerning freedom and self-determination that put an obstacle in the way of unrestrained exploitation of superior strength. But here the best of intentions are eroded in the long run by the inner logic of dominion. This inner logic finds expression in two fields: within the context of a given area of imperialistic influence and in the larger context of the international relations of imperial powers.

Concerning the first, the decisive determinant at the working level — as distinguished from the level of plans and intentions — is the instability of any relationship of unequal power. In the long run, the weaker party will never accept his inferiority, first because of the material disadvantages it entails, but even more because of the humiliation it imposes. In return, the stronger party must ceaselessly concern itself with the security of its position. Hence this imperialism of the "turbulent frontier" so well described by John Galbraith: each strong point requires outposts to defend it, and each outpost calls for new ones beyond it.[26] The spiral of increasing commitments and "obligations" is limited only by the balance of power.

This pattern of pressure or the threat of pressure from the weak side and response from the strong has its counterpart in initiatives from the strong side and responses from the weak. Whatever may be the policy of the imperial nation, however restrained it may be in its application of power, its citizens — businessmen, missionaries, soldiers of fortune — exploit on their own initiative the opportunities offered. Moreover, there is no necessity here of concerted action. The situation is analogous to a market in which equilibrium may be upset by the action of only one competitor. All that is needed is one man to place the prestige of the dominant group in the scales or put its security in jeopardy, and corrective action is inevitable. It may occasionally take the form of restoring the previous equilibrium, but it will not do this indefinitely. Sooner or later the fatal words will be pronounced: "We're going to get no rest until. . . ."

In the second or international arena, an analogous situation prevails. It matters not what the intentions; each nation operates in a universe peopled by other nations, and its actions are determined as much by their moves as by its own objectives. Under the circumstances, principle and morality must yield to tactical necessity — on a small scale, as in mid-century Egypt, where Britain found herself obliged to follow the example of the other European powers in extorting advantages for her nationals, if only to maintain her prestige in the area;[27] or on a large scale, as when the transpiring ambitions of other European powers led Britain in the 1880s to adopt the policy of preemptive veto on the acquisition of any of the unclaimed areas of the world.

So if one seeks to understand the imperialism of the nineteenth century, one must take into account not only stronger economic motives, among others, but even more those technological changes that increased the disparity of force between Europe and the rest of the world and created the opportunity for and possibility of dominion. It is no coincidence that the Araucanian Indians of South America repeatedly defeated and humiliated the Spanish invaders in the eighteenth century (as they had the Incas earlier) but succumbed to Chilean troops in the nineteenth, while at the same time, but thousands of miles away, settlers from the north succeeded in subduing the Plains Indians of the southwestern United States, where the Spanish and Mexicans had failed. The key to conquest in both cases was essentially improved firepower through the introduction of repeating weapons.[28]

In this sense, the expansion of the nineteenth century is only the last phase of a millennial explosion that goes back to the turning point of the Middle Ages when the peoples of Europe, long compressed and pierced by stronger enemies, halted their incursions and beat them back—on the plateau of Castile, on the east Elbian plain, along the shores of the Mediterranean. The explosion is not even or continuous; the frontier of dominion retreats as well as advances. But in the long run the great tide swells inexorably, for it expresses a fundamental and continuing shift in the balance of power between Europe and the rest of the world. And power, like nature, abhors a vacuum.

Notes

1. The definition does not comprise the range of phenomena covered by François Perroux's concept of economic domination. This includes involuntary as well as voluntary subordination by one economic entity of another, whether at the level of enterprises, national economics, or regional groups of economies; there may or may not be control or constraint. Such a concept is at once more comprehensive than imperialism as defined above, in that it embraces all interrelationships of strong and weak economic units, whether or not there is dominion; and at the same time less comprehensive, in that it does not include imperialism of noneconomic origin or character. See F. Perroux, "Esquisse d'une théorie de l'économie dominante," *Economie appliquée* 1 (1948):243-300.

2. R. Koebner, "The Concept of Economic Imperialism," *Econ. Hist. Rev.,* 2d

Ser., 2 (1949):5.

3. These points are phrased by Lenin. The edition used is that of E. Varga and L. Mendelsohn (eds.), *New Data for V. I. Lenin's "Imperialism, the Highest Stage of Capitalism"* (New York: International Publishers, n.d.), pp. 174, 182.

4. Commander Popham took it upon himself to sail his squadron from African waters to Buenos Aires in time of war. When His Majesty's Navy took umbrage at this and instituted court-martial proceedings, Popham saved himself by rallying the British mercantile community to his defense. See H. S. Ferns, *Britain and Argentina in the Nineteenth Century* (Oxford: Clarendon Press, 1960), ch. 1. Note that Britain's interest in new markets in this period was much stimulated by the commercial dislocations of war. Even before the formal institution of the Continental Blockade, the rich European market had become precarious and costly of access — a foretaste of things to come. See F. Crouzet, *L'économie britannique et le blocus continental* (1806-1813), 2 vols. (Paris: Presses Universitaires, 1958). On Raffles, there is abundant literature. See especially the article by H.R.C. Wright, "The Anglo-Dutch Dispute in the East, 1814-1824," *Econ. Hist. Rev.*, 2d ser., 3 (1950):229-39; also the highly critical Dutch viewpoint of Bernard H. M. Vlekke, *Nusantara: A History of the East Indian Archipelago* (Cambridge: Harvard University Press, 1945), ch. 12.

5. S. B. Saul, "The Economic Significance of 'Constructive Imperialism,'" *The Journal of Economic History* 17, no. 2 (June 1957):184-186; Wong Lin Ken, "Western Enterprise and the Development of the Malayan Tin Industry to 1914" (mimeographed paper presented to the Study Group on the Economic History of Southeast Asia of the School of Oriental and African Studies, University of London, July 1961).

6. The point is to distinguish between relationships real or latent in any market situation and those specific to imperialism, that is, to separate out from the range of phenomena embraced by the concept of the *économie dominante* those deriving from the exercise or threat of superior force. The two definitions most current in the economic literature will not do this. One — payment to labor of less than its marginal product — relates to any deviation from perfect competition; the second — payment of less than marginal revenue product — is relevant to cases of *monopsony or collusion.* A third definition, the Marxian one, is based on a normative judgment of social deserts: the appropriation by employers of the so-called surplus value of labor. Because of its tautological character — exploitation is built into the Marxian definition of capitalism — it is neither susceptible to verification or disproof nor applicable to exploitation by noncapitalist systems.

7. Thus the Dutch gave their officials a portion of the proceeds of the system; and crops that required processing, such as sugar, were turned over to factories managed by Europeans or Chinese and worked for or financed by the government. J.A.M. Caldwell, "Indonesian Export Production from the Decline of the Culture System to the First World War" (mimeographed paper presented to the Study Group on the Economic History of the East and Southeast Asia of the School of Oriental and African Studies, University of London, July 1961); C. Day, *The Policy and Administration of the Dutch in Java* (New York: Macmillan Company, 1904), chs. 7-9.

8. Cf. Persia C. Campbell, *Chinese Coolie Emigration to Countries within the British*

Empire (London: P. S. King, 1923); also Watt Stewart, *Chinese Bondage in Peru: A History of the Chinese Coolie in Peru, 1849-1874* (Durham: Duke University Press, 1951).

9. A. Cabaton, *Java, Sumatra, and the Other Islands of the Dutch East Indies* (New York: Scribners; London: T. Fisher Unwin, 1911), pp. 301 f.

10. S. O. Biobaku, *The Egba and Their Neighbours*, 1842-1872 (Oxford: Clarendon Press, 1957), p. 40. (Ironically, the Dahomi were famous—or infamous—throughout West Africa for their women soldiers.)

11. A. B. Ellis, *A History of the Gold Coast of West Africa* (London, 1893), pp. 117 f.

12. There is material on this in the archives of the banking house of S. Bleichröder, graciously lent me by Mr. F. H. Brunner, of Arnhold and S. Bleichröder, New York. Among the numerous but scattered printed sources, see H. Feis, *Europe, the World's Banker, 1870-1914* (New Haven: Yale University Press, 1930); and G. Diouritch, *L'expansion des banques allemandes à l'étranger* (Paris: A. Rousseau, 1909), pp. 738-763.

13. Again there is information in the Bleichröder archive on Leopold's efforts to draw in German capital. The story of the reserved reaction of the Belgian business community remains to be examined in detail. Cf. P. A. Roeykens, *La période initiale de l'oeuvre africaine de Léopold III* [Memoires de l'Académie Royale des Sciences Coloniales, Brussels, Classe des Sciences Morales et Politiques, Nouvelle Série in – 8°, Tome III, fasc. 3] (Brussels, 1957), p. 85.

14. B. Schnapper, "La politique des 'points d'appui' et la fondation des comptoirs fortifiés dans le golfe de Guinée (1837-1843)," *Revue historique* 225 (1961):99-120.

15. W. O. Henderson, "British Economic Activity in the German Colonies, 1884-1914." *Econ. Hist. Rev.* 15 (1945):56-66. In the case of the Congo, it was Leopold's declared intention from the start to establish a free-trade area, not only because any other policy would have alienated potential support from abroad, but because this was the way to maximize return from what was intended to be the biggest personal domain of the age (or the ages). At the same time, he wooed his countrymen by stressing the contribution the Congo would make to Belgian prosperity, without, however, making any promises of special treatment. This all-things-for-all-men technique is closely analogous to that employed by Lesseps in his promotion of the Suez canal.

16. Even with those colonies that clearly paid, however, the historian must take care not to overestimate their contribution to the economy of the imperial country, the more so as this contribution hardly requires exaggeration. It was greater for small nations like Belgium and Holland. It was less important for Britain. It is an article of faith among many Indian historians that the Indian market was the key to British industrial growth and prosperity; indeed, that the "exploitation" of India accounts for the Industrial Revolution. In fact, it was not until after 1815 that exports of British manufacturers to the East began their rapid growth. Thus in 1814 less than one million yards of cotton cloth were sent to ports east of Suez, or less than one half of 1 percent of the total exports. By 1830 the figure was 57 million; by 1860, 825 million to India alone. At the last date, British shipments accounted for perhaps 35 percent of the consumption of the Indian market, as against some 4 percent in the early thirties, and almost a third of total British exports of cloth. In the

course of these years, therefore, Indian production for home consumption actually increased; but Indian exports were virtually driven from the world market. Th. Ellison, *The Cotton Trade of Great Britain* (London, 1886), p. 63; S. B. Saul, *Studies in British Overseas Trade, 1870-1914* (Liverpool: Liverpool University Press, 1960), p. 14 and n. 2.

17. A. J. MacDonald, *Trade, Politics and Christianity in Africa and the East* (London: Longmans, Green, 1916), p. 114.

18. S. Gwynn and G. M. Tuckwell, *The Life of the Rt. Hon. Sir Charles W. Dilke,* 2 vols. (London: J. Murray, 1917), 2:86.

19. Thus Britain made repeated efforts to defend the government of Egypt in the 1850s and 1860s against the extortions of foreign businessmen, adventurers, and confidence men, extortions condoned and connived at by the consular representatives of the European powers and effected thanks to a system of extraterritorial privilege and the threat of superior force; to no avail. See D. S. Landes, *Bankers and Pashas* (London: Heinemann, 1958), ch. 3, especially the sources cited in p. 94, n. 3.

20. Gwynn and Tuckwell, *Life of Dilke,* 2:87.

21. P. Masson, *Marseille et la colonisation française* (Marseilles: Barlatier, 1906), p. 387.

22. Roland Oliver, *Sir Harry Johnston and the Scramble for Africa* (New York: St. Martin's, 1958), pp. 198 f.

23. The records of the Service du Movement des Fonds of the French Ministry of Finance are full of evidence of this subordination of banking to politics. The dossiers on Rumania (Archives Nationales, F^{03} 327) are particularly suggestive, not only for what they show of government attitudes, but also for the evidence they offer of the ability of the state to impose its will on reluctant enterprises in a nominally free economy. The Deutsches Zentral Archiv in Potsdam contains similar material on German lending policy, among other things, on Bismarck's famous decision to cut off credit to Russia in 1887 in order to bring pressure on the Tsarist government.

24. J. Gallagher and R. Robinson, "The Imperialism of Free Trade," *Econ. Hist. Rev.,* 2d ser., 6 (1953):1-15.

25. Ibid., p. 15.

26. J. S. Galbraith, "The 'Turbulent Frontier' as a Factor in British Expansion," *Comparative Studies in Society and History* 2 (1960):150-68.

27. Thus in the enforcement in 1868-1869 of British claims against the Egyptian government in the liquidation of the Société Agricole. F. O. 78-2166 and 2167, especially F. O. 78-2167, Clarendon to Stanton, teleg. 23-4-1869, letter 30-4-1869.

28. On the Araucanian Indians, see R. C. Padden, "Cultural Changes and Military Resistance in Araucanian Chile, 1550-1730," *Southwestern Journal of Anthropology* 13 (1957):103-121. On the Plains Indians of North America, the discussion of Walter P. Webb, *The Great Plains* (Boston: Ginn and Co., 1931), chs. 4 and 5, is a classic. Eric A. Walker, *A History of Southern Africa* (London: Longmans, Green, 1957), p. 429, has a ghastly phrase about the effect of military technology on British dominion over the Matabele: "The machine guns, a novelty in warfare in those days [1893], worked wonders at Shangani and Imbembezi, and the volunteers entered the ruins of Bulawayo to find the king fled." Compare the change in British

fortunes (and policy) in the Sudan, from the days of Gordon (fall of Khartum, 1885) to those of Kitchener (battle of Omdurman, 1898). It is one of the ironies of history that the machine gun, which long met with skepticism in the planning rooms of European war ministries, was proved and perfected in combat with the colonial peoples of the world, so that when World War I came, with its trench warfare, the now much improved weapon was able to slaughter the children of its European developers. Cf. G. S. Hutchison, *Machine Guns: Their History and Technical Employment* (London: Macmillan, 1938).

18
A Structural Theory of Imperialism

Johan Galtung

Introduction

This theory takes as its point of departure two of the most glaring facts about this world: the tremendous inequality, within and between nations, in almost all aspects of human living conditions, including the power to decide over those living conditions; *and* the resistance of this inequality to change. The world consists of Center and Periphery nations; and each nation, in turn, has its centers and periphery. Hence, our concern is with the mechanism underlying this discrepancy, particularly between the center in the Center, and the periphery in the Periphery. In other words, how to conceive of, how to explain, and how to counteract inequality as one of the major forms of *structural violence*.[1] Any theory of liberation from structural violence presupposes theoretically and practically adequate ideas of the dominance system against which the liberation is directed; and the special type of dominance system to be discussed here is *imperialism*.

Imperialism will be conceived of as a dominance relation between collectivities, particularly between nations. It is a sophisticated type of dominance relation which cuts across nations, basing itself on a bridgehead which the center in the Center nation establishes in the center of the Periphery nation, for the joint benefit of both. It should not be confused with other ways in which one collectivity can dominate another in the sense of exercising power over it. Thus, a military occupation of B by A may seriously curtail B's freedom of action, but is not for that reason an imperialist relationship unless it is set up in a special way. The same applies to the *threat* of conquest and possible occupation, as in a balance of power relationship. Moreover, *subversive* activities may also be brought to a stage where a nation is dominated by the pinpricks exercised against it from below, but this is clearly different from imperialism.

Thus, imperialism is a species in a genus of dominance and power rela-

Reprinted by permission of the publisher from Johan Galtung, "A Structural Theory of Imperialism," *Journal of Peace Research* 8 (1971):81-117.

tionships. It is a subtype of something and has itself subtypes to be explored later. Dominance relations between nations and other collectivities will not disappear with the disappearance of imperialism; nor will the end to one type of imperialism (e.g., political or economic) guarantee the end to another type of imperialism (e.g., economic or cultural). Our view is not reductionist in the traditional sense pursued in Marxist-Leninist theory, which conceives of imperialism as an economic relationship under private capitalism, motivated by the need for expanding markets, and which bases the theory of dominance on a theory of imperialism. According to this view, imperialism and dominance will fall like dominoes when the capitalistic conditions for economic imperialism no longer obtain. According to the view we develop here, imperialism is a more general structural relationship between two collectivities and has to be understood at a general level in order to be understood and counteracted in its more specific manifestations—just like smallpox is better understood in a context of a theory of epidemic diseases, and these diseases better understood in a context of general pathology.

Briefly stated, imperialism is a system that splits up collectivities and relates some of the parts to each other in relations of *harmony of interest,* and other parts in relations of *disharmony of interest,* or *conflict of interest.*

Defining "Conflict of Interest"

"Conflict of interest" is a special case of conflict in general, defined as a situation where parties are pursuing incompatible goals. In our special case, these goals are stipulated by an outsider as the "true" interests of the parties, disregarding wholly or completely what the parties themselves say explicitly are the values they pursue. One reason for this is the rejection of the dogma of unlimited rationality: actors do *not* necessarily know, or they are unable to express, what their interest is. Another, more important, reason is that rationality is unevenly distributed, that some may dominate the minds of others, and that this may lead to "false consciousness." Thus, learning to suppress one's own true interests may be a major part of socialization in general and education in particular.

Let us refer to this true interest as LC, *living condition.* It may perhaps be measured by using such indicators as income, standard of living in the usual materialistic sense—but notions of *quality of life* would certainly also enter, not to mention notions of *autonomy.* But the precise content of LC is less important for our purpose than the definition of conflict of interest:

There is *conflict,* or *disharmony of interest,* if the two parties are coupled together in such a way that the LC *gap* between them is *increasing;*

There is *no conflict,* or *harmony of interest,* if the two parties are coupled together in such a way that the LC *gap* between them is *decreasing down to zero.*

Some points in this definition should be spelled out.

First, the parties have to be coupled together, in other words *interact.* A difference between mutually isolated parties does not in itself give rise to problems of interest. There was neither harmony, nor disharmony of interest between the peoples in Africa, Asia, and America before the white Europeans came — there was *nothing.*

Second, the reference is to *parties,* not to actors. In the theory of conflict of *interests,* as opposed to the theory of conflict of *goals,* there is no assumption that the parties (better: categories) have crystallized into actors. This is what they may have to do after they see their own situation more clearly, or in other words: the conflict of interest may have to be transformed into a conflict of *goals.* Thus, if in a nation the center, here defined as the "government" (in the wide sense, not the "cabinet") uses its power to increase its own LC much more than does the rest of the nation, then there is disharmony of interest between government and people according to this definition. This may then be used as a basis for defining the government as illegitimate — as opposed to the usual conception where illegitimacy is a matter of opinion, expressed in the legislature or in the population. The trouble with the latter idea is that it presupposes a level of rationality, an ability of expression and political consciousness and party formation that can only be presupposed at the center of the more or less vertical societies in which human beings live. It is a model highly protective of the center as a whole, however much it may lead to rotation of groups within the center, and hence protective of vertical society.

Third, there is the problem of what to do with the case of a *constant gap.* The parties grow together, at the same rate, but the gap between them is constant. Is that harmony or disharmony of interest? We would refer to it as disharmony, for the parties are coupled such that they will not be brought together. Even if they *grow* parallel to each other it is impossible to put it down as a case of harmony, when the distribution of value is so unequal. On the contrary, this is the case of disharmony that has reached a state of equilibrium.

Fourth, this definition has the advantage of enabling us to talk about *degrees of harmony and disharmony* by measuring the angle between the two trajectories, perhaps also taking speed into account. Thus we avoid the difficulty of talking simplistically in terms of polar opposites, harmony versus disharmony, and can start talking in terms of weak and strong harmony and disharmony.

Fifth, there is an implicit reference to *time* in the two terms "increasing" and "decreasing." We have not been satisfied with a time-free way of operationalizing the concept in terms of static LC gaps. It is much more easy with conflict of *goals,* as we would then be dealing with clearly demarcated actors whose values can be ascertained, and their compatibility or incompatibility likewise: there is no need to study the system over time. To understand conflict of *interest* it looks as if at least a bivariate, diachronic analysis should be carried out to get some feel of how the system operates.

But we should obviously make a distinction between the *size* of the gap, and what happens to the gap over time. If we only had access to static, synchronic data, then we would of course focus on the magnitude of the gap and talk about *disharmony of interest if it is wide, harmony of interest if it is narrow or zero.*

As a first approximation this may not be too bad, but it does lead us into some difficulties. Thus, how do we rank these combinations in terms of increasing disharmony of interest? As we see from Table 18.1, the only doubt would be between combinations B and C. We would favor the alphabetical order for two reasons: first, becoming is more important than being (at least if the time-perspective is reasonably short), and second, the diachronic relationship probably reveals more about the coupling between them. For example, the gap in living condition between Norway and Nepal in 1970 is not significant as an indicator of any imperialism. If it keeps on increasing there may be a bit more basis for the suspicion, but more evidence is needed to state the diagnosis of imperialism. The crucial word here is "coupling" in the definition. The word has been put there to indicate some type of social causation in interaction relation and interaction structure which will have to be demonstrated, over and above a simple correlation.

Let us conclude this discussion by pointing out that a gap in living condition, or at least one important kind, is a necessary, if not sufficient, condition for conflict or disharmony of interest. If in addition the gap can be observed over time, a more satisfactory basis for a diagnosis in terms of imperialism may emerge.

TABLE 18.1   Four Types of Harmony/
Disharmony of Interest

| | | gap | |
		decreasing	increasing
gap	narrow	A	C
	wide	B	D

And then, in conclusion, it is clear that the concept of interest used here is based on an ideology, or a *value premise of equality*.[2] An interaction relation and interaction structure set up such that inequality is the result is seen as a coupling not in the interest of the weaker party. This is a value premise like so many other value premises in social science explorations, such as "direct violence is bad," "economic growth is good," "conflict should be resolved," etc. As in all other types of social science, the goal should not be an "objective" social science freed from all such value premises, but a more honest social science where the value premises are made explicit.

Defining "Imperialism"

We shall now define imperialism by using the building blocks presented in the preceding two sections. In our two-nation world, imperialism can be defined as one way in which the Center nation has power over the Periphery nation, so as to bring about a condition of disharmony of interest between them. Concretely, *Imperialism* is a relation between a Center and a Periphery nation so that[3]

1. there is *harmony of interest* between the *center in the Center* nation and the *center in the Periphery* nation,
2. there is more *disharmony of interest* within the Periphery nation than within the Center nations,
3. there is *disharmony of interest* between the *periphery in the Center* nation and the *periphery in the Periphery* nation.

Diagrammatically it looks something like Figure 18.1. This complex definition, borrowing largely from Lenin,[4] needs spelling out. The basic idea is, as mentioned, that the center in the Center nation has a bridgehead in the Periphery nation, and a well-chosen one: the center in the Periphery nation. This is established such that the Periphery center is tied to the Center center with the best possible tie: the tie of harmony of interest. They are linked so that they go up together and down, even under, together. How this is done in concrete terms will be explored in the subsequent sections.

Inside the two nations there is disharmony of interest. They are both in one way or another vertical societies with LC gaps — otherwise there is no possibility of locating a center and a periphery. Moreover, the gap is not decreasing, but is at best constant. But the basic idea, absolutely fundamental for the whole theory to be developed, is that *there is more disharmony in the Periphery nation than in the Center nation*. At the simplest static level of description this means there is more inequality in the Periphery than in the Center. At the more complex level we might talk in terms of the gap open-

FIGURE 18.1   The Structure of Imperialism

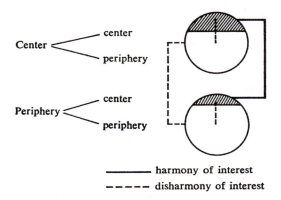

ing more quickly in the Periphery than in the Center, where it might even remain constant. Through welfare state activities, redistribution takes place and disharmony is reduced for at least some LC dimensions, including income, but usually excluding power.

If we now would capture in a few sentences what imperialism is about, we might perhaps say something like this:

In the Periphery nation, the center grows more than the periphery, due partly to how interaction between center and periphery is organized. Without necessarily thinking of economic interaction, the center is more enriched than the periphery — in ways to be explored below. However, for part of this enrichment, the center in the Periphery only serves as a transmission belt (e.g., as commercial firms, trading companies) for value (e.g., raw materials) forwarded to the Center nation. This value enters the Center in the center, with some of it drizzling down to the periphery in the Center. Importantly, there is less disharmony of interest in the Center than in the Periphery, so that *the total arrangement is largely in the interest of the periphery in the Center*. Within the Center the two parties may be opposed to each other. But in the total game, the periphery see themselves more as the partners of the center in the Center than as the partners of the periphery in the Periphery — and this is the essential trick of that game. Alliance formation between the two peripheries is avoided, while the Center nation becomes more and the Periphery nation less cohesive — and hence less able to develop long-term strategies.

Actually, concerning the three criteria in the definition of imperialism as given above it is clear that no. 3 is implied by nos. 1 and 2. The two centers are tied together and the Center periphery is tied to its center: that is the whole essence of the situation. If we now presuppose that the center in the Periphery is a smaller proportion of that nation than the center in the Center, we can also draw one more implication: *there is disharmony of interest between the Center nation as a whole and the Periphery nation as a whole.* But that type of finding, frequently referred to, is highly misleading because it blurs the harmony of interest between the two centers and leads to the belief that imperialism is merely an international relationship, *not a combination of intra- and international relations.* [5]

However, even if the definition given above purports to define the pure case of imperialism, we may nevertheless fruitfully think in terms of degenerate cases. Thus, the first point in the definition about harmony between the two centers is obviously the most important one. If the second point does not hold, and consequently not the third point either, it may still be fruitful to talk about imperialism. But in this degenerate case the two peripheries may more easily find each other, since they are now only kept apart by geographical distance (assuming that the two nations are nation-states, often even located far apart), not in addition by disharmony of interest. Thus, if the relationship between the two peripheries and their centers should become more similar, periphery alliance formation might easily be the result, and the two centers would have to resort to more direct means of violence rather than, or in addition to, the delicate type of structural violence that characterizes the pure type of imperialistic relationship.

But what if there is no distinction between center and periphery in the two nations; what if they are completely horizontal societies? In that case, we should not talk about the dominance relationship whereby the Center nation extracts something from the Periphery nation as an imperialistic one, but rather as something else — looting, stealing, etc. Where there is no bridgehead from the Center nation in the center of the Periphery nation, there cannot be any imperialism by this definition.

From this an important methodological remark may follow. Imagine we now start from the other end and discover that over time some nations increase their living conditions more than other nations — the "increasing gap" so often referred to today — and that there seems to be some kind of structure to this, some kind of invariance. As mentioned, this does not in itself constitute proof of any diagnosis in terms of imperialism, but should prompt the researcher to look for data in that direction. More particularly, we should try to study the precise nature of the interaction between the nations or groups of nations, and see whether the nations can be differentiated in terms of centers and peripheries that relate to each other in the way indicated. But to do this in at all a concrete manner, we must make our definition of imperialism much less abstract. To this we now turn, in successive stages, exploring two *mechanisms,* five *types,* and three *phases* of imperialism.

The Mechanisms of Imperialism

The two basic mechanisms of imperialism both concern the *relation* between the parties concerned, particularly between the nations. The first mechanism concerns the *interaction relation* itself, the second how these relations are put together in a larger interaction structure:

  1. the principle of *vertical interaction relation;*
  2. the principle of *feudal interaction structure.*

The basic point about interaction is, of course, that people and nations have different values that complement each other, and then engage in exchange. Some nations produce oil, other nations produce tractors, and they then carry out an exchange according to the principles of comparative advantages. Imagine that our two-nation system has a prehistory of no interaction at all, and then starts with this type of interaction. Obviously, both will be changed by it, and more particularly a gap between them is likely to open and widen if the interaction is cumulatively asymmetric in terms of what the two parties get out of it.

To study whether the interaction is symmetric or asymmetric, on equal or unequal terms, *two* factors arising from the interaction have to be examined:

  1. *the value-exchange between the actors — inter-*actor effects
  2. *the effects inside the actors — intra-*actor effects

In *economic* relations the first is most commonly analyzed, not only by liberal but also by Marxist economists. The inter-actor flow can be observed as flows of raw material, capital, and financial goods and services in either direction, and can literally be measured at the main points of entry: the customs houses and the national banks. The flow both ways can then be compared in various ways. Most important is the comparison in terms of *who benefits most,* and for this purpose intra-actor effects also have to be taken into consideration.

In order to explore this, the interaction budget indicated in Table 18.2 may be useful. In the table the usual exchange pattern between a "developed" nation A and a "developing" nation B, where manufactured goods are exchanged for raw materials, is indicated. Whether it takes place in a barter economy or a money economy is not essential in a study of exchange between completely unprocessed goods like crude oil and highly processed goods like tractors. There are negative intra-actor effects that accrue to both parties, indicated by the terms "pollution" for A and

TABLE 18.2   An Interaction Budget

	A ('developed')		B ('developing')	
	inter-actor effects	intra-actor effects	inter-actor effects	intra-actor effects
positive (in)	raw materials	spin-offs	manufactured goods	little or nothing
negative (out)	manufactured goods	pollution, exploitation	raw materials	depletion, exploitation

"depletion" for B, and "exploitation" for either. So far these negative spin-off effects are usually not taken systematically into account, nor the positive spin-off effects for A that will be a cornerstone in the present analysis.

It is certainly meaningful and important to talk in terms of unequal exchange or asymmetric interaction, but not quite unproblematic what its precise meaning should be. For that reason, it may be helpful to think in terms of three stages or types of exploitation, partly reflecting historical *processes* in chronological order, and partly reflecting types of *thinking* about exploitation.

In the first stage of exploitation, A simply engages in looting and takes away the raw materials without offering anything in return. If he steals out of pure nature there is no human interaction involved, but we assume that he forces "natives" to work for him and do the extraction work. It is like the slave owner who lives on the work produced by slaves — which is quantitatively not too different from the landowner who has landworkers working for him five out of seven days a week.

In the second stage, A starts offering something "in return." Oil, pitch, land, etc., is "bought" for a couple of beads — it is no longer simply taken away without asking any questions about ownership. The price paid is ridiculous. However, as power relations in the international systems change, perhaps mainly by bringing the power level of the weaker party up from zero to some low positive value, A has to contribute more: for instance, pay more for the oil. The question is now whether there is a cutoff point after which the exchange becomes equal, and what the criterion for that cutoff point would be. Absence of subjective dissatisfaction — B says that he is now content? Objective market values or the number of man-hours that have gone into the production on either side?

There are difficulties with all these conceptions. But instead of elaborating on this, we shall rather direct our attention to the shared failure of all these attempts to look at *intra*-actor effects. Does the interaction have enriching or impoverishing effects *inside* the actor, or does it just lead to a standstill? This type of question leads us to the third stage of exploitation, where there may be some balance in the flow between the actors, but great differences in the effect the interaction has within them.[6]

As an example let us use nations exchanging oil for tractors. The basic point is that this involves different levels of processing, where we define "processing" as an activity imposing culture on nature. In the case of crude oil the product is (almost) pure nature; in the case of tractors it would be wrong to say that it is a case of pure culture, pure *form* (like mathematics, music). A transistor radio, an integrated circuit, these would be better examples because nature has been brought down to a minimum. The tractor is still too much iron and rubber to be a pure case.

The major point now is the *gap in processing level* between oil and tractors and the differential effect this gap will have on the two nations. In one nation the oil deposit may be at the waterfront, and all that is needed is a derrick and some simple mooring facilities to pump the oil straight into a ship — e.g., a Norwegian tanker — that can bring the oil to the country where it will provide energy to run, among other things, the tractor factories. In the other nation the effects may be extremely far-reaching due to the complexity of the product and the connectedness of the society.

There may be ring effects in all directions, and in Table 18.3 we have made an effort to show some types of spin-off effects. A number of comments are appropriate in connection with this list, which, needless to say, is very tentative indeed.

First, the effects are rather deep reaching if this is at all a correct image of the situation. And the picture is hardly exaggerated. It is possible to set up international interaction in such a way that the positive intra-actor effects are practically nil in the raw material delivering nation, and extremely far-reaching in the processing nation.[7] This is not in any sense strange either: if processing is the imprint of culture on nature, the effects should be far-reaching indeed, and strongly related to development itself.

Second, these effects reinforce each other. In the nine effects listed in Table 18.3, there are economic, political, military, communications, and cultural aspects mixed together. Thus, the nation that in the international division of labor has the task of providing the most refined, processed products — like Japan with its emphasis on integrated circuits, transistors, miniaturization, etc. (or Eastern Europe's Japan: the DDR, with a similar emphasis) — will obviously have to engage in research. Research needs an infrastructure, a wide cultural basis in universities, etc., and it has obvious spill-over effects in the social, political, and military domains. And so on; the list may be examined and all kinds of obvious types of cross-fertilization be explored.

Third, in the example chosen, and also in the formulations in Table 18.3,

TABLE 18.3   Intra-Actor Effects of Interaction Across Gaps in Processing Levels

Dimension	Effect on center nation	Effect on periphery nation	Analyzed by
1. Subsidiary economic effects	New *means of production* developed	Nothing developed, just a hole in the ground	Economist
2. Political position in world structure	Central position reinforced	Periphery position reinforced	International relationists
3. Military benefits	*Means of destruction* can easily be produced	No benefits, wars cannot be fought by means of raw materials	
4. Communication benefits	*Means of communication* easily developed	No benefits, transportation not by means of raw materials	Communication specialists
5. Knowledge and research	Much needed for higher levels of processing	Nothing needed, extraction based on being, not on becoming	Scientists, Technicians
6. Specialist needed	Specialists in *making*, scientists, engineers	Specialist in *having*, lawyers	Sociologists of knowledge
7. Skill and education	Much needed to carry out processing	Nothing needed, just a hole in the ground	Education specialists
8. Social structure	Change needed for ability to convert into mobility	No change needed, extraction based on ownership, not on ability	Sociologists
9. Psychological effects	A basic psychology of self-reliance and autonomy	A basic psychology of dependence	Psychologists

we have actually referred to a very special type of gap in processing level: the case when one of the nations concerned delivers raw materials. But the general point here is the *gap*, which would also exist if one nation delivers semifinished products and the other finished products. There may be as much of a gap in trade relations based on exchange between textiles and transistors as one based on exchange between oil and tractors. However, and this seems to be basic, we have looked in vain for a theory of economic trade where this gap is meaningfully operationalized so that the theory could be based on it. In fact, *degree of processing,* which is the basic variable behind the spin-off effects, seems absent from most thinking about international exchange.

This, and that is observation number *four,* is not merely a question of analyzing differences in processing level in terms of what happens inside the factory or the extraction plant. It has to be seen in its social totality. A glance at the right-hand column of Table 18.3 immediately gives us some clues as to why this has not been done: academic research has been so divided that nowhere in a traditional university setup would one come to grips with the totality of the effects of an interaction process. Not even in the most sophisticated inter-, cross-, or transdisciplinary research institute has that type of research been carried so far that a meaningful operationalization has been offered. Yet this is indispensible for a new program of trade on equal terms to be formulated: *trade, or interaction in general, is symmetric, or on equal terms, if and only if the total inter- and intra-actor effects that accrue to the parties are equal.* [8]

But, and this is observation number *five*, why has the idea of comparing the effects of interaction only at the points of exit and entry been so successful? Probably basically because it has always been natural and in the interest of the two centers to view the world in this way, not necessarily consciously to reinforce their position in the center, but basically because interaction looks more like "*interaction only*" to the center. If the center in the Periphery has based its existence on being rather than becoming, on ownership rather than processing, then the interaction has been very advantageous to them. What was formerly nature is through the "beneficial interaction" with another nation converted into money, which in turn can be converted into many things. *Very little effort was needed:* and that this was precisely what made the exchange so disadvantageous, only became clear after some time. Japan is, possibly, the only nation that has really converted the absence of raw materials into a blessing for the economy.

Some implications of the general principle of viewing intra-actor in addition to inter-actor effects can now be spelled out.

One is obvious: *asymmetry cannot be rectified by stabilizing or increasing the prices for raw materials.* Of course, prices exist that could, on the surface, compensate for the gap in intra-actor effects, convertible into a corresponding development of subsidiary industries, education industry, knowledge industry, and so on (although it is hard to see how the psychology of self-reliance can be bought for money). Much of this is what raw material producing countries can do with the money they earn. But this is not the same. One thing is to be *forced* into a certain pattern of intra-actor development *in order to* be able to participate in the inter-actor interaction, quite another thing is to be free to make the decision without having to do it, without being forced by the entire social machinery.

The second implication is also obvious, but should still be put as a question to economists. Imagine that a nation A gives nation B a loan L, to be repaid after n years at an interest rate of p % p. a. There is only one condition in addition to the conditions of the loan: that the money be used to procure goods at a high level of processing in A. Each order will then have deep repercussions in A, along the eight dimensions indicated, in addition to the direct effect of the order itself. The value of these effects is certainly not easily calculated, but in addition A also gets back from B, if B has not gone bankrupt through this process in the meantime, $L(1 + p)^n$ after n years. If procurement is in terms of capital goods rather than consumer goods (usually for consumption by the center in the Periphery mainly) there will also have been intra-actor effects in B. In all likelihood the intra-actor effects of the deal in A are more far-reaching, however, for two reasons: the effects of the interaction process enter A at a higher level of processing than B, and A has already a socioeconomic-political structure enabling it to absorb and convert and redirect such pressures for maximum beneficial impact.

Imagine now that n is high and p is low; the loan is said to be "on generous terms." The question is whether this generosity is not deceptive, *whether it would not have paid for A to give L for eternity, at no interest,* i.e., as a grant. Or even better, it might even have paid for A to persuade B to take on L with negative interest, i.e., to pay B for accepting the loan, because of all the intra-actor effects. The situation may be likened to a man who pays some people a certain sum on the condition that they use the money to pay him for an article on, say, imperialism. By having to produce, by having obligations to fulfill, the man is forced to create and thereby expand, and consequently forced to enrich himself.[9]

In short, we see vertical interaction as the major source of the inequality of this world, whether it takes the form of looting, of highly unequal exchange, or highly differential spin-off effects due to processing gaps. But we can also imagine a fourth phase of exploitation, where the modern King Midas becomes a victim of his own greed and turns his environment into muck rather than gold, by polluting it so strongly and so thoroughly that the negative spin-off effects from processing may outstrip all the positive effects. This may, in fact, place the less developed countries in a more favorable position: the lower the GNP, the lower the Gross National Pollution.

But this phase is still for the (near?) future. At present what we observe is an inequality between the world's nations of a magnitude that can only be explained in terms of the cumulative effect of *strong* structural phenomena over time, like the phenomena desribed here under the heading of imperialism. This is not to deny that other factors may also be important, even decisive, but no analysis can be valid without studying the problem of development in a context of vertical interaction.

If the first mechanism, the *vertical interaction relation,* is the major factor behind inequality, then the second mechanism, the *feudal interaction structure,* is the factor that maintains and reinforces this inequality by protecting it. There are four rules defining this particular interaction structure:[10]

1. interaction between Center and Periphery is *vertical*
2. interaction between Periphery and Periphery is *missing*
3. multilateral interaction involving all three is *missing*
4. interaction with the outside world is *monopolized* by the Center, with two implications:

a. Periphery interaction with other Center nations is *missing*
b. Center as well as Periphery interaction with Periphery nations belonging to other Center nations is *missing*.

This relation can be depicted as in Fig. 18.2. As indicated in the figure, the number of Periphery nations attached to any given Center nation can, of course, vary. In this figure we have also depicted the rule "if you stay off my satellites, I will stay off yours."

Some important *economic* consequences of this structure should be spelled out. First and most obvious is the *concentration on trade partners*. A Periphery nation should, as a result of these two mechanisms, have most of its trade with "its" Center nation. In other words, empirically we would expect high levels of *import concentration* as well as *export concentration* in the Periphery, as opposed to the Center, which is more free to extend its trade relations in almost any direction—except in the pure case, with the Periphery of other Center nations.

Second, and not so obvious, is the *commodity concentration:* the tendency for Periphery nations to have only one or very few primary products to export. This would be a trivial matter if it could be explained entirely in terms of geography, if, for example, oil countries were systematically poor as to ore, ore countries poor as to bananas and coffee, etc. But this can hardly be assumed to be the general case: nature does not distribute its riches that way. There is a historical rather than a geographical explanation to this. A territory may have been exploited for the raw materials most easily available and/or most needed in the Center, and this, in turn, leads to a certain social structure, to communication lines to the deposits, to trade structures, to the emergence of certain center groups (often based on

FIGURE 18.2   A Feudal Center-Periphery Structure

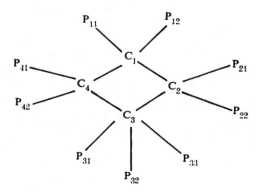

ownership of that particular raw material), and so on. To start exploiting a new kind of raw material in the same territory might upset carefully designed local balances; hence, it might be easier to have a fresh start for that new raw material in virgin territory with no bridgehead already prepared for imperialist exploits. In order to substantiate this hypothesis we would have to demonstrate that there are particularly underutilized and systematically underexplored deposits precisely in countries where one type of raw material has already been exploited.

The combined effect of these two consequences is a *dependency* of the Periphery on the Center. Since the Periphery usually has a much smaller GNP, the trade between them is a much higher percentage of the GNP for the Periphery, and with both partner and commodity concentration, the Periphery becomes particularly vulnerable to fluctuations in demands and prices. At the same time the center in the Periphery depends on the Center for its supply of consumer goods. Import substitution industries will usually lead to consumer goods that look homespun and unchic, particularly if there is planned obsolescence in the production of these goods in the Center, plus a demand for equality between the two centers maintained by demonstration effects and frequent visits to the Center.[11]

However, the most important consequence is political and has to do with the systematic utilization of feudal interaction structures as a way of protecting the Center against the Periphery. The feudal interaction structure is in social science language nothing but an expression of the old political maxim *divide et impera,* "divide and rule," as a strategy used systematically by the Center relative to the Periphery nations. How could—for example—a small foggy island in the North Sea rule over one quarter of the world? By isolating the Periphery parts from each other, by having them geographically at sufficient distance from each other to impede any real alliance formation, by having separate deals with them so as to tie them to the Center in particularistic ways, by reducing multilateralism to a minimum with all kinds of graded membership, *and* by having the mother country assume the role of window to the world.

However, this point can be much more clearly seen if we combine the two mechanisms and extend what has been said so far for relations between Center and Periphery *nations* to relations between center and periphery *groups* within nations. Under an imperialist structure the two mechanisms are used not only between nations but also within nations, but less so in the Center nation than in the Periphery nation. In other words, there is vertical division of labor within as well as between nations. And these two levels of organization are intimately linked to each other (as A. G. Frank always has emphasized) in the sense that the center in the Periphery interaction structure is also that group with which the Center nation has its harmony of interest, the group used as a bridgehead.

Thus, the combined operation of the two mechanisms at the two levels builds into the structure a subtle grid of protection measures against the major potential source of "trouble," the periphery in the Periphery. To summarize the major items in this grid:

1. the general impoverishment of pP brought about by vertical division of labor within the Periphery nation, and particularly by the high level of inequality (e.g., differential access to means of communication) and disharmony of interest in the Periphery nation;
2. the way in which interaction, mobilization, and organization of pP are impeded by the feudal structure *within* Periphery nations;
3. the general impoverishment of the Periphery nation brought about by vertical division of labor, particularly in terms of means of destruction and communication;
4. the way in which interaction, mobilization, and organization of the Periphery nations are impeded by the feudal interaction structure *between* nations
   a. making it difficult to interact with other Periphery nations "belonging" to the same Center nations,
   b. making it even more difficult to interact with Periphery nations "belonging" to other Center nations;
5. the way in which it is a fortiori difficult for the peripheries in Periphery nations to interact, mobilize, and organize
   a. intranationally because of 1 and 2,
   b. internationally because of 3 and 4,
   c. in addition: because the center in the Periphery has the monopoly on international interaction in all directions and cannot be counted on to interact in the interest of its own periphery;
6. the way in which pP cannot appeal to pC or cC either because of the disharmony of interest.

Obviously, the more perfectly the mechanisms of imperialism within and between nations are put to work, the less overt machinery of oppression is needed and the smaller can the center groups be, relative to the total population involved. *Only imperfect, amateurish imperialism needs weapons; professional imperialism is based on structural rather than direct violence.*

The Types of Imperialism

We shall now make this more concrete by distinguishing between five types of imperialism depending on the *type* of exchange between Center and Periphery nations:

1. economic
2. political
3. military
4. communication
5. cultural

The order of presentation is rather random: we have no theory that one is more basic than the others, or precedes the others. Rather, this is like a pentagon or a Soviet Star:[12] imperialism can start from any corner. They should all be examined regarding the extent to which they generate interaction patterns that utilize the two *mechanisms* of imperialism so as to fulfill the three *criteria* of imperialism, or at least the first of them.

The most basic of the two mechanisms is *vertical* interaction, which in its modern form is conceived of as interaction across a gap in processing level. In other words, what is exchanged between the two nations is not only not the same things (which would have been stupid) but things of a quite different kind, the difference being in terms of where the most complex and stimulating operations take place. One tentative list, expanding what has been said about economic interaction, might look like Table 18.4. The order of presentation parallels that of Table 18.3, but in that table cultural imperialism was spelled out in more detail as spin-off effects from economic imperialism.

The vertical nature of this type of *economic* interaction has been spelled out in detail above since we have used that type of imperialism to exemplify definition and mechanisms. Let us look more at the other types of vertical interaction.

The *political* one is clear: the concept of a "mother" country, the Center nation, is also an indication of how the decisionmaking center is dislocated, away from the nation itself and towards the Center nation. These decisions

TABLE 18.4   The Five Types of Imperialism

Type	Economic	Political	Military	Communication	Cultural
Center nation provides	processing, means of production	decisions models	protection means of destruction	news, means of communication	teaching, means of creation – autonomy
Periphery nation provides	raw materials, markets	obedience, imitators	discipline, traditional hardware	events, passengers, goods	learning, validation – dependence

may then affect economic, military, communication, and cultural patterns. Important here is the division of labor involved: some nations produce decisions, others supply obedience. The decisions may be made upon application, as in "bilateral technical assistance," or in consultation — or they may simply emerge by virtue of the model-imitator distinction. Nothing serves that distinction quite so well as unilinear concepts of "development" and "modernization," according to which Center nations possess some superior kind of structure for others to imitate (as long as the Center's central position is not seriously challenged), and which give a special aura of legitimacy to any idea emanating from the Center. Thus, structures and decisions developed in the "motherland of liberalism" or in the "fatherland of socialism" serve as models by virtue of their place of origin, not by virtue of their substance.

The *military* implications or parallels are also rather obvious. It cannot be emphasized enough that the economic division of labor is also one which ensures that the Center nations economically speaking also become the Center nations in a military sense: only they have the industrial capacity to develop the technological hardware — and also are often the only ones with the social structure compatible with a modern army. He who produces tractors can easily produce tanks, but he who delivers oil cannot defend himself by throwing it in the face of the aggressors. He has to depend on the tank producer, either for protection or for acquisition (on terms dictated by the Center). And just as there is a division of labor with the Center nation producing manufactured goods on the basis of raw materials extracted in the Periphery nation, there is also a division of labor with the *Center nations processing the obedience provided by the Periphery nations into decisions that can be implemented.* Moreover, there is also a division of labor with the Center providing the protection (and often also the officers or at least the instructors in "counterinsurgency") and the Periphery the discipline and the soldiers needed — not to mention the apprentices of "military advisors" from the Center.

As to the fourth type, *communication* imperialism, the emphasis in the analysis is usually turned towards the second mechanism of imperialism: the feudal interaction structure. That this largely holds for most world communication and transportation patterns has been amply demonstrated.[13] But perhaps more important is the vertical nature of the division of labor in the field of communication/transportation. It is trivial that a high level of industrial capacity is necessary to develop the latest in transportation and communication technology. The preceding generation of *means of communication/transportation* can always be sold, sometimes secondhand, to the Periphery as part of the general vertical trade/aid structure, alongside the *means of production* (economic sector), the *means of destruc-*

tion (military sector), and the *means of creation* (cultural sector). The Center's planes and ships are faster, more direct, look more reliable, and attract more passengers and goods. And when the Periphery finally catches up, the Center will for a long time have dominated the field of communication satellites.

One special version of this principle is a combination of cultural and communication exchange: *news communication*. We all know that the major agencies are in the hands of the Center countries, relying on Center-dominated, feudal networks of communication.[14] What is not so well analyzed is how Center news takes up a much larger proportion of Periphery news media than vice versa, just as trade with the Center is a larger proportion of Periphery total trade than vice versa. In other words, the pattern of partner concentration as something found more in the Periphery than in the Center is very pronounced. The Periphery nations do not write or read much about each other, especially not across bloc borders, and they read more about "their" Center than about other Centers — because the press is written and read by the center in the Periphery, who want to know more about that most "relevant" part of the world — for them.

Another aspect of vertical division of labor in the news business should also be pointed out. Just as the Periphery produces raw material that the Center turns into processed goods, *the Periphery also produces events that the Center turns into news.*[15] This is done by training journalists to see events with Center eyes, and by setting up a chain of communication that filters and processes events so that they fit the general pattern.

The latter concept brings us straight into *cultural* imperialism, a subtype of which is scientific imperialism. The division of labor between teachers and learners is clear: it is not the division of labor as such (found in most situations of transmission of knowledge) that constitutes imperialism, but the location of the teachers, and of the learners, in a broader setting. If the Center always provides the teachers and the definition of that worthy of being taught (from the gospels of Christianity to the gospels of technology), and the Periphery always provides the learners, then there is a pattern which smacks of imperialism. The satellite nation in the Periphery will also know that nothing flatters the Center quite so much as being encouraged to teach, and being seen as a model, and that the Periphery can get much in return from a humble, culture-seeking strategy (just as it will get little but aggression if it starts teaching the Center anything — like Czechoslovakia, who started lecturing the Soviet Union on socialism). For in accepting cultural transmission the Periphery also, implicitly, validates for the Center the culture developed in the center, whether that center is intra- or international. This serves to reinforce the Center as a center, for it will then continue to develop culture along with transmitting it, thus creating lasting demand for the latest innovations. Theories, like cars and fashions, have their life cycle, and whether the obsolescence is planned or not there will always be a time lag in a structure with a pronounced difference between center and periphery. Thus, the tram workers in Rio de Janeiro may carry banners supporting Auguste Comte one hundred years after the center of the Center forgot who he was.

In science we find a particular version of vertical division of labor, very similar to economic division of labor: the pattern of scientific teams from the Center who go to Periphery nations to collect data (raw material) in the form of deposits, sediments, flora, fauna, archeological findings, attitudes, behavioral patterns, and so on for data processing, data analysis, and theory formation (processing, in general) in the Center universities (factories), so as to be able to send the finished product, a journal or a book (manufactured goods), back for consumption in the center of the Periphery — after first having created a demand for it through demonstration effect, training in the Center country, and some degree of low-level participation in the data collection team.[16] This parallel is not a joke, it is a *structure*. If in addition the precise nature of the research is to provide the Center with information that can be used economically, politically, or militarily to maintain an imperialist structure, the cultural imperialism becomes even more clear. And if to this we add the *brain drain* (and body drain) whereby "raw" brains (students) and "raw" bodies (unskilled workers) are moved from the Periphery to the Center and "processed" (trained) with ample benefits to the Center, the picture becomes complete.

The Phases of Imperialism

We have mentioned repeatedly that imperialism is *one* way in which one nation may dominate another. Moreover, it is a way that provides a relatively stable pattern: the nations are linked to each other in a pattern that may last for some time because of the many stabilizing factors built into it through the mechanism of a feudal interaction structure.

The basic idea is that the center in the Center establishes a bridgehead in the Periphery nation, and more particularly, in the center of the Periphery nation. Obviously, this bridgehead does not come about just like that: there is a phase preceding it. The precise nature of that preceding phase can best be seen by distinguishing between three phases of imperialism in history, depending on what type of concrete method the center in the Center has used to establish the harmony of interest between itself and the center in the Periphery. This is enumerated in Table 18.5.

From the table we see that in all three cases, the Center nation has a hold

TABLE 18.5   Three Phases of Imperialism in History

Phase	Period	Form	Term
I	Past	*Occupation*, cP physically consists of cC people who engage in *occupation*	Colonialism
II	Present	*Organization*, cC interacts with cP via the medium of international *organizations*	Neo-colonialism
III	Future	*Communication*, cC interacts with cP via international communication	Neo-neo-colonial-ism

over the center of the Periphery nation. But the precise nature of this grip differs and should be seen relative to the means of transportation and communication. No analysis of imperialism can be made without a reference to these means that perhaps are as basic as the means of production in producing social dynamics.

Throughout the overwhelming part of human history, transportation (of human beings, of goods) did not proceed at a higher speed than that provided by pony expresses and quick sailing ships; and communication (of signals, of meaning) not at higher speed than that provided by fires and smoke signals which could be spotted from one hilltop to another. Precise control over another nation would have to be exercised by physically transplanting one's own center and grafting onto the top of the foreign body—in other words, colonialism in all its forms, best known in connection with "white settlers." According to this vision, colonialism was not a discovery of the Europeans subsequent to the Great Discoveries: it could just as well be used to describe great parts of the Roman Empire that through textbooks and traditions of history writing so successfully has dominated our image of racial and ethnical identity and national pride.[17]

Obviously, the quicker the means of transportation could become, the less necessary would this pattern of permanent settlement be. The break in the historical pattern came when the steam engine was not only put into the factory to provide new *means of production* (leading to conditions that prompted Marx to write *Das Kapital*) but also into a vessel (Fulton) and a locomotive (Stephenson): in other words, *means of transportation* (the book about that is not yet written). This gave Europeans a decisive edge over peoples in other regions, and colonialism became more firmly entrenched. Control could be accurate and quick.

But decolonialization also came, partly due to the weakening of cC, partly due to the strengthening of cP that might not challenge what cC did, but want to do so itself. Neocolonialism came; and in this present phase of imperialism, control is not of the direct, concrete type found in the past. It is mediated through the means of transportation (and, of course, also communication) linking the two centers to each other. The control is less concrete: it is not physical presence, but a link; and this link takes the shape of international organizations. The international organization has a certain permanence, often with physical headquarters and a lasting general secretary in the mother country. But above all it is a medium in which influence can flow, with *both* centers joining as members and finding each other. Their harmony of interest can be translated into complete equality within the international organization, and vice-versa. Their identity is defined relative to the organization, not to race, ethnicity, or nationality. But with differential disharmony *within* nations, this actually becomes an instrument of disharmony *between* nations.

These organizations are well known for all five types of imperialism. For the economic type, the private or governmental multinational corporations (BINGOs) may serve;[18] for the political type, many of the international governmental organizations (IGOs); for the military type, the various systems of military alliances and treaties and organizations (MIGOs?);[19] for communication the shipping and air companies (CONGOs?), not to mention the international press agencies, offer ample illustration; and for cultural imperialism, some of the international nongovernmental organizations (INGOs) may serve as the conveyor mechanisms. But this is of course not to say that international organizations will necessarily serve such purposes. According to the theory developed here, this is an empirical question, depending on the degree of division of labor inside the organization and the extent to which it is feudally organized.

Next, the third phase. If we now proceed even further along the same line of decreasingly concrete (but increasingly effective?) ties between the two centers, we can envisage a phase where even the international organizations will not only go into disrepute, but dissolve. What will come in their place? *Instant communication,* whereby parties who want to communicate with each other set up ad hoc communication networks (telesatellites, etc.) that form and dissolve in rapid succession, changing scope and domain, highly adjustable to external circumstance, guided by enormous data banks and idea banks that permit participants to find their "opposite numbers" without having them frozen together in a more permanent institutional network that develops its own rigidities.[20]

In other words, we envisage a future where very many international organizations will be threatened in two ways. First, they will be exposed to increasing criticism as to their function as a tie between two centers, communicating and coordinating far above the masses in either country, which will in itself lead to a certain disintegration. Second, this does not mean that the centers, if they are free to do so, will cease to coordinate their action, only that they will do so by other means. Instead of going to ad hoc or annual conventions, or in other ways instructing a general secretary and his staff, they may simply pick up their videophone and have a long distance conference organized, where the small group of participants can all see and talk to each other — not like in a conference, but in the more important adjoining lobbies, in the coffee houses, in private quarters — or wherever they prefer to carry out communication and coordination.[21]

To penetrate more deeply into the role of international organization as an instrument of imperialistic dominance, let us now distinguish between five phases in the development of an international organization. As example we take one economic organization, General Motors Corporation (GMC), and one political organization, the International Communist Movement (ICM) — at present not organized formally as an international. The stages are indicated in Table 18.6. Needless to say, these two are taken as *illustrations* of economic and political imperialism — this is not a *study* of GMC and ICM respectively.

In the beginning, the organization exists only within national boundaries. Then comes a second phase when it sends representatives, at that stage usually called "agents," abroad. This is a critical stage: it is a question of gaining a foothold in another nation, and usually subversive, from below. If the other nation is completely new to this economic or political pattern, the "agents" often have to come from the "mother country" or the "fatherland" upon the invitation of dissatisfied individuals who find their own mobility within the system blocked *and* who think that the present system does not satisfy the needs of the population. But this phase is not imperialist, for the center in the mother country has not established any bridgehead in the *center* of the offspring country — yet.

TABLE 18.6   Stages in the Development of an International Organization

	General Motors Corporation (GMC)	International Communist Movement (ICM)
Phase 1: National only	in one country only ('mother country')	in one country only ('fatherland')
Phase 2: National goes abroad	*subsidiary*, or branch office, established by 'agents'	*subversive* organization, established by 'agents'
Phase 3: Multi-national, asymmetric	other national companies started, with 'mother country' company dominating	other national parties established, with 'fatherland' party dominating
Phase 4: Multi-national, symmetric	total network becomes symmetric	total network becomes symmetric
Phase 5: Global, or transnational organization	national identities dissolve	national dissolve

The agents may be highly instrumental of social change. They may set into motion patterns in economic life that may reduce significantly the power of feudal landlords and introduce capitalist patterns of production; or they may set into motion patterns in political life that may reduce equally significantly the power of industrialists and introduce socialist patterns of production. Both activities are subversive of the social order, but not imperialist, and are, consequently, examples of other ways in which one nation may exercise influence over another.[22]

But in phase 3 this development has gone a significant step further. The agents have now been successful, so to speak: national companies/parties have been established. Elites have emerged in the Periphery nations, strongly identified with and well harmonizing with the Center elites. The whole setting is highly asymmetric; what we have identified as mechanisms and types of imperialism are now discernible.

There is *division of labor:* the "daughter" company in the Periphery nation is particularly concerned with making raw materials available and with securing markets for the mother company in the Center nation. If it enters into processing, then it is often with a technology already bypassed by "development" in the Center country, or only leading to semifinished products. Correspondingly, the company/party in the mother country makes more decisions and the parties in the Periphery provide obedience and secure markets for the implementation of orders. Thus, in both cases the implicit assumption is always that the top leadership of the international organization shall be the top leadership of the company/party in the Center country. Headquarters are located there and not elsewhere; this location is not but rotation or random choice.[23]

Further, the *general interaction structure is clearly feudal:* there is interaction along the spokes, from the Periphery to the Center hub; but not along the rim, from one Periphery nation to another. There may be multilateral meetings, but they are usually very heavily dominated by the Center, which takes it for granted that it will be in the interest of the Periphery to emulate the Center. And this then spans across all five types of interaction, one way or the other—in ways that are usually fairly obvious.

We have pointed to what seem to be basic similarities between the two international organizations (GMC and ICM). Precisely because they are similar, they can do much to impede each other's activities. This similarity is not strange: they both reflect the state of affairs in a world that consists of (1) nation-states, of (2) highly unequal power and level of development along various axes, and is (3) too small for many nation-states to stay within their bonds—so they spill over with their gospels, and patterns are established that are imperialist in nature. *For phase 3 is clearly the imperialist phase;* and because so many international organizations are in this third phase, they at present stand out as vehicles of asymmetric forms of center-center cooperation.[24]

This is the present state of most international organizations. Most are extensions of patterns developed first in one nation, and on assumptions that may have been valid in that country. They are usually the implementation in our days of the old missionary command (Matthew 28:18-20): "Go ye all forth and make all peoples my disciples." This applies not only to economic and political organizations, but to the other three types as well. Typical examples are the ways in which cultural patterns are disseminated. In its most clear form, they are even handled by official or semiofficial institutions more or less attached to the diplomatic network (such as USIS, and the various cultural activities of the Soviet and Chinese embassies in many countries; and to a lesser extent, the British Council and Alliance Française). But international organizations are also used for this purpose by Center nations who firmly believe that their patterns are good for everybody else because they are good for themselves.

However, the Periphery does not necessarily rest content with this state of affairs. There will be a dynamism leading to changes towards phase 4, so far only brought about in very few organizations. It will probably have its roots in the division of labor, and the stamp as second-class members given to the Periphery in general, and to heads of Periphery companies and parties in particular. Why should there be any written or unwritten law that GMC and ICM heads are located in the United States and the Soviet Union, respectively?[25] Why not break up the division of labor completely, distribute the research contracts and the strategic planning evenly, why not rotate the headquarters, why not build up interaction along the rim and build down the interaction along the spokes so that the hub slowly fades out and the resulting organization is truly symmetric? This is where the Norwegian GMC president and the Rumanian ICM general secretary have, in a sense, common interests — and we predict that this movement will soon start in all major international organizations following some of the very useful models set by the UN and her specialized agencies. It should be noted, however, that it is not too difficult to obtain equality in an international organization where only the elites participate, since they already to a large extent harmonize with each other.

But this is not the final stage of development; nothing is. The multinational, symmetric form will always be artificial for at least two reasons: the nations are not symmetric in and by themselves — some contribute more than others — and they form artificial pockets relative to many of the concerns of the organizations. Any multinational organization, however symmetric, is a way of reinforcing and perpetuating the nation-state. If nation-states are fading out in significance, much like municipalities in many parts of the world, multinational organizations will also fade out because they are built over a pattern that is becoming less and less salient. What will come in its place? The answer will probably be what has here been called a hypothetical phase 5—*the global* or *world organization*, but we shall not try to spell this out here.

From Spin-off to Spill-over: Convertibility of Imperialism

We have now presented a theory of imperialism based on *three* criteria, *two* mechanisms, *five* types, and *three* phases. In the presentation, as is usually done in any presentation of imperialism, economic imperialism was used for the purpose of illustration. However, we tried to carry the analysis further: for economic imperialism, exploitation was not only defined in terms of unequal exchange because A gives less to B than he gets from B, but also in terms of differential intra-actor or spin-off effects. Moreover, it is quite clear from Tables 18.3 and 18.4 that these spin-off effects are located in other areas in which imperialism can also be defined. Vertical economic interaction has political spin-offs, military spin-offs, communication spin-offs, and cultural spin-offs; and vice versa, as we shall indicate.

For that reason we shall now make a distinction between *spin-off* effects and *spill-over* effects. When a nation exchanges tractors for oil it develops a tractor-producing capacity. One possible spin-off effect is a tank-producing capacity, and this becomes a spill-over effect the moment that capacity is converted into military imperialism, for instance in the form of *Tank-Kommunismus* or *Tank-Kapitalismus*. Of course, this does not become military imperialism unless exercised in cooperation with the ruling elite in the Periphery nation. If it is exercised against that elite, it is a simple *invasion*—as distinct from an *intervention* that is the product of cC-cP cooperation.

A glance at Tables 18.3 and 18.4 indicates that the road from spin-off to spill-over is a short one, provided that there are cooperating or even generalized elites available both in the Center and the Periphery nations. It is not necessary for the same person in Center and Periphery to be on top on both the economic, political, military, communication, and cultural organizations—that would be rather superhuman! Many would cover two or three such positions, few would command four or five. But if the five elites defined through these five types of exchange are *coordinated* into generalized upper classes based on a rich network of kinship, friendship, and association (not to mention effective cooperation), then the basis is laid for an extremely solid type of *generalized imperialism*. In the extreme case there would be rank concordance in both Center and Periphery, which means that there would not even be some little disequilibrium present in either case to give some leverage for a revolutionary movement. All groups would have learned, in fact been forced, to play generalized roles as dominant and dependent, respectively.

For this rank concordance to take place, gains made from one type of imperialism should be readily convertible into the other types. The analytical instrument here could be what we might call the *convertibility matrix,* given in Table 18.7.

The numbers in the first row correspond to the spin-off effects for vertical division of labor in economic transactions, as indicated in Table 18.3. A more complete theory of imperialism would now try to give corresponding spin-off effects, convertible into spill-over effects, for the other four types with regard to all five types. We shall certainly not engage fully in this taxonomic exercise but only pick one example from each row.

Thus, it is rather obvious how political imperialism can be converted into economic imperialism by dictating terms of trade, where the latter are not seen so much in terms of volume as trade composition.[26]

Correspondingly, military imperialism can easily be converted into communication imperialism by invoking the need for centralized command over communication and transportation facilities. It is no coincidence that the capital in so many Center countries is located inland and well protected, whereas the capital in most Periphery countries is a port, easily accessible from the Center country, and with a feudal interaction network inland facilitating the flow of raw materials to the capital port and a trickling of consumer goods in the other direction (most of it being absorbed in the capital port itself). Precise command of territory may be necessary to establish a communication network of this type, but once established, it is self-reinforcing.

Similarly, to take another example: communication imperialism may be converted into cultural imperialism by regulating the flow of information, not only in the form of news, but also in the form of cheaply available books, etc., from the Center country.

TABLE 18.7   Convertibility of Types of Imperialism

	Economic	Political	Military	Communication	Cultural
Economic	1	2	3	4	5–9
Political					
Military					
Communication					
Cultural					

Finally, cultural imperialism is convertible into economic imperialism in ways very commonly found today: by means of technical assistance processes. A technical assistance expert is not only a person from a rich country who goes to a poor country and stimulates a demand in the poor country for the products of the rich country.[27] He is also a man who goes to the poor country in order to establish a routine in the poor country, reserving for himself all the benefits of the challenges of this entrepreneurial activity. He *writes* the SOP (standard operating procedure); it is for his "counterpart" to *follow* the SOP. That this challenge is convertible into more knowledge (more culture) and eventually also into economic benefits upon the return of the technical assistance expert is hardly to be doubted in principle, but it is another question whether the Center country understands this and fully utilizes the resource.

Convertibility could now be studied at two levels: the extent to which the nation as such can use such spin-offs from one type and direct them towards consolidation of another type, and the extent to which an individual may do so. If an individual can, the result is some type of rank concordance; if the nation can, we might perhaps talk of imperialism concordance.

But the only point we want to make here is that the convertibility matrix seems to be complete. It is hard to imagine any cell in Table 18.7 that would be empty in the sense that there could be no spill-over effects, no possibility of conversion. If everything can be bought for money, obtained by political control, or ordered by military imposition, then that alone would take care of the first three horizontal rows. Correspondingly, most authors would talk about economic, political, and military imperialism, but we have added the other two since they seem also to be primordial. Perhaps the first three will build up more slowly along the lines established by division of labor in communication and cultural organizations, but it is very easy to imagine scenarios as well as concrete historical examples.

The completeness of the convertibility matrix, more than anything else, would lead us to reject the assumption of one type of imperialism as more basic than the others. It is the mutual reinforcement, the positive feedback between these types rather than any simple reductionist causal chain, that seems the dominant characteristic. If economic, political, and military imperialism seem so dominant today, this may be an artifact due to our training that emphasizes these factors rather than communication and cultural factors. Belief in a simple causal chain is dangerous because it is accompanied by the belief that imperialism can be dispensed with forever if the primary element in the chain is abolished, e.g., private capitalism. The more general definition of imperialism presented here directs our search towards the two mechanisms as well as the particular criteria of exploitation within and between nations.

In order to talk about imperialism, not only economic inequality but also political, military, communication, and cultural inequality should be distributed in an inegalitarian way, with the periphery at the disadvantage. Are they? We think yes. The not-so-blatantly-unequal access to acquisite power, to some *political* power through voting, to some control over the *use of violence* (through political power, through civilian control of the military, and through equality of opportunity as to access to ranking positions in the military), to *communication* (usually via access to acquisitive power, but also via denser, less feudal communication networks linking periphery outposts more directly together in Center nations), and to *cultural* goods (through widespread literacy and equality in access to educational institutions) — all these are trademarks of what is referred to as a liberal democracy. And that form of sociopolitical life is found in the Center rather than the Periphery of the world.

This leads to an important point in the theory of imperialism. *Instead of seeing democracy as a consequence or a condition for economic development within certain nations, it can (also) be seen as the condition for exercising effective control over Periphery nations.* Precisely because the Center is more egalitarian and democratic than the Periphery, there will be more people in the Center who feel they have a stake in the present state of affairs, since the fruits of imperialist structures are more equally shared on the top than on the bottom. And this will make it even less likely that the periphery in the Center will really join with the periphery in the Periphery against the two centers. Rather, like Dutch workers they will oppose the independence of Indonesia, and like U.S. workers they will tend to become hardhats over the Indochina issue.

It is now relatively clear what would be the perfect type of imperialism. In perfect imperialism, regardless of phase, we would assume all three criteria, both mechanisms, and all five types to be completely operative. This would mean complete harmony between the centers, with the elites in the Periphery nations almost undistinguishable from the elites in the Center nations where living conditions are concerned; much better distribution in the Center nations than in the Periphery nations; a perfectly vertical division of labor along all five types of exchange, and a perfectly feudal interaction network.

Where in the world, in space and/or in time, does one find this type of relations? The answer is perhaps not only in the colonial empires of the past, but also in the neocolonial empires of the present using international organizations as their medium. To what extent it is true is an empirical question, and all the factors mentioned above can be operationalized. In other words, what is often called "positivist" methodology can be brought to bear on problems of structuralist or even Marxist analyses. A crude and limited exercise in this direction will be given in the following section.

Suffice it here only to say that no system is perfect, and no system is a perfect copy of some ideal-type model. It may be that the neocolonial empire the United States had in Latin America in the 1950s and into the 1960s was a relatively perfect case,[29] and that this also applies to the relation between the EEC countries and the Associated States.[30] But it does not apply to the United States in Western Europe, nor to the Soviet Union in Eastern Europe, to the Soviet Union in the Arab world, or to Japan in Southeast Asia. This is not to deny that the United States in Western Europe and the Soviet Union in Eastern Europe are at the summit of military organizations that seem to satisfy all conditions, although the parallel is not entirely complete. But both of the superpowers are peripheral to the communication networks, their cultures are largely rejected in Western and Eastern Europe respectively, and where economic penetration is concerned there is a vertical division of labor in favor of the United States relative to Western Europe, but in favor of Eastern Europe (in general) relative to the Soviet Union — with the Soviet Union as a provider of raw materials for, for instance, high level processing in the DDR. But it may then be argued that what the Soviet Union loses in economic ascendancy it compensates for in a political organization with strong feudal components.[31]

Similar arguments may be advanced in connection with the Soviet Union in the Arab world, and with Japan in Southeast Asia. Where the latter is concerned there is no doubt as to the economic imperialism, but there is neither political, military, communication, nor cultural ascendancy.[32]

And this, then, leads to the final conclusion in this section. Imperialism is a question of degree, and if it is perfect it is a perfect instrument of structural violence. When it is less than perfect something must be substituted for what is lost in structural violence: direct violence, or at least the threat of direct violence. This is where the military type of imperialism becomes so important, since it can be seen as a potential to be activated when the other types of imperialism, particularly the economic and political types, show important cracks in the structure. This does not, incidentally, necessarily mean that direct violence only has to be applied in Periphery nations; it may also be directed against the periphery in Center nations if there is a danger of their siding with the periphery in the Periphery. The structural conditions for this would be that criterion no. 2 in the definition does not hold, in other words that there is not less, but possibly even more, inequality in the Center than in the Periphery.[33]

Some Empirical Explorations

The theory developed above is too complex in its empirical implications to be tested in its entirety. But some data can at least be given for economic imperialism, not because we view this as the basic type of imperialism, but because it is the type for which data are most readily available.

Everybody knows that there is the gap in GNP per capita, that there are rich nations and poor nations. From one point of view this gap poses a problem, the answer to which is in terms of *redistribution*. But from the structuralist point of view taken here the gap poses a problem that can only be answered in terms of *structural change*. It may be that redistribution can contribute to this change; but it may also be that it only serves to postpone the solution because symptoms rather than the disease itself is cured.

The claim, therefore, is that when some nations are rich and some nations are poor, when some nations are developed and some nations are underdeveloped, this is intimately related to the structure within and between nations. To explore this in line with the theory developed above we shall make use of the following seven variables shown in Table 18.8.[34]

The first two variables place the nation in the international ranking system using two types of development variables that are, of course, highly but not completely correlated. The next two variables, the Gini indices, say something about the internal structure of the nation, whereas the last three variables say something about the structure of the relations between them. Of these three, the first one relates to the first mechanism of imperialism and the other two to the second mechanism of imperialism. More precisely, the trade composition index is based on the following formula:[35]

Trade composition index

$$\frac{(a + d) - (b + c)}{(a + d) + (b + c)}$$

where:
a is value of raw materials imported
b is value of raw materials exported
c is value of processed goods imported
d is value of processed goods exported

There is no doubt that this index is a crude measure, among other reasons because the variable *degree of processing,* so crucial to the whole analysis, has here been dichotomized in "raw materials" vs. "processed goods" neglecting completely the problem of degree, *and* because the basis for dichotomization is the division made use of in UN trade statistics. However, despite its shortcomings it serves to sort nations apart. The highest ranking nation on this variable is Japan with an import consisting almost entirely of raw materials and an export consisting almost entirely of processed goods. Correspondingly, at the bottom according to this index

TABLE 18.8   Seven Structural Variables

Development variables:	1.	GNP/cap
	2.	Percentage employed in non-primary sectors
Inequality variables:	3.	Gini index, income distribution
	4.	Gini index, land distribution
Vertical trade variable:	5.	Trade composition index
Feudal trade variables:	6.	Partner concentration index
	7.	Commodity concentration index

are the nations that export raw materials and import processed goods only; but the relative position of several countries in between may certainly be disputed.

As to the last two variables, they are simply the ratios between the proportion of the export going to the *one* most important partner, or consisting of the *three* most important commodities relative to the total export, respectively.[36]

According to our general theory we should now expect some countries to be developed and to be on top of the vertical trade index but low in terms of inequality and position on the feudal trade index — whereas other countries would be undeveloped and low on the vertical trade index but on the other hand high in terms of inequality and position on the feudal trade index. The correlation structure should be something like Figure 18.3 where the solid lines indicate positive relations and the broken lines negative relations, and the numbers in parentheses are the numbers of indicators for each dimension.

Thus, of the twenty-one bivariate correlations we predict six positive and twelve negative correlations. In addition there are the three correlations between indicators of the same dimension: we expect them to be positive, but not too positive since that would reduce the usefulness for independent testing of the hypotheses.

Because of the grave doubts as to the validity and reliability of all variables we decided to dichotomize them, either at the point where there is a "natural" cut (a large interval between one country and the next) or at the median cut. The correlation coefficient used was Yule's Q, and the results were as shown in Table 18.9. All correlations are in the expected direction, most of them rather substantial. There are only three low correlations, and two of them are between indicators of the same dimension. Hence we regard the hypothesis as very well confirmed.

Of course, this is only a test of a theory along the edges of that theory; it

FIGURE 18.3   The Correlation Pattern According to the Imperialism Hypothesis

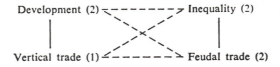

TABLE 18.9   A Test of the Hypothesis of Economic Imperialism (Yule's Q)

	1	2	3	4	5	6	7
1 GNP/cap		0.79	− 0.90	− 0.80	0.89	− 0.52	− 0.89
2 % non-primary			− 1.00	− 0.83	0.77	− 0.72	− 0.87
3 Gini income				0.20	− 0.83	0.80	0.86
4 Gini land					− 0.95	0.21	0.85
5 Trade comp.						− 0.69	− 0.97
6 Partner concentration							0.35
7 Commodity concentration							

does not in itself prove that the system is in fact working as described above. But if these findings had not come out so strongly as they do, we would have been forced to conclude that the imperialist model cannot possibly be a good model of the world system today. Hence, as a test of the hypotheses the findings provide positive confirmation, but as a test of a theory only the negative support that a theory would have to be rejected if the findings had been in the opposite direction.[37]

We should also add that the theory in itself is so rich in implications that it provides ample basis for empirical research, within liberal and Marxist schools of thought, and employing synchronic statistical methods as well as diachronic case studies. It would be sad if ideological and other types of conflicts between adherents of different schools should lead to any systematic neglect as to mobilizing general social science for a deeper understanding of how this system works.

Further Theoretical Explorations

Let us then make use of the results of the theoretical and empirical explorations to go somewhat more deeply into four problems.

Defining "Center" and "Periphery"

We are now in a better position to define our basic terms, "center" and "periphery" (loosely introduced previously), whether they refer to relations between or within nations.[38] Actually, implicit in what has been said above are three approaches when it comes to defining these terms:

1. in terms of *absolute properties* (e.g., development variables): center is high on rank dimensions, periphery is low
2. in terms of *interaction relation* (e.g., trade composition index): center enriches itself more than the periphery
3. in terms of *interaction structure* (e.g., partner and commodity concentration index): center is more centrally located in the interaction network than the periphery — the periphery being higher on the concentration indices.

Empirically it may not matter that much which of these three dimensions is used to define center and periphery, since Table 18.9 shows them highly correlated — at least today. According to one type of theory this is because no. 1 above is primordial, basic: the richer, more educated, stronger nation (individual) is able to place itself in the world structure (social structure) so that it can be on top of a vertical interaction relation and in the center of a feudal interaction structure. According to another type of theory, nos. 2 or 3 are basic: if an individual or nation is able to place itself on top of a vertical relation, and possibly, in addition, in the center of a feudal interaction structure, it will also be able to climb higher on the dimensions on which nations (individuals) climb — whatever they might be.

We find it difficult to be dogmatic about these two theories. Rather, they seem to complement each other. One nation (individual) may have gotten an edge over another in one way or another and been able to convert that into an advantageous interaction position, as the Europeans did after the Great Discoveries. Or — it may have come into an advantageous interaction position by some lucky circumstance, e.g., in a communication network — and been able to convert this into some absolute value for itself, and so on.

In general, we think there are reasons to say that the relative significance of the three *aspects* of the center-periphery distinction varies with time and space, with historical and geographical circumstances. For that reason we would prefer to view them precisely as three different *aspects* of that distinction. Thus, we define center vs. periphery as nations (individuals) that satisfy no. 1 *or* 2 *or* 3; "or" taken in the usual sense of and/or. This may lead to confusion, but since both theories above would lead to the same conclusion we do not worry so much about that. Rather, the definition should be accompanied with a warning to the analyst: he should always be sensitive to possible cases of divergence, that a nation (individual) may be in the center relative to one aspect and in the periphery relative to another, and so on. That this in itself would provide rich sources for theories about dynamism, about how a center position of one kind can be converted into a center position of the other kind, is obvious. And in that connection the second aspect, the relation itself, may perhaps be more basic, since it provides, through accumulation, a constant flow of resources towards the center. The advantage of this aspect is that it is so *concrete*. According to this aspect the sorting into center and periphery is not only an operation carried out by the analyst, it takes place, *in concreto,* in the interaction process itself. The two actors "sort" themselves away from each other by participating in vertical interaction, and become increasingly unequal in the process.[39]

Generalization to Three Nations and Three Classes

So far we have operated with a simple scheme involving two nations and two classes; time has now come to break out of that limitation. Here we shall only offer some remarks in that connection, not carry the analysis through in detail.

Thus, the introduction of a middle class between the center and the periphery would be entirely consistent with thinking in most social science schools. Whether the center is defined in terms of economic, political, military, communication, or cultural interaction, a strict dichotomy between center and periphery will often be too crude. The alternative to a dichotomy may be a continuum, but on the way towards that type of thinking a trichotomy may also be useful. Strict social dichotomies are usually difficult to obtain unless hedged around by means of highly visible and consensual racial, ethnic, or geographical distinctions. A country composed of three races may therefore provide a stable three-class structure; if there is only one race, the continuous model may be more useful.

However, it is difficult to see that this should significantly affect our theory. Whether there are two or three classes or a continuum from extreme center to extreme periphery does not invalidate descriptions of the nation in terms of averages (such as GNP/capita) and dispersions (such as Gini indices). Nor will it invalidate the comparisons between the nations in such terms. In fact, there is nothing in this theory that presupposes a dichotomous class structure since the theory is not based on a dichotomy like owner vs. nonowner of means of production.

More interesting results can be obtained by interspersing a third nation between the Center and Periphery nations. Such a nation could, in fact, serve as a go-between. Concretely, it would exchange semiprocessed goods with highly processed goods upwards and semiprocessed goods with raw materials downwards. It would simply be located in between Center and Periphery where the degree of processing of its export products is concerned. Moreover, such go-between nations would serve as an intermediate layer between the extreme Center and the extreme Periphery in a feudal interaction structure. And needless to say, the intranational centers of all three nations would be tied together in the same international network, establishing firm ties of harmony of interest between them.

In another version of the same conception the go-between nation would be one cycle behind the Center as to technology but one cycle ahead of the Periphery;[40] in line with its position as to degree of processing. This would also apply to the means of destruction and the means of communication.

If the United States is seen as *the* Center nation in the world (with Japan as an extremely dangerous competitor precisely in terms of degree of processing), then several such chains of nations suggest themselves, as shown in Table 18.10.

Just as for the generalization to three classes, this could also be generalized to a continuous chain which would then serve to make for considerable distance between the extreme Center and the extreme Periphery.

Generalizations to More than One Empire

So far all our thinking has been within one empire, except for passing references to countries outside the empire that the Periphery is prevented from interacting with. But the world consists of more than one empire, and any realistic theory should see an empire in its context — especially since

TABLE 18.10 Some Hypotheses about Go-Between Relations

Center	Go-Between	Periphery
USA	Western Europe	Eastern Europe
USA	Canada	Anglo-America (Trinidad, etc.)
USA	Mexico Argentina Brazil	Central America
USA	Japan	Southeast Asia
Japan	South Korea Taiwan	Southeast Asia (and North America)
Western Europe	Eastern Europe	Soviet Union

direct violence is to relations between empires what structural violence is within empires.

Clearly, relations between empires are above all relations between the centers of the Centers; these relations can be negative, neutral, or positive. Two capitalistic empires may be in competition, but they may also subdivide the world between them into spheres of interest so perfectly that the relations become more neutral. In this first phase one empire may fight to protect itself in the competition with another capitalist empire, but in a second phase they may join forces and more or less merge to protect not this or that particular capitalist empire, but the system of capitalism as such. And we could also easily imagine a third phase where noncapitalist empires join with capitalist empires in the pattern of "united imperialism," for the protection of imperialism as such.

All this is extremely important from the viewpoint of the Periphery nations. A world with more empires, which above all means a world with more Center nations, is at least potentially a world with more possibilities. To explore this in more detail, let us assume that we have Center and Periphery nations, vertically related to each other. For each type of nation there are three cases: one nation alone, two nations either very low on interaction or hostile to each other, and two nations in so friendly cooperation as to constitute one actor. The result is shown in Figure 18.4, which permits us to recognize many and politically very important situations (the arrows in Figure 18.4 stand for relations of vertical interaction).

Here, situations *a, b,* and *c* take place within one empire and lead to a situation with a certain element of defeudalization: horizontal interaction has been established between the two Periphery nations.

In situations *d, e,* and *f,* Periphery nations are able to interact with more than one Center nation, possibly even play one against the other because of their hostile relationship. In this situation the Periphery will have a vested interest in protracting the Center conflict, and may even join forces (model *f*) to make optimum gains from the conflict.

In situations *g, h,* and *i,* it is the Center side that cooperates, for instance by establishing a "consortium" whereby several rich nations join together to help one or more poor nations, singly or combined.[41]

Importantly, none of these strategies will lead to any changes in the vertical interaction *relation*, only to some changes in the feudal interaction *structure*. As such they attack only one aspect of imperialism, not the other, possibly more important aspect. And if we look more closely at model *i*, this is nothing but model *a* writ large, as when EEC rather than France alone stands in a relationship of vertical interaction with eighteen Associated States rather than with one of them alone. It is difficult to see that im-

FIGURE 18.4 Possible Relations in a Multiempire World

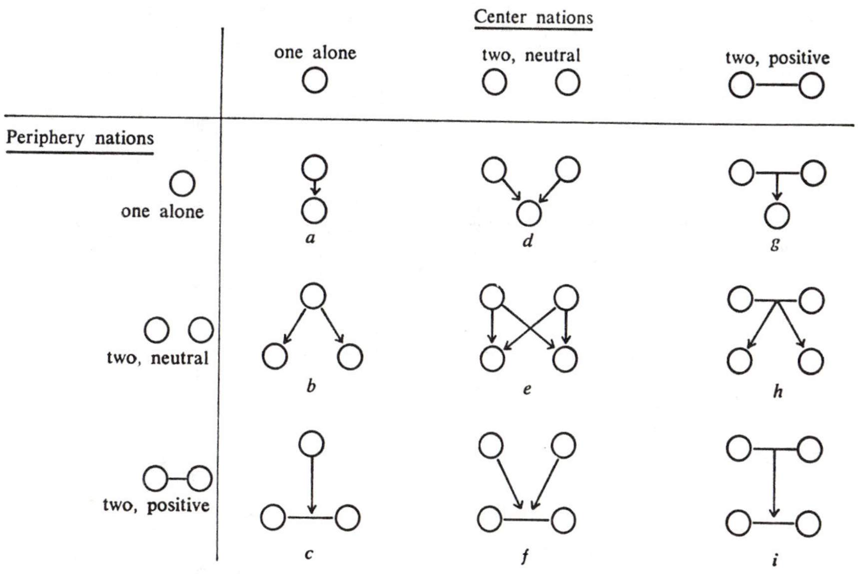

perialistic relationships become less imperialistic by being established between super-Center and a super-Periphery rather than between the original Center and Periphery nations (we should add that h rather than i is a more correct model of the relationship between EEC and the Associated States).

This factor notwithstanding, there is no reason to deny that a multi-empire world not only creates more bargaining possibilities, but also is a more realistic model of the world in which mankind lives—at present.

Generalization to Nonterritorial Actors

We have defined nonterritorial actors above, in Table 18.5, phases 3, 4, and 5—where phases 3 and 4 refer to multinational or international nonterritorial actors and phase 5 to transnational actors. These are collectivities, they consist of human beings, they have more often than not a vertical division of labor within, and there is little reason why they should not also often have vertical division of labor between and be chained together in imperialistic relationships. Thus, there may be a division of labor between governmental and nongovernmental international organizations, with the more far-reaching decisions taken by the former and some of the implementations carried out by the latter. For this system to function well, the governmental organizations will have to harmonize the policymaking centers of the nongovernmental organizations with themselves, and one concrete way of doing this would be to have a member on the council or executive committee. This article is not the occasion to spell this point out in any detail or with empirical examples, but we should point out that imperialism as a structure is not at all tied to territorial actors alone.[42]

Conclusion: Some Strategic Implications

From a general scheme, we cannot arrive at more than general policy implications that can serve as guidelines, as strategies. More concreteness is needed to arrive at the first tactical steps. But theory developed in peace research should lead to such guidelines; if it merely reflects what is empirical, not what is potential, then it is not good theory.

Our point of departure is once more that the world is divided into have's and have not's, in have and have-not nations. To decrease the gap,[43] one aspect of the fight against structural violence, redistribution by taking from the have's and giving to the have not's, is not enough: the structure has to be changed. The imperialist structure has international as well as intranational aspects and will consequently have to be changed at both levels.

However, let us start with the international changes needed, for a point of departure. Following closely the analysis of the mechanisms of imperialism in order to establish antimechanisms, we get Table 18.11.

TABLE 18.11   Strategies for Structural Change
of the International Dominance System

I. HORIZONTALIZATION

1. *Horizontalization Center-Periphery*

a. *exchange on more equal terms,* either by reducing the division of labor, or by more horizontal division of labor that would equalize spin-off effects. Concretely this would mean that Center nations would have to start importing processed products from Periphery nations, and engage in intra- rather than inter-sector trade, and even intra- rather than inter-commodity trade.

b. *reduction of vertical interaction,* down to total de-coupling in case exchange on more equal terms is unacceptable or does not work.

c. *self-reliance,*[44] partly in order to develop import substitutes, and partly in order for Periphery nations to define themselves what products they need rather than adapting the preference scales developed in the Center.

II. DEFEUDALIZATION

a. *exchange on equal terms,* intra- rather than inter-sector, but obviously at a lower level where degree of processing is concerned than under 1.a. above. It may imply exchanges of raw materials, or exchanges of semi-processed goods. Obviously, which Periphery country should interact horizontally with which other Periphery countries would depend on the nature of the economic exchange and the concrete geo-political situation.

b. *development of viable organization of Periphery countries for international class conflict.* Such organizations seem to depend for their viability not only on commitment to an ideology (rejection of past and present as well as visions for the future), but also seem to function better if they are built around an exchange relation of the type indicated in 2.a. The exact purpose of the organization would be to force Center nations to change their policies in the direction of 1.a., and also to command a better redistribution of capital and technology from the Center. This would also be the organization that could organize a strike on the delivery of raw materials in case Center nations do not conform with these types of structural changes, as an analogy to the denial of human manpower typical of intra-national strikes.

3. *Multilateralization Center-Periphery*

a. *multinational, symmetric organization should be established wherever possible,* the system of international organizations should be taken out of phase 3 and moved towards phase 4. These organizations would serve as concrete instruments for horizontal relationships between Center and Periphery, and between Periphery and Periphery.

b. *destruction of multi-national asymmetric organizations* if they do not change in the direction of 3.a. above by withdrawal of Periphery participation.

c. *self-reliance with the Periphery itself building multinational symmetric organizations,* retaining some contact with the Center for conflict articulation. This pattern might also apply to the UN and the UN Agencies unless they pursue policies of the types indicated above.

d. *establishment of global or trans-national organizations* that could serve to globalize the world's means of communication and means of production in order to establish a universally accessible communication network and a production system that would give top priority to the needs of the periphery of the Periphery.

4. *Extra-bloc activity*

a. *Periphery-Center contacts extended to other Centers,* but in accordance with the program indicated in 1.a. and 1.b. above.

b. *Periphery-Periphery contacts extended to other Periphery countries,* but in accordance with points 2 and 3 above. For the latter the Algiers Group of 77 would be an important, although weak model, and the conferences of non-aligned states another. At the first conference in Beograd in 1961 there were 25 participants, at the second in 1964 in Cairo 47 participants, and at the 1970 Lusaka conference there were 54 participants (the number of observers was 3, 10, and 12 respectively).

Again, at this general level it is impossible to indicate the first steps that would lead from vertical, feudal interaction towards horizontalization and defeudalization. These are guidelines only. And their implementation should certainly not be seen as a sufficient condition for a process of genuine development to start in the Periphery, with the possible result that the gap between Center and Periphery may be decreasing again, but as a necessary condition. Very many of the findings in "liberal" development theory may become valid precisely when today's periphery nations become autonomous through structural change. Hence, the basic formulas of horizontalization and defeudalization are necessary conditions, not panaceas.

But another question that certainly has to be asked is what this presupposes in terms of intranational strategies. In one sense the answer is simple: Table 18.11 also applies to the relation between center and periphery within a nation, not only between nations. As such it gives four general guidelines for a revolutionary process that would abolish the exploitation of the periphery by the Center.

But this is too abstract, so let us return to the question in more concrete terms. The major difficulty with the international strategies in Table 18.11 is obviously that these would not be in the interest of the center in the Periphery. Nothing in these strategies would guarantee them the living conditions they already enjoy, very often on par with (or even above) the living conditions of the center in the Center. They would have all reasons to resist such changes. In fact, from a purely human point of view this group is perhaps the most exposed group in the whole international system, on the one hand the pawn and instrument of the center in the Center and on the other hand the exploiters of the periphery in the Periphery. In such a cross pressure it seems reasonable to expect that the group will sooner or later have to choose sides. Either it will have to relocate and join the center in the Center, or it will have to stand in solidarity with the periphery in the Periphery.

We can now, building on the *criteria* of imperialism, formulate a new set of strategies that would have more immediate domestic implications and support the international strategies of Table 18.11, as is shown in Table 18.12.

At this point we choose to stop. These strategies will be explored in much more detail elsewhere. They are only presented here in brief outline in order to indicate what to us seems to be a crucial criterion against which any theory should be tested: Is it indicative of a practice, does it indicate who the actors behind that practice could be? A theory should not only be evaluated according to its potential as a reservoir of hypothesis implications to be tested against present reality (data), but as much — or perhaps more — as a reservoir of policy implications to be tested against potential reality (goals, values). What we have tried to do here is an effort in both directions.

TABLE 18.12 Strategies for Structural Change of the Intranational Dominance System

I. REDUCED HARMONY BETWEEN THE CENTERS

1. *Reduction to neutral or no relationship*

This type of situation arises often when there is a crisis in the center of the Center, for instance due to internal war in the Center or external war between two or more Center nations. In this situation the Periphery attains some kind of autonomy because the Center can no longer exercise minute control — as seems to be the case for many countries in Latin America during the Second World War.

2. *Change to negative relationship between the centers*

In the general theory it has been postulated that there is 'harmony' between the two centers, but social relations being complex such a harmony is hardly ever complete. There may be some privileges that cC reserve for themselves (such as taxation *without* representation) or some privileges that cP reserve for themselves (such as the right to maintain a slavery or racist society). In general tensions may arise precisely because the model of complete harmony and similarity is not realized. The result may be a *nationalist* fight for liberation from the Center country, and this fight may even attain a populist character if cP can manage to interpret the conflict as a threat to the Periphery nation as a whole, not only to its center. If the Center engages in destructive behavior against the Periphery, such as economic warfare (with economic sanctions as a special case) or even military warfare, a homogenization of the Periphery may occur, sufficient to conceal the disharmony of interest built into the Periphery.

II. REDUCED DISHARMONY IN THE PERIPHERY

3. *Violent revolution in the Periphery*

According to this formula the internal disharmony of interest is eliminated by eliminating cP as a class, by using means of force. This can be done partly by killing them, partly by means of imprisonment, and partly by giving them the chance to relocate, for instance by using their ties with cC so as to settle where they really belong — in the Center.[45] A new regime is then introduced which perhaps may have its center, but certainly not a center that is tied with relations of harmony to the old cC.

4. *Non-violent revolution in the Periphery*

In this approach cP are not eliminated as persons, but as a part of the Periphery structure because the rest of the Periphery nation refuses to interact with them. They become non-functional socially rather than eliminated in a physical sense. To give them new tasks in a new society becomes an important part of the non-violent revolution.

5. *Cooperation between the peripheries in the Periphery*

Since international relations are so dominated by the centers in the Periphery, more of international relations has to be carried out by the peoples themselves in patterns of non-governmental foreign policy. The Havana-based *Tricontinental* (OSPAAAL) is an important example.

But in general we would believe more in Periphery-generated strategies than in the Center-generated ones, since the latter may easily lead to a new form of dependence on the Center.

III. CHANGES IN THE CENTER

6. *Increased disharmony in the Center*

In this case pC may no longer side with cC as it should according to nationalist ideology in the Center, but find that the Periphery nation in general and pP in particular is the natural ally. It is difficult to see how this can have consequences that could be beneficial to the Periphery unless the two countries are contiguous, or unless this might be a factor behind the types of development outlined in I,1 and I,2 above.

7. *Changes in the goals of the Center*

In this case there is no assumption of changes in the level of internal disharmony in the Center. The Center might itself choose to stop imperialist policies, not because it is forced to do so from below (the Center by the Periphery, or cC by pC as above), but out of its own decision. Thus, cC might see that this is a *wrong* policy to pursue, e.g., because of the exploitation it leads to, because of the dangers for world peace, because of relations to other nations, etc. Or, there may be internal reasons: the Center might reduce its economic growth and change towards a politics of justice. Anti-centers, or the periphery in the Center might decide to boycott further economic growth because of its consequences in terms of negative spin-off effects (pollution, exploitation of man). There are many possibilities, and they may combine into quite likely contributions towards a disruption of the system. But in general we would believe more in Periphery-generated strategies than in Center-generated ones, since the latter may easily lead to a new form of dependence on the Center.

APPENDIX: Some Data on Economic Relations Within and Between Nations

	1	2	3	4	5	6	7
Nation	GNP/cap.	Non-Primary %	GINI (i)	GINI (l)	Trade Composition Index	Partner Concentration	Commodity Concentration
Argentina	670	82.2	0.45	0.863	− 0.667	16.5	51.5
Australia	2 035	90.6	0.35	0.929	− 0.576	18.4	50.9
Austria	1 287	79.9	−	0.740	0.021	20.1	29.2
Belgium	1 761	94.5	−	0.587	0.175	22.4	34.1
Brazil	273	48.4	−	0.837	− 0.510	32.0	59.3
Canada	2 505	87.9	−	0.497	− 0.258	57.5	26.7
Ceylon	145	51.1	0.50	−	− 0.375	29.3	93.4
Colombia	305	52.8	0.50	0.849	− 0.710	47.3	84.8
Congo, D.R.	85	86.4	−	−	− 0.062	32.3	65.5
Costa Rica	421	50.9	−	0.892	− 0.989	50.0	65.1
Denmark	2 109	83.4	0.42	0.458	− 0.270	22.5	34.8
Ecuador	223	44.4	−	0.864	− 0.766	54.7	75.2
El Salvador	273	39.7	0.45	0.828	− 0.529	25.7	68.3
Finland	1 747	64.5	−	0.599	− 0.039	20.8	60.5
France	1 922	83.4	−	0.583	0.158	18.7	23.8
W. Germany	1 977	90.0	0.44	0.674	0.418	11.3	24.7
Ghana	288	42.0	−	−	− 0.750	22.0	78.1
Guatemala	322	34.6	0.48	0.860	− 0.659	32.9	68.0
Guyana	−	70.4	−	−	− 0.675	−	−
Honduras	225	33.2	−	0.757	− 0.759	56.9	67.9
India	102	27.1	0.57	0.522	− 0.044	19.0	54.8
Iran	270	53.1	−	−	− 0.812	17.3	92.8
Ireland	951	69.2	−	0.598	− 0.322	70.7	42.3
Israel	1 407	88.0	−	−	− 0.076	14.9	52.4
Italy	1 100	76.7	0.40	0.803	0.384	20.1	22.5
Ivory Coast	285	13.6	−	−	− 0.703	37.5	83.1
Jamaica	516	63.9	−	0.820	0.480	37.4	76.5
Japan	870	79.4	−	0.470	0.707	29.7	36.1
Jordan	237	64.7	−	−	− 0.241	15.0	59.9
S. Korea	99	48.2	−	−	− 0.114	27.3	26.8
Kuwait	−	98.9	−	−	− 0.486	−	−
Liberia	280	19.1	−	−	− 0.754	38.7	91.2
Libya	705	64.3	−	0.700	− 0.871	19.0	98.8
Mexico	482	45.2	0.53	−	− 0.608	55.0	35*)
Morocco	196	43.7	−	−	− 0.335	42.8	45.2
Netherland	1 532	91.7	0.43	0.605	− 0.077	27.2	18.5
New Zealand	2 025	86.9	−	0.772	− 0.733	46.4	81.0
Nicaragua	325	40.3	−	0.757	− 0.783	29.5	65.2
Niger	91	3.1	−	−	− 0.688	−	−
Norway	1 907	81.5	0.39	0.669	− 0.207	18.9	26.4
Pakistan	97	31.2	0.38	−	− 0.337	12.8	61.7
Panama	517	53.8	−	0.737	− 0.524	55.9	89.4
Peru	372	50.3	−	0.875	− 0.545	41.8	58.7
Philippines	156	47.3	−	0.564	− 0.608	43.1	72.7
Poland	−	52.3	−	−	0.037	−	−
Portugal	400	66.5	−	−	− 0.068	−	25*)
Sierra Leone	159	25.2	−	−	− 0.108	65.7	82.7
S. Africa	590	70.5	−	−	− 0.386	−	−
Spain	600	67.2	−	0.780	− 0.131	−	35*)

*) Estimate

	1	2	3	4	5	6	7
Nation	GNP/cap.	Non-Primary %	GINI (i)	GINI (l)	Trade Composition Index	Partner Concentration	Commodity Concentration
Sudan	103	14.2	–	–	– 0.718	14.4	69.7
Sweden	2 487	89.9	0.42	0.572	– 0.012	13.8	28.6
Switzerland	2 301	92.2	–	0.498	0.152	15.8	28.5
Syria	228	43.0	–	∠	– 0.449	36.5	64.9
Thailand	129	18.0	–	–	– 0.606	19.4	56.3
Turkey	279	28.8	–	–	– 0.705	17.2	38.3
UAR	159	43.4	–	–	– 0.275	50.8	63.0
UK	1 790	96.9	0.38	0.710	0.424	10.8	22.2
USA	3 536	95.0	0.36	0.705	0.101	20.2	15.6
Venezuela	971	67.7	–	0.909	– 0.893	35.5	99.6
Yugoslavia	–	43.1	–	–	– 0.045	–	–

Sources:

GNP/Cap.: Hagen & Hawlyryshyn, 1969: Analysis of World Income and Growth, 1955–65, *in Economic Development and Cultural Change*, Vol. 18, No. 1 part II, October 1969.
% Non-primary: The PRIO Nation Data File. Compiled from ILO and OECD sources. Year: 1967.
GINI (i): Weisskopf, T. E. 1970: Underdevelopment, Capitalistic Growth and the Future of the Poor Countries. Preliminary Draft, Harvard University, April 1970.
GINI (l): Russett, B. et al., *World Handbook of Social and Political indicators*
Trade comp.: Computed from, *UN Yearbook of International Trade Statistics*, 1967.
Partner conc.: Hagen & Hawlyryshyn, op.cit.
Comm. conc.: Hagen & Hawlyryshyn, op.cit.

Notes

This is a revised version of a paper originally prepared for the International Political Science Association World Conference in München, September 1970, under the title "Political Development and the International Environment. An Essay on Imperialism." I am grateful to Ali Mazrui for having solicited the paper, and for all other colleagues in the World Order Models Project under the direction of Saul Mendlovitz for penetrating and stimulating discussions — particularly Osvaldo Sunkel, Stephen Hymer, and Otto von Kreye. The paper has also been presented at the International Peace Academy in Vienna, July and September 1970; at the University of Lund, December 1970; at the College of Europe, Bruges, and University of Groningen, January 1971, and at the PRIO Theory Weeks, January 1971. I am grateful to discussants at all places, and particularly to Lars Dencik, Egil Fossum, Tord and Susan Høivik and Knut Hongrø. The article can be identified as PRIO-Publication no. 27-1 from the International Peace Research Institute, Oslo.

1. For an exploration of this concept, see Galtung, J., 1969, Violence, Peace and Peace Research, *Journal of Peace Research* 6:167-191.

2. This equality premise may be formulated in terms of distribution, or

redistribution, of values generated by the society in liberal theory, or as absence of exploitation in Marxist theory. The two approaches have in common the idea that a party may have an interest even if it does not proclaim that it has this interest, but whereas the liberal approach will keep the social structure but carry out some redistribution along the road, the Marxist approach will change the social structure itself. In both cases one may actually also make a further distinction as to whether harmony is to be obtained by equalization of what the society produces of material and spiritual value, or equalization when it comes to the power to decide over what the society produces. But imperialism as a structure cuts across these distinctions and is, in our view, based on a more general concept of harmony and disharmony of interests.

3. No attempt will be made here to explore similarities and dissimilarities between this definition of imperialism and that given by such authors as Hobson, Luxemburg, Lenin, Hilferding, and very many others. This definition has grown out of a certain research tradition, partly inductively from a long set of findings about international interaction structures, and partly deductively from speculations relating to structural violence in general and the theory of inequality in particular.

4. Particularly one aspect of Lenin's conception of imperialism has been picked up in our definition: the general idea of a labor aristocracy. Lenin quotes Engels when he says that "quand aux ouvriers, ils jouissent en toute tranquillité avec eux du monopole colonial, de l'Angleterre et de son monopole sur le marché mondial." (*L'impérialisme: Stade supreme du Capitalisme*, [Moscow, 1969], p. 139.) The same idea is expressed by L. S. Senghor: "Les prolétaires d'Europe ont bénéficié du régime colonial; partant, ils ne s'y sont jamais réellement, je veux dire efficacement, opposés." (*Nation et voie africaine du socialisme*, p. 51.) And T. Hopkins in Third World Modernization in Transnational Perspective (*The Annals* [1969], pp. 126-136) picks up the other angle of this: "There are strong indications that in most Third World Countries, internal inequality is increasing. The educated are markedly more advantaged; urban workers are relatively well-off; unemployment is high and increasing; rural populations are poor."

5. Thus, international statistics should not be given only for national aggregates since this conceals the true nature of the relations in the world. It would be much more useful if statistics were given for the four groups defined in our definition. In general we would assume such statistics over time to show that cC and cP grow most quickly and more or less together, then follows pC and at the bottom is pP that is not only located much below the other two, but also shows very little growth or none at all. The more numerous the group, the lower the growth: it is the accumulated work from these vast masses that permits the growth of the dominating minorities. One highly stimulating analysis in this direction is given by Th. E. Weisskopf who tries to disaggregate the growth rates and is led to the conclusion that the growth in the developing countries has taken place in the upper and middle strata of the population, in the secondary sector of economic production, and in the urban areas. The growth rates in these parts of the developing nations are not too different from growth rates in corresponding parts in developed nations, but due to the absence of mechanisms for redistribution this leaves the vast periphery of the developing nations with close to zero or even negative growth. Weisskopf, T. E., "Underdevelop-

ment, Capitalistic Growth and the Future of the Poor Countries," World Order Models Project, 1970.

6. This argument is carried much further for the case of interindividual rather than international interaction in Galtung, J., "Structural Pluralism and the Future of Human Interaction," paper presented at the Second International Future Research Conference, Kyoto, April 1970; and Galtung, J., "Perspectives on Development: Past, Present and Future," paper presented at the International Sociological Association Conference, Varna, September 1970.

7. The basic point here is that a demand generates a chain of demands. Economists have made some estimates in this connection. For instance, H. B. Chenery and T. Watanabe conclude, "In the four industrial countries studied here (United States, Japan, Norway, and Italy), between 40% and 50% of total domestic demands for goods and services comes from other productive sectors rather than from final users" (International Comparisons of the Structure of Production, *Econometrica* [1958], p. 504). The more connected the economy of a country, the more will a demand proliferate. Other social scientists should have tools corresponding to the input-output analyses of the economists in order to study the degree of connectedness of a society. Characteristic of a traditional society is precisely the low level of connectedness: the spread effect into other branches of economic activity and into other districts is much lower. Also see Stirton-Weaver, F., "Backwash, Spread and the Chilean State," *Studies in Comparative International Development* 5, no. 12; and Hirschman, A. O., *The Strategy of Economic Development* (New Haven: Yale University Press, 1958), especially his discussion of backward and forward linkages (pp. 100-119).

8. It is this equality that we stipulate to be in the interest of both parties, both for the exploiter and the exploited. Obviously, there are two approaches: the interaction structure can be changed so that the inter- and intra-actor effects are equal, and/or redistribution can take place. But if this interaction structure has been in operation for a long time and has already generated considerable differences in living conditions then both methods may have to be used, a point to be further elaborated below. For highly stimulating discussions of unequal exchange, see Casanova, P. G., *Sociología de la Explotación* (Mexico: Siglo Veintiuno, 1969); and Arghiri, Emmanuel, *L'exchange inégal* (Paris: Maspero, 1969).

9. What we have in mind here, concretely, is of course all the various forms of development assistance based on the idea that grants are given to poor countries on the condition that they use them to procure capital goods in developed countries. In an excellent article, "Prospectives for the Third World," S. Sideri summarizes much of the literature showing how well development assistance pays. However, these analyses are by no means complete since only some aspects of the economic spin-off effects are considered, not all the others that may also, incidentally, be convertible into economic effects, at least in the long run.

10. For an analysis of social status systems using feudal interaction as the basic concept, see Galtung, J., "Feudal Systems, Structural Violence and the Structural Theory of Revolutions," in *Proceedings of the IPRA Third General Conference,* I (Van Gorcum, Assen, 1970), pp. 110-188.

11. For a penetrating analysis of the relation between dependency and develop-

ment, see Cardoso, F. H., and Faletto, E., *Dependencia y desarrollo en America Latina* (Mexico: Siglo Veintiuno, 1969). One important difference between that book and the present analysis lies in the warning the authors give against generalization beyond the concrete case. While sympathetic to this, we nevertheless feel there is considerable virtue in general theory, as a baseline for understanding the concrete case.

Another basic analysis of this type of relationship is, of course, Frank, A. G., *Capitalism and Underdevelopment in Latin America* (New York: Monthly Review Press, 1967). The basic key to Frank's analysis is the structure that "extends from the macrometropolitan system center of the world capitalist system 'down' to the most supposedly isolated agricultural workers, who, through this chain of interlinked metropolitan-satellite relationships, are tied to the central world metropolis and thereby incorporated into the world capitalist system as a whole" (p. 16), and he goes on (p. 17) to talk about "the exploitation of the satellite by the metropolis or . . . the tendency of the metropolis to expropriate and appropriate the economic surplus of the satellite." All this is valid as general formulas, but too little emphasis is given to the type of exploitation referred to here as "asymmetric distribution of spin-offs" and the special organization referred to as "feudal interaction structure." And economists with no Marxist inclination at all are certainly not helpful when it comes to reflecting imperialistic types of relations. Thus, in Jan Tinbergen, *The Design of Development* (Baltimore: Johns Hopkins, 1966), development is discussed throughout the book as if the government in a developing country is free to make its decisions. And in T. Haavelmo, *A Study in the Theory of Economic Evolution* (Amsterdam: North-Holland Publ. Co., 1954) it is difficult to see that any theory at all based on *relations* between nations is offered to explain the tremendous disparities in this world; just to mention two examples. And even Myrdal's *Asian Drama* has little to say on international relations, as pointed out by Lars Rudebeck in an excellent review article (*Cooperation and Conflict,* 1969, pp. 267-281).

12. One book that gives a fairly balanced account of Soviet dominance patterns is *The New Imperialism,* by Hugh Seton-Watson (New York: Capricorn Books, 1961). Andre Amalrik's analysis *Will the Soviet Union Survive Until 1984* (New York: Harper & Row, 1970) also deserves reading, not so much for its apocalyptic scenario as for its penetrating analysis of the internal dominance system. The question of whether the total Soviet system should be referred to as imperialism remains open, however, among other reasons because the Soviet Union does not enjoy spin-offs from processing of raw materials and because the internal inequality is hardly lower than in dependent countries. But the elite harmonization criterion will probably hold to a large extent mediated through the cooperation between party elites.

Comparative studies of imperialistic structures, in the tradition of Helio Jaguaribe, comparing different types of empires in this century as well as long-time historical comparisons bringing in, for instance, the Roman Empire, would be highly useful to shed more light over this particular international structure. At present this type of exercise is hampered by the tendency to use "imperialism" as an abusive term, as a category to describe the other camp. We have preferred to see it as a technical term, which does not mean that he who struggles for peace will not have to struggle against imperialism regardless of what shape it takes.

13. For an analysis of international air communication, see Gleditsch, N. P., "Trends in World Airline Patterns," *JPR* 1967, pp. 366-408.

14. For an analysis of the role of the international press agencies, see Østgaard, E., "Factors Influencing the Flow of News," *Journal of Peace Research 2*:39-63.

15. For an analysis of this, see Galtung, J., and Ruge, M. H., "The Structure of Foreign News: The Presentation of the Congo, Cuba and Cyprus Crises in Four Norwegian Newspapers," *Journal of Peace Research 2*:64-91.

16. For an analysis of this, see Galtung, J., "After Camelot," in Horowitz, I. L. (ed.), *The Rise and Fall of Project Camelot* (Cambridge, Mass.: M.I.T. Press, 1967).

17. As one example, and a very explicit one, may serve the following quotation: "Can we discharge our responsibility to God and to man for so magnificent, so populous a proportion of the world? . . . Our answer is off hand ready and simple. We are adequate. We do discharge our responsibilities. We are a conquering and imperial race. All over the world we have displayed our mettle. We have discovered and annexed and governed vast territories. We have encircled the globe with our commerce. We have penetrated the pagan races with our missionaries. We have innoculated the Universe (sic!) with our institutions. We are apt indeed to believe that our soldiers are braver, our sailors hardier, our captains, naval and military, skilfuller, our statesmen wiser than those of other nations. As for our constitution, there is no Briton at any hour of the day or night who will suffer it to be said that any approaches it." From Lord Boseberry, "Questors of Empire 1900," in *Miscellanies, Literary and Historical, vol. II* (London: Hodder & Stoughton, 1921). I am indebted to Fiona Rudd for this remarkable reference.

18. This is extremely clearly expressed in a report of a U.S. presidential mission to the Western Hemisphere (the Rockefeller report): "Just as the other American republics depend upon the United States for their capital equipment requirements, so the United States depends on them to provide a vast market for our manufactured goods. And as these countries look to the United States for a market for their primary products whose sale enables them to buy equipment for their development at home, so the United States looks to them for raw materials for our industries, on which depend the jobs of many of our citizens." (Quality of Life in the Americas, Agency for International Development, August 1969, pp. 5-113.) The paragraph is as if taken out of a textbook on imperialism, emphasizing how the Center countries provide capital equipment and manufactured goods, and the Periphery countries raw materials and markets. The only interesting thing about the quotation is that it is still possible to write like this in 1969.

19. One example is the Brezhnev Doctrine. Speaking in Warsaw on November 12, 1968, to the Fifth Congress of the Polish United Workers Party, Brezhnev emphasized the need for "strict respect" for sovereignty of other socialist countries, and added: "But when internal and external forces that are hostile to Socialism try to turn the development of some socialist country towards the restoration of a capitalist regime, when socialism in that country and the socialist community as a whole is threatened, it becomes not only a problem of the people of the country concerned, but a common problem and concern of all Socialist countries. Naturally an action such as military assistance to a fraternal country designed to avert the threat to the social system is an extraordinary step, dictated by necessity." Such a step, he added,

"may be taken only in case of direct actions of the enemies of Socialism within a country and outside it, actions threatening the common interests of the Socialist camp." (*Keesing's Contemporary Archives*, 1968, p. 23027.) Its similarity to the Monroe Doctrine has often been pointed out, but there is the difference that the U.S. sometimes seems to be acting as if it had a Monroe Doctrine for the whole world.

Without implying that the following is official Soviet policy, it has nevertheless appeared in *International Affairs* (April 1970):

> The socialist countries, united in the Warsaw Treaty Organization, are profoundly aware that the most reliable guarantee that their security will be preserved and strengthened is allround cooperation with the Soviet Union, including military cooperation. They firmly reject any type of anti-Soviet slander and resist attempts by imperialism and the remnants of domestic reaction to inject into the minds of their people any elements of anti-Sovietism, whether open or veiled.
>
> With the two worlds—socialist and capitalist—in global confrontation, any breach of internationalist principles, any sign of nationalism, and especially any toleration, not to say use, of anti-Sovietism in policy turns those who pursue such policies into an instrument of imperialist strategy and policy, regardless of whether their revisionist slogan is given a Right or ultra-Left twist, regardless of the subjective intentions of the advocates and initiators of the course. And whether it is very big or very small, it remains nothing but an instrument in the hands of imperialism and in either case retains its ignominious essence, which is incompatible with truly revolutionary socialist consciousness. (V. Razmerov, "Loyalty to Proletarian Internationalism—Fundamental Condition for Success of All Revolutionary Forces").

What this quotation says is in fact that not only hostile deeds, but also all hostile words are to be ruled out. It is also interesting to note that the types of attitudes that are not to be expressed are referred to as "anti-Soviet." In other words, the reference is to the Center country in the system, not even to the masses of that country, nor to antisocialism.

20. In general, international contacts between ministries seem to become increasingly transnational. Where the minister of defense in country A some time ago would have to use a channel of communication involving at least one embassy and one ministry of foreign affairs to reach his opposite number in country B, direct telecommunication would now be the adequate channel. What this means in terms of cutting out filtering effects and red tape is obvious. It also means that transnational ties may be strengthened and sometimes be posted against the nation state. Obviously, this system will be expanding, for instance with a system of telesatellites available for elite communication between Center and Periphery countries within a bloc. For the Francophone countries the projected satellite Symphonie may, perhaps, be seen as a step in this direction, although it is targeted on audiences rather than on concrete, specific persons. The NATO satellite communication system is another example.

21. Very important in this connection is, of course, the quick development of the telephone concept from essentially bilateral (one person talks with one other person, possibly with some others listening in at either end, or in the middle!) towards the telephone as a multilateral means of communication. Bell Telephone Company can

now organize conferences over the telephone by connecting a number of subscribers. Obviously, if combined with a videoscreen the conversation may be more orderly because participants may also react on nonverbal, visual cues such as facial expressions, etc. More particularly, they may raise a finger and ask for the "floor."

22. The battle between the two types of imperialism is perhaps more important in the imagination of those who try to uphold one of the types than in social reality. Thus, what happened in the Dominican Republic in 1965 was interpreted by those who are upholding a pattern of economic imperialism as an attempt by "the other bloc" to establish political imperialism; just as the events in Czechoslovakia in 1968 were interpreted by the servants of political military imperialism as an effort by "the other bloc" to introduce economic imperialism. Whatever history's judgement may be in terms of these two hypotheses it is obvious that two types of imperialism, directed from antagonistic blocs, cannot at the same time be in the same phase. One pattern would be that the dominant type is in phase 3 and the competitive type is in phase 1 — and that is what was claimed by the Center countries in the two cases.

23. The best analysis we have read of division of labor in multinational corporations is by Stephen Hymer ("The Multi-national Corporation and the Law of Uneven Development," to appear in Bhagwati, J. N. (ed.), *Economics and World Order* [New York: World Law Fund, 1970]).

24. This is not a random event: international organizations are in that phase because they reflect the relationships between national actors, that in the present stage of development are the major carriers of these relations.

25. Thus, when Stalin died in 1953 there must have been great expectation in China that Mao Tse-tung would be the next head of the international communist movement. His revolution was more recent, the country in which the revolution had taken place was by far the biggest, and he was also older as a revolutionary fighter in a leading position than possible competitors. Nevertheless, it was quite clear that the Soviet conception was that the leader of the international communist movement would have to be the leader of what they interpreted as the leading communist nation: the Soviet Union herself.

26. This is a major difference between liberal and structuralist peace theory. It is hardly unfair to interpret liberal peace theory as somehow stating that "peace" is roughly proportionate to the volume of trade, possibly interpreted as an indicator of the level of interdependence, whereas structural peace theory would bring in the factor of equality and ask for the composition as well as the volume of trade. If structural theory is more correct and if the present world trade structure is such that only the Center nations can enjoy both high level of interdependence and high level in equality in exchange, then "peace" is one extra benefit that will accrue to the Center layer of the world.

27. Another concept would be the frequently quoted saying that "technical assistance is taken from the poor man in the rich country and given to the rich in the poor country." The model of the world implied by the dominance theory would certainly not contradict this quite elegant statement: technical assistance is to a large extent paid for by taxpayers' money, not to mention by the surplus produced by the masses working in the rich countries, and given via public channels for investment

in infrastructures in poor countries, often for the benefit of the layers in the poor countries that have a consumption structure compatible with a production structure that the rich countries can offer.

28. Galtung, J., "International Relations and International Conflicts: A Sociological Approach," *Transactions of the Sixth World Congress of Sociology* (International Sociological Association, 1966), pp. 121-161.

29. E.g., Magdoff, H., *The Age of Imperialism,* (New York: Monthly Review, 1969).

30. Research on this is currently in progress at the International Peace Research Institute, Oslo.

31. But it is still an open question whether this should really be referred to as imperialism, since so many of the criteria do not seem to be fulfilled. Once more this seems to bring up the importance of seeing imperialism as a special case of a wider set of social relationships, conveniently lumped together under the heading "domination."

32. Relations between Soviet Union and the Arab world, and Japan and Southeast Asia, are being explored at the International Peace Research Institute, Oslo, by Tormod Nyberg and Johan Galtung respectively.

33. This type of structural reasoning seems particularly important in the Soviet case. It can hardly be claimed that the Soviet periphery participates more in the decisionmaking made by the Soviet center than the Czech periphery participated in the decisionmaking made by the Czech center in the months prior to the invasion in August 1968. On the contrary, the opposite hypothesis seems more tenable. And if this is the case the Soviet center could no longer necessarily count on the allegiance of its own periphery, particularly not on the Ukrainian periphery, bordering Czechoslovakia not only geographically, but also linguistically and culturally (and apparently listening attentively to broadcasts). This means that what happened in Czechoslovakia became a threat to the Soviet center, perhaps more than to the Soviet Union as a Center nation.

34-35. See Appendix for data for sixty nations on these seven variables (but missing for most of the nations for Gini i, and for many of the nations for Gini 1). The trade composition index was developed by Knut Hongrø after some suggestions by the present author. It may, however, well be that the index

$$\frac{(a + d) - (b + c)}{(a + d) + (b + c)}$$

would be better, since values of trade are usually added, not multiplied, and since this would attain the value 1 not when b *or* c equals 0, but when b *and* c equals 0. (Galtung, J., "Vertical and Horizontal Trade Relation: A Note on Operationalization," WOMP, 1970).

36. References are given in the Appendix.

37. In this connection it should be pointed out that the theory of imperialism would not be disconfirmed if these correlation coefficients had been much lower. It is only the theory as a model for the concrete empirical world here and now that would have been disconfirmed, not imperialism as one factor in systems of collec-

tivities, and particularly as a factor that together with other factors may rise to the constellation known in the present world. What Table 18.8 seems to indicate is that the theory of imperialism as presented here is not a bad map of orientation in the contemporary world.

38. For one exposition of the center-periphery theory for individuals see Galtung, J., 1964, "Foreign Public Opinion as a Function of Social Position," *Journal of Peace Research* 1:206-231.

39. This, of course, would also be true interindividually: division of labor may be organized in such a way that it is personality expanding for some actors and personality contracting for others so that they "sort" themselves away from each other by participating in this type of vertical interaction.

40. See the article by Stephen Hymer referred to in note 23 above.

41. We are thinking particularly of the Pakistan consortium and the India consortium.

42. Thus, center-periphery theory in connection with nonterritorial actors should perhaps not be stated so much in terms of size or age of organizations, as in terms of whether they are able to establish bridgeheads in other nonterritorial actors, and whether they are able to organize systematically some vertical type of division of labor. Thus, the system of "consultative status" clearly indicates who is to decide and who to be consulted.

43. It should be pointed out that no strategy seems to exist for reducing the gap. There is not even any strategy for reducing the increase of the gap, the only strategy that perhaps may be said to exist is a strategy for improving the level of poor nations. A strategy for reducing the gap does not necessarily imply a basic change of the structure of the relations between rich and poor nations, however. It might also come about by reducing significantly the growth in the rich nations.

44. New statesmen seem to have put this point more strongly than Julius Nyerere in the famous Arusha Declaration: "If every individual is self-reliant the ten-house cell will be self-reliant; if all the cells are self-reliant the whole ward will be self-reliant, then the Region is self-reliant, and if the Regions are self-reliant, then the whole Nation is self-reliant and this is our aim." In this there is of course also an implicit theory: self-reliance has to be built from the very bottom, it can only be basically a property of the individual, not of the nation. And Kenneth Kaunda has this to add (*Humanism in Zambia,* Lusaka, 1968): "We all know that a man who has developed a genuine sense of self-reliance will not in any way wish to exploit his fellow men" (p. 50).

45. In the present phase of imperialism, cP would use their good contacts with cC through international organizations to get resettled in the Center. This seems to work for businessmen in the capitalist world as well as for high-ranking party officials in the communist world. For the latter, "reasons of health" are often invoked.

Part 7
Decisionmaking Inquiries

Introduction

In reviewing the study of war by political scientists from antiquity to the eve of World War II, Quincy Wright (1965:1376-1381) identified six schools of thought: (1) the classical school; (2) the practical school; (3) the juristic school; (4) the psychological school; (5) the institutional school; and (6) the statistical school. However, the study of war by contemporary political scientists of behavioral and interdisciplinary orientation has generally focused on causal linkages joining international conflict, crisis, and war.

Specifically, conflict research by international relations specialists has centered on international crises. International crises represent critical thresholds between nonviolent conflict management (peace) and violent conflict management (war). Situated in an intermediate zone between war and peace, international crises serve as the empirical and logical point of departure for probing the age-old question on the causes of war: Why or under what conditions do some crises escalate into war while others are resolved nonviolently? Political scientists have approached this question from two different perspectives: decisionmaking and (international) systemic. This part deals with the former while Part 8 will deal with the latter.

Not surprisingly, there is no consensus as to the definition of crisis on the part of the decisionmaking and systemic perspectives. The most widely accepted and cited definition of crisis relied upon by the decisionmaking perspective emphasizes the properties of *threat, time,* and *surprise* and is formulated as a situation "that (1) threatens high-priority goals of the decision-making unit, (2) restricts the amount of time available for response before the decision is transmitted, and (3) surprises the members of the decision-making unit by its occurrence" (Hermann 1972:13). For our purposes, however, the definition operationalized by Glenn H. Snyder and Paul Diesing (1977:6), who in their recent landmark study advanced a theory of international crisis behavior by integrating the systems, bargaining, and decisionmaking theories, is more suitable: "An international crisis is a sequence of interactions between the governments of two or more sovereign states in severe conflict, short of actual war, but involving the perception of a dangerously high probability of war."

The concept of foreign policy decisionmaking in the study of international relations was first introduced by Richard C. Snyder and his collaborators at Princeton University in the early 1950s. The advent of this new concept quickly generated considerable excitement and popularity in a variety of inquiries in political science research and then lost its momentum in the 1960s, lacking theory building, empirical inquiry — Glenn D. Paige's (1968) study stands out as an exception in this regard — and sustained interest in the relevance or utility of the concept. In the 1970s, however, decisionmaking analysis embodying a variety of models has made a major comeback, as evidenced in the works of Graham Allison (1971), Ole Holsti (1972), Charles Hermann (1972), Morton Halperin (1974), Robert Axelrod (1976), Robert Jervis (1976), Irvin L. Janis and Leon Mann (1977), and Glenn Snyder and Paul Diesing (1977).

Decisionmaking inquiries into the causes of war are mainly concerned with the war-prone foreign policy behavior of individual nation-states rather than with the dynamics of the international system. The question as to why war occurs in the international system or why nations go to war is being reformulated into the question as to why — and under what conditions — decisionmakers empowered to make authoritative allocation of resources decide to go to war. War making is thus conceptualizd as a deliberate choice, a decision outcome. However, decisionmaking analysis focuses on *process variables,* a host of antecedent variables leading to decision outcomes. The main objective in the decisionmaking approach is to identify the relationship of causal variables — psychological, communicational, organizational, and political — and how these variables affect decision behavior of a foreign policy elite in a crisis situation. As a study of elite decision behavior, decisionmaking analysis transcends any rigid disciplinary autonomy in social science as it draws upon data and theories of psychology, social psychology, biology, cybernetics, public administration, and political sociology.

Beyond the agreement on the level and unit of analysis, however, the decisionmaking perspective has produced three broad theoretical approaches based upon distinct — and at times mutually incompatible — methodological assumptions. *The rational actor theory* as a derivative of game theory in mathematical economics conceptualizes decisionmaking as a deliberate and rational process of maximizing expected utility. Deterrence theory is a rational actor theory *par excellence;* it rests on the assumption that both deterrers and deterrees will reach a decision guided by rational calculations of costs and benefits, accurate definitions of the situation, and dispassionate assessments of relative capabilities and intentions, most prominently in the area of nuclear strategy, sometimes conventionally crystallized as MAD (Mutual Assured Destruction). Herman Kahn's (1965) analysis of the intensification of conflict between nuclear adversaries through an elaborate construction of the forty-four rungs on the nuclear escalation ladder represents an extreme version of the rational actor theory of decisionmaking.

The bureaucratic politics theory shies away from the model of a value-maximizing decisionmaker. It rejects the notion that the decisionmaker is a unitary actor in rational pursuit of a single goal or objective. Instead, this theory sees decisionmaking as a political process of building a majority coalition among key policymakers in different bureaus and departments within the national security bureaucracy with different roles, interests, goals, information sources, and bargaining powers. "Rather than through grand decisions on grand alternatives," noted Roger Hilsman (1967:5), reflecting on his own experience as a participant in the foreign-policy making process of the Kennedy administration, "policy changes seem to come through a series of slight modifications of existing policy, with the new policy emerging slowly and haltingly by small and usually tentative steps, a process of trial and error in which policy zigs and zags, reverses itself, and then moves forward in a series of incremental steps." David Braybrooke and Charles E. Lindblom (1963) have aptly characterized the above model of decisionmaking as "disjointed incrementalism."

Finally, *the perceptual theory* is based on the assumption that the decisionmakers' images constitute the most crucial link in the decisionmaking process. Applying theories and findings of social psychology, especially cognitive psychology, to decisionmaking, this theoretical model focuses on the intellectual process by which certain policies acquire their structure and content. Robert Jervis's (1976) interdisciplinary study of decisionmakers' perception and misperception and of their causes and consequences impinging on foreign policy decisionmaking process stands out as a model of this approach. A new variant of the perceptual theory is the "cognitive mapping" approach. Based on the premise that foreign policy of any given nation is strongly influenced by the belief systems of its key decisionmakers, this approach attempts to provide a graphic representation of a decisionmaker's belief system (a cognitive map) and to assess its influence on the decisionmaking process as well as on its policy outcomes (Axelrod 1976; Hart 1977).

The chapter by Robert Jervis, our first selection, is an elaborate sociopsychological inquiry into the intellectual process of foreign policy decisionmaking. The fourteen hypotheses on misperception in the chapter together show how decisionmakers' images of reality impose severe constraints on the working of the rational actor model; they shed light on the difficulties that one nation's decisionmakers have in transmitting undistorted signals and messages to those of another nation. The rigidity and inflexibility of decisionmakers' images also pose an enormous obstacle in the way of a constructive role in the part of a dissenting minority (a devil's advocate) whose view or perception of reality does not conform to the prevailing images of the majority. Note that Jervis carefully avoids the hazards of over-psychologizing by paying greater attention to cognitive factors than to emotional or idiosyncratic factors and also by drawing more on a wide range of historical cases than on laboratory experiments. Unfortunately, Jervis does not fully explain whether his hypotheses on misperception can be applied to both crisis and noncrisis decisionmaking.

Our next selection by Ole Holsti convincingly demonstrates some crucial differences in variables between crisis and noncrisis decisionmaking processes. Drawing largely on the findings and theories in experimental psychology, Holsti explores the possible consequences of crisis-induced stress on the behavior of key foreign policy decisionmakers. Since crisis decisionmaking typically involves only the core decisional group of slightly over a dozen individuals, as will be further noted below, Holsti's conceptual focus on the types, functions, and effects of the biological and psychological variables affecting the behavior of decisionmakers in a crisis situation seems appropriate.

The evidence Holsti marshals clearly suggests that crisis-induced stress significantly hampers the rational performance of involved decisionmakers by activating and aggravating a variety of maladaptive and dysfunctional variables in human behavior. To cite only a few notable examples, decisionmakers under crisis-induced stress exhibit reduced toleration for ambiguity, increased selective perception (misperception), impaired intellectual ability to process information or to discriminate between sense and nonsense, and reduced cognitive power to separate the dangerous from the trivial and the relevant from the irrelevant. Holsti's study thus effectively rebuts the sanguine assumption of nuclear deterrence theory — that is, the presumed rational and predictable behavior of strategic decisionmakers in a nuclear crisis. One methodological problem in such biopsychological analysis of decisionmaking concerns, as Holsti himself admits in the chapter, the moral and practical requirements of drawing largely on laboratory experiments or simulations rather than on actual cases.

The last chapter, by Glenn D. Paige, persuasively demonstrates the empirical and theoretical utility of a comparative case study in explaining crisis decisionmaking. It lays to rest the popular myth among the systems theorists that case studies can contribute little to theory building in the study of international crises. Paige illuminates major similarities and differences between the Korean and Cuban crisis decisions — the former was a deliberate choice to participate in a remote war and the latter a deliberate war-provoking act (blockade) on the calculated probability of "somewhere between one out of three and even" of setting in motion a nuclear exchange between the two superpowers — focusing on organizational, informational, and normative variables.

One of Paige's key findings with far-reaching implications for decision-making inquiries into the causes of war deserves mentioning here. In both crisis decisions Paige confirms our common-sense observation that foreign policy crisis decisions are made in secrecy by small, *ad hoc* decisional units. Note here that the core decisional groups in the Korean and Cuban cases numbered respectively fourteen and about sixteen; in comparison, the Politburo of the Soviet Union, the core decisional unit of Soviet crisis management, consisted as of January 1, 1978, of fourteen full members. In light of this, the UNESCO's peace formula could be revised as follows: "Since wars begin in the minds of men in the core decisional groups of the nation-states, it is in the minds of those men that the defenses of peace must be constructed." Of course, underneath such an assertion is whether these individuals are primarily agents of deeper social forces or are capable of acting rather independently within the confines of their roles.

In critically reading and evaluating the three selections below, the reader should be sensitive to some unresolved problems and questions in decision-making inquiries into the causes of war. First, there is the question of how much generalization can be made about elite crisis behavior based on the studies of decisionmaking systems of the Western countries in general and of the United States in particular. Second, there are data problems. Some may question whether laboratory simulations can really approximate actual stress behavior of decisionmakers. On the other hand, empirical and historical data relating to crises are not readily available and are notoriously self-serving when available.

Finally and most importantly, most decisionmaking inquiries purport to be value free following the mainstream of contemporary social science research predicated on the assumptions that the distinction between facts and values is logically possible, theoretically necessary, and axiologically essential. However, the problem of reciprocal interaction between actor values and observer values was most perceptively illustrated in an unusual "confessional essay" by Glenn D. Paige, author of the much admired study, *The Korean Decision* (1968). Since the decisionmaking approach did not require acceptance of a violent or nonviolent value position, Paige took a "value-neutral" approach by treating normative issues independently of empirical description. However, a shift of his own value position from violence accepting to violence rejecting made him aware that his case study had implicitly encouraged the acceptance of proviolence value assumptions and that "actor values were given explicit attention," while observer values "were left to vary with the professional conscience of the researcher" (Paige 1977:1604). Reexamination of *The Korean Decision* from a nonviolent value premise led Paige to drastically revise one of the main conclusions of his original study. The reader would do well in following Paige's example of scholarly integrity in their critical reading of the following chapters.

19

Hypotheses on Misperception

Robert Jervis

In determining how he will behave, an actor must try to predict how others will act and how their actions will affect his values. The actor must therefore develop an image of others and of their intentions. This image may, however, turn out to be an inaccurate one; the actor may, for a number of reasons, misperceive both others' actions and their intentions. In this research note I wish to discuss the types of misperceptions of other states' intentions which states tend to make. The concept of intention is complex, but here we can consider it to comprise the ways in which the state feels it will act in a wide range of future contingencies. These ways of acting usually are not specific and well-developed plans. For many reasons a national or individual actor may not know how he will act under given conditions, but this problem cannot be dealt with here.

Previous Treatments of Perception in International Relations

Although diplomatic historians have discussed misperception in their treatments of specific events, students of international relations have generally ignored this topic. However, two sets of scholars have applied content analysis to the documents that flowed within and between governments in the six weeks preceding World War I. But the data have been put into quantitative form in a way that does not produce accurate measures of perceptions and intentions and that makes it impossible to gather useful evidence on misperception.[1]

The second group of theorists who have explicitly dealt with general questions of misperception in international relations consists of those, like Charles Osgood, Amitai Etzioni, and, to a lesser extent, Kenneth Boulding and J. David Singer, who have analyzed the cold war in terms of a spiral of misperception.[2] This approach grows partly out of the mathematical

Robert Jervis, "Hypotheses on Misperception," *World Politics* 20, no. 3 (April 1968). Copyright © 1968 by Princeton University Press. Reprinted by permission of the author and Princeton University Press.

theories of L. F. Richardson[3] and partly out of findings of social and cognitive psychology, many of which will be discussed in this research note.

These authors state their case in general, if not universal, terms, but do not provide many historical cases that are satisfactorily explained by their theories. Furthermore, they do not deal with any of the numerous instances that contradict their notion of the self-defeating aspects of the use of power. They ignore the fact that states are not individuals and that the findings of psychology can be applied to organizations only with great care. Most important, their theoretical analysis is for the most part of reduced value because it seems largely to be a product of their assumption that the Soviet Union is a basically status-quo power whose apparently aggressive behavior is a product of fear of the West. Yet they supply little or no evidence to support this view. Indeed, the explanation for the differences of opinion between the spiral theorists and the proponents of deterrence lies not in differing general views of international relations, differing values and morality,[4] or differing methods of analysis,[5] but in differing perceptions of Soviet intentions.

Theories — Necessary and Dangerous

Despite the limitations of their approach, these writers have touched on a vital problem that has not been given systematic treatment by theorists of international relations. The evidence from both psychology and history overwhelmingly supports the view (which may be labeled Hypothesis 1) that decisionmakers tend to fit incoming information into their existing theories and images. Indeed, their theories and images play a large part in determining what they notice. In other words, actors tend to perceive what they expect. Furthermore (Hypothesis 1a), a theory will have greater impact on an actor's interpretation of data (a) the greater the ambiguity of the data and (b) the higher the degree of confidence with which the actor holds the theory.[6]

For many purposes we can use the concept of differing levels of perceptual thresholds to deal with the fact that it takes more, and more unambiguous, information for an actor to recognize an unexpected phenomenon than an expected one. An experiment by Bruner and Postman determined "that the recognition threshold for . . . incongruous playing cards (those with suits and color reversed) is significantly higher than the threshold for normal cards."[7] Not only are people able to identify normal (and therefore expected) cards more quickly and easily than incongruous (and therefore unexpected) ones, but also they may at first take incongruous cards for normal ones.

However, we should not assume, as the spiral theorists often do, that it is necessarily irrational for actors to adjust incoming information to fit more closely their existing beliefs and images. ("Irrational" here describes acting under pressures that the actor would not admit as legitimate if he were conscious of them.) Abelson and Rosenberg label as "psycho-logic" the pressure to create a "balanced" cognitive structure—i.e., one in which "all relations among 'good elements' [in one's attitude structure] are positive (or null), all relations among 'bad elements' are positive (or null), and all relations between good and bad elements are negative (or null)." They correctly show that the "reasoning [this involves] would mortify a logician."[8] But those who have tried to apply this and similar cognitive theories to international relations have usually overlooked the fact that in many cases there are important logical links between the elements and the processes they describe which cannot be called "psycho-logic." (I am here using the term "logical" not in the narrow sense of drawing only those conclusions that follow necessarily from the premises, but rather in the sense of conforming to generally agreed-upon rules for the treating of evidence.) For example, Osgood claims that psycho-logic is displayed when the Soviets praise a man or a proposal and people in the West react by distrusting the object of this praise.[9] But if a person believes that the Russians are aggressive, it is logical for him to be suspicious of their moves. When we say that a decisionmaker "dislikes" another state this usually means that he believes that that other state has policies conflicting with those of his nation. Reasoning and experience indicate to the decisionmaker that the "disliked" state is apt to harm his state's interests. Thus in these cases there is no need to invoke "psycho-logic," and it cannot be claimed that the cases demonstrate the substitution of "emotional consistency for rational consistency."[10]

The question of the relations among particular beliefs and cognitions can often be seen as part of the general topic of the relation of incoming bits of information to the receivers' already established images. The need to fit data into a wider framework of beliefs, even if doing so does not seem to do justice to individual facts, is not, or at least is not only, a psychological drive that decreases the accuracy of our perceptions of the world, but is "essential to the logic of inquiry."[11] Facts can be interpreted, and indeed identified, only with the aid of hypotheses and theories. Pure empiricism is impossible, and it would be unwise to revise theories in the light of every bit of information that does not easily conform to them.[12] No hypothesis can be expected to account for all the evidence, and if a prevailing view is supported by many theories and by a large pool of findings it should not be quickly altered. Too little rigidity can be as bad as too much.[13]

This is as true in the building of social and physical science as it is in policymaking.[14] While it is terribly difficult to know when a finding throws serious doubt on accepted theories and should be followed up and when instead it was caused by experimental mistakes or minor errors in the theory, it is clear that scientists would make no progress if they followed Thomas Huxley's injunction to "sit down before fact as a mere child, be prepared to give up every preconceived notion, follow humbly wherever nature leads, or you will learn nothing."[15]

As Michael Polanyi explains, "It is true enough that the scientist must be prepared to submit at any moment to the adverse verdict of observational evidence. But not blindly. . . . There is always the possibility that, as in [the cases of the periodic system of elements and the quantum theory of light], a deviation may not affect the essential correctness of a proposition. . . . The process of explaining away deviations is in fact quite indispensable to the daily routine of research," even though this may lead to the missing of a great discovery.[16] For example, in 1795, the astronomer Lalande did not follow up observations that contradicted the prevailing hypotheses and could have led him to discover the planet Neptune.[17]

Yet we should not be too quick to condemn such behavior. As Thomas Kuhn has noted, "There is no such thing as research without counter-instances."[18] If a set of basic theories — what Kuhn calls a paradigm — has been able to account for a mass of data, it should not be lightly trifled with. As Kuhn puts it: "Lifelong resistance, particularly from those whose pro-ductive careers have committed them to an older tradition of normal science [i.e., science within the accepted paradigm], is not a violation of scientific standards but an index to the nature of scientific research itself. The source of resistance is the assurance that the older paradigm will ultimately solve all its problems, that nature can be shoved into the box the paradigm provides. Inevitably, at times of revolution, that assurance seems stubborn and pigheaded as indeed it sometimes becomes. But it is also something more. That same assurance is what makes normal science or puzzle-solving science possible."[19]

Thus it is important to see that the dilemma of how "open" to be to new information is one that inevitably plagues any attempt at understanding in any field. Instances in which evidence seems to be ignored or twisted to fit the existing theory can often be explained by this dilemma instead of by il-logical or nonlogical psychological pressures toward consistency. This is especially true of decisionmakers' attempts to estimate the intentions of other states, since they must constantly take account of the danger that the other state is trying to deceive them.

The theoretical framework discussed thus far, together with an examina-tion of many cases, suggests Hypothesis 2: scholars and decisionmakers are apt to err by being too wedded to the established view and too closed to new information, as opposed to being too willing to alter their theories.[20] Another way of making this point is to argue that actors tend to establish their theories and expectations prematurely. In politics, of course, this is often necessary because of the need for action. But experimental evidence indicates that the same tendency also occurs on the unconscious level. Bruner and Postman found that "perhaps the greatest single barrier to the recognition of incongruous stimuli is the tendency for perceptual hypotheses to fixate after receiving a minimum of confirmation. . . . Once there had occurred in these cases a partial confirmation of the hypothesis . . . it seemed that nothing could change the subject's report."[21]

However, when we apply these and other findings to politics and discuss kinds of misperception, we should not quickly apply the label of cognitive distortion. We should proceed cautiously for two related reasons. The first is that the evidence available to decisionmakers almost always permits several interpretations. It should be noted that there are cases of visual perception in which different stimuli can produce exactly the same pattern on an observer's retina. Thus, for an observer using one eye the same pattern would be produced by a sphere the size of a golf ball which was quite close to the observer, by a baseball-sized sphere that was further away, or by a basketball-sized sphere still further away. Without other clues, the observer cannot possibly determine which of these stimuli he is presented with, and we would not want to call his incorrect perceptions examples of distortion. Such cases, relatively rare in visual perception, are frequent in international relations. The evidence available to decisionmakers is almost always very ambiguous since accurate clues to others' intentions are surrounded by noise[22] and deception. In most cases, no matter how long, deeply, and "objectively" the evidence is analyzed, people can differ in their interpretations, and there are no general rules to indicate who is correct.

The second reason to avoid the label of cognitive distortion is that the distinction between perception and judgment, obscure enough in individual psychology, is almost absent in the making of inferences in international politics. Decisionmakers who reject information that contradicts their views — or who develop complex interpretations of it — often do so consciously and explicitly. Since the evidence available contains contradictory information, to make any inferences requires that much information be ignored or given interpretations that will seem tortuous to those who hold a different position.

Indeed, if we consider only the evidence available to a decisionmaker at the time of decision, the view later proved incorrect may be supported by as much evidence as the correct one — or even by more. Scholars have often been too unsympathetic with the people who were proved wrong. On closer examination, it is frequently difficult to point to differences between those who were right and those who were wrong with respect to their openness to new information and willingness to modify their views. Winston Churchill, for example, did not openmindedly view each Nazi action to see if the explanations provided by the appeasers accounted for the data better than his own beliefs. Instead, like Chamberlain, he fitted each bit of ambiguous information into his own hypotheses. That he was correct should not lead us to overlook the fact that his methods of analysis and use of theory to produce cognitive consistency did not basically differ from those of the appeasers.[23]

A consideration of the importance of expectations in influencing perception also indicates that the widespread belief in the prevalence of "wishful thinking" may be incorrect, or at least may be based on inadequate data. The psychological literature on the interaction between affect and perception is immense and cannot be treated here, but it should be noted that phenomena that at first were considered strong evidence for the impact of affect on perception often can be better treated as demonstrating the influence of expectations.[24] Thus, in international relations, cases like the United States' misestimation of the political climate in Cuba in April 1961, which may seem at first glance to have been instances of wishful thinking, may instead be more adequately explained by the theories held by the decisionmakers (e.g., Communist governments are unpopular). Of course, desires may have an impact on perception by influencing expectations, but since so many other factors affect expectations, the net influence of desires may not be great.

There is evidence from both psychology[25] and international relations that when expectations and desires clash, expectations seem to be more important. The United States would like to believe that North Vietnam is about to negotiate or that the USSR is ready to give up what the United States believes is its goal of world domination, but ambiguous evidence is seen to confirm the opposite conclusion, which conforms to the United States' expectations. Actors are apt to be especially sensitive to evidence of grave danger if they think they can take action to protect themselves against the menace once it has been detected.

Safeguards

Can anything then be said to scholars and decisionmakers other than "Avoid being either too open or too closed, but be especially aware of the latter danger"? Although decisionmakers will always be faced with ambiguous and confusing evidence and will be forced to make inferences about others which will often be inaccurate, a number of safeguards may be suggested which could enable them to minimize their errors. First, and most obvious, decisionmakers should be aware that they do not make "unbiased" interpretations of each new bit of incoming information, but rather are inevitably heavily influenced by the theories they expect to be verified. They should know that what may appear to them as a self-evident and unambiguous inference often seems so only because of their preexisting beliefs. To someone with a different theory the same data may appear to be unimportant or to support another explanation. Thus many events provide less independent support for the decisionmakers' images than they may at first realize. Knowledge of this should lead decisionmakers to examine more closely evidence that others believe contradicts their views.

Second, decisionmakers should see if their attitudes contain consistent or supporting beliefs that are not logically linked. These may be examples of true psycho-logic. While it is not logically surprising nor is it evidence of psychological pressures to find that people who believe that Russia is aggressive are very suspicious of any Soviet move, other kinds of consistency are more suspect. For example, most people who feel that it is important for the United States to win the war in Vietnam also feel that a meaningful victory is possible. And most people who feel defeat would neither endanger U.S. national security nor be costly in terms of other values also feel that we cannot win. Although there are important logical linkages between the two parts of each of these views (especially through theories of guerrilla warfare), they do not seem strong enough to explain the degree to which the opinions are correlated. Similarly, in Finland in the winter of 1939, those who felt that grave consequences would follow Finnish agreement to give Russia a military base also believed that the Soviets would withdraw their demand if Finland stood firm. And those who felt that concessions would not lead to loss of major values also believed that Russia would fight if need be.[26] In this country, those who favored a nuclear test ban tended to argue that fallout was very harmful, that only limited improvements in technology would flow from further testing, and that a test ban would increase the chances for peace and security. Those who opposed the test ban were apt to disagree on all three points. This does not mean, of course, that the people holding such sets of supporting views were necessarily wrong in any one element. The Finns who wanted to make concessions to the USSR were probably correct in both parts of their argument. But decisionmakers should be suspicious if they hold a position in which elements that are not logically connected support the same conclusion. This condition is psychologically comfortable and makes decisions easier to reach (since competing values do not have to be balanced off against each other). The chances are thus considerable that at least part of the reason why a person holds some of these views is related to psychology and not to the substance of the evidence.

Decisionmakers should also be aware that actors who suddenly find themselves having an important shared interest with other actors have a tendency to overestimate the degree of common interest involved. This tendency is especially strong for those actors (e.g., the United States, at least before 1950) whose beliefs about international relations and morality imply that they can cooperate only with "good" states and that with those states there will be no major conflicts. On the other hand, states that have either a tradition of limited cooperation with others (e.g., Britain) or a strongly held theory that differentiates occasional from permanent allies[27] (e.g., the Soviet Union) find it easier to resist this tendency and need not devote special efforts to combating its danger.

A third safeguard for decisionmakers would be to make their assumptions, beliefs, and the predictions that follow from them as explicit as possible. An actor should try to determine, before events occur, what evidence would count for and against his theories. By knowing what to expect he would know what to be surprised by, and surprise could indicate to that actor that his beliefs needed reevaluation.[28]

A fourth safeguard is more complex. The decisionmaker should try to prevent individuals and organizations from letting their main task, political future, and identity become tied to specific theories and images of other actors.[29] If this occurs, subgoals originally sought for their contribution to higher ends will take on value of their own, and information indicating possible alternative routes to the original goals will not be carefully considered. For example, the U.S. Forest Service was unable to carry out its original purpose as effectively when it began to see its distinctive competence not in promoting the best use of lands and forests but rather in preventing all types of forest fires.[30]

Organizations that claim to be unbiased may not realize the extent to which their definition of their role has become involved with certain beliefs about the world. Allen Dulles is a victim of this lack of understanding when he says, "I grant that we are all creatures of prejudice, including CIA officials, but by entrusting intelligence coordination to our central intelligence service, which is excluded from policy-making and is married to no particular military hardware, we can avoid, to the greatest possible extent, the bending of facts obtained through intelligence to suit a particular occupational viewpoint."[31] This statement overlooks the fact that the CIA has developed a certain view of international relations and of the cold war which maximizes the importance of its information-gathering, espionage, and subversive activities. Since the CIA would lose its unique place in the government if it were decided that the "back alleys" of world politics were no longer vital to U.S. security, it is not surprising that the organization interprets information in a way that stresses the continued need for its techniques.

Fifth, decisionmakers should realize the validity and implications of

Roberta Wohlstetter's argument that "a willingness to play with material from different angles and in the context of unpopular as well as popular hypotheses is an essential ingredient of a good detective, whether the end is the solution of a crime or an intelligence estimate."[32] However, it is often difficult, psychologically and politically, for any one person to do this. Since a decisionmaker usually cannot get "unbiased" treatments of data, he should instead seek to structure conflicting biases into the decisionmaking process. The decisionmaker, in other words, should have devil's advocates around. Just as, as Neustadt points out,[33] the decisionmaker will want to create conflicts among his subordinates in order to make appropriate choices, so he will also want to ensure that incoming information is examined from many different perspectives with many different hypotheses in mind. To some extent this kind of examination will be done automatically through the divergence of goals, training, experience, and information that exists in any large organization. But in many cases this divergence will not be sufficient. The views of those analyzing the data will still be too homogeneous, and the decisionmaker will have to go out of his way not only to cultivate but to create differing viewpoints.

While all that would be needed would be to have some people examining the data trying to validate unpopular hypotheses, it would probably be more effective if they actually believed and had a stake in the views they were trying to support. If in 1941 someone had had the task of proving the view that Japan would attack Pearl Harbor, the government might have been less surprised by the attack. And only a person who was out to show that Russia would take objectively great risks would have been apt to note that several ships with especially large hatches going to Cuba were riding high in the water, indicating the presence of a bulky but light cargo that was not likely to be anything other than strategic missiles. And many people who doubt the wisdom of the administration's Vietnam policy would be somewhat reassured if there were people in the government who searched the statements and actions of both sides in an effort to prove that North Vietnam was willing to negotiate and that the official interpretation of such moves as the Communist activities during the Têt truce of 1967 was incorrect.

Of course all these safeguards involve costs. They would divert resources from other tasks and would increase internal dissension. Determining whether these costs would be worth the gains would depend on a detailed analysis of how the suggested safeguards might be implemented. Even if they were adopted by a government, of course, they would not eliminate the chance of misperception. However, the safeguards would make it more likely that national decisionmakers would make conscious choices about the way data were interpreted rather than merely assuming that they can be seen in only one way and can mean only one thing. Statesmen would thus be reminded of alternative images of others just as they are constantly reminded of alternative policies.

These safeguards are partly based on Hypothesis 3: actors can more easily assimilate into their established image of another actor information contradicting that image if the information is transmitted and considered bit by bit than if it comes all at once. In the former case, each piece of discrepant data can be coped with as it arrives and each of the conflicts with the prevailing view will be small enough to go unnoticed, to be dismissed as unimportant, or to necessitate at most a slight modification of the image (e.g., addition of exceptions to the rule). When the information arrives in a block, the contradiction between it and the prevailing view is apt to be much clearer and the probability of major cognitive reorganization will be higher.

Sources of Concepts

An actor's perceptual thresholds—and thus the images that ambiguous information is apt to produce—are influenced by what he has experienced and learned about.[34] If one actor is to perceive that another fits in a given category he must first have, or develop, a concept for that category. We can usefully distinguish three levels at which a concept can be present or absent. First, the concept can be completely missing. The actor's cognitive structure may not include anything corresponding to the phenomenon he is encountering. This situation can occur not only in science fiction, but also in a world of rapid change or in the meeting of two dissimilar systems. Thus China's image of the Western world was extremely inaccurate in the mid-nineteenth century, her learning was very slow, and her responses were woefully inadequate. The West was spared a similar struggle only because it had the power to reshape the system it encountered. Once the actor clearly sees one instance of the new phenomenon, he is apt to recognize it much more quickly in the future.[35] Second, the actor can know about a concept but not believe that it reflects an actual phenomenon. Thus Communist and Western decisionmakers are each aware of the other's explanation of how his system functions, but do not think that the concept corresponds to reality. Communist elites, furthermore, deny that anything *could* correspond to the democracies' description of themselves. Third, the actor may hold a concept, but not believe that another actor fills it at the present moment. Thus the British and French statesmen of the 1930s held a concept of states with unlimited ambitions. They realized that Napoleons were possible, but they did not think Hitler belonged in that category. Hypothesis 4 distinguishes these three cases: misperception is most difficult to correct in the case of a missing concept and least difficult to correct in the case of a recognized but presumably unfilled concept. All other things being equal (e.g., the degree to which the concept is central to the actor's cognitive structure), the first case requires more cognitive reorganization than does the second, and the second requires more reorganization than the third.

However, this hypothesis does not mean that learning will necessarily be slowest in the first case, for if the phenomena are totally new the actor may make such grossly inappropriate responses that he will quickly acquire information clearly indicating that he is faced with something he does not understand. And the sooner the actor realizes that things are not — or may not be — what they seem, the sooner he is apt to correct his image.[36]

Three main sources contribute to decisionmakers' concepts of international relations and of other states and influence the level of their perceptual thresholds for various phenomena. First, an actor's beliefs about his own domestic political system are apt to be important. In some cases, like that of the USSR, the decisionmakers' concepts are tied to an ideology that explicitly provides a frame of reference for viewing foreign affairs. Even where this is not the case, experience with his own system will partly determine what the actor is familiar with and what he is apt to perceive in others. Louis Hartz claims, "It is the absence of the experience of social revolution which is at the heart of the whole American dilemma. . . . In a whole series of specific ways it enters into our difficulty of communication with the rest of the world. We find it difficult to understand Europe's 'social question'. . . . We are not familiar with the deeper social struggles of Asia and hence tend to interpret even reactionary regimes as 'democratic.'"[37] Similarly, George Kennan argues that in World War I the Allied powers, and especially America, could not understand the bitterness and violence of others' internal conflicts: "The inability of the Allied statesmen to picture to themselves the passions of the Russian civil war [was partly caused by the fact that] we represent . . . a society in which the manifestations of evil have been carefully buried and sublimated in the social behavior of people, as in their very consciousness. For this reason, probably, despite our widely traveled and outwardly cosmopolitan lives, the mainsprings of political behavior in such a country as Russia tend to remain concealed from our vision."[38]

Second, concepts will be supplied by the actor's previous experiences. An experiment from another field illustrates this. Dearborn and Simon presented business executives from various divisions (e.g., sales, accounting, production) with the same hypothetical data and asked them for an analysis and recommendations from the standpoint of what would be best for the company as a whole. The executives' views heavily reflected their departmental perspectives.[39] William W. Kaufmann shows how the perceptions of Ambassador Joseph Kennedy were affected by his past: "As befitted a former chairman of the Securities Exchange and Maritime Commissions, his primary interest lay in economic matters. . . . The revolutionary character of the Nazi regime was not a phenomenon that he could easily grasp. . . . It was far simpler, and more in accord with his own premises, to explain German aggressiveness in economic terms. The Third Reich was dissatisfied, authoritarian, and expansive largely because her economy was unsound."[40] Similarly it has been argued that Chamberlain was slow to recognize Hitler's intentions partly because of the limiting nature of his personal background and business experiences.[41] The impact of training and experience seems to be demonstrated when the background of the appeasers is compared to that of their opponents. One difference stands out: "A substantially higher percentage of the anti-appeasers (irrespective of class origins) had the kind of knowledge which comes from close acquaintance, mainly professional, with foreign affairs."[42] Since members of the diplomatic corps are responsible for meeting threats to the nation's security before these grow to major proportions and since they have learned about cases in which aggressive states were not recognized as such until very late, they may be prone to interpret ambiguous data as showing that others are aggressive. It should be stressed that we cannot say that the professionals of the 1930s were more apt to make accurate judgments of other states. Rather, they may have been more sensitive to the chance that others were aggressive. They would then rarely take an aggressor for a status-quo power, but would more often make the opposite error.[43] Thus in the years before World War I the permanent officials in the British Foreign Office overestimated German aggressiveness.[44]

A parallel demonstration in psychology of the impact of training on perception is presented by an experiment in which ambiguous pictures were shown to both advanced and beginning police-administration students. The advanced group perceived more violence in the pictures than did the beginners. The probable explanation is that "the law enforcer may come to accept crime as a familiar personal experience, one which he himself is not surprised to encounter. The acceptance of crime as a familiar experience in turn increases the ability or readiness to perceive violence where clues to it are potentially available."[45] This experiment lends weight to the view that the British diplomats' sensitivity to aggressive states was not totally a product of personnel selection procedures.

A third source of concepts, which frequently will be the most directly relevant to a decisionmaker's perception of international relations, is international history. As Henry Kissinger points out, one reason why statesmen were so slow to recognize the threat posed by Napoleon was that previous events had accustomed them only to actors who wanted to modify the existing system, not overthrow it.[46] The other side of the coin is even more striking: historical traumas can heavily influence future perceptions. They can either establish a state's image of the other state involved or can be used as analogies. An example of the former case is provided by the fact that for at least ten years after the Franco-Prussian War most of Europe's statesmen felt that Bismarck had aggressive plans when in fact his main goal was to protect the status quo. Of course the evidence was ambiguous. The post-1871 Bismarckian maneuvers, which were designed to keep peace, looked not unlike the pre-1871 maneuvers designed to set the stage for war. But that the post-1871 maneuvers were seen as indicating aggressive plans is largely attributable to the impact of Bismarck's earlier actions on the statesmen's image of him.

A state's previous unfortunate experience with a type of danger can sensitize it to other examples of that danger. While this sensitivity may lead the state to avoid the mistake it committed in the past, it may also lead it mistakenly to believe that the present situation is like the past one. Santayana's maxim could be turned around: "Those who remember the past are condemned to make the opposite mistakes." As Paul Kecskemeti shows, both defenders and critics of the unconditional surrender plan of the Second World War thought in terms of the conditions of World War I.[47] Annette Baker Fox found that the Scandinavian countries' neutrality policies in World War II were strongly influenced by their experiences in the previous war, even though vital aspects of the two situations were different. Thus "Norway's success [during the First World War] in remaining nonbelligerent though pro-Allied gave the Norwegians confidence that their country could again stay out of war."[48] And the lesson drawn from the unfortunate results of this policy was an important factor in Norway's decision to join NATO.

The application of the Munich analogy to various contemporary events has been much commented on, and I do not wish to argue the substantive points at stake. But it seems clear that the probabilities that any state is facing an aggressor who has to be met by force are not altered by the career of Hitler and the history of the 1930s. Similarly the probability of an aggressor's announcing his plans is not increased (if anything, it is decreased) by the fact that Hitler wrote *Mein Kampf*. Yet decisionmakers are more sensitive to these possibilities, and thus more apt to perceive ambiguous evidence as indicating they apply to a given case, than they would have been had there been no Nazi Germany.

Historical analogies often precede, rather than follow, a careful analysis of a situation (e.g., Truman's initial reaction to the news of the invasion of South Korea was to think of the Japanese invasion of Manchuria). Noting this precedence, however, does not show us which of many analogies will come to a decisionmaker's mind. Truman could have thought of nineteenth-century European wars that were of no interest to the United States. Several factors having nothing to do with the event under consideration influence what analogies a decisionmaker is apt to make. One factor is the number of cases similar to the analogy with which the decisionmaker is familiar. Another is the importance of the past event to the political system of which the decisionmaker is a part. The more times such an event occurred and the greater its consequences were, the more a decisionmaker will be sensitive to the particular danger involved and the more he will be apt to see ambiguous stimuli as indicating another instance of this kind of event. A third factor is the degree of the decisionmaker's personal involvement in the past case — in time, energy, ego, and position. The last-mentioned variable will affect not only the event's impact on the decision-maker's cognitive structure, but also the way he perceives the event and the lesson he draws. Someone who was involved in getting troops into South Korea after the attack will remember the Korean War differently from someone who was involved in considering the possible use of nuclear weapons or in deciding what messages should be sent to the Chinese. Greater personal involvement will usually give the event greater impact, especially if the decisionmaker's own views were validated by the event. One need not accept a total application of learning theory to nations to believe that "nothing fails like success."[49] It also seems likely that if many critics argued at the time that the decisionmaker was wrong, he will be even more apt to see other situations in terms of the original event. For example, because Anthony Eden left the government on account of his views and was later shown to have been correct, he probably was more apt to see as Hitlers other leaders with whom he had conflicts (e.g., Nasser). A fourth factor is the degree to which the analogy is compatible with the rest of his belief system. A fifth is the absence of alternative concepts and analogies. Individuals and states vary in the amount of direct or indirect political experience they have had which can provide different ways of interpreting data. Decisionmakers who are aware of multiple possibilities of states' intentions may be less likely to seize on an analogy prematurely. The perception of citizens of nations like the United States which have relatively little history of international politics may be more apt to be heavily influenced by the few major international events that have been important to their country.

The first three factors indicate that an event is more apt to shape present perceptions if it occurred in the recent rather than the remote past. If it occurred recently, the statesman will then know about it at first hand even if he was not involved in the making of policy at the time. Thus if generals are prepared to fight the last war, diplomats may be prepared to avoid the last war. Part of the Anglo-French reaction to Hitler can be explained by the prevailing beliefs that the First World War was to a large extent caused by misunderstandings and could have been avoided by farsighted and nonbelligerent diplomacy. And part of the Western perception of Russia and China can be explained by the view that appeasement was an inappropriate response to Hitler.[50]

The Evoked Set

The way people perceive data is influenced not only by their cognitive structure and theories about other actors but also by what they are concerned with at the time they receive the information. Information is evaluated in light of the small part of the person's memory that is presently active—the "evoked set." My perceptions of the dark streets I pass walking home from the movies will be different if the film I saw had dealt with spies than if it had been a comedy. If I am working on aiding a country's education system and I hear someone talk about the need for economic development in that state, I am apt to think he is concerned with education, whereas if I had been working on, say, trying to achieve political stability in that country, I would have placed his remarks in that framework.[51]

Thus Hypothesis 5 states that when messages are sent from a different background of concerns and information than is possessed by the receiver, misunderstanding is likely. Person A and person B will read the same message quite differently if A has seen several related messages that B does not know about. This difference will be compounded if, as is frequently the case, A and B each assume that the other has the same background he does. This means that misperception can occur even when deception is neither intended nor expected. Thus Roberta Wohlstetter found not only that different parts of the United States government had different perceptions of data about Japan's intentions and messages partly because they saw the incoming information in very different contexts, but also that officers in the field misunderstood warnings from Washington: "Washington advised General Short [in Pearl Harbor] on November 27 to expect 'hostile action' at any moment, by which it meant 'attack on American possessions from without,' but General Short understood this phrase to mean 'sabotage.'"[52] Washington did not realize the extent to which Pearl Harbor considered the danger of sabotage to be primary, and furthermore it incorrectly believed that General Short had received the intercepts of the secret Japanese diplomatic messages available in Washington which indicated that surprise attack was a distinct possibility. Another implication of this hypothesis is that if important information is known to only part of the government of state A and part of the government of state B, international messages may be misunderstood by those parts of the receiver's government that do not match, in the information they have, the part of the sender's government that dispatched the message.[53]

Two additional hypotheses can be drawn from the problems of those sending messages. Hypothesis 6 states that when people spend a great deal of time drawing up a plan or making a decision, they tend to think that the message about it they wish to convey will be clear to the receiver.[54] Since they are aware of what is to them the important pattern in their actions, they often feel that the pattern will be equally obvious to others, and they overlook the degree to which the message is apparent to them only because they know what to look for. Those who have not participated in the endless meetings may not understand what information the sender is trying to convey. George Quester has shown how the German and, to a lesser extent, the British desire to maintain target limits on bombing in the first eighteen months of World War II was undermined partly by the fact that each side knew the limits it was seeking and its own reasons for any apparent "exceptions" (e.g., the German attack on Rotterdam) and incorrectly felt that these limits and reasons were equally clear to the other side.[55]

Hypothesis 7 holds that actors often do not realize that actions intended to project a given image may not have the desired effect because the actions themselves do not turn out as planned. Thus even without appreciable impact of different cognitive structures and backgrounds, an action may convey an unwanted message. For example, a country's representatives may not follow instructions and so may give others impressions contrary to those the home government wished to convey. The efforts of Washington and Berlin to settle their dispute over Samoa in the late 1880s were complicated by the provocative behavior of their agents on the spot. These agents not only increased the intensity of the local conflict, but led the decisionmakers to become more suspicious of the other state because they tended to assume that their agents were obeying instructions and that the actions of the other side represented official policy. In such cases both sides will believe that the other is reading hostility into a policy of theirs which is friendly. Similarly, Quester's study shows that the attempt to limit bombing referred to above failed partly because neither side was able to bomb as accurately as it thought it could and thus did not realize the physical effects of its actions.[56]

Further Hypotheses From the Perspective of the Perceiver

From the perspective of the perceiver several other hypotheses seem to hold. Hypothesis 8 is that there is an overall tendency for decisionmakers to see other states as more hostile than they are.[57] There seem to be more cases of statesmen incorrectly believing others are planning major acts against their interest than of statesmen being lulled by a potential aggressor. There are many reasons for this which are too complex to be treated here (e.g., some parts of the bureaucracy feel it is their responsibility to be suspicious of all other states; decisionmakers often feel they are "playing it safe" to believe and act as though the other state were hostile in questionable cases; and often, when people do not feel they are a threat to others, they find it difficult to believe that others may see them as a threat). It should be noted, however, that decisionmakers whose perceptions are described by this hypothesis would not necessarily further their own values by trying to correct for this tendency. The values of possible outcomes as well as their probabilities must be considered, and it may be that the probability of an unnecessary arms-tension cycle arising out of misperceptions, multiplied by the costs of such a cycle, may seem less to decisionmakers than the probability of incorrectly believing another state is friendly, multiplied by the costs of this eventuality.

Hypothesis 9 states that actors tend to see the behavior of others as more centralized, disciplined, and coordinated than it is. This hypothesis holds true in related ways. Frequently, too many complex events are squeezed into a perceived pattern. Actors are hesitant to admit or even see that particular incidents cannot be explained by their theories.[58] Those events not caused by factors that are important parts of the perceiver's image are often seen as though they were. Further, actors see others as more internally united than they in fact are and generally overestimate the degree to which others are following a coherent policy. The degree to which the other side's policies are the product of internal bargaining,[59] internal misunderstandings, or subordinates' not following instructions is underestimated. This is the case partly because actors tend to be unfamiliar with the details of another state's policymaking processes. Seeing only the finished product, they find it simpler to try to construct a rational explanation for the policies, even though they know that such an analysis could not explain their own policies.[60]

Familiarity also accounts for Hypothesis 10: because a state gets most of its information about the other state's policies from the other's foreign office, it tends to take the foreign office's position for the stand of the other government as a whole. In many cases this perception will be an accurate one, but when the other government is divided or when the other foreign office is acting without specific authorization, misperception may result. For example, part of the reason why in 1918 Allied governments incorrectly thought "that the Japanese were preparing to take action [in Siberia], if need be, with agreement with the British and French alone, disregarding the absence of American consent,"[61] was that Allied ambassadors had talked mostly with Foreign Minister Motono, who was among the minority of the Japanese favoring this policy. Similarly, America's NATO allies may have gained an inaccurate picture of the degree to which the American government was committed to the Multilateral Force (MLF) because they had greatest contact with parts of the government that strongly favored the MLF. And states that tried to get information about Nazi foreign policy from German diplomats were often misled because these officials were generally ignorant of or out of sympathy with Hitler's plans. The Germans and the Japanese sometimes purposely misinformed their own ambassadors in order to deceive their enemies more effectively.

Hypothesis 11 states that actors tend to overestimate the degree to which others are acting in response to what they themselves do when the others behave in accordance with the actor's desires; but when the behavior of the other is undesired, it is usually seen as derived from internal forces. If the *effect* of another's action is to injure or threaten the first side, the first side is apt to believe that such was the other's *purpose*. An example of the first part of the hypothesis is provided by Kennan's account of the activities of official and unofficial American representatives who protested to the new Bolshevik government against several of its actions. When the Soviets changed their position, these representatives felt it was largely because of their influence.[62] This sort of interpretation can be explained not only by the fact that it is gratifying to the individual making it, but also, taking the other side of the coin mentioned in Hypothesis 9, by the fact that the actor is most familiar with his own input into the other's decision and has less knowledge of other influences. The second part of Hypothesis 11 is illustrated by the tendency of actors to believe that the hostile behavior of others is to be explained by the other side's motives and not by its reaction to the first side. Thus Chamberlain did not see that Hitler's behavior was related in part to his belief that the British were weak. More common is the failure to see that the other side is reacting out of fear of the first side, which can lead to self-fulfilling prophecies and spirals of misperception and hostility.

This difficulty is often compounded by an implication of Hypothesis 12: when actors have intentions that they do not try to conceal from others, they tend to assume that others accurately perceive these intentions. Only rarely do they believe that others may be reacting to a much less favorable image of themselves than they think they are projecting.[63]

For state A to understand how state B perceives A's policy is often difficult because such understanding may involve a conflict with A's image of itself. Raymond Sontag argues that Anglo-German relations before World War I deteriorated partly because "the British did not like to think of themselves as selfish, or unwilling to tolerate 'legitimate' German expansion. The Germans did not like to think of themselves as aggressive, or unwilling to recognize 'legitimate' British vested interest."[64]

Hypothesis 13 suggests that if it is hard for an actor to believe that the other can see him as a menace, it is often even harder for him to see that issues important to him are not important to others. While he may know that another actor is on an opposing team, it may be more difficult for him to realize that the other is playing an entirely different game. This is especially true when the game he is playing seems vital to him.[65]

The final hypothesis, Hypothesis 14, is as follows: actors tend to overlook the fact that evidence consistent with their theories may also be consistent with other views. When choosing between two theories we have to pay attention only to data that cannot be accounted for by one of the theories. But it is common to find people claiming as proof of their theories data that could also support alternative views. This phenomenon is related to the point made earlier that any single bit of information can be interpreted only within a framework of hypotheses and theories. And while it is true that "we may without a vicious circularity accept some datum as a fact because it conforms to the very law for which it counts as another confirming instance, and reject an allegation of fact because it is already excluded by law,"[66] we should be careful lest we forget that a piece of information seems in many cases to confirm a certain hypothesis only because we already believe that hypothesis to be correct and that the information can with as much validity support a different hypothesis. For example, one of the reasons why the German attack on Norway took both that country and England by surprise, even though they had detected German ships moving toward Norway, was that they expected not an attack but an attempt by the Germans to break through the British blockade and reach the Atlantic. The initial course of the ships was consistent with either plan, but the British and Norwegians took this course to mean that their predictions were being borne out.[67] This is not to imply that the interpretation made was foolish, but only that the decisionmakers should have been aware that the evidence was also consistent with an invasion and should have had a bit less confidence in their views.

The longer the ships would have to travel the same route whether they were going to one or another of two destinations, the more information would be needed to determine their plans. Taken as a metaphor, this incident applies generally to the treatment of evidence. Thus as long as Hitler made demands for control only of ethnically German areas, his actions could be explained either by the hypothesis that he had unlimited ambitions or by the hypothesis that he wanted to unite all the Germans. But actions against non-Germans (e.g., the takeover of Czechoslovakia in March 1938) could not be accounted for by the latter hypothesis. And it was this action that convinced the appeasers that Hitler had to be stopped. It is interesting to speculate on what the British reaction would have been had Hitler left Czechoslovakia alone for a while and instead made demands on Poland similar to those he eventually made in the summer of 1939. The two paths would then still not have diverged, and further misperception could have occurred.

Notes

I am grateful to the Harvard Center for International Affairs for research support. An earlier version of this research note was presented at the International Studies Association panel of the New England Political Science Association in April 1967. I have benefited from comments by Robert Art, Alexander George, Paul Kecskemeti, Paul Leary, Thomas Schelling, James Schlesinger, Morton Schwartz, and Aaron Wildavsky.

1. See, for example, Ole Holsti, Robert North, and Richard Brody, "Perception and Action in the 1914 Crisis," in J. David Singer, ed., *Quantitative International Politics* (New York, 1968). For a fuller discussion of the Stanford content analysis studies and the general problems of quantification, see my "The Costs of the Quantitative Study of International Relations," in Klaus Knorr and James N. Rosenau, eds., *Contending Approaches to International Politics* (forthcoming).

2. See, for example, Osgood, *An Alternative to War or Surrender* (Urbana, 1962); Etzioni, *The Hard Way to Peace* (New York, 1962); Boulding, "National Images and International Systems," *Journal of Conflict Resolution* 3 (June 1959):120-131; and Singer, *Deterrence, Arms Control, and Disarmament* (Columbus, 1962).

3. *Statistics of Deadly Quarrels* (Pittsburgh, 1960) and *Arms and Insecurity* (Chicago, 1960). For nonmathematicians a fine summary of Richardson's work is Anatol Rapoport's "L. F. Richardson's Mathematical Theory of War," *Journal of Conflict Resolution* 1 (September 1957):249-299.

4. See Philip Green, *Deadly Logic* (Columbus, 1966); Green, "Method and Substance in the Arms Debate," *World Politics* 16 (July 1964):642-667; and Robert A. Levine, "Fact and Morals in the Arms Debate," *World Politics* 14 (January 1962):239-258.

5. See Anatol Rapoport, *Strategy and Conscience* (New York, 1964).

6. Floyd Allport, *Theories of Perception and the Concept of Structure* (New York, 1955), 382; Ole Holsti, "Cognitive Dynamics and Images of the Enemy," in David Finlay, Ole Holsti, and Richard Fagen, *Enemies in Politics* (Chicago, 1967), 70.

7. Jerome Bruner and Leo Postman, "On the Perceptions of Incongruity: A Paradigm," in Jerome Bruner and David Krech, eds., *Perception and Personality* (Durham, N.C., 1949), 210.

8. Robert Abelson and Milton Rosenberg, "Symbolic Psycho-logic," *Behavioral Science* 3 (January 1958):4-5.

9. P. 27.

10. Ibid., 26.

11. I have borrowed this phase from Abraham Kaplan, who uses it in a different but related context in *The Conduct of Inquiry* (San Francisco, 1964), 86.

12. The spiral theorists are not the only ones to ignore the limits of empiricism. Roger Hilsman found that most consumers and producers of intelligence felt that intelligence should not deal with hypotheses, but should only provide the policymakers with "all the facts" (*Strategic Intelligence and National Decisions* [Glencoe, 1956], 46). The close interdependence between hypotheses and facts is overlooked partly because of the tendency to identify "hypotheses" with "policy preferences."

13. Karl Deutsch interestingly discusses a related question when he argues, "Autonomy . . . requires both intake from the present and recall from memory, and selfhood can be seen in just this continuous balancing of a limited present and a limited past. . . . No further self-determination is possible if either openness or memory is lost. . . . To the extent that [systems cease to be able to take in new information], they approach the behavior of a bullet or torpedo: their future action becomes almost completely determined by their past. On the other hand, a person without memory, an organization without values or policy . . . — all these no longer steer, but drift: their behavior depends little on their past and almost wholly on their present. Driftwood and the bullet are thus each the epitome of another kind of loss of self-control" (*Nationalism and Social Communication* [Cambridge, Mass, 1954], 167-168). Also see Deutsch's *The Nerves of Government* (New York 1963), 98-109, 200-256. A physicist makes a similar argument: "It is clear that if one is too attached to one's preconceived model, one will miss all radical discoveries. It is amazing to what degree one may fail to register mentally an observation which does not fit the initial image. . . . On the other hand, if one is too open-minded and pursues every hitherto unknown phenomenon, one is almost certain to lose oneself in trivia" (Martin Deutsch, "Evidence and Inference in Nuclear Research," in Daniel Lerner, ed., *Evidence and Inference* [Glencoe 1958], 102).

14. Raymond Bauer, "Problems of Perception and the Relations Between the U.S. and the Soviet Union," *Journal of Conflict Resolution* 5 (September 1961):223-229.

15. Quoted in W.I.B. Beveridge, *The Art of Scientific Investigation,* 3rd ed. (London, 1957), 50.

16. *Science, Faith, and Society* (Chicago, 1964), 31. For a further discussion of this problem, see ibid., 16, 26-41, 90-94; Polanyi, *Personal Knowledge* (London, 1958), 8-15, 30, 143-168, 269-298, 310-311; Thomas Kuhn, *The Structure of Scientific Revolution* (Chicago, 1964); Kuhn, "The Function of Dogma in Scientific Research," in A. C. Crombie, ed., *Scientific Change* (New York, 1963), 344-369; the comments on Kuhn's paper by Hall, Polanyi, and Toulmin, and Kuhn's reply, ibid., 370-395. For a related discussion of these points from a different perspective, see Norman Storer, *The Social System of Science* (New York, 1960), 116-122.

17. "He found that the position of one star relative to others . . . had shifted. Lalande was a good astronomer and knew that such a shift was unreasonable. He crossed out his first observation, put a question mark next to the second observation, and let the matter go" (Jerome Bruner, Jacqueline Goodnow, and George Austin, *A Study of Thinking* [New York, 1962], 105).

18. *The Structure of Scientific Revolution,* 79.

19. Ibid., 150-151.

20. Requirements of effective political leadership may lead decisionmakers to voice fewer doubts than they have about existing policies and images, but this constraint can only partially explain this phenomenon. Similar calculations of political strategy may contribute to several of the hypotheses discussed below.

21. P. 221. Similarly, in experiments dealing with his subjects' perception of other people, Charles Dailey found that "premature judgment appears to make new data harder to assimilate than when the observer withholds judgment until all data are seen. It seems probable . . . that the observer mistakes his own inferences for facts" ("The Effects of Premature Conclusion Upon the Acquisition of Understanding of a Person," *Journal of Psychology* 30 [January, 1952]:149-150). For other theory and evidence on this point, see Bruner, "On Perceptual Readiness," *Psychological Review* (March 1957):123-152; Gerald Davidson, "The Negative Effects of Early Exposure to Suboptimal Visual Stimuli," *Journal of Personality* 32 (June 1964):278-295; Albert Myers, "An Experimental Analysis of a Tactical Blunder," *Journal of Abnormal and Social Psychology* 69 (November 1964):493-498; and Dale Wyatt and Donald Campbell, "On the Liability of Stereotype or Hypothesis," *Journal of Abnormal and Social Psychology* 44 (October 1950):496-500. It should be noted that this tendency makes "incremental" decisionmaking more likely (David Braybrooke and Charles Lindblom, *A Strategy of Decision* [New York, 1963]), but the results of this process may lead the actor further from his goals.

22. For a use of this concept in political communication, see Roberta Wohlstetter, *Pearl Harbor* (Stanford, 1962).

23. Similarly, Robert Coulondre, the French ambassador to Berlin in 1939, was one of the few diplomats to appreciate the Nazi threat. Partly because of his earlier service in the USSR, "he was painfully sensitive to the threat of a Berlin-Moscow agreement. He noted with foreboding that Hitler had not attacked Russia in his *Reichstag* address of April 28. . . . So it went all spring and summer, the ambassador relaying each new evidence of the impending diplomatic revolution and adding to his admonitions his pleas for decisive counteraction" (Franklin Ford and Carl Schorske, "The Voice in the Wilderness: Robert Coulondre," in Gordon Craig and Felix Gilbert, eds., *The Diplomats,* Vol. III [New York, 1963]:573-574). His hypotheses were correct, but it is difficult to detect differences between the way he and those ambassadors who were incorrect, like Neville Henderson, selectively noted and interpreted information. However, to the extent that the fear of war influenced the appeasers' perceptions of Hitler's intentions, the appeasers' views did have an element of psycho-logic that was not present in their opponents' position.

24. See, for example, Donald Campbell, "Systematic Error on the Part of Human Links in Communications Systems," *Information and Control* 1 (1958):346-350; and Leo Postman, "The Experimental Analysis of Motivational Factors in Perception," in Judson S. Brown, ed., *Current Theory and Research in Motivation* (Lincoln, Neb., 1953), 59-108.

25. Dale Wyatt and Donald Campbell, "A Study of Interviewer Bias as Related to Interviewer's Expectations and Own Opinions," *International Journal of Opinion and Attitude Research* 4 (spring 1950):77-83.

26. Max Jacobson, *The Diplomacy of the Winter War* (Cambridge, Mass., 1961), 136-139.

27. Raymond Aron, *Peace and War* (Garden City, 1966), 29.

28. Cf. Kuhn, *The Structure of Scientific Revolution,* 65. A fairly high degree of knowledge is needed before one can state precise expectations. One indication of the lack of international relations theory is that most of us are not sure what "naturally" flows from our theories and what constitutes either "puzzles" to be further explored with the paradigm or "anomalies" that cast doubt on the basic theories.

29. See Philip Selznick, *Leadership in Administration* (Evanston, 1957).

30. Ashley Schiff, *Fire and Water: Scientific Heresy in the Forest Service* (Cambridge, Mass., 1962). Despite its title, this book is a fascinating and valuable study.

31. *The Craft of Intelligence* (New York, 1963), 53.

32. P. 302. See Beveridge, 93, for a discussion of the idea that the scientist should keep in mind as many hypotheses as possible when conducting and analyzing experiments.

33. *Presidential Power* (New York, 1960).

34. Most psychologists argue that this influence also holds for perception of shapes. For data showing that people in different societies differ in respect to their predisposition to experience certain optical illusions and for a convincing argument that this difference can be explained by the societies' different physical environments, which have led their people to develop different patterns of drawing inferences from ambiguous visual cues, see Marshall Segall, Donald Campbell, and Melville Herskovits, *The Influence of Culture on Visual Perceptions* (Indianapolis, 1966).

35. Thus when Bruner and Postman's subjects first were presented with incongruous playing cards (i.e., cards in which symbols and colors of the suits were not matching, producing red spades or black diamonds), long exposure times were necessary for correct identification. But once a subject correctly perceived the card and added this type of card to his repertoire of categories, he was able to identify other incongruous cards much more quickly. For an analogous example — in this case, changes in the analysis of aerial reconnaissance photographs of an enemy's secret weapons-testing facilities produced by the belief that a previously unknown object may be present — see David Irving, *The Mare's Nest* (Boston, 1964), 66-67, 274-275.

36. Bruner and Postman, 220.

37. *The Liberal Tradition in America* (New York, 1955), 306.

38. *Russia and the West Under Lenin and Stalin* (New York, 1962), 142-143.

39. DeWitt Dearborn and Herbert Simon, "Selective Perception: A Note on the Departmental Identification of Executives," *Sociometry* 21 (June 1958):140-144.

40. "Two American Ambassadors: Bullitt and Kennedy," in Craig and Gilbert, 358-359.

41. Hugh Trevor-Roper puts this point well: "Brought up as a business man, successful in municipal politics, [Chamberlain's] outlook was entirely parochial. Educated Conservative aristocrats like Churchill, Eden, and Cranborne, whose families had long been used to political responsibility, had seen revolution and revolutionary leaders before, in their own history, and understood them correctly;

but the Chamberlains, who had run from radical imperialism to timid conservatism in a generation of life in Birmingham, had no such understanding of history or the world: to them the scope of human politics was limited by their own parochial horizons, and Neville Chamberlain could not believe that Hitler was fundamentally different from himself. If Chamberlain wanted peace, so must Hitler" ("Munich — Its Lessons Ten Years Later," in Francis Loewenheim, ed., *Peace or Appeasement?* [Boston, 1965], 152-153). For a similar view see A. L. Rowse, *Appeasement* (New York, 1963), 117.

But Donald Lammers points out that the views of many prominent British public figures in the 1930s do not fit this generalization (*Explaining Munich* [Stanford, 1966], 13-140). Furthermore, arguments that stress the importance of the experiences and views of the actors' ancestors do not explain the links by which these influence the actors themselves. Presumably Churchill and Chamberlain read the same history books in school and had the same basic information about Britain's past role in the world. Thus what has to be demonstrated is that in their homes aristocrats like Churchill learned different things about politics and human nature than did middle-class people like Chamberlain and that these experiences had a significant impact. Alternatively, it could be argued that the patterns of child rearing prevalent among the aristocracy influenced the children's personalities in a way that made them more likely to see others as aggressive.

42. Ibid., 15.

43. During a debate on appeasement in the House of Commons, Harold Nicolson declared, "I know that those of us who believe in the traditions of our policy, . . . who believe that one great function of this country is to maintain moral standards in Europe, to maintain a settled pattern of international relations, not to make friends with people who are demonstrably evil . . . — I know that those who hold such beliefs are accused of possessing the Foreign Office mind. I thank God that I possess the Foreign Office mind" (quoted in Martin Gilbert, *The Roots of Appeasement* [New York, 1966], 187). But the qualities Nicolson mentions and applauds may be related to a more basic attribute of "the Foreign Office mind" — suspiciousness.

44. George Monger, *The End of Isolation* (London, 1963). I am also indebted to Frederick Collignon for his unpublished manuscript and several conversations on this point.

45. Hans Toch and Richard Schulte, "Readiness to Perceive Violence as a Result of Police Training," *British Journal of Psychology* 52 (November 1961):392 (original italics omitted). It should be stressed that one cannot say whether or not the advanced police students perceived the pictures "accurately." The point is that their training predisposed them to see violence in ambiguous situations. Whether on balance they would make fewer perceptual errors and better decisions is very hard to determine. For an experiment showing that training can lead people to "recognize" an expected stimulus even when that stimulus is in fact not shown, see Israel Goldiamond and William F. Hawkins, "Vexierversuch: The Log Relationship Between Word-Frequency and Recognition Obtained in the Absence of Stimulus Words," *Journal of Experimental Psychology* 56 (December 1958):457-463.

46. *A World Restored* (New York, 1964), 2-3.

47. *Strategic Surrender* (New York, 1964), 215-241.

48. *The Power of Small States* (Chicago, 1959), 81.

49. William Inge, *Outspoken Essays,* First Series (London, 1923), 88.

50. Of course, analogies themselves are not "unmoved movers." The interpretation of past events is not automatic and is informed by general views of international relations and complex judgments. And just as beliefs about the past influence the present, views about the present influence interpretations of history. It is difficult to determine the degree to which the United States' interpretation of the reasons it went to war in 1917 influenced American foreign policy in the 1920s and 1930s and how much the isolationism of that period influenced the histories of the war.

51. For some psychological experiments on this subject, see Jerome Bruner and A. Leigh Minturn, "Perceptual Identification and Perceptual Organization," *Journal of General Psychology* 53 (July 1955):22-28; Seymour Feshbach and Robert Singer, "The Effects of Fear Arousal and Suppression of Fear Upon Social Perception," *Journal of Abnormal and Social Psychology* 55 (November 1957):283-288; and Elsa Sippoal, "A Group Study of Some Effects of Preparatory Sets," *Psychology Monographs* 66, no. 210 (1935):27-28. For a general discussion of the importance of the perceiver's evoked set, see Postman, 87.

52. Pp. 73-74.

53. For example, Roger Hilsman points out, "Those who knew of the peripheral reconnaissance flights that probed Soviet air defenses during the Eisenhower administration and the U-2 flights over the Soviet Union itself . . . were better able to understand some of the things the Soviets were saying and doing than people who did not know of these activities" (*To Move a Nation* [Garden City, 1967], 66). But it is also possible that those who knew about the U-2 flights at times misinterpreted Soviet messages by incorrectly believing that the sender was influenced by, or at least knew of, these flights.

54. I am grateful to Thomas Schelling for discussion on this point.

55. *Deterrence Before Hiroshima* (New York, 1966), 105-122.

56. Ibid.

57. For a slightly different formulation of this view, see Holsti, 27.

58. The Soviets consciously hold an extreme version of this view and seem to believe that nothing is accidental. See the discussion in Nathan Leites, *A Study of Bolshevism* (Glencoe, 1953), 67-73.

59. A. W. Marshall criticizes Western explanations of Soviet military posture for failing to take this into account. See his "Problems of Estimating Military Power," a paper presented at the 1966 Annual Meeting of the American Political Science Association, 16.

60. It has also been noted that in labor-management disputes both sides may be apt to believe incorrectly that the other is controlled from above, either from the international union office or from the company's central headquarters (Robert Blake, Herbert Shepard, and Jane Mouton, *Managing Intergroup Conflict in Industry* [Houston, 1964], 182). It has been further noted that both Democratic and Republican members of the House tend to see the other party as the one that is more disciplined and united (Charles Clapp, *The Congressman* [Washington, 1963], 17-19).

61. George Kennan, *Russia Leaves the War* (New York, 1967), 484.

62. Ibid., 404, 408, 500.

63. Herbert Butterfield notes that these assumptions can contribute to the spiral of "Hobbesian fear. . . . You yourself may vividly feel the terrible fear that you have of the other party, but you cannot enter into the other man's counter-fear, or even understand why he should be particularly nervous. For you know that you yourself mean him no harm, and that you want nothing from him save guarantees for your own safety; and it is never possible for you to realize or remember properly that since he cannot see the inside of your mind, he can never have the same assurance of your intentions that you have" (*History and Human Conflict* [London, 1951], 20).

64. *European Diplomatic History 1871-1932* (New York, 1933), 125. It takes great mental effort to realize that actions which seem only the natural consequence of defending your vital interests can look to others as though you are refusing them any chance of increasing their influence. In rebutting the famous Crowe "balance of power" memorandum of 1907, which justified a policy of "containing" Germany on the grounds that she was a threat to British national security, Sanderson, a former permanent undersecretary in the Foreign Office, wrote, "It has sometimes seemed to me that to a foreigner reading our press the British Empire must appear in the light of some huge giant sprawling all over the globe, with gouty fingers and toes stretching in every direction, which cannot be approached without eliciting a scream" (quoted in Monger, 315). But few other Englishmen could be convinced that others might see them this way.

65. George Kennan makes clear that in 1918 this kind of difficulty was partly responsible for the inability of either the Allies or the new Bolshevik government to understand the motivations of the other side: "There is . . . nothing in nature more egocentrical than the embattled democracy. . . . It . . . tends to attach to its own cause an absolute value which distorts its own vision of everything else. . . . It will readily be seen that people who have got themselves into this frame of mind have little understanding for the issues of any contest other than the one in which they are involved. The idea of people wasting time and substance on any *other* issue seems to them preposterous" (*Russia and the West*, 11-12).

66. Kaplan, 89.

67. Johan Jorgen Holst, "Surprise, Signals, and Reaction: The Attack on Norway," *Cooperation and Conflict*, No. 1 (1966):34. The Germans made a similar mistake in November 1942 when they interpreted the presence of an Allied convoy in the Mediterranean as confirming their belief that Malta would be resupplied. They thus were taken by surprise when landings took place in North Africa (William Langer, *Our Vichy Gamble* [New York, 1966], 365).

20

Crisis, Stress, and Decisionmaking

Ole R. Holsti

"What is relevant for policy" in times of crisis, according to President Nixon's principal foreign policy adviser, "depends not only on academic truths but also on what can be implemented under stress."[1] Observations by others who have experienced or studied international crises vary widely. Consider the following:

"Hence, a decision-maker may, in a crisis, be able to invent or work out easily and quickly what seems in normal times to both the 'academic' scholar and the layman to be hypothetical, unreal, complex or otherwise difficult."[2]

"In every case, the decision [to go to war] is based upon a careful weighing of the chances and of anticipating consequences. . . . In no case is the decision precipitated by emotional tensions, sentimentality, crowd-behavior, or other irrational motivations."[3]

"We have faith that man, who has been endowed with the wit to devise the means of his self-destruction, also has enough wit to keep those means under effective control."[4]

"We create and enjoy crises. . . . Why? I don't know. I wish I knew. But all of us like them. I know I enjoy them. . . . There is a sense of elation that comes with crises."[5]

"You see a poor, rather stupid fellow behind a desk and you wonder why he couldn't do better than that [in crisis situations]. Unfortunately, that picture comes up too often."[6]

"I saw first-hand, during the long days and nights of the Cuban crisis, how brutally physical and mental fatigue can numb the good sense as well as the senses of normally articulate men."[7]

"That kind of [crisis-induced] pressure does strange things to a human being, even to brilliant, selfconfident, experienced men. For some it brings out characteristics and strengths that perhaps they never knew they had,

Ole R. Holsti, "Crisis, Stress and Decision-Making," *International Social Science Journal* 23, no. 1, © UNESCO, 1971. Reproduced by permission of UNESCO and the author.

and for others the pressure is too overwhelming."[8]

How do individuals and groups respond to the pressures and tensions of a crisis? Do we tend to approach such situations with high motivations, a keen sense of purpose, extraordinary energy, and enhanced creativity? Is necessity, as Kahn suggests, the mother of invention? Or, is our capacity for coping with the problem reduced, perhaps even to the point of serious impairment? When under intense pressure do we characteristically take the more cautious path, or are we more prone to taking high risks? Is our sense of what constitutes risk in any way altered?

The answers to these questions are always important for persons who find themselves faced with a crisis. They assume extraordinarily wide significance when the individuals are national leaders and the context is that of a contemporary international crisis: the ability of national leaders to cope with situations of intense stress may affect the lives of millions, if not the future of mankind. Despite the importance of these questions, many descriptive or prescriptive theories of international politics either ignore them or assume that the answers are self-evident. Consider, for instance, some of the basic premises of deterrence theories: that decisions by both the deterrer and the deterree will be based on dispassionate calculations of probable costs and gains, accurate evaluations of the situation, and careful assessments of relative capabilities; that the value hierarchies of both the deterrer and the deterree are similar at least to the point that each places the avoidance of war at or near the top; and that both sides maintain tight centralized control over decisions which might involve or provoke the use of force.

Deterrence thus presupposes rational and predictable decision processes. No system of deterrence, however powerful the weapons, is likely to prove effective against a nation led by a trigger-happy paranoid, or by one seeking personal or national self-destruction or martyrdom, or by decision-makers willing to play a form of international Russian roulette, or by leaders whose information about and communication with an adversary are so incomplete that their decisionmaking processes are largely dominated by guesswork, or by those who regard the loss of most of their nation's population and resources as a "reasonable" cost for the achievement of foreign policy goals.

Clearly the assumptions of deterrence are valid most of the time and under most circumstances, even in relationships of considerable enmity such as "cold wars." Otherwise, we would be at war almost continuously. Most deterrence theories further assume, however, that threats and ultimatums are not only effective for influencing an adversary's behaviour but also that they will enhance calculation, control, and caution while inhibiting recklessness and risk taking. There may be a recognition that "the rationality upon which deterrence must be based is frangible,"[9] but there is also a tendency to assume that these rationalistic premises require little if any modification for crisis situations. Deterrence theorists tend to be sanguine about the creativity of policymakers under stress.[10] To be sure, they often recognize some special features of crisis—for example, the difficulties of normal communication between adversaries.[11] But the lesson drawn from such examples is usually that lack of control over the situation may be used as a bargaining asset to force the adversary into a disadvantageous position, not only once, but in repeated encounters.

Clearly this summary is a grossly oversimplified view of the rich literature on deterrence. Nevertheless, there is a substantial element of truth in a critic's assertion that "the theory of deterrence, however, first proposes that we should frustrate our opponents by frightening them very badly and that we should then rely on their cool-headed rationality for our survival."[12]

The more general question is how crisis—defined here as a situation of unanticipated threat to important values in which decision time is short[13]—is likely to affect policy processes and outcomes. What are the probable effects of crisis upon abilities which are generally considered essential to effective decisionmaking? These include the ability to: (a) identify major alternative courses of action; (b) estimate the probable costs and gains of alternative policy choices; (c) distinguish between the possible and the probable; (d) assess the situation from the perspective of other parties; (e) discriminate between relevant and irrelevant information; (f) tolerate ambiguity; (g) resist premature action; and (h) make adjustments to meet real changes in the situation (and, as a corollary, to distinguish real from apparent changes).

This list is by no means exhaustive. Nor does it unrealistically portray the model of the omniscient official.[14] It does, however, give us a check list against which we can evaluate the probable consequences of stress on aspects of human performance relevant to foreign policy decisions.

The most important aspect of crises for our purposes is that these situations are characterized by high stress for the individuals and organizations involved. That a threat to important values is stress-inducing requires little elaboration. The element of surprise is also a contributing factor; there is evidence that unanticipated and novel situations are generally viewed as more threatening.[15] Finally, crises are often marked by almost around-the-clock work schedules, owing to both the severity of the situation and the absence of extended decision time. During the Cuban missile confrontation, for instance, many American officials slept in their office for the duration of the crisis: "We had to go on a twenty-four hour basis here in the Department of State."[16] Premier Khrushchev also appears to have had little sleep during that week: "I must confess that I slept one night in my studio fully dressed on the sofa. I did not want to be in the position of one Western diplomat who, during the Suez crisis, rushed to the telephone without his trousers."[17] Even during the much less intense Middle East situation created by the "Six Day War" in 1967, the Soviet Politburo had at least one all night meeting.[18] Lack of rest and excessively long working hours are likely to magnify the stresses inherent in the situation.

Stress and Performance: The Evidence from Psychology

The central concern of this article is to explore the possible consequences of crisis-induced stress on those aspects of individual and organizational performance that are most likely to affect the processes and outcomes of foreign-policymaking. As a starting point we shall turn to the rich and voluminous body of theory and evidence from experimental psychology. The advantages of precise measurement, easy replication, and tight control over the experimental variables have permitted psychologists to probe many aspects of human performance in various types of situations. Some emphasis will be placed on the consequences of stress for the identification of alternatives and processes of choosing from among them, assessments of time factors and patterns of communication. We shall also consider how time pressure, alternatives, and communications may effect the level of stress in a situation, as well as other relationships between these variables — for example, between patterns of communications and iden-tification of alternatives.

Some degree of stress[19] is an integral and necessary precondition for in-dividual or organizational problem solving; in its absence we lack any motivation to act. Low levels of pressure alert us to the presence of a situa-tion requiring our attention, increase our vigilance, and our preparedness and ability to cope with it. Increasing stress to moderate levels may heighten our propensity and ability to find a satisfactory solution to the problem. A study of research scientists revealed, for example, that an environment of moderate stress, characterized by "uncertainty without anxiety," is the most conducive to creative work.[20] Indeed, for some elementary tasks a rather high degree of pressure may increase per-formance, at least for limited periods of time. If the problem is qualitatively simple and performance is measured by quantitative criteria, stress can in-crease output. A crisis period of limited duration might result in improved performance by the foreign office clerical staff.

Our present concern, however, is with the effects of crisis on top-ranking foreign policy officials. Under the best of circumstances foreign policy issues tend to be marked by complexity, ambiguity, and the absence of stability; they usually demand responses which are judged by qualitative rather than quantitative criteria. It is precisely these qualitative aspects of performance that are most likely to suffer under high stress.[21]

Most research findings indicate a curvilinear relationship between stress and the performance of individuals and groups. At moderate levels, anxiety can be facilitating, but at higher levels it disrupts decision processes.[22] On the basis of a series of experiments, Birch determined that inter-mediate — rather than high or low motivation — was most conducive to effi-cient solution of both insightful and noninsightful problems. These results are supported by other studies.[23] Lanzetta, in an analysis of group behaviour, found that "under increased stress there was a decrease in ini-tiating behaviors, mainly in terms of 'diagnoses situation, makes interpreta-tion' kinds of behavior; and an increase in more 'general discussions of the task' kind of behavior."[24] Following their analysis of the effects of stress on perception, Postman and Bruner concluded: "Perceptual behaviour is disrupted, becomes less well controlled than under normal conditions, and hence is less adaptive. The major dimensions of perceptual function are af-fected: selection of percepts from a complex field becomes less adequate and sense is less well differentiated from nonsense; there is maladaptive ac-centuation in the direction of aggression and escape; untested hypotheses are fixated recklessly."[25]

Other effects of stress which have been found in experimental research include: increased random behaviour; deterioration of verbal perfor-mance; increased rate of error; regression to simpler and more primitive modes of response; problem-solving rigidity; diminished tolerance for am-biguity; reduction in the focus of attention, both across time and space; reduced ability to discriminate the dangerous from the trivial; diminished scope of complex perceptual activity; loss of abstract ability; and disorienta-tion of visual-motor coordination.[26] A finding of special relevance for inter-national crises is that toleration for ambiguity is reduced under high stress. Under these conditions individuals made decisions before adequate infor-mation was available, with the result that they performed much less capably than those working under normal conditions. The combination of stress and uncertainty leads some persons to feel that "the worst would be better than this."[27]

In summary, in situations of high stress "there is a narrowing of the cognitive organization at the moment; the individual loses broader perspec-tive, he is no longer able to 'see' essential aspects of the situation and his behavior becomes, consequently, less adaptive."[28]

Some experimental studies have been criticized on both conceptual and methodological grounds, but the general conclusion that high stress inhibits rather than facilitates most aspects of human performance appears to be unassailable. Moreover, the capabilities which may be enhanced by moderate-to-high stress tend to have limited relevance in formulating foreign policy, whereas those which are inhibited under these conditions are usually crucial for such complex tasks.

A related aspect of international crises is the existence of time pressures which may become accentuated if either party believes that there are advantages to acting first. It should be pointed out that time pressure is not only a matter of clock time, but also of the task to be accomplished. Given five minutes within which to choose between playing golf or mowing the lawn on Sunday a person may feel no particular pressure, but a five-week deadline for deciding whether to change jobs may give rise to intense feelings of short decision time. Moreover, it is apparently the perceptions of time that are crucial: "The effects of a time limit appear to be due to perceived pressure rather than actual pressure brought on by an impossible time limit."[29]

Time perspectives are affected by high stress. For example, the ability to judge time is impaired in situations which increase anxiety.[30] Thus there appears to be a two-way relationship between time and stress. On the one hand the common use during crisis of such techniques as ultimatums and threats with built-in deadlines is likely to increase the stress under which the recipient must operate. On the other hand, increasing levels of stress tend to heighten the salience of time and to distort judgements about it. The expression that "a watched pot never boils" is a common way of stating the relationship between stress and distorted time perspective. It has been found in "real-life" crisis situations as well as experimentally that as danger increases there is a significant overestimation of how fast time is passing.[31] This suggests not only that short decision time distinguishes crises from other types of situations,[32] but also that increasing stress will further heighten the perceived salience of time.

Foreign policy issues are rarely, if ever, analogous to the familiar multiple-choice question in which the universe of options is neatly outlined. The theoretically possible choices far exceed the number that can or will be considered. Especially in unanticipated situations such as crises it is necessary to search out and perhaps create alternatives. Perceived time pressure affects the search for alternatives in several ways. A number of studies indicate that some time pressure can enhance creativity as well as the rate of performance, but most of the evidence suggests that beyond a moderate level it has adverse effects. Because complex tasks requiring feats of memory and inference suffer more from time pressure,[33] its effects on foreign policy decisions — which are usually marked by complexity — are likely to be particularly harmful. In such situations there is a tendency to fix upon a single approach to problem solving and to continue using it whether or not it proves effective.[34]

Experimental research has shown that under severe time pressure, normal subjects produce a schizophrenic-like type of error. Another study revealed that, although a moderate increase in time pressure can increase group productivity, an increase from low to high pressure has an adverse effect. Mackworth and Mackworth report that increasing the number of decisions required in a given period of time by a factor of five led to a fifteen-fold rise in decision errors. There is, in addition, evidence that time pressure increases the propensity to rely upon stereotypes, disrupts both individual and group problem solving, narrows the focus of attention, and impedes the use of available information. Finally, short decision time tends to create early group agreement, thereby reducing incentives to search for and weigh other options.[35]

When decision time is short, the ability to estimate the range of possible consequences arising from a particular policy choice is likely to be impaired. Both experimental and field research indicate that stress produces a constricted future outlook.[36] There are several reasons why severe stress is likely to give rise to almost undivided concern for the present and immediate future at the sacrifice of attention to longer-range considerations. The uncertainties attending severe crisis make it exceptionally difficult to follow outcomes from a sequence of actions and responses very far into the future. The tendency of increasing stress to narrow the focus of attention also limits perceptions of time to the more immediate future. During the Korean War, for instance, it was observed that combat troops "cannot exercise complex functions involving the scanning of a large number of factors or long-term foresight because the stress is too massive and time too short for anything but the immediately relevant."[37] Moreover, if the present situation is perceived as extremely dangerous, the more distant future may appear to have little or no relevance unless a satisfactory solution can be found for the immediate problems. This may well be true and placing a priority on the immediate often makes sense. After a drowning man has been pulled out of icy waters it would be foolish to take medical steps directed at warding off the longer-range dangers of pneumonia before giving artificial respiration to revive the victim.

There are also potential difficulties, however, in an overdeveloped sense of concern for the immediate. Present actions alter future options and decisions which provide immediate advantages may carry with them unduly heavy costs later. The price may be worth paying but the balance sheet can scarcely be evaluated effectively if attention is fixed solely on the short-run benefits. There is also something seductively appealing about the belief that "if I can just solve the problem of the moment the future will take care of itself." This reasoning appears to have contributed to both Neville

Chamberlain's actions during the Czech crisis of 1938 and to Lyndon Johnson's policies during the war in Viet Nam.

Sustained time pressure may also give rise to significant changes in goals. The authors of a bargaining experiment concluded that "the meaning of time changed as time passed without the bargainers reaching an agreement. Initially the passage of time seemed to place the players under pressure to come to an agreement before their costs mounted sufficiently to destroy their profit. With the continued passage of time, however, their mounting losses strengthened their resolution not to yield to the other player. They comment: 'I've lost so much I'll be damned if I give in now. At least I'll have the satisfaction of doing better than he does.'"[38] This comment and its underlying rationale are remarkably similar to one of Kaiser Wilhelm's marginal notes when he finally recognized that his hopes of British neutrality in the rapidly approaching war were a delusion: "If we are to bleed to death, England shall at least lose India."[39]

The rate of search for satisfactory solutions to a problem depends in part on the belief that the environment is benign and that such options in fact exist. But it is in the nature of crisis that most, if not all, policy alternatives are likely to be perceived as undesirable. The frying pan and the fire rather than Burian's ass (who starved to death when unable to choose between equally delectable bales of hay) is the proper metaphor for choices in an international crisis. As noted earlier, when stress increases problem solving tends to become more rigid: the ability to improvise declines, previously established decision rules are adhered to more tenaciously, and the ability to "resist the pull of closure" is reduced.[40] These findings suggest the paradox that an increasingly severe crisis tends to make creative policymaking both more important and less likely.

Identification of alternatives can also be related to the element of surprise in crises. Snyder has suggested that more options will be considered when the decision is anticipated rather than occasioned by the environment.[41] By the definition used here, crises are unanticipated, for at least one of the parties. Thus this attribute of the situation will itself restrict inquiry and, as the crisis deepens and stress increases, the search for options is likely to be further constricted. In a situation such as existed after the attack on Pearl Harbor in 1941 one would not expect a lengthy review of potential responses by decisionmakers. Even in the Korean crisis of 1950, in which the situation was somewhat more ambiguous, only a single alternative course of action was considered: "the decision-making process in the Korean case was not characterized by the consideration of multiple alternatives at each stage. Rather a single proposed course of action emerged from the definition of the situation."[42]

The extreme situation occurs when only a single option is perceived and the policymaking process is reduced to resigning oneself to the inevitable. If decisionmakers perceive that their options are reduced to only those with potentially high penalties — for example, "We have no alternative but to go to war" — considerable dissonance may be generated. The dissonance between what the decisionmaker does (pursues policies that are known to carry a high risk of war) and what he knows (that war can lead to disaster) can be reduced by absolving himself from responsibility for the decision. This solution has been described by Festinger: "It is possible, however, to reduce or even eliminate the dissonance by revoking the decision psychologically. This would consist of admitting to having made the wrong choice *or insisting that really no choice had been made for which the person had any responsibility.* Thus, a person who has just accepted a new job might immediately feel he had done the wrong thing and, if he had it to do over again, might do something different. Or he might persuade himself that *the choice had not been his; circumstances and his boss conspired to force the action on him.*"[43] This process may also be related to the widespread inability to perceive and appreciate the dilemmas and difficulties of others: "The grass is always greener on the other side of the fence." This has been noted with respect to the motives, general capabilities, and military strength ascribed to the adversary.[44]

One method of dissonance reduction is to believe that the only options which offer a way out of the dilemma rest with the enemy — only the other side can prevent the impending disaster. For example, during the frantic last-minute correspondence between the German Kaiser and the Russian Tsar in July 1914, Wilhelm wrote: "The responsibility for the disaster which is now threatening the whole civilized world will not be laid at my door. In this moment it still lies in your [Nicholas] power to avert it."[45] Although it may at times be difficult to appreciate fully the dilemmas and difficulties of friends[46] there is likely to be greater empathy with allies than with enemies. In summary, then, a likely means of coping with dissonance is to persuade oneself that the enemy is free from the very situational constraints which restrict the options available to self and allies.

What, finally, is the relationship among crisis-induced stress, communication, and policymaking? The adequacy of communication both in the physical sense of open channels of communication and in the sense of "pragmatics" — the correspondence between the sender's intent and the recipient's decoding — has been a major concern in decisionmaking studies. In this respect Heise and Miller have found that "the performance of a small group depends upon the channels of communication open to its members, the task which the group must handle, and the stress under which they work."[47]

Inadequate communications have received the greatest share of attention, in crisis studies, with less concern for the effects of information overload.[48] Study of the latter appears to have been confined to the laboratory rather than to historical situations. Yet information overload does appear to be an important consideration. The inception of crisis usually gives rise to a sharply increased pace of individual and bureaucratic activities, virtually all of which are likely to increase the volume of diplomatic communication.

We noted earlier that high-stress situations tend to increase selective perception and to impair the ability to discriminate between sense and nonsense, the relevant and the irrelevant. Aside from the effects of stress, there are limits on our ability to process information.[49] As the volume of information directed at policymakers rises, the search for information within the communication system will tend to become less thorough, and selectivity in what is read, believed, and retained takes on increasing importance. Unpleasant information and that which does not support preconceived beliefs is most likely to fall by the wayside. The experimental finding that selective filtering is often used at levels ranging from cells to human groups to cope with an unmanageable amount of information[50] is apparently also valid for governmental organizations: "All Presidents, at least in modern times, have complained about their reading pile, and few have been able to cope with it. There is a temptation, consequently, to cut out all that is unpleasant."[51] Thus, more communication may in fact result in less useful and valid information available to policymakers.

Although the volume of communication may rise during crises, the increase is likely to be uneven; there may be considerable disruption of communication with potential adversaries. In a simulation study, Brody found that as perceived threat rose, the proportion of intraalliance communication—as compared to interalliance messages—increased.[52] At the same time, both incoming and outgoing messages are likely to reflect increasingly simple and stereotyped assessments of the situation. If these expectations regarding changes, patterns, and content of communication in crisis are valid, the number of options which decisionmakers will consider is correspondingly restricted.

Certain other aspects of communications in a crisis may restrict the search for alternatives. There is a general tendency for a reduction in size of decisionmaking groups in such situations.[53] Technological and other factors have reduced decision time to a point where broad consultation with legislatures and other important groups may be virtually impossible. The limited membership of the "Excom," in which the decisions regarding missiles in Cuba were made, is a case in point. Decision bodies in the crises concerning Korea in 1950, Indochina in 1954, and others, were similarly limited in size.[54]

There may be, moreover, a tendency to consult others less as the pressure of time increases, as well as to rely more heavily upon those who reinforce preexisting stereotypes. In his study of a governmental department, Pruitt found a significant reduction in the number of people consulted by persons responsible for solving problems when time pressure increased.[55] One of the crucial decisions in the crisis leading up to the First World War — the German decision to grant Vienna a "blank cheque" in support of the plan to punish Serbia — was made without any extended consultation.

> On 5 July the Kaiser went for a stroll in the park at Potsdam with his chancellor, that bearded, sad-eyed giant Theobald von Bethmann-Hollweg, whom irreverent young officers called "Lanky Theobald," and Under-Secretary Zimmermann of the Foreign Office. By the time the walk was over, the Kaiser had made up his mind.
>
> Not another man had been consulted. The Foreign Minister was on his honeymoon and had not been recalled. The experienced, too subtle, too slippery ex-chancellor Bernhard von Bülow had not been called in. There in the park with Bethmann-Hollweg, whose judgment he despised, and Zimmermann, an official, the Kaiser reached his decision. He told the Austrian ambassador in Berlin that Germany would cover Austria should Russia intervene.[56]

Similarly, during the Suez crisis of 1956, John Foster Dulles made the crucial decision to cancel a loan for the Aswan Dam virtually on his own. He refused to consult with, much less accept the advice of, the American Ambassador to Egypt, Henry Byroade, whose assessment of the situation — a correct one as it turned out — did not correspond to his own. A more recent example is President Nixon's decision to send American troops into Cambodia, a project which appears to have been undertaken without the counsel of many top-ranking foreign-policy advisers.

Increasing stress may produce one potentially counteracting change in communication. In his studies of information overload, Miller found that one of the widely used coping mechanisms is the use of parallel channels of communication, particularly in higher-level systems such as groups or organizations, as opposed to cells, organs, or individuals.[57] Decisionmakers may seek to bypass both the effects of information input overload and of distortion of content in transmission by the use of improvised ad hoc channels of communication. These may take many forms, including direct communication between heads of governments and employment of special emissaries, or mediators.

It has been noted at various points that the rate of diplomatic and other activities tends to increase sharply during a crisis.[58] It remains to consider whether high stress increases risk taking, aggressiveness, and related aspects of foreign policy. Are we led to a position closely akin to the frustration-aggression hypotheses? The evidence is mixed. In some instances stress has resulted in higher risk taking; in other cases persons in such situations have become more cautious because they demanded greater certainty before committing themselves.[59] Assessments of what constitutes high and low risk may, however, change in circumstances of severe stress. Consider British foreign policy during 1938-1939. What no doubt appeared as the low-risk strategy (at least in the short run) scarcely contributed to stability and peace. Or, to cite a more recent example, Dean Acheson, William Fulbright, and Richard Russell argued in October 1962 that President Kennedy's decision to blockade Cuba represented a far higher risk than their preferred strategy of bombing or invading to remove the Soviet missiles.

Thus, high stress situations may result in more aggressive policy choices, but the evidence presented here suggests a somewhat more complex process: crisis-induced stress gives rise to certain changes in perceptions of time, definition of alternatives, and patterns of communication. These, in turn, may reduce the effectiveness of both decisionmaking processes and the consequent policy choices, but not necessarily in the direction of higher risk taking.

Conclusion

In summary, then, the evidence suggests that policymaking under circumstances of crisis-induced stress is likely to differ in a number of respects from decisionmaking processes in other situations. More important, to the extent that such differences exist, they are likely to inhibit rather than facilitate the performance of those engaged in the complex tasks of making foreign-policy choices.[60] Certainly this conclusion is consistent with the findings from experimental research.

While this literature is not lacking in empirical and quantitative findings, it is not wholly free from conceptual and operational problems. It cannot merely be assumed, for example, that results obtained with student subjects are necessarily valid for persons of different age, culture, experience, and the like.[61] Nor is the usual experimental technique of asking subjects to find the best answer to a problem or puzzle quite analogous to the task of the policymaker who may be confronted with a situation in which there is no single, correct answer.

Perhaps an even more important question might be raised about the experimenter's ability to create a truly credible situation of high stress.[62] When human subjects are used, the stress situation in the laboratory must of necessity be relatively benign and of short duration. It is usually induced by leading the subject to believe that he has failed at his assigned task. In contrast, a foreign-policy official may perceive a crisis situation as a genuine threat to the continued existence of self, family, nation, or even mankind. Clearly, the ethical experimenter cannot create an identical situation in the laboratory.

In short, these experimental findings suggest some questions about the "conventional wisdom" underlying several aspects of strategy and diplomacy in crises. But the answers can only be found in the real world of international crises, not in the laboratory. Research along these lines has begun and there are strong indications of significant convergences between findings derived from laboratory experiments, simulations, and historical analyses.[63]

Notes

I gratefully acknowledge the financial support of the Canada Council for my research on crisis.

1. Henry A. Kissinger, "Domestic Structure and Foreign Policy," in: James N. Rosenau (ed.), *International Politics and Foreign Policy*, p. 265, rev. ed. (New York: The Free Press, 1969).

2. Herman Kahn, *On Escalation: Metaphors and Scenarios*, p. 38 (New York: Praeger, 1965).

3. Theodore Abel, "The Element of Decision in the Pattern of War," *American Sociological Review* 4 (1941):855.

4. John Foster Dulles, "The Problem of Disarmament," *State Department Bulletin*, 12 March 1956, p. 416.

5. Unidentified diplomat, quoted in Chris Argyris, *Some Causes of Organizational Ineffectiveness within the Department of State*, p. 42 (Washington, D.C.: Center for International Systems Research, Department of State, 1967), Publication no. 8180.

6. Dwight D. Eisenhower, Address to *Washington Post* Book and Author Lunch, quoted in *Palo Alto Times*, 1 October 1965.

7. Theodore C. Sorensen, *Decision-Making in the White House*, p. 76 (New York: Columbia University Press, 1964).

8. Robert F. Kennedy, "Thirteen Days: The Story About How the World Almost Ended," *McCalls*, November 1968, p. 148.

9. Bernard Brodie, quoted in Philip Green, *Deadly Logic: The Theory of Nuclear Deterrence*, p. 159 (New York: Schocken Books, 1966).

10. See, for example: Thomas C. Schelling, *Arms and Influence*, p. 96 (New Haven, Conn.: Yale University Press, 1966); Kahn, *On Escalation*, pp. 37-38; Albert Wohlstetter and Roberta Wohlstetter, *Controlling the Risks in Cuba* (London: Institute of Strategic Studies, April 1965), Adelphi paper no. 17.

11. See especially Thomas C. Schelling, *The Strategy of Conflict* (New York: Ox-

ford University Press, 1963).

12. Karl Deutsch, *The Nerves of Government*, p. 70 (New York: The Free Press, 1963).

13. This definition of crisis is taken from Charles F. Hermann, "Some Consequences of Crisis which Limit the Viability of Organization," *Administrative Science Quarterly* 8 (1963):61-82. There are many usages of the term "crisis." For extensive critical reviews of these, see: Charles F. Hermann, *Crises in Foreign Policy* (Indianapolis, Ind.: Bobbs-Merrill, 1969); James A. Robinson, "Crisis: An Appraisal of Concepts and Theories," in: Charles F. Hermann (ed.), *Contemporary Research in International Crisis* (New York: The Free Press [in press]); Kent Miller and Ira Iscoe, "The Concept of Crisis: Current Status and Mental Health Implications," *Human Organization* 22 (1963):195-201.

14. For a much more demanding list, see J. David Singer and Paul Ray, "Decision-making in Conflict: From Inter-personal to Inter-national Relations," *Bulletin of the Menninger Clinic* 30 (1960):303.

The literature on the limits of rationality in decisionmaking is extensive. See, for example: Herbert A. Simon, *Administrative Behavior* (New York: Macmillan, 1957); James G. March and Herbert A. Simon, *Organizations* (New York: John Wiley & Sons, 1958); Richard Snyder, H. W. Bruck, and Burton Sapin, *Foreign Policy Decision Making* (New York: The Free Press, 1962).

15. Sheldon J. Korchin and Seymour Levine, "Anxiety and Verbal Learning," *Journal of Abnormal and Social Psychology* 54 (1957):238.

16. Dean Rusk, "Interview of Secretary Rusk by David Schoenbrun of CBS News," in: David Larson, *The 'Cuban Crisis' of 1962*, p. 268 (Boston, Mass.: Houghton Mifflin, 1963).

17. *New York Times*, 27 June 1967.

18. *San Francisco Chronicle*, 9 June 1967.

19. It should be noted that there is a lack of consensus on definitions of stress among psychologists. For example, some define it as the stimulus (e.g., a severe threat), whereas others view it as the perceptual and behavioural responses to threat. For a further discussion, see: Raymond B. Cattell and Ivan H. Scheier, "Stimuli Related to Stress, Neuroticism, Excitation, and Anxiety Response Patterns," *Journal of Abnormal and Social Psychology* 60 (1960):195-204; Richard S. Lazarus, *Psychological Stress and the Coping Process* (New York: McGraw-Hill, 1966); Margaret G. Hermann, "Testing a Model of Psychological Stress," *Journal of Personality* 34 (1966):381-396.

20. Cited in Kurt Back, "Decisions Under Uncertainty: Rational, Irrational, and Non-rational," *American Behavioral Scientist* 4 (February 1961):14-19. Unless a specific study is cited, I have relied on two extensive reviews of the literature: Richard S. Lazarus, James Deese, and Sonia F. Osler, "The Effects of Psychological Stress Upon Performance," *Psychological Bulletin*, Vol. IL (1952):293-317; F. E. Horvath, "Psychological Stress: A Review of Definitions and Experimental Research," in L. von Bertalanffy and Anatol Rapoport (eds.), *General Systems Yearbook*, Vol. IV (Ann Arbor, Mich.: Society for General Systems Research, 1959).

21. Alfred Lowe, "Individual Differences in Reaction to Failure: Modes of Cop-

ing with Anxiety and Interference Proneness," *Journal of Abnormal and Social Psychology* 62 (1961):303-308; Sara B. Kiesler, "Stress, Affiliation and Performance," *Journal of Experimental Research in Personality* 1 (1966):227-235.

22. S. J. Korchin et al., "Visual Discrimination and the Decision Process in Anxiety," *A.M.A. Archives of Neurology and Psychiatry* 78 (1957):424-438; Robert E. Murphy, "Effects of Threat of Shock, Distraction, and Task Design on Performance," *Journal of Experimental Psychology* 58 (1959):134-141.

23. Herbert G. Birch, "Motivational Factors in Insightful Problem-Solving," *Journal of Comparative Psychology* 37 (1945):295-317; R. M. Yerkes, "Modes of Behavioral Adaptation in Chimpanzees to Multiple Choice Problems," *Comparative Psychological Monographs* 10 (1934):1-108.

24. John T. Lanzetta, "Group Behavior under Stress," *Human Relations* 8 (1955):47-48.

25. Leo Postman and Jerome S. Bruner, "Perception under Stress," *Psychological Review* 55 (1948):322.

26. E. Paul Torrance, "The Behavior of Small Groups under the Stress Conditions of 'Survival,'" *American Sociological Review* 19 (1954):751-755; Sheldon J. Korchin, "Anxiety and Cognition," in: Constance Sheerer (ed.), *Cognition: Theory, Research, Promise,* p. 67 (New York: Harper & Row, 1964); H. Kohn, cited in Enoch Callaway and Donald Dembo, "Narrowed Attention," *A.M.A. Archives of Neurology and Psychiatry* 79 (1958):85; L. T. Katchmas, S. Ross, and T. G. Andrews, "The Effects of Stress and Anxiety on Performance of a Complex Verbal-Coding Task," *Journal of Experimental Psychology* 85 (1958):562; Ernst G. Beier, "The Effects of Induced Anxiety on Flexibility of Intellectual Functioning," *Psychological Monographs* 65, no. 326 (1951):19.

27. C. D. Smock, "The Influence of Psychological Stress on the 'Intolerance of Ambiguity,'" *Journal of Abnormal and Social Psychology* 50 (1955):177-182; B. B. Hudson, quoted in Stephen B. Whithey, "Reaction to Uncertain Threat," in George W. Baker and Dwight W. Chapman (eds.), *Man and Society in Disaster,* p. 118 (New York: Basic Books, 1962).

28. D. Krech and R. S. Crutchfield, quoted in Korchin, "Visual Discrimination," p. 63.

29. Roland L. Frye and Thomas M. Stritch, "Effects of Timed vs. Nontimed Discussion Upon Measures of Influence and Change in Small Groups," *Journal of Social Psychology* 63 (1964):139-143. For an intriguing discussion of "subjective time," see John Cohen, "Psychological Time," *Scientific American* (November 1964), pp. 116-124.

30. Samuel I. Cohen and A. G. Mezey, "The Effects of Anxiety on Time Judgment and Time Experience in Normal Persons," *J. Neurol. Neurosurg. Psychiatry* 24 (1961):266-268.

31. Harry B. Williams and Jeannette F. Rayner, "Emergency Medical Services in Disaster," *Medical Annals of the District of Columbia* 25 (1956):661; Jonas Langer, Seymour Wapner, and Heinz Werner, "The Effects of Danger Upon the Experience of Time," *American Journal of Psychology* 74 (1961):94-97.

32. See the definition of "crisis" on page 55.

33. Jerome Bruner, Jacqueline J. Goodnow, and George A. Austin, *A Study of*

Thinking, p. 147 (New York: John Wiley & Sons, 1956).

34. Abraham S. Luchins, "Mechanization in Problem-Solving," *Psychological Monographs* 54, no. 248 (1942).

35. George Usdansky and Loren J. Chapman, "Schizophrenic-like Response in Normal Subjects under Time Pressure," *Journal of Abnormal and Social Psychology* 60 (1960):143-146; Pauline N. Pepinsky, Harold B. Pepinsky, and William B. Pavlik, "The Effects of Task Complexity and Time Pressure Upon Team Productivity," *Journal of Applied Psychology* 44 (1960):34-38; N. H. Mackworth and J. F. Mackworth, "Visual Search for Successive Decisions," *British Journal of Psychology,* Vol. IL (1958):210-221; Birch, "Motivational Factors"; Bruner et al., *A Study of Thinking;* Peter Dubno, "Decision Time Characteristics of Leaders and Group Problem Solving Behavior," *Journal of Social Psychology* 59 (1963):259-282; Horvath, "Psychological Stress"; Donald R. Hoffeld and S. Carolyn Kent, "Decision Time and Information Use in Choice Situations," *Psychological Reports* 12 (1963):68-70; Frye and Stritch, "Effects."

36. Robert J. Albers, "Anxiety and Time Perspectives," *Dissertation Abstracts* 26 (1966):4848; James D. Thompson and Robert W. Hawkes, "Disaster, Community Organization, and Administrative Process," in Baker and Chapman (eds.), *Man and Society in Disaster,* p. 283.

37. David Rioch, quoted in Korchin, "Visual Discrimination," p. 63.

38. Morton Deutsch and Robert M. Krauss, "The Effects of Threat Upon Interpersonal Bargaining," *Journal of Abnormal and Social Psychology* 61 (1960):189.

39. Max Montgelas and Walther Schücking (eds.), *Outbreak of the World War, German Documents Collected by Karl Kautsky,* no. 401 (New York: Oxford University Press, 1924).

40. Korchin, "Visual Discrimination," pp. 65-67; J. W. Moffitt and Ross Stagner, "Perceptual Rigidity and Closure as a Function of Anxiety," *Journal of Abnormal and Social Psychology* 52 (1956):355; S. Pally, "Cognitive Rigidity as a Function of Threat," *Journal of Personality* 23 (1955):346-355; Sheldon J. Korchin and Harold Basowitz, *Journal of Psychology* 38 (1954):501.

41. Richard C. Snyder, *Deterrence, Weapons and Decision-Making,* p. 80 (China Lake, Calif.: U.S. Naval Ordnance Test Station, 1961).

42. Richard C. Snyder and Glenn D. Paige, "The United Nations Decisions to Resist Aggression in Korea: The Application of an Analytical Scheme," *Administrative Science Quarterly* 3 (1958):245; Glenn D. Paige, *The Korean Decision* (New York: The Free Press, 1968). See also March and Simon, *Organizations,* pp. 154 ff.

43. Leon Festinger, *A Theory of Cognitive Dissonance,* pp. 43-44 (Evanston, Ill.: Row, Peterson & Co., 1957). Italics added.

44. See, for example: Kenneth Boulding, "National Images and International Systems," *The Journal of Conflict Resolution* 3 (1959):120-131; Charles E. Osgood, "Suggestions for Winning the Real War with Communism," *The Journal of Conflict Resolution* 3 (1959):295-325; Raymond A. Bauer, "Problems of Perception and the Relations Between the United States and the Soviet Union," *The Journal of Conflict Resolution* 5 (1961):223-229; Samuel F. Huntington, "Arms Races," in Carl Friedrich and Seymour Harris (eds.), *Public Policy, 1958* (Cambridge, Mass.: Harvard University Press, 1958).

45. Montgelas and Schücking, *Outbreak of the World War,* no. 480.

46. Ole R. Holsti and Robert C. North, "The History of Human Conflict," in Elton B. McNeil (ed.), *The Nature of Human Conflict,* pp. 165-166 (Englewood Cliffs, N.J.: Prentice-Hall, 1965).

47. George A. Heise and George A. Miller, "Problem Solving by Small Groups Using Various Communication Nets," *Journal of Abnormal and Social Psychology* 46 (1951):335.

48. For exceptions, see Charles F. Hermann, "Some Consequences of Crisis," and James G. Miller, "Information Input Overload," *Self Organizing Systems — 1962,* n.p.; James G. Miller, "Information Input Overload and Psychopathology," *The American Journal of Psychiatry* 116 (1960):695-704; Harry B. Williams, "Some Functions of Communication in Crisis Behavior," *Human Organization* 16 (1957):15-19; Richard L. Meier, "Information Input Overload and Features of Growth in Communication-Oriented Institutions," in Fred Massarik and Philburn Ratoosh (eds.), *Mathematical Explorations in Behavioral Science* (Homewood, Ill.: Irwin-Dorsey, 1965).

49. George A. Miller, "The Magical Number Seven Plus or Minus Two: Some Limits on Our Capacity for Processing Information," *Psychological Review* 63 (1956):81-97.

50. James G. Miller, "Information Input Overload and Psychopathology," *The American Journal of Psychiatry* 116 (1960):695-704.

51. Sorensen, *Decision-Making in the White House,* p. 38.

52. Richard A. Brody, "Some Systemic Effects of the Spread of Nuclear Weapons Technology: A Study Through Simulation of a Multi-Nuclear Future," *The Journal of Conflict Resolution* 7 (1963):663-753.

53. This aspect of crisis may, however, actually improve certain aspects of decision processes: "The greater the emergency, the more likely is decision-making to be concentrated among high officials whose commitments are to the over-all system. Thus it may be, paradoxically, that the model of means-ends rationality will be more closely approximated in an emergency when the time for careful deliberation is limited. Though fewer alternatives will be considered the values invoked during the decision period will tend to be fewer and more consistent, and decisions will less likely be the result of bargaining within a coalition." Sidney Verba, "Assumptions of Rationality and Non-rationality in Models of the International System," *World Politics* 14 (1961):115.

54. Richard C. Snyder and Glenn D. Paige, "The United States Decision to Resist Aggression in Korea: Application of an Analytical Scheme," *Administrative Science Quarterly* 3 (1958):341-378; Glenn D. Paige, *The Korean Decision* (New York: The Free Press, 1968); C. M. Roberts, "The Day We Didn't Go to War," *The Reporter,* 14 September 1954.

55. Dean G. Pruitt, "Problem Solving in the Department of State," Northwestern University, 1961 (unpublished paper cited in Charles F. Hermann, "Some Consequences of Crisis.").

56. George M. Thomson, *The Twelve Days: July 24 to August 4, 1914,* pp. 44-45 (New York: G. P. Putnam's Sons, 1964).

57. James G. Miller, "Information Input Overload."

58. Paul Smoker, "Sino-Indian Relations: A Study of Trade, Communication and Defence," *Journal of Peace Research,* no. 2 (1964):65-76.

59. Amia Lieblich, "Effects of Stress on Risk Taking," *Psychon. Sci.* 10 (1968):303-304; Korchin and Levine, "Anxiety and Verbal Learning," p. 238; Leonard Berkowitz, "Repeated Frustration and Expectations in Hostility Arousal," *Journal of Abnormal and Social Psychology* 40 (1960):422-429; Bruce Dohrenwend, "The Social Psychological Nature of Stress," *Journal of Abnormal and Social Psychology* 62 (1961):294-302.

60. An alternative view is that "decision-makers do not perceive or behave differently in a crisis"; that is, "they do not perceive hostility where none exists, and they express hostility directly in terms of their perception of hostility." Dina A. Zinnes, Joseph Zinnes, and R. D. McClure, "Hostility in Diplomatic Communication: A Study of the 1914 Crisis," in Charles F. Hermann (ed.), *Contemporary Research in International Crisis* (New York: The Free Press [in press]). This does not demonstrate, however, that many other aspects of perception and behaviour may not change in crisis situations. Moreover, their conclusion does not rule out the possibility that mutual perception of hostility may be sustained and magnified beyond their original causes.

61. Nor, of course, can it be assumed that they are not valid, or that the converse of the experimental findings is true.

62. For a further development of this point, see Horvath, "Psychological Stress."

63. See, for example: Charles F. Hermann, *Crises in Foreign Policy* (Indianapolis, Ind.: Bobbs-Merrill, 1969); Charles F. Hermann (ed.), *Contemporary Research in International Crisis* (New York: The Free Press [in press]); and my *Crisis, Escalation and War* (in press).

21
Comparative Case Analysis of Crisis Decisions: Korea and Cuba

Glenn D. Paige

The methodology of theory-oriented case studies of foreign policy decision making is still in its infancy. Although a fruitful conceptual framework for the study of foreign policy making has been suggested by Snyder, Bruck, and Sapin,[1] and although an application of this framework has been attempted in a single case,[2] much work remains to be done before the method becomes a reliable intellectual tool and before greater degrees of confidence are warranted in the propositions produced by this kind of analysis.

The principal task of the present chapter is to attempt to contribute to the . . . goals of clarifying concepts, methods, and findings in the study of international crises by means of a comparative case analysis of the Korean and Cuban decisions. At the same time it represents an effort to explore the usefulness of the Snyder, Bruck, and Sapin decisionmaking framework in comparative inquiry.

The empirical bases of the comparison are narrative reconstructions of the Korean decision (June 24-30, 1950)[3] and of the Cuban decision (October 15-28, 1962).[4] For purposes of this inquiry the period of decision in each case is taken as the interval between initial receipt of information about the precipitating event and the first public announcement by the president of military measures to be taken in response to it. For the Korean decision this includes the sixty-four-hour period from 8:00 P.M., Saturday, June 24, 1950, to 12:00 noon, Tuesday, June 27. In the Cuban decision

Reprinted with permission of Macmillan Publishing Co., from *International Crises: Insights from Behavioral Research,* by Charles F. Hermann, ed., pp. 41-55. Copyright © 1972 by The Free Press, a Division of The Macmillan Company.

this is a period of seven days (168 hours) between 7:00 P.M., Monday, October 15, and 7:00 P.M., Monday, October 22, 1962. Although some reference will be made to antecedent and consequent events, the main focus of attention will be on these periods. It will be noted that this analytical choice means that the period of the Cuban decision was a little over two and a half times that of the Korean decision.

Four preexisting elements were combined to produce the present analysis: the Snyder, Bruck, and Sapin conceptual framework for the study of foreign policy decisions;[5] a narrative reconstruction of the Korean decision based on that framework;[6] a set of propositions induced from the Korean decision;[7] and reconstructions of the Cuban decision prepared without reference to the decisionmaking framework.[8] The sequence of investigation was as follows. First, the Cuban case materials were studied in the light of the decisionmaking frame of reference but there was no explicit attempt to "test" or to relate to this decision the propositions derived from the Korean decision. In this way it was hoped to maximize the probability of appreciating new features and relationships among variables. Thus the Cuban case materials were first studied with the following general questions in mind: What relationships among organizational, informational, and normative variables does this case suggest? What similarities and differences are suggested through general comparison with the Korean decision? A second step was to review a list of about fifty propositions based on the Korean decision for the purpose of identifying those that seemed supported, contradicted, or needful of modification on the basis of the Cuban materials. This review of the emerging inventory of decisionmaking propositions for relevance to the Cuban case was done intuitively. It might better have been accomplished by a panel of judges employing explicit criteria of relevance. Third, the implications of the comparison for the Hermann crisis variables were examined. Finally, an attempt was made to reflect more broadly upon the significance of the comparison for understanding crisis decisions in international politics and for the further development of decisionmaking analysis.

Before presenting some of the results of this inquiry, it will be helpful to recall the principal event structure of the two decisions under study. Both decisions seem to meet the three criteria for a "crisis decision" that have been suggested by Hermann: short decision time, high perceived threat to values, and surprise.[9]

The Korean Decision

On Saturday, June 24, 1950 (Washington time), the North Korean People's Army invaded the Republic of Korea without warning. The news reached Washington at 8:00 P.M. against a background of vigorous domestic political criticism of the administration's China policies, but with relatively little attention devoted to Korea. That night the president, who was then home in Missouri, approved the recommendation of the secretary of state and a small working group at the State Department that the United States bring the matter before the United Nations Security Council. This was done on the afternoon of Sunday, June 25, when a resolution was obtained calling for a cease-fire and a North Korean withdrawal. The president returned to Washington as the Security Council met. En route to the capital the president asked the secretary of state to assemble a group of advisers to confer with him upon arrival at Blair House. Subsequently, a core group of thirteen advisers met with the president in two major conferences held on the evenings of June 25 and June 26. The group included eight officials from the Department of Defense (the secretary of defense, the service secretaries, and the joint chiefs of staff) and five officials from the Department of State (the secretary of state, the under secretary of state, the assistant secretary of state for United Nations affairs, the assistant secretary of state for Far Eastern affairs, and an ambassador-at-large). As the North Koreans rapidly advanced, it became clear that only direct military assistance would save the Republic of Korea. The decisionmakers were unanimous in their belief that acceptance of a successful North Korean Communist invasion of the Republic would constitute intolerable "appeasement" that would surely lead to World War III, just as unopposed aggressions of the 1930s had led to World War II. They hoped by positive action — affirmation of the principle of "collective security against aggression" — to help strengthen the newly established United Nations. They calculated that neither Soviet nor Chinese Communist counterintervention was probable and that the United States held a margin of military superiority over its principal potential opponent — the Soviet Union. The secretary of state took the lead in proposing courses of action for approval by the president. There was no division among the president's advisers over competing alternatives. Thus, on the evening of June 26, the president decided to commit American air and naval forces to combat in the area south of the thirty-eighth parallel, to deter an anticipated Chinese Communist invasion of Taiwan by committing the Seventh Fleet to its defense, and to increase military assistance to the Philippines and to Indochina. These decisions were announced on June 27. By June 30 the president had authorized air and naval operations into North Korea and had approved the commitment of two infantry divisions to combat. Thus the United States became engaged in a war that lasted for three years — measured in terms of casualties this became the fifth most costly war in American history.

The Cuban Decision

On Monday, October 15, 1962, at about 7:00 P.M., it was reported to the higher levels of the Kennedy administration that photoanalysts of the Defense Intelligence Agency had discovered preparations for the emplacement of Soviet medium-range ballistic missiles in Cuba. This report came against a background of American warnings against the emplacement of offensive nuclear weapons in Cuba, of Soviet denials that they intended to deploy them there, and of vociferous Republican charges that the Russians already had done so. The President was informed of the results of the photographic interpretation on the morning of October 16. He immediately requested that a group of fifteen advisers meet with him to consider the situation. This group consisted of five close associates of the president (three presidential assistants, the attorney general, and the secretary of the treasury), four officials from the Department of State (the secretary and under secretary of state, the assistant secretary for inter-American affairs, and an ambassadorial specialist on Soviet affairs), four officials from the Department of Defense (the secretary and deputy secretary of defense, the assistant secretary for international security affairs, and the chairman of the Joint Chiefs of Staff), the vice president, and the deputy director of the Central Intelligence Agency (later, the director). This group of "fourteen or fifteen men,"[10] with slight changes and supplemented by the president's consultations with three respected private citizens (a former secretary of state, a former secretary of defense, and a former high commissioner to Germany), served as the core decisionmaking body throughout the period of choice. Only on October 22, nearly a week after its formation, was the group formally designated as the Executive Committee of the National Security Council. In deciding upon an appropriate response to the Soviet military action, the president and his advisers considered at least five alternatives: to do nothing; to lodge a complaint with the United Nations; to establish a military embargo and naval blockade of Cuba; to destroy the missile sites by precision bombing; and to invade Cuba with ground forces. In a prolonged evaluation of these alternatives, extending over the week preceding the public announcement of intended action, the President's advisers divided in favor of two responses: a naval blockade or "quarantine," and an air attack. There was some disagreement over the degree of increased military threat to the United States posed by the missiles in Cuba, but there was a strong immediate consensus that their presence was an intolerable threat to the principles of the Monroe Doctrine. No dominant analogy with the past was perceived; the Soviet action in stationing nuclear weapons outside its own territory was unprecedented except at sea.

On occasion, the president deliberately absented himself from the discussions of his advisers. His brother, the attorney general, tended to emerge as the informal discussion leader, eliciting alternatives and challenging proponents to defend them. After an initial inclination to follow a preexisting plan of direct military action against Cuba,[11] the president finally decided upon a naval blockade that seemed to be favored by a majority of his advisers. But he assured those advisers who had argued strongly for an air attack that their proposal would be made a part of contingency planning. The president's decision was announced on October 22. At that time he estimated the probability of aggressive Soviet counteraction to be "somewhere between one out of three and even."[12] On October 28 the Soviet Union agreed to remove the objectionable weapons from Cuba on the condition that the United States would agree not to invade Cuba.

Some Major Similarities and Differences

Crisis decisions, like personalities, can be compared either as a whole or in part. A general comparison reveals many similarities and differences. Some salient ones are the following.

The Korean and Cuban decisions were similar in that the precipitating event came to the decisionmakers by surprise even though there had been unconfirmed reports that it would indeed happen. In both cases the event seems to have been the product of mutual miscalculation; neither side apparently foresaw accurately what the other side would do. Both precipitating events were perceived as threatening deeply held values: no appeasement of aggression in the Korean case: the inviolability of the Monroe Doctrine in the Cuban decision. There was a strong sense of foreshortened time imposed by the rapidly changing objective situation: the Republic of Korea would be overrun within hours; the Soviet missiles in Cuba would be operational within one week. At the time of the crises both American administrations were under strong domestic political attack for failure to take more resolute counteractions against the extension of Communist power and influence. In each case the initial inclination of the President was to adopt a firm posture of resistance against the threat; this sense of resolve was shared by his advisers. In both cases the President decided to act without obtaining prior congressional authorization and without engaging members of the Congress in the decisionmaking process. In both cases efforts were made to keep contemplated responses secret, to avoid alarming the American public, to obtain international organizational legitimation for actions taken, and to inform preferentially key domestic and international political figures of contemplated action prior to public announcement. In each case the President legitimated a consensus, or at least a majority opinion, reached by his advisers. In each case the decisionmakers seemed ready to engage their opponents in expanded conflict if their initial effort to remove the perceived threat failed. In both cases the decisionmakers initially attempted to provide an opportunity for voluntary opponent withdrawal.

There were also many marked differences. Cuba was at the forefront of domestic American political debate when the precipitating event occurred; Korean policy was not a major domestic issue when the North Korean attack took place. In the Cuban crisis the precipitating event was secret; in Korea it was generally known throughout the world. For coping with a Soviet military threat from Cuba there was a preexisting plan for direct military counteraction; in Korea there was nothing except a standard plan for the evacuation of citizens in the event of an outbreak of hostilities. In the Cuban decision the United States was directly confronted by Soviet military power, vastly increased over 1950 by the addition of nuclear weapons; in the Korean case the United States, favored by a near monopoly of atomic weapons, faced the Soviet Union indirectly in the actions of a close Soviet ally. American military security was a much more salient value in the Cuban decision than in the Korean case. In the Cuban decision there was sharp conflict among the President's advisers who advocated two different courses of action; in the Korean decision there was group consensus around a single action proposal. The Korean decision did not contain contingency plans; the Cuban decision envisaged escalating application of military measures. In the Korean case legitimating international support preceded, but the Cuban case followed, the American military action. In the Korean decision the United States obtained the support of a "universal" international organization (the United Nations); the Cuban action was supported by a regional international organization (the Organization of American States).

Comparison and Decisionmaking Analysis

If we narrow attention to specific analytical aspects of foreign policy decisions and compare the two cases in terms of decisionmaking variables and propositions derived from the Korean decision, the following principal findings are suggested.

Organizational Variables

Investigation of the Cuban case reveals strong support for the Korea-derived hypothesis that *crisis decisions tend to be made by small, ad hoc decisional units*. It will be recalled that the decisional unit in the Korean case numbered fourteen officials; in the Cuban case, about sixteen. That this size group may be optimum for high-level decisions under existing psychological and technological conditions is further suggested by the fact that the contemporary ruling Presidium of the Communist Party of the Soviet Union now numbers thirteen officials. An especially important point to note is that these crisis decisional units are of an ad hoc nature. Neither the formal National Security Council nor the cabinet was used in either case. It is to be noted also that the units vary in their ad hoc qualities. Some official roles were constant across the two cases—that is, the president, the secretaries of state and defense, and the chairman of the Joint Chiefs of Staff (four roles). Even if the roles of regional assistant secretary of state and of experienced ambassador are considered as functional equivalents in the two cases, still less than half the members of the decisional units occupy the same roles in the two decisions (a total of six roles). This suggests that the ad hoc properties of crisis decisional units are well worth close attention. So also does a report from Moscow that during all-night deliberations connected with the Israeli-Arab crisis of June 1967, the Soviet Presidium was joined by at least one nonregular member—Foreign Minister Andrei Gromyko.[13]

A comparison of the composition of the Korean and Cuban decisional units reveals a majority of military-related roles in the former and a plurality of special presidential advisers in the latter. The full-scale representation of the top leaders of the military establishment in 1950 may have been correlated with the newness of the Department of Defense; their absence in 1962 may have been related to the department's strength and to the president's confidence in its leadership. The absence and presence of the head of the Central Intelligence Agency may be related to similar considerations. But, in any event, the president has been seen in two instances to have exercised wide latitude in deciding who should participate in determining the nation's response to crisis. By comparison, the Korean unit seems much more formal and hierarchical; the Cuban unit seems more diverse and reflective of different presidential needs.

Evidence to support another proposition derived from the Korean decision also seemed to be found in the Cuban case; that is, *the greater the crisis, the more the leader solicitation of subordinate advice.* This was originally suggested by President Truman's practice in the Blair House conferences of asking each of his advisers, in turn, what he thought of the situation. President Kennedy went beyond this in 1962. Not only did he withdraw from deliberations among his advisers so that they might freely express their views without distortions occasioned by his presence (it was found, for example, that departmental subordinates were less inclined to challenge the views of their own superiors in the president's presence),[14] but he sought the advice of experienced officials then outside government. At a late stage of decision, on October 21, he even sounded out the views of the British ambassador, a long-time friend.[15] If the Cuban crisis is regarded as of greater magnitude than that in Korea, the differential search for advice might then be explained on the basis of objective characteristics of the situation. On the other hand, perhaps the somewhat different pattern of advice seeking can be explained on grounds of different presidential personalities. One of the tasks of the further development of decisionmaking analysis will be to devise means for separating such factors and arriving at judgments about their relative importance.

A third proposition suggested by the Korean-Cuban comparison was one not originally entertained: *the greater the crisis, the greater is the clarity of differentiation between task leadership and emotional affect leadership roles.* In both decisions one official, who regarded himself and was recognized by others as having especially close affective ties with the president, seemed to emerge into a salient position as the adviser who contributed most to clarifying a recommended course of action to lay before the president for decision. In the Korean decision the task of presenting courses of action for decision by the president was performed by the secretary of state; in the Cuban decision it was performed outstandingly, but not exclusively, by the president's brother, the attorney general. In both cases it was true, of course, that the president himself ultimately had to decide — to think through and to be ultimately responsible for the measures proposed for the task of crisis management. But at the same time his emotional affect role (or perhaps, better, his authoritative decision or legitimating role) was perhaps even more salient. "He pulled us all together" was the way one participant of the Blair House conferences explained President Truman's role. And it may well be imagined that President Kennedy's reassurance to the air strike advocates that their course of action was not completely out of the question did much to preserve the cooperative behavior and satisfaction with group performance among his advisers after hours of conflict among advocates of different alternatives. If such enhanced role differentiation proves characteristic of crisis decisions in international politics, then an important link can be made with analogous findings of small group research in social psychology with interesting mutual implications.

Informational Variables

Two propositions from the Korean decision pertaining to information and communication variables were also seen reflected with some modification and with deepened appreciation of their significance as a result of comparison with the Cuban decision. These were that *crisis tends to be accompanied by increased search behaviors for new information about the threatening event* and *the greater the crisis, the more information about it tends to be elevated to the top of the organizational hierarchy.* These two propositions describe a pattern of search and centralization of new information in organizational behavior under crisis conditions. They were suggested by persistent requests for new information from Korea after the first press report of the invasion, by President Truman's orders to all American missions throughout the world to provide him with any new information about possible Soviet moves, and by the speed and directness with which essential information was brought to his attention (including delivery of a report from General MacArthur at 5:00 A.M. on June 30). The same pattern of intensified search for new information was observed in the Cuban decision where the president immediately authorized more aerial reconnaissance missions to verify the findings of early photographic analysis. Although such flights involved risk, the president was willing to take it for the needed information.

Both the Korean and Cuban decisions saw temporary exceptions to the second proposition cited above: the sleeping General MacArthur in Tokyo was not informed of initial reports of the North Korean invasion during the early morning hours of June 25 until his aides had confirmed that the news was really serious; President Kennedy was not informed of the initial discovery of the Cuban missile sites on the evening of October 15 until the next morning because an adviser wished to protect his health by allowing him a good night's sleep after arduous travel to prepare for the difficult days ahead.

Both of these stoppages on the upward path of information were temporary and in these cases did not have a significant effect upon the decisions taken. However, the attention given to them, especially the latter, underscores the widely appreciated necessity for relevant information to reach speedily the highest decisional levels under crisis conditions. This pattern of behavior, if it proves general, has very important implications for crisis management; for it means that decisionmakers under crisis are not to be viewed as impervious to new informational inputs but are, on the contrary, to be seen as actively seeking news of relevance. This means that knowledge of criteria of relevance and channels of communication would permit placing information from outside sources into the search and centralization pattern of the organization responding to crisis.

Another proposition based on the Korean case held that *the greater the crisis, the greater is the propensity to supplement information about the objective state of affairs with information drawn from past experience.* This was suggested by the fact that decisionmakers in 1950 tended to view the North Korean invasion as having the same significance as the German, Japanese, and Italian aggressions of the pre–World War II period. The Cuban decision was different; the Russians had never done what they were found to be doing in Cuba — never before had they stationed nuclear weapons on foreign soil. Somehow, no historical analogy came readily to mind. But one Leninist maxim, identical to one cited in the course of the Korean decision, was recalled out of the past: the advice that "if you strike steel, pull back, if you strike mush, keep going."[16] This maxim was introduced into the deliberations of the President's advisers, as it was in the Korean decision, in the absence of more direct knowledge as information bearing upon Soviet motivations and probable responses to American actions. Comparative analysis thus aids appreciation of the kinds of information that can be added from past experience: historical analogy and asserted codes of behavior. Where one is not readily available, the other may be invoked.

A new proposition suggested by the Cuban case is that *the more the flow of past unconfirmed warnings that the crisis-precipitating event will occur, and the more the face-to-face assurances by an opponent that the action is not contemplated, the greater is the emotional shock when the event takes place.* This proposition combines two elements: frequency of unconfirmed prior reports and mode of communicating denial of intended action. In both the Korean and Cuban cases there were rumors and reports that what did happen would happen. But only in the Cuban case were there explicit denials by Soviet spokesmen to the president and to other high American officials that the Soviet Union did not intend to deploy offensive nuclear weapons in Cuba. When the undeniable evidence finally emerged, the President and his advisers seemed especially "angry" at Soviet duplicity; there was a sense of betrayal.[17] In the Korean decision there were no such direct Soviet assurances of non-threatening behavior; the president and his advisers seemed to react with less emotion to the surprise attack. One suspects, however, that most crisis situations will be characterized by a rather strong emotional tone and that prior warnings and direct reassurances are intensifying rather than prerequisite conditions for emotional arousal. In the Korean decision, for example, Soviet leaders seem to have been shaken by the American action even though the two factors noted above were not present from the Soviet point of view. As Andrei Vyshinsky said to a Korean decision participant just prior to the former Soviet diplomat's death, "We can't believe anything you Americans say. You led us to believe that you wouldn't do anything in Korea and then you did."

Normative Variables

A basic proposition concerning values from the Korean decision that seems supported in the Cuban case is that *crisis tends to evoke a dominant goal-means value complex that persists as an explicit or implicit guide to subsequent responses.* In the Korean decision this proposition was suggested by the immediate response of the American officials to try to secure their goal of a cessation of North Korean aggression through collective action within the framework of the United Nations. Their first thought was not of direct military counteraction and there was no prepared plan for it. In the Cuban decision the first response of American officials was that the United States would have to take some kind of military action to attain the goal of withdrawal of Soviet missiles from Cuba;[18] there were, in fact, plans ready for military action against the island.[19] Although there is no information about the president's initial reaction to the reported presence of the missiles, an authoritative account of the first conference indicates measures involving air, naval, or ground action were salient in the discussions of his advisers from the outset. And one of the first directives given by the president as a result of this conference was that the armed forces should prepare for military action against Cuba within a week. Thus in Korea the initial American response was a diplomatic one with military overtones; while in Cuba it was a military move with diplomatic correlates. Both cases suggest the importance of the initial frame of normative reference (desired goals and preferred means of achieving them) that emerges in a crisis situation.

A proposition suggested by the Cuban case enables new appreciation of related behaviors in the Korean decision. This is that *moral persuasion can lead to changes in preferred courses of action by at least some officials*. In the Cuban decision, following an eloquent argument by the attorney general that a surprise attack was not in the American tradition, the secretary of the treasury changed his preference from air attack to naval blockade.[20] On the other hand, the same moral appeal was rejected as irrelevant by former Secretary of State Acheson who continued to favor the air attack alternative. Nevertheless, the potency of moral suasion in at least one case suggests a new appreciation of President Truman's moral commitment to the United Nations revealed at the very outset of the Korean decision. Movingly, before the first formal deliberations began, the president was heard to say, "We can't let the U.N. down." Although there was no record of conflict over alternatives or changes of preference associated with values in the Korean case, the shared desire to avoid world war by strengthening the United Nations takes on new importance as an explanation for the strong consensus behind military resistance in Korea in 1950.

Interestingly, the Korean-Cuban comparison suggests the proposition that *in international crisis decisionmaking there is a taboo against explicit general discussion of the domestic political implications of the event or of intended action* — at least in the American case. An intriguing finding of the Korean case was that there was no discussion of domestic politics in the two Blair House conferences. When the under secretary of state tried to begin such a discussion at the end of the first conference, he apparently so annoyed the President that he was excluded from the second meeting. In the Cuban decision the only record of consideration of such matters was a note passed surreptitiously to presidential assistant Theodore Sorensen by a Republican air strike proponent who warned that unless effective action were taken to remove the missiles a Republican House of Representatives would be elected in the impending mid-term elections. The private transmittal of this note seems to underscore the sensed impermissibility of open discussion of such issues. The derivation of this proposition illustrates how a fact perceived in one case comes to be perceived as part of a possibly significant general pattern only on the basis of inquiry in other cases. The qualification that this may apply only to American experience has been added; crossnational studies of foreign policy crisis decisions will be required before this proposition will merit more general confidence.

Organizational Process, Intellectual Process, and Decisional Outcome

The primary tasks of decisionmaking analysis are to describe and to explain decisionmaking processes and outcomes. In pursuing these tasks, two main processes can be separated analytically: an organizational process and an intellectual process. It is further assumed that these two processes are in a relationship of mutual influence. In the first process organizational roles are mobilized for decision; information is received, gathered, and recalled; and relevant values are given, identified, or newly thrust upon the decisionmakers. In the second kind of process the main elements of decision are identified, evaluated, combined, and selected in group activity. The outcomes — the chosen alternatives, the plans for implementation, and the contingency plans — are thought of as being the product of the interaction of the organizational and intellectual processes.

The comparison of the Korean and Cuban decisions permits a somewhat clearer understanding of the importance of organizational and intellectual processes for decisional outcomes than was possible on the basis of the Korean decision alone. One factor — intellectual task leadership — seems to stand out with greater importance as a key element in explaining the nature of decisions taken in response to crisis. The Korean and Cuban decisions differ in their antecedent conditions, organizational processes, intellectual processes, and decisions taken. In the Korean decision there was no a priori contingency plan for military action; yet a decision was taken to engage in military combat. In the Cuban case plans for a military attack on Cuba were in existence, but a limited blockade short of direct attack was chosen. Compared with the Cuban decision, the organizational roles engaged in the Korean decision were less heterogeneous, there was more formality in organizational structure, the information available to the decisionmakers was less comprehensive and accurate, and the values perceived to be threatened were less complex. In terms of intellectual process, the Korean decision was characterized by commentary upon a single proposed course of action; the Cuban decision was marked by contention over preferred alternatives. The Korean decisional outcome was limited in the scope of its anticipation of subsequent events. It was not a composite of the various courses of action proposed — a composite that envisioned increasingly costly commitments to action, as was represented by the Cuban decision where possible Soviet countermoves had been hypothesized. The Korean decision was undertaken with less perceived risk of Soviet counteraction than was the Cuban decision. Both decisions were similar, however, in the strong initial agreement among the officials that the course of events perceived as taking place in the international environment had by some means to be reversed. What remained at issue was how and when.

Now no single factor explanation will be sufficient to account for these similarities and differences in process and outcome; indeed, a basic assumption of decisionmaking analysis is that appreciation of the *interaction* of the multiple variables to which attention is called by the framework is a more adequate approach to understanding. Yet, as empirical research proceeds in the case study of decisions, undoubtedly some factors will come to be perceived as more directly and importantly contributive to outcomes than others. On the basis of the Korean-Cuban comparison the exceptional importance of the president's style of leadership can be seen. His choice of who should advise him in the crisis is a vitally important element of organizational process. Furthermore, his choice — either explicitly made or implicitly accepted — of the process by which alternative courses of action are to be identified, evaluated, and presented to him is an element of high importance for the intellectual process of decision. In the Korean decision the president supported the intellectual leadership of the secretary of state and the latter fulfilled his responsibility according to his own definition: an adviser should present the president a set of considered recommendations that are the product of staff work involving interdepartmental coordination. The tone of the two Blair House conferences was not one of group creativity in identifying and evaluating proposed courses of action; in fact, some participants and close observers noted the lack of exploration in depth of the implications of the decision. This is not to say that the president inhibited the free expression of views; he did not. In fact he called for them. But the relationship between the president and the secretary of state was so intimate, the intellectual style of the secretary was of such a nature, and relationships with the secretary of defense were so avoidant, that no truly wide-ranging exploration of the issues raised by the attack was made. Thus a decision to fight was taken without explicit plans for possible ground intervention or for measures to be taken in response to Soviet counterintervention if it should occur. By contrast, President Kennedy chose his advisers in part in terms of intellectual intimacy. He encouraged creative group problem-solving processes. No one adviser was his "first minister," but he allowed his brother to lead intellectually an extended exploration of alternatives in nearly a week of questioning. The product was a decision that foresaw a great many contingencies and was prepared for multiple courses of action. The difference in time available for the two decisions, of course, was a variable of high importance, but the significance of both organizational and intellectual task leadership seems striking when the two decisions are compared.

Comparison and the Concept of Crisis

Another approach to the comparative analysis of the two decisions is to examine their implications for the three components of crisis that have been suggested by Hermann and to explore their implications for crisis management.

Time as an Independent Variable

The Cuban decision took place over a longer period of time than did the Korean decision. Thus it may be possible to identify some of the more important correlates of long versus short decision time by comparing the two decisions. It may be argued that it is tautologically or at least trivially true to say that "the longer the time, the longer the something" because "something" in this case can mean "anything." And yet out of the infinite universe of anything that might happen during the longer time of the Cuban decision as compared with the Korean decision, only some things thrust themselves before our attention as potentially significant. It is these that we will note briefly here, ordering them in terms of categories of the decisionmaking framework. Thus our comparison suggests for *organization* that the longer the decision time, the greater the conflict within decisional units and the greater the investment of emotional affect in policy and personal differences; the greater the needs for affective leadership within decisional units; the greater the achievement of decisional unit consensus through processes of changes in individual positions and withdrawal of dissenters; the greater the efforts to secure decisional reversals by proponents of different courses of action; the greater the consultation with persons outside the core decisional unit; the greater the proliferation of functionally specific subordinate organizations designed to provide the decisionmakers with premises for choice; and the greater the probability that the dominant leader will seek confirmation of the soundness of his choices from trusted friends before public commitment. For *information,* extended decision time implies greater inputs of written versus oral information and interpretation; and greater probability of information disclosures that may facilitate unfavorable opponent counteraction. In *normative* matters, it is to be expected that long decision time will be accompanied by shifts in the value bases designed to legitimate the crisis responses — for example, in the Cuban decision it was decided to legitimate American action under Articles 6 and 8 of the Rio Treaty rather than under the United Nations Charter as first contemplated. In relationships with the *external* and *internal settings,* longer decision time implies greater efforts to communicate with allies on a face-to-face basis (e.g., Mr. Acheson's mission to Europe to inform NATO allies of the American position), and greater frequency of public deception to conceal information about the way in which the crisis is perceived and about the probable costs of coping with it. In terms of *intellectual process* it is to be expected that the longer the decision time, the more the alternative courses of action considered.

Aside from the above hypothesized empirical correlates of longer decision time, comparison of the two cases suggests some strategies for manipulating the variable of time in producing crisis conditions. At least three techniques are possible: creating short decision time by ultimatum; pursuing rapid deprivational action; and overloading the problem-solving capacities of the decisionmakers so that they can devote but little attention to the problem at hand. Conversely, to provide more extended time for crisis decision deliberations one would avoid issuance of an ultimatum, act slowly in relation to opponent values, and minimize other problems thrust upon his attention.

Threat to Values as an Independent Variable

Comparison of the Korean and Cuban decisions suggests that it may be fruitful to begin to create a typology of the kinds of values perceived as threatened in crisis situations. Both crises suggest that there is a tendency to perceive one central value as severely threatened and then to distinguish many other important values related to it. In the Korean case the main value seemed to be that of protecting the United Nations as an instrument of peace by successfully carrying out a collective security response to aggression: thus world war would be averted. Related values were the confidence of allies in American assurances of support and the security of Japan. The North Korean invasion was not perceived as an immediate threat to the military security of the United States. By contrast, in the Cuban decision the military security of the United States was the central value. The viability of the principles of the Monroe Doctrine and the confidence of American allies in Latin America and elsewhere were related values.

Thus, building upon the kinds of values seen threatenened in the two decisions, a typology might be suggested that includes at least: threats to military security (immediate and long-range), threats to asserted universal principles of international order, threats to regional stability and integrity (proximate and distant), and threatened loss of international political support.

In terms of crisis management the Korean-Cuban comparison suggests that the sense of increased threat to values can be manipulated by targeting on values of high priority in the opponent's normative hierarchy, by threatening many values simultaneously, by evoking past threats to values (as the North Korean invasion unwittingly did), and by acting close in psychological space (as the Russians did in Cuba). Lesser threat to values can be achieved by avoiding such behaviors.

Surprise as an Independent Variable

Comparison of the two decisions reveals a different quality of surprise in each case that may well be worth considering further in studies of crisis. The type of surprise represented in the Korean case can be defined as AGUS surprise (Anticipated Generally but Unanticipated Specifically). In the spring of 1950, American intelligence analysts had anticipated that something unusual of a military nature was about to happen along the Soviet periphery but they were unable to pinpoint the exact location. Korea was generally discounted as their analysis focused upon the Middle East and Europe. They also expected a Chinese Communist invasion of Taiwan in the summer of 1950, but they did not expect correlated Korean action. Thus the Korean attack occurred within a context of expected military action somewhere along the periphery of the Communist countries. The surprising thing was that it came in Korea.

The kind of surprise involved in the Cuban decision was somewhat different. It might be termed BATO surprise (Betrayed Assurances to the Opposite). In this kind of surprise the event is anticipated, even specifically, but the opponent gives explicit reassurances that the action will not be taken. In fact, the prelude to the Cuban decision presents a classic paradigm for this kind of surprise: The actor warns the opponent not to do it. The opponent says he has not done it. The opponent says he will not do it. The opponent has actually never done it in the past. The opponent says that he can gain his goals in other ways. The actor agrees that the opponent can achieve his goals in other ways. The opponent offers plausible explanations of facts that might suggest he will do it. There are numerous unconfirmed reports that the opponent has done or is doing it. The opponent does it. Surprise!

The principal difference in the effect of AGUS versus BATO surprise is that the latter seems to produce a much stronger emotional reaction. Americans will recall that national indignation over the attack on Pearl Harbor was much greater because Japanese diplomats were "talking peace" in Washington at the time it occurred, something that wartime commentators almost never failed to emphasize. Whether higher degrees of emotionality in crisis responses will lead to perceptual distortions or to greater propensity for risk taking is something that will have to be explored in further studies of crisis decisionmaking. A seeming difference in the emotional quality of surprise in the two decisions studied can only be mentioned here.[21]

With respect to crisis management, the above paradigm might be followed to produce an emotional quality of surprise in adversaries — or might be avoided to diminish that quality.

Conclusions: Developing Case Studies of Crisis Decisions

The analysis presented above by no means exhausts the potentialities for comparative analysis of the Korean and Cuban decisions. Since there is a hypothetically infinite variety of analytical aspects that can be created to describe a concrete social object, much more extended inquiry into the two cases is warranted both within the decisionmaking framework and from other perspectives.

But, in addition to further analytical efforts employing existing frameworks for case studies on available materials, several other lines of development for decisionmaking case analysis have been suggested by the present inquiry. The first is greater refinement of single case and comparative case study methods. The case study method is well known for its diagnostic usefulness in probing complex relationships among variables, in identifying important variables that may be overlooked in less deep immersion in events, and in achieving comprehension of the unity and integration of political action. But can it also become a reliable tool for cumulative development of theory through comparative analysis?

A second important need is to raise the question through comparative analysis as to whether capacities for coping with foreign policy crises at the national level improve over time. Such a study would raise issues similar to those studies in the fields of political and administrative development. It would benefit enormously from advances in the study of organizational learning. An important early task would be to develop criteria for effective crisis coping and then to compare at least two decisions made within the same national context on these dimensions over time. External theory and research could be introduced to suggest desirable directions for developing crisis-coping capacities.

A third essential study will be to reconstruct "normal" decisions and to compare them with crisis decisions. A suggestion of methodological perspective for such studies may be taken from the findings of the study of personality development through research on letters written by the individual to various correspondents. It has been found that a much more adequate understanding of the individual has been obtained by studying the letters written to a stable set of correspondents over a long period of time than by analysis of a series of letters to the same individual or fragmentary letters to various correspondents, either concentrated or scattered in time.[22] This suggests that a much better understanding of crisis decisions and of foreign policy decisionmaking in general will be achieved when the behavior of the decisionmakers can be viewed in the context of normal activities of directing the national or international organizational course in international politics.

A fourth essential task, very high in terms of priority, will be to introduce into the analysis of case study materials interpretive hypotheses derived from the other behavioral science disciplines. The very nature of the decisionmaking framework encourages this kind of approach to understanding since it calls for data bearing upon theories of organizational behavior, information theory, and theories of motivation in individual and group psychology. Strategies may well be devised for relating theories of learning, change, conflict, control, creativity, and other social science perspectives. Except for the pioneering work of de Rivera,[23] this has not been seriously attempted for case studies and remains a worthy challenge.

A continuing task will be to relate the findings of crisis case studies to those obtained by laboratory simulations, experiments, documentary studies, mathematical analyses, and attitude surveys. Somehow, the scattered resources of more or less reliable propositions about crisis decision making will have to be inventoried and subjected to a constant process of integration-evaluation-selection-reintegration in the pursuit of deeper understanding. Comparative case studies of crisis decisions offer only one approach — but a challenging one — toward that end.

Notes

1. Richard C. Snyder, H. W. Bruck, and Burton Sapin, *Foreign Policy Decision Making* (New York: The Free Press, 1962).

2. Richard C. Snyder and Glenn D. Paige, "The United States Decision to Resist Aggression in Korea," *Administrative Science Quarterly* 3 (December 1958), 341-378; and Glenn D. Paige, *The Korean Decision* (New York: The Free Press, 1968).

3. Ibid., chaps. 4-11.

4. Theodore C. Sorensen, *Kennedy* (New York: Bantam Books, 1966), chap. 24; and Elie Abel, *The Missile Crisis* (New York: Bantam Books, 1966).

5. Snyder, Bruck, and Sapin, *Foreign Policy,* pp. 14-185.

6. Paige, *Korean Decision,* chaps. 4-11.

7. Ibid., chap. 12.

8. Sorensen, *Kennedy;* and Abel, *Missile Crisis.*

9. Charles F. Hermann, *Crises in Foreign Policy* (Indianapolis: Bobbs-Merrill, 1969).

10. Sorensen, *Kennedy,* p. 760.

11. The President is quoted as saying, "We'll have to do something quickly. . . . I suppose the alternatives are to go in by air and wipe them out, or to take other steps to render the weapons inoperable," Sorensen, *Kennedy,* p. 36.

12. Ibid., p. 795.

13. *New York Times,* June 9, 1967, p. 8.

14. Sorensen, *Kennedy,* pp. 765-766.

15. Abel, *Missile Crisis,* p. 89.

16. Sorensen, *Kennedy,* p. 763.

17. Ibid., p. 759.

18. Abel, *Missile Crisis,* p. 36.

19. Ibid., p. 21.

20. Ibid., p. 67.

21. A third type of surprise situation is also worth investigating—NEATA surprise (Not Expected At All).

22. Hedda Bolgar, "The Case Study Method," in Benjamin B. Wolman, ed., *Handbook of Clinical Psychology* (New York: McGraw-Hill, 1965), pp. 33ff.

23. Joseph H. de Rivera, *The Psychological Dimension of Foreign Policy* (Columbus: Merrill, 1968).

Part 8
International Systemic Inquiries

Introduction

Since the concept of an international system was first introduced in 1957 by Morton Kaplan in his *System and Process in International Politics,* systemic (or systems) analysis has emerged as one of the two dominant approaches (the other being decisionmaking analysis as already noted in Part 7) to the study of international relations in general and of international conflicts and crises in particular. An international system is a theoretical or heuristic concept for the study of international relations; it refers to the assembly of independent but interacting political entities whose relationship is marked by certain recurring patterns of behavior on a continuum ranging from the pole of peace to the pole of war. The systemic level of analysis is the most comprehensive of all the levels in the study of war as it encompasses the totality of all elements encompassed by the field.

Specifically, systemic analysis is concerned with describing and explaining (1) the boundaries of the system, (2) the component political units making up the system, (3) the structures (or types) of the system, (4) the forms or patterns of interaction in the system, and (5) the rules and norms governing the process of the system. Within this general framework, however, international systemic inquiries have diverged into different paths focusing on different systemic variables and their linkages to international violence. Still, the common methodological assumption underlying systemic inquiries is that the causes of international violence may be found in a macroanalysis of the structural and behavioral dynamics of the international system qua system. The central question is directed as to what variables contribute in what manner to systemic instability.

The contrast between decisionmaking and systemic inquiries into the causes of war is evident in the conceptualization of international crisis. Oran R. Young (1967:10) provided one of the most complete systemic definitions of crisis in the following terms: "An international crisis, then, is a set of rapidly unfolding events which raises the impact of destabilizing forces in the general international system or any of its subsystems substantially above 'normal' (i.e., average) levels and increase in the likelihood of international violence occurring in the system." According to such systemic definition of crisis, many local wars or even such regional wars as the 1962 Sino-Indian Border War and the 1979 Sino-Vietnamese War may not qualify as international crises since their destabilizing impact on the international system was not significantly above normal levels.

Much of systems analysis has centered on exploring reciprocal influence of structural and process variables upon the stability of the international system. What are the possible effects of the structures or types of the international system on the forms of interaction between the most dominant units, namely, sovereign states? What are the possible effects of certain behaviors of state actors (revolutionary challenge, status quo defense, or hegemonic expansion) on the structural transformation of the international system? Kaplan's pioneering study specified six types of international systems (the balance of power system, the loose bipolar system, the tight bipolar system, the universal system, the hierarchical system, and the unit veto system) in terms of their equilibrium (stabilizing) potential. From the vantage point of a "billiard ball" perspective, systemic analysis seeks to grapple with the question of what kinds of structure and process in the international system are more (or less) prone to destabilizing international violence.

Our first selection, by Kenneth E. Boulding, presents a sophisticated systems analysis based on the dynamics of the hostility matrix. Boulding is focusing on the intellectual process of interaction between nation-states. Boulding sees the incompatibility of various national images as contributing to the long-run tendency of an international system toward hostility, crisis, and war. He analyzes these national images along three dimensions — geographical space, hostility or friendliness, and strength or weakness — and concludes that such imaging is the last great stronghold of unsophistication. It is impregnated with cognitive, affective, and evaluative distortions that help induce national behavior incompatible with peaceful systemic maintenance or change. In short, Boulding makes a cogent argument to the effect that our national images have now become maladaptive, threatening the very existence of life on earth. His prescription for peace is "the rapid growth of sophistication, especially at the level of the images of the powerful."

The chapter by Melvin Small and J. David Singer, our second selection, presents in a convenient summary form an empirical overview of the patterns of international warfare in the modern international system. It draws heavily on the findings of the Correlates of War Project at the University of Michigan, large portions of which were elaborated by the same authors in *The Wages of War 1816-1965: A Statistical Handbook* (1972). This study makes a systemic search for the factors which account for the incidence of international war by identifying and correlating in a most rigorous empirical manner the variables that are most frequently associated with the onset of war in modern times. The authors have identified ninety-three international wars as having satisfied their three specific criteria for inclusion: (1) wars fought within the temporal scope of 1815-1965; (2) wars fought by members of the international system; and (3) wars whose battle-connected deaths for all systemic combatants taken together exceeded 1,000.

Several key findings of the study that deserve the reader's close and critical attention are as follows: (1) that there is no upward or downward trend in the incidence of international warfare; (2) that there is a strong tendency toward periodicity (war cycles) in the system's war experience; (3) that major powers were the most war prone; and (4) that more than half the nations (77 out of 144 members of the international system throughout the period) managed to escape international war entirely. Given the revolutionary change in weapons systems, the reader might question the generalizability of these findings in relation to contemporary conditions. The unduly restrictive criteria that Small and Singer employed led them to identify only 93 international wars, in striking contrast with the 120 armed conflicts which qualified as wars in the 32-year period, 1945-1976, in a recent study, in which war is operationalized in terms of three broader — and in our opinion more realistic and updated — criteria (Kende 1978:227).

The third selection by Bruce M. Russett takes an imaginative case study approach to the causes of World War I from a systemic perspective. Russett adapts an accounting scheme originally designed to identify the causes of automobile accidents. Russett makes the assumption that no belligerent in any particular war really wanted a global war; hence, such a war was an "accidental" consequence of a series of limited acts of commission and omission. The general war-producing process of the international system on the eve of World War I is conceptually analogized by Russett to an interstate traffic system in which a half dozen stages (remote causes, mediate causes, surprise, no escape, direct cause, and key event) are analyzed to depict the accident-making process.

The period between "surprise" and "no escape" deserves our critical attention because, as Russett points out, surprise as to the danger of war preceded its point of no escape for every belligerent. In a word, this is the period of crisis management. Whether intended or not, the importance of integrating the systemic and decisionmaking approaches comes through clearly in this study, for the point of surprise was "to a great extent determined by the development and perceptiveness of one's intelligence services, and by the perceptiveness of top policy-makers." Russett's main conclusion reinforces Boulding's main thesis about incompatible national images operating as a primary cause of international hostility. For war prevention (or accident avoidance), however, Russett suggests lengthening the period of crisis management between surprise and no escape so as to enable decisionmakers to explore possible preventive measures. This seems to be a somewhat short-sighted technical solution designed more to deal with symptoms rather than with germs of war. At any rate, the reader should read this piece as one way of conceptualizing and analyzing the causes of war employing a case study method. The reader should also keep in mind that the international system has changed substantially in all of its systemic dimensions since World War I.

By way of conclusion, some unresolved issues and problems in systemic inquiries into the causes of war can be specified. First, the systemic perspective leads to an unduly homogenized image of national actors in the international system. To change the metaphor, this approach has the bias that "every tree or every billiard ball is more or less the same." Relatively little attention is devoted to the individual peculiarities and idiosyncracies of national foreign policies. Second, systemic inquiries, despite repeated lip service, have not sufficiently taken into account the roles of non-nation-state actors (supranational, subnational, and extranational actors) in the interaction process of the contemporary international system. To cite one example, dominant systemic inquiries have not paid sufficient attention to the role of the United Nations in the reformulation of the rules and norms governing behavioral processes in the international system. Nor have systemic inquiries done an adequate job of defining and redefining the boundaries of the international system in a constant state of flux.

Third, systemic inquiries are too preoccupied with the interaction process of the superpowers. Given the destructive and system destroying capability of the superpowers, this emphasis can be defended to a certain extent. However, this preoccupation with superpower politics has caused a failure to devote sufficient attention to the implications of the structural change in the system from bipolar to multipolar direction, on the one hand, and of the substantive change in the system from geopolitical to ecopolitical direction, on the other. Emphasizing superpower politics also leads to the neglect of integrative or cooperative patterns of interaction in the international system. Functionalism or the functional approach to world order seems to be a weak link in dominant systemic inquiries.

Fourth, there is the question as to whether the international system theory really corresponds to the empirical reality it purports to describe and explain. Note for illustrative purposes the pervasive mixture of descriptive and prescriptive statements that make up the Chinese three-worlds theory of geopolitics. Such mixture of empirical and normative analyses is not immune from scholarly systemic inquiries. Finally, systemic inquiries have shown a normative bias in favor of stability. Stability or equilibrium is inherent in the concept of system. But the reader might well ask: stability for what and for whom? Of the three contending approaches to world order — system maintaining, system enhancing, and system transforming

(Falk 1977) — system-maintaining bias appears to be the underlying normative assumption of dominant systemic inquiries into the causes of war. Systemic inquiries need a more explicit clarification of the definition of world order in order to realize their potential in empirical research and normative research, or even possibly to undergird a normative science of international relations.

22
National Images and
International Systems

Kenneth E. Boulding

An international system consists of a group of interacting behavior units called "nations" or "countries," to which may sometimes be added certain supranational organizations, such as the United Nations.

Each of the behavior units in the system can be described in terms of a set of "relevant variables." Just what is relevant and what is not is a matter of judgment of the system builder, but we think of such things as states of war or peace, degrees of hostility or friendliness, alliance or enmity, arms budgets, geographic extent, friendly or hostile communications, and so on. Having defined our variables, we can then proceed to postulate certain relationships between them, sufficient to define a path for all the variables through time. Thus we might suppose, with Lewis Richardson,[1] that the rate of change of hostility of one nation toward a second depends on the level of hostility in the second and that the rate of change of hostility of the second toward the first depends on the level of hostility of the first. Then, if we start from given levels of hostility in each nation, these equations are sufficient to spell out what happens to these levels in succeeding time periods. A system of this kind may (or may not) have an *equilibrium* position at which the variables of one period produce an identical set in the next period, and the system exhibits no change through time.

Mechanical systems of this kind, though they are frequently illuminating, can be regarded only as very rough first approximations to the immensely complex truth. At the next level of approximation we must recognize that the people whose decisions determine the policies and actions

The original version of this article appeared under the title "National Images and International Systems," by Kenneth E. Boulding, published in *Journal of Conflict Resolution* 3, no. 2 (June 1959):120-131, and is reprinted herewith by permission of the publisher, Sage Publications, Inc., and of the author.

of nations do not respond to the "objective" facts of the situation, whatever that may mean, but to their "image" of the situation. It is what we think the world is like, not what it is really like, that determines our behavior. If our image of the world is in some sense "wrong," of course, we may be disappointed in our expectations, and we may therefore revise our image; if this revision is in the direction of the "truth" there is presumably a long-run tendency for the "image" and the "truth" to coincide. Whether this is so or not, it is always the image, not the truth, that immediately determines behavior. We act according to the way the world appears to us, not necessarily according to the way it "is." Thus in Richardson's models it is one nation's image of the hostility of another, not the "real" hostility, which determines its reaction. The "image," then, must be thought of as the total cognitive, affective, and evaluative structure of the behavior unit, or its internal view of itself and its universe.[2]

Generally speaking, the behavior of complex organizations can be regarded as determined by *decisions,* and a decision involves the selection of the most preferred position in a contemplated field of choice. Both the field of choice and the ordering of this field by which the preferred position is identified lie in the image of the decisionmaker. Therefore, in a system in which decisionmakers are an essential element, the study of the ways in which the image grows and changes, both of the field of choice and of the valuational ordering of this field, is of prime importance. The image is always in some sense a product of messages received in the past. It is not, however, a simple inventory or "pile" of such messages but a highly structured piece of information capital, developed partly by its inputs and outputs of information and partly by internal messages and its own laws of growth and stability.

The images which are important in international systems are those which a nation has of itself and of those other bodies in the system which constitute its international environment. At once a major complication suggests itself. A nation is some complex of the images of the persons who contemplate it, and as there are many different persons, so there are many different images. The complexity is increased by the necessity for inclusion, in the image of each person or at least of many persons, his image of the image of others. This complexity, however, is a property of the real world, not to be evaded or glossed over. It can be reduced to simpler terms if we distinguish between two types of persons in a nation—the powerful, on the one hand, and the ordinary, on the other. This is not, of course, a sharp distinction. The power of a decisionmaker may be measured roughly by the number of people which his decisions potentially affect, weighted by some measure of the effect itself. Thus the head of a state is powerful, meaning that his decisions affect the lives of millions of people; the ordinary person is not powerful, for his decisions affect only himself and the lives of a few people around him. There is usually a continuum of power among the persons of a society: thus in international relations there are usually a few very powerful individuals in a state — the chief executive, the prime minister, the secretary of state or minister of foreign affairs, the chiefs of staff of the armed forces. There will be some who are less powerful but still influential — members of the legislature, of the civil service, even journalists, newspaper owners, prominent businessmen, grading by imperceptible degrees down to the common soldier, who has no power of decision even over his own life. For purposes of the model, however, let us compress this continuum into two boxes, labeled the "powerful" and the "ordinary," and leave the refinements of power and influence for later studies.

We deal, therefore, with two representative images, (1) the image of the small group of powerful people who make the actual decisions which lead to war or peace, the making or breaking of treaties, the invasions or withdrawals, alliances, and enmities which make up the major events of international relations, and (2) the image of the mass of ordinary people who are deeply affected by these decisions but who take little or no direct part in making them. The tacit support of the mass, however, is of vital importance to the powerful. The powerful are always under some obligation to represent the mass, even under dictatorial regimes. In democratic societies the aggregate influence of the images of ordinary people is very great; the image of the powerful cannot diverge too greatly from the image of the mass without the powerful losing power. On the other hand, the powerful also have some ability to manipulate the images of the mass toward those of the powerful. This is an important object of instruments as diverse as the public education system, the public relations departments of the armed services, the Russian "agitprop," and the Nazi propaganda ministry.

In the formation of the national images, however, it must be emphasized that impressions of nationality are formed mostly in childhood and usually in the family group. It would be quite fallacious to think of the images as being cleverly imposed on the mass by the powerful. If anything, the reverse is the case: the image is essentially a mass image, or what might be called a "folk image," transmitted through the family and the intimate face-to-face group, both in the case of the powerful and in the case of ordinary persons. Especially in the case of the old, long-established nations, the powerful share the mass image rather than impose it; it is passed on from the value systems of the parents to those of the children, and agencies of public instruction and propaganda merely reinforce the images which derived essentially from the family culture. This is much less true in new nations which are striving to achieve nationality, where the family culture frequently does not include strong elements of national allegiance but rather stresses allegiance to religious ideals or to the family as such. Here the powerful are frequently inspired by a national image derived not from family tradition but from a desire to imitate other nations, and here they frequently try to impose their images on the mass of people. Imposed images, however, are fragile by comparison with those which are deeply internalized and transmitted through family and other intimate sources.

Whether transmitted orally and informally through the family or more formally through schooling and the written word, the national image is essentially a *historical* image — that is, an image which extends through time, backward into a supposedly recorded or perhaps mythological past and forward into an imagined future. The more conscious a people is of its history, the stronger the national image is likely to be. To be an Englishman is to be conscious of "1066 and All That" rather than of "Constantine and All That," or "1776 and All That." A nation is the creation of its historians, formal and informal. The written word and public education contribute enormously to the stability and persistence of the national images. The Jews, for instance, are a creation of the Bible and the Talmud, but every nation has its bible, whether formed into a canon or not — noble words like the Declaration of Independence and the Gettysburg Address — which crystallize the national image in a form that can be transmitted almost unchanged from generation to generation. It is no exaggeration to say that the function of the historian is to pervert the truth in directions favorable to the images of his readers or hearers. Both history and geography as taught in national schools are devised to give "perspective" rather than truth: that is to say, they present the world as seen from the vantage point of the nation. The national geography is learned in great detail, and the rest of the world is a fuzzy outline; the national history is emphasized and exalted; the history of the rest of the world is neglected or even falsified to the glory of the national image.

It is this fact that the national image is basically a lie, or at least a perspective distortion of the truth, which perhaps accounts for the ease with which it can be perverted to justify monstrous cruelties and wickednesses. There is much that is noble in the national image. It has lifted man out of the narrow cage of self-centeredness, or even family-centeredness, and has forced him to accept responsibility, in some sense, for people and events far beyond his face-to-face cognizance and immediate experience. It is a window of some sort on both space and time and extends a man's concern far beyond his own little lifetime and petty interests. Nevertheless, it achieves these virtues usually only at the cost of untruth, and this fatal flaw constantly betrays it. Love of country is perverted into hatred of the foreigner, and peace, order, and justice at home are paid for by war, cruelty, and injustice abroad.

In the formation of the national image the consciousness of great *shared* events and experiences is of the utmost importance. A nation is a body of people who are conscious of having "gone through something" together. Without the shared experience, the national image itself would not be shared, and it is of vital importance that the national image be highly similar. The sharing may be quite vicarious; it may be an experience shared long ago but constantly renewed by the ritual observances and historical memory of the people, like the Passover and the Captivity in the case of the Jews. Without the sharing, however, there is no nation. It is for this reason that war has been such a tragically important element in the creation and sustenance of the national image. There is hardly a nation that has not been cradled in violence and nourished by further violence. This is not, I think, a necessary property of war itself. It is rather that, especially in more primitive societies, war is the one experience which is dramatic, obviously important, and shared by everybody. We are now witnessing the almost unique phenomenon of a number of new nations arising without war in circumstances which are extremely rare in history, for example — India, Ghana, and the new West Indian Federation, though even here there are instances of severe violence, such as the disturbances which accompanied partition in India. It will be interesting to see the effect, if any, on their national images.

We now come to the central problem of this chapter, which is that of the impact of national images on the relations among states, that is, on the course of events in international relations. The relations among states can be described in terms of a number of different dimensions. There is, first of all, the dimension of simple geographical space. It is perhaps the most striking single characteristic of the national state as an organization, by contrast with organizations such as firms or churches, that it thinks of itself as occupying, in a "dense" and exclusive fashion, a certain area of the globe. The schoolroom maps which divide the world into colored shapes which are identified as nations have a profound effect on the national image. Apart from the very occasional condominium, it is impossible for a given plot of land on the globe to be associated with two nations at the same time. The territories of nations are divided sharply by frontiers carefully surveyed and frequently delineated by a chain of customs houses, immigration stations, and military installations. We are so accustomed to this arrangement that we think of it as "natural" and take it completely for granted. It is by no means the only conceivable arrangement, however. In primitive societies the geographical image is not sharp enough to define clear frontiers; there may be a notion of the rough territory of a tribe, but, especially among nomadic peoples, there is no clear concept of a frontier and no notion of a nation as something that has a shape on a map. In our own society the shape on the map that symbolizes the nation is constantly drilled into the minds of both young and old, both through formal teaching in schools and through constant repetition in newspapers, advertisements, cartoons, and so on. A society is not inconceivable, however, and might even be desirable, in which nations governed people but not territories and claimed jurisdiction over a defined set of citizens, no matter where on the earth's surface they happened to live.

The territorial aspect of the national state is important in the dynamics of international relations because of the *exclusiveness* of territorial occupation. This means that one nation can generally expand only at the expense of another; an increase in the territory of one is achieved only at the expense of a decrease in the territory of another. This makes for a potential conflict situation. This characteristic of the nation does not make conflict inevitable, but it does make it likely and is at least one of the reasons why the history of international relations is a history of perpetual conflict.

The territorial aspect of international relations is complicated by the fact that in many cases the territories of nations are not homogeneous but are composed of "empires," in which the populations do not identify themselves with the national image of the dominant group. Thus when one nation conquers another and absorbs the conquered territory into an empire, it does not thereby automatically change the culture and allegiances of the conquered nation. The Poles remained Polish for a hundred and twenty-five years of partition between Germany, Austria, and Russia. The Finns retained their nationality through eight hundred years of foreign rule and the Jews, through nearly two thousand years of dispersion. If a nation loses territory occupied by disaffected people, this is much less damaging than the loss of territory inhabited by a well-disposed and loyal population. Thus Turkey, which was the "sick man of Europe" as long as it retained its heterogeneous empire, enjoyed a substantial renewal of national health when stripped of its empire and pushed back to the relatively homogeneous heartland of Anatolia. In this case the loss of a disaffected empire actually strengthened the national unit.

The image of the map shape of the nations may be an important factor affecting the general frame of mind of the nation. There is a tendency for nations to be uneasy with strong irregularities, enclaves, detached portions, and protuberances or hollows. The ideal shape is at least a convex set, and there is some tendency for nations to be more satisfied if they have regularly round or rectangular outlines. Thus the detachment of East Prussia from the body of Germany by the Treaty of Versailles was an important factor in creating the fanatical discontent of the Nazis.

A second important dimension of the national image is that of hostility or friendliness. At any one time a particular national image includes a rough scale of the friendliness or hostility of, or toward, other nations. The relationship is not necessarily either consistent or reciprocal—in nation A the prevailing image may be that B is friendly, whereas in nation B itself the prevailing image may be one of hostility toward A; or again in both nations there may be an image of friendliness of A toward B but of hostility of B toward A. On the whole, however, there is a tendency toward both consistency and reciprocation—if a nation A pictures itself as hostile toward B, it usually also pictures B as hostile toward it, and the image is likely to be repeated in B. One exception to this rule seems to be observable: most nations seem to feel that their enemies are more hostile toward them than they are toward their enemies. This is a typical paranoid reaction; the nation visualizes itself as surrounded by hostile nations toward which it has only the nicest and friendliest of intentions.

An important subdimension of the hostility-friendliness image is that of the stability or security of the relationship. A friendly relationship is frequently formalized as an alliance. Alliances, however, are shifting; some friendly relations are fairly permanent, others change as the world kaleidoscope changes, as new enemies arise, or as governments change. Thus a bare fifteen or twenty years ago most people in the United States visualized Germany and Japan, even before the outbreak of the war, as enemies, and after Hitler's invasion of Russia, Russia was for a while regarded as a valuable friend and ally. Today the picture is quite changed: Germany and Japan are valuable friends and allies; Russia is the great enemy. We can roughly classify the reciprocal relations of nations along some scale of friendliness-hostility. At one extreme we have stable friendliness, such as between Britain and Portugal or between Britain and the Commonwealth countries. At the other extreme we have stable hostility—the "traditional enemies" such as France and Germany. Between these extremes we have a great many pairs characterized by shifting alliances. On the whole, stable friendly relations seem to exist mainly between strong nations and weaker nations which they have an interest in preserving and stable hostile relations between adjacent nations each of which has played a large part in the formation of the other.

Another important dimension both of the image and of the "reality" of the nation-state is its strength or weakness. This is, in turn, a structure made up of many elements—economic resources and productivity, political organization and tradition, willingness to incur sacrifice and inflict cruelties, and so on. It still makes some kind of sense to assess nations on a strength-weakness scale at any one time. Strength is frequently thought of in military terms as the ability to hurt an opponent or to prevent one's self from being hurt by him. There are also more subtle elements in terms of symbolic loyalties and affections which are hard to assess but which must be included in any complete picture. Many arrays of bristling armaments have been brought low by the sheer inability of their wielders to attract any lasting respect or affection. No social organization can survive indefinitely unless it can command the support of its members, and a continuing sense of the significance of the organization or group as such is much more durable a source of support than is the fleeting booty of war or monopoly. The Jews have outlasted an impressive succession of conquerors. These questions regarding the ultimate sources of continuing strength or weakness are difficult, and we shall neglect them in this chapter.

In order to bring together the variables associated with each nation or pair of nations into an international system, we must resort to the device of a matrix, as in Figure 22.1. Here the hostility-friendliness variable is used as an example. Each cell, a_{ij}, indicates the degree of hostility or friendliness of nation I (of the row) toward nation J (of the column). For purposes of illustration, arbitrary figures have been inserted on a scale from 5 to -5, -5 meaning very hostile, 5 very friendly, and 0 neutral.[3] A matrix of this kind has many interesting properties, not all of which can be worked out here but which depend on the kind of restraints that we impose on it. If we suppose, for instance, that the relations of nations are reciprocal, so that I's attitude toward J is the same as J's toward I, the matrix becomes symmetrical about its major diagonal — that is, the lower left-hand triangle is a mirror image of the upper right-hand triangle. This is a very severe restriction and is certainly violated in fact: there are unrequited loves and hates among the nations as there are among individuals. We can recognize a *tendency,* however, for the matrix to become symmetrical. There is a certain instability about an unrequited feeling. If I loves J and J hates I, then either J's constant rebuff of I's affections will turn I's love to hate, or I's persistent wooing will break down J's distaste and transform it into affection. Unfortunately for the history of human relations, the former seems to be the more frequent pattern, but the latter is by no means unknown.[4]

The sum totals of the rows represent the overall friendliness or hostility of the nation at the head of the row; the sum totals of the columns represent the degree of hostility or friendliness *toward* the nation at the head of the column. The sum of either of these sums (which must be equal, as each represents a way of adding up all the figures of the matrix) is a measure of the overall friendliness or hostility of the system. In the example of Figure 22.1, B is evidently a "paranoid" nation, feeling hostile toward everyone and receiving hostility in return; D is a "neutral" nation, with low values for either hostility or friendliness; E is a "friendly" nation, reciprocating B's general hostility but otherwise having positive relations with everyone. In this figure it is evident that A, C, and E are likely to be allied against B, and D is likely to be uncommitted.

In the matrix of Figure 22.1 no account is taken of the relative size or

FIGURE 22.1   Hostility/Friendliness Matrix (two nations)

	A	B	C	D	E	Totals
A		−5	+3	0	+2	0
B	−3		−2	−1	−2	−8
C	+2	−4		0	+1	−1
D	−1	−1	0		0	−2
E	+4	−3	+2	0		+3
Totals	+2	−13	+3	−1	+1	−8
X	2	−5	4	+1	−2	0
Y	1	−10½	1	−1½	2	−8

power of the different nations. This dimension of the system can easily be accommodated, however. All that is necessary is to take the power of the smallest nation as a convenient unit and express the power of the others in multiples of this unit. Then in the matrix we simply give each nation a number of places along the axes equal to the measure of its power. Thus in Figure 22.2 we suppose a system of three nations, where B is twice as powerful as C and A is three times as powerful as C; A is then allotted three spaces along the axes, B two, and C one. The analysis of the matrix proceeds as before, with the additional constraint that all the figures in the larger boxes bounded by the lines which divide the nations should be the same, as in the figure.

The difference between the sum of a nation's column, representing the

FIGURE 22.2   Hostility/Friendliness Matrix (three nations)

	A	A	A	B	B	C
A				−5	−5	4
A				−5	−5	4
A				−5	−5	4
B	−4	−4	−4			−2
B	−4	−4	−4			−2
C	2	2	2	−1	−1	

general degree of support or affection it *receives,* and the sum of a nation's row, representing the sum of support or affection it *gives,* might be called its *affectional balance.* This is shown in the row X in Figure 22.1. It is a necessary property of a matrix of this kind that the sum of all these balances shall be zero. They measure the relative position of each nation in regard to the degree of support it can expect from the international system as a whole. Thus in Figure 22.1 it is clear that B is in the worst position, and C in the best position, vis-à-vis the system as a whole. Another figure of some interest might be called the *affectional contribution,* shown in the line Y. This is the mean of the column and row totals for each nation. The total affectional contribution is equal to the total of all the figures of the matrix, which measures the general hostility or friendliness of the whole system. The affectional contribution is then a rough measure of how much each nation contributes to the general level of hostility of the whole system. Thus in the example of Figure 22.1 we see that nation B (the paranoid) actually contributes more than 100 percent to the total hostility of the system, its extreme hostility being offset to some extent by other nations' friendliness.

One critical problem of an international system, then, is that of the *dynamics* of the hostility matrix. We can conceive of a succession of such matrices at successive points of time. If there is a system with a "solution," we should be able to predict the matrix at t_1 from the knowledge we have of the matrix at t_0 or at various earlier times. The matrix itself will not, in general, carry enough information to make such predictions possible, even though it is easy to specify theoretical models in which a determinate dynamic system can be derived from the information in the matrix alone.[5]

The difficulty with "simple" systems of this nature is that they are very much more simple than the reality which they symbolize. This is because, in reality, the variables of the system consist of the innumerable dimensions of the images of large numbers of people, and the dynamics of the image are much more complex than the dynamics of mechanical systems. This is because of the structural nature of the image; it cannot be represented simply by a set of quantities or variables. Because of this structural nature, it is capable occasionally of very dramatic changes as a message hits some vital part of the structure and the whole image reorganizes itself. Certain events — like the German invasion of Belgium in 1914, the Japanese attack on Pearl Harbor in 1941, the American use of the atom bomb at Hiroshima and Nagasaki, the merciless destruction of Dresden, and the Russian success with Sputnik I — have profound effects and possibly long-run effects on reorganizing the various national images. The "reorganizing" events are hard both to specify and to predict; they introduce, however, a marked element of uncertainty into any dynamic international system which does not exist, for instance, in the solar system!

In spite of this difficulty, which, oddly enough, is particularly acute in short-term prediction, one gets the impression from the observation of history that we are in the presence of a true system with a real dynamic of its own. We do observe, for instance, cumulative processes of hostility. If we had some measures of the hostility matrix, however crude, it would be possible to identify these processes in more detail, especially the "turning points." There is an analogy here with the business cycle, which also represents a system of cumulative stochastic processes subject to occasional "reorganizations" of its basic equations. Just as we can trace cumulative upward and downward movements in national income, the downward movements often (though not always) culminating in financial crisis and the upward movements often leading to inflation and a subsequent downturn, so we can trace cumulative movements in the hostility matrix. We have "prewar" periods corresponding to downswings, in which things go from bad to worse and hostility constantly increases. The total of all the hostility figures (e.g., -8 on Fig. 22.1) is a striking analogue of the national-income concept. It might be called the "international temperature." Just as there is a certain critical point in a deflation at which a financial crisis is likely to ensue because of the growing insolvency of heavily indebted businesses, so there is a critical point in the rise of hostility at which war breaks out. This critical point itself depends on a number of different factors and may not be constant. Some nations may be more tolerant of hostility than others; as the cost of war increases, the tolerance of hostility also increases, as we see today in the remarkable persistence of the "cold war." A deflation or downturn, however, *may* reverse itself without a crisis, and a "prewar" period may turn into a "postwar" period without a war. Indeed, in the period since 1945 we might identify almost as many small international cycles as there have been business cycles! The "upturn" may be a result of a change of government, the death of certain prominent individuals, or even a change of heart (or image!) on the part of existing rulers. The catharsis of a war usually produces the typical "postwar" period following, though this is often tragically short, as it was after the end of World War II, when a "downturn" began after the revolution in Czechoslovakia. The downturn is often the result of the reassertion of a persistent, long-run character of the system after a brief interlude of increasing friendliness. There seems to be a certain long-run tendency of an international system toward hostility, perhaps because of certain inescapable flaws in the very concept of a national image, just as there also seems to be a long-run tendency of an unregulated and undisturbed market economy toward deflation.

In considering the dynamics of an international system, the essential properties of the image matrix might be summed up in a broad concept of "compatibility." If the change in the system makes for greater compatibility the system may move to an equilibrium. The "balance-of-power" theory postulates the existence of an equilibrium of this nature. The record of history, however, suggests that, in the past at least, international systems have usually been unstable. The incompatibility of various national images has led to changes in the system which have created still greater incompatibility, and the system has moved to less and less stable situations until some crisis, such as war, is reached, which represents a discontinuity in the system. After a war the system is reorganized; some national units may disappear, others change their character, and the system starts off again. The incompatibility may be of many kinds, and it is a virtue of this kind of rather loose model that the historian can fill in the endlessly various details in the special situations which he studies. The model is a mere dress form on which the historian swathes the infinite variations of fashion and fact.

In the model we can distinguish two very different kinds of incompatibility of images. The first might be called "real" incompatibility, where we have two images of the future in which realization of one would prevent the realization of the other. Thus two nations may both claim a certain piece of territory, and each may feel dissatisfied unless the territory is incorporated into it. (One thinks of the innumerable irredenta which have stained the pages of history with so much blood!) Or two nations may both wish to feel stronger than, or superior to, each other. It is possible for two nations to be in a position where each is stronger than the other *at home,* provided that they are far enough apart and that the "loss of power gradient" (which measures the loss of power of each as we remove the point of application farther and farther from the home base) is large enough. It is rarely possible, however, for two nations each to dominate the other, except in the happy situation where each suffers from delusions of grandeur.

The other form of incompatibility might be called "illusory" incompatibility, in which there exists a condition of compatibility which would satisfy the "real" interests of the two parties but in which the dynamics of the situation or the illusions of the parties create a situation of perverse dynamics and misunderstandings, with increasing hostility simply as a result of the reactions of the parties to each other, not as a result of any basic differences of interest. We must be careful about this distinction: even "real" incompatibilities are functions of the national images rather than of physical fact and are therefore subject to change and control. It is hard for an ardent patriot to realize that his country is a mental, rather than a physical, phenomenon, but such indeed is the truth! It is not unreasonable to suppose, however, that "real" incompatibilities are more intractable and less subject to "therapy" than illusory ones.

One final point of interest concerns what might be called the impact of "sophistication" or "self-consciousness" on national images and the international system. The process of sophistication in the image is a very general one, and we cannot follow all its ramifications here. It occurs in every person in greater or less degree as he grows into adult awareness of himself as part of a larger system. It is akin almost to a Copernican revolution: the unsophisticated image sees the world only from the viewpoint of the viewer; the sophisticated image sees the world from many imagined viewpoints, as a system in which the viewer is only a part. The child sees everything through his own eyes and refers everything to his own immediate comfort. The adult learns to see the world through the eyes of others; his horizon extends to other times, places, and cultures than his own; he learns to distinguish between those elements in his experience which are universal and those which are particular. Many grown people, of course, never become adults in this sense, and it is these who fill our mental hospitals with themselves and their children.

The scientific subculture is an important agency in the sophistication of images. In the physical world we no longer attribute physical phenomena to spirits analogous to our own. In the social sciences we have an agency whereby men reach self-consciousness about their own cultures and institutions and therefore no longer regard these as simply given to them by "nature." In economics, for instance, we have learned to see the system as a whole, to realize that many things which are true of individual behavior are not true of the system and that the system itself is not incapable of a modicum of control. We no longer, for instance, regard depressions as "acts of God" but as system-made phenomena capable of control through relatively minor system change.

The national image, however, is the last great stronghold of unsophistication. Not even the professional international relations experts have come very far toward seeing the system as a whole, and the ordinary citizen and the powerful statesman alike have naïve, self-centered, and unsophisticated images of the world in which their nation moves. Nations are divided into "good" and "bad" — the enemy is all bad, one's own nation is of spotless virtue. Wars are either acts of God or acts of the other nations, which always catch us completely by surprise. To a student of international systems the national image even of respectable, intellectual, and powerful people seems naïve and untrue. The patriotism of the sophisticated cannot be a simple faith. There is, however, in the course of human history a powerful and probably irreversible movement toward sophistication. We can wise up, but we cannot wise down, except at enormous cost in the breakdown of civilizations, and not even a major breakdown results in much loss of knowledge. This movement must be taken into account in predicting the future of the international system. The present system as we have known it for the past hundreds or even thousands of years is based on the widespread acceptance of unsophisticated images, such as, for instance, that a nation can be made more secure *merely* by increasing its armaments. The growth of a systems-attitude toward international relations will have profound consequences for the dynamics of the system itself, just as the growth of a systems attitude in economics has profound consequences for the dynamics of the economic system.

If, as I myself believe, we live in an international system so unstable that it threatens the very existence of life on earth, our main hope for change may lie in the rapid growth of sophistication, especially at the level of the images of the powerful. Sophistication, of course, has its dangers also. It is usually but a hair's breadth removed from sophistry, and a false sophistication (of which Marxism in some respects is a good example) can be even more destructive to the stability of a system than a naïve image. Whichever way we move, however, there is danger. We have no secure place to stand where we are, and we live in a time when intellectual investment in developing more adequate international images and theories of international systems may bear an enormous rate of return in human welfare.

Notes

This paper was presented to a meeting of the American Psychological Association in Washington, D.C., on August 30, 1958.

1. See Anatol Rapoport, "Lewis F. Richardson's Mathematical Theory of War," *Journal of Conflict Resolution* 1 (September 1957):249, for an excellent exposition.
2. See K. E. Boulding, *The Image* (Ann Arbor: University of Michigan Press, 1956), for an exposition of the theory on which this paper is based.
3. The problem of the measurement of hostility (or friendliness) is a very interesting one which we cannot go into extensively here but which is not so hopeless of solution as might at first sight appear. Possible avenues are as follows: (1) An historical approach. Over a period of years two nations have been at war, threatening war, allied, bound by treaty, and so on. Each relation would be given an arbitrary number, and each year assigned a number accordingly: the average of the years' numbers would be the index. This would always yield a symmetrical matrix — that is, the measure of I's relation to J would be the same as J's relation to I, or $a_{ij} = a_{ji}$. (2) An approach by means of content analysis of public communications (official messages, newspaper editorials, public speeches, cartoons, etc.). This seems likely to be most immediately useful and fruitful, as it would give current information and would also yield very valuable dynamic information about the *changes* in the matrix, which may be much more important than the absolute figures. The fact that any measure of this kind is highly arbitrary is no argument against it, provided that it is qualitatively reliable — that is, moves generally in the same direction as the variable which it purports to measure — and provided also that the limitations of the measure are clearly understood. It would probably be advisable to check the second type of measure against the more objective measures derived from the first method. The difficulty of the first method, however, is the extreme instability of the matrix. The affections of nations are ephemeral!
4. George F. Kennan once said: "It is an undeniable privilege of every man to prove himself in the right in the thesis that the world is his enemy; for if he reiterates it frequently enough and makes it the background of his conduct, he is bound eventually to be right" ("The Roots of Soviet Conduct," *Foreign Affairs,* July 1947). If for "enemy" we read "friend" in this statement, the proposition seems to be equally true but much less believed.
5. As a very simple example of such a system, let $(a_{ij})t$ be a cell of the matrix at time t and $(a_{ij})t + 1$ be the corresponding value at time $t + 1$. Then if for each cell we can postulate a function $(a_{ij})_{t + 1} = F(a_{ij})_t$, we can derive the whole $t + 1$ matrix from the t matrix. This is essentially the dynamic method of Lewis F. Richardson, and in fairly simple cases it provides an interesting way of formulating certain aspects of the system, especially its tendency toward *cumulative* movements of hostility (arms races) or occasionally of friendliness.

23
Patterns in International Warfare, 1816-1965

Melvin Small
and J. David Singer

Since Thucydides, scholars and statesmen have speculated about the causes and consequences of conflict between nation-states. Despite the earnest efforts of countless generations of investigators, it is only within the past several decades that any promising attack on the problem of the causes of war has been mounted. In our judgment, the important turning point in man's long quest to understand this recurrent phenomenon occurred in the 1930s, when Quincy Wright and Lewis Richardson began to employ operational, quantitative techniques in the description and analysis of the most pernicious product of international relations.[1]

Inspired by the work of these pioneers, and borrowing many of their methodological and theoretical innovations, we have initiated a project whose major objective is to identify the variables that are most frequently associated with the onset of war, from the Congress of Vienna to 1965.[2] Our first requirement was to describe and measure the dependent variable, and ascertain the trends and fluctuations in the frequency, magnitude, severity, and intensity of war during that period. This task has now been completed and the data base we have developed allows us to generalize with some degree of confidence about patterns in international violence over the last century and a half.[3] Before we turn to such generalizations, however, we should explain briefly the data acquisition and coding procedures employed in our study.

Reprinted by permission of the publisher and authors from Melvin Small and J. David Singer, "Patterns in International Warfare, 1816-1965," *The Annals of the American Academy of Political and Social Science* 391 (September 1970):145-155.

Identifying the Wars

Most major studies of war suffered from an absence of methodological precision and an invisibility of coding rules.[4] These practices often resulted in the impressionistic analysis by anecdote of a few famous and large wars by political theorists, or the hyperempirical analysis of every conceivable sort of violence by scholars with a mathematical orientation. Aware of the pitfalls inherent in both approaches, we have adopted criteria and rules which we feel allow maximum practicality and efficiency but which do not violate intellectual standards of reliability and validity.

Thus, we began by delimiting the system in which we were interested. Although it would be useful to know something about violence in all polities for all recorded time periods, such an approach would find us laboring far into the foreseeable future in the often barren vineyards of historiography. The period since 1815, which is manageable in terms of the availability of historical sources, satisfies our need both for systemic continuity and for a time span long enough to allow for any permutations in the level of violence to evidence themselves. Within these temporal bounds, we were concerned with wars fought by members of the international system against fellow members (interstate wars) and against independent or colonial entities which did not qualify for membership in the system (extrasystemic wars). To qualify for membership in the international system, a state needed to have a population of at least 500,000 and diplomatic recognition from legitimizers within the international community.[5] In the period after 1920, membership in the League of Nations or the United Nations was used as an alternate criterion in some cases. The adoption of such a scheme results in a system with 23 members in 1816, 34 in 1870, 61 in 1920, and 124 in 1965.

As for the wars themselves, we gathered data on those conflicts in which the battle-connected deaths for all systemic combatants taken together surpassed 1,000. A slightly more complicated procedure was used to determine the inclusion or exclusion of some extra-systemic wars.[6] (Civil wars, even those with foreign intervention, were not considered in this stage of the project.) All the qualifying wars were codified in terms of severity (or battle deaths of system-member participants) and magnitude (or total number of nation-months that system-member participants spent in combat). The ninety-three wars which met our criteria are listed in chronological order in Table 23.1, with the fifty interstate wars shown in italics. Alongside each war is its rank position in terms of battle deaths, nation-months, and a simple intensity measure—number of battle deaths divided by number of nation-months.[7]

TABLE 23.1   Basic List of International Wars, 1816-1965 (N = 93)

NAME OF WAR	RANK POSITION		
	BATTLE DEATHS	NATION MONTHS	BATTLE DEATHS PER NATION MONTH
British-Maharattan, 1817–1818	73.5	70	68.5
Greek Independence, 1821–1828	37.5	12	70
Franco-Spanish, 1823	89	52.5	90.5
First Anglo-Burmese, 1823–1826	37.5	29	52
Dutch-Javanese, 1825–1830	37.5	17	70
Russo-Persian, 1826–1828	58	45	67
Navarino Bay, 1827	69	86.5	24.5
Russo-Turkish, 1828–1829	9	26.5	11
First Polish Insurrection, 1831	37.5	66	22
First Syrian, 1831–1832	46.5	52.5	46
Texan-Mexican, 1835–1836	89	70	83
First British–Afghan, 1838–1842	30	18	59
Second Syrian, 1839–1840	46.5	78.5	20
Peruvian-Bolivian, 1841	89	91	35
First British–Sikh, 1845–1846	78.5	83	54.5
Mexican-American, 1846–1848	34	19	60.5
Austro-Sardinian, 1848–1849	50.5	62.5	40
First Schleswig–Holstein, 1848–1849	55	47	62.5
Hungarian Revolution, 1848–1849	17.5	58	9
Second British–Sikh, 1848–1849	78.5	78.5	66
Roman Republic, 1849	73.5	70	68.5
La Plata, 1851–1852	82	56.5	85
First Turco-Montenegran, 1852–1853	58	81	26.5
Crimean, 1853–1856	6	6	17
Anglo-Persian, 1856–1857	73.5	65	72.5
Sepoy Mutiny, 1857–1859	66	35.5	82
Second Turco-Montenegran, 1858–1859	69	56.5	71
Italian Unification, 1859	26	70	14
Spanish-Moroccan, 1859–1860	46.5	62.5	35
Italo-Roman, 1860	89	91	35
Italo-Sicilian, 1860–1861	89	75	79.5
Franco-Mexican, 1862–1867	30	7	75.5
Second Polish Insurrection, 1863–1864	58	50	64.5
Ecuadorian-Columbian, 1863	89	91	35
Second Schleswig–Holstein, 1864	61	59.5	62.5
La Plata, 1864–1870	11	5	41.5
Spanish-Chilean, 1865–1866	89	47	92.5
Seven Weeks, 1866	23	49	16
Ten Years, 1868–1878	12	8	41.5
Franco-Prussian, 1870–1871	7	30	8
Dutch-Achinese, 1873–1878	55	16	87
Balkan, 1875–1877	46.5	38	57
Russo-Turkish, 1877–1878	5	43	3
Bosnian Insurrection, 1878	66	83	31
Second British Afghan, 1878–1880	63.5	43	72.5
British-Zulu, 1879	66	75	50
Pacific, 1879–1883	41	4	88.5
Franco-Indochinese, 1882–1884	61	31	75.5
Mahdist Insurrection, 1882–1885	30	21	54.5
Sino-French, 1884–1885	42	33	54.5
Central American, 1885	89	91	35
Serbo-Bulgarian, 1885	73.5	91	18
Sino-Japanese, 1894–1895	37.5	47	38.5
Franco-Madagascan, 1894–1895	55	64	48
Cuban Revolution, 1895–1898	20	24.5	28
Italo-Ethiopian, 1895–1896	50.5	61	43

TABLE 23.1 (continued)

NAME OF WAR	RANK POSITION		
	BATTLE DEATHS	NATION MONTHS	BATTLE DEATHS PER NATION MONTH
First Philippine Insurrection, 1896–1898	73.5	35.5	88.5
Greco-Turkish, 1897	73.5	75	64.5
Spanish-American, 1898	46.5	67	30
Second Philippine Insurrection, 1899–1902	61	20	85
Boer, 1899–1902	27	28	47
Russo-Japanese, 1904–1905	9	22.5	13
Central American, 1906	89	75	79.5
Central American, 1907	89	75	79.5
Spanish-Moroccan, 1909–1910	46.5	43	51
Italo-Turkish, 1911–1912	30	32	45
First Balkan, 1912–1913	15	39.5	10
Second Balkan, 1913	16	80	4
World War One, 1914–1918	2	2	5
Russian Nationalities, 1917–1921	20	22.5	29
Hungarian-Allies, 1919	43	55	44
Greco-Turkish, 1919–1922	20	13	49
Riffian Revolt, 1921–1926	25	15	60.5
Druze Rebellion, 1925–1926	63.5	35.5	75.5
Manchurian, 1931–1933	17.5	26.5	20
Chaco, 1932–1935	9	14	20
Italo-Ethiopian, 1935–1936	30	52.5	26.5
Sino-Japanese, 1937–1941	4	9	7
Russo-Japanese, 1939	33	59.5	23
World War Two, 1939–1945	1	1	1
Russo-Finnish, 1939–1940	14	70	6
Indonesian Rebellion, 1945–1946	81	35.5	92.5
Indochinese Rebellion, 1945–1954	13	10	38.5
Madagascan Rebellion, 1947–1948	78.5	39.5	90.5
First Kashmir, 1947–1949	78.5	52.5	85
Palestine, 1948–1949	52	41	58
Korean, 1950–1953	3	3	12
Algerian Revolution, 1954–1962	37.5	11	79.5
Tibetan Revolt, 1956–1959	22	24.5	32
Russo-Hungarian, 1956	24	86.5	2
Sinai, 1956	69	86.5	24.5
Sino-Indian, 1962	89	86.5	54.5
Second Kashmir, 1965	53	83	15

Trends and Cycles

After the basic data were reordered according to the amount of war begun, under way, and terminated each year, we were able to search for secular trends and periodicity over the past century and a half. Looking first at secular trends, contrary to what might have been expected, no trend, either upward or downward, is evident. That is, whether we concentrate upon frequencies, magnitudes, severities, or intensities, we do not find appreciably more or less war in any of the subepochs covered. Of course, there were more battle deaths in the twentieth century than in the nineteenth (thanks to the impact of the two world wars and the Korean conflict), but when the figures are normalized for the number of nations in the system, this trend disappears. International war, therefore, appears to be neither waxing nor waning. It is true, however, that extrasystemic wars have been decreasing in frequency; but this is entirely a product of the liquidation of formal colonial empires and the expansion of the international system to include all independent entities.

While such findings might cheer those who intuitively feared that we have been experiencing an ever-increasing amount of war as we approach the apocalypse, they must be balanced with the more dismal finding that there appears to be a strong tendency toward periodicity in the system's war experiences. Although cycles are not apparent when we examine the amount of war beginning in each year or time period, a discernible periodicity emerges when we focus on measures of the amount of war under way. That is, discrete wars do not necessarily come and go with regularity but with some level of interstate violence almost always present; there are distinct and periodic fluctuations in the amount of that violence. The twenty-year cycle in the amount of nation-months of war under way can be seen in the graph in Figure 23.1.

Others have discerned similar cycles which could be related, among other things, to the time needed for a generation to "forget" the last bloody conflict.[8] It must be remembered that such analyses assume an interdependence between the martial activities of all system members, and that, for example, the incidence of war in the Balkans presumably affects the incidence of war on the Iberian Peninsula or even in Southeast Asia. In-

FIGURE 23.1   Annual Amount (in Nation-Months) of International War Under Way, 1816-1965

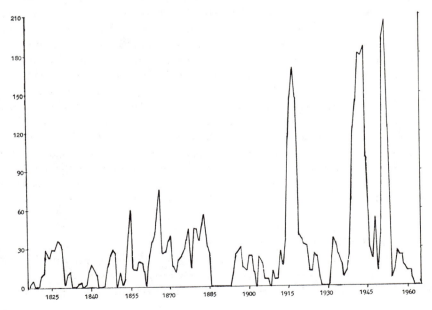

terestingly, no cyclical patterns are apparent when we examine the military experiences of the individual nations which participated in several wars. Thus, we must be rather tentative in affirming the existence of periodicity in the incidence of war, for our one strong pattern shows up only when we isolate one set of variables among many. Much more work needs to be done before we can accept completely the notion of a twenty-year cycle, although these preliminary findings suggest the direction in which this work should go.

Seasons and Wars

Another way to approach the temporal variable is to examine the relationship between season and month and the incidence of war. According to the folklore, the onset and termination of war should be determined, in part, by climatological conditions which might affect military mobility and efficiency, and the growing and harvesting seasons which might, in turn, affect provisioning and recruiting an army. Some contemporary analysts would expect most wars to begin between March 22 and April 20 under the sign of bellicose Aries, and the fewest to begin between September 24 and October 23 when the gentle Libra is dominant.

To some degree, our data support the common folklore although the verdict is mixed for the astrologists. Of the 93 wars, 64 began in either spring or autumn and only 29 in summer and winter. Moreover, this pattern does not change much over time; for example, 11 of the 21 wars fought since 1920 began in autumn. As for specific months, April and October saw the initiation of 28 of the 93 conflicts, while long and bloody wars tended to begin in July and September. No one season or month stands out when it comes to the termination of war. This latter finding, when compared to the onset patterns, lends credence to the thesis that policymakers are influenced by the season when they consider a war/no-war decision, but that once the war is under way, more nonrational factors militate against weather or supplies playing such a crucial role. Of course, much of this is conjecture. Before we can attest with certainty to the proposition that weather and climate weigh heavily with the decisionmaker, we must compare similar sets of crises, which did and did not terminate in war, with specific seasonal variables.

The War Proneness of Nations

Whereas systemic patterns of international violence are most interesting to the political theorist, the record of individual nations' martial activities has long fascinated historians. Many have argued that some nations (perhaps during certain periods) are more aggressive than others, or that some ethnic groups are naturally warlike whereas others are naturally pacific. At the same time, repeated involvement in war may not necessarily relate to any innate characteristic but merely to the misfortune of being geographically proximate to predatory powers. By computing the number and severity of wars experienced by each nation during its tenure in the system, we can obtain a more accurate indication of the distribution of wars among the nations, and whether, indeed, certain nations, or certain classes thereof, are more prone to war involvement than others.

In terms of the sheer number of international wars, France and England lead the field with 19 each, Turkey participated in 17, Russia 15, and Italy (including its predecessor, Sardinia) 11. All of these nations were members of the system for the full 150 years. Spain, which fought in 9 wars, and the United States, which fought in 6, are two other charter members of the system with significant war experience. Those with a shorter tenure are led by Austria-Hungary with participation in 8 wars, Greece and Japan with 7, and Germany (including its predecessor, Prussia) with 6. As might be expected, many of these nations also sustained the most battle deaths, with Russia, Germany, China, France, Japan, England, Austria-Hungary, Italy, and Turkey, in that order, all suffering 750,000 or more. Moreover, 39 percent of all the system's nation-months of war were accounted for by 5 nations — France, England, Turkey, Spain, and Russia — whereas 39 of the 43 extrasystemic wars were fought by 7 states — England 12, France 7, Turkey 6, Russia 5, Spain 4, Holland 3, and Austria-Hungary 2.

Obviously, major powers were the most war prone, with Turkey, Spain, and Greece the only nonmajors to appear in this firmament.[9] No major powers were able to escape this scourge, which may, in fact, turn out to be a prerequisite for achievement of that exalted status. On the other hand, most of the smaller states, and especially those in extra-European regions, enjoyed a fairly pacific record in terms of international war. Many of these, of course, experienced long and bloody civil conflicts. Still, the fact that more than half the nations (77 out of 144) which were at one time or another members of the system were able to escape international war entirely, suggests that military conflict between nations is not so common a systemic activity as some have posited.

National Military Achievement

Although some nations have fought in more wars than others, they have done so with varying degrees of success. Indeed, success in warfare might predict to frequency of involvement. A nation which loses several wars might behave with great circumspection in order to avoid the necessity of

having to go to war again. Alternately, a military loss might foster a re-
vanchist spirit, or worse yet, it could tempt a third power which felt it could
easily defeat the nation whose military record was less than impressive. The
data upon which one might base such generalizations are offered in Table
23.2, which shows each nation's record of victories and defeats in all international wars, followed by its record for interstate wars only.[10] Experiences
in the one stalemate (the Korean war) have been excluded from this tabula-
tion.

Thanks to their choice of enemies and allies, as well as their military
capabilities and skills, most of the major powers have done rather well. The

TABLE 23.2   National Performances in International War, 1816-1965

Nation Name	All Wars	Interstate Wars	Nation Name	All Wars	Interstate Wars
England	16–2	6–0	China	3–4	2–4
Russia	13–2	8–2	Bulgaria	1–3	1–3
France	14–4	9–2	India	1–2	0–2
Italy (Sardinia)	8–3	8–2	Mexico	1–2	1–1
United States	5–0	4–0	Peru	1–2	1–1
Brazil	3–0	2–0	Salvador	1–2	1–2
Japan	5–2	5–2	Ecuador	0–1	0–1
Yugoslavia (Serbia)	4–1	4–0	Hanover	0–1	0–1
Rumania	4–1	4–1	Hesse Electoral	0–1	0–1
Austria-Hungary	5–3	3–3	Hesse Grand Ducal	0–1	0–1
Belgium	2–0	2–0	Iraq	0–1	0–1
Chile	2–0	2–0	Jordan	0–1	0–1
Germany (Prussia)	4–2	4–2	Lebanon	0–1	0–1
Greece	4–2	4–2	Mecklenburg-Schwerin	0–1	0–1
Holland	3–1	1–0	Persia	0–1	0–1
Israel	2–0	2–0	Saxony	0–1	0–1
Mongolia	2–0	2–0	Syria	0–1	0–1
Spain	5–4	2–3	Bolivia	0–2	0–2
Australia	1–0	1–0	Denmark	0–2	0–2
Canada	1–0	1–0	Finland	0–2	0–2
Colombia	1–0	1–0	Honduras	0–2	0–2
Czechoslovakia	1–0	1–0	Morocco	0–2	0–2
New Zealand	1–0	1–0	Papal States	0–2	0–2
Nicaragua	1–0	1–0	U.A.R. (Egypt)	0–2	0–2
Norway	1–0	1–0	Hungary	0–3	0–3
Pakistan	1–0	1–0	Turkey	5–11	4–6
Paraguay	1–0	1–0			
Portugal	1–0	1–0			
Poland	1–0	1–0			
South Africa	1–0	1–0			
Baden	1–1	1–1			
Bavaria	1–1	1–1			
Ethiopia	1–1	1–1			
Guatemala	1–1	1–1			
Two Sicilies	1–1	1–1			
Württemberg	1–1	1–1			
Argentina	1–1	0–1			

nine nations which were at one time or another major powers hold six of the first seven positions and eight of the first thirteen in terms of won-lost records. The one major power absent from this galaxy, China, achieved its poor record while it was a minor power—since 1950 China has won two wars and tied in another. Turkey, as was expected, has a dismal history in this realm, but the Italians, often maligned for their legendary military ineptitude, nevertheless emerged victorious in eight of their eleven engagements.

The Initiation of Interstate War

A history of involvement in international war is a necessity but not suffi-cient indication of a nation's bellicosity. The determination of the initiator of military conflict, however, may tell us a bit more about a nation's ag-gressive proclivities. When we speak of initiation here, we are merely iden-tifying the nation(s) which made the first attack on an opponents' armies or territories. Clearly, initiator and aggressor are not always identical, as a participant might provoke its adversary into military action by mobiliza-tion or other aggressive diplomatic or economic actions. But the designa-tion of the initiator of military aggression should nevertheless provide some tentative clues as to the relative belligerency of system members.

In examining the 49 interstate wars in which we were able to make this designation, we find that Italy was the actual initiator (or on the side of the initiator) on 8 occasions, France played that role on 6 occasions, Germany and Japan on 5, and Austria-Hungary, Russia, and Bulgaria on 4.[11] But when we turn from sheer number of initiations to the frequency of initia-tion compared to the total number of war experiences, some of the nations on this infamous list look a little less bellicose. Whereas Italy initiated or fought on the side of the initiator in 8 of her 10 interstate wars, Germany in 5 of her 6, Japan in 5 of her 7, Austria-Hungary in 4 of her 6, and Bulgaria in all of her 4, France initiated only 6 of her 12 interstate wars, and Russia only 4 of her 10. Among those nations with significant war experience which are absent from this list and therefore, perhaps, more pacific, are: the two "sick men" of Asia, Turkey and China; three Balkan states, Greece, Rumania, and Yugoslavia; and the two Anglo-Saxon major powers, England and the United States.

The decision to initiate hostilities is related, in part, to the expectation of victory. Few governments would move first militarily unless they expected that such preemption had a high probability of victory or, at least, of national survival. Not surprisingly, then, we find that initiators emerged victorious in 34 of the 49 interstate wars although they lost 14 times and ex-perienced one stalemate. As for battle fatalities, in 36 of those 49, the initiators lost fewer men than their opponents, and they were victorious in 6 of those 13 wars in which their losses were greater than their opponents'. This is an impressive record when one considers that an attacking force is generally assumed to lose more men than a defending force in a given engagement.

Of course, in almost 40 percent of the cases, the initiator turned out to be a major power attacking a minor power. Of the 19 wars which saw such a one-sided confrontation, the major power initiated hostilities on 18 occasions and won 17 of those 18 contests.[12] When minors fought minors, the initiator won 14 times and lost 7, but when majors fought majors, the initiators won 3 times and lost 5. Thus, initiation of hostilities appears to have been a major advantage to the combatants, but an advantage which decreased in importance when the two sides were more nearly equal in power.

Traditional Enmities and Friendships

A nation's record of participation, as well as of success and of failure, in war has something to do with its historic long-term relationship to other nations. Historians and political scientists have written about the importance of traditional enmities and friendships between nations, and speculated as to whether similar governments, religions, ethnicity, or stages of economic development affect the propensity of nations to war against, or ally with, one another. Moreover, the experience of conflict against or alliance with a state in one war should affect future relations with that state in other wars and crises. In the *Statistics of Deadly Quarrels,* Richardson reported that 48 percent of the pairs who fought on opposite sides in all wars from 1820 to 1949 fought against each other on more than one occasion. But he also found that 29 percent of those pairs who had been allies in one war had already fought against each other in an earlier experience.[13] Looking at our more restricted set of wars, we find somewhat less evidence for the prevalence of historical enmities and alliances.

Of the 209 pairs who fought opposite each other in our 50 interstate wars, only 19 percent had fought against each other before, while 21 percent had been allies in an earlier war. As for those pairs with more than one experience in war (136), of the 95 pairs with some experience as opponents, 77 of them also fought at least once on the same side.

Thus, in terms of war experience, few friendships or enmities have held up throughout our 150-year period. When we look only at those nations with 3 or more experiences as allies and none as opponents in that period, we find that France and England have been partners on 6 occasions, Greece and Yugoslavia on 4, and Belgium, England and France, Greece and

England, Holland and England, and the United States, England, and France on 3. As for historical enmities, those with 3 or more experiences as opponents and none as allies are Russia and Turkey with 5 conflicts, Austria-Hungary and Italy, and China and Japan with 4, and Germany and France with 3. While these listings conform to the historians' generalizations, the large number of possible dyadic relationships requires us to conclude that the notion of enduring and traditional relationships in war applies only to a limited number of famous pairs.

Conclusion

The above figures provide a brief, and necessarily superficial, overview of the incidence of war in the modern international system. While they are of some intrinsic interest, their major value is more instrumental in nature. That is, with such data as summarized here (and reported more fully in our *Wages of War*) an accelerated assault on the problem of the causes of war becomes feasible. A variety of researchers, reflecting diverse disciplines and numerous theoretical orientations, can now undertake a systematic search for the factors which account for this organized tribal slaughter. Whether the focus be on economic or strategic, psychological or technological phenomena, the dependent variable data are now at hand. Our major purpose was to make such research possible, and as we explore the problem from our particular point of view, we hope others will do likewise. Although the odds do not seem particularly favorable, we might just unravel the mystery of war's regularity before we stumble into its final occurrence.

Notes

1. Quincy Wright, *A Study of War,* 2 vols. (Chicago: University of Chicago Press, 1942); Lewis F. Richardson, *Statistics of Deadly Quarrels* (Chicago: Quadrangle, 1960). In the third volume of his *Social and Cultural Dynamics* (New York: American Book, 1937), Pitirim A. Sorokin also applied empirical techniques to a longitudinal study of warfare.

2. For a complete description of the project, see J. David Singer, "Modern International War: From Conjecture to Causality," in Albert Lepawsky et al., *Essays in Honor of Quincy Wright* (in press).

3. Most of the material in this article is reported in other forms in J. David Singer and Melvin Small, *The Wages of War, 1816-1965: A Statistical Handbook* (New York: John Wiley, 1970).

4. Even Wright and Richardson's pathbreaking works suffer from these shortcomings to some degree. Except for the most recent period, Wright did not order his study of wars in terms of magnitude or severity, nor did he present operational criteria for defining his universe. For his part, Richardson did not distinguish be-

tween the status of political entities engaged in conflict, nor was he interested in the casualties suffered by the separate participants in the wars he studied.

5. A complete explanation of membership criteria is found in J. David Singer and Melvin Small, "The Composition and Status Ordering of the International System, 1815-1940," *World Politics* 18, no. 2 (January 1966):236-282.

6. Because many nineteenth-century imperial conflicts achieved a casualty level of 1,000 battle deaths only after five or ten years, we decided that such a conflict had to average 1,000 battle deaths a year for the system member in order to qualify for inclusion in our list.

7. Battle-death and nation-month scores for extrasystemic wars reflect only the war experiences of system members. Many of these wars would have ranked considerably higher on all indices had we included nonmember battle deaths and nation-months.

8. See, for example, Frank H. Denton, "Some Regularities in International Conflict, 1820-1949," *Background* 9, no. 4 (February 1966):283-296; Frank H. Denton and Warren Phillips, "Some Patterns in the History of Violence," *Journal of Conflict Resolution* 12, no. 2 (June 1968):182-195; Edward R. Dewey, *The 177 Year Cycle in War, 600 B.C.–A.D. 1957* (Pittsburgh: Foundation for the Study of Cycles, 1964); J. S. Lee, "The Periodic Recurrence of Internecine Wars in China," *The China Journal* 14, no. 3 (March 1931):111-115, 159-162.

9. Our major powers (reflecting the historians' consensus) were England 1815-1965, France 1815-1940, 1945-1965, Germany 1815-1918, 1925-1945, Russia 1815-1917, 1921-1965, Austria-Hungary, 1815-1918, Italy 1860-1943, United States 1899-1965, Japan 1895-1945, and China 1950-1965.

10. In some cases, the distinction between victor and vanquished was difficult to make, but in the end we "declared" a victor in all but one of the wars. For our purposes, nations like Poland and Belgium in World War II, while defeated in the initial stages of the war, were considered victors since they emerged at war's end on the side of the winning coalition.

11. The one case which we did not include in this analysis was the Navarino Bay incident of 1827. In several other wars, the labeling of one side as initiator came only after long and troubled consideration.

12. In seventeen of these wars, the major power shared a border with the minor power.

13. Richardson, *Statistics of Deadly Quarrels,* 196-199.

24

Cause, Surprise, and No Escape

Bruce M. Russett

A Conceptual Scheme

What causes a war? For as long as there have been wars and historians to write about them, controversy has raged over what the precise factors were which resulted in a particular war. Explanations have ranged from simplistic "war guilt" accusations to the despairing answer that wars have myriad causes and we can never hope to untangle the web of causation. Many of the difficulties, however, stem from the lack of a systematic framework of analysis to apply to the problem. The usefulness of such conceptual frameworks is being demonstrated to an increasing extent in other areas of political science, particularly comparative government.[1]

In this chapter we shall attempt once again to assess the causes of World War I, using the classic study by Sydney Bradshaw Fay as a starting point.[2] In an effort to clarify the problem we shall employ an accounting scheme originally designed to identify the causes of an automobile accident.[3] It is hoped that this analysis will be useful in suggesting similar ways to study other periods of international tension, and to build a body of comparative data. In the final section of the chapter we shall use the conceptual scheme and analysis as springboards to consider some possible ways in which the conflict might have been avoided, and to discuss the relevance of the analysis to contemporary problems. Particularly, we shall attempt to identify opportunities for improved strategic intelligence, and areas where such intelligence might contribute to current inquiries into problems of credibility and predictability in an age of nuclear war. The examination is, of course, in no sense intended as definitive, but rather as a discussion to promote further thought and research.

The use of an "accident" accounting scheme obviously implies certain assumptions about the origins of the war. Specifically, it assumes that the outbreak of war, at least on a scale involving several major powers, was an

Reprinted by permission of the publisher and author from Bruce M. Russett, "Cause, Surprise, and No Escape," *Journal of Politics* 24 (1962):3-22.

accident rather than the result of a deliberate aggressor's plot. "War guilt" is rejected. This was Fay's major contribution, for by identifying the numerous interwoven causes of the world war and showing that the Central Powers neither wanted a European war nor, for quite a while at least, realized how close they were to having one, he eliminated war guilt as a satisfying explanation. Instead we assume that, as in an automobile accident, no power wanted a general conflict — a driver does not usually deliberately run his car into a tree. Rather, the war or accident arises because of numerous acts of commission and of neglect, acts whose probable consequences were not foreseen at the time. Thus there are numerous causes, a point of sudden surprise when the seriousness of the consequences becomes known, and a point when those consequences can no longer be avoided. We do not deny that there have been instances when a war was deliberately planned for the achievement of specific aims. But this does not appear to be such a case; if it were, a quite different system of analysis would be required.

The accounting scheme we shall employ is as follows:

Cause: This will refer only to those events or factors about which we can say, "If it had not existed, there is an overwhelming probability that the war would not have occurred." There is naturally an element of imprecision in the term "overwhelming probability." We shall use it, however, because of the impossibility of absolute certainty that its absence would have prevented the outbreak. At the same time, we wish it to be clear that the factor in question seems almost certain to have been essential, thus eliminating mere "contributing factors" from the analysis. When possible we shall use Fay's interpretation as to whether a particular factor was necessary to produce the final catastrophe. Where he is ambiguous we must be somewhat arbitrary. Some arbitrariness, while regrettable, cannot be avoided in such a brief analysis, and does not hinder its usefulness for illustration. Finally, a cause, while seemingly necessary, need not be a sufficient factor.

Remote cause: We shall use this term to describe any condition which made possible the chain of events leading directly to the outbreak of hostilities. Thus we mean conditions of neglect or factors such as those binding one country to the support of another. In short, it means any condition which either made the occurrence of an "incident" very likely, or which made it very difficult to correct short of war any such incident once it had occurred.

Mediate cause: Three types may be distinguished: (1) Conditions which exist in the period immediately preceding the outbreak of hostilities and which affect the actors involved; (2) The acts or neglect which leads quickly up to surprise; (3) The acts after surprise which make the situation worse, or the failure to take action to mitigate the seriousness of the accident.

Direct cause: The behavior of an actor which leads directly to the *key event*. It thus refers to a single act only. Furthermore, it need be in no way autonomous, as it may be wholly determined by factors up to and including the point of *no escape*.

Key event: The actual declaration of war or the commencement of hostilities on a large scale, whichever should occur first. One qualification, not applicable to this situation, might be made regarding the declaration of war. In some cases, as the period of "phoney war" in 1939-1940, large-scale hostilities do not follow the declaration of war for some time. In the "phoney war," for example, a number of political leaders seem to have hoped for several months that an agreement might be reached, and each side avoided provoking the other.[4] Under such circumstances the *key event* occurred only with the German invasion of the Low Countries, and the point of *no escape* may have followed rather than preceded the declarations of war in September 1939. This situation, however, is not applicable to 1914. With the possible exception of England, each of the major powers was engaged in large-scale conflict almost immediately after the declaration of war. Germany, for instance, hastened the declaration lest German troops enter France before this formality had been met.

Point of surprise: The moment when those controlling the foreign policy of a state realize that something is going wrong and is likely to involve their state in war. While the awareness may exist to some degree for a very long period before the *key event,* there is usually a point which can be identified as signalling a sharp increase in the awareness of danger. It is not the moment when the danger actually develops, as it may develop before the actors are aware of it.

Point of no escape: That point in time after which the war cannot be prevented. Nothing the actors can do will save them from hostilities. It may also be argued that there is a second point of *no escape* when the military situation gets out of hand. Thus both sides in the Korean War undoubtedly expected a far more limited war than they eventually were forced to conduct. (The North Koreans certainly did not expect a massive injection of United States ground forces, and the Americans in turn ignored Chinese threats to intervene.) In World War I it is safe to assume that none of the participants expected to conduct a four-year war of attrition. While this would be an extremely important matter to investigate, it lies beyond Fay's work and the analysis of this study. We shall limit the discussion to the events leading to the opening of hostilities.

An examination of the pattern of events suggests that the analysis can best be carried on by dividing those events into four stages. The first concerns the war between Serbia and Austria, which did not spread to include the other powers until four days after the Austrian declaration. In this case the chain of events producing the conflict is necessarily the same for both parties. Thus a war is different from an automobile accident, which requires only one participant even though it may, of course, include more. A second stage concerns the events which culminated in the German declaration of war on Russia. This resulted in the addition of two more belligerents, again with the same causal chain. We shall also analyze separately the events leading France, and finally England, into the war. Fay makes no mention of the declarations of war between Austria and the Entente powers, but given the situation and the Austro-German alliance, Austria's wider participation necessarily followed Germany's.

We thus shall deal separately with the events resulting in the broadening of hostilities at each stage. Naturally those events which caused the original (Austria-Serbia) conflict are also causes of the war engulfing other states; they must be understood as such even though we shall not repeat them for each actor. While logically there is no reason why a cause may not be unique to a single stage, in fact the involvement of each power in World War I was contingent on the inclusion of all those who entered earlier. England, for example, would not have gone to war if the Austria-Serbia conflict had not spread to Russia, Germany, and France. The image of a row of falling dominoes is particularly appropriate.

We may note also that the point of *surprise* may be different for every actor; it need not, for instance, have been the same for Austria as for Serbia. Although it was identical for a local war between the two, the point of *surprise* for a European war occurred appreciably sooner for Serbia than for Austria. Where there are more than two antagonists the point of *no escape* also need not be the same for every one of the ultimate participants. In cases of ambiguity we shall note the actors to whom a particular event applies, as SURPRISE^A_E indicates the point when *Austria* became aware of the acute danger of a *European* war involving at least one other great power.

The Scheme Applied: World War I

AUSTRIA-HUNGARY—SERBIA

REMOTE CAUSES

- Frictions and irritations among all powers, due in turn to the arms races, alliances, nationalism, economic imperialism, and irresponsible newspaper activities. No one of these, however, seems essential to this friction

- Failure to comprehend the severity of the consequences of a general European war
  - Progressive decay of the Ottoman Empire, particularly in the Balkans
  - Serbian nationalism
  - Pan-Slavism, and Russian encouragement to Serbian nationalism
  - Presence of many Serbs in parts of Austria, thus making Serbian nationalism a threat to Austria's national integrity
  - Hungarian oppression of Serbs in Austria
  - Lack of plan or leader in Austria to accommodate Slavs in country
  - Decline of Austria's power and prestige
  - Serbian government's long-standing toleration of agitation against Austria
  - Serb certainty of Russian support in any conflict with Austria
  - Conspicuous failure of London Conference on Albania in 1913 and equally conspicuous success of Austria's unilateral ultimatum to Serbia. Thus, conviction in Austria that Serbia could be dealt with only unilaterally
  - German need for Austria as her one dependable ally (See RUSSIA-GERMANY for causes of this)

MEDIATE CAUSES: Serbian government's failure either to take action to prevent the attack on Archduke Franz Ferdinand or adequately to warn Austria of the plot

SURPRISE^{AS}
SURPRISE$^{S}_{A}$: Assassination of Franz Ferdinand
SURPRISE$^{S}_{E}$

MEDIATE CAUSES

- Serbian government's failure to deprive Austria of excuse by itself taking prompt action to apprehend all involved in assassination plot
- Russian military weakness but growing strength, therefore,
- Austrian conviction that an immediate war with Serbia could be localized whereas a later one could not
- Austrian conviction that strong action could restore prestige as a great power
- Germany fails to restrain Austria; instead assures support for whatever action Austrians deem necessary to deal with Serbs
- Austria decides to use assassination as excuse to crush Serbia

- Austria issues Serbia an ultimatum which is designed to be unacceptable, war to follow if all points not accepted
- France and Russia refuse to participate in mediation
- Serbian government fails to comply with ultimatum

NO ESCAPE[A-S]: Germany rejects Grey's conference proposal

DIRECT CAUSE[A-S]: Austria declares war on Serbia (or possibly, Austrian bombardment of Belgrade)[5]

SURPRISE[A_E]: News of Russian military preparations (before mobilization) reaches Austria

NO ESCAPE[E]
DIRECT CAUSE[E]: See events under RUSSIA-GERMANY
KEY EVENT[E]

RUSSIA-GERMANY

REMOTE CAUSES

- Frictions and irritations among all powers
- Failure to comprehend the severity of the consequences of a general European war
- Pan-Slavism and Russian encouragement to Serbian nationalism
- Failure to maintain Re-Insurance Treaty between Russia and Germany
- Russian-Austrian antagonism in the Balkans
- Alliance with France and entente with England
- French conviction alliance is essential to her interests (see FRANCE);
- English conviction that entente must be maintained (see ENGLAND); thus,
- Russian confidence of support from France and England
- Previous Russian humiliations and defeats, giving "need" to restore prestige
- Growing Russian military capabilities and confidence, as evidenced by contemplation of "preventive war" on Turkey in early 1914
- Military advantages of being first nation to mobilize in war and serious handicap of being attacked before own mobilization is complete
- Technical military reasons why mobilization, once begun, could not be halted short of war
- Russian military's failure to plan for partial mobilization, which could be directed at Austria only, without weakening German front
- Major role of military in Russian government

- Tsar's personal weakness; follows advice of the last adviser who speaks with him
- Enmity of France toward Germany (see FRANCE)
- German failure to accept proffered alliance with England
- German-English friction, due to combination (no one essential) of English opposition to Baghdad Railway, naval rivalry, formation of entente, Boer War, and competition for colonies
- Fear of encirclement and need for Austria as Germany's one dependable ally

MEDIATE CAUSES: Absence of moderate and conciliatory men like Kokovtsev from Russian cabinet

SURPRISE^R: Austrian ultimatum to Serbia:

MEDIATE CAUSES

- Overwork, worry, and fatigue of leaders
- Because of Pan-Slavism and earlier encouragement to Serbs, feeling that Russia could not abandon Serbia if she were attacked
- French failure to restrain Russia, and promise of support
- English failure either to restrain Russia or to warn Germany she would not be neutral in a European war (see ENGLAND)
- Russian distrust of German motives; conviction that Germany was egging Austria on rather than restraining her
- Military leaders declare partial mobilization against Austria, which only leaves Russia at the mercy of Germany in the event of a general war

SURPRISE^G: Only one day before Austrian declaration of war on Serbia:

MEDIATE CAUSES

- Austria declares war on Serbia
- Austria fails to accept "pledge plan" to halt at Belgrade and not crush Serbia
- Russian military leaders decide war is inevitable
- Tsar approves order for general mobilization
- Russian general mobilization begun

NO ESCAPE: German government decides delay would be fatal, must declare war immediately if Russia does not halt mobilization

DIRECT CAUSE: Russia refuses to rescind mobilization order

KEY EVENT: Germany declares war on Russia

FRANCE

REMOTE CAUSES

- Frictions and irritations among all powers
- Failure to comprehend the severity of the consequences of a general European war
- Franco-Prussian War, and German annexation of Alsace-Lorraine
- Recurrent irritations and bad feelings toward Germany
- Passionate French desire for *revanche*
- French fear of having to face Germany alone in another war
- Alliance with Russia, and conviction that it must be maintained
- French entente with England (see ENGLAND)
- Anglo-French military and naval conversations, and subsequent impression of English "moral commitment" in case France had to fight a nonaggressive war
- French firm expectation of English support in case of such a war
- German geographical position and inferiority in troops to Russia and France combined, giving a military decision, if general war seemed certain, to crush France quickly, then turn on Russia

MEDIATE CAUSES

- All events leading to Russian general mobilization
- Overwork, worry, and fatigue of leaders

SURPRISE[F]: Probably the Austrian ultimatum to Serbia

NO ESCAPE

- German government decides delay would be fatal, must declare war immediately if Russia does not halt mobilization
- Germany asks French if they will stay neutral in case of a German-Russian war
- France declares she will "respect her obligations"
- Russia refuses to rescind mobilization order

DIRECT CAUSE: Germany declares war on Russia

KEY EVENT: Germany declares war on France

ENGLAND

REMOTE CAUSES

- Frictions and irritations among all powers

- Failure to comprehend the severity of the consequences of a general European war
- German rejection of proffered alliance with England
- German-English antagonism (naval rivalry, colonies, etc.). English distrust of Germany and German militarists
- English fear that a German victory over France would upset the continental balance of power
- Desire to maintain solidarity of entente (which would prevent England from putting firm pressure on either France or Russia in case of danger)
- Anglo-French military and naval conversations, and subsequent "moral commitment" to aid France
- English form of government, which made it impossible for leaders with any certainty to warn another power that a particular action would lead to war

MEDIATE CAUSES

- All events leading to German declaration of war on France. Note specifically England's failure to warn either Germany or Russia against precipitate action.
- Overwork, worry, and fatigue of leaders

SURPRISE[E]: Austrian ultimatum to Serbia

MEDIATE CAUSES

- Grey decides England is morally bound to fight with France if war develops
- Germany decides it must declare war on France and Russia

NO ESCAPE: Unionist Party assures Grey of its support if he decides for war with Germany

DIRECT CAUSE: Germany declares war on France. (Note: We do not consider the German violation of Belgian neutrality as either the direct cause or the point of *no escape.*[6])

KEY EVENT: England declares war on Germany

Avoiding Accidents

At this point we shall evaluate some of these events to discover possible ways of avoiding the outbreak of war. We shall move from the analytical scheme to areas where prewar strategic intelligence can be improved.

Perhaps the matter which deserves most attention is the period between *surprise* and *no escape*. Note that in the above analysis, *surprise* for a war precedes its point of *no escape* for every actor. In each case, therefore, it was possible for the leaders of the nation to pull back after they had discerned the immediate danger. Yet *surprise* did not occur at the same moment for each power, indicating that the point of *surprise* is to a great extent determined by the development and perceptiveness of one's intelligence services, and by the perceptiveness of top policymakers.[7] For Serbia, Russia, France, and England, news of the Austrian ultimatum to Serbia seems to have introduced *surprise* for a general European war; until then the danger of a major war did not appear great. For Germany, however, *surprise* probably did not occur until just before the Austrian declaration of war on Serbia — three days after *surprise* for the other powers. This delay made it much harder to reverse the trend toward war. The Austrian point of *surprise* for a general European war, however, only occurred after the declaration of war on Serbia and the arrival of news about Russian military preparations. Thus the point of *no escape* from a war with Serbia had already passed, and while that for a general war had not yet occurred, time was very short and many serious irreversible moves had been made.

Even for those states in the most favorable circumstances, the period between *surprise* and *no escape* was only six days, or between the arrival of news of the Austrian ultimatum and Germany's decision that it could not tolerate Russian mobilization (for France and Russia). Although England had three more days before she was irrevocably committed to war herself, a continental war was inescapable after the German decision. It was, in fact, extremely difficult to avoid after Russian mobilization had begun. The period within which action could be taken was therefore very short for all powers concerned. And insofar as we have listed overwork, fatigue, and worry as a cause of the war for all participants (except perhaps for Austria), the short time becomes even more important. A final factor that can be very important when there is such a short span of time is overload of the decisionmaking system. England's attention was seriously diverted by the smoldering Irish situation, and while this was not listed above because it did not seem *necessary* to produce English belligerency, the diversion of attention at this vital time was certainly a major contributing factor in preventing a peaceful solution.

One of the primary causes of the war was the growth of nationalism, particularly in the Balkans. We now have measures which enable us to identify areas where nationalist tensions are strong and the rate at which they are increasing.[8] Such measures need not be listed in detail here, but their use might have been extremely beneficial to the Austrians. With them they might have more accurately identified the dangers in the Balkans, both within and without the Dual Monarchy, and might then have taken proper steps to alleviate tension.

Cause, Surprise, and No Escape
                                                                573

Another important cause was the failure of the powers to recognize the nature of the ties among the major states. Had the Central Powers been certain that England would not stay neutral it is improbable that they would have acted so precipitately. Nor would Austria likely have decided to crush Serbia in 1914 had she known the degree to which the Russians felt committed to Serbia's support. And Germany would not have been so quick to reject the proffered English alliance much earlier had she known of the likelihood of an understanding between England and France and Russia.[9]

Fay refers to one possible means of identifying such close ties when he marks the great influx of Englishmen to the Paris World's Fair as the beginning of the Anglo-French entente. Other now familiar methods of analyzing communications flows, such as trade, mail, travel, and migration,[10] would have been of great use, particularly in warning Germany despite the lack of an explicit warning of England's intentions. In addition to identifying current directions and long-term trends, it seems possible that discontinuities or sudden shifts in the direction of a nation's policy could be predicted by looking for sudden shifts in its attention pattern. For example, five of six countries experiencing "neutralist" shifts in foreign policy between 1955 and 1959 showed a marked increase in trade with the Soviet bloc either in the year of the shift or up to three years before.[11] In each case exports to the bloc increased by 85 percent or more from one year to the next, exports to the Communist area totalled at least 6 percent of the nation's total exports, and this percentage was higher than that of 1952, showing that the increase was not merely a recovery from a bad year. Even though in some cases the shift in trade did not occur until the year of the political shift, the Communist nations usually deal through trade agreements, which must be concluded up to a year before the goods begin to flow. Thus on-the-spot observers in these countries, watching the flow of goods and the progress of trade negotiations, could have predicted the change in foreign policy before it occurred.

Similarly, an analysis of newspapers, both elite and mass, in terms of some sort of ratio of favorable/unfavorable editorial comment toward particular states would have helped discern a nation's probable moves even before its leaders had made a decision. Possibly also the relative frequency of references to "peace and/or neutrality" vs. "solidarity with allies" (admittedly a very crude measure; better ones could be suggested by clues in the content of the papers) would be a useful predictive tool. Insofar as certain editorials in elite papers can be identified as government-inspired their importance increases, as possibly the dependence on quantitative analytical techniques decreases.

Another very useful measure applicable to newspaper editorials might be something on the order of a "frustration ratio." Three of the participants in

World War I had felt frustrated in the achievement of several major aims of foreign policy. Thus the crisis after Sarajevo offered an opportunity to wipe away previous frustrations through a military or diplomatic victory which would raise their self-esteem and their prestige in the eyes of others. While none of them deliberately created a major war, their feelings of frustration made them more willing to incur the risk. A "frustration ratio" might measure column inches in newspaper editorials referring to the achievement of goals of national foreign policy as the denominator, and inches referring to the frustration of perceived goals, either by foreign powers or by domestic ineptitude, as the numerator. A particularly high frustration ratio might warn of a sudden desperate move (as is sometimes alleged to have been the case with the Anglo-French attack on Suez). A particularly low ratio, on the other hand, might warn of an appetite that grows with the eating. As with all these measures, it is important to watch trends in the ratio, not just the absolute level at any time.

Yet another possible use of newspaper scrutiny would be a warning when *surprise* has occurred for other actors. In most cases, when a government decides war may be imminent it takes action to prepare the attitudes of its public. It may begin violent denunciation of the prospective enemy, or place special stress on its own virtue and readiness to defend itself. Awareness of such a sharp shift in others' expectations should induce *surprise* in the mind of the analyst.[12]

Finally, improved military intelligence might have warned Austria that Russia was not as weak militarily as the Central Powers believed, and at the same time warned Russia that her relative military power was not yet sufficient to allow her to defeat Austria. In this way a mutual inspection system, by providing a more realistic assessment of the other side's capabilities, might have prevented hasty moves. Several other possible consequences of arms inspection must be considered, however. (1) By providing one side with information about the other's pehaps temporary weakness, it may stimulate an immediate "preventive war" attack. (2) It may, on the contrary, give the weaker side an incentive to catch up before its weakness becomes serious. (3) It may reduce those tensions which stem from a fear that the opponent may have some secret weapon giving him a great qualitative advantage. A properly operating inspection scheme would make the presence or absence of any such weapon known. In general, it is unlikely that inspection would cause an arms race or exacerbate an existing one. An arms race proceeds best where there is some information on the opponent's capabilities but where that information is inadequate. The Anglo-German naval rivalry before World War I is an excellent example. Had both sides possessed more complete information the rivalry probably would have been less serious rather than more so.[13]

Though the discussion so far has been largely in terms of the world of 1914, the problem is very much a current one. Military technology has changed immeasurably since World War I, but war by mistake remains a distinct possibility. In 1914 each of the continental powers had a mobilization scheme that called for the immediate dispatch of great numbers of troops to the frontiers and into the other country, using split-second railroad scheduling. To allow the enemy to mobilize without doing so oneself meant leaving one's frontiers undefended. Yet once mobilization had actually begun, it was impossible to stop it without creating utter chaos with fragmented units scattered across the country's railways. Thus once either side was convinced that the other had begun to mobilize, conflict was inevitable. The point of *no escape* was passed.

The present situation is analogous. With the advent of nuclear-weapon-carrying missiles a premium attaches to identifying an enemy attack immediately, and launching retaliation without delay, for delay could under certain circumstances result in the loss of the ability to retaliate. If an attack seems to be in progress, the defender's soft missiles must be in the air before the enemy's strike. But once launched they cannot be called back.[14] The points of *surprise* and *no escape* thus become practically simultaneous. If the attack is real, *no escape* actually precedes surprise for the attacked party. But if there really is no attack, *no escape* can follow almost immediately on the heels of *surprise*. The "attacked" party has little time to evaluate the ambiguous evidence, and if it decides to "retaliate" war is on. The system may be very vulnerable to false alarms, which could launch "retaliation" merely because certain signals (meteors on the radar scope) were misinterpreted.

The danger of such an event rises during periods of international tension, such as that over Quemoy. Each major power may fear that events are likely to get out of hand and that the other may launch a deliberate or a preemptive attack. Because of this fear, each may instruct its radar operators to be less cautious in their interpretations of possibly hostile moves. On seeing ambiguous blips they would be less likely to interpret them as normal benign occurrences than they would be in a period of lesser tension. Therefore the "threshold," or the amount of provocation necessary to trigger a "retaliatory" attack, is dependent not only on weapons development and the adequacy of the warning system, but also on the general tension level; that is, the degree to which either side holds it probable that the other will attack unexpectedly.

Measures to prevent this sort of occurrence can be classified either as attempts to hasten the advent of *surprise* or to postpone the point of *no escape*. There have been a number of suggestions for improving intelligence so as to hasten surprise. Kissinger and Schelling have suggested means for exchanging information about capabilities or for making it possible to determine the extent of each other's preparations for launching a surprise attack.[15] The now very much outdated open-skies proposal fell into this category, as in some respects do unilateral measures like the use of reconnaissance satellites.[16] Proposals for crash arms control, whereby in a great crisis both sides might temporarily find it worthwhile to accept far-reaching inspection, are highly stimulating. One can easily imagine circumstances under which a power would be desperately anxious not only to assure himself that the enemy was not planning to strike, but to offer his enemy tangible proof of his own intentions and so prevent mistaken preemption.[17] Schelling also offers provocative comments on procedure in the so-called co-ordination game, where both powers try to devise means to communicate to the other the stakes they consider important and worth fighting for, thus preventing the other from unknowingly stepping over the line to unavoidable war.[18]

Alternatively, we might concentrate on postponing the point of *no escape.* In terms of the 1914 situation, limited progress has been made in this area, with improved machinery for consultation and mediation, as well as changes in military procedures and the requirements of mobilization. Had any of the proposals for conference or mediation been accepted, for example, World War I might have been prevented. Note that German rejection of Grey's conference proposal was given as the point of *no escape* for an Austro-Serbian conflict. Even though the participants had decided for war, hostilities might have been prevented by the action of a third party.

In a thermonuclear world, an additional set of measures is required. To some extent they may be undertaken unilaterally rather than only by negotiation or explicit understanding. *No escape* may be postponed or avoided by hardening missile bases or making them mobile. If one can be sure that a substantial number can survive an enemy first strike, one may wait, after *surprise,* for indisputable evidence that one has been attacked. A complementary result can be obtained by the large-scale construction of fallout shelters, or the evacuation of one's metropolitan population in time of great crisis.[19] These measures provide some protection not only against imagining an attack when there is in fact none, but the possibility of "catalytic" war.[20] The last is where a small, adventurous power attacks a larger one with the intention of creating a conflict among the major powers. If the attacked nation can take time to ascertain the source of a few missiles which have just hit it, the chance of a mistaken retaliation is reduced.[21]

It should be noted that several suggestions for stabilizing the military environment need not necessarily have the desired effects. A huge shelter program in one country, ostensibly for stabilizing purposes, might actually tempt the other power to make a preemptive attack before the program was complete, for afterward the sheltered power might be in a position to risk nuclear war without losing too great a proportion of its civilian population. Similarly, suppose that a program of mass evacuation from its cities was worked out by the Soviet Union, and one day the Russians announced that they were testing the system. Once the evacuation was complete, they would then be in an extremely advantageous position to blackmail the United States. The position might be so dangerous to America, in fact, that it might consider preempting before the evacuation was complete. The Soviets might actually be testing their system in complete good faith, but one could well imagine situations where the United States would not dare to trust them. Finally, despite all the recent attention to problems of arms control and inspection, there has been little careful discussion of what is to be done if a violation of the arms control agreement should be detected.[22] If the violation was well advanced and seriously disequilibrating, it is possible that the violator might elect to attack immediately on his exposure. Or if he had the capabilities to do so, the discoverer might under certain circumstances prefer to preempt rather than publicly expose the violation. The purpose of these points is not to disparage fallout shelters, civil defense, or arms control agreements, but to urge more thorough examination of the consequences.

We have dwelt largely on situations where no major power wants war, even though under some conditions it would initiate one in order to avoid being attacked. When considering a war launched with a large measure of deliberate planning and calculation the problems of inducing surprise at an earlier moment become quite different, and in many ways easier to solve. Almost all of the above measures could be adapted to this purpose, and many others added.[23]

We do not, therefore, contend that all wars are of the "accidental" variety, and so amenable to the kind of cooling-off treatment which can take place between the points of *surprise* and *no escape*. Hitler in 1939 consciously ran at least the high risk of war for the achievement of certain aims, and the resulting conflict was not "accidental." It may further be contended that there is at least one other type of war-producing situation—one where a crisis drags on for some time and where, despite the early advent of *surprise*, either the situation is not amenable to diplomatic procedures or the possible steps are not taken. Perhaps the present long-term crisis over Berlin, which first alarmed a number of responsible officials in the State Department in the spring of 1959, is such a case. At the time this paper was written little of consequence had been done to relieve the situation, and one might even argue that no permanent solution is possible short of near capitulation by one side. The conceptual scheme might well be modified to cover such a case, possibly by distinguishing two separate points of *surprise*. The first would be when responsible officials become acutely aware of the danger, and the second when certain identifiable steps to avert it are begun. In any case, it is not argued that lengthening the period between *surprise* and *no escape* necessarily prevents war. It merely provides an opportunity to explore possible preventive measures. Yet this does suggest ways in which the framework can be adapted to apply to more than one type of war-producing instance. Further inquiry will determine the degree to which such adaptation is possible and the kinds of modification needed.

Much of this discussion has dealt with means of making certain actions of one power more readily predictable to other powers, and particularly to prospective opponents. This is in sharp contrast to much of traditional diplomacy, with its frequent emphasis on keeping the opponent off balance by being unpredictable. But by appraising each side of the other's desire to avoid general war, and furnishing tangible evidence of intentions, part of the edge can be removed from the present hair trigger. By reducing the danger of "accidental" war, all powers can gain.

Notes

I wish to express my gratitude to Karl W. Deutsch and W. W. Kaufmann for their most valuable suggestions.

1. For instance, see Gabriel A. Almond, "Comparative Political Systems," *Journal of Politics* 18, 3 (August 1956), pp. 391ff.; Gabriel Almond and James Coleman, *Politics of the Developing Areas* (Princeton: Princeton University Press, 1960); Roy C. Macridis, *The Study of Comparative Government* (Garden City: Doubleday, 1954); and Edward Shils, *Political Development in the New States,* Agenda Paper, Conference on Political Modernization, Committee on Comparative Politics of the Social Science Research Council.

2. *The Origins of the World War,* 2 volumes (New York: Macmillan, 1928). While some of Fay's interpretations have since been challenged and new material made available, we shall not attempt to reevaluate his conclusions in the light of this new evidence. The question of his accuracy is not directly relevant to the purpose of this paper, which is to offer a possible system of analysis.

3. Adapted from J. Stannard Baker, "A Framework for the Assessment of Causes of Automobile Accidents," reprinted in Paul F. Lazarsfeld and Morris Rosenberg, *The Language of Social Research* (Glencoe, Illinois: Free Press, 1955), pp. 438-48.

4. Winston S. Churchill, *The Second World War,* I, *The Gathering Storm* (Boston: Houghton Mifflin,), pp. 484-85, 582-83.

5. It might even be contended that we should not regard the key event as occurring until the Austrian invasion of Serbia was begun; that is, after the other powers had been brought into the war. In this instance it is not an important distinction, however, as once the Austrian government was firmly resolved to invade, and the other powers for one reason or another had refused mediation or conference, it is

most difficult to see how that invasion might have been forestalled.

6. It is somewhat inaccurate to label a decision, such as that of the Unionist party to support Grey, as the point of *no escape*. As long as the decision has not been implemented by military or diplomatic moves it can, in principle, still be reversed. The Tsar's first order for general mobilization was, in fact, rescinded in time, even if only to be repeated a day later. Yet in the English case it seems that Grey's mind was made up, and once he was assured of parliamentary support it is very unlikely that anything could have changed his decision. For this reason we do not call the invasion of Belgium either the point of *no escape* or the direct cause. Grey had already decided to fight, according to Fay. The German invasion made it easier for Grey to justify his decision to the public, but did not cause it. Also because of Grey's decision to fight we do not treat the actual commitment of English forces on the continent as a relevant *key event*.

7. Note the conclusion of Benno Wasserman ("The Failure of Intelligence Prediction," *Political Studies* 8, 2 (June 1960), p. 165) that in very many cases "the *failure of intelligence prediction is due to faulty evaluation and not to lack of available information*" (author's italics).

8. See. K. W. Deutsch, *Nationalism and Social Communication* (New York: Technology Press of M.I.T. and John Wiley & Sons, 1953), especially chapter 5.

9. It is doubtful whether threatening policy statements alone could correct misapprehensions of this sort. The recent decline in American willingness to depend solely on a strategy of massive retaliation illustrates some of the difficulties involved in making a threat credible. "Over-advertisement" of one's readiness to go to war can, if not believed, create as much dangerous uncertainty as the "under-advertisement" of 1914.

10. See especially K. W. Deutsch et al., *Political Community and the North Atlantic Area* (Princeton: Princeton University Press, 1957), pp. 144-46; and Deutsch, "Toward an Inventory of Basic Trends and Patterns in Comparative and International Politics," *American Political Science Review,* LIV, 1 (March 1960), pp. 34-57.

11. The shifts that could have been "predicted" by this test were: Yugoslavia (rapprochement with Soviets — 1955), Egypt (arms purchase — 1955, the first clear indication of a change in Egyptian policy), Syria (arms purchase — 1956), Iceland (Communist election gains and near expulsion of the United States from its NATO base — 1956), and Lebanon (revolution — 1958). No such trade increase was associated with the Iraq revolution of 1958, in part because approximately 90 percent of the country's exports are controlled by the Western-owned oil companies. The proposed test would also give a few false positives, but as in a hypothetical cancer test it is far more important that the test locate most actual cases than that it identify *only* true cases of cancer.

Data from United Nations, Statistical Papers, Series T, Vol. X, No. 8, *Direction of International Trade* (New York, 1958).

12. Ithiel de Sola Pool ("Public Opinion and the Control of Armaments," *Daedalus,* Fall 1960, p. 996) has pointed out that the frequent reiteration of one's peaceful intentions to a domestic audience may make one's own troops undependable in any attempt to launch a first strike. Yet a sudden shift to warlike propaganda may surrender the advantages of surprise.

13. See Samuel P. Huntington, "Arms Races: Prerequisites and Results," in Carl J. Friedrich and Seymour E. Harris, *Public Policy* (Cambridge: Harvard University Press, 1958), pp. 41-86, for a further examination of these problems. See also Malcolm W. Hoag, "On Stability in Deterrent Races," *World Politics,* XIII, 4 (July 1961), pp. 505-27, and Anatol Rapoport, *Fights, Games, and Debates* (Ann Arbor: University of Michigan Press, 1960).

14. Theoretically they might be destroyed in the air, but since any power which believed itself under attack would expend a great many missiles in the first shot, it might find itself practically defenseless if it then destroyed them.

15. Henry A. Kissinger, "Arms Control, Inspection, and Surprise Attack," *Foreign Affairs,* XXXVIII, 4 (July 1960), and T. C. Schelling, "Reciprocal Measures for Arms Stabilization," *Daedalus,* Fall 1960, pp. 892-914.

16. See Albert Wohlstetter, "The Delicate Balance of Terror," *Foreign Affairs,* XXXVII, 2 (January 1959), for demolition of the notion that aerial inspection could detect an imminent surprise attack with current weapons.

17. T. C. Schelling, "Arms Control: Proposal for a Special Surveillance Force," *World Politics,* XIII, 1 (October 1960), pp. 1-18.

18. *The Strategy of Conflict* (Cambridge: Harvard University Press, 1960). Just this kind of communication failure seems to have occurred in Korea during the fall of 1950, especially in the American failure to take seriously Chinese warnings about advancing into North Korea. By the time the Americans became seriously alarmed, China had committed herself to enter the war. (*No escape* preceded *surprise.*) See Allen S. Whiting, *China Crosses the Yalu* (New York: Macmillan, 1960).

19. Getting one's missiles off the ground is of course no way to protect one's population from a first blow if the enemy is already attacking, but it can prevent their death in a second strike, or at least make the difference between winning and losing a war. On the principle that "winning" and "losing" are not necessarily wholly inappropriate to nuclear warfare see Herman Kahn, *On Thermonuclear War* (Princeton: Princeton University Press, 1960).

20. Arthur L. Burns, *The Rationale of Catalytic War,* Research Monograph No. 3, Center for International Studies (Princeton, 1959).

21. Aaron Wildavsky has suggested in an unpublished manuscript that chances of international military stability may actually be *increased* by the spread of nuclear weapons to additional powers. While the possibility of a deliberate or accidental explosion is increased by such a spread, it may induce restraint in retaliation. Under present conditions if a major power saw a nuclear explosion on its territory it would "know" where it came from, but if many nations had nuclear capabilities it would be more alert to the possibility of hoax or accident. For other arguments about the possible stabilizing effects of nuclear dispersal see the debate on a NATO capability and Morton Kaplan's discussion of the "unit veto" system (*System and Process in International Politics* [New York: John Wiley & Sons, 1957], pp. 50-52).

22. Fred Iklé, "After Detection-What?" *Foreign Affairs,* XXXIX, 2 (January 1961), pp. 208-20, is the most thorough discussion of these matters at present, but it leaves many questions. See also Robert Bowie, "Basic Requirements for Arms Control," and Lewis B. Sohn, "Adjudication and Enforcement in Arms Control," *Daedalus,* Fall 1960, pp. 708-22 and 879-91.

23. Seymour Melman, ed., *Inspection for Disarmament* (New York: Columbia University Press, 1958), remains the most complete published examination of detection methods. See also Bernard T. Feld, "Inspection Techniques of Arms Control," *Daedalus,* Fall 1960, pp. 860-78, and the references there.

Evidence of the usefulness of the kinds of quantitative techniques suggested earlier for predictive purposes is still somewhat scanty, but there have been a number of studies which indicate that they can substantially increase the reliability of forecasts. Alexander George (*Propaganda Analysis,* Row Peterson, Evanston, 1959) used content analysis quite successfully to predict Axis moves during World War II, and Ithiel de Sola Pool, *Symbols of Internationalism* (Stanford: Stanford University Press, 1951), showed a high correlation between the degree of favorableness of elite newspaper editorials and more intuitive post hoc judgements about relations between a number of pairs of countries at various periods. Richard L. Merritt (*Symbols of American Nationalism,* Ph.D. dissertation, Yale University, in progress) shows the relationship between newspaper content and the emergence of feelings of separateness and commonality in colonial America. Similar results to Pool's, using data like that cited in note 10, will be presented by Karl W. Deutsch and I. Richard Savage (*Regionalism, Trade, and Political Community,* forthcoming). For the relation of about thirty indices of communication and transaction to trends in Anglo-American relations see my forthcoming book (*Testing Political Community: Britain and America Since 1890*).

Part 9
Normative Inquiries

Introduction

For more than one hundred years there has been a continual effort to regulate war by means of moral and legal norms, although throughout this period there have been moments of hope and long intervals of skeptical disregard. The character and effectiveness of these norms are fit subjects for scholarly inquiry. As might be expected, this subject matter stimulates controversy as to value and effectiveness. Part of the controversy concerns whether norms in international society can ever have more than a peripheral effect on statesmen faced with the realities of power. After all, there are no means of enforcing norms in an impartial, effective manner. Put differently, international society lacks a sanctioning process, at least of a kind associated with the internal order of a modern state. Perhaps more important is the primacy of national interests in diplomacy leading those with the power of decision to set norms of constraint in situations of international conflict.

At the same time, large-scale war has become widely acknowledged as mutually destructive under modern circumstances. Among major states there is a reciprocal interest of the highest kind in preventing the outbreak of war and of minimizing its scope and duration should it occur. Norms have grown up to reinforce and preserve these shared interests.

Unfortunately, however, the war system itself is not seriously challenged as possessing endemic dangers of general warfare among leading countries. General norms prohibiting recourse to force except in self-defence are widely subscribed to by governments, and yet their formulation and interpretation are so vague that there is a limited restrictive impact on governmental behavior. As has been traditional, some specific norms within the sphere of war are generally observed, such as those dealing with treatment of prisoners of war, with soldiers wounded in combat, and with civilians.

The question posed by our first chapter, written by Stanley Hoffmann, is related to the scope of international law, given the geopolitical realities of the war system. On the one side is the fruitlessness of formal prohibitions that enjoy the status of law and yet have no behavioral impact on governmental statecraft. On the other side is the cynical tendency to call any persisting pattern of behavior "law" so that there will not appear to be too large a gap between what the law prescribes and what states do. We need to strike a balance between the prescriptive function of law to set standards and the reality of law in a decentralized system of states where compliance with rules by governments is largely voluntary. That is, compliance emerges out of perceptions of self-interest, including convenience, moral rectitude, and possibly some feeling for long-term stability. In a central respect, then, the traditional realm of normative discourse involves an appraisal of the role of international law, both with respect to its relevance and to what degree of regulation it is reasonable to achieve in this sort of system.

International law works least impressively in the setting of war as the issues of choice that face leaders relate so directly to the dynamics of power, placing an premium on effectiveness whatever the normative status of particular acts. And yet it is the public pressure to do something about "the scourge of war" that stretches the credibility of international law past its breaking point. That is, international law is made to bear a burden of public hopes that is too great given the poor prospects for inducing states to comply.

One way to meet this problem of realistic expectations is to shift the locus of inquiry to the nature of international society. Hedley Bull does this in the second chapter by comparing two differing views of international society, each of which gives rise to an appropriate role for law in relation to war. The first, associated with the outlook of the great Dutch jurist Hugo Grotius ([1625] 1962), views international society as a potential human community, with governments of states acting really as agents of their people. The Grotian view endorses efforts to build up a normative tradition of regulating war, condemning recourse to aggressive war, punishing the leaders of states who violate legal norms of restraint, and building up the authority and capability of international institutions as rapidly as possible.

The other view, associated with the writing of Lassa Oppenheim and the tradition of legal positivism, believes that state sovereignty is the main ordering logic of the world order system. As such, it regards efforts to pass normative judgment as fundamentally incompatible with promoting restraint in international relations as it seems to challenge the principle of state sovereignty. The Grotian approach is criticized as overstating the community dimension of the world system. In contrast, the Oppenheim view suggests that states are the self-regulating units and that it serves no useful function to condemn their behavior by external procedures. If these procedures operate they tend to exacerbate conflict through processes of condemnation that mainly reflect the preferences of a political configuration of states, and are not even trustworthy guides as to the content of the relevant legal norms. In effect, this positivist approach to norms is a plea for modesty, arguing that governments can't and won't participate seriously in the international legal order unless reassured about their sovereign prerogatives. Of course, the Grotian response here is that such reassurance is exactly what must be avoided, that wars of ghastly proportions will be frequent in international society until state sovereignty is effectively challenged and curbed.

The debate over contending perspectives underlies recent divergent evaluations of the United Nations, especially the General Assembly. The Grotians virtually concede that the General Assembly can generate norms on behalf of the world community. The Oppenheimians contend that the General Assembly is little more than a boisterous debating society without any competence to intrude on national sovereignty.

The final chapter, by Falk, carries the inquiry into war to its outer horizon — the sustainability of the world order system now dominated by sovereign states. In this context the problem of war is intertwined with issues of population growth, world poverty, pollution and ecological decay, and patterns of social and political injustice. Either one can present this mixture of trends in the neutral fashion of analyst or one can contend that the trends make out a normative case for human intervention; that is, if things go on the quality of our life will deteriorate and a crackup is likely to occur. Since something must be done, it can and should be. It is this line of affirmative thinking that underlies the world order movement — not merely to understand the world, but to change it.

As such, it presents an exciting challenge to social science inquiry: How can we use what we know to shape what we do? As such, the objective canons of observation and explanation are supplemented by the subjective canons of values and action. Under the abstract contention that war can be studied and state behavior appraised lies the conviction that the human species requires a different type of world order system in the decades ahead if it is to adapt and evolve. Future world order will need to combine ideas about human solidarity with the provision of basic needs for all people in political arrangements that protect cultural and political diversity while finding ways to wage and resolve conflict that do not depend on large-scale, high-technology violence. In short, the proper study of war these days inclines inquiry in a radical direction, toward proposals and approaches aimed at the abolition of the war system.

25
International Law and the Control of Force

Stanley Hoffmann

A vigorous discussion is taking place, among international lawyers and political scientists, about the proper place and possibilities of international law. It may be strange for the coeditor of a volume on the relevance of international law to contribute an essay that could, with only a little flippancy, be taken as an attempt to show the irrelevance of international law. However, my primary purposes are of a different sort. First, I want to show why and where the plight of international law in the present international milieu is particularly serious. Secondly, I will try to indicate why the relevance of legal rules to the control of the use of force among states will, in my opinion, remain limited in the near future.

I

There have been recent chivalrous attempts to minimize or deny the plight of international law either by pointing out that the flaws which allegedly plague it affect other bodies of law as well, or by stressing ways of looking at the functions of international law that somehow remove its weaknesses from the angle of vision. Both approaches may succeed in making one feel better. But I doubt that they go to the heart of the problem.

To be sure, one must begin by indicating what the problem is not. It is not the recurrent failure of the subjects to observe the rules 100 percent. By definition (but it is a definition that some schools of legal or political theory have tended to obfuscate) a legal system is a normative one, i.e., it is — just like an ethical code — a set of rules *for* human behavior, and not merely the transcription of empirical rules *of* human behavior. We may suppose that if men in society behaved in a perfect way, from the viewpoint of both moral

Reprinted by permission of the publisher and author from Stanley Hoffmann, "International Law and the Control of Force," in Karl Deutsch and Stanley Hoffmann, eds., *The Relevance of International Law* (New York: Anchor Books, 1971), pp. 34-66.

order and sociopolitical order, there would be no need for moral and legal rules. Unfortunately, they do not; moreover there is no unanimity on what constitutes the good moral or social life. Therefore not only is there need for normative rules, but there is also an inevitable discrepancy between how men or groups actually behave, and how the codes prescribe that they ought to behave. As Richard Falk has put it most succinctly, "Perfect compliance suggests the triviality of a rule. . . . If there is no pressure on the rule, there would be no social function for it."[1] To demand that international law adjust to political reality is therefore "to miss the point," not at all, as one writer has suggested,[2] because international law is a part of reality,[3] but because any legal system, while reflecting either a general consensus about reality or the law makers' image of reality, also tries to a varying extent to change reality in such a way as to produce the minimum of discrepancy between rules *of* and rules *for* behavior through a transformation of the former.

The problem of international law, which is sui generis, is therefore not the inevitable tension with political reality, but the *nature* and *scope* of this tension. The plight of international law does not stem from a temporary divorce between what the group does and what the law says it ought to do, it stems from the fact that the group permanently behaves in such a way that the divorce can be reduced to "ordinary," i.e., manageable, nonscandalous proportions only if the law's reforming ambitions are kept extremely low—and this, precisely in a milieu whose conduct seems, from the viewpoint of moral as well as social order, to require a maximum of normative correction. This plight is particularly severe at present because of the current proportions of the gap between the chaotic implications of the group's behavior and the requirements of order.

In a domestic legal system, when the tension between the requirements of law and actual behavior (or general aspirations frustrated by those requirements) is too great, two kinds of resolutions are conceivable: a revision of the law that brings it closer to (although never identical with) actual behavior or those aspirations, or a tightening of enforcement—i.e., constraint—that forces people to act in accordance with their legal obligations. Both kinds may involve a large amount of violence—against delinquents (which may be whole groups) in the latter case, against the legal system if the revision, in the former case, takes the form of a revolution. But two points are important: First, there is no reason inherent in the group that is being regulated (i.e., domestic society) why the inevitable tensions between the legal system and the code of behavior actually practiced or desired by the group should necessarily and recurrently flare into violence: indeed, violence is the symptom of a serious disease of the domestic sociolegal systems. Secondly, the tension that is endemic does not necessarily lead either to the destruction or to the abdication of the legal system. In the case of international law, however, the nature of the group—i.e., a fragmented, competitive coexistence of rival societies—is such that the resort to violence is of the essence of the group: violence is the outcome of its structure; and the tensions between actual or desired behavior and the legal system tend to destroy or to cripple the latter.

It will be said that such a view is unduly pessimistic about international law—indeed, isn't the bulk of the rules faithfully observed by the governments? Doesn't the view of large-scale, perpetual trouble between legal order and political order mistake a very small proportion of the rules for the whole? A few words must be said here, in reply to and in criticism of the view according to which international law does not function so differently from other kinds of law. For that view, in my opinion, ignores the peculiarities of the milieu which international law pretends to regulate.

One formulation of this view stresses the functions of international law other than "a direct constraint on political action,"[4] or than a direct "restraint on behavior."[5] It is of course true that there are other functions, in particular that of providing "a medium for precise communication between international actors."[6] It is an "institutional device for communicating to the policy-makers of various states a consensus on the nature of the international system."[7] But first, our proper and fashionable concern for communication systems should not make one forget who the communicators are, or what is being communicated: In the international milieu, some communicators have the might to force others to accept messages on which there is no consensus or the might to reject messages they don't like, and the communicators tend to agree on exchanging only such messages as enshrine their actual habits or serve their convenience. Secondly, and consequently, this implies that the very nature of the international milieu should stop one from deemphasizing the problem of restraint. For unless behavior is restrained, the communications will be, if not empty, at least always fragile in their efficacy and limited in their scope. When the consensus that is being communicated is one that maintains the group in a situation of latent anarchy, and when the consensus disappears, the communication function shrinks or dies because the constraining function failed.

Another formulation denies that the group is in a situation of latent anarchy, and instead of offering a consoling view of the legal system, presents a reassuring one of the milieu. It analyzes international politics as a "primitive system," which, like primitive societies, depends essentially on self-help and deterrence for the maintenance of order, and in which law—just as much a product of custom and bargaining as in primitive societies—is enforced by self-help.[8] Now, it is true that there is no more formal, central government in the world than in a primitive society, and that the legal systems of those two kinds of societies are marked by a very low degree of institutionalization. But otherwise the parallel is entirely misleading. International law is the law of a group whose component units have highly institutionalized legal systems and differentiated political institutions; primitive law is the law of a group whose components have neither; in other words, the meaning of the low degree of institutionalization of international law is not at all the same as that of the low degree of institutionalization of primitive law. Primitive law is the law of a society that is highly integrated—which helps explain why it can subsist without a differentiated central power and why self-help both often suffices to preserve order and tends to maintain rather than to disrupt the social fabric. International law is the law of a milieu that has no central power because of the fragmentation and will to fragmentation of its parts, and where self-help, while capable at times of giving to international anarchy an appearance of order, often threatens to plunge the milieu into sheer chaos. Self-help is indeed the mark of primitive legal systems—primitive from the viewpoint of institutionalization, but the lack of institutionalization can be found, so to speak, at the two extremes on the scale of group integration; at one extreme, it confirms integration, at the other, it confirms nonintegration and may promote further disintegration. For the significance of violence in the two kinds of societies is completely different. Violence within a primitive society (I refer here to feuds rather than wars) is comparable to private violence within a civilized one, rather than to war. Wars among primitive societies are more comparable to our wars; they too tend to integrate the fighting communities; yet they usually fail to disrupt the "ordered anarchy" of the primitive milieu because they do not have the elements that make "modern" war so original—the rational calculations of ends and means, and the technological means of destruction.

It is once again the uniqueness of the international milieu and the seriousness of the problem of violence in this milieu that oblige one to take a dim view of the role of law in ordering such a group. It is true that "the horizontality of the international legal order implies a range of interpretative discretion by nations that impedes the growth of highly specific rules of restraint. This is simply an attribute of the system"; but it does not follow that it is "not an occasion for lament."[9] When sporadic, endemic violence does little harm to a group, or integrates the respective fighting units without threatening the overall milieu with destruction, one may well be satisfied with, or resigned to, a legal system that uses violence (in the form of self-help) as a prop rather than seeing it in an enemy, and imposes no constraint against the resort to force. But in the international milieu one simply cannot be so reassured. Here we must turn to the notion of restraint. Legal norms never constrain all by themselves. Behavior is restrained (1) either by self-restraint arising out of a sense of duty pure and simple — a categorical imperative: when the citizens of a nation obey the law even if it goes against their interests and although they have no fear of sanctions, the constraint is achieved by the combination of legal norms and *conscience;* (2) or by self-restraint due to the calculation of interest — I obey because my respect for the legal norm will bring a gain, or my disrespect will entail a deprivation; the legal norm is backed and buttressed by the subjects' *expectations* or by *deterrence* of the subjects' antilegal inclinations; the constraint operates through a combination of legal norms and power considerations; (3) or by the actual use of force on behalf of the norm: here we have *coerced* restraint.

The trouble with international law, permanently, is, each time the more important interests of the members are in play, (1) that the nature of the group rules out the first form of constraint, for, to use Raymond Aron's categories, the international milieu cannot practice the ethics of law alone: it has, at best, to find a compromise between those ethics and the ethics of combat, between Kant and Machiavelli. Only a group in which violence is effectively outlawed can afford to be guided by Kant alone; (2) that the second form of constraint, which is frequent (indeed it is the regulative principle of international relations), does not always coincide with the imperatives of international law, i.e., calculations of power and commands of law, instead of converging, tend to live on separate planes; (3) that coercion — through "self-help" — again has often nothing to do with the enforcement of law. In other words, international law as a system of constraint is weak law, in the one milieu in which the restraint on behavior happens to be the crucial issue. For it is when such restraint is no longer an issue, i.e., when behavior is easily constrained in one of the three ways I have described, that the legal analyst is at liberty to minimize that function and to stress the other functions of law. But when the restraining function is not performed, those other functions, even when (as in the case of international law) they are performed quite well, remain essentially fragile, always threatened or undermined by the fiasco of the restraining function. Let us go back to the "indirect restraint" of the communication function. Law as a system that coordinates expectations and communicates claims is supposed to provide the subjects with a zone of predictability. But such predictability presupposes the effectiveness of constraints on misbehavior. The nature of the international milieu makes the coordination of expectations both essential and precarious: essential because of the milieu's decentralization, precarious because of the unsolved problem of restraint. The subjects' right (or might) to resort to violence and the absence of a central constraining power result in a very low degree of certainty as soon as one enters the critical zone in which state interests are at stake. For (a) the way in which international law is made is such that at any given moment the normative air is filled with principles ("legitimacy," "self-determination," not to mention such flytraps as democracy or human dignity) whose legal status is unclear, and with practices that may or may not be in the process of becoming customs and that can in the meanwhile be analyzed either as inchoate new law that replaces, retouches, amends the old, or as violation of established law; (b) the nature of the group as well as the law-making process leads to two other kinds of weaknesses. On the one hand, the legal fabric is full of holes—zones which the units refuse to regulate, zones about which they "communicate" to each other a determination to stay unfettered, a claim to arbitrary action; on the other hand, many of the norms agreed upon are sufficiently vague or contradictory to allow the maximum of twisting and require the minimum of outright violation for comfort. To say this is neither to attack international law, nor to expect international law to do the impossible: it is merely to state that, indeed, the role law *can* play in domestic systems (and assuredly does not always play); it cannot play effectively at all here because of the unique features of the international milieu.

The failure of the constraining function has always been at the heart of the weakness of international law. But this failure takes on a new dimension, and constraint a new urgency, at a time when the free resort to violence means the possibility of total war. As long as states observed, in their resort to force, some restraints on ends and means (not primarily involving law) the weakness of international law was not a matter of life and death. But we have entered an age of revolutionary international politics and, while restraints have obviously been observed, the nature of many states' ends and the scope of the new means of destruction make one rather uncomfortable about the solidity of those restraints. It is perfectly normal that in a world of limited wars and developing techniques of adjudication, theorists should have envisaged progress merely in terms of "more of same" as Oppenheim did just before World War I. And it is perfectly normal for theorists writing in the age of nuclear weapons and mushrooming sovereignties to think that the maintenance of order in the world requires a drastic transformation in the conditions of the use of force and that international order will provide the security, flexibility, and consensus required only if it becomes an effective legal order.

However, the very seriousness of the problem of force in a world whose fundamental structure has not changed, i.e., which still lives in a state of nature, is also the reason why legal attempts at constraint have so far been in vain. There is no better example of what I have described earlier as perpetual large-scale trouble between political realities and the law, and of the destruction of the latter by the former, than the area of the control of force. It would be too easy as well as banal to tell once more the story of what happened to the provisions of the Covenant in the 1930s. It is more interesting to say a few words about the fate of the system of the Charter, precisely because, by contrast with the thirties, international politics in the nuclear age have been marked by far greater restraint, based on the one discernible common end—survival.

The legal system of the Charter had three main elements: the individual ban of article 2, paragraph 4, which limits the ends for which force can be used or threatened and for practical purposes rules out the use or threat of force as an instrument of national policy; the collective monopoly of force in the hands of the world organization, in the case of threats to peace, breaches of peace and acts of aggression; the exception of article 51—individual or collective self-defense against an armed attack until the Security Council has had the time to act. The basis of this system was a certain conception of international relations, a certain model of crises—the "sin" to be abolished, the evil to be prevented was the crossing of a border by the armed forces of a state, the model was that of 1914 and 1939, the daemon to be exorcised was the annexionist or expansionist state. Ironically, what has made this system unworkable is not the fury of contemporary violence—it is on the contrary the insidious pervasiveness of low-scale violence in the nuclear age which has made the model of the cataclysmic spasm irrelevant. The tripwire function which law can play when it is effective is, with regard to nuclear war and to large-scale, interstate war, played not by the legal ban but by the fear of nuclear weapons. But when peace has been endangered by postwar violent clashes, the legal system has proven to be of little direct relevance.

For political reality has witnessed what I would call the prevalence of marginal situations over the clear-cut case envisaged by the Charter. This can be shown from two viewpoints. From the viewpoint of the *initiation* of force, the ban has been violated or (more usually) undermined in two kinds of cases. On the one hand, force has often been used or threatened, but in such a way that the act did not clearly fall under the prohibition of article 2, paragraph 4. The notion of a resort to force "against the political independence or territorial integrity" of a state presupposes the existence of a well-defined state, with clear-cut boundaries. What has happened again and again is that the boundary itself has been the question mark—not because (as in the model) one side coveted a territory that clearly belonged to another party, but either because the limits of the contending states had not been clearly drawn and were at stake (Kashmir, Arab-Israeli dispute, African border claims), or because violence broke out between two halves of a partitioned country (Vietnam today).

On the other hand, there have been innumerable acts of violence short of armed attack or of the threat of armed attack—the countless varieties of subversion, "indirect aggression," intervention, that evade the "ban of the Charter" either because they remain hidden within the territory of the violator (training of subversives, radio broadcasts) or because they take the form of meddling in a civil strife so as not to violate the independence or integrity of a state but to determine its internal regime. To be sure, although such acts do not fall squarely under the prohibition of the "new" international law of the Charter, they should come under the rules of the "old" international law; but as Richard Falk has recently shown,[10] those rules have been widely disregarded because they are grossly inadequate. For they were based, first, on a presumption in favor of the status quo (i.e., foreign governments could support the government in trouble, at least in cases of mere rebellions, but were never authorized to support the rebels); secondly, on the assumption that conflicts of domestic legitimacy should not become the source of international strife — i.e., that such conflicts, like wars among nations, could be insulated and treated as momentary interruptions of peace: hence the rigor with which these rules prescribed neutrality for third parties as soon as the civil strife had reached the proportions of internal war. Such norms are obviously untenable at a time when there is literally no status quo to start from, and when the logic of competition in a shrunken world rules out nonintervention. As a result, the old ban on help to rebels has been violated by all (in Vietnam and Laos, Algeria and Yemen, Cyprus and Malaysia, Congo and Cuba, etc.). The old rule that allows third parties to help the government in power — a rule that covers the United States in Lebanon and Vietnam, the British in Greece and Jordan — has only served to justify interventions that shored up either highly controversial regimes or besieged central forces long after the rebellion had reached insurgency or belligerency proportions; the circumstances of its use have thus helped those who intervened on the side of the rebels to rationalize their own violations of the law. The old rule also assumed that there would be a clear-cut distinction between the government in power and the challengers, but that distinction has often collapsed, just as the visible boundary between established states: and two most spectacular interventions, those of the Soviets in Hungary and of the United States in the Dominican Republic, took place precisely in chaotic circumstances in which the governments in power were yesterday's rebels, and still shaky.

From the viewpoint of the *response* to another party's use of force, the postwar world has witnessed the indefinite stretching of the notion of self-defense — what was supposed to be an exception not much larger than a needle's eye has become a loophole through which armies have passed. Insofar as an armed attack had taken place, self-defense has been used to cover retaliatory measures quite out of proportion with the original blow (Israel 1956, India 1965). Insofar as no armed attack had occurred, the notion has nevertheless been used to justify a resort to force or the threat of force against all kinds of acts short of the one article 51 had listed. Either a long-lasting situation such as Portugal's occupation of Goa was termed tantamount to armed aggression, or else it has been argued that modern technology rules out retaliatory self-defense (which might come too late) and requires anticipatory, preemptive self-defense. Or else it has been stated that the provisions of article 51 did not abolish the pre-1945 international law of self-defense, and that next to the "self-defense against armed attack" singled out by the Charter and limited in scope because of the assumption of a UN monopoly in cases of armed attack, there is an inalienable right of self-defense in cases in which there exists no such monopoly, for instance in order to protect one's nationals (Britain and France at Suez, Belgium in the Congo, the United States in Santo Domingo), or in order to protect one's interests against someone else's intervention.[11]

Perhaps the best case study of the inadequacy of existing law to the present kinds of conflicts is provided by the United States' action in the Cuban crisis of 1962. The data are simple: the decision to impose a quarantine on certain kinds of shipping raised two legal issues — that of the freedom of the high seas, that of the compatibility of the U.S. threat of force with article 2, paragraph 4. The legal case of the United States rested not on the concept of pacific blockade (clearly inapplicable since it is supposed to cover reprisals against an illegal act, to be proportional to that act and to follow the failure of other remedies), but on the Rio treaty and on its connection with the UN Charter. The Rio treaty refers to joint measures, including the use of armed force, against aggression or any other factor or situation that endangers the peace of the Americas; the Charter recognizes regional arrangements for peace and security, if they are consistent with the purposes and principles of the Charter and if any enforcement action decided by them gets Security Council endorsement. It was argued here that no enforcement action was involved, for the Organ of Consultation of the OAS merely "recommended" measures, that the sanctioning power of the Security Council had become atrophied anyhow, and that the U.S. action was not inconsistent with the purposes and principles of the Charter since the Charter's chapter VIII recognizes the validity of regional arrangements.[12]

The debate provoked by the U.S. government's decision and by the arguments its legal advisers produced reveals clearly the weaknesses or uncertainties mentioned above, and proves Jean Giraudoux's witty point about international law being the most powerful training ground for imagination.[13] Some lawyers have declared America's action illegal, for the Rio procedure merely followed America's initiative instead of preceding it, and ended in enforcement action; moreover the language of article 51 has to be interpreted plainly. Others, on the contrary, criticized U.S. officials for the timidity of their arguments: one claimed that the Soviet offensive missiles amounted to an armed attack against which self-defense under article 51 was permissible, another gave to article 51 an extraordinarily elastic interpretation, justly and wittily denounced by Leo Gross,[14] thanks to the magical Lasswellian categories that are assured of giving to whoever uses them whatever result he wants to reach.[15] The significance of this debate is all too clear: One, the law as it stands is inadequate to a situation of this sort; i.e., one in which the initial crisis-provoking act is perfectly legal in itself (sending weapons to a government that has requested or accepted them) but tends to perform a radical transformation in the distribution of powers—and in which the response is a threat of force of dubious legality, but the alternatives to which would have been either even more illegal and far more brutal acts, or else a perfectly lawful abstention amounting to appeasement with possibly disastrous political effects. Two, in a clash between inadequate law and supreme political interests, law bows—and lawyers are reduced to serve either as a chorus of lamenters with fists raised at sky and state or as a clique of national justifiers in the most sophisticatedly subservient or sinuous fashion. Law bows because, as Acheson—a lawyer—put it in unforgettably blunt terms, it raises a "moral" rather than a "real" issue—i.e., law is *so* inadequate, tries to reform behavior in so unrealistic a way that it ceases being "part of political reality"; if "the survival of states is not a matter of law,"[16] if furthermore the international system is one which raises problems of survival incessantly, then we are left with the sad conclusion that in the last analysis, in this crucial area, the states are still above the law.

II

I may be accused of undue pessimism again. After all, the only thing I proved is that the *present* law of force is inadequate to the conditions in which force is so frequently used or agitated. But why could one not devise an international law more appropriate to those conditions; one that would address itself to actual behavior and try to reform it as much as the international system allows, in particular by exploiting the political foundations and manifestations of restraint which have kept the world away from chaos, and so as to produce the kind of convergence of legal norms and power calculations or coercion that operates in other legal systems?

I would be the last to argue that such a task is impossible. Indeed, I see it as both possible and indispensable. But it is inordinately difficult. Let us go back to the various forms of restraint. I am afraid that in international politics the "germ of universal conscience" is still too small to make restraints based on duty alone either frequent or solid — I doubt that a state capable of annihilating its enemy would refrain from doing so unless it were afraid of the consequences for itself.

As for coerced restraint, it is of course much less inconceivable; one could imagine the superpowers agreeing not only on a treaty against nuclear proliferation, but also on a procedure for joint enforcement. However, the nature of the contemporary international system makes collective enforcement[17] more rather than less unlikely. On the one hand, the competition among the superpowers, as well as their fear of what would happen to their respective alliances if they should act too closely together as great powers with joint responsibility rather than act as rivals, seems to rule out institutionalized joint enforcement action (although not occasional "collusion"). On the other hand, even if, through some miracle, a return to a multipolarity of militarily powerful states were accompanied by a cooling of the competition among them, the problem of enforcement would remain difficult: for in a world in which the great are mighty largely thanks to weapons they do not want to use, and in which the small, who profit from that partial "impotence of power," are both endowed with splendid nuisance possibilities, and busily engaged in acquiring means of power of their own, the relative equalization of power that follows complicates the prospects of enforcement through the big powers or international organization. There is little reason to believe that the experience of the United Nations will not be relevant in the near future: the militant enforcement-minded system of chapter VII has been for all practical purposes abandoned — not only because of the cold war — and the United Nations has preferred instead to rely on "fire-extinguishing" techniques; attempts at collective enforcement — in Korea and in some stages of the Congo affair — have proven disruptive rather than precedent making. Given the nature of the international system, the "universal actor" is led to concentrate on the prevention and on the stopping of "self-help" rather than on enforcement;[18] the major powers whenever they do not deter one another either resort to self-help but on behalf of their policies rather than of international law, or, more frequently, refrain from using force due to deterrence. There is a certain logic that operates here, even if it complicates the task of world order: as long as the use of force did not pose a threat of chaos, the enforcement of international law by force was perfectly acceptable. Once the use of force has become the major problem and fear of mankind, assuring compliance with legal norms by force becomes a formidable problem and peril of its own, as long as the world remains one of fragmented sovereignties, i.e., differs fundamentally from the ideal type of domestic communities.[19]

Those who advocate, for the promotion of international law, the "emergence of effective supranational management on a regional and universal basis" of the use or threat of force, i.e., a more centralized world society,[20] are right in pointing out what would ideally be needed. But they skip much too fast over two sets of problems: (1) What kind of "supranational" management? Would it be a world still divided into multiple states, albeit with an international police at their disposal—in which case we would be faced with formidable problems of control and command?[21] Would it be a world of separate states but with a much reduced level of national armaments as well as a police—in which case, should that force be greater than that of any one state, it could become a formidable instrument of domination, which would incite a permanent contest for control? Would it be a world government, in which case the problem of enforcement would be the same as within a state in which consensus and central power are weak? (2) Since any one of these solutions represents a leap from a present in which sovereignty is indeed transformed in its substance by the new conditions of nuclear interdependence, but rarely transferred to any agency independent of the state, into a future in which there would be new agencies superseding the states, how will one get the states to move in this direction? If world conquest by one state is ruled out, if what I have called elsewhere sanity at the brink of a holocaust[22] is averted, there remain only the traditional processes of international politics. In other words an institutionalized centralization of enforcement will have to be preceded either by enforcement through self-help, made less likely for the reasons just given, or by self-restraint based on power considerations, to which we come now.

What are the prospects for a development of legal controls of force, by exploiting those calculations which lead states to refrain from various resorts to violence out of a fear of loss or a hope of gain? Could one not arrive at a legal system that would codify those restraints and replace both the obsolete rules of pre-1914 international law and the premature international law of Charter variety? A study of postwar international relations shows that a number of restraints have been consistently observed: the abstention from the use and even the offensive threat of nuclear weapons, the observance of cease-fires at the request of the United Nations and the acceptance of UN observation or peace forces, the limitation of "escalation" measures in interbloc clashes, etc. (see note 19). Indeed, some restraints have been enshrined in law, such as the test ban. Is it not time to recognize the inadequacy of the Charter model, understand that deterrence and self-deterrence rule out large-scale, classical war, realize that the very riskiness of such war encourages the resort to "subconventional" uses of force—and try to devise a legal system that tries to fight the evil where it is? This system would regulate such wars in order to limit their destructiveness and the perils they create for peace; it would also reinforce the inhibitions against "classical" war, lest they become weakened by nuclear proliferation, by the uncertainties of deterrence, and by the multiplication of states.

I must repeat: this is indeed the way, but it is a narrow one. To be sure, there are many rules of behavior that have developed over the past twenty years. But not every rule of behavior is fit to become a rule *for* behavior. Some are not fit because they are too fragile; some are not, because if the purpose of law is — as it must be — to restrain behavior with respect to force, then these rules are simply not restraining enough to justify their enshrinement in law. Let us start with the latter kind of "pattern of national behavior." Does one really want to sanctify, say, the imposition of quarantines or the conduct of underground tests or the experimenting of weapons in the high seas or the orbiting of "spies in the sky" merely because they are wide practices that have not been widely opposed? The lack of timidity of opposition is a form of restraint, but the practice itself, far from being one, is an extension of state control. There are certain sectors of international law in which it makes sense to accept such extensions as law (continental shelf, territorial sea, sovereignty over air space immediately above the earth), on behalf of security and predictability. But in the area of force, while a case could be made for requesting that states at which blockades or tests or "spies in the sky" are aimed be *obliged* to respect such measures, for otherwise their reactions would be destabilizing, a case can also be made for leaving the initiation of such measures in a legal no-man's-land. They are to be tolerated both insofar as they themselves are not destabilizing, and as an outright ban would be, once again, unlikely to stick; for it would be unenforceable except at a great risk to peace, and conflict with the power calculations of the initiator. But these practices are not to be turned into customs. A distinction should be kept between a recognition of the *possibility* of certain state actions, and an explicit grant of authority. For not every practice, turned into *a* rule of law, is a fitting contribution to *the* rule of law; the latter expression refers to a certain conception (or perhaps ideology) of the role of law;[23] but not every legal code serves this conception, far from it. One could conceive of an international order in which highly abusive practices would receive the explicit blessing of international law — indeed, many already have it, for instance in the area of nationality, just as many domestic codes have aims quite different from that of restraining the power of the mighty. But this is not exactly the kind of order both the champions of international law and critics or skeptics like myself have in mind. Richard Falk has suggested that "the traditional criteria used to support the recognition of belligerent status" being inadequate, they be replaced with the criterion of "substantial participation in the internal war by private or public groups external to the society";[24] as a result (contrary, incidentally, to the old law of belligerency that provided for the neutralization, not the intervention, of outside parties) a state would have the right to "counterintervene" against the intervention of such groups. Here again, the legal codification of a prevailing practice, far from necessarily inciting restraint, would amount to a simple abdication to reality—i.e., a retreat from the normative concern of law—and could amount to giving legal blessing to political chaos. Would anyone suggest that the so far unopposed practice of using tear gas and napalm in Vietnam ought to be recognized as part of the new international law?

As for those rules of behavior that are indeed instances of self-restraint, from any angle (i.e., because they cannot be analyzed as anyone's extension of control), their elevation into law is often handicapped by the particular acuteness that the tension between law's striving for predictability and the states' jealous defense of their "right to be unpredictable"[25] presents in revolutionary international systems. We must turn from the interest of the law to the interests of the states. In order to assess the prospects of a further legalization of adequate restraints, we must evaluate the efficiency of such controls in the present and near future, i.e., start by observing how states behave in the presence of such controls, and in the absence of a sense of duty and of outside coercion. We saw earlier that restraints could be effective in such circumstances, when they were buttressed by considerations of gains and losses—expectations and deterrence. The question thus raised is double: when, in general, does a state calculate that it is in its interest to obey the law, i.e., under what conditions is international law effective? Are these conditions met in the present international system?

We must look at international law from the viewpoint of the policymakers: Where and when do the respect and application of its rules fit in their constellation of policies? Various sets of distinctions are of use here. First, the distinction between long-term and short-term interests may provide a preliminary criterion. International law tries to define with a certain solemnity the political framework of international relations and establishes rights and duties designed to give a measure of stability and certainty to those relations. One can say that it expresses a kind of long-range consensus on the limits, rights, duties, and possibilities of joint action by states, and that it will be effective whenever statesmen calculate that their long-term interest in maintaining this consensus exceeds any short-term losses the observance of the law, or any short-term gains the violation of the law, could bring.

Secondly, however, one can get a less vague approximation by using Arnold Wolfers' excellent distinction between "possession" and "milieu" goals,[26] and observe that the respect and enforcement of international law is typically a milieu goal, corresponding to a state's desire to pursue its "possession" policies in an atmosphere of stability and predictability, either in the long run (this applies primarily to the international law of reciprocity) or even in the short run (especially if we deal with the law of the political framework).[27] International law will be effective whenever statesmen calculate that their long-term or even short-term interest in preserving such a milieu exceeds the gains which the pursuit of their possession goals at law's expense, or the losses for their possession goals which the respect for law, would bring.

Thirdly, one can get a clearer idea of the cases in which the last generalization applies by distinguishing between the national visions, i.e., overall conceptions of what the world, and one's place in it, ought to be and to become. There are on the one hand revolutionary and revisionist visions which aim either at a radical transformation of the international milieu or at a radical improvement of one's status in it. There are on the other hand conservative and reformist visions, which aim either at the preservation of the status quo or at the adoption by regular, nondestabilizing methods of measures designed to improve cooperation among states. It is clear that the "milieu goal" of restraint is more likely to be given priority over conflicting possession goals by statesmen with conservative or reformist visions than by statesmen with revolutionary or revisionist ones: for, as a milieu goal, international law corresponds to the belief that international "society," for all its competitiveness, should also entail orderly cooperation.

Finally, we must observe that the respect and enforcement of international law may well be a possession goal, usually, but not necessarily, for the short run. A state will tend to respect and enforce rules of law when those rules buttress a concrete political asset that the violation or obsolescence of the norm could endanger: the very solemnity of international law reinforces, and is frequently used to reinforce and to highlight a political position that one wants to maintain (cf. peace treaties); such norms, seen from the viewpoint of the interested party, are extensions, or defenses, of control rather than restraints. But respect for law is a possession goal not only when one *expects* to preserve a gain or prevent a loss thereby, but also when one is *deterred* from violating a norm that hinders one's interests by the fear of inducing thereby one's opponent to disregard in turn a norm that protects one of one's own political assets, which one judges more important than the gain one's violation would permit or than the loss one's violation could prevent. As a restraining possession goal, international law corresponds to the belief that even the competitive part of international relations can take the form of ordered mutuality rather than that of unbounded conflict.

It would be of considerable theoretical interest to study the instances in which international law is effective because the international system is one in which conservative or reformist visions prevail, milieu goals at the service of such visions are given precedence in the hierarchy of goals, or the most essential possession goals of states are served rather than obstructed by international law. Within the scope of this essay, all that is possible and needed is to show why the present international system does not allow for such efficiency. The way the problem is posed to the statesmen is not: "Shall we respect international law," in a general way; the typical situation is that of the foreign policy that leads the statesmen to envisage a move that contradicts or violates a certain treaty provision or departs from a specific custom. The question arises: "Should we observe the restraint required by this norm, or pursue our immediate goal?" There are various reasons why the answer, at present, is only rarely favorable to law.

1. The first reason is the prevalence or abundance of "armed visions" in the international system: there is no room for the respect of international law as a milieu goal in such visions. For it is only when a state has long-term expectations of a convergence or harmony of interests among nations, or when its conception of the future, although one of victory for one's cause, envisages that this victory will come automatically, without any need for drastic unilateral action on its part (a most unlikely case), that the respect for international law can become a long-term or short-term milieu goal. When the state not only sees the world as a struggle between good and evil but also promotes the victory of the former, its reasoning in a crisis will tend to be as follows: "My disrespect for international law may bring about a loss in predictability, stability, etc. . . . but my cause is not that of stability, and my respect for law would entail a loss for my cause, or prevent a gain for it; whatever short-term interest I myself may have in a modicum of order cannot be put in balance with my long-term interest in changing the world or my place in it." Thus many of the new nations that have promoted subversion elsewhere, not to mention the Communist states, have often sacrificed an already mediocre or miserable present to the hope of a better future. A revolutionary or revisionist state rationalizes its disregard for present law by hoping for and acting toward a revision or overhaul of law along more acceptable lines. Today's world is full of such visions; in other words, a system agitated by these visions tends to put the competitively important above even the cooperatively urgent.

2. A second reason concerns, not the impact of certain visions on the competition, but the pressure of the competition on state goals. Even for those states whose visions entail the respect of international law as a long-term or short-term milieu goal, the intensity of the contest leads to the downgrading of this goal. For in the crisis situation assumed above, respect for law would triumph only if the leaders gave precedence to a long-term interest in a world order based on lawful behavior and reciprocity, over a short-term interest in preserving or improving their position in the contest, or if a short-term interest in an orderly milieu overrode this short-term

"possession goal." This is not a theoretical impossibility — the national interest can be defined in a variety of ways, ranging from the most short-term selfish and competitive, to the most loftily long-term and cooperative. However, whether the latter definition prevails or not depends on the intensity of the contest, i.e., on the nature of the international system; and the present one is marked by a competition so intense as to prevent the triumph of the more enlightened version. The pressures of the contest, as well as the domestic fragility of so many contestants, assure either that short-term possession goals will override conflicting milieu goals, or that the leaders will deem their short- or long-term milieu goals reachable only if their immediate possession goals are achieved. A crisis-ridden system tends to put the competitively urgent above the cooperatively important; statesmen fear that any other, "wiser" conduct on their part would only put them out of the running, or out of existence in the international milieu, or sometimes in their internal jungles. It has been pointed out that "in our current age of mass politics . . . the language of interest is becoming drowned out by the language of international public bargaining."[28] The language of interest to which this quotation refers is that of relaxed calculations — long-term considerations or "enlightened" short-term ones; the language of public bargaining is that of the frequent tests of wills that upset such calculations, yet inevitably mark a contest which is fierce in scope and fortunately limited in its means. For in such tests, the statesmen tend to reason as follows:

a. "Even though my disregard for the law may lead to a long- or short-term loss in order and certainty, my respect for the law would entail for me a short-term loss so serious that my whole position in the contest would suffer." This is at the root of Britain's and France's action in Suez, of America's escalation measures in Vietnam, of Israel's action in June 1967.

b. "Even though my disrespect for the law may lead to a long-term or short-term 'milieu' loss, it will lead to a 'possession' gain for myself and my cause, and I cannot betray the latter and neglect the former." This has been the reasoning behind many of the interventions in civil wars — and for instance Soviet help to North Vietnam, at a time when the Soviet Union's loss of revolutionary fervor was denounced by China, and when Soviet intervention could be seen as restoring Soviet positions and prestige in the underdeveloped countries.

One is justified in denouncing the all-pervasiveness of the "bargaining rhetoric" and the prevalence of the game of chicken, but one must also realize that in the present conditions of the international system the alternative to the game is more likely to be large-scale violence than moderation.

3. Armed visions and the intensity of the contest converge in weakening

the hold that legal restraints buttressing political positions of states—i.e., international law as a possession goal—may have on policy. In the kind of situation described above, in which the statesmen assess the pros and cons of respect for a norm as against the pursuit of an immediate goal, the case we have now come to can be formulated as follows: "Shall we respect the norm because our violation could incite our rival to disregard a rule that protects our interests, or reject the norm because it is an obstacle to our policy?" In this kind of conflict, international law as a possession goal tends to be displaced by the other, conflicting goals, in two sets of circumstances.

a. In the case of the "armed visions," international law as an immediate possession goal yields to the combative milieu goals that serve those visions. For instance, many of the new nations that have intervened in internal wars all over the globe, or resorted to expropriations in violation of international law, did so in full awareness of the "possession losses" their acts could entail, for instance in the form of cuts in economic aid.

b. In the case of the other visions, what we are envisaging here is a conflict of possession goals—the protection of the interest covered by the norm vs. the promotion or defense of an interest hindered by it. What tends to displace international law as a possession goal is, again, the intensity of the competition: in the crisis which raises the question of their respect for a rule, the statesmen tend to address themselves to the emergency at hand and to deal with what is certain—the promotion or defense of the interest to which the rule is an obstacle—rather than with what is seen as uncertain—the rival's retaliation—and manageable by other means should such retaliation come. Thus the United States has decided to bomb North Vietnam despite the prospects of increased Soviet or Chinese involvement, both because the crisis in South Vietnam required emergency measures,[29] and because such intervention could be "handled" by a combination of diplomatic and military means. The United States imposed a quarantine in October 1962 despite the risk of a Soviet reaction in Berlin, because of the certainty of colossal losses in case of inaction in Cuba as against the uncertainty of a Berlin crisis. Egypt challenged free passage through the straits of Tiran in order to help its Syrian ally and its own prestige and power position, despite the risk of Israeli retaliation. Thus in this group of cases, competitiveness through conflict prevails over competitiveness through mutuality.

We find therefore that the present conditions are unfavorable to legal restraints, while favorable to empirical restraints achieved by trial and error and ultimately based on the fear of holocaust. We find that the existence of legal restraints in the area of force frequently results in violations, and even more frequently submits the states to the kinds of conflicts of goals analyzed above. We must conclude that the chances of getting a further expansion of controls accepted by states are dim: for the transformation of empirical into legal restraints would put the statesmen into a position in which they do not like to be; even though, in a crisis, legal restraints prove to be fragile indeed, the statesmen do not enjoy being pushed to the point where they may have to demonstrate this fragility. An empirical norm of restrained behavior is flexible enough to be easily revised when the need arises, again by trial and error: what is communicated by such a norm is a tactical agreement, subject to testing and informal tampering. A legal norm communicates a solemn commitment, and establishes a trip wire that begs for, and can set off, a conspicuous crisis when crossed. A legal restraint is one that paints a line in shrill colors, beyond which states are not supposed to go without drastic consequences. It is a fact that, despite their "customary behavior" of crossing legal lines when their visions and policies seem to require it, states are reluctant to do so openly and deliberately—precisely because they understand the relevance of international law to long-term predictability, or fear that the outright violation of a norm that hinders them may lead a rival to violate a norm whose respect happens to serve them. States tend to behave in such a way as not to maximize difficulties for their future—so as to minimize their own pain, if you like. Hence their reluctance to agree on disarmament, to negotiate explicit arms control agreements, to establish an international military force: all such devices could still, in a world of states, be broken, but at a cost; why, therefore, run the risk of finding one's hands so tied that breaking the chain would cut them? Hence also the states' unwillingness to paint lines they may have to cross, or they may then feel obliged not to cross at the cost of a sacrifice of immediate "possession" interests, which the absence of a rule could help one avoid.

Thus, although no nuclear power has resorted to nuclear weapons, a treaty through which the first use of those weapons would be repudiated by all their possessors could oblige them, in a major crisis, to face the tragic choice between a violation of a solemn treaty (with all the precedent-making aspects of this kind of violation) and obedience at the cost of defeat. Although, until Vietnam, states that favored "subversion" by intervening on the rebels' behalf in a civil strife had always been treated as "privileged sanctuaries," a treaty that would have ratified this practice would have put the United States in the uncomfortable position of having to choose between granting impunity to an adversary unwilling to negotiate, and a deliberate violation that it would have been rather more difficult for the Chinese and Russians to treat as serenely as they have—precisely because legal norms are as visible as lightning rods. Turning into a "nonaggression treaty" the empirical norm of abstention from resort to force in order to change the European status quo would raise for the United States grave difficulties in its relations with its West European allies. Hence a sad but understandable tendency to abstain from commitments that may become millstones around the statesmen's necks. For states want both a modicum of predictability, and the opportunity to change the rules if the game goes against them.

Moreover, not only is it not always in the states' interests to legalize observed restraints, but the nature of some of the contests makes such legalization most difficult. We are faced with one more paradox: the new destructiveness of force has led to abstention not only from unrulable total war but also from the kind of conventional war that nineteenth-century international law regulated in part. The combination of the "repression" of force with the revolutionary conditions in many parts of the world has led to the proliferation of internal wars, wars for the allegiance of societies rather than for the annexation of someone else's domain. Those wars happen to be particularly hard to regulate because the traditional grip of international law—interest in reciprocity—is here so hard to apply. Conventional wars are, to a large extent, symmetrical; unconventional war is not. It is an absolute war in the sense of ends—a fact that always condemns regulation to fragility. It is fought on both sides with limited means, but means that are so different that the notion of proportionality seems irrelevant. Is a B-52 raid a proportional reply to a terrorist bombing of a restaurant? Is a tank invasion of Pakistan an inappropriate reply to large-scale infiltration behind Indian lines in Kashmir? When both sides use swords, common rules are conceivable; when one uses the poisoned sting and the other the sledgehammer, who shall say where the common restraint should be?

Thus the nature of the present experience of states shows their restraints to be too fragile or too unmatched for a simple transformation into a formal code of expectations, since the states know also that all too often expediency would force them to rock those expectations. Empirical restraints are a necessary condition for effective legal ones. They are neither a sufficient condition, nor a pressing invitation. In the area of force, a fundamental distinction must be observed.

1. It is wise and useful to plead for the development of international law whenever the rules proposed would clearly be in the long-term "milieu" interests perceived by their subjects, as well as not in contradiction with their short-term possession goals (for instance, the preservation of their alliances). This means, at this stage of international politics,

a. that there are extremely few rules on which *all* states could formally agree, beyond those already accepted, say, in the Geneva conventions. We find lined up against the development of international law not only the conditions of competition described above, but also the conditions of modern technology. In a revolutionary period, restrictions on the ends states are allowed to serve are likely to be twisted or broken, even though they appear indispensable. But restrictions on the means—the traditional approach of international law—suffer from the fact that such restraints are unlikely to be observed whenever the means are not equally shared by the contestants, and one of them may therefore hope to "prevail" in a tight squeeze by using whatever he has in greater abundance: be it nuclear weapons, tanks, planes, or saboteurs.

b. that there are greater chances of *partial* legalization, i.e., along regional lines (we know that certain states have a revolutionary vision for the world at large, but quite conservative goals for their own region), or among those states that wish to give a solemn (if limited) recognition to their determination to reduce the heat, or the scope, of their competition. The test ban (which left out the challengers, France and China) was an example of such a development. A nonproliferation treaty could follow, should a solution or device be found to reassure simultaneously the West Germans and the Soviets. A partial ordering of the use of force is better than none.

2. It would, however, be unwise and useless to push for more than the traffic can safely bear. Those who are interested in the preservation and prevalence of international law should be the first to realize that the rule of law would be the main victim of a proliferation of norms belonging to one of the two following families. One is the family of norms that would turn into explicit grants of authority practices that nations may well have both to promote and to tolerate because and as long as the international system raises life and death issues for so many states, and because any other form of conduct would lead either to suicidal abnegation or to homicidal escalation. To give a solemn normative recognition to a necessary but temporary evil is a folly, for it would give a good conscience to those who should, in the very interest of ultimate order, resort to the inevitable only with fear and trembling, pursued by the flies of their bad conscience, willing to purge themselves of sin as soon as the international system would no longer penalize virtue, and determined to redeem their more shabby, yet necessary, moves through acts aimed at transforming the system into one that provides incentives for good behavior. The other family is that of norms too frail to live. To ask for rules that the pressures of the system would force states either to pervert or to support only at a cost that would in the long run prove detrimental to their future willingness to accept legal restraints is also a folly. It is in the interest of international law itself to put states' consciences neither to sleep nor to torture.

What I suggest is the difficulty, not to say the incapacity, for international law in revolutionary systems to avoid the Charybdis of subservience to state ambitions and the Scylla of excessive pretentions of restraint. But I also suggest that it is better to recognize this dilemma as a fact of a certain kind of life, and to concentrate on the reform of this life through other means, than on attempts at using international law for this purpose. For the most likely results would be political failure and the discrediting of law. In the control of force, international law can only ratify, and so to speak "miniaturize" a preexisting consensus; it cannot create one, nor should it ratify a temporary consensus on behavior that can and should be seen as a temporary reflection of upheaval. It is essential to preserve the idea of an effective international law. That idea has to be safeguarded against attempts at disguising the ratification of highly debatable (if restrained from the viewpoint of total war) rules of behavior as the development of new rules *for* behavior. It must also be preserved against attempts at pushing law too far ahead of behavior. For in that case one only provides states (obligingly served by their legal glossarians) with new clubs with which to hit one another and with a better arsenal for mutual recrimination; and one only leads the believers in law and order down the road to an international Miltown, in which they will be run over by the players of the game of chicken, but die happy in the conviction that those players had agreed to enshrine common values and concerns in common verbiage.

This is no counsel of despair. For on the one hand, what applies to the control of force does not obtain in other sectors of international behavior, where the development of international law can indeed proceed on the basis either of a stable reciprocity of state interests in certainty and security, or of a growing transnational society of individuals. The "changing structure of international law" takes these facts already into large account. On the other hand, in the legal no-man's-land that I recommend for the area of force, I do not suggest passivity. I am in favor of a multiplication of contacts, signals, messages between actors, designed to communicate an understanding of restraints, and a multiplication of UN practices not only for peacemaking but also for issue settling (not a very successful subject matter so far, again for structural reasons). I simply suggest that we leave for the time being all these practices in a kind of gray area (comparable to that in which we find moral-political principles of legitimacy that aren't quite law but are more than aspirations): such practices, like those values, should be seen as something less than legally binding; they are modes of behavior corresponding to the needs of the situation. Both those practices and those notions could be seen as quasilaw: "ultralaw" in the case of the latter (which define aims toward which positive law will tend), de facto law in the case of the former, a substitute for and perhaps, if the system quietens down, a prelude of genuine law.

Such a position leaves one free to concentrate not only on the strengthening of those modes of conduct but also on the improvement of the situation — on the transformation of the system into one that allows states to assess their long-term interests in convergent ways, to analyze their short-term possession goals as compatible with a long-term interest in order, to subordinate their short-term possession goals to short-term milieu goals, and to allow for the pursuit of possession goals through the channels of legal reciprocity.

What is required is not merely the spread of techniques of restraint — for they are always fragile when the underlying conditions in the world breed recurrent crises and prevent substantive settlements. What is needed is much more: on the one hand, the success of deterrence, to prevent the "crime" of force from paying, and — alas — the tolerance of self-help against force as long as there is no effective collective way of stopping it, but at low levels of violence so as not to rock the very boat one tries to stabilize. On the other hand, in a world in which the individual initiation of force would thus be repressed or suppressed, the erosion of "armed visions" should be expected not only from the frustration of their offensive designs, but also from the success of efforts at improving as much as possible the local conditions that give rise to internal wars and to outside interventions. Only when the international system will be less heterogeneous than it is now, when there will be more "poles" of power, fewer ideological passions, less unevenness in development, greater internal stability in the new states, will one be able to turn the ad hoc management of conflicts — kept moderate only by the fear of holocaust — into a legalized restraint on force arising out of basic social and political forces of moderation. The transformation of a system that owes its relative moderation to technology alone, into a genuinely, organically stable one is a long enterprise. In its accomplishment, international law has a modest role, principally outside the realm of force. Once the task is accomplished, it will have a bigger and better role in the realm of force as well.

Notes

1. In James N. Rosenau, ed., *International Aspects of Civil Strife* (Princeton, 1964), p. 230.

2. William D. Coplin, "International law and assumptions about the state system," *World Politics,* Vol. XVII, No. 4, July 1965, pp. 615-634, at p. 633.

3. True enough — as long as one recognizes that at any given point reality equals status quo plus attempts at, or ideas about, changing it.

4. Coplin, "International Law," p. 633.

5. Richard A. Falk, "Janus tormented: The international law of internal wars," in Rosenau, op. cit., p. 210.

6. Falk, ibid., p. 211.

7. Coplin, "International Law," p. 617.

8. See Roger D. Masters, "World politics as a primitive political system," *World Politics,* Vol. XVI, No. 4, July 1964, pp. 595-619.

9. Falk, op. cit., p. 211.

10. Ibid., pp. 197-209.

11. I will not discuss here the fate of the "third branch" of the Charter System, the UN monopoly. See I. L. Claude, "The U.N. and the use of force," *International Conciliation,* No. 532, March 1961.

12. See Abram Chayes, "Law and the quarantine of Cuba," *Foreign Affairs,* Vol. 41, No. 3, April 1963, pp. 550-557.

13. In *Tiger at the Gates.*

14. See his "Problems of international adjudication and compliance with international law; some simple solutions," *American Journal of International Law,* Vol. 59, No. 1, January 1965, pp. 48-59, at pp. 52-54.

15. See the *American Journal of International Law,* Vol. 57, 1963, pp. 373-377, 515-565, 588-603, and *Proceedings, American Society of International Law,* 1963, pp. 1-17, 147-172.

16. Acheson, *Proceedings,* p. 14.

17. One could argue that in the decentralized international milieu coercion on behalf of international law can still be performed against a violator by self-help, i.e., individual enforcement (usually by the victims). However, (1) unless one is clearly in a case of "self-defense against armed attack," or unless the enforcer has a collective mandate, such self-help strikes me as being of dubious legality; (2) the conditions of the use of force in the nuclear age tend to discourage states from "taking the law into their hands," without a mandate; or else, when they act alone, it is usually in the pursuit of political interests from which the present law has very little to gain.

18. Witness the minimization of the notion of enforcement action in the World Court's advisory opinion on the financing of UN peacekeeping operations.

19. These remarks are elaborated further in "Terror in theory and progress," in the author's *State of War* (New York: Praeger, 1965), and in "Nuclear proliferation and world politics," in Alistair Buchan (ed.), *A world of nuclear powers?* (Englewood Cliffs: Prentice-Hall, 1966).

20. Falk, op. cit., p. 234. The term supranational is, alas, a masterpiece of legal and political ambiguity. Falk acknowledges both the dangers of leaving "regional" problems to regional organizations (e.g., the Palestine problem, or the Congo or Kashmir) and the risk of conflicts between regional and universal agencies. But these are not the only headaches: all those agencies, until now, are merely emanations of the states, i.e., they have no independent powers, and consequently, especially when they try to deal with the issue of force, i.e., when they try to act as powers, they are themselves the stakes of battles for control.

21. See "Erewhon or Lilliput," in Lincoln Bloomfield et al., *International Military Forces* (Boston: Little, Brown, 1964), pp. 187-211.

22. "Roulette in the basement," in the *State of War.*

23. See Judith N. Shklar's brilliant book, *Legalism* (Cambridge: Harvard University Press, 1964).

24. Op. cit., p. 223.

25. I. L. Claude, *Power and International Relations* (New York: Random House, 1962), p. 121.

26. *Discord and Collaboration* (Baltimore: Johns Hopkins Press, 1962), chapter 5.

27. On the distinction between the law of reciprocity and the law of the political framework, see "International systems and international law" in the *State of War.*

28. Karl W. Deutsch and Morton A. Kaplan, in Rosenau, *International Aspects of Civil Strife,* p. 179.

' 29. Whether bombing the North was politically and militarily intelligent is another matter. We are trying here to reconstruct the reasoning of the statesmen.

26
The Grotian Conception of International Society

Hedley Bull

I

Underlying a great deal of the theory and practice of international relations since the First World War there is a certain conception of international society, whose imprint may be traced in the Covenant of the League of Nations, the Paris Pact, the United Nations Charter and the Charter of the International Military Tribunal at Nuremberg. It is widely taken to contain within itself an adequate formula for orderly and just international conduct, such that the disparity between it and the actual course of events since 1919 may be ascribed to the failure of states or statesmen to behave in accordance with it, rather than to its own inherent defects. The purpose of this chapter is, at the risk of losing sight of its many varieties and nuances, to state the essence of this doctrine; and to consider the adequacy of its prescriptions.

The conception of international society I have in mind may be called the Grotian conception. The reason for giving it this name does not lie in the part which the writings of Grotius have played in bringing about this twentieth-century doctrine, although this has been by no means negligible; but simply in the measure of identity that exists between the one and the other. We shall have occasion to consider the difference as well as the resemblances between Grotius himself and the twentieth-century neo-Grotians; but the resemblances are remarkable enough to warrant our treatment of *De Jure Belli ac Pacis* as containing the classical presentation of the same view. Two important studies, to which reference will be made, have discerned a return to Grotius in this century, and along with it a reversal of the previous trend of international legal thought, which from the seventeenth century to the early twentieth, had been away from him. The

Hedley Bull, "The Grotian Conception of International Society," in Herbert Butterfield and Martin Wight, eds., *Diplomatic Investigations* (London: George Allen & Unwin Ltd., 1966), pp. 51-73. Reproduced herewith by permission of the publisher.

first of these studies, by Cornelius van Vollenhoven, was written in the summer of 1918 and looked forward to the resuscitation of Grotian doctrines, for which the world war seemed to have set the stage.[1] The second was published by the late Sir Hersch Lauterpacht in 1946, by which time he was able to record the penetration by these doctrines into positive international law.[2] Both these writers are concerned to contrast the position shared by Grotius and the twentieth-century neo-Grotians with representative thinkers of the intervening period, Vollenhoven taking Vattel to exemplify a position contrary to that of Grotius, and Lauterpacht referring in this connection to the work of the nineteenth-century international legal positivists. Vollenhoven and Lauterpacht, it should be noted, themselves embrace the broad Grotian position. It shall be our purpose, while exploring the conflict between this position and that alternative conception of international society to which Vattel and the nineteenth-century positivists may be said to have contributed, to consider whether the return to Grotius does indeed constitute that advance which Vollenhoven and Lauterpacht take it to be.

The central Grotian assumption is that of the solidarity, or potential solidarity, of the states comprising international society, with respect to the enforcement of the law. This assumption is not explicitly adopted and defended by Grotius, but, it will be argued, the rules which he propounds for international conduct are such as to presuppose that it is made. In the conception of international society which stands opposed to the Grotian doctrine the contrary assumption is made that states do not exhibit solidarity of this kind, but are capable of agreeing only for certain minimum purposes which fall short of that of the enforcement of the law. In the view it takes of the area of actual or potential agreement among the member states of international society it may be called pluralist where the Grotian doctrine is solidarist; and the rules it prescribes for relations among them are such as to reflect this difference.

The issues which divide the Grotian or solidarist conception from the pluralist[1] one may be stated with greater precision by contrasting the doctrine of Grotius himself with that of a particular representative of the latter school, Lassa Oppenheim, the first edition of whose *International Law* was published in 1905 and 1906.[3] Three aspects of the disagreement between them are especially relevant to our inquiry. The first concerns the place of war in international society. The second is about the sources of the law by which the member states of international society are bound. And the third turns upon the status in the society of states of individual human beings.

II

On what is perhaps the most fundamental question of the theory of international relations, Grotius and Oppenheim (and indeed, the two schools of thought they illustrate) are at one. Both assert the existence of an international society and of laws which are binding on its member states in their relations with one another. Both are opposed to the tradition of *Realpolitik,* according to which there is no international society but rather an international state of nature in which states are without binding obligations in their relations with one another. And both are hostile also to that doctrine according to which the standards to which appeal may be made in international politics enjoin not the preservation of international society, but its subversion and replacement by a universal empire or cosmopolitan society.[4]

For anyone who upholds, as Grotius and Oppenheim do, the idea of international society, the fact of war presents a difficulty. In domestic society the private use of force, apart from certain residual rights of self-defence, is proscribed; and the legitimate exercise of violence is the monopoly of the community. If the private use of force has the same significance in relations among states that it has within them, then the fact of war must be taken to indicate that international society does not exist. If their theories are to take account of war and not merely ignore it, those who seek to show that there is a society of states must therefore demonstrate that in international relations the private use of force has a meaning altogether different from that which attaches to it within the confines of the state. They must present international society as a society of a different sort from that formed by individual men; as one with whose functioning the private use of force may be consistent. It is a point of departure common to Grotius and Oppenheim that war of a certain sort plays a part in international society; and that so far from indicating its absence, it provides evidence of its working. They are concerned to show, therefore, that while some kinds of war are contrary to the law of international society, other kinds may be sanctioned by it.

On the question of the legitimacy of war there are three possible positions. There is first the view of the pacifist that no war or act of war is legitimate. There is secondly the view, sometimes called that of the militarist, that any war or act of war is legitimate. And there is the view that a distinction should be drawn between some wars, or acts of war, and others; that some are legitimate while others are not. It is upon this third position that Grotius and Oppenheim both take their stand. The pacifist and militarist positions are alike inimical to the idea of international society: the former because it rejects that violence which is necessary to uphold the international order against attempts to subvert it; the latter because it admits violence of a sort that must destroy the international order; and both because, in asserting that war stands beyond the reach of law, they are denying the relevance of international law to a large area of international

experience. Grotius is expressing a doctrine common to all those who embrace the conception of an international society when he writes: "For both
extremes, then, a remedy must be found, that men may not believe either
that nothing is allowable or that anything is."[5]

Here, however, the agreement between Grotius and Oppenheim ends.
There are two ways in which the attempt may be made to distinguish just
war from unjust. Either we may say that a just war is one fought for a just
cause. Or we may say that it is one conducted in a just or lawful way.
Whereas Oppenheim holds the law to be concerned exclusively with determining what constitutes lawful conduct in war, Grotius believes it also to
distinguish just from unjust causes of war, and to insist that war be waged
only for the former.

According to Oppenheim, although it is a part of ethics to distinguish
just from unjust causes of war it is no part of international law. War, on his
view, is the prerogative right of sovereign states; and the law is concerned
simply to take account of the fact of war when it occurs, and to regulate the
way in which it is conducted. Before 1919 the international law arising from
custom and treaty was wholly in accord with Oppenheim's view. It had
evolved certain rules concerning the observance of due form in beginning
and ending a war; the legal consequences for states and individuals of the
existence of a state of war; the proper limits of violence in war; and the relations between belligerent and nonbelligerent states. But it did not seek to
infringe the right of states to undertake war.

Grotius, by contrast, insists that it is the province of the law to determine
the proper causes for which war may be fought. His basic criterion of just
war is that it be fought in order to enforce rights: "No other cause for
undertaking war can there be excepting injury received."[6] In elaborating
this doctrine Grotius confines the just causes of war to three: defence, the
recovery of property, and the infliction of punishment. Since the First
World War the Grotian doctrine of a distinction between just and unjust
causes of war, and of the limitation of lawful causes of war to the former,
has been written into positive international law. The League of Nations
Covenant, the Paris Pact, and the United Nations Charter all reject the
older doctrine of an unqualified prerogative of states to resort to war; and
all present war as something which can be legitimate only when it is the
means by which the law is upheld, whether such war is undertaken on the
independent decision of particular states or on the authority of bodies, such
as the United Nations Security Council, deemed to represent the society of
nations as a whole.

The drawing of a distinction between just and unjust causes of war may
be said to have two effects. It excludes one kind of war; but at the same time
it sanctifies another and enhances its dignity. Grotius was clearly intent

that his doctrine should have the first effect, of excluding occasions of war. It is worth remarking how restrictionist he is in defining the boundaries of what is permissible. His proposition that "war ought not to be undertaken except to enforce rights" is one that permits war only the function of conserving a fixed system of rights, or responding to infringements of them; it does not admit of war to change the system of rights.[7] He devotes a chapter to enumerating unjust causes of war.[8] In elaborating the right of self-defence he rejects the claims of preventive war, insisting that we must be certain not only regarding the power of our neighbour but also regarding his intent. The desire for richer lands furnishes no just cause of war; nor the refusal of marriage, where there is an abundance of marriageable women; nor "the desire to rule others against their will on the pretext that it is for their good";[9] nor "the discovery of things previously taken over by others."[10] Consistently with his acceptance of the legitimacy of a society of sovereign states he rejects the title of emperor or church to universal empire as providing a just cause of war. Wars cannot justly be waged, either against those who refuse to accept the Christian religion or who err in its interpretation. Not even the desire of a subject people for freedom furnishes them with a just cause of war.

Moreover, Grotius is hesitant to endorse resort to war even where there does exist a just cause. He devotes a chapter to the consideration of "Doubtful Causes of War" and stipulates that in addition to a just cause there must exist a conviction in the mind of the doer of its justice; in cases of doubt we must refrain from war.[11] In another chapter of "Warnings not to Undertake War Rashly" he urges that war ought not to be undertaken for every just cause, and in particular that "war is not to be undertaken, unless of necessity."[12] All these restrictions are consonant with the purpose Grotius states in the prolegomena for undertaking to write on the subject: that he had observed throughout the Christian world "a lack of restraint in relation to war, such as even barbarous races should be ashamed of; I observed that men rush to arms for slight causes, or no cause at all."[13]

At the same time Grotius is concerned that the distinction he has drawn will have the second effect also, that of sanctifying war which is waged on behalf of international society rather than against it or in disregard of it. War in the Grotian system derives its legitimacy from the service it renders to international society as a whole; the king or people going to war to redress an injury received are entitled to regard themselves as the instruments of a general purpose. Their aims in war include not merely reparation for the damage they have suffered, but also the infliction of punishment. Grotius rejects the view of Vitoria and others that punishment may be inflicted only by those who have civil jurisdiction over the wrongdoer. The natural law, he argues, does require that punishment be inflicted by one who is superior; but a state which has committed a crime has thereby made itself inferior to others, and may be punished by them, so long as they are not equally guilty of the same offence. The waging of just war to obtain reparation from the criminal king or people and inflict punishment upon it, moreover, is not confined to the state which is the victim of the crime. It is one of the central Grotian theses that "the causes . . . which are just in relation to the person whose interest is at stake are just also in relation to those who give assistance to others."[14] There is therefore a general right of participation in just war, conferred by "the mutual tie of kinship among men, which of itself affords sufficient ground for rendering assistance."[15] Grotius even goes so far as to say that it is more honourable to avenge the wrongs of others than one's own.

Thus, although Grotius and Oppenheim both contend that war may be conducted within the bounds of international law and society, they differ as regards the place they assign to it. For Oppenheim war is a political act, and the attitude of the law towards the purposes for which it is waged is one of indifference. For Grotius war is either an infringement of the law or an act of law enforcement; and the interest of international society is not merely that the rules of war should be observed but also that the side upholding the law should triumph. It should be noted that each thinker, while stating his distinctive view, displays some awareness of the contrary position. Thus, Oppenheim does recognize that one of the reasons a state may have for going to war is the enforcement of its rights; and indeed his claim that the rules he is expounding have the status of law is founded upon the proposition that they are enforced by "self-help and the help of other states which sympathize with the wronged one."[16] He contends, however, that states also go to war for purely "political causes" and that this is the fact of which the law needs to take account. Grotius appears to concede something to the position contrary to his own when he recognizes that, although a war cannot be just on both sides it can be just on neither side, so that there may exist a situation in which international society, as it were, is indifferent as to the outcome. Nevertheless there remains a fundamental contrast in their approaches; and it has important consequences for a wide range of their respective systems of thought.

III

The first of these concerns the rights and duties of belligerent states in relation to one another during the course of a war. The tendency of the Grotian doctrine that war be waged only for a just cause is to weaken the rules of customary and treaty law, requiring that it be conducted in a just way. For Oppenheim, who holds the law to make no distinction between just and unjust causes of war, it is a natural conclusion that the rules of war apply equally to both parties in a conflict. For Grotius, however, the question arises whether the party fighting for the law should suffer the same inhibitions as the side fighting against it.

There is no logical inconsistency in holding both that war should be fought only for a just cause and that it should be carried on in a just way. Yet in their application to social life there is clearly a certain tension between these two doctrines. If international society is to regard war as a contest in which one side is seeking to uphold the law and the other to undermine it, it would seem desirable that no obstacle be placed in the way of the former. On the other hand, if the prime consideration is to ensure that war, for whatever reason it breaks out, is conducted according to the rules, then the duty to abide by the laws of war must be made reciprocal, for it is only on the understanding of reciprocity that any prospect exists of their being observed.

Grotius does not reject the idea of laws of war; on the contrary *De Jure Belli ac Pacis* is as much concerned with upholding *jus in bello* as it is with defining *jus ad bellum*; and almost the whole of book III is devoted to the former subject. What he rather does is attempt to reconcile the two conceptions. In asking himself what is permissible in war he begins by considering the matter from the standpoint of natural law, which he regards as the chief source of international law and in terms of which his theory of the just causes of war has been primarily worked out. From this viewpoint, Grotius considers just conduct in war to be something deriving from the justice of the cause for which it is fought: for "in a moral question things which lead to an end receive their intrinsic value from the end itself."[17] Moreover, given a right to self-defence, the recovery of property, or the infliction of punishment, all use of force which is necessary to enforce that right is permissible. From such a viewpoint no rights are enjoyed by the unjust party and no obligations bind the just, apart from that of remaining within the bounds of necessity.

Grotius goes on, however, to consider the matter from the standpoint of the law of nations, the law arising from the will of nations or of many nations. From this viewpoint any war which is waged on behalf of a sovereign power and is preceded by a declaration of war, is a lawful war; and whatever the cause for which it is undertaken, acts performed in it may be said to have "a legal effect." The laws of war of the early seventeenth century, which Grotius goes on to expound, were extremely permissive by comparison with what they had become by the time of Oppenheim. For example, according to Grotius's account the law of nations permitted belligerents to kill and injure all who are in enemy territory, including women and children; to destroy and pillage enemy property, even that which is held sacred; to kill captives and hostages; and to make slaves of prisoners of war (although it strictly forbade the use of poison). Grotius however, makes clear his dissent from the existing state of the law by saying that it prescribes merely what is permissive in the sense that it is done with impunity, even though it might "deviate from the rule of right."[18] He then adds a series of pleas for modernization in the exercise of what the law permits.

It is noteworthy also that Grotius displays considerable understanding of the functions performed in international society by a system of law of war which disregards the causes for which a war is fought. He considers why it is that the law of nations insists upon a declaration of war, and concludes that it is so that "the fact might be established with certainty that war was being waged not by private initiative but by the will of each of the two peoples."[19] He asks why nations should have approved a rule allowing both belligerents the right to kill, and gives these reasons: "To undertake to decide regarding the justice of a war has been dangerous for other peoples, who were on this account involved in a foreign war. . . . Furthermore, even in a lawful war, from external indications it can hardly be adequately known what is the just limit of self-defence, of recovering what is one's own, or of inflicting punishments; in consequence it has seemed altogether preferable to leave decisions in regard to such matters to the scruples of the belligerents rather than to have recourse to the judgments of others."[20]

But although he admits the idea of laws for the conduct of war that do not discriminate among the belligerents with regard to the causes they pursue, Grotius weakens its force by stating alongside it the contrary doctrine he derives from natural law. If we treat *De Jure Belli ac Pacis* as the exposition of a system of law, rather than as a contribution to philosophy or political theory, it has the grave weakness which Lauterpacht has remarked, that while it tells us what is said about international relations by various laws (the Roman law, natural law, the law of nations, divine law, canon law, the moral law) it nowhere forges these into a system by stating unambiguously what is *the* law.[21] In his discussion of what is permissible in war Grotius states what the natural law and the law of nations each contains on this subject, and criticizes both from the standpoint of love and Christian charity; but he leaves us without guidance as to which of these constitutes the law in cases of conflict. It is difficult to decide, therefore, how the clash between the natural law and the law of nations with regard to what is permissible in war is reconciled in Grotius's account. Setting aside the question of the law, however, we can form some impressions of what he thought should be done and of what kind of rules he thought international society requires.

It is clearly not the view of Grotius that those who are fighting for an unjust cause thereby place themselves *outside* international society, where they enjoy no rights. Although it is suggested by some of his language, such a conception is foreign to Grotius's fundamental assertion of the universality of international society, the participation of all mankind in *magna communitas gentium*. It derives not from the theory of just war but from the doctrine of a holy war, the conception of a struggle between completely incompatible systems, against which the main thrust of the idea of international society was directed. To make war against a state in order to compel it to conform to the rules, even to punish it in the severest way for having broken them, is still to treat it as part of the system.

Moreover, Grotius urges that the party equipped with a just cause should practice moderation towards the enemy. There is a limit to vengeance and punishment; punishment may often be justly remitted even to enemies who deserve death; women, children, farmers, merchants, prisoners, even the guilty, if their number is very great, should, if possible, be spared for "the rules of love are broader than the rules of law."[22] Good faith must always be observed with the enemy, not only with an unjust king or people, but even with tyrants and pirates and with those who are faithless.

Grotius, however, nowhere says that the privileged position afforded by natural law to the just parity is overridden by the law of nations. And while he employs arguments drawn from the higher moral law to plead moderation in the exercise of these privileges, he also uses such arguments to show that the acts of a king or people fighting an unjust war, even if they conform to the laws of war, are morally wrong. Those with a just cause, moreover, are specifically afforded the privilege of violating neutral territory in case of necessity.[23] Those who have given others cause for just war are denied the right of self-defence against the just invader of the territory; the argument that "few are satisfied with exacting vengeance in proportion to the injury suffered" Grotius dismisses on the ground that "fear of an uncertainty cannot confer the right to resort to force."[24]

The progress after 1919 of the doctrine that war should be fought only for a just cause has confronted the twentieth-century neo-Grotians with the same problem of reconciling this with the tradition of laws of war, so much less permissive by this time as the result of changes brought about by both custom and treaty. Like Grotius they have not felt able to deny the unjust party all rights in war. The view of the United States Military Tribunal at Nuremberg in the Weizsäcker case that the Paris Pact "implicitly authorized the other nations of the world to take such measures as they might deem proper or necessary to punish the aggressor," and that it "placed the transgressor outside the society of nations," was untypical.[25] Lauterpacht in his view that "any application to the actual conduct of war of the principle *ex injuria jus non oritur* would transform the contest into a struggle which is subject to no regulation at all" is giving expression to the same hesitancy which

Grotius experienced when faced with the implications of the just war doctrine.[26] At the same time, like Grotius, Lauterpacht seeks to salvage something of the idea of discrimination in favour of the just party, while shrinking before its full consequences.

The second important consequence of the disagreement between Grotius and Oppenheim about the just war concerns the relationship between the states immediately involved in the war and the remainder of international society. Oppenheim's theory, since it treats the causes for which the war is waged as irrelevant from the point of view of the law, extends no invitation to other states to enter the conflict on the side of the just party. Although in his system any state not immediately involved may, by exercising its prerogative of making war, decide to join in the conflict, it is also true that such a state is not encouraged by the law to regard the causes of other states as its own. Moreover, according to Oppenheim, having once embarked upon the policy of neutrality a state has, in return for enjoying the rights of this status, the duty of absolute impartiality as between the belligerents. Grotius, however, holds that when a war breaks out, one party may be seen to have a just cause; and it is his view also, as we have noted, that the causes which are just in relation to the person whose interest is at stake are just also when adopted by those who render him assistance.[27] In Grotius's view, therefore, if a war breaks out in which one party has a just cause, all other states have the right to join in the struggle. Moreover, if they choose instead to remain neutral, that status does not oblige them to adopt an attitude of impartiality but requires them instead to exercise a qualified discrimination in favour of the just party.

Grotius rejects the idea that third states have a *duty* to go to war on the side of the just party.[28] He upholds the rights of "those who are of neither side in war" against the tendency of belligerent states to infringe them. Indeed, he undoubtedly contributed to the development of the idea of neutrality as a regular status. Such a notion had no place in the systems of Vitoria and Suarez, and although Gentili among theorists of law had upheld it before him, Grotius was among the first to provide an analysis of it. But at the same time his concern for the victory of the just party in war leads him to subordinate the objective of limiting the number of participants in a conflict, which later writers such as Vattel were to regard as the chief object of a status of neutrality. In asserting the right of third states to enter the war on the side of the just party, and in reinforcing this with the idea of the nobility of fighting for causes in which one's own interests are not involved, Grotius was diluting the idea of a right to be neutral with the earlier (and later) notion of the solidarity of the community in relation to a struggle between right and wrong. His definition of the duties attaching to a status of neutrality, moreover, reflected the same kind of dilution. While those who wish not to participate in the war, and to have this wish respected by the belligerents, may do so, in Grotius's view they must also refrain from hindering the just party or from assisting the unjust party (what Grotius had in mind was especially the extension to belligerents of the right of passage across neutral territory and the supply to them of provisions).

The just war doctrines contained in the League Covenant, the Paris Pact, and the United Nations Charter also have the consequence of weakening the right to remain neutral, and of transforming the duty of neutrals to be impartial into one of "qualified neutrality" or "nonbelligerency."

A third consequence of the disagreement between Grotius and Oppenheim concerning just war concerns the obligation of alliances. Oppenheim does insist that immoral obligations cannot be the object of a treaty; and that an alliance for the purpose of attacking a third state without provocation is not binding. But he does admit that "the question as to what is immoral is often controversial";[29] and he does not insist that a state is obliged to assist its ally only if it has a just cause. Grotius, by contrast, insists that the principle that war be fought only for a just cause must override the obligations of a treaty of alliance.

The twentieth-century equivalent of Grotius's doctrine is the principle that the justice of the case, defined in relation to the purposes of international society as a whole, must override partial alliances. The disparagement of alliances, the international counterpart of Rousseau's disparagement of factions as coming between the individual and the general will, is a feature of the solidarist ideology, engendered by the League of Nations and the United Nations. According to this ideology alliances, since they come between the individual state and international society as a whole, distort its judgement of "the merits of the issue." They constitute in themselves a source of tension and discord; not a device for coping with it. Criticism of the French system of alliances in the interwar years exemplified this solidarist view. After the Second World War the solidarist view itself became an important ingredient in the Indian doctrine of nonalignment.

A fourth consequence concerns the right of states to territorial sovereignty and their corresponding duty not to intervene in one another's internal affairs. For Oppenheim the existence inside the boundaries of a state of a civil conflict in which one party may be said to have a just cause cannot be taken to qualify the duty of states to refrain from dictatorial intervention in foreign domestic conflicts. Oppenheim does recognize that intervention of this sort sometimes occurs in order to uphold minimum standards of humanity; and he concedes also that, as in the case of the intervention of the European powers in Turkey so as to uphold the rights of Christian subjects, this may be accompanied by the support of public opinion. He is also able to conceive, furthermore, that a time may arise when the law of nations will provide for humanitarian intervention, so long as this takes the form of the collective intervention of the powers (it is likely that he had in mind the collective European intervention in China at the time of the Boxer Rebellion). But he rejected any notion that a right of military intervention to enforce standards of conduct was already part of the law, his position being that the right of territorial and personal sovereignty and the duty of nonintervention were part of the constitution of international society; and that the only purposes for which they could be overridden were that of self-preservation and that of the maintenance of the balance of power. For Grotius, on the other hand, the right of a sovereign state to take up arms for a just cause applies to civil conflicts as well as international ones; kings, as well as being responsible for the safety and welfare of their subjects, are burdened with the guardianship of human rights everywhere. Although Grotius denies, along with Hobbes, that subjects may themselves justly rebel against their ruler, he holds that "nevertheless it will not follow that others may not take up arms on their behalf."[30]

It would not be possible to find much support at the present time for the view that international law confers upon international society a right of humanitarian intervention by war, still less that it bestows such a right upon particular states. Nor would there be general assent to the more general presupposition of Grotius, from which his right of humanitarian intervention is derived: that individual human beings are subjects of international law and members of international society in their own right. On the other hand a number of developments in international theory and practice in this century indicate the progress of such conceptions: on the one hand the assertion of human rights in the United Nations Charter, the Charter of the International Military Tribunal at Nuremberg, and the Declaration of Human Rights; and on the other hand, the view of some international legal theorists that individual human beings are themselves subjects of international law, or even that international law conceived as a law regulating the relations of sovereign states is ceasing to exist and is in process of giving place to a universal law of mankind.[31]

A fifth and final consequence concerns the obligation of individual human beings to bear arms on behalf of their ruler or state. For Oppenheim, who takes the view that only states are members of international society and subjects of international law, the duty of the citizen to bear arms is something upon which international law cannot have anything to say. Grotius, however, contends that if an individual subject believes the cause of the war in which he is ordered to bear arms to be unjust, he should refuse. There is no ground for contending that such a principle has become part of international law in this century. At Nuremberg the view was rejected that German soldiers, apart from being charged with having committed unjust acts in the course of the war, could be held culpable merely for having taken part in an unjust war. Such a notion is tantamount to the equation of war with murder and to the obliteration of the whole convention that there exists a society of states.

IV

The disagreement between Grotius and Oppenheim concerning the place of war in international society may be characterized in a different way. Oppenheim's theory clearly rejects the view that international society is like domestic society; and it upholds the contrary doctrine that states form a society which is unique. The theory of Grotius, by contrast, hesitates between the one view and the other.

Within the modern state there exists a government exercising a virtual monopoly of force. Above states no such government exists. If the only kind of political society that obtains is that represented by the modern state, then it may be argued that states do not form a political society; and that such prospects as may exist for the establishment of a political society on a universal scale depend upon the dismantling of the system of states and its replacement by a single, universal state. Those who have maintained that sovereign states *do* constitute a political society have done so by rejecting the model of the modern state and demonstrating that the society formed by states is one with its own special institutions and ways of working. Grotius and Oppenheim both contend that there is an international society, and they are both concerned to reject the domestic analogy. But while Oppenheim's system is free of the domestic analogy, the Grotian system makes important concessions to it.

In domestic society when violence is legitimately exercised it is as an act of law enforcement; and the rules which are recognized in relation to the use of force are calculated to place no obstacle in the path of the victory of the side representing the law. When the champions of the law clash with criminals, it is not expected that rules for the conduct of violent conflict will be observed, applying equally to both parties. Bystanders have the right to assist the victim of the crime, and the duty not to aid the criminal or to hinder the police. The chief loyalty of the citizen is to the state; in the event of a conflict between loyalty to the state and some more partial allegiance, the former must take priority. In international society as conceived by Oppenheim, however, the analogy with police action and crime is rejected. Since war is taken to be a legitimate political act of states, the consideration which informs the rules governing its conduct is not that of ensuring the victory of a just party but that of limiting the dimensions of the conflict so that the international order is not destroyed by it. The duty to observe the laws of war, the right of neutrality, the obligation of alliances, the right of sovereignty and duty of nonintervention, the silence of international law concerning the private duty to bear arms are devices for the limitation of conflict.

The position of Grotius is one of hesitancy between the domestic model and the international one. On the one hand Grotius embraces the notion that war is an act of law enforcement, substituting the idea of enforcement by particular members of society for that of enforcement by a central authority. But on the other hand he recognizes that war is a recurrent phenomenon; and that international society may be threatened by the way in which it is conducted as well as by the failure of the side representing the law to achieve victory. Thus he recognizes such institutions as the laws of war, neutrality, alliances, and nonintervention, but at the same time seeks to circumscribe their operation with qualifying clauses drawn from his doctrine of the just war.

However, although Grotius's view of international relations concedes so much more to the domestic analogy than does that of Oppenheim, it may be argued that his own originality, his "contribution," was to have assisted the movement of thought in a direction opposite to this. The place of the domestic model in *De Jure Belli ac Pacis* may be seen as a medieval residue; its novelty as lying in the stirrings it contains towards the conception of international society as a unique society, that is fully defined only by the writers of the eighteenth and nineteenth centuries. From this perspective what is remarkable in Grotius is not that he "qualified" such notions as those of the laws of war, neutrality, alliances, and sovereignty with the solidarist doctrine of just war which he inherited and adapted from the Catholic tradition. What is noteworthy is rather that he recognized these notions at all, at a time when their position had not yet become assured.

In this respect the positions of Grotius and of the twentieth-century neo-Grotians are quite distinct. Grotius stands at the birth of international society and is rightly regarded as one of its midwives. For him the terminology of a universal state is what is still normal, and the language of international relations can be spoken only with an effort. The neo-Grotians, however, have three more centuries of the theory and practice of international society behind them; their novelty lies not in moving away from the domestic model in international relations, but in moving back towards it.

A second aspect of the disagreement between Grotius and Oppenheim which may be briefly mentioned concerns the sources from which the law of nations is derived. For Oppenheim international law is the law arising from custom and treaty, and may be equated with what Grotius called the law of nations in the sense of the law arising from the will of nations or of many nations.[32] Natural law, in Oppenheim's view, forms no part of international law; and indeed he holds in addition that it does not exist. For Grotius, however, natural law is not merely a source of the law governing relations between states, alongside divine law and voluntary law; it is even taken to have a kind of primacy among the sources of the law of nations. He does not adopt the position of Pufendorf that natural law alone governs the relations between states. But he places it in a central position by arguing, on the one hand, that natural law is valid independently of divine law and cannot be overruled by it; and on the other hand that natural law is the ultimate source of the validity of voluntary law, and is itself a direct source of international law, when the positive law is silent.

For Oppenheim, then, the law judged to be binding in international society may be gauged empirically by ascertaining the rules to which the states members of that society have given their express or their tacit consent. The prescriptions of international law in the positivist view display a certain broad conformity with the movement of historical events. It is for this reason that Oppenheim takes states to be united in international society only for certain minimum purposes; and that he considers international society not to be universal, but to be limited to those states which share a certain civilization whose standards are in origin Christian and European. But for Grotius the ascertaining of the law is not merely a matter of empirical observation but, insofar as it involves the natural law, a matter of "certain fundamental conceptions which are beyond question, so that no one can deny them without doing violence to himself. For the principles of that law, if only you pay strict heed to them, are in themselves manifest and clear, almost as evident as are the things which we perceive by the external senses."[33] In the understanding of Grotius, therefore, international law need not be in conformity with the movement of events but may utter a protest against them. Thus Grotius may prescribe rules for an international society united by an area of agreement much wider than any to which it has given its consent; and he may take international society to be universal in scope, denying the distinction drawn by the expositors of the positive international law between relations among member states of international society and relations between these and barbarians. Whereas for Oppenheim the question whether or not the law distinguishes just from unjust causes of war is a matter to be determined by observation, for Grotius it is a matter settled in advance by the dictates of right reason. Moreover, whereas for Oppenheim it is an empirical question whether in any given case agreement exists as to which is the just party in a war, for Grotius the results of such an inquiry cannot alter the principle that each individual is equipped for the making of such a distinction.

A third aspect of the disagreement we have been considering concerns the membership of international society. For Oppenheim international society is composed of states, and only states possess rights and duties in international law. Individuals, in his view, may be regarded as objects of international law, as when rights and duties are conferred upon them by international agreements regarding diplomatic immunities or extradition; but these are rights and duties in the domestic law of the country concerned and do not render the recipients of them members of international society in their own right. Individuals can and do have rights and duties in other systems of rules; but in the conversation among the powers there is a convention of silence about the place in their society of their human subjects, any interruption of which is a kind of subversion. In Grotius's system, however, the members of international society are ultimately not states but individuals. The conception of a society formed by states and sovereigns is present in his thought; but its position is secondary to that of the universal community of mankind, and its legitimacy derivative from it. Grotius states in the prolegomena that he wishes to expound that body of law "which is concerned with the mutual relations among states or rulers of states,"[34] but the natural law, to which he affords primacy as a source of this law, is one which binds all human beings. The rights and duties of individuals may therefore be directly asserted in transactions between states, as we have noted in connection with the right of humanitarian intervention and the right to bear arms. Grotius's use of the conception *magna communitas humani generis* is one calculated to buttress the idea of a society of states. By asserting the bonds of natural law binding the persons who ruled states and the communities of persons of whom they are composed he sought to fill the vacuum left by the declining force of divine or ecclesiastical law and the rudimentary character of existing voluntary or positive law. At the same time the conception of a universal community of mankind is potentially destructive of the society of sovereign states, for it may be employed not only to support the rules of international society but also to assert others that undermine it.

V

The Grotian conception of international society is upheld by Vollenhoven and Lauterpacht on the ground that sovereign states cannot permit one another an unrestricted right to undertake war. According to these writers international society, different though it is from domestic, can and should be modelled upon it at least to this extent: that in it, violence is regarded as either police action or crime. The pluralist conception, which we have taken Oppenheim to exemplify and which Vattel did a great deal to establish, they dismiss as one which amounts to the admission that international society does not exist; or as one which, while asserting the existence of international society, does not allow it to be capable of that further development which in the twentieth century it can and must undergo.[35] If the Grotian conception is said to be a scheme set over and against the facts, then the reply of its defenders is that the pluralist doctrine is a cowardly submission to them. "For what is the nature of Vattel's success?" asks Vollenhoven, seeking to account for popularity of *Le Droit des Gens*. "The success of a mother who suffers herself to be bullied by her children; of a schoolmaster who abolished homework; of a cabinet minister who grants and puts down in the Estimates whatever the members of parliament come to ask of him."[36] "In the assertion of 'reason of State' and of the double standard of morality," Lauterpacht writes, "the claim to an unrestricted right of war is the most important. It is not the dagger or the poison of the hired assassin or the sharp practice of the realistic politician which expresses most truly, upon final analysis, the ideas of *'raison d'état.'* It is the infliction, without a shadow of a specific right and without a claim to any particular right, of the calamities and indignities of war and of the territorial mutilation and the very annihilation of statehood following upon defeat in war. Prior to the changes introduced by the Covenant of the League of Nations, the Pact of Paris of 1928, and the Charter of the United Nations, that central idea of 'reason of State' formed part of international law. States claimed — and had — the right to resort to war not only in order to defend their legal rights but in order to destroy the legal rights of other states."[37]

The question at issue between the Grotians and the pluralists is not one as to what is contained in the law. It is a question as to what kind of legal rules are most appropriate to the working of the international order; a matter not of international law but of international political science. The central assumption of the Grotians, as was mentioned at the outset of our inquiry, is that there exists solidarity in international society with regard to the enforcement of the law. If in fact a consensus may be reached as to the nature of the distinction between just and unjust causes of war; if the international community can be brought to agree in a particular case as to which side is engaging in police action and which in crime; if the claims of the former to represent international society as a whole are in fact given credence by the active or passive support of a preponderance of states, then it may well be that it is upon Grotian principles that the international order should be shaped. But if, on the other hand, no solidarity on these matters obtains; if international society finds itself unable to agree as to the criterion of just war; if the outbreak of war typically finds international society at large, as well as the belligerents themselves, divided as to which side embodies the just cause, then our conclusion must be a different one. It may be argued of the Grotian conception in this event not merely that it is unworkable but that it is positively damaging to the international order; that by imposing upon international society a strain which it cannot bear, it has the effect of undermining those structures of the system which might otherwise be secure. And it may be said of the pluralist doctrine that so far from constituting a disguised form of *Realpolitik,* it presents a set of prescriptions more conducive to the working of the international order than those of the Grotians.

International society will be able to enforce its law only if it can mobilize superior power in its support. The existence of a system of rules favouring the victory of the just party may facilitate the imposition of the law, as the work of the police within a modern state is assisted by the legal principles we have discussed.[38] But they will not suffice to call into being a coalition with will and force sufficient to ensure victory, where these elements are lacking. That they have been lacking in the years since the First World War, and that the provisions of the Covenant, the Paris Pact, and the Charter facilitating the victory of the just party in war have not been acted upon by an international community with solidarity enough to make a reality of them, is today well enough understood.

What is less appreciated is that the Grotian doctrine may have, and perhaps has had, an influence positively detrimental to international order. For to the extent that it influences the course of events, the doctrine that war should be fought only for a just cause is injurious to the institutions with which international society had equipped itself for the limitation of war. The qualifications that the Grotian doctrine attaches to its endorsement of institutions are such as to impede their working. If one side in an armed conflict regards itself as specially privileged by the laws of war, then reciprocal observance of these laws, which is a basic condition of their efficacy, is undermined. If a state which wishes to remain neutral nevertheless discriminates in favour of one party, then unless it does so from a position of superior strength, as did the United States when it pursued a policy of "qualified neutrality" in 1940-1941, it cannot expect to have the belligerent which suffers discrimination respect its wish. If the obligations of an alliance are to be qualified by the justice of the cause, this latter being something subjectively or arbitrarily determined, then an impediment exists to the conclusion or to the maintenance of alliances, which in the absence of a system of collective law enforcement may be held to be essential devices for the maintenance of security and order. If a right of intervention is proclaimed for the purpose of enforcing standards of conduct, and yet no consensus exists in the international community governing its use, then the door is open to interventions by particular states using such a right as a pretext, and the principle of territorial sovereignty is placed in jeopardy.

To show how in the twentieth century the influence of Grotian conceptions has in fact impeded the working of these institutions for the limitation of conflict would take us far afield. Three episodes may be mentioned, however, as having been especially influenced by the neo-Grotian doctrine. The first is the action of the League of Nations in imposing economic sanctions against Italy in 1935. The second is the trial and punishment of German and Japanese citizens by the International Military Tribunal of Nuremberg and that of the Far East, on charges of having begun an unjust war. The third is the war conducted in the name of the United Nations in Korea. None of these events could be regarded as having been brought about by the neo-Grotian doctrine; but each assumed the particular character it did in part because of that influence. The effects of these three episodes on the structure of international order were manifold and even contradictory; and it is possible to derive all sorts of lessons from them. But it might be argued in each case that the Grotian influence served to weaken devices for the limitation of conflict.

The view of the pluralists is not to be dismissed as a mere rationalization of state practice; it is a conception of international society founded upon the observation of the actual area of agreement between states and informed by a sense of the limitations within which in this situation rules may be usefully made rules of law. It seeks not to burden international law with a weight it cannot carry; and to have it leave room for the operation of those political forces, beyond the control of law, on which the existence of international society also depends. Thus although Oppenheim's exposition of the law allows war to be fought for any cause whatever, the political theory he presents does include a doctrine of just war; and it is partly in deference to this that he rejects the Grotian position. "The assertion that whereas all wars waged for political causes are unjust, all wars waged for international delinquencies are just, if there be no other way of getting reparation and satisfaction, is certainly incorrect in its generality. The evils of war are so great that, even when caused by an international delinquency, war cannot be justified if the delinquency was comparatively unimportant and trifling. And, on the other hand, under certain circumstances and conditions many political causes of war may correctly be called just causes. Only such individuals as lack insight into history and human nature can, for instance, defend the opinion that a war is unjust which has been caused by the desire for national unity or by the desire to maintain the balance of power which is the basis of all International Law."[39] It may be held one of the weaknesses of the Grotian and neo-Grotian doctrines that they do not take account of the theory of the balance of power, nor face up to the question of the relationship between the prescriptions emanating from this theory and the presciptions of international law.

Grotius is, I believe, fundamentally correct in his perception that international society cannot survive if it is to tolerate resort to war for any purpose whatever. The difference between Grotius and Oppenheim is partly explicable in terms of the fact that during the Thirty Years' War all sorts of claims were being advanced, hostile to the emergence of a society of sovereign states and a reality to its first great theoretician, that in the opening years of the twentieth century seemed remote and improbable. War to enforce the right to universal empire and war to impose a religion cannot be comprehended under the heading of "war for political causes" which Oppenheim thought international society could tolerate; and if these dangers did not seem real enough in 1905 to be worthy targets of protest, it was nevertheless still true that international society rested on the rejection of them. There is in Grotius also an awareness of a threat to international society more deadly even than these, and seeming still more remote within the confines of European international society in 1905: the war of barbarians. Grotius recognizes in addition to causes for war which are justifiable and causes which are merely persuasive (in the sense that though just causes are stated for them, these are only pretexts) a third category of causes of war which are neither justifiable nor persuasive but "wars of savages" fought without a cause of any sort.[40] Vattel also is conscious of this possible dimension of international experience and speaks of those who begin war without pretext of any kind as "monsters unworthy of the name of men," whom nations may unite to suppress.[41] If Oppenheim is correct in taking the divisions in international society to be too great to warrant an attempt to write a theory of just war into international law, it is also true that international society in his own time displayed on more fundamental matters a solidarity so great that it did not occur to him to call it in question.

But it is one thing to appreciate that international society presupposes abstention from war directed at certain ends and another to say that rules enjoining such abstention can usefully be made rules of law. Oppenheim's approach to the question of the place of law in international society was accompanied by an attitude of complacency about war and its use as an instrument of national policy which is rightly rejected today. But it may still be held that the method he employed, of gauging the role of law in international society in relation to the actual area of agreement between states is superior to one which sets up the law over and against the facts. And although the solidarity exhibited by international society may increase in the future, just as it may decrease, it can still be argued that in the twentieth century the Grotian conception has proved premature.

Notes

1. Cornelius van Vollenhoven, *The Three Stages in the Evolution of the Law of Nations* (The Hague, Nijhoff, 1919). See also his "Grotius and Geneva," *Bibliotheca Visseriana,* vol. vi, 1926.

2. Sir Hersch Lauterpacht, "The Grotian Tradition in International Law," *British Yearbook of International Law,* 1946.

3. L. Oppenheim, *International Law,* vol. i, *Peace* (Longmans, 1905), vol. ii, *War and Neutrality* (Longmans, 1906). All subsequent references are to this first edition.

4. However, one way of describing the difference between Grotius and Oppenheim would be to say that while Grotius, in his conception of international society, leans toward the doctrine that would replace it with a universal state, Oppenheim leans toward the position of *Realpolitik.*

5. *De Jure Belli ac Pacis,* translated by Francis W. Kelsey (Oxford: Clarendon Press, 1925), Prolegomena, para. 29. Cf. below, p. 91.

6. Book II, ch. i, section i. 4.

7. Prolegomena, para. 25.

8. Book II, ch. xxii.

9. Book II, ch. xxii, section xii.

10. Book II, ch. xxii, section ix.

11. Book II, ch. xxiii, especially section vi.

12. Book II, ch. xxiv, section viii.

13. Prolegomena, para. 28.

14. Book II, ch. xxv, section i. 1.

15. Book II, ch. xxv, section vi.

16. Oppenheim, *International Law,* vol. i, p. 13.

17. Grotius, book III, ch. i, section ii. 1.

18. Book III, ch. x, section i. 1.

19. Book III, ch. iii, section xi.

20. Book III, ch. iv, section iv.

21. Lauterpacht, "The Grotian Tradition," p. 5.

22. Grotius, book III, ch. xiii, section iv. 1.

23. Book II, ch. ii, section x.

24. Book II, ch. i, section xviii. 1.

25. Quoted by H. Lauterpacht in "Rules of Law in an Unlawful War," in *Law and Politics in the World Community,* ed. G. A. Lipsky (University of California Press, 1953), p. 97.

26. Ibid., p. 92.

27. Ibid., p. 56.

28. Grotius, book II, ch. xxv, section vii.

29. Oppenheim, *International Law,* vol. i, p. 528.

30. Grotius, book II, ch. xxv, section viii. 3. Cf. below, p. 119.

31. For the former view see H. Lauterpacht, *International Law and Human Rights* (Stevens, 1950). For the latter view, C. Wilfred Jenks, *The Common Law of Mankind* (Stevens, 1958).

32. Grotius uses the term *ius gentium* in two senses. The first or broad sense com-

prises all the laws governing relations between sovereigns or peoples, from whatever source they are derived. The second, narrow sense entails the law arising from the will of nations or of many nations, and may be roughly equated with what is now called positive international law.

33. Grotius, Prolegomena, para. 39.

34. Para. 1.

35. Vattel's theory bears superficial resemblances to that of Grotius but in spirit is closer to that of Oppenheim. Thus although he held the law to insist that war be fought only for a just cause, he holds that what constitutes a just cause for a particular state it alone can decide.

36. Vollenhoven, *Three Stages in the Evolution of the Law of Nations,* p. 33.

37. Lauterpacht, "The Grotian Tradition in International Law," *British Yearbook of International Law,* 1946, p. 36.

38. Ibid., p. 65.

39. Oppenheim, *International Law,* vol. ii, p. 71.

40. Grotius, book II, ch. xxii, section ii.

41. *Le Droit des Gens,* book III, ch. iii, section 34.

27

Unravelling the Future of World Order

Richard A. Falk

Albert Camus put it well back in 1946: "Living against a wall is a dog's life." Many of us are disturbed about the patterns of behavior that dominate life on earth. We approach the year 2000 as if it were a wall. To avoid despair we need to be hopeful about the future. Genuine hope, however, must rest upon an understanding of present problems of the planet and a sense of confidence abouut how to deal with them.

Such genuine hope is not very evident these days. Many people approach the destiny of the human species in a spirit of complacency, assuming that someone else will deal with them, perhaps the government, if they are or become really serious. Others are more fatalistic and have grown disgusted or frustrated by their efforts and have turned inward toward private concerns, in some cases "dropping out" altogether. Still others feel overwhelmed, awestruck by the sheer magnitude of the dangers to life on earth and are immobilized by their own impotence to act in response or by their irrelevance to the forces that dominate the world scene.

Because of these difficulties of finding a basis for response there is also a tendency for individuals to become concerned with a particular issue, as if it could be torn out of the social and political fabric of our national and global existence. To avoid beating one's head against a wall or just standing still with a dumb stare while the world crumbles around one there is a lot of action and organization that has developed around specific issues: for instance, population control, energy policy, environmental quality, conservation of nature and resources, peace, economic cooperation, social welfare, human rights, and many others. Each of these undertakings has led civic-minded people of talent and commitment to do hard work, to feel active in relation to real problems, and to seek specific social goals.

The point of this chapter is that these separate efforts can become much

Reprinted by permission of the publisher and author from Richard A. Falk, *Unravelling the Future of World Order* (pamphlet) (New York: The Fund for Peace, 1974).

more effective and satisfying if bonded in a more common strategy. One of the prime features of our world is its growing interdependence. This interdependence brings mankind closer together creating a novel awareness of the planet as a whole and of our shared dependence on its successful stewardship. The most lasting benefit of the Apollo program is likely to be its photographs of the earth as an island spinning in space, an island on which the political boundaries that have been the cause of such bloodshed and suffering seem artificial. So the idea of the unity of mankind and the oneness of the planet is sinking into our political imagination, although not yet often reflected in our behavior.

But interdependence also creates a new vulnerability as well. "The limits to growth" debate centers on the capacity of the life support systems of the earth to sustain the basic industrial ethos of continuous growth. "How much longer?" is a question on many lips. Energy resources are in short supply. An awareness of our dependence on the resources of the planet is growing, and with it, the belief, to borrow a phrase, that we live in a time of "affluence in jeopardy." Interdependence includes a sense of our belonging to nature, subject to natural forces and capacities in a very fundamental sense that we had nearly forgotten in our enchantment with the wonders of industrialization and the miracles of technology. The sweeps of flu across the planet are an expression of this interdependence with its vulnerability, and who is to say that the next sweep will not involve a lethal strain?

It suggests the potency of well-conceived disruption, whether planned by desperate men or evoked by an abused natural habitat. Hijacking, blackouts, and nuclear blackmail are examples of this new vulnerability. Ecological catastrophes associated with polluted air and water are also familiar expressions of the negative side of this interdependence.

There is a sense, as well, that the planet needs a better system of management if it is to serve mankind well in the future. Many of us feel that the earth is too crowded, that its resources are being used up too quickly, that its air, water, and land are being abused, that man's political habits associated with nationalism and war are regressive cultural traits that imperil the species, that we need a new charter for mankind that works to achieve minimum economic, social, and political rights for people everywhere. This agenda of needs is formidable and real progress depends on a set of coordinated responses. Otherwise the knot of interdependence gets pulled tighter, despite the best will in the world.

A first step is to understand that the social and political dynamics of the planet give a particular prominence to four linked sets of concerns:

- population pressure;

- environmental decay, including both pollution and the depletion of resources;
- economic, social, and political misery associated with poverty, discrimination, and repression;
- war as a human institution that appropriates valuable resources, that generates attitudes of hate, hostility, and fear, and that causes destruction and suffering.

To build a future that makes us hopeful will require a common strategy to deal with these four sets of concerns, the main strands in the world order knot. Separate groups devoted to each strand—without adequate communication and collaboration with other groups devoted to the other three concerns—overlook the vital reality of interdependence. As such, no solution can be forthcoming, and a sense of despair and impotence will eventually emerge, and the underlying distress will not be alleviated.

To assert interdependence is not, of course, to demonstrate it. We shall give some examples that may suggest the basic contours of our analysis:

- a factory on one side of the border discharges wastes into a river that flows downstream through other countries;
- farmers in the interior of India use DDT as a cheap insecticide which washes out into the oceans imperiling the food chain of many varieties of marine life;
- nuclear radiation released in the Pacific enters a mother's milk in Greenland;
- a hydroelectric dam built in Egypt deprives the soil of nutrients, causes disease-bearing snails to breed, and brings at least as much grief as relief;
- blacks in South Africa or Palestinian refugees face a life of degradation and poverty unless they join a liberation movement;
- repressive governments in many countries torture dissenters and political opponents to keep a dissatisfied population intimidated and at bay;
- the U.S. government justifies it high defense budget on the military spending and capabilities of the Soviet Union, which does the same in reverse; and so do other countries in relation to their rivals at home or abroad;
- individuals, corporations, communities, and nations all seek to increase their incomes so as to consume more and have more wealth and status and are not disposed to share with the less privileged or to limit their take in relation to long-run conservation considerations.

These examples suggest certain traits of life as it has evolved on the planet. These problems exhibit some common features that need to be taken into account:

- there is great *inequality* in living standards within and among national societies;
- there is a strong tendency to pursue *growth* and to *maximize power, wealth,* and *prestige* at all levels of social organization;
- there is a willingness and a perceived need to defend what one has and acquire what one wants or believes in by *force of arms,* including threats to destroy and kill.

Such patterns are increasingly dangerous. We are approaching ecological limits on a local, regional, and global scale. We have very complex interrelationships that are growing especially vulnerable to disruption. We have an increasing number of people who are excluded from the benefits of power, wealth, and prestige, resent this exclusion, and are prepared to act in a desperate manner if it persists. Such a condition of latent discontent stimulates efforts to prevent its activation. Rulers grow nervous. Police capabilities and prerogatives increase. Surveillance and repression become attractive options even in societies with long democratic traditions. That is, there is a link between desperation and repression, a cumulative and intensifying cycle in which each turn of events encourages a further turn. The outcome is either a police state or a bloody revolution, or possibly both in sequence. It hardly matters whether we end up gripped by fears of chaos or undermined by an orchestrated conformism. The choice between Big Brother and the hijacker as the archetype of the future is hardly worth making, at least for anyone who values the human spirit, the promise of a free society of citizens, or the potentiality of a commonwealth of nations.

On a global scale certain patterns of behavior are no longer conducive to human welfare:

- violent resolution of conflict; more broadly, "the war system" as the basis of national security and the fundamental ground of dispute settlement and grievance satisfaction;
- laissez-faire and free-market attitudes toward population policy, resource use, and environmental protection;
- attitudes based on notions of national destiny, racial superiority, and "chosen people" that vindicate inequality and missions of expansion and domination and associate honor and virtue with "winning" and "victory."

These patterns of behavior are not easy to alter and reflect very deeply engrained values that have evolved over centuries. The basic world order challenge is whether we can evolve new values that allow us to adapt to the new problems confronting mankind in this age of heightened interdependence and complexity. We do not know how much time is available to evolve these new values that will generate more suitable patterns of behavior and more sensible arrangements of power and wealth. We believe, however, that it would be much more constructive to evolve the values we need for the future by voluntary change that takes place as naturally as possible. Alternative processes of adjustment will involve trauma and breakdown of old patterns of order. We can imagine very new institutional arrangements taking shape after World War III or IV; we would assume that "the death of the oceans" or a global famine would induce a new approach to resource use, population policy, and international cooperation. Such adjustments would be exceedingly painful to experience, and would entail much destruction. We believe it is possible to work toward peaceful transitions that are not dependent on reactions to catastrophe, but only if we understand the challenge and take it seriously. There must be a link between the medication and the disease. So far as world order doctors we have been treating secondary and tertiary symptoms. Such medicine may temporarily relieve the most acute pain of the patient, but it offers no hope for a recovery. If the earth is our patient, then it is time we stopped treating it like a terminal case. We already have doctors able to diagnose the disease. We are in the midst of a crash program of research on how to achieve a lasting recovery by the quickest and most painless means. No inquiry man has made is more important than this one, because the whole future of the human species and the destiny of the planet is at stake. Can we learn how to live peacefully and justly on the planet? Can we learn soon? Can we translate our learning into behavior? Can we engender new patterns of behavior without enduring a terrifying war between the forces wedded to the old order of things and the new forces dedicated to meeting this survival challenge?

The key to success is whether we can *learn* what is needed soon enough and *persuade* most people. In a societal sense what is needed is a change in values, or at least a change in priorities with respect to how we organize our lives at all levels, from individual existence to global relations. We in the United States are wonderfully situated to participate in this great drama of the future of the human race. Our power and affluence, our technological prowess, the openness, diversity, and size of our society, and our pride as a nation all endow us with an extraordinary opportunity to embody a new order of planetary existence in our individual lives and in our social and political arrangements. Others have commented on this hopeful possibility, noting the vitality of "the counterculture," the use of environmental awareness, and the widespread experimentation with new life-styles.

But America is also a place where the challenge assumes such terrifying proportions. In our decaying, drugged, and violent cities with their frequent halos of poison and with their invariable neon wastelands of stores and services catering an automobile-obsessive culture, we can experience the challenge in its most concentrated form. But, as well, with our silos of missiles targeted to destroy distant hostage cities we can sense the mindlessness of what we call "security." These realities are the excesses of earlier strengths. We developed a powerful and successful society by allowing individuals to pursue their self-interest with maximum freedom and by rewarding them with power and prestige to the extent of their success. "Winners" were the true heroes; "growth" was the dynamic both of *progress* for the society as a whole and of *justice* by making more available simultaneously for all social sectors and all needs. Government was entrusted with keeping this system working smoothly and in making sure that our people and their land were not imperiled by external enemies. Of course, this is a simplification, but it expresses the basic character of the social contract between the governers and the governed. So long as there was space to expand and resources to fuel the dynamism of the economy such a system was basically a remarkable success. Surely, there were wastes and costs, "depressions" in the economy and wars abroad, but the integrity of the country and its forward momentum seemed assured and definite.

The very success gave rise to the dangers that now beset us. Too much industrial capacity has overloaded the environment in numerous ways; as well, industrial expansion entails a drain on resource stocks and there are signs that critical limits are being approached very rapidly. We can understand the notion of limits when we visit national parks and museums that grow more crowded each year. At some level of use the crowds grow so dense that the resource loses its value. The Soviet Union after having preached for years about culture for the masses as a free good in a socialist society faces a profound crisis. The famed collection in the Hermitage Museum is being damaged by the number of visitors and by the moisture of their breath. So a decision must be made: either jeopardize the paintings or terminate the policy of open admission. In a sense this choice faces the whole planet. We need more planning, more sense of limits, more prudence and restraint, more disposition toward compromise and moderation if we are to save the planet from decay and imminent catastrophe.

We need to develop rapidly the values of this kind of new global context. We need to use the technological resources at our disposal to lengthen the time available for value change by evolving pollution-free technologies and by gaining access to ocean resources, new energy sources, and cheaper ore grades. But *technological innovation* is no substitute for *value change*. We can no more leave the future of the planet to technical experts than we can leave it to the government.

Nor can we assume that new economic structures will automatically adapt to the requirements of the modern age. The multinational corporation—in all of its manifoldness—is a wonderfully exciting extension of economic activity. Indeed, the multinational managers may be "the new globalists" who aspire out of self-interest to a unified world order, or at least, are driven to prefer a world without boundaries to the anarchic state system that we have been struggling to keep in being these last several decades. This corporate universalism is a powerful force available to neutralize nationalism and statism in the non-Communist world. As such, it gives world order reformers a potency that never existed when the world without boundaries was nothing more than a gleam in a dreamy head. At the same time, the corporation is organized, above all, around profits and growth. Although the record is mixed, there is no reason to assume a sense of corporate responsibility with respect to the social, political, and ecological needs of life on the planet. The multinational corporation is part of the problem, as well as the solution, and neither impact should be overlooked. Often we find apologists looking to corporate universalism as the agent of rescue and critics considering the expansion of multinational business as the shoals of shipwreck.

In this time of complexity and specialization there is a great impulse to isolate some single factor as the fundamental need. Some are convinced that the root of the problem is population pressure, that we should mobilize all our energy to turn off the population bomb before its time fuse ticks to the moment of ignition. Others counsel a life of austerity, alleging that it is the way we live that forces up the GNP and per-capita energy consumption to such high levels. Still others argue that we need disarmament, an end to war, or else we will blow ourselves up. Some contend that we must first get rid of misery and deprivation or else people will not stop having children or renounce reliance on desperate tactics of reform. We argue that there is no fundamental factor, that each of these concerns is part of the misfit that now exists between man's life-style and arrangements of power and wealth and his longer-term well-being as a species, that we have a knot of many strands that must be unravelled altogether.

Population will not decisively decline or stabilize until people feel that life is worth living, that problems of poverty have been largely solved. Similarly, the deprived (and hence the privileged) will not renounce the instruments or dispositions toward violence until some sense of social justice exists and nonviolent procedures of change are established. War is the other face of peaceful change. Life cannot be frozen into a status quo.

On a planet of limits and scarce resources there is a need to stabilize consumption at some level. The idea of growth is positive so long as it is not rigidly linked to material output. Indeed, we want to discover ways of growth appropriate to our postindustrial condition, but we also need to be sure that curtailed growth by the rich does not enmire the poor in permanent poverty. In adjusting to limits we seek both an equilibrium with nature and a new social contract that acknowledges the *dignity* of all people and provides the *equity* that is a necessary precondition of dignity.

In other words, values associated with a peaceful, just, and ecologically viable world are very closely linked. We do not yet have enough information and knowledge to assess the full extent or proximity of danger, nor to prescribe the exact shape of social, economic, and political arrangements needed to sustain the planet, but we do know about the values and orientation that can get us started in the right direction.

What is needed now, above all else, is a concert of action to build a social consensus around this orientation and its values. Such a concert would be immeasurably strengthened by the acceptance of this goal by all individuals and groups dedicated at present to the pursuit of some separate, specialized aspect of the whole. We believe that not only is the whole greater than the sum of its parts, but that the parts will become much stronger because of their link to the whole. Thus for groups in the area of population policy, peace studies, environmental and resource policy, development aid and social welfare, and human rights to join together in their affirmation of their interdependence of concerns and their endorsement of some new directions in human values would mark a dramatic step in the history of human enlightenment, a possible Magna Carta for the long difficult work of bringing to people genuine hope in the future of mankind and in the viability of peaceful and just patterns of life on the planet. Without a fundamental ethical reorientation other efforts at planetary reform will fail. Anything more at this stage would risk plunging the world into some new flaming realm of oppression. We need to cooperate with one another to build a strong movement for individual, community, national, and global reform, which forsakes neither the urgency of its mission nor the preciousness of human guidance. Only so can we unravel the knot of many folds that now has roped us into a false bind.

Selected Bibliography

This bibliography is deliberately short, listing only important books under a general category as well as under nine topical categories following the structure of the book. Scholarly articles, with a few exceptions that are cited in the text of the introductory essays, are excluded. A work already listed under one category is not repeated under another category. The reader should consult a variety of references quoted or listed in each of the chapters in the book.

General Works

Alcock, N. Z. 1972. *The War Disease*. Oakville, Ontario: Canadian Peace Research Institute Press.

Allport, Gordon W. 1968. *The Person in Psychology*. Boston: Beacon Press.

Beitz, C. B., and Theodore, H., eds. 1973. *Peace and War*. San Francisco: W. H. Freeman and Co.

Blainey, G. 1973. *The Causes of War*. New York: Free Press.

Bramson, L., and Goethals, G. W., eds. 1968. *War: Studies from Psychology, Sociology, Anthropology*. New York: Basic Books.

Choucri, N., and North, R. 1975. *Nations in Conflict*. San Francisco: W. H. Freeman and Co.

Clausewitz, Carl. 1976. *On War*. Edited and translated by Michael Howard and Peter Paret. Princeton: Princeton University Press.

Falk, R. A., and Mendlovitz, S. H., eds. 1966. *The Strategy of World Order: Toward a Theory of War Prevention*, vol. 1. New York: World Law Fund.

Fisher, R., ed. 1964. *International Conflict and Behavioral Science*. New York: Basic Books.

Haas, M. 1974. *International Conflict*. Indianapolis and New York: The Bobbs-Merrill Co.

McNamara, R. S. 1968. *The Essence of Security*. New York: Harper & Row.

McNeil, E. B., ed. 1965. *The Nature of Human Conflict*. Englewood Cliffs, N.J.: Prentice-Hall.

Millis, W., and Real, J. 1963. *The Abolition of War.* New York: Macmillan.

Prosterman, R. L. 1972. *Surviving to 3000.* Belmont, Calif.: Duxbury Press.

Pruitt, D. G., and Snyder, R. C., eds. 1969. *Theory and Research on the Causes of War.* Englewood Cliffs, N.J.: Prentice-Hall.

Richardson, L. F. 1960a. *Arms and Insecurity.* Pittsburgh: Boxwood Press.

_____. 1960b. *Statistics of Deadly Quarrels.* Pittsburgh: Boxwood Press.

Singer, J. D., and Small, M. 1972. *The Wages of War 1816-1965: A Statistical Handbook.* New York: John Wiley & Sons.

Shawcross, W. 1979. *Sideshow: Kissinger, Nixon, and the Destruction of Cambodia.* New York: Simon & Schuster.

Snyder, G. H., and Diesing, P. 1977. *Conflict Among Nations.* Princeton: Princeton University Press.

Sorokin, P. A. 1937. *Social and Cultural Dynamics,* vol. 3. New York: American Book Co.

Waltz, K. N. 1959. *Man, the State and War.* New York: Columbia University Press.

Wright, Q. 1965. *A Study of War.* 2nd ed. Chicago: University of Chicago Press.

Moral and Philosophical Inquiries

Bainton, R. H. 1960. *Christian Attitudes Toward War and Peace.* New York: Abingdon Press.

Bennett, J. C. 1962. *Nuclear Weapons and the Christian Conscience.* New York: Scribner.

Bondurant, J. V., ed. 1971. *Conflict: Violence and Nonviolence.* Chicago and New York: Aldine-Atherton Press.

_____. 1971. *Conquest of Violence: The Gandhian Philosophy of Conflict.* Rev. ed. Berkeley: University of California Press.

Brandt, R. B. 1973. *War and Moral Responsibility.* Princeton: Princeton University Press.

Camus, A. 1960. *Resistance, Rebellion and Death.* New York: Random House.

Erikson, E. H. 1969. *Gandhi's Truth.* New York: W. W. Norton & Co.

Gallie, W. B. 1978. *Philosophers of Peace and War.* New York: Cambridge University Press.

Gray, J. G. 1970. *On Justifying Violence Philosophically.* New York: Harper & Row.

Johnson, J. T. 1975. *Ideology, Reason, and the Limitation of War.* Princeton: Princeton University Press.

Kant, I. 1914. *Eternal Peace and Other International Essays.* Translated by W. Hastie. Boston: The World Peace Foundation.

Mao Tse-tung. 1966. *Selected Military Writings of Mao Tse-tung.* Peking: Foreign Languages Press.

Osgood, R. E., and Tucker, R. W. 1967. *Force, Order, and Justice.* Baltimore: Johns Hopkins University Press.

Peannock, J. R., and Chapman, J. W., eds. 1978. *Anarchism.* New York: New York University Press.

Potter, R. B. 1969. *War and Moral Discourse.* Richmond, Va.: John Knox Press.

Ramsey, P. 1968. *The Just War.* New York: Scribner.

Sharp, G. 1970. *Exploring Nonviolent Alternatives.* Boston: Porter Sargent, Publisher.

Tucker, R. W. 1960. *The Just War: A Study of Contemporary Doctrine.* Baltimore: The Johns Hopkins University Press.

Walzer, M. 1977. *Just and Unjust Wars: A Moral Argument with Historical Illustrations.* New York: Basic Books.

Wasserstrom, R., ed., 1970. *War and Morality.* Belmont, Calif.: Wadsworth.

Zahn, G. C. 1967. *War, Conscience and Dissent.* New York: Hawthorn Books.

Ethological and Psychological Inquiries

Ardrey, R. 1966. *The Territorial Imperative.* New York: Atheneum.

Bandura, A. 1973. *Aggression: A Social Learning Analysis.* Englewood Cliffs, N.J.: Prentice-Hall.

Bandura, A., and Walters, R. H. 1959. *Adolescent Aggression.* New York: Ronald Press.

———. 1963. *Social Learning and Personality Development.* New York: Holt, Rinehart & Winston, Inc.

Berkowitz, L. 1962. *Aggression: A Social Psychological Analysis.* New York: McGraw-Hill Book Co.

Buss, A. H. 1961. *The Psychology of Aggression.* New York: Wiley.

Carthy, J. D., and Ebling, F. J., eds. 1964. *Natural History of Aggression.* London: Academic Press.

Dollard, J., et al. 1939. *Frustration and Aggression.* New Haven: Yale University Press.

Dunn, F. 1950. *War and the Minds of Men.* New York: Harper & Row.

Durbin, E.F.M., and Bowlby, J. [1939] 1968. Personal Aggressiveness and War. In *War,* ed. L. Bramson and G. W. Goethals. New York: Basic Books.

Eibl-Eibesfeldt, I. 1970. *Ethology: The Biology of Behavior.* New York: Holt, Rinehart & Winston.

———. 1972. *Love and Hate: The Natural History of Behavior Patterns.* Tr. G. Strachan. New York: Holt, Rinehart & Winston.

Freedman, J. L. 1975. *Crowding and Behavior.* San Francisco: W. H. Freeman and Co.

Freud, S. 1968. Why War? In *War,* ed. L. Bramson and G. W. Goethals. New York: Basic Books.

———. 1962. Civilization and Its Discontents. Tr. and ed. J. Strachey. New York: W. W. Norton & Co.

Fornari, F. 1974. *The Psychoanalysis of War.* New York: Anchor Books.

Fromm, E. 1973. *The Anatomy of Human Destructiveness.* New York: Holt, Rinehart & Winston.

Klineberg, O. 1950. *Tensions Affecting International Understanding: A Survey of Research.* New York: Social Science Research Council.

———. 1964. *The Human Dimension in International Relations.* New York: Holt, Rinehart & Winston.

Lorenz, K. 1966. *On Aggression.* New York: Harcourt, Brace & World.

Montagu, A., ed. 1973. *Man and Aggression.* 2nd ed. New York: Oxford University Press.

Osgood, C. E. 1962. *Alternative to War or Surrender.* Urbana: University of Illinois Press.

Scott, J. P. 1958. *Aggression.* Chicago: University of Chicago Press.

Storr, A. 1970. *Human Aggression.* New York: Bantam Books.

Tiger, L. 1970. *Men in Groups.* New York: Vintage Books.

Toch, H. 1969. *Violent Men: An Inquiry into the Psychology of Violence.* Chicago: Aldine.

Wilson, E. O. 1975. *Sociobiology: The New Synthesis.* Cambridge: Harvard University Press.

_____. 1978. *On the Human Nature.* Cambridge: Harvard University Press.

Cultural and Anthropological Inquiries

Benedict, R. 1946. *The Chrysanthemum and the Sword.* Boston: Houghton Mifflin.

Bohannon, P., ed. 1967. *Law and Warfare: Studies in the Anthropology of Conflict.* Garden City, N.Y.: The Natural History Press.

Boulding, K. E. 1967. Am I a Man or a Mouse—or Both? *War/Peace Report,* (March), pp. 14-17.

Chagnon, N. A. 1968. *Yanomamö: The Fierce People.* New York: Holt, Rinehart & Winston.

Fried, M.; Harris, M.; and Murphy, R. 1968. *War: The Anthropology of Armed Conflict and Aggression.* Garden City, N.Y.: The Natural History Press.

Givens, R. D., and Nettleship, M. A. 1976. *Discussions on War and Human Aggression.* The Hague: Mouton Publishers.

Gluckman, M. 1963. *Order and Rebellion in Tribal Africa.* New York: Free Press.

Harris, M. 1977. *Cannibals and Kings.* New York: Random House.

Melko, M. 1969. *52 Peaceful Societies.* Oakville, Ontario: Canadian Peace Research Institute Press.

Montagu, A., ed. 1974. *Culture and Human Development.* Englewood Cliffs, N.J.: Prentice-Hall.

_____. 1976. *The Nature of Human Aggression.* New York: Oxford University Press.

Narroll, R. 1966. Does Military Deterrence Deter? *Trans-Action* 3:14-20.

Nettleship, M. A.; Givens, R. D.; and Nettleship, A. 1975. *War, Its Causes and Correlates.* The Hague: Mouton Publishers.

Otterbein, K. F. 1970. *The Evolution of War: A Cross-Cultural Study.* New Haven: Human Relations Area Files Press.

Turney-High, H. H. 1949. *Primitive War: Its Practice and Concepts.* Columbia: University of South Carolina Press.

UNESCO. 1973. *International Repertory of Institutions for Peace and Conflict Research.*

Sociopsychological Inquiries

Adorno, T., et al. 1950. *The Authoritarian Personality.* New York: Harper & Row.

Allport, G. 1954. *The Nature of Prejudice.* Cambridge: Addison-Wesley.

Buchanan, W., and Cantril, H. *How Nations See Each Other: A Study in Public Opin-*

ion. Urbana: University of Illinois Press.

Cantril, H., ed. 1950. *Tensions That Cause Wars.* Urbana: University of Illinois Press.

Durbin, E.F.M., and Bowlby, J. 1939. *Personal Aggressiveness and War.* London: Kegan Paul.

Frank, J. 1968. *Sanity and Survival.* New York: Vintage Books.

Gurr, T. R. 1970. *Why Men Rebel.* Princeton: Princeton University Press.

Janis, I. L. 1972. *Victims of Groupthink.* Boston: Houghton Mifflin.

Kelman, H. C., ed. 1965. *International Behavior: A Social-Psychological Analysis.* New York: Rinehart & Winston.

Larsen, K. S. 1976. *Aggression: Myths and Models.* Chicago: Nelson-Hall.

Lasswell, H. D. 1935. *World Politics and Personal Insecurity.* New York: McGraw-Hill.

Singer, J. D., ed. 1965. *Human Behavior and International Politics: Contributions from the Social-Psychological Sciences.* Chicago: Rand McNally.

Thomas, W. I. 1928. *The Child in America.* New York: Knopf.

White, R. K. *Nobody Wanted War.* New York: Doubleday.

Williams, R. M. 1947. The Reduction of Intergroup Tensions. *SSRC Bulletin* 57.

Sociological Inquiries

Barnet, R. J. 1972. *Roots of War.* New York: Atheneum.

Bernard, J. 1957. The Sociological Study of Conflict. In *The Nature of Conflict: Studies on the Sociological Aspects of International Tensions,* pp. 33-117. Paris: UNESCO.

Coser, L. 1956. *The Functions of Social Conflict.* New York: Free Press.

Dahrendorf, R. 1959. *Class and Class Conflict in Industrial Society.* Rev. and enl. ed. Stanford: Stanford University Press.

Eckstein, H., ed. 1964. *Internal War.* New York: Free Press.

Gluckman, M. 1956. *Custom and Conflict in Africa.* Glencoe, Ill.: Free Press.

Graham, H. D., and Gurr, T. R. 1969. *Violence in America.* Washington, D.C.: Government Printing Office.

Haas, M. 1968. Social Change and National Aggressiveness, 1900-1960. In *Quantitative International Politics,* ed. J. D. Singer, pp. 215-244. New York: Free Press.

Merton, R. K. 1949. *Social Theory and Social Structure.* Glencoe, Ill.: Free Press.

Millis, C. W. 1956. *The Power Elite.* New York: Oxford University Press.

National Commission on the Causes and Prevention of Violence. 1969. *To Establish Justice, to Insure Domestic Tranquility.* Washington, D.C.: Government Printing Office.

Parsons, T. 1951. *The Social System.* Glencoe, Ill.: Free Press.

Rosenau, J. N., ed. 1969. *Linkage Politics.* New York: Free Press.

Rummel, R. J. 1963. Testing Some Possible Predictors of Conflict Behavior Within and Between Nations. *Peace Research Society Papers* 1:79-111.

_____. 1968. The Relationship Between National Attributes and Foreign Conflict Behavior. In *Quantitative International Politics,* ed. J. D. Singer, pp. 187-214. New York: Free Press.

_____. 1973. Dimensions of Conflict Behavior Within and Between Nations. In

Conflict Behavior & Linkage Politics, ed. J. Wilkenfeld, pp. 59-106. New York: David McKay Co.

Simmel, G. 1955. *Conflict: The Web of Group Affiliations.* Glencoe, Ill.: Free Press.

Surgeon General's Scientific Advisory Committee on Television and Social Behavior. 1972. *Television and Growing Up: The Impact of Televised Violence.* Washington, D.C.: Government Printing Office.

Tanter, R. 1966. Dimensions of Conflict Behavior Within and Between Nations, 1958-1960. *Journal of Conflict Resolution* 10:41-64.

UNESCO. 1957. *The Nature of Conflict: Studies on the Sociological Aspects of International Tensions.* Paris: UNESCO.

United States Kerner Commission Report. 1968. Washington, D.C.: U.S. Government Printing Office.

United States President's Commission on Law Enforcement and Administration of Justice. 1967. *The Challenge of Crime in a Free Society.* Washington, D.C.: U.S. Government Printing Office.

Weber, J. 1978. *Economy and Society* (edited by Guenther, Roth, and Wittich). Berkeley: University of California Press.

Wilkenfeld, J., ed. 1973. *Conflict Behavior and Linkage Politics.* New York: David McKay Co.

Socioeconomic Inquiries

Amin, S. 1973. *L'échange inégal et la loi de la valeur.* Paris: Anthropos.

———. 1976. *Unequal Development.* New York: Monthly Review Press.

———. 1977. *Imperialism and Unequal Development.* New York: Monthly Review Press.

Benoit, E., ed. 1967. *Disarmament and World Economic Interdependence.* New York: Columbia University Press.

———, and Boulding, K. E., eds. 1963. *Disarmament and the Economy.* New York: Harper & Row.

Boulding, K. E., ed. 1970. *Peace and the War Industry.* New Brunswick: Transaction Books.

———, and Gleason, A. H. 1965. War As an Investment: The Strange Case of Japan. *Peace Research Society Papers* 3:1-17.

———, and Mukerjee, T., eds. 1972. *Economic Imperialism.* Ann Arbor: University of Michigan Press.

Burin, F. S. 1963. The Communist Doctrine of the Inevitability of War. *American Political Science Review* 62:334-354.

Cardoso, F. H. 1973. Associated-Dependent Development: Theoretical and Practical Implications. In *Authoritarian Brazil,* ed. A. Stepan, pp. 142-176. New Haven: Yale University Press.

Cohen, B. J. 1973. *The Question of Imperialism.* New York: Basic Books.

Fann, K. T., and Hodges, D. C., eds. 1971. *Readings in U.S. Imperialism.* Boston: Porter Sargent, Publisher.

Frank, A. G. 1967. *Capitalism and Underdevelopment in Latin America.* New York: Monthly Review Press.

————. 1975. *On Capitalist Underdevelopment.* New York: Oxford University Press.

Galtung, J. 1978. *Peace and Social Structure.* Copenhagen: Christian Ejlers.

Hobson, J. [1902] 1948. *Imperialism: A Study.* 3rd ed. London: Allen & Unwin.

Hu Sheng. 1955. *Imperialism and Chinese Politics.* Peking: Foreign Languages Press.

Jalée, P. 1972. *Imperialism in the Seventies.* Tr. R. and M. Sokolov. New York: The Third Press.

Kemp, T. 1967. *Theories of Imperialism.* London: Dobson Books.

Lenin, V. I. [1917] 1947. *Imperialism: The Highest Stage of Capitalism.* Moscow: Foreign Languages Publishing House.

Lichtheim, G. 1971. *Imperialism.* New York: Praeger.

Magdoff, H. 1969. *The Age of Imperialism.* New York: Monthly Review Press.

Melman, S. 1970. *The War Economy.* New York: Oxford University Press.

————. 1974. *The Permanent War Economy.* New York: Simon and Schuster.

Rhodes, R. I., ed. 1970. *Imperialism and Underdevelopment.* New York: Monthly Review Press.

Robbins, L. 1939. *The Economic Causes of War.* London: Cape.

Rosen, S., ed. 1973. *Testing the Theory of the Military-Industrial Complex.* Lexington, Mass.: D. C. Heath.

————, and Kurth, J., ed. 1974. *Testing the Theory of Economic Imperialism.* Lexington, Mass.: D.C. Heath.

Russett, B. M. 1970. *What Price Vigilance?* New Haven: Yale University Press.

Sarkesian, S., ed. 1972. *The Military-Industrial Complex: A Reassessment.* Beverly Hills: Sage Publications.

Schumpeter, J. [1919] 1951. *Imperialism and Social Classes.* New York: Kelley.

Thayer, G. 1969. *The War Business.* New York: Simon and Schuster.

Winslow, E. M. 1948. *The Pattern of Imperialism.* New York: Columbia University Press.

Wolfe, M. 1972. *The Economic Causes of Imperialism.* New York: Wiley.

Decisionmaking Inquiries

Allison, G. 1971. *The Essence of Decision.* Boston: Little, Brown.

Axelrod, R., ed. 1976. *Structure of Decision.* Princeton: Princeton University Press.

Bobrow, D. B.; Chan, S.; and Kringen, J. A. 1979. *Understanding Foreign Policy Decisions: The Chinese Case.* New York: Free Press.

Braybrooke, D., and Lindblom, C. E. 1963. *A Strategy of Decision: Policy Evaluation as a Social Process.* New York: Free Press.

Halperin, M. 1974. *Bureaucratic Politics and Foreign Policy.* Washington, D.C.: Brookings.

Hart, J. A. 1977. Cognitive Maps of Three Latin American Policy Makers. *World Politics* 30:115-140.

Hermann, C. F. 1969. *Crises in Foreign Policy: A Simulation Analysis.* Indianapolis: Bobbs-Merrill.

————, ed. 1972. *International Crises: Insights from Behavioral Research.* New York: Free Press.

Hilsman, R. 1967. *To Move a Nation: The Politics of Foreign Policy in the Administration of John F. Kennedy.* Garden City, N.J.: Doubleday.

Holsti, O. R. 1972. *Crisis, Escalation, War.* Montreal and London: McGill-Queen's University Press.

Janis, I. L., and Mann, L. 1977. *Decision Making: A Psychological Analysis of Conflict, Choice, and Commitment.* New York: Free Press.

Jervis, R. 1970. *The Logic of Images in International Relations.* Princeton: Princeton University Press.

_____. 1976. *Perception and Misperception in International Politics.* Princeton: Princeton University Press.

Paige, G. D. 1968. *The Korean Decision.* New York: Free Press.

_____. 1977. *On Values and Sciences:* The Korean Decision Reconsidered. *American Political Science Review* 71:1603-1609.

Snyder, R. C.; Bruck, H. W.; and Sapin, B. 1954. *Decision-Making as an Approach to the Study of International Politics.* Foreign Policy Analysis Series No. 3. Princeton University Organizational Behavior Section.

Snyder, R. C., et al., eds. 1962. *Foreign Policy Decision-Making: An Approach to the Study of International Politics.* New York: Free Press.

von Neumann, J., and Morgenstern, O. 1944. *Theory of Games and Economic Behavior.* 3rd ed. New York: Wiley.

Whiting, A. S. 1960. *China Crosses the Yalu: The Decision to Enter the Korean War.* New York: Macmillan.

International Systemic Inquiries

Aron, R. [1962] 1968. *Peace and War: A Theory of International Relations.* Tr. R. Howard and A. B. Fox. New York: Praeger.

Burton, J. W. 1969. *Conflict and Communication: The Use of Controlled Communication in International Relations.* New York: Free Press.

Butterworth, R. L. 1976. *Managing Interstate Conflict, 1945-74: Data with Synopses.* University Center for International Studies: University of Pittsburgh.

Falk, R. A. 1977. Contending Approaches to World Order. *Journal of International Affairs* 31:171-98.

Kahn, H. 1960. *On Thermonuclear War.* Princeton: Princeton University Press.

_____. [1965] 1968. *On Escalation.* Baltimore: Penguin Books.

Kaplan, M. A. 1957. *System and Process in International Politics.* New York: Wiley.

Kende, I. 1978. Wars of Ten Years (1967-1976). *Journal of Peace Research* 15:227-241.

Knorr, K. E., and Verba, S., eds. 1961. *The International System: Theoretical Essays.* Princeton: Princeton University Press.

McClelland, C. A. 1966. *Theory and the International System.* New York: Macmillan.

Midlarsky, M. I. 1975. *On War: Political Violence in the International System.* New York: Free Press.

Rosecrance, R. 1963. *Action and Reaction in World Politics: International Systems in Perspective.* Boston: Little, Brown.

_____. 1973. *International Relations: Peace or War?* New York: McGraw-Hill.

Rosen, S., ed. 1969. *A Survey of World Conflicts.* Pittsburgh: University of Pittsburgh

Center for International Studies Preliminary Paper.

Russett, B. C., ed. 1972. *Peace, War and Numbers*. Beverly Hills: Sage Publications.

————. 1974. *Power and Community in World Politics*. San Francisco: W. H. Freeman and Co.

Schelling, T. C. 1963. *The Strategy of Conflict*. New York: Oxford University Press.

Singer, J. D., and Small, M. 1972. *The Wages of War, 1816-1965: A Statistical Handbook*. New York: Wiley.

Smoke, R. 1977. *War: Controlling Escalation*. Cambridge: Harvard University Press.

Wallace, M. D. 1973. *War and Rank Among Nations*. Lexington, Mass.: D. C. Heath.

Young, O. R. 1967. *The Intermediaries: Third Parties in International Crisis*. Princeton: Princeton University Press.

Normative Inquiries

Beres, L. R., and Targ, H. R. 1977. *Constructing Alternative World Futures*. Cambridge: Schenckman Publishing Co.

Bull, H. 1977. *The Anarchical Society: A Study of Order in World Politics*. New York: Columbia University Press.

Black, C. E., and Falk, R. A., eds. 1969-1972. *The Future of International Legal Order*, vols. 1-4. Princeton: Princeton University Press.

Chayes, A. 1974. *The Cuban Missile Crisis*. New York: Oxford University Press.

Clark, G., and Sohn, L. B. 1966. *World Peace Through World Law*. 3rd ed. Cambridge: Harvard University Press.

Deutsch, K., and Hoffman, S., eds. 1971. *The Relevance of International Law*. New York: Anchor Books.

Falk, R. A. 1968. *Legal Order in a Violent World*. Princeton: Princeton University Press.

————. 1970. *The Status of Law in International Society*. Princeton: Princeton University Press.

————. 1975. *A Study of Future Worlds*. New York: Free Press.

————, ed. 1967-1976. *The Vietnam War and International Law*, vols. 1-4. Princeton: Princeton University Press.

————, and Mendlovitz, S., eds. 1966. *The Strategy of World Order*, vols. 1-4. New York: World Law Fund.

Grotius, H. [1625] 1962. *The Law of War and Peace: De jure belli ac pacis*. Tr. F. W. Kelsey. Indianapolis: Bobbs-Merrill.

Hoffman, S. 1978. *Primary or World Order*. New York: McGraw-Hill.

Kelsen, H. (rev. by Tucker, R. W.) 1966. *Principles of International Law*. 2nd ed. New York: Holt, Rinehart & Winston.

Lepawsky, A., ed. 1971. *The Search for World Order*. New York: Appleton Century-Crofts.

Mendlovitz, S., ed. 1975. *On the Creation of a Just World Order*. New York: Free Press.

McDougal, M. S., and Feliciano, F. P. 1961. *Law and Minimum World Public Order*.

New Haven: Yale University Press.

Mische, G., and Mische, P. 1977. *Toward a Human World Order*. New York: Paulist Press.

Moore, J. N., ed. 1974. *Law and Civil War in the Modern World*. Baltimore: Johns Hopkins University Press.

Northedge, F. S., ed. 1974. *The Use of Force in International Relations*. New York: Free Press.

Reisman, W. M., and Weston, B. H., eds. 1976. *Toward World Order and Human Dignity*. New York: Free Press.

Report to the Club of Rome, 1976. *Reshaping the International Order*. New York: E. P. Dutton.

Sivard, R. L. 1978. *World Military and Social Expenditures 1978*. Leesburg, Va.: WMSE Publications.

Stone, J. 1958. *Aggression and World Order*. Westport, Conn.: Greenwood Press.

————. 1954. *Legal Controls of International Conflict*. Sydney, Aust.: Maitland Publications.

Vincent, R. J. 1974. *Nonintervention and International Order*. Princeton: Princeton University Press.

Books Written Under the Auspices of the Center of International Studies, Princeton University, 1952-1979

Gabriel A. Almond, *The Appeals of Communism* (Princeton University Press, 1954).

William W. Kaufmann, ed., *Military Policy and National Security* (Princeton University Press, 1956).

Klaus Knorr, *The War Potential of Nations* (Princeton University Press, 1956).

Lucian W. Pye, *Guerrilla Communism in Malaya* (Princeton University Press, 1956).

Charles De Visscher, *Theory and Reality in Public International Law,* trans. by P. E. Corbett (Princeton University Press, 1957; rev. ed., 1968).

Bernard C. Cohen, *The Political Process and Foreign Policy: The Making of the Japanese Peace Settlement* (Princeton University Press, 1957).

Myron Weiner, *Party Politics in India: The Development of a Multi-Party System* (Princeton University Press, 1957).

Percy E. Corbett, *Law in Diplomacy* (Princeton University Press, 1959).

Rolf Sannwald and Jacques Stohler, *Economic Integration: Theoretical Assumptions and Consequences of European Unification,* trans. by Herman Karreman (Princeton University Press, 1959).

Klaus Knorr, ed., *NATO and American Security* (Princeton University Press, 1959).

Gabriel A. Almond and James S. Coleman, eds., *The Politics of the Developing Areas* (Princeton University Press, 1960).

Herman Kahn, *On Thermonuclear War* (Princeton University Press, 1960).

Sidney Verba, *Small Groups and Political Behavior: A Study of Leadership* (Princeton University Press, 1961).

Robert J. C. Butow, *Tojo and the Coming of the War* (Princeton University Press, 1961).

Glenn H. Snyder, *Deterrence and Defense: Toward a Theory of National Security* (Princeton University Press, 1961).

Klaus Knorr and Sidney Verba, eds., *The International System: Theoretical Essays* (Princeton University Press, 1961).

Peter Paret and John W. Shy, *Guerrillas in the 1960's* (Praeger, 1962).

George Modelski, *A Theory of Foreign Policy* (Praeger, 1962).

Klaus Knorr and Thornton Read, eds., *Limited Strategic War* (Praeger, 1963).

Frederick S. Dunn, *Peace-Making and the Settlement with Japan* (Princeton University Press, 1963).

Arthur L. Burns and Nina Heathcote, *Peace-Keeping by United Nations Forces* (Praeger, 1963).

Richard A. Falk, *Law, Morality, and War in the Contemporary World* (Praeger, 1963).

James N. Rosenau, *National Leadership and Foreign Policy: A Case Study in the Mobilization of Public Support* (Princeton University Press, 1963).

Gabriel A. Almond and Sidney Verba, *The Civic Culture: Political Attitudes and Democracy in Five Nations* (Princeton University Press, 1963).

Bernard C. Cohen, *The Press and Foreign Policy* (Princeton University Press, 1963).

Richard L. Sklar, *Nigerian Political Parties: Power in an Emergent African Nation* (Princeton University Press, 1963).

Peter Paret, *French Revolutionary Warfare from Indochina to Algeria: The Analysis of a Political and Military Doctrine* (Praeger, 1964).

Harry Eckstein, ed., *Internal War: Problems and Approaches* (Free Press, 1964).

Cyril E. Black and Thomas P. Thornton, eds., *Communism and Revolution: The Strategic Uses of Political Violence* (Princeton University Press, 1964).

Miriam Camps, *Britain and the European Community 1955-1963* (Princeton University Press, 1964).

Thomas P. Thornton, ed., *The Third World in Soviet Perspective: Studies by Soviet Writers on the Developing Areas* (Princeton University Press, 1964).

James N. Rosenau, ed., *International Aspects of Civil Strife* (Princeton University Press, 1964).

Sidney I. Ploss, *Conflict and Decision-Making in Soviet Russia: A Case Study of Agricultural Policy, 1953-1963* (Princeton University Press, 1965).

Richard A. Falk and Richard J. Barnet, eds., *Security in Disarmament* (Princeton University Press, 1965).

Karl von Vorys, *Political Development in Pakistan* (Princeton University Press, 1965).

Harold and Margaret Sprout, *The Ecological Perspective on Human Affairs, With Special Reference to International Politics* (Princeton University Press, 1965).

Klaus Knorr, *On the Uses of Military Power in the Nuclear Age* (Princeton University Press, 1966).

Harry Eckstein, *Division and Cohesion in Democracy: A Study of Norway* (Princeton University Press, 1966).

Cyril E. Black, *The Dynamics of Modernization: A Study in Comparative History* (Harper & Row, 1966).

Peter Kunstadter, ed., *Southeast Asian Tribes, Minorities, and Nations* (Princeton University Press, 1967).

E. Victor Wolfenstein, *The Revolutionary Personality: Lenin, Trotsky, Gandhi* (Princeton University Press, 1967).

Leon Gordenker, *The UN Secretary-General and the Maintenance of Peace* (Columbia University Press, 1967).

Oran R. Young, *The Intermediaries: Third Parties in International Crises* (Princeton University Press, 1967).

James N. Rosenau, ed., *Domestic Sources of Foreign Policy* (Free Press, 1967).

Richard F. Hamilton, *Affluence and the French Worker in the Fourth Republic* (Princeton University Press, 1967).

Linda B. Miller, *World Order and Local Disorder: The United Nations and Internal Conflicts* (Princeton University Press, 1967).

Henry Bienen, *Tanzania: Party Transformation and Economic Development* (Princeton University Press, 1967).

Wolfram F. Hanrieder, *West German Foreign Policy, 1949-1963: International Pressures and Domestic Response* (Stanford University Press, 1967).

Richard H. Ullman, *Britain and the Russian Civil War: November 1918–February 1920* (Princeton University Press, 1968).

Robert Gilpin, *France in the Age of the Scientific State* (Princeton University Press, 1968).

William B. Bader, *The United States and the Spread of Nuclear Weapons* (Pegasus, 1968).

Richard A. Falk, *Legal Order in a Violent World* (Princeton University Press, 1968).

Cyril E. Black, Richard A. Falk, Klaus Knorr, and Oran R. Young, *Neutralization and World Politics* (Princeton University Press, 1968).

Oran R. Young, *The Politics of Force: Bargaining During International Crises* (Princeton University Press, 1969).

Klaus Knorr and James N. Rosenau, eds., *Contending Approaches to International Politics* (Princeton University Press, 1969).

James N. Rosenau, ed., *Linkage Politics: Essays on the Convergence of National and International Systems* (Free Press, 1969).

John T. McAlister, Jr., *Viet Nam: The Origins of Revolution* (Knopf, 1969).

Jean Edward Smith, *Germany Beyond the Wall: People, Politics and Prosperity* (Little, Brown, 1969).

James Barros, *Betrayal from Within: Joseph Avenol, Secretary-General of the League of Nations, 1933-1940* (Yale University Press, 1969).

Charles Hermann, *Crises in Foreign Policy: A Simulation Analysis* (Bobbs-Merrill, 1969).

Robert C. Tucker, *The Marxian Revolutionary Idea: Essays on Marxist Thought and Its Impact on Radical Movements* (W. W. Norton, 1969).

Harvey Waterman, *Political Change in Contemporary France: The Politics of an Industrial Democracy* (Charles E. Merrill, 1969).

Cyril E. Black and Richard A. Falk, eds., *The Future of the International Legal Order.* Vol. I: *Trends and Patterns* (Princeton University Press, 1969).

Ted Robert Gurr, *Why Men Rebel* (Princeton University Press, 1969).

C. Sylvester Whitaker, *The Politics of Tradition: Continuity and Change in Northern Nigeria 1946-1966* (Princeton University Press, 1970).

Richard A. Falk, *The Status of Law in International Society* (Princeton University Press, 1970).

John T. McAlister, Jr., and Paul Mus, *The Vietnamese and Their Revolution* (Harper & Row, 1970).

Klaus Knorr, *Military Power and Potential* (D. C. Heath, 1970).

Cyril E. Black and Richard A. Falk, eds., *The Future of the International Legal Order.*

Vol. II: *Wealth and Resources* (Princeton University Press, 1970).

Leon Gordenker, ed., *The United Nations in International Politics* (Princeton University Press, 1971).

Cyril E. Black and Richard A. Falk, eds., *The Future of the International Legal Order*. Vol. III: *Conflict Management* (Princeton University Press, 1971).

Francine R. Frankel, *India's Green Revolution: Economic Gains and Political Costs* (Princeton University Press, 1971).

Harold and Margaret Sprout, *Toward a Politics of the Planet Earth* (Van Nostrand Reinhold Co., 1971).

Cyril E. Black and Richard A. Falk, eds., *The Future of the International Legal Order*. Vol. IV: *The Structure of the International Environment* (Princeton University Press, 1972).

Gerald Garvey, *Energy, Ecology, Economy* (W. W. Norton, 1972).

Richard H. Ullman, *The Anglo-Soviet Accord* (Princeton University Press, 1973).

Klaus Knorr, *Power and Wealth: The Political Economy of International Power* (Basic Books, 1973).

Anton Bebler, *Military Rule in Africa: Dahomey, Ghana, Sierra Leone, and Mali* (Praeger Publishers, 1973).

Robert C. Tucker, *Stalin as Revolutionary 1879-1929: A Study in History and Personality* (W. W. Norton, 1973).

Edward L. Morse, *Foreign Policy and Interdependence in Gaullist France* (Princeton University Press, 1973).

Henry Bienen, *Kenya: The Politics of Participation and Control* (Princeton University Press, 1974).

Gregory J. Massell, *The Surrogate Proletariat: Moslem Women and Revolutionary Strategies in Soviet Central Asia, 1919-1929* (Princeton University Press, 1974).

James N. Rosenau, *Citizenship Between Elections: An Inquiry Into The Mobilizable American* (Free Press, 1974).

Ervin Laszlo, *A Strategy for the Future: The Systems Approach to World Order* (George Braziller, 1974).

R. J. Vincent, *Nonintervention and International Order* (Princeton University Press, 1974).

Jan H. Kalicki, *The Pattern of Sino-American Crises: Political-Military Interactions in the 1950s* (Cambridge University Press, 1975).

Klaus Knorr, *The Power of Nations: The Political Economy of International Relations* (Basic Books, Inc., 1975).

James P. Sewell, *UNESCO and World Politics: Engaging in International Relations* (Princeton University Press, 1975).

Richard A. Falk, *A Global Approach to National Policy* (Harvard University Press, 1975).

Harry Eckstein and Ted Robert Gurr, *Patterns of Authority: A Structural Basis for Political Inquiry* (John Wiley & Sons, 1975).

Cyril E. Black, Marius B. Jansen, Herbert S. Levine, Marion J. Levy, Jr., Henry Rosovsky, Gilbert Rozman, Henry D. Smith, II, and S. Frederick Starr, *The Modernization of Japan and Russia* (Free Press, 1975).

Leon Gordenker, *International Aid and National Decisions: Development Programs in Malawi, Tanzania, and Zambia* (Princeton University Press, 1976).

Carl von Clausewitz, *On War,* edited and translated by Michael Howard and Peter Paret (Princeton University Press, 1976).

Gerald Garvey and Lou Ann Garvey, *International Resource Flows* (D. C. Heath, 1977).

Walter F. Murphy and Joseph Tanenhaus, *Comparative Constitutional Law: Cases and Commentaries* (St. Martin's Press, 1977).

Gerald Garvey, *Nuclear Power and Social Planning: The City of the Second Sun* (D. C. Heath, 1977).

Richard E. Bissell, *Apartheid and International Organizations* (Westview Press, 1977).

David P. Forsythe, *Humanitarian Politics: The International Committee of the Red Cross* (Johns Hopkins University Press, 1977).

Paul E. Sigmund, *The Overthrow of Allende and the Politics of Chile, 1964-1976* (University of Pittsburgh Press, 1977).

Henry S. Bienen, *Armies and Parties in Africa* (Holmes and Meier, 1978).

Harold and Margaret Sprout, *The Context of Environmental Politics: Unfinished Business for America's Third Century* (University Press of Kentucky, 1978).

Samuel S. Kim, *China, the United Nations, and World Order* (Princeton University Press, 1979).

S. Basheer Ahmed, *Nuclear Fuel and Energy* (D. C. Heath, 1979).

Robert Johansen, *The National Interest and the Human Interest: An Analysis of U.S. Foreign Policy* (Princeton University Press, 1979).